CHRIST AMONG US

SIXTH REVISED EDITION

Christ Among Us

A Modern Presentation
of the Catholic Faith for Adults

Anthony Wilhelm

HarperOne
An Imprint of HarperCollinsPublishers

HarperOne

HarperCollins books may be purchased for educational, business, or sales promotional use. For information please write: Special Markets Department, HarperCollins Publishers, 10 East 53rd Street, New York, NY 10022.

HarperCollins Web site: http://www.harpercollins.com

HarperCollins®, ■®, and HarperOne™ are trademarks of HarperCollins Publishers.

Library of Congress Cataloging-in-Publication Data
Wilhelm, Anthony J.
Christ among us : a modern presentation of the Catholic faith for adults / Anthony Wilhelm. — 6th rev. ed.
Includes bibliographical references and index.
ISBN: 978–0–06–069349–7
1. Catholic Church—Doctrines.   I. Title.
BX1754.W47   1996
230'.2—dc20   96–15096

09 10 11 RRD(H) 30 29 28 27

Contents

Preface

In the history of humankind there have been a few truly unique moments and special places—occasions when people of stature claimed an encounter with one who is beyond, a divine, transcendent reality.

On these occasions great movements have started that have affected billions of human lives and changed our world. They have given people hope, courage, compassion, and led them to dream of life beyond.

This is the story of the furthest-reaching claim to contact with divinity in human history. It is a story of real people and actual events—some of the most striking people and most moving events of all time. It is particularly the story of the one who has been called history's outstanding personality, Jesus Christ.

We offer here that to which countless billions, like St. Paul, have dedicated their lives:

> To announce the secret hidden for long ages and through many generations, but now disclosed to God's people . . . to make known how rich and glorious it is among all nations. The secret is this: *Christ in you—among you the hope of glory to come* (Colossians 1, 26–27).

This story of Christ among us is a study of the Catholic faith. Catholicism had a Council in the 1960s, a four-year gathering of its leaders—the bishops from throughout the world—that greatly changed it. We hope that the image and personality of Christ now shines more clearly through us poor humans who are the Church.

Today while some feel that God is a dead issue in their lives, others believe that this story can—and has—changed their lives. Many of these feel that the Church is now in its most unsettling but promising period since the beginning of institutional Christianity. Perhaps the reader (particularly one who has heard the story before) will find in this contemporary presentation a new hope and a new purpose.

For one who comes to this book seeking something, only two things are necessary: an open mind and a willingness to take a risk. An open mind because unless one is open and true to oneself, life is a waste. A willingness to take a risk because one may come to believe. The believer becomes changed. Many things may have to be renounced and life itself staked upon something unseen. Friends, even loved ones, often do not understand. This can be deeply upsetting. But unless it is tried, one will never know the fulfillment it can bring.

The sensation of a swim in cool water cannot be explained to someone who is unwilling to plunge in. A beautiful house cannot be appreciated by looking at it only from a distance. The experience of love can never be had by one who is unwilling to risk loving. So, too, the deep joys of belief and divine love come only to one who is willing to try—to read, to persevere, to practice as best one can.

SOME WORDS ABOUT USING THIS BOOK . . .

The initial sentences or phrases in bold print give a summary of the paragraph following; one who wants merely to skim can read these. The ordinary print following these is the main text of the book, usually concerning generally accepted Catholic teachings and practices.

The indented paragraphs in smaller print are for those who want to go more deeply into a particular subject. These give more detailed explanations of teachings, practical Catholic pastoral practices, and particular theological viewpoints.

The index should be consulted by those seeking information on a particular subject. For this Sixth Revised Edition it has been done in even greater detail to make it more comprehensive and easier to use.

Since the Bible is the basic source of Christ's teachings, to get the most out of this book, the use of a Bible with it is strongly recommended. The "Read" references to Scripture given throughout the book are for this purpose. The Revised Standard Version (1952, with 1957 Apocrypha) and the New Revised Standard Version (1989, with Apocrypha) are used for most of the biblical references and sometimes an amalgam of the two versions in an effort to use inclusive language.

The liturgy—the Church's ceremonies and rituals—is the great way Catholics make contact with God and share with one another. Sections called "**In the Liturgy**" are incorporated throughout the book so that the reader can see how our worship expresses itself.

Near the end of each chapter, a section called "**Daily Living**" gives practical applications of the chapter's teaching. The moral teaching of the Church is integrated into these sections instead of being left in its entirety to the end of the book.

The "**Discussion**" section near the end of each chapter is meant not only to help the reader grasp the points made in the chapter but to help stimulate—and share—further insights and experiences from daily life. The "**Personal Reflection**" that ends each chapter is meant to help the reader ponder, pray over, and do something about what he or she has read.

The sections at the end of each chapter entitled "**Further Reading**" and "**Further Viewing/Listening**" give suggestions for current books, films, and cassettes pertaining to the chapter's subject matter. A book title marked by one bullet means that it is a good general treatment for anyone; two bullets mark books for those who want to go deeper.

Regarding Sources: the teachings of Vatican Council II (1962–65) are the highest authority for what the Catholic Church teaches. The Council's documents form the basis for what is presented here—when they are quoted or referred to, the name and section of the particular document is given in parentheses.

The *Catechism of the Catholic Church* (1994), the latest official presentation of Catholic teachings, is also excerpted herein: references to it, also in parentheses, are sometimes given simply as *Catechism,* followed by the relevant section. The 1985 Code of Canon (Church) Law, pertinent papal documents, as well as those of the American bishops—and of some mainstream theologians—are also used.

For Whom This Is Meant: This book from its inception has been meant primarily for those on a journey toward the Catholic Church. Today that journey takes place within the Rite of Christian Initiation of Adults.

This Rite is described in detail in chapter 13, and the appendix also has practical suggestions for those using this book as they go through it.

This book has also been found helpful by many who are returning to the Church and/or those who simply want to update themselves on the Church's doctrinal and moral teachings as well as its ritual and other practices.

As with previous editions, every effort has been made to faithfully and accurately present the Church's teachings. This book is meant primarily for adult-level seekers, for more mature, often widely questioning minds seeking understanding. It aims both to present doctrinal truths and moral norms and to explore the theological possibilities and practical pastoral concerns of mainstream Catholics in our culture.

This is not a theologian's book, giving all possible viewpoints, looking as much at dissent as at doctrine. But while it tries to focus on accepted Catholic teaching and practices, it is for inquiring minds and hearts who are seeking in mainstream Catholicism for reasons and possibilities, for hope and a reason for living, for relevance and to clarify misunderstandings—and to find the living God. The author, incidentally, would be very grateful for any comments or suggestions for improvement—and he is deeply thankful to all who have added to what was in previous editions.

With Gratitude: As with previous editions, the author has had the help of many competent and wonderfully inspiring people. Without them this book would never have been possible:

The many Paulist Fathers who have been friends and colleagues for most of my life and who were cocreators of this book from its start; the priests, religious, and laypeople of Minneapolis and St. Paul, of San Francisco, Oakland, and Berkeley, who have been constant contributors; Rev. Paul Carlson, who has again updated his chapter on the Bible; the people of Berkeley's Newman Hall—especially of its catechumenate and Homecoming programs; Mike McGarry, C.S.P., for his contributions to the sections on Judaism and Christianity; Tom West, Ph.D., of St. Catherine's College, St. Paul, for his insights and contributions throughout; Bob Rowden, M.D., for his help with the sections on bioethics; Paulist Press and Margo LeBert of RENEW for help "Breaking Open the Catechism of the Catholic Church"; Bruno Barnhart, O.Cam., the Camaldolese hermits of Immaculate Heart Monastery, and Rev. Clifford and Ethel Elizabeth Crummey, who are still always there; above all, Pamela, for her always confident, prodding love; and finally, Tom Grady, Mimi Kusch, Laura Harger, and the others of HarperSanFrancisco, who have made yet another edition a reality.

Our Life and God

What is life all about? Is there a God? If there is a God, does he care about us? Can I make contact with God? To answer these questions, we begin with something all people seek . . .

SOMETHING TO LIVE FOR

If there is one thing that people seek from life, it is fulfillment. We need a purpose, something to live for, a goal that will truly fulfill us and bring us happiness.

Many live for a successful marriage and a good home; some want a pleasant job with financial security; some seek power, or a life of pleasure and leisure, or friends and social position.

Many today, including many younger people, find their purpose in the service of others. In this age of great social change and consequent confusion these highly motivated individuals have brought about great good in our world.

Yet we must acknowledge that none of these things can completely satisfy our aspirations. No matter what we have, there is always something else we want. We also realize that these things cannot give us lasting and secure happiness, nor a lasting sense of accomplishment, for human weakness, tragedy, or death can destroy what we have. "Human beings are like a breath; their days like a passing shadow" (Psalm 144, 4).

The conviction of the Christian believer is that two thousand years ago Jesus Christ revealed to us an ultimate purpose to our life: to

live forever with God after death. We know that our greatest happiness in this life comes from love. From childhood everyone has an insatiable desire to love and be loved. Our happiness in human love, Christ tells us, is but a dim reflection of the immense, unending joy of loving God and being loved by him forever.

Jesus told us that this unending life of happiness after death is such that we could not even begin to dream of it. It is as if someone lived in a closed room, never seeing or hearing anything outside. Then one day someone opened the door to the outside to display the world with its marvels. Christ did this for us, but he revealed that our destiny is infinitely more wonderful—so staggering that we can grasp it only bit by bit.

Jesus told us that we begin our life of love and happiness with God while still here on earth. But this happiness is different from what many people think. It does not come from satisfying our desire for pleasure or material things or social achievement. It comes from truly loving and often involves suffering and sacrifice. It is realistic. It brings not freedom from pain but a deep peace and sense of fulfillment even in the midst of pain.

Jesus showed us how to get along with others and how to bear sufferings and frustration. He told us and showed us what we can do about our loneliness and fears, our guilt and uneasiness, and how to have true peace and security.

Jesus revealed that God has a plan by which we are to share in his love and happiness, in other words, that there is a meaning to human history. He told us not only that we have a place in God's plan but that (as is becoming more apparent today) the working out of this plan depends on us, on our free cooperation with God as coauthors of history. Jesus' great follower, St. Paul, put it this way:

> To me, though I am the very least of all the saints, this grace was given, to preach to the Gentiles the news of the boundless riches of Christ, and to make all humanity see what is the plan of the mystery hidden for ages in God who created all things; that through the Church the wisdom of God in its rich variety might now be made known. . . . This was according to the eternal purpose which he has realized in Christ Jesus our Lord (Ephesians 3, 8–11).

The unique claim that Jesus made for his teaching was that he has a special knowledge of God and his plan for us, and that he alone can lead us to God. He said that he was sent by God, and is, in fact, God's only Son: "I am the way, and the truth, and the life. No one comes to the Father but through me" (John 14, 5).

Therefore the story of Jesus' teaching and God's plan begins with God himself . . .

HOW PEOPLE COME TO KNOW GOD

People come to a realization of God in countless ways. These are some of them:

Some have grown from childhood with a knowledge of God, are accustomed to pray and to make God a part of their thoughts and decisions.

Some reflect on the course of their life and have an unshakable conviction of God's providence over them. Particularly in times of crisis, they realize, someone was there who heard and understood.

Some find God's presence in nature. In hills and mountains, a peaceful lake, an expanse of sky, there comes the conviction of someone. A few might come closest while caught up in a moving piece of music, in the contemplation of an art masterpiece, or something similar.

Some are convinced that they have personally experienced God—a deeply moving, joyous, and unifying experience, giving great peace, clarity, and certainty, profoundly affecting their lives yet unexplainable to others. Many who testify to this—and it is usually with reluctance that they do so—are otherwise balanced and credible people.

> For others, experiencing God is not as intense. It may be an experience of our human limitations or "boundaries," a sense of wonder that we exist at all, and a hint of an otherness that lies beyond. It may be a glorious sunset, the sweep of stars in a clear nighttime sky, a look from a loved one or a touch of an understanding hand, a child's laughter, an unexpected joy—all these tell of another that sustains, gives hope, and is always there.

Some come to God through their desire for perfect love. We know that everyone, from childhood, has a strong need for understanding and affection, perhaps accentuated by suffering or continual frustration. Yet we know that every human love has weaknesses and will eventually disappoint us. We then look to someone, beyond this life, who will never fail us, who can perfectly understand us and fulfill our aspirations and our desire for love.

Some are helped by demonstrations from reason of God's reality. For example, an enormously complicated space satellite cannot make itself and launch itself into orbit. It has to be designed, built, launched, and sustained by intelligent humans. Our world and the countless star systems act according to amazingly consistent laws in a universe that is far more complicated than any satellite. The vast universe must, therefore, have been planned, made, and is being sustained by one of supreme intelligence and power. This one we call God.

> Reasoning like this, "circumstantial evidence," might show some the need for a limitless, timeless force sustaining the universe. But God himself must give us an insight into himself if we are ever to know him as close, personal, interested, loving.

Some are helped by those they love who are lovers of God. The example of the deep faith of a friend or beloved, its effect on that person's life, and the generous love it seems to produce may gradually open the seeker to the divine lover.

Many cannot express why they believe in God or what God is to them. They are instinctively dumb before this unfathomable mystery. Even a master of language like Cardinal Newman said of this, "Words are such poor vehicles for what my mind holds and my heart believes." Perhaps the greatest obstacle a believer encounters in expressing belief to an unbeliever—or even to him- or herself—is the inability to communicate in understandable concepts.

> Seeking God is for many like peering through a fog to see if there is a house at a particular spot; often all we catch is a glimpse, confused, uncertain. We never see God. But most of us reach certainty about him by a "cumulation of converging probabilities," which can give not just an opinion but the deepest conviction (*Catechism,* no. 31). Some never attain this deepest conviction but seem permitted by God to remain in a state of constant quest. In the search for truth it is perhaps not important how many fragments of the stag-

gering whole one manages to perceive during one's lifetime, but the courage and openness with which one continues the search.

As we move toward truth we may come to realize that we are as much being sought as seeking, that the truth we seek, the God we would love, is already deeply within us, soliciting our love. We come to realize our conviction of this all along: one who becomes convinced of God could never recognize him unless one had somehow known him before.

WHAT IS NECESSARY TO KNOW GOD

As in any honest pursuit, we must be open to truth, not only the truth of absolute values but also the truth about ourselves, who we are and what we ultimately want from the experience of life. This requires courage, a willingness to be threatened by often unpleasant realities. Those who are self-sufficient or self-satisfied will have no reason to push out beyond themselves in search of a higher good.

We must be willing to take time to question, observe, reflect. In our achievement-oriented society, particularly, it is hard for one to devote time to reflecting on ultimate values. Even when the satisfaction of achievement fails one and all one's striving seems useless, the consideration of a possible God behind it all is often rejected as a demeaning crutch.

We must be open to our fellow humans and treat them as our conscience demands, with dignity and justice. The mature person sees that in each individual there is a spark, however dim, of enduring goodness. This spark is the divine within each person, and if one is ever to find God one must recognize and respect this spark in others. One who uses others or demeans them, who seeks only one's own good, will inevitably find only oneself.

Christians believe that God has revealed—and is revealing—himself to humankind and that one must investigate this claim of revelation if one is to find God as he has shown himself to us. This seems logical to the Christian; if there is an infinite one, we who are finite cannot grasp him unless he reveals himself to us. Thus, although not everyone will find God's revelation, it is the highest logic to search for it.

However, to meet God as he has revealed himself—to realize he is there—he must give us faith, the power to recognize him, the intuitive grasp of his reality. Ultimately whether one is a believer or not depends not only on one's openness but on God. This explains why some find God while others of equal intelligence and good will do not.

Today many feel that God is missing from our world, or at least silent. For some, caught up by scientific advances and a technology by which humankind seems able to solve its own problems, a search for God seems irrelevant, meaningless.

The great majority of people in our culture, however, express belief in God. Some testify to experiencing God. Others are disposed to seek an experience of God—they know they need a source of security, meaning, or fulfillment in their lives. Yet often God is not evident or present in any felt, tangible way. They turn to him when they need him, but he is not there. He seems to keep eluding them.

Why does not God make himself unmistakably known to all people? We can only speculate about this, but a reason might lie in the Christian view of God: far from being a Supreme One who imposes himself on us, demanding that we acknowledge him and give him our obeisance, God is one who is among us, loving us with great and intimate tenderness, soliciting our free response of love.

Why are many people unable to find God? Some seem unable to detach themselves from the pursuit of modern false gods: money, social status, power, pleasure. As long as a person primarily seeks these, he or she will never find the living and true God.

Even the person of great good will who is continually occupied with material things—for example, the world of science or business—must expect difficulty in coming to realize spiritual reality, however noble his or her daily pursuits may be. To come to realize God takes time and persevering effort.

Some project a distorted image of God that pictures him as a disinterested power, perhaps capricious, even vengeful. These people usually have not had the proper kind of love in their lives, may have experienced much seemingly meaningless suffering, and so cannot accept a loving God. They have never experienced the love they have been told God is—and perhaps they have experienced the unlovingness of those who claim to be friends of God.

The Vatican Council says of this:

Some . . . seem more inclined to affirm [humanity] than to deny God. Again, some form for themselves such a fallacious idea of God that when they repudiate this figment, they are by no means rejecting the God of the Gospel. . . . Moreover, atheism results not rarely from a violent protest against the evil in this world. . . . Believers can have more than a little to do with the birth of atheism. To the extent that they neglect their own training in the faith, or teach erroneous doctrine, or are deficient in their religious, moral or social life, they . . . conceal rather than reveal the authentic face of God and religion (Vatican Council II, *The Church in the Modern World,* no. 19).

One perceptive modern author writes:

One of the greatest obstacles to belief in God is the complacency of believers. It is not the adulterers, the takers of bribes, the licentious, whose conduct induces disbelief. It is the righteous, the solid citizens, the people of good reputation in the community. Such believers show few signs of ever having encountered the terrifying God; nor do they appear to live in that cold night of belief in which he is most truly found. Their god seems to be an idol, the idol of habit, routine, sentiment, and self-congratulation. By their words and actions, they treat God as a vague guarantor of the good order which makes them secure (Novak, *Belief and Unbelief,* p. 182).

It seems that after a certain point in life one does not change one's basic position from belief to unbelief, or from unbelief to belief. This point seems to be the late teens or early twenties, or it may be even earlier, by the time of adolescence. Some believers may doubt after this, even consider themselves unbelievers, but this is usually a temporary state.

Many young people must go through a rejection—or better, a testing—of the authority structures of their life: their home, their religion, their belief in God, and so on. This experience seems necessary for most thinking young people, and some older ones as well, that they might arrive at a more mature faith and one to which they are personally committed.

It is the believer's conviction that many seek God—and find him in the depths of their being—without realizing it: some through their unrelenting pursuit of truth, justice, the good of the community, or another humanitarian ideal—and many through their insatiable thirst for love. They are never satisfied. Through their total commitment to a transcendent idea they are, to the believer, reaching the absolute that we call God.

Some have a radical dissatisfaction with any human accomplishment, are unfulfilled by any human love. Nothing any longer impresses them. Even the wonderful interchange and intimacy of human love at its deepest level only elicits in them a further desire, one that cannot be satisfied.

Sometimes, perceiving no end to their quest, they lapse into a seeming cynicism, take refuge in flippancy, or strike out against the believer—but to the discerning believer their reaction is only the measure of their unknowing love, a love that might be far greater than the believer's own. The believer must always pray, "O God, some know and serve you as truth, honor, integrity, service . . . as well as I, and perhaps better. . . . "

It seems, too, that unbelievers have a providential role toward believers, one of challenging them to consider aspects of God that they might otherwise forget: God is truly inaccessible and incomprehensible; we are totally dependent on his revelation of himself and can never take for granted that we know much at all about him and his will for us.

The committed believer and unbeliever then have much in common. Both are dedicated seekers of truth. Both seek in darkness—to both God is an absence, one who is not there, for he is not an object to be found. Yet he is there, for both believer and unbeliever have an objective in their lifelong striving—though called different names, conceptualized differently, by each. To both, then, God is a presence and an absence, one who is there and one who is not there.

The constant temptation of the believer is to fabricate a God with whom he or she is comfortable, a God who will not disturb one's life and with whom one can come to terms once and for all. When doubts come, or new and unsettling views about God and his will, this type of believer becomes confused, perhaps resentful that his or her faith should be a struggle as well as a secure refuge. Some of these who consider themselves believers, it is evident, have simply never known the living God.

We cannot believe in God once-for-all any more than we can exist once-for-all. Faith must always realize itself, and yet must always remain unrealized. If so, it must *beware* of seeking rest if it should feel the fatigue of self-exertion, as must he who, tired of existence, imagined he could find repose outside it (Dewart, *The Future of Belief,* p. 65).

Doubts about God, then, must be expected even by believers who try to know and love him faithfully. Faith must grow, and growth is often uncertain, painful. Those who tell us of overwhelming, rapturous experiences of God also testify to states of "darkness" and terrible doubt during which God is no longer a reality. God is utterly silent—and such a state may last for years.

Believers must try to deepen their faith, learn more, live their faith more fully, or else they might lose their ability to experience belief. Believers cannot consider themselves superior to their unbelieving friends, as if their own faith could never slip away. They should recognize that their faith is a free gift of God to which they continually and freely commit themselves. Humbly each must say daily, "Lord, I do believe—help my unbelief!"

WHAT CAN WE SAY ABOUT GOD?

We can learn something about God from examining the universe about us. As we learn of the skill of an artist or builder by examining his or her work, so we can learn about God through the universe he has made. We can grasp something of his power, limitlessness, beauty, his care for the tiniest particle as well as the vast whole. St. Paul put it: "Ever since the creation of the world his invisible nature . . . has been clearly perceived in the things that have been made" (Romans 1, 20).

The Judeo-Christian belief is that God has himself told us something about himself, revealed himself to us. He has done this in many ways, but particularly to the Israelites of the Old Testament. For example, over three thousand years ago he revealed himself to Moses as the living, all-pervading God: **Read Exodus 3, 2-6 and 13-14.**

God is "wholly other," transcendent, infinitely holy. Those to whom he has revealed himself have often testified to a feeling of utter awe, wonderment, profound abasement, a sort of "holy terror" in his presence. Thus the Jewish prophet Isaiah tried to describe his experience of God: **Read Isaiah 6, 1-7.** Moses' experience is also primitive but striking: **Read Exodus 33, 18-23.**

God has revealed that he is a loving, "personal" God, concerned with each of us. He loves each of us, believer and unbeliever, in a way that he loves nothing else in creation. We will see how he shows himself to be good, kind, patient, and faithful. As the Jews of the Old Testament came to realize this, they compared God to a shepherd who carefully guides his helpless sheep, to a good king, a loving father, a mother: "Can a woman forget her sucking child, that she should have no compassion on the son of her womb? Even these may forget, yet I will not forget you" (Isaiah 49, 15).

God's ultimate revelation of himself was through his own Son, Jesus Christ. This is the uniquely Christian view of God—that he has a Son, Jesus Christ, and that this Son has come among us as a human. "In many and various ways God spoke of old to our fathers by the prophets, but in these last days he has spoken to us by a Son . . . " (Hebrews 1, 1–2).

Jesus teaches us what God is by calling him our Father. He is a Father who has not only given us life but who loves each of us with a limitless love, cares for us each day, and wants us to live happily with him forever. He is a merciful Father, always ready with his forgiveness for us—as long as we are willing to forgive others. The Lord's Prayer, taught us by Jesus, beautifully expresses this:

> **Our Father, who art in heaven, hallowed be thy name. Thy kingdom come, thy will be done on earth as it is in heaven. Give us this day our daily bread, and forgive us our trespasses as we forgive those who trespass against us. And lead us not into temptation, but deliver us from evil. Amen.**

In calling God "Father" Jesus uses the language of the patriarchal (i.e., male-dominated) society of his day. God, of course, has no gender—and we will see that Jesus rejects the widespread male notions of dominance and power. Jesus is telling us that God is a divine Parent who has the best qualities of an ideal Mother as well as Father: One who has given us life, nurtures us, and is intimately close to us—tender as well as strong, just but always accepting, suffering with us and rejoicing with our achievements, gently but firmly drawing us toward maturity and fulfillment.

Some today wonder why all the fuss about the use of only male images for God. The use of this imagery, we will see, gives an incomplete, often distorted picture of the God Jesus revealed. And, as a saying among theologians today puts it, "when God is male, the male becomes God"—religion becomes patriarchal, male dominated. Seen more positively, the more metaphors—male, female, whatever—we use for God, the more we might begin to get some slight sense of the infinite, boundless Mystery that God in fact is.

God reveals himself, we shall see later, as a loving "family" of three Persons who draw us to themselves, to share their happiness. God is not just Father but also Son and Holy Spirit, to each of whom we have a special relationship of love. This paradox of one God who is yet three Persons is the mystery of the Trinity, discussed in chapter 7.

God respects each of us—our freedom, our dignity, our person—because he loves each of us. Though many are not yet aware of this, God enters into a most intimate "I-Thou" relationship with each of us. He calls each of us by our own name. Rather than absorbing us into himself, the God of our Judeo-Christian revelation enables each of us to develop to our utmost as a person—even as he unites us most intimately with himself. To this paradox the greatest mystics testify.

God has revealed that even the sufferings of innocent people somehow work out for the eventual happiness of us all. Though we cannot yet understand how, the wars, crimes, and terrible injustices of human history are in some way encompassed by God's plan for sharing with us his love and happiness. We cry out for an explanation when suffering strikes, but then we remind ourselves that our vision is finite, that we see only the moment of this life—next to nothing, really, when compared to an eternity of happiness. This, of course, is no answer, but for one who believes it can be a beginning of a meaning.

God himself is somehow involved in our suffering—because he loves us he suffers with us. As people mature they realize that love, if it means anything, means suffering (as well as rejoicing) with one's beloved. Some, however, find this difficult to apply to God. Later, when we consider Jesus and his great work for us, we will see more about the meaning of suffering.

The mind-boggling view of God represented by process theology says, in part, that God experiences with us the daily working out of our life, with all its hopes and fears, its unknowns and vulnerabilities, its joys, sorrows, and triumphs. God by his own inner necessity is fully involved with us—and nowhere more so than when we are poor or afflicted. Instead of existing in splendid, isolated self-sufficiency, God relates in love to his creatures in limitless, unsuspected, unimaginable ways.

Ultimately, while we can know that God is—that we are in contact with him, that he is present to us—we cannot know what he is. We seek him, try to apply to him our poor human categories, and experience his loving involvement with us. But, paradoxically, he is also "totally other," and all our speculations must ultimately end in awesome ignorance—as some mystics have said, "learned ignorance." He is always a hidden God.

Therefore we must expect to find mysteries in our study of God and religion—things about which we can know very little, or that make little sense to us. When we think that we understand him, or when we confidently predict his actions, then we are in trouble.

> O the depth of the riches and wisdom and knowledge of God! How unsearchable are his judgments and how inscrutable his ways! For who has known the mind of the Lord . . . (Romans 11, 33–34).

DAILY LIVING: PRAYER—OUR CONTACT WITH GOD

To come to know God as he really is, and to experience his love for us, it is absolutely necessary to try to contact him. This is prayer . . .

It is necessary for each sincere seeker to try to pray. Others might testify about their knowledge of God, what he is like, but each of us must form our own acquaintance with God. We might hear descriptions about a wonderful woman from those who have met her, but we will never really know that person until we have met her and communicated with her ourselves.

Just as every genuine human love relationship is unique and can be fully experienced only by the lovers themselves, so each person's love relationship with God is unique, can be achieved by her or him alone, and cannot be communicated adequately to anyone else. If we remain aloof, waiting for God to come without trying to reach God, we will never know God any more than we could know another person whom we treated in this way.

The few whose persistent prayer has led them to experience a love affair with the living God know that it can be a terrifying, totally demanding, unbelievably fulfilling, fantastically wonderful thing. Most of us will not—perhaps cannot—bring ourselves to risk such an experience. But if we are wise we will not reject what these experiencers of the divine have to say. We will listen to their insights, for they might be of immense help to us as we struggle enmeshed in our human condition. They are unanimous in telling us that our moments of prayer are the most alive moments of all, that when we pray we are on the threshold of a life and beauty and joy that are utterly unimaginable.

Prayer is simply talking with God, trying to put ourselves in touch with him, contacting and becoming aware of him. By prayer, "something out there" becomes someone personal, close, concerned. We can never be sure there is a God, nor come to know what he is like, unless we pray. When we refuse to try to pray, "the world becomes our jail."

God loves us and respects our freedom. He wants our mature love. He will never force himself upon us. We must try to reach out to him, freely, by prayer.

The reason we pray is not to tell God something he does not know, nor to change his mind. Rather, prayer makes us aware of God, opens us to perceive his love and his desires for us. Prayer gradually makes us realize our complete dependence on God, our radical need of him. It makes us appreciate, bit by bit, how we are utterly bound to him by love. It also makes us realize the great power we have to better our human condition. When one prays, the happenings of life, the joys as well as the agonies, begin to take on a meaning.

God always answers a sincere prayer, but not always in the way we expect. We tend to complain of unanswered prayers, but perhaps we were not open to God as he tried to "get through" with an answer. We might be praying for something that, however hard to believe now, would ultimately be harmful, or we might be expecting God to do what is within our own power to bring about. Sometimes a lack of imaginative faith—perhaps together with narrowing pain of body or spirit—makes us close off options God is trying to get us to see.

We should pray for ourselves and for others, including our enemies. Prayer for ourselves need not be selfish—on the contrary, it is usually an acknowledgment of our total human inadequacy. Prayer for others helps them to be open to God's love and our love and helps us to be open to them. We shall see more later about the power of prayer.

Some suggestions about how to pray: We can simply talk to God as to our best and most understanding friend, our loving Father or Mother. The best prayer is from our heart, in our own words. If we wish, we can use words someone else has composed, or we might say nothing, content just to be in God's presence, thinking about him, about ourselves, our loved ones, our life.

We can pray anywhere, anytime. But it is good to set aside a special time—perhaps in the morning and evening—and a special place, away from distractions. We read about Christ: "And in the morning, a great while before day, he rose and went out to a lonely place, and there he prayed. . . . And after he had taken leave of them, he went into the hills to pray" (Mark 1, 35; 6, 46).

We need not say much. Christ warns us against imitating those who "think that by talking much they will be heard" (Matthew 6, 8). Reading, especially the Bible, is food for prayer; people often cannot pray because they know so little about God, his actions and teachings.

Prayer can be difficult. But to try to pray, is to pray. One can feel utterly helpless when trying it for the first time, or returning to it as an adult. One wonders: How should I go about it? Will I be heard? Isn't there a danger of self-hypnosis? It can be like talking into a phone with no one on the other end of the line. One should expect these problems in trying to reach for an Infinite One. But we must be willing to risk, to try.

If we persevere, gradually, perhaps very slowly and painfully, the conviction grows that there is Someone. Things begin to fall into place. We long for more contact, to know more, to have more help, to give ourselves to him. Mysteriously, the bond of love grows.

SOME SUGGESTIONS FOR . . .

DISCUSSION

How would you describe what you perceive as your purpose in life?

How do you conceive of God—what, for you, is God like?

Can you understand why all-male images of God might cause problems for some people?

What best makes God's presence real in your life? What could you do to be more aware of God's presence?

What would most cause you to doubt God's goodness and love? How do you best experience God in prayer?

FURTHER READING

- *Meeting the Living God,* O'Malley (Paulist Press, 1983)—New edition of an excellent book, especially for students; frank, current, realistic. Also on video.
- *Dreams: God's Forgotten Language,* Sanford (Harper & Row, 1989)—An excellent, clearly written book by a Jungian analyst and Episcopal priest on how our dreams can reveal God and his guidance to us.
- •• *She Who Is: The Mystery of God in Feminist Theological Discourse,* Johnson (Crossroad, 1993)—Discusses how to talk about God and different ways of looking at God: as Wisdom or Sophia, as Mother, and so on. Probably the best single-volume presentation on this subject to date.
- *The Silence of God,* Carse (HarperSanFrancisco, 1995)—Paperback edition of a particularly good book regarding our not getting a sign or answer when we need it most.
- •• *The Divine Relativity,* Hartshorne (Yale University Press, 1948)—A small, older book on process theism, this may still be the best concise explanation of this way of looking at our relationship with God.
- •• *Stubborn Fact and Creative Advance,* Hosinski (Rowman & Littlefield, 1993)—Subtitled "An Introduction to the Metaphysics of Alfred North Whitehead," this is probably the best introduction to process theology to be published in recent years.
- *Beginning to Pray,* Bloom (Paulist Press, 1982)—A second edition of a beautifully helpful book on prayer by a Russian Orthodox archbishop.

PERSONAL REFLECTION

I am always in the presence of God, my loving Father. Each morning and evening I might offer this simple, expressive prayer:

"O God, help me to know what to do,
and give me the courage to do it."

God's Plan for Us Begins with Creation

How did the human race begin? Is there a conflict between science and the Bible? What is humankind's place in the universe? Will we survive after death? What of other worlds, angels, devils?

THE SOURCE OF OUR STORY

To answer the basic questions of our origin, we look to God's own record of his unfolding plan, history's all-time best-seller, the Bible . . .

The Bible, or Sacred Scripture, is a collection of books inspired by God, revealing himself and his plan for our salvation. God is considered the principal author of the Bible in that he influenced those who wrote the books—even though they wrote freely and may not have been aware of his guidance—and so we say it was inspired by God. It expresses his revelation of himself to humankind and is therefore called his written "Word." The *Catechism of the Catholic Church* says, "In Sacred Scripture God speaks to [us] in a human way" (109).

The Bible is a religious book whose purpose is to tell of God and his plan for us, especially his great deeds on our behalf and his teaching about how to live and attain heaven. Since its authors were writing religious history, they related historical events only as a means of instructing and inspiring their readers. Sometimes they embellished their accounts with imaginative details, illustrated a point by a fictitious story, or omitted things that would detract from their religious purpose.

The Bible is a miniature library containing all sorts of writing. It contains poetry, prayers, hymns, love songs, riddles, fables, allegories, various kinds of historical narratives, folklore, biographies, prophecies, letters, and more. Each biblical author used the type of literature, or literary form, that best suited the author's purpose. Each literary form must be interpreted properly if the author is to be understood, as we today interpret poetry differently than we do a newspaper editorial, and a fairy tale still differently. These ancient oriental literary forms are often hard for us to understand, since they were the expressions of the people of another time and culture.

For example, a visitor to earth from another planet, understanding our language but nothing more about us, might read a newspaper and consider everything in it equally true—news columns, ads, comics, letters to the editor, and so on—whereas we know that each style of writing must be interpreted differently.

Thus the biblical authors often used myths to convey what they were trying to say. It is important to understand what is meant here by "myth." To most people "myth" means something not real, something that was once believed but is now seen to be untrue, not scientifically or historically verifiable. Actually a historical myth is a story told in ancient humankind's symbolic language whose structure and details were not literally true, but that had a central point that was true. Myths were—and are—ways of expressing real events or facts of our human experiences, especially our universal, worldwide, or "archetypal" experiences.

An example of a myth in which most of us find meaning is the Santa Claus story. This has its origin in a real individual, an early Christian bishop, St. Nicholas, who secretly gave money to poor girls as a dowry for a husband. There are other versions of the secret gift-giver in almost every culture of the world. Thus, the Santa Claus story we tell our children today has a real truth behind it: loving parents everywhere delight in surprising their children with gifts. And its most basic meaning is that God—our almighty and ceaselessly loving Parent—takes care of us with his gifts, ever surprising us with his help, if we are open, humble, and trustful enough to recognize his Presence.

Especially in ancient times, the myth-story expressed humankind's deepest experiences, particularly religious ones. Later, as humankind became more accustomed to abstract thinking, the Church tried to set down in understandable terms the God-experiences of Judaism and of the Christian community. Since this experiencing involved God, there was always much more to it than they could ever express.

So when people's religious experiences are recorded, as in the Bible, we expect them to use symbolic language to express what they have experienced as profoundly real and true. Symbols or symbolic "language"—we shall see—always "stands for" something more than is immediately apparent. Religious language or terminology, because it tries to express our experiences of the limitless "beyond," of God himself, is especially symbolic; there is always vastly more to it than the words convey at first sight.

Just as people's backgrounds, their learning, insights, prejudices, and so on, affect what they report as real, just as scientists' reports of their experiments and deductions are affected by their prior theories, their personal paradigms, and their own involvement in the experimental process, and just as our personal "bias," acknowledged or not, affects what we report as true and how we relate it, so with the biblical stories of the God-experiences of Judaism and of Christianity. The more we can "enter into" what is set down and the more we openly and seekingly read with our intuitions and imaginations as well as with our reasoning, the more it will "come alive" for us in our lives.

The Bible is the story of how God enters the lives of those open to him. We believe that God today will communicate, in some way, with anyone who reads the Bible story with an open, seeking mind. The Bible was written by and about people like us whose lives were changed by their experiences with God. They are the great, "foundational" religious experiences of our Western civilization—and the deeds and experiences related in the Bible can have as much of an effect on us today as they did upon the people to whom they originally happened. It is the conviction of the Christian believer that these experiences were meant to help all men and women throughout history. If we truly try to "relate" these great experiences and deeds to the situations of our life with an open and seeking mind, God can use this story to bring us to himself.

The Bible is divided into the Old Testament—the Jewish Scriptures, the story of God's revelation of himself and his plan up to the coming of Christ—and the New Testament, a kind of outline of Christ's

life and teachings. The Old Testament, forty-five books in the Catholic version, was written by many authors and centers on the Jewish people. The Middle Eastern traditions in the first five books—the Torah or Pentateuch (Greek for "five books")—go back to the time of Moses (thirteenth century B.C.E.—i.e., before the common Judeo-Christian era) and beyond. These were first woven together on a major scale about the tenth century B.C.E. The last book to be written, Wisdom, was set down about 50 B.C.E.

The first book of the Old Testament, Genesis, begins with the story of the origin of the world and of humankind . . .

HUMAN BEGINNINGS

The story came to us in this way: Over three thousand years ago, a band of exslaves found themselves wandering in the Sinai desert after a dramatic escape from pagan Egypt. In this remote place, God spoke to Moses, their leader, and made them his chosen people, promising them great blessings. But the people, conscious of their vague past and uncertain future and aware of their weaknesses, began to ask Moses questions: How did it all start? What was this God of theirs like? Was he really an all-powerful God? If so, why did he choose them? Where did they come from, and who were their ancestors?

The answer Moses and others gave—the story of the beginning of God's plan for our world—was elaborated over the centuries. Eventually it was written down as Genesis, the first book of the Bible: **Read Genesis 1, 1–2, 24.**

This story of creation is meant to teach us that God made everything that exists and that everything he has made is good. Genesis speaks of creation in six days to help its primitive audience better understand that God made everything, even the things worshiped by other peoples; the picture of God creating for six days and resting on the seventh is meant to teach a Jewish audience that they should rest on the sabbath.

Humankind is at the peak of creation, in some way like God himself, and is given everything in the world for its use. "What are human beings that you are mindful of them, mortals that you care for them? Yet you have made them a little lower than God, and crowned them with glory and honor" (Psalm 8, 4–5).

The Bible's account of creation can fit in perfectly with science's teaching on the evolution of the universe, even though, as we said, the Bible is not meant to be a scientific text. God brings the world to realization, not by continual interventions—stepping in to "make" this or that—but in such a way that the higher emerges from the lower, by evolution. He is continually creating as he activates the whole, gigantic, unfolding process.

By the description of the creation of woman as man's "helper and partner," the biblical author is emphasizing women's dignity, that they are human beings equal to men. This stands in sharp contrast to the common ancient view of a woman as merely something to be used by a man. This description can also be seen as the origin of marriage—a wonderfully intimate union begun by God himself as a part of his unfolding plan for humankind.

> The biblical story of human origins has been interpreted until relatively recently as meaning one original couple (monogenism). Many current biblical scholars take a broader view and point out that monogenism is not necessarily part of God's revelation. One says, "Studies in exegesis and conciliar history lead us to ask whether the intention of the author of Genesis, of St. Paul, and of the . . . Council of Trent was really directed at the strict unity of origin of the human race and not rather at the universality of 'sin'" (Dubarle, *The Biblical Doctrine of Original Sin,* p. 228).

WHAT ARE WE?

Christianity, building on God's revelation to us, has reached certain conclusions about us humans:

Each of us is composed of soul, or spirit, and materiality. With the help of God's further revelation we can see this in the story of humans made "in the image of God" and of "the dust of the earth." These are the two "aspects" of a human being, two "powers," two ways in which we can act.

By our soul, or spiritual aspect, we are "like God," persons, free, immortal, able to reflect on ourselves and realize ourselves. "[Humankind] outstrips the whole sum of mere things . . . surpasses the material universe . . . and shares in the light of the divine mind" (*Church in the Modern World,* no. 14).

By our materiality, or material aspect—our bodies—we are connected with and dependent upon other things, limited, mortal, but capable of perfecting our universe. We are not angels or pure spirits. Our bodies are good and also relate us to God.

Each of us is a single, unified person. Our soul and materiality are not two "parts," but rather two aspects of the one person who does everything. Our spirit depends upon our materiality—upon our brain, senses, and so on—that we might think and act. Whether we have the loftiest "spiritual" thoughts or engage in the most basic "animal" actions, it is we ourselves, single persons, who do these things.

Our soul, or spiritual power, is just as real as the materiality we can see and feel. It is the core of our being, our conscious self, our innermost "me." It infuses every part of us that is alive. It enables us to think and make free choices and love. When we think, we call this power our intellect or mind; when we make free choices and love, we call it our free will.

We can be sure that we have this spiritual aspect, or soul, even aside from God's teaching about it. We have nonmaterial or spiritual ideas, such as truth, love, and so on. We can conceive and carry out plans for the future; we can reflect on our past actions. We make abstract judgments; we produce culture, art, and poetry, study philosophy and religion—all having little or nothing to do with our material survival.

The existence of the human spirit is often best shown when we triumph over inhumanity, suffering, and death. The diary of Anne Frank, a Jewish teenager's writings discovered in her Amsterdam hideout after her cruel death at the hands of the Nazis, is a striking modern testimony to the power of the spirit.

Each person's soul, or spiritual power, comes specially from God, but not by God's intervening and putting something in us from the outside. Our soul does not exist before we do as a person. Each person's soul is a special "aspect" of God's continuing creation of the universe—an individual spiritual power that comes about by the evolutionary process that God began, working itself out in each of us. In the thinking of the great priest-paleontologist

Teilhard de Chardin, and others, the human soul first came about at the critical point of evolution when a primate became able to reflect on itself—and hence became human, free, and immortal, able to think and choose, however primitively, and to relate to others and to God.

Each of us is specially related to God in a unique way. We might sometimes wonder, "How can the infinite God be concerned about me?" And yet he is, in a relationship with each one of us that is most intimate and will never be duplicated. The mystics say that God calls each of us by a secret name, lovingly, constantly, intimately.

Christ's great teaching is that because of our soul we will go on living forever after death. Before Christ came, humankind could not have the certainty of this immortality that he brought. He stated emphatically, "Truly, truly, I say to you, whoever keeps my word will never see death" (John 8, 51). The *Catechism of the Catholic Church* calls the soul "the seed of eternity we bear within ourselves" (34).

Humankind generally has believed in some sort of survival after death. Our instincts and desires lead us to yearn for this perfection of happiness. "Unless humans are immortal the universe is a stairway leading nowhere," said Plato. If death completely destroys the human personality, then the peak of creation as we know it is left unfinished. God would be like a half-witted artist, amusing himself with creatures that have no ultimate meaning, creating people and wiping them out. But God's whole revelation of himself is that he is good, just, and loving.

Historian Arnold Toynbee summed up human belief in a personal immortality in the face of modern unbelievers: "For human beings who have once tasted the hope of personal immortality, the loss of this hope takes much of the light out of life. . . . If I have lost a dearly beloved wife or husband or child or parent, what consolation is it to me that the sacred rights of the community have been vindicated, or that a spaceman has landed on the moon? . . . Collective human triumphs are very fine, but they do not bring the dead back to life, and do not console me for my human losses. . . . "

Each of us is responsible for what happens to us after death. Though our genetic inheritance as well as our environment may impinge on our freedom, all of us are basically free in God's image, and God will never interfere with our freedom. At the end of our life we will have to give an account of it—of the good we have done and the evil as well—in perfect honesty, before God, without any deception or delusion. Christ reminds us pointedly, "What will it profit them to gain the whole world and forfeit their life?" (Mark 8, 36).

Each year on Ash Wednesday it is a Catholic custom to have our foreheads marked with ashes by the Church's minister, who says, "Remember that you are dust and to dust you shall return." It is a striking reminder at the beginning of the forty days' Lenten penance that our material body is perishable and we should live for immortality.

In God's plan all people are brothers and sisters, one human family, working and sharing together. The story of our common first parents makes clear that we are all essentially the same and all have a right to share in the world's goods. Discrimination and prejudice insert themselves into humankind later as a result of sin.

God is continually creating. Rather than considering creation as something over and done with, we should think of it as a process that is continually developing, something like a magnificent painting that is gradually taking form and will be complete only at the end of time.

God's plan is for us to be "cocreators" with him, to develop our world in partnership with him. Thus God said, "Let them have dominion over the fish of the sea. . . . Be fruitful and multiply and fill the earth and subdue it. . . . " It is becoming increasingly apparent that God so loves us that he associates us most intimately and powerfully with himself and his works. We, by our achievements in making a better world, work "in the presence of God" to carry out the plan for the perfection of all things that he has left us to develop.

Today we are realizing that we must be respectful of the rest of creation, attentive to nature's balance, to preserving rather than exploiting nature and careful in using our growing powers to "improve" on it. We especially realize that when we abuse nature it is to our own ultimate detriment.

All of creation, then, is interrelated and interdependent. We humans are a part of creation, as well as at its peak. Our "dominion" over inanimate and other living beings is not absolute, says the *Catechism of the Catholic Church*, but must be limited by a concern for the quality of life of our neighbor, including generations to come: "It requires a religious respect for the integrity of creation" (2415).

Regarding animals, the *Catechism* says further that while experimentation on them is morally acceptable since it contributes to the welfare of human lives, "it is contrary to human dignity" to cause them to suffer or die needlessly. It is also "unworthy" of us to spend money on animals that should as a priority go to the relief of human misery (2417–18).

Love is the whole reason for creation, for us, and for everything that exists. Experience tells us that goodness tends to diffuse itself, that a truly good person tends to share happiness, to show love to others. God's revelation of himself, we shall see, is that he is limitless love and goodness. Thus he is impelled by his very nature to share his happiness, the happiness of loving on a level unimaginable to us—and so he creates in order to share his love. The universe gives us a glimpse of his beauty, and the height of human love a tiny taste of his love for us.

OTHER WORLDS, ANGELS, AND DEVILS

In our space age, humankind has become aware that it is only a tiny part of a vast universe. Other creatures, angels, are mentioned numerous times in Scripture. Our society today has seen a remarkable revival of interest in them.

Angels, in Catholic tradition, are good spirits who worship God, act as his messengers, and guard and pray for us. As intermediaries or messengers between God and us, they were conceived of as moving with great swiftness, and thus are often pictured as winged (cf. Revelation 12, 11–12; Psalm 103, 20).

The story of the angels, as traditionally conceived, is that God created them and gave them great happiness; he offered them an opportunity to show their gratitude to him, and in return he would give them even greater happiness in heaven. But some of them, led by Lucifer, or the devil, ungratefully refused to love God, and in fact wanted to take over God's position in heaven. Fixed forever on evil, they were relegated to hell, the state of eternal suffering and separation from God (cf. Revelation 12, 7–9; Isaiah 14, 12ff.).

The concept of demons came originally from the religions of cultures surrounding the Jews. Belief in a supreme evil spirit came late into Jewish beliefs. Called the devil, from the Greek *diabolos,* a translation of the Hebrew "Satan," meaning accuser, he is seen early on as a kind of prosecutor, accusing us before God of our sins. Later he becomes one enticing us to sin.

Today theology is examining in more depth the place of angels and devils in our world. They are part of the biblical milieu and its story of God's revelation. As elsewhere in the story, mythology plays a part here, especially regarding angelic forms, numbers, varieties, and such.

For some today, angels can be guiding, comforting presences—as the devil is a deceitful, disruptive one. Whatever their form and function they are finite creatures of God, as are we, and are not beings that rival God in producing good or evil in our world.

In a time of simpler religious belief, the devil became for some a convenient, excusing cause of their own sins. And yet it is hard to dismiss the reality of an evil, superhuman intelligence, so firmly rooted is it in the long tradition and liturgy of the Church, and in the experience of many individuals—as well as perhaps influencing the massive evils of our own day, such as the Holocaust, the Cambodian genocide, and the "ethnic cleansing" in the former Yugoslavia, among others.

"Possession" is the taking over of a person's body by the devil or evil spirits; "obsession" is the inhabiting of a place or objects by them. Many such cases can be explained naturally, as parapsychology particularly has shown. For some theologians today, possession is simply the coalescing of the very real evil that proceeds from humans, concentrated in a certain person or place, and the ritual of exorcism ("driving out the evil spirit[s]") opposes this with God's all-powerful love. When the gospels tell of Christ driving out evil spirits, we today might speak of epilepsy or mental illness.

In any event, the concept of angelic creatures has served to bridge the gap between God and humankind and to remind us of unseen spiritual realities, the dangers of sin, and of God's ever-present help, which overcomes any "power" of darkness (cf. 1 Corinthians 15, 24). Also, today, when we face the possibilities of life in space, references to angels should remind us how little we really know of God's creation.

Obviously, then, there could be other rational creatures in the universe. They, too, would have been created by God and be loved and cared for by him. They would show forth other aspects of his infinite wisdom and love, perhaps some that humankind cannot. If there are such, it would surely be good for us to reach out lovingly toward them, for the same loving God would have made us all in some sense brothers and sisters.

Contemplating the possibility of humans one day standing face-to-face with other rational creatures should make us realize how ridiculous are our petty human divisions, our wars, and other conflicts. Much of the science fiction of our time has attempted to tell us this. At any rate, our concern in this book is with God's revelation to us in this world, staggering and limitless in itself.

DAILY LIVING: WORSHIPING OUR CREATOR

When we realize that God is our Creator and that we are completely dependent on him, our most natural feelings are of awe and reverence and awareness of our nothingness before him. From ancient times humans have always felt this way before the vast mystery of God. We want to know more about God, to pay him homage, and yet we know how very limited we are.

Worship is the way we express our feelings toward God and try to be united with him. Just as a child expresses dependence on and love for her or his human mother and father, and desires to be with them, so it is natural for us to express our feelings toward God. Worship comes from "worthship," showing what God is worth to us, how we revere, need, and love him.

And as it is unnatural for a daughter or son to ignore a good parent, so it is unnatural for us to ignore God, who gives us all we have and who, unlike any human parent, is continually there for us. Not being able to express how we feel about God can leave us, in an often indefinable way, unfulfilled, yearning, restless, searching on a very profound level.

We humans have the ability to respond to God's love. The rest of creation—to the extent we know it—cannot experience God's love as we do. We are free to accept his love and to love in return.

God loves each of us infinitely, intimately, personally, with all-powerful love, and he wants our personal love in return. He has an intimate, loving interest in each of us. Christ says, "Why even the hairs of your head are all numbered" (Luke 12, 7).

Instead of an infinite number of possible people, God created you and me, and he guides us through life to an endless eternity with himself. Each of us is loved uniquely and each of us has a unique contribution: we can love God and we can give love to the universe in a way no one else can. Worship gradually makes us aware of God's incredible, tender, personal love.

We can worship God by ourselves, silently honoring him in our thoughts. Worship must be interior and sincere, or else it is a mockery: "They who worship must worship in spirit and truth," says Christ (John 4, 24).

It is also natural to express our worship with others, as anyone in love will openly express feelings about his or her beloved. We are members of one human family, and it is as natural to join with others in worship as in any meaningful experience.

We worship, then, as full human beings when we read, speak, sing, stand, sit, or kneel in reverence. And we join with all God's creation in worship, and so we use things such as water, oil, fire, stone, bread and wine, branches of trees, ashes, and so on. "And God saw everything that he had made and behold, it was very good" (Genesis 1, 31).

Ceremonies or rituals of worship are signs that express our spiritual feelings. A handshake is a simple ceremony; a person seeing it knows from this sign that two people are friends. A kiss between husband and wife is a sign of their love: done frequently it can be a ritual between them that has deep meaning. So, too, religious ceremonies and rituals are the Church's "sign language" expressing our beliefs. Each time we take part in them we deepen our beliefs.

Some will feel closer to God while alone, perhaps when out amid nature's wonders, when listening to music, and so on. God is infinite beauty, and when we enter into things of beauty we are being drawn to him. Some feel God's presence more in these moments than in church, in humankind's organized religious assemblies. They may find formal worship difficult, meaningless.

These should then seek God where they can find him—but they should also try to appreciate the meaning of religious worship because one's personal contacts with God can remain vague and meaningless unless one seeks God in union with others. Conversely, a formal worship might become a delusion unless it is interior and sincere.

We must remember that if we are to approach the infinite God (even if we are not sure an infinite one is there) we must do so in a reverent setting. We would certainly prepare well for an interview with a president or other important person. Yet we often casually, sporadically approach the infinite God—and then are surprised when nothing comes of it. Worship should be something regular, consistent, given a special time and place in our life.

Christians believe that God has shown us a way to join together and worship him. As people in love want to show their love in the best possible way, so people have always wanted to worship God adequately. Our conviction is that God has come to our aid and told us how. Catholics believe that the Mass, given us by Christ himself, is a special way God has given us to worship him.

Worship, then, is an integral part of the study of Catholic Christianity. The official public worship of the Catholic Church is called the sacred liturgy. To aid this presentation from now on, appropriate ceremonies of the liturgy will be noted in sections called **"In the Liturgy."**

SOME SUGGESTIONS FOR . . .

DISCUSSION

Does the use of myths in religion make sense?

What, for you, is the most moving in the Bible's account of creation? What is not?

Are angels a reality for you? Is the demonic, the devil?

How does the mystic teaching that God calls each of us by a secret name strike you?

A scientist at a meeting of Catholic university faculty said that in our technological age we have lost our sense of awe, wonder, and mystery. How are you best aware of God's wondrous presence in creation?

What do you think of the Christian notion of humankind's exalted, eternal place in the universe?

FURTHER READING

- • *Harper's Bible Commentary,* ed. Mays (HarperSanFrancisco, 1988)—A superb, thirteen-hundred-page, chapter-and-verse explanation of the whole Bible that can be used with any English translation; it has an excellent introduction to the Bible and to each book. It is cross-referenced with *Harper's Bible Dictionary* (HarperSanFrancisco, rev. ed., 1996).

- • *Reading the Old Testament,* Boadt (Paulist Press, 1984)—An excellent introduction to both the setting of the Old Testament and its various books.

- • *How to Interpret the Bible,* Montague (Liturgical Press, 1982)—This seven-page "gem" is a simple yet very informative guide for beginners.

- • *How to Understand the Bible,* Langenbrunner (Catholic Update 0382, St. Anthony Messenger Press)—A very brief, excellent guide to the way Scripture scholars work.

- • • *The Universe, God, Science, and the Human Person,* Ford (Twenty-third Publications, 1987)—An excellent treatment of the subjects given in the title and a fine overall view of God's creation, set in a scientific context.

- • • *Science and Religion: From Conflict to Conversation,* Haught (Paulist Press, 1995)—In a very fine presentation, a theologian and writer in the area of science reflects on the conflicts as well as the agreements between scientists and religious believers.

- • • *Gaia and God: An Ecofeminist Theology of Earth Healing,* Ruether (HarperSanFrancisco, 1992)—A veteran Catholic feminist theologian compares three creation stories in the light of modern science and, with ecological sensitivity, sees all life as interrelated from its origin.

- • • *The Body of God: An Ecological Theology,* McFague (Fortress Press, 1993)—Another ecologically sensitive view of creation by a mainstream feminist theologian: it sees creation as "organic," with individuality and differences as well as interrelatedness and interdependence among everything that is.

•• *The Divine Milieu* and *The Hymn of the Universe,* De Chardin
  (Harper & Row, 1967)—For an open, intuiting mind these books can
  be experiences, sharing a vision with an outstanding Christian, scientist, and mystic.

PERSONAL REFLECTION

I might make some private, sincere act of worship each day.

This Sunday, the Lord's day, I might join with others in worshiping God.

Each Sunday Catholics worship by taking part in the Mass, and
everyone is welcome to come and take part. When one first attends, it is
natural to be somewhat confused by the ceremonies, the priest's clothing,
and so on. These will be explained later.

Since the Mass is so central to Catholicism, and since it takes time to
familiarize oneself with it, we recommend that those seriously studying
Catholicism begin to attend Mass.

If you wish to attend, you might ask a Catholic friend to accompany
you. You might stand, sit, or kneel when everyone else does. Or, if you
wish, just sit and watch—or read and sing along from the booklets or program sheets usually provided.

**Those in an inquiry/precatechumenate or catechumenate pro-
gram** might attend with someone who could later be their sponsor or
godparent. Doing this, of course, implies no commitment whatsoever to
join the Church. Chapter 13 and the appendix, on the Rite of Christian
Initiation of Adults, tell of this in greater detail.

One might say the Lord's Prayer with the congregation. It is the basic
and central Christian prayer (cf. p. 10).

❧ 3 ❧

God's Gift of Himself and Our Rejection of Him

What is God's plan for us? How do we usually respond to God? Why are we drawn to sinful things and actions of which we are ashamed? How does God help us overcome our weaknesses?

GOD'S GREAT GIFT AND HIS DESIRE FOR HUMANKIND

People in love want to share their happiness with the ones they love. A man in love with a woman wants to be with her to make her happy. God loves us. He made us to be happy with him in heaven forever.

But we could not exist for a moment in God's presence, much less speak with him and love him. We would be annihilated by even a glimpse of him. So God does something for us, to enable us to live with and love him forever. He gives us a great gift: **Read Matthew 13, 44–46.**

Christ was trying to describe something wonderful when he spoke of this "hidden treasure," the "pearl of great value" for which a man sells all he has. It is the greatest gift that God can give us, sanctifying grace.

Sanctifying grace is God's life and love within us, God's presence loving each of us. It is the way God lives within us and possesses us—the intimate, personal relationship of God to me. It is God himself giving me his friendship, his love, his very life—so we call it God's grace-presence within us.

"Sanctifying" means to make holy or like God. This new life truly makes us like God. "Grace" means a gift—we have no right to it whatsoever.

To understand this, consider the various personal relationships we have with others: Some we know slightly, as mere acquaintances; with others our mutual appreciation is growing, and with yet others we have a deep love, perhaps the love of friendship or that of a man and a woman, sharing love, strength, and inspiration on a profound level. There is also the relationship of parents to their children—a mother, for instance, communicating life to the child within her. Writers today speak of relationships as "I-it" and "I-thou," according to their meaningfulness. By grace we are most profoundly a "thou" in the eyes of the infinite God.

Sanctifying grace is the closest possible relationship between God and his human creatures. It is God's gift of himself in love to us—the closest possible love. It is also a love that gives us life itself, not just human life but the fullest possible sharing in the limitless life of God.

An orphan's adoption by a millionaire happens only rarely in our world, but by sanctifying grace the infinite God "adopts" us to live with him and share his wealth, his very life forever. "See what love the Father has given us, that we should be called children of God; and so we are" (1 John 3, 1; cf. Galatians 4, 7). We are "born again" into this new life (John 3, 5), and have a completely new relationship with God, that of a son to his Father (Romans 8, 14–17); we are a "new creation" (2 Corinthians 5, 17).

This presence has been called "supernatural" life, that is, greater than our ordinary natural life, a sharing in God's own life, beyond this life in heaven. Through sanctifying grace we actually begin the life of heaven here on earth; we can begin to know and love God person-to-person and be loved by him.

This is a living love, a relationship that grows and develops as any love must—or else it dies. God's love continually presses us. We either grow in it or we fall back. We shall see that this love, constantly increasing, never ceases but grows for eternity.

We cannot normally "feel" grace within us. But we shall see that Christ gave us ways to be sure of having this life-presence.

This most personal love of God for each of us has many wonderful aspects: his condescension, continually open to me, and indeed desirous of my constant communication with him; his mercy, continually forgiving me; his protection, unceasingly doing good things, somehow arranging the plan of the universe for me; his unending faithfulness to me, no matter how I treat him—unless I reject him entirely, and even then he wants to return to me.

We know how even a human love relationship can transform people. Often people's lives are made or broken by whether or not they have someone who truly loves them. As love develops, one is raised beyond oneself, taking on more and more the characteristics of one's friend or beloved.

If human love can so change one, we can imagine what God's continual look of love must be doing to us. Unfortunately, we are hardly ever aware of this because it is so staggering, so beyond human comprehension. An unshielded look into an atomic pile could blind or kill, such is its power of radiation; one in grace has such interior beauty that if God ever permitted a glimpse of the person as he or she really is, the beholder would be torn apart in ecstasy.

God's grace-presence gives us the power to transform everything we do into eternal happiness for ourselves and others. It expands us, giving us the possibility of life beyond our wildest dreams and enabling us to share this with others. It is as if everything we touched turned into gold—except that by grace we can turn our every contact into unending, unimaginable happiness for all.

God's plan was that humankind would develop so that we could have his grace-presence, grow in it, and be with him forever in heaven. He would send his Son, Jesus Christ, to earth when we were ready, to fill us with a superabundance of his grace-presence. But we humans are weak, and God's plan now had to take account of our hesitancy, our inability to trust ourselves to this infinite love.

HUMANKIND'S REJECTION OF GOD'S LOVE

When we honestly face ourselves, we are aware of our failings. We are all drawn to do things we later regret. We hurt ourselves and others, even those we love. This is sin, a dreary and inevitable fact over which humans have puzzled for centuries.

The ancient Hebrews also pondered the fact that all people are sinners. But unlike their pagan contemporaries—who often thought of the gods as cruel, arbitrary, jealous of humans—they could not believe that God had originally formed us in such a state of wretchedness and sin. It would be unreconcilable with God's whole revelation of himself as good and loving.

The biblical author looked back to the beginning of the human race and set down the story of how people had sinned from their origin. The background of the story we recall from chapter 2 of Genesis. The first humans are pictured in a luxurious garden, with power over the rest of creation; man and woman are intimately united, of "one flesh." "The man and his wife were both naked and were not ashamed," that is, they have complete confidence, openness, esteem for each other. Above all they are intimate friends of God, who speaks to them with love and concern. Then comes tragedy: **Read Genesis, chapter 3.**

The first couple chose their own way over God's. They had to make a choice like everyone who was to follow them: to give themselves to God or to rely on their own human power. They chose their own way and rejected God's proffered love. "In one person all have sinned," says St. Paul. We all are affected by this sin, and in turn sin ourselves.

This story is symbolic, mythical, so its precise details are unimportant. We do not know what the sinful action of the first humans actually was. The serpent is a symbol of evil, some malevolent power outside of man; the serpent was also worshiped as a deity by some of the Israelites' neighbors. Eating the forbidden fruit signifies humankind's choosing its own way over God's. The effects of this sin can be attested to by the experience of anyone who has ever done serious wrong.

Is God revealing that Adam and Eve were perfect specimens of humankind? No, we need only believe that they had true human liberty. Is God saying that they were created in a state of sublime happiness and grace from which there was a "fall"? This has been the traditional view, but today many theologians also view the biblical imagery as referring to a future fulfillment in Christ

The worst effect of their sin is that man and woman no longer have confident access to God's friendship. They are pictured as hiding from God and are finally put out of the garden. They also notice they are naked: they have lost trust in their fellow humans, have difficulty communicating, and are subject to social conventions and shame. Man's labor and woman's motherhood—their typical roles for the author—are made difficult, full of anxieties. Woman's cooperation with man becomes servitude. They no longer have access to the tree of life: death now comes as a brutal, painful experience. Humankind's struggle against the serpent, against evil, becomes constant and difficult.

Work has become more burdensome because of this sin, but work itself is natural, necessary, and our privilege, fashioning the universe as "cocreators" with God himself. After the first sin we read, "Cursed is the ground because of you; in toil shall you eat of it all the days of your life . . . in the sweat of your face you shall eat bread." But from the beginning humans were to work with God, to "fill the earth and subdue it. . . . " It is our attitude toward work that sin changes.

The whole physical world has somehow become involved in humankind's sin. Our "dominion" over nature is now burdensome and often exploitative. But the universe is still good, and as we shall see, redeemed humankind must work with God to preserve it and bring it to perfection.

This description of sin is a masterful presentation of the way in which we all encounter evil: the temptation, first rejected, then dallied with—then the fall. Our sin, too, is basically one of pride, trying to "be like God," putting our judgment over his. Afterward we are ashamed, but God seeks us out through our unrelenting conscience. We must face the consequences of our sin. Yet God is always willing to give us a fresh start, promising that we can overcome the serpent of evil with his help.

Why did God let humankind sin? Why did he not make us so we could not sin? We have no complete answer, but perhaps, analogously to human love, we could not enjoy the reward of God's love unless we knew that we had done our part to freely earn it. This means there must be the possibility of not earning it, of not loving, of sinning, and this is what we humans used our freedom to do.

Further, consider what sin costs God. What is more incredible than that God should subject himself to continual refusals, possibly an eternal refusal, by his creatures? To tolerate such a rebuff God must infinitely love and desire humans just as they are. Sin thus proves God's great love, respect, and solicitude for each of us.

This is the heart of the matter: God's incredible love wishes to exalt us to himself. But we must freely respond to his love and cooperate in his plan for us. He allows our disobedience because he respects our freedom, our dignity as a person, our true lovableness. No matter how we strike out at him he still respects and loves us. Even when we do not respect ourselves, the infinite God does.

The evil of sin must also be seen in perspective. God puts us on earth so we can freely choose his love, and this is such a brief moment of choice when compared to eternity! It is like asking a child to spend a few minutes alone in a dark room, and in return giving the child a lifetime of tremendous joy—except that for our brief trust God gives us eternal joy.

As humankind developed, we continued to sin, and each generation was affected by the faults of its predecessors. The story of Cain and Abel ("sons" of Adam and Eve in the sense that any of us are) shows how evil humans could become: **Read Genesis 4, 1-18.** In this story we see the basic sin in all human relationships: selfish individualism. "Am I my brother's keeper?" should sound familiar to all of us.

The story of the flood and Noah's Ark (Genesis, chapters 6-9) is another symbolic story showing the widespread evil of humans and how God continued to bless the few who served him. After the flood, the ages of people decrease, an ancient literary device to show humankind's gradual moral deterioration. Then comes the incident of the tower of Babel (Genesis 11, 1-9), another symbolic story showing how humans tried to defy God, ended in confusion, and brought disastrous effects upon future generations. As time passed, Adam's sin went on snowballing.

This, then, is original sin: the effect of the sin of the first humans plus the accumulated sin of humankind. We all inherit this accumulation of humankind's defects, its lack of love, its ignorance and corruption. Each of us adds to this common burden of sin by his or her own sinful acts. Because of it we have a proneness to sin ("concupiscence") passed on from parents to children.

Just as heredity and environment transmit certain defects to an infant, so everyone from the womb grows in a sinful moral environment. We experience not only love but what it is to be unloved, and therefore we will be unloving in return. We unconsciously adopt the unloving attitudes and values of our society—for example, the pervading notion that money and material success are the important goals of one's life.

This "sin" is "original," then, because it afflicts all of us at our origin—as well as having its inception at the origin of the human race. It is "sin" for us only in an analogous sense because we have not willed it. It is part of our original state or condition rather than an action of ours—a tendency, despite our basic goodness, toward alienation from God and others, a proneness to willful sins of our own.

FACING OUR SINS

From this story of sin we see that our sins are rejections of God's love and of our fellow human beings. They are refusals to respond, to let ourselves be loved by God. Adam's sin is typical: God's love surrounds us in countless ways, and to sin we must hide from him, turn away from his loving care. In doing this we also turn away from our fellow humans. We turn in on ourselves, choosing our way over God's and our neighbor's.

We all have a conscience that must be followed, by which we know right and wrong. Our mind judges that some actions are good, and therefore should be done, and other things are wrong and must be avoided. If we are not true to these judgments, we are untrue to ourself and can never expect real happiness.

> *Conscience is really our center of awareness, the innermost "place" within us where God leads us to awareness of ourselves and others.* It is where God opens my awareness to look honestly at myself in relation to others—the needs of others, my effect on others, my duty to others in love. The more I allow God to "come through," and the more I am in touch with this core of myself, the more sensitive I will be to others, to their dignity, needs, and hopes. Then, hopefully, I will follow my conscience-awareness and be more loving toward them, and toward God.

Our conscience must be guided by God because only he is infinitely wise and sees what is truly right and wrong. Just as we make mistakes in other things, so we sometimes form a mistaken sense of morality. We must investigate to make sure that our conscience agrees with God's loving plan for us. We shall see that he has given us concrete moral guides, particularly through Christ's teaching. Reflection on Christ's teaching through the centuries has shown us certain things about this:

Some sins are worse than others because they deliberately reject love and cut us off from God's grace-presence and our fellow humans. In a serious matter we might freely and deliberately choose to reject God and our fellow humans, to follow our own selfish way. Obviously we should avoid all sin, but particularly serious sin of this sort. Only when we are truly sorry and are forgiven can we enjoy God's grace-presence once more. Later we shall consider this further.

These normally are serious sins against love: deliberately refusing to open oneself to God; seriously injuring another physically or with slander; refusing to help another in serious need; serious offenses of sexual immorality, scandal, stealing, drunkenness, refusing to use our talents, prejudice or discrimination against others.

Each sin of ours, and especially serious sin, makes it harder for us to know God's truth and follow it. Obviously the grossly immoral person—one seeking primarily one's own pleasure, power, or wealth—will never be able to accept God's teachings. Most people, of course, are not such deliberate sinners. But even their occasional sins make it harder for them to accept God's teachings and follow them.

Each sin of ours adds to the burden of sin in the world and blocks the spread of God's love to our fellow humans. Each sin causes us to draw away from others; we fail to do our part to spread love and happiness.

GOD'S PLAN OF GREATER LOVE

Though humankind went on sinning, God did not abandon our race. We might have expected God to reject humankind, considering history's accumulated sin—the endless wars, crimes, cruelty, and terrible injustices that we have inflicted on ourselves. Some philosophers and observers of the human scene have said that, if there is a God, he must have long since left us to our own devices.

But God is limitless love and compassion—he sees in each of us a goodness, beauty, and potential that we are unable to see in ourselves. If he looks at us with sadness, his look of hope and love and desire for us is far stronger.

God used humankind's sins to show even greater love. He promised that he would save us from our sins. His promise to save us is described as the curse that he put on the serpent; there will be a constant battle with evil, and it can hurt us, but eventually it will be overcome by the offspring of the woman: "I will put enmity between you and the woman, and between your seed and her seed; he shall bruise your head, and you shall bruise his heel" (Genesis 3, 15).

Then God gradually unfolded his plan: Despite our sin, and in fact because of it, God would send his own Son into the world to give us his grace-presence and love beyond measure. Christ, the offspring of the woman, would crush the power of evil and bring us overwhelming grace. This is why each year during the Easter vigil service the Church says of Adam's sin: "O happy fault, that merited such a redeemer!" Out of the great evil of sin God has brought far greater good.

IN THE LITURGY

The texts of the Mass are filled with allusions to our sinfulness and our need of grace: "I confess to almighty God," "Lord, have mercy, Christ, have mercy," "Forgive us our trespasses," "Lamb of God, you take away the sins of the world, have mercy on us," and others.

DAILY LIVING: GOD'S CONSTANT HELPS

Because we are weak and prone to sin we need God's constant help. By his grace-presence God continually gives us many promptings to know what to do and strength to do it. These constant helps are called his actual graces.

Actual graces are the continuous ways in which God's grace-presence prompts us to do good or avoid evil. They come for particular "acts." They are the innumerable little ways in which God within us makes his presence known. If we are sensitive to them, we will recognize them many times a day: a prompting comes to do some good act, to pray, to help someone, to avoid a sinful situation, or to realize more clearly a truth about God or ourselves, to see another with greater appreciation, and so on.

Our every good thought or action is initiated and supported by God's actual graces. We cannot do a thing to reach heaven without his help. "For it is God who of his good pleasure works in you both the will and the performance" (Philippians 2, 13).

God continually gives these promptings, makes these overtures, even to those not yet related to him by sanctifying grace. He constantly and lovingly "prods" even the worst sinners. He invites them in all sorts of ways to make their free commitment of love to him, to let him possess them and love them by his grace-presence.

God gives us these helps particularly if we ask for them, and even more so if we are determined to follow them when he gives them. We need much prompting from God's actual graces, especially as we study religion, to know and follow his truth sincerely and courageously.

SOME SUGGESTIONS FOR . . .

DISCUSSION

Can you grasp something of the transforming power of God's grace-presence within us?

Can you understand the snowballing of sin down through history?

Does it make sense that sin would inhibit our knowing God and his desires for us? What have you found most effective in dealing with your particular proneness to sin?

Can you recall some instances of God's actual graces coming into your daily life?

FURTHER READING

- •• *Original Sin: Two Major Trends in Contemporary Roman Catholic Reinterpretation,* Vandervelde (University Press of America, 1981)— For those who wish to look at the history and development of this teaching.
- • *Original Blessing,* Fox (Bear & Co., 1983)—A different interpretation of the human condition stressing God's blessing of humankind rather than its sinfulness; this author has some devoted followers.

PERSONAL REFLECTION

Sin from the start began "snowballing," cut our whole race off from God, and brought the horrors of death, wars, crime, cruelty, and untold suffering into our world. This is the terrible, cumulative effect of sin. My personal sins can also cut me off from God and can affect many others, causing unhappiness and pain of which I may not even be aware.

My sins also make it more difficult, and sometimes impossible, to know and believe in Christ's teachings. Christ said, "Anyone who resolves to do the will of God will know whether the teaching is from God . . . " (John 7, 17). I should honestly and sincerely think over my sins, especially my serious sins—perhaps during my evening prayer. I will determine to do all in my power to avoid them, especially the one that does the most harm to others.

ण⠀

4

God's Plan Unfolds in the Old Testament

Has God ever shown his concern with human affairs? Can we see God's plan at work anywhere in history? What is the unique importance of the Jewish people?

THE GREAT PEOPLE OF THE COVENANT

The story of humankind after the first sin is a dreary one of continuing infidelity to God. Sin seems to dominate everywhere. But God is silently at work, and when people are ready, he steps into human history. He selects a tiny group of people and with them begins his new plan for the salvation of the world.

The Old Testament tells the story of God's relationship with his people before the coming of Jesus Christ. It is also called the Hebrew Scriptures because it tells of God's special revelation of himself to the Hebrews, later called the Jewish people. It is concerned with only this one people, the Jews. Other nations are mentioned only incidentally. It does not even give a complete history of the Jewish people, but only of the events that directly concern God's plan.

We should note especially that the main themes of the Old Testament look forward to completion in the New Testament. God's people of the Old Testament are the forerunners and basis of his people of the New Testament, Christ's Church. Vatican Council II said this clearly and gratefully:

The Church of Christ acknowledges that . . . the beginnings of her faith and her election are found already among the patriarchs, Moses and the prophets . . . that all who believe in Christ are included in Abraham's call, and that the salvation of the Church is mysteriously foreshadowed by the chosen people's exodus. . . . The Church, therefore, cannot forget that she received the revelation of the Old Testament through the people with whom God in his inexpressible mercy concluded the ancient covenant. Nor can she forget that she draws sustenance from the root of that well-cultivated olive tree onto which have been grafted the wild shoots, the Gentiles (*Declaration on the Relationship of the Church to Non-Christian Religions,* no. 4).

We should try to "enter into" the events of this story, since it was written as much for us as for the people of two or three thousand years ago. It is the Christian conviction that this story is meant for everyone, that it is the high point of humankind's relationship with God. It tells of the great events that have profoundly influenced our human situation and particularly our Western civilization. If we read of these events sympathetically and openly, trying to understand their meaning, they can tell us much about the meaning of our life and our relationship with God and other people. Countless millions have become deeper, better human beings through this story—and so can we.

These events are part of an epic story or saga, a combination of actual history and symbolic stories or myths. Most scholars today hold that while these patriarchs and matriarchs are historical figures, most of the stories are mythical, transformed in hindsight to convey truths about God's revelation.

God stepped into human history by making himself known to Abraham, the first of the patriarchs, about nineteen hundred years before Christ. Abraham was probably a raiser of livestock, the leader of his seminomadic tribe, living at Ur (in modern Iraq). God changed his name from Abram and made him great promises: **Read Genesis 12, 1-3.**

God then made a covenant—an agreement or testament—with Abraham. A covenant is the ancient way by which two parties solemnly bound themselves together. It was a contract, a promise, or pledge, and those making it called down punishment on themselves if they should break it.

A covenant was made by some visible sign or ceremony signifying the internal union of the parties concerned. When Abraham asked for a sign of the covenant, God told him to cut in half several animals and lay the pieces opposite each other. Then, "as the sun was setting, Abram fell into a deep sleep; and terror came upon him, a great darkness. The Lord said to Abram, 'Know for certain . . . ' [and] when the sun had set and it was dark, a smoking fire pot and a flaming torch passed between the pieces. On that day the Lord made a covenant with Abram . . . " (Genesis 15, 8ff.).

The ceremony or ritual was sometimes, as in Abraham's case, for both parties to pass between the divided parts of an animal; sometimes there was a shedding of blood, considered the sacred principle of life by the ancients; sometimes it was an exchange of gifts, or eating and drinking together the "covenant meal."

Today we often make agreements in this way: a treaty signed by representatives of two nations; a business contract concluded at a meal and then signed by the parties; a bet made with a handshake; in particular, an agreement based on love, such as an exchange of wedding vows symbolized by an exchange of rings.

The covenant with Abraham is described in Genesis: Read Genesis 17, 1-12. By this covenant God promised Abraham great posterity, a fruitful land, and extraordinary blessings on his descendants and through them on all humankind. Abraham and his descendants for their part were to serve God and have faith in his promises. Circumcision was to be the sign of the covenant.

This is the first great and extraordinary sign of God's love: he binds himself by a covenant with humankind—and, further, he is faithful to it even when we are not. Now a new relationship of intimacy, a truly personal union, begins between God and us. We see how great is our worth and dignity to God—a unique concept when compared to other beliefs in which the soul often loses its identity, and where the individual means little.

Abraham was outstanding for his faith in God, so much so that he was ready to obey God's command to sacrifice his only son, Isaac. His obedience began to reverse the trend begun by Adam's disobedience:

"Take your son, your only son Isaac, whom you love, and go to the land of Moriah, and offer him there as a burnt offering upon one of the mountains of which I shall tell you. . . . " Abraham built an altar there, and laid the wood in order, and bound his son Isaac, and laid him on the altar, upon the wood. Then Abraham put forth his hand, and took the knife to slay his son. But the angel of the Lord called to him from heaven, and said, "Abraham, Abraham." And he said, "Here am I." He said, "Do not lay your hand on the lad or do anything to him; for now I know that you fear God, seeing you have not withheld your son, your only son, from me" (Genesis 22, 2, 9–12).

God's covenant with Abraham was renewed with his son, Isaac, and with his grandson, Jacob, or Israel, from whose twelve sons came the twelve tribes of the Jewish nation. The family had now settled in the land to which God had directed them, present-day Israel. Like Abraham, Jacob's name was changed to fit his new role in God's plan:

And God said to him, "Your name is Jacob; no longer shall your name be called Jacob, but Israel shall be your name." So his name was called Israel. And God said to him, "I am God Almighty: be fruitful and multiply; a nation and a company of nations shall come from you, and kings shall spring from you. The land which I gave to Abraham and Isaac I will give to you, and I will give the land to your descendants after you" (Genesis 35, 10–12).

The Scriptures tell how Joseph, Israel's son, went to Egypt and became a leader of that country. Some Hebrews followed, and they increased in numbers and wealth. But then the Egyptians began to enslave them. God, however, was watching over his people and raised up their greatest leader, Moses, to lead them out of bondage.

Moses was the great Israelite leader chosen by God to deliver his people out of Egypt. We saw earlier his great experience of God, how the Lord came to him in a burning bush and revealed that he was the living God of the patriarchs:

"Do not come near; put off your shoes from your feet, for the place on which you are standing is holy ground." And he said, "I am the God of your father, the God of Abraham, the God of Isaac, and the God of Jacob." And Moses hid his face, for he was afraid to look at God (Exodus 3, 5–6).

Then God gave Moses his mission:

"Say this to the people of Israel, 'The Lord, the God of your fathers, the God of Abraham, the God of Isaac, the God of Jacob, has sent me to you. . . . I have observed you and what has been done to you in Egypt; and I promise that I will bring you up out of the affliction of Egypt, to the land of the Canaanites . . . a land flowing with milk and honey'" (Exodus 3, 15–17).

Moses went to Pharaoh and demanded that he let the Israelites leave Egypt, but was refused. This Pharaoh is thought to be the famous and egotistical Rameses II, whose images cover Egypt and whose mummy can be seen today in the Egyptian National Museum in Cairo. In the records of his reign we find nothing about the Israelites, but we know that Semite slaves worked on his great store cities, and the Israelites at this time were a small, unorganized group, probably scarcely noticed in the continual migrations across Egypt's borders.

After a series of plagues—natural yearly occurrences that could be interpreted as divine interventions—Pharaoh still would not let them go. Finally, God told Moses that on a particular night each Israelite family was to slaughter a lamb, put some of its blood on the doorposts of their houses, and eat it with unleavened bread and bitter herbs: **Read Exodus 12, 1–14.**

This was the Passover or Pasch, begun by the paschal meal. It began the events leading up to the old covenant. Later Christ will eat this meal to begin his new covenant. The story continues, telling in figurative, hyperbolic language (typical of this epic style of writing) of what was probably the death of Pharaoh's firstborn son: **Read Exodus 12, 29–32.**

Saved by the blood of the lamb, the Israelites fled from Egypt and with God's help passed through the waters of the Red Sea—most probably a passage through the marshy "Sea of Reeds" and aided by favorable winds, which later brought the high waters in which Pharaoh's pursuing soldiers were drowned. By this natural event, God again aided his people—and gave a prophetic sign of what his new people would do in Christian baptism, passing through water to salvation and freedom.

This is the Exodus, the deliverance of the Israelites from Egypt. A series of remarkable events that took place over a number of years, it is celebrated as the central event of Jewish history, the striking proof of God's intervention on behalf of his people, and the foundation of their hope that he would one day do so again. Strikingly unlike their pagan neighbors, the Jews retold this greatest event of their history year after year, century after century—and still recount it—as proof of God's intervention on their behalf.

THE MAKING OF THE OLD COVENANT

Free of their enemies, the Israelites now journeyed some three hundred miles through the harsh, debilitating Sinai desert. Finally they came to the Sinai mountains near the tip of the peninsula, a desolate, silent, awesome place even today.

At Mount Sinai, God made his great covenant with the Israelites: Read Exodus 19, 1–6.

This was the old covenant, or Old Testament. Moses is the mediator of this old covenant, a figure of Christ who will mediate the new and perfect covenant. Moses alone can enter God's awesome presence: **Read Exodus 19, 16–25.**

By this covenant the promises made to Abraham and his descendants are extended to all the Israelites who are now made God's own people. Here the straggling, motley, and probably terrified band of ex-slaves are formed into a great people. Circumcision is a sign of their unique destiny.

In return for making the Israelites his own people, God asked them to keep their part of the covenant, summarized in the Ten Commandments. This simple moral code was known throughout the Middle East at that period, particularly in the famous Code of Hammurabi—except that Israel's concept of God, as we shall see, was unique: **Read Exodus 20, 1–17 or see pages 51–52.**

The Ten Commandments were supplemented by a whole set of other laws organizing and administering the life of the people. Thus the first five books of the Old Testament are called the Torah—Hebrew for "the Law"—and much of it is concerned with property and criminal laws, rules of daily prayer, worship and sacrifice, regulations about health and marriage, and so on. It guided every aspect of life, was pondered, debated, and commented upon at length.

The Torah should not be seen as a series of endless regulations, but as it was for the Jews—a way of fulfilling their covenant with God. We will see that Christ condemned abusing it, living by its letter while overlooking its spirit, but he reverenced it as did any devout Jew.

Then Moses "sealed" or accepted the covenant on behalf of the people by a sacrifice culminating in the sprinkling of an animal's blood: Read Exodus 24, 3–8. We have seen that important covenants were often made by some such sign or ceremony. Later Christ will inaugurate the new, perfect covenant by shedding his blood for us in sacrifice.

This is the "church" of the Old Testament, God's people, the Israelites gathered together. This is what "church" originally meant—God's people called together by him, under the authority of their leaders, his representatives, to receive his teaching and show their acceptance of it by sacrifice.

Israel's whole future was to be judged by whether or not she kept this covenant, but almost immediately the people broke it, idolatrously worshiping a golden calf. God pardoned and spared his people through Moses' intercession, after he had fasted for forty days in reparation—here again we see Moses as the savior of his people. These violations of the covenant were to happen repeatedly. After the first enthusiastic acceptance of the covenant the people grew restless, dissatisfied. So God kept them in the desert for a whole generation, toughening and disciplining them until they forgot the "fleshpots" of Egypt.

The Israelites wandered for forty years through the desert, but God gave them many signs of his presence and protection: a cloud during the day, the fire of lightning by night, a discovery of water when they most needed it, and the food of the desert manna tree to sustain them.

By these events, God reveals but also conceals himself, since such events can always admit of a natural explanation. As with the signs of the Exodus—the plagues, passing over the Sea of Reeds, the thunder and lightning and earthquake of Sinai—it takes faith to realize God is acting. God is always a hidden God. "No [one] can see my face and live," he told Moses. And so it is with all his actions through history, and with us today.

But the story of the forming of Israel, and particularly Israel's concept of God, is strikingly unique in history. Most of Israel's culture came from surrounding cultures, but her religion, the heart of her national life, was opposed in every way to that of her neighbors. The surrounding gods were very human, fighting, lustful, often cruel, capricious, and unpredictable, needing to be placated by magic or human sacrifice, whose cults often glorified war, pillage, the degradation of women, incest, and so on.

Israel's God is wholly different from humans, always takes the initiative, fills us with awe, can be neither controlled by magic nor manipulated by sacrifice; he demands our total submission. He is the Lord of all history, but yet is loving, good, always faithful to his people. Israel's unique concept of Yahweh, their God, can be summed up in two poignant passages: **Read Exodus 15, 11-16 and Deuteronomy 7, 6-12.**

> Israel's relationship with God is expressed in the prayer called (from its first word) the "Shema": "Hear, O Israel, the Lord your God is one" (Deuteronomy 6, 4-5). It expresses Israel's monotheism and its realization that its God was God of all creation.

Moses died within sight of the Promised Land, and Joshua was selected by God to lead the people across the Jordan river and into Canaan. They "passed over" the Jordan into the Promised Land. This was the land to which Abraham had been led by God centuries before; today, it is, roughly, the State of Israel or Palestine. Eventually, with God's constant help, they are pictured in epic fashion as conquering the land and dividing it among the twelve tribes. Judges were placed as rulers over the tribes.

> *Some people, reading of the bloody conquest of the Promised Land (the books of Joshua and Judges, apparently divinely authorized in Deuteronomy 20), wonder at the cruel deity portrayed there*—he is certainly infinitely remote from the God of Jesus. Israel thought of its God at this relatively primitive period as a purely nationalistic deity, a God of Battles whose power was chiefly shown in the prosecution of Holy War. God would gradually manage to expand their moral consciousness over the succeeding centuries, and they would get a much different picture of him. But we might well ask today, after two World Wars, Vietnam, and Bosnia, if we are much better.
>
> *Also, when we read of God "punishing" his people, taking "vengeance" on them, and so on,* we should remember that the Hebrews had a strong sense of God being present and involved in their everyday actions and continually

using people and events to bring about his purposes. They would attribute their own sometimes unworthy motives to God or see God behind what we today would call chance or ascribe to human causality.

The Exodus was over. God had kept his promise. He had given the Israelites a home of their own. But they were still unfaithful to him.

The Israelites broke the covenant again and again, but God was always faithful. His people worshiped pagan gods and adopted immoral pagan customs. The Old Testament then portrays God as allowing disasters to come upon them—war, famine, plague, conquest, exile—in order to bring them back to repentance. He continually forgave them and allowed them to renew the covenant.

A touching description of God's love for his unfaithful people is Hosea's tragic story of his marriage with the prostitute Gomer. After the birth of their three children, Gomer takes up with other men, leaves Hosea, and again becomes a prostitute. Because he still loves her, Hosea seeks her out and takes her back. Thus God loves his unfaithful people and takes them back—including us today:

> She decked herself with her rings and jewelry, and went after her lovers, and forgot me, says the Lord. . . . Therefore, behold, I will allure her, and bring her into the wilderness, and speak tenderly to her. . . . And in that day, says the Lord, you will call me "My husband," and no longer will you call me, "My Baal" [false god] (cf. Hosea, chapters 1–3).

IN THE LITURGY

At Mass the first Scripture reading is normally a passage from the Old Testament, recounting some part of this great story for our benefit today.

During the first official eucharistic prayer, the priest asks God to accept our offerings "as once you accepted the gifts of your servant Abel, the sacrifice of Abraham, our father in faith, and the bread and wine offered by your priest Melchisedech."

In the Litany for the Dying, the Church asks Abel, Abraham, and the patriarchs and prophets to pray for us, and then petitions: "Deliver, O Lord, the soul of your servant, as you delivered Abraham from Ur of the

Chaldees . . . as you delivered Isaac from becoming a sacrifice at the hand of his father, Abraham . . . as you delivered Moses from the power of Pharaoh, King of Egypt. . . . "

And in the burial service the Church prays: "May the angels lead you to the bosom of Abraham [heaven]."

During the Easter Vigil Service, the high point of the Church's year, the great Easter hymn is chanted, pointing out the connection between Christ and Moses, and Christ and the paschal lamb:

> Jesus Christ, our Lord, paid to the eternal Father the whole debt of Adam, blotting out the bond that still held us forfeit, with his dear blood. The paschal feast is this! Here the lamb is slain, with whose blood the doors of his faithful people are made holy. This night long ago thou didst rescue the sons of Israel, our fathers, out of Egypt.

DAILY LIVING: THE TEN COMMANDMENTS— RELATING TO GOD AND OUR NEIGHBOR

The Ten Commandments have been a handy summary of morality for Christians as well as Jews through the centuries. There are various ways of numbering them—the traditional Catholic numbering is given here. More important than their numbering—or memorizing them—is entering into their spirit:

They are only a framework, for Christian love carries us far beyond them. But they are ways of fulfilling our covenant of love with God—the first three directly, and the last seven through the love of our neighbor. The following is the essence of the commands of Exodus 20, 1–17:

1. I am the Lord your God. . . . You shall have no other Gods before me. . . .
2. You shall not take the name of the Lord your God in vain. . . .
3. Remember the sabbath day, to keep it holy. . . .
4. Honor your father and your mother. . . .
5. You shall not kill.
6. You shall not commit adultery.
7. You shall not steal.
8. You shall not bear false witness against your neighbor.

9. You shall not covet your neighbor's house; you shall not covet your neighbor's wife.

10. or his manservant, or his maidservant, or . . . anything that is your neighbor's.

Jesus gives this summary of the law: "You shall love the Lord your God with all your heart, and with all your soul, and with all your mind. You shall love your neighbor as yourself" (Matthew 22, 34–40). Jesus picks these summary statements—in Deuteronomy 6, 5 and Leviticus 19, 18—and joins them together. For Jesus, we will see, love is the fulfillment of the law—it is his "new law" that covers all situations and circumstances.

SOME SUGGESTIONS FOR . . .

DISCUSSION

Can you appreciate the naturalness of covenants? Of God making one with humankind?

Does Israel's continually breaking its covenant with God sound personally familiar? Is there one thing you might do, however small, to be more faithful?

Is there a "desert experience" like Israel's of utter needfulness and dependence on God that has happened in your life? In retrospect, might it have been in some way necessary?

Which commandments have particular relevance for you as you journey through life?

FURTHER READING

- • *Reading the Old Testament: An Introduction,* Boadt (Paulist Press, 1984)—An excellent, one-volume companion for a journey through the Old Testament; both scholarly and well written.
- • *Covenant in the Old Testament,* Guinan (Franciscan Herald Press, 1975)—An easily readable, fine treatment of the various covenants in the Old Testament and their significance and meaning for us today.
- • *A Theology of the Old Testament,* McKenzie (University Press of America, 1986)—An excellent study of the Old Testament as the his-

tory of Yahweh's (God's) special people, and their dynamic, living relationship with him.

- *The Man Who Wrestled with God*, Sanford (Paulist Press, 1981)—
  This popular author, a Jungian analyst and Episcopalian priest, skillfully uses significant early stories of the Old Testament to help us arrive today at a well-rounded personhood through our own wrestlings or struggles.

PERSONAL REFLECTION

A "passing over" from slavery and suffering, through the desert, to freedom and happiness was necessary for the Israelites. Later, Christ will accomplish his great work by passing over from suffering and death to life. So anyone who would find God today must undergo suffering in order to enter eternal joy.

In the desert Israel was alone before God: there were no distractions, no places to run and hide. Their decision was whether to live or die. If they wanted to survive, there was only one way: total submission to God's will. Realizing that God alone could save them, Israel enthusiastically accepted his covenant.

Sometimes God must bring us "into the desert," make us realize our total inadequacy, so that we will give ourselves to him. I should ask for the faith to recognize him in my suffering and inadequacies.

5

Priests, Kings, and Prophets Prepare the Way

SACRIFICES, PRIESTS, AND KINGS

After Sinai, God dwelt among his people with an extraordinary familiarity. He was present especially above the Ark of the Covenant, a small gold-covered chest containing the commandments, which was placed in the tabernacle, a portable temple-tent (Exodus, chapters 25–27). From here God communicated with Moses and his other representatives among the people. In this, we have a prelude to our practice of reserving the eucharist, Christ's special presence among us, in the tabernacles of our churches.

As God's people came to know him they worshiped him, to show their feelings toward him, to give themselves to him and be united with him. They wanted to show their recognition that he was their God and to express their obligations to him. As with any growing love, they also wished to be transformed, united with him.

They worshiped God particularly by sacrifice—by publicly offering gifts to him. Just as people have always expressed their feelings toward one another by giving gifts, so they offered gifts to the deity.

The great events of life are celebrated by giving gifts, expressing many things, particularly a desire to be united with one we love. We give birthday presents and wedding gifts, we exchange gifts at Christmas, and so on. Gifts express love, praise, thanks, repentance, and they often implicitly ask for something. A gift stands for the giver—accepting the gift means acceptance of the one who gave it, as when a young woman accepts a young man's ring. Above all, then, a gift expresses our desire to be united in love with the one to whom we give it.

Sacrifice meant offering a gift, by a priest, changing it in some way, and eating of it. People would take some gift that represented themselves and offer it to God by means of their representative, a priest. He would change or transform the gift to signify that they were giving it to God, that it no longer belonged to them—often he would kill a living gift, or victim—and then he would burn it to further show God's acceptance and possession of it. Sometimes there would be a meal or banquet, a communion, to further signify union with God by eating of what was now divine.

Abel had offered sacrifice to God, as had Noah, and Abraham had been ready to sacrifice his only son. After one of Abraham's victories, the mysterious figure of Melchisedech offered bread and wine to God in thanksgiving, a foreshadowing of what Christ and the Christian priesthood would do.

> And Melchisedech, king of Salem, brought out bread and wine; he was priest of God most high and he blessed him and said, "Blessed be Abram by God most high, maker of heaven and earth. . . . " (Genesis 14, 18–20).

A sacrifice had sealed the old covenant, and the Israelites were guided by God to lay down definite norms for sacrifices. These were offered by the priests at an altar set aside for this in the tabernacle (Leviticus, chapters 1–7). As when any group offers a gift, one person, the priest, made the offering.

The priests were specially chosen to offer sacrifice and to bring God's blessings to the people. They were essentially mediators, "gobetweens." God chose Aaron, Moses' brother, as his first priest, and his descendants were to carry on the work of the priesthood. They were made priests at a special ceremony during which they were anointed with oil and clothed in special garb.

> "Then bring near to you Aaron your brother, and his sons with him, from among the people of Israel, to serve me as priests. . . . And you shall make

holy garments for Aaron your brother, for glory and for beauty . . . and you shall take the anointing oil, and pour it on his head and anoint him" (Exodus 28, 1–2; 29, 7).

Later Christ will offer his life as the perfect sacrifice to begin the new covenant, and the elements of sacrifice will then be brought to perfection. All the sacrifices before Christ prepared the way for his perfect sacrifice, which would attain the perfect union of humankind with God.

In the most solemn and significant Hebrew ritual, the Sacrifice of Atonement, the high priest once a year sacrificed a bull and goat outside the sanctuary, then took their blood into the Holy of Holies, and sprinkled it over the covering of the Ark where Yahweh dwelt. Since their life was considered to be in their blood, these victims representing the people were united with God as far as it was possible to do so. Later, New Testament writers will show how Christ shed his blood, as he sacrificed his life to bring all humankind "once for all" into God's presence in heaven.

The Israelites also wanted a king, and God inspired Samuel to anoint Saul. When he was killed, David was anointed king (c. 1000 B.C.E.). The job was evidently too much for Saul, and he went slowly mad. The shepherd boy, David, was brought in to soothe Saul with his music, became a popular hero after he killed the giant Goliath, and then had to flee the paranoid ruler. Upon Saul's tragic death, David was chosen king by popular acclaim and made Jerusalem the capital city, bringing there the Ark of the Covenant. The biblical books 1 and 2 Samuel tell of this period.

David sinned but repented, and God promised that someday a king would come from his descendants whose kingdom would last forever. When the prophet Nathan excoriated David for his adultery with Bathsheba and his murder of her husband, he became a great figure of true repentance; then through Nathan God made him his great promise: Read 2 Samuel 7, 12–16.

Solomon, David's son, succeeded him and built the magnificent temple in Jerusalem in which he placed the Ark of the Covenant. There sacrifices to God took place daily. Solomon had a reign of great splendor, the high point of Israelite power and influence. But like many of his people he sinned by greed and idolatry, and eventually rebellion arose, in the midst of which Solomon died. The two biblical books of Kings tell of this and the following periods.

Because of their sinfulness, Israel was now split into the northern kingdom, Israel, and the southern kingdom, Judah, whose people came to be called "Jews." The latter, the two tribes of Judah and Benjamin, would contain the tiny "remnant" that would eventually fulfill God's promises. It is more than coincidental that as God's people of the Old Testament were split because of their sinfulness, so it was to be with his people of the New Testament: when Christendom became widely corrupted, its unity was also destroyed.

However, God did not abandon his people but sent them in their degeneration another outstanding group, the prophets.

THE PROPHETS

The prophets were specially called by God to speak in his name, his spokespersons to his people for several hundred years. They were one of the most amazing groups in history. Herders, priests, nobles, migrant workers, they shared one thing: a burning desire to return their people to faithfulness to the covenant and to deepen their understanding of it. They were the conscience of Israel. Through them Israel's religion was gradually purified and developed.

By their lives of total dedication and their outstanding deeds, the prophets gained acceptance in Israel—though, like forthright people, they were usually unpopular, and not infrequently they were murdered by the people.

The great Elijah, for instance, whose cave can be seen today on Mount Carmel above the modern city of Haifa, had to contend with the weak and degenerate king Ahab and his infamous queen, Jezebel, and with the attraction of Baal-worship and its human sacrifice and other gross immoralities. In epic fashion, the first book of Kings tells how Elijah pitted his sacrifice-offering against that of the prophets of Baal: God sent down lightning, "the fire of the Lord," to dramatically consume his offering, and the prophets of Baal were disgraced and slain. Jezebel then vowed she would kill Elijah. He fled into the Sinai desert, weak and weary, wanting to die where God had first revealed himself to Israel. There God came to him and reassured him: **Read 1 Kings 19, 1-18.**

Then there is Amos, probably a migratory worker, a forceful man who castigated the wealthy for their oppression of the poor: "They sell the righteous for silver, and the needy for a pair of shoes—they that trample the head of the poor into the dust of the earth, and turn aside the way of the afflicted . . . " (Amos 2, 6-7).

Amos particularly condemned their smug pride over their status, which would eventually destroy them: **Read Amos 3, 1-2; 4, 1-5.**

In predicting the coming disaster, he spoke of the "remnant" that would be preserved faithful to the Lord:

> Thus says the Lord, "As the shepherd rescues from the mouth of the lion two legs, or a piece of an ear, so shall the people of Israel who dwell in Samaria be rescued, with the corner of a couch and part of a bed" (Amos 3, 12).

Isaiah was the longest-lived of the prophets, and even as he foretold the destruction to come, he touchingly reminded the people of God's love:

> But Zion said, The Lord has forsaken me, my Lord has forgotten me, Can a woman forget her sucking child, that she should have no compassion on the son of her womb? Even these may forget, yet I will not forget you (Isaiah 49, 14-15).

The prophets' predictions of destruction were largely ignored by the sinful people. Then the blow fell: First the northern kingdom was destroyed by the Assyrians, who swept over the country and deported many of the people. Then the kingdom of Judah fell in 587 B.C.E., and the people were deported to Babylon. But the prophets consoled them, and many of the most beautiful psalms (religious hymns) are from this period. From this time on many of the Jews would be scattered "among the nations," in the diaspora, eventually providing bases for the spread of Christ's teachings.

At this critical time God promised a new, more perfect covenant. Jeremiah gives this great promise (cf. also Ezekiel 36, 24ff.): **Read Jeremiah 31, 31-34.**

The prophets' teaching now gradually converged toward the Messiah who was to come. These prophecies were given at different times and are scattered throughout the Old Testament. Many are obscure and seemingly contradictory, and evidently the prophets themselves did not understand exactly how they would be fulfilled; only when we study the life of Christ do we see how Jesus fulfilled them.

Many of the prophecies concerned a new age, "the day of the Lord." Joel, for instance, saw it first of all as a time of judgment upon Israel:

> Let all the inhabitants of the land tremble for the day of the Lord is coming, it is near, a day of darkness and gloom, a day of clouds and thick darkness! (Joel 2, 1–2).

But it will also be a time of great blessings, when God's spirit is "poured out on all flesh." Peter's Pentecost sermon, the first announcement of the Christian message, will quote this: Read Joel 2, 28–29.

The "Messiah" or "Christ" means the one anointed with holy oil, as were the priests, kings, and prophets. The word *Messiah* meant particularly the king who would fulfill Israel's destiny. While the prophecies are often obscure, one looking at them with the help of faith can discern many characteristics of Jesus as the Messiah who would begin this new age: Read Isaiah 35, 3–6.

The Messiah would be a great king of David's lineage whose rule would never end. This, we saw, was predicted by Nathan. We should note that the ideal king in those days was Yahweh's instrument, the one through whom he saved his people, who protected them from external enemies and from oppression by the powerful. A few centuries later the prophet Isaiah also told of the kingly Messiah who would be a descendant of David; his best-known prophecies concern Emmanuel, "God-with-us" (chapters 7–11). We shall see that Christ is this kingly descendant of David: Read Isaiah 9, 2–7.

A mysterious "Son of Man" also appears in connection with the messianic hopes of God's people. Christ will later relate this title to himself:

> I saw in the night visions, and behold, with the clouds of heaven there came one like the son of man, and he came to the Ancient of Days and was presented

before him. And to him was given dominion and glory and kingdom, that all peoples, nations, and languages should serve him . . . (Daniel 7, 13–14; cf. Psalm 110).

The "suffering servant" is perhaps the best-known figure of the Messiah, given by the prophet known as Second Isaiah. He stressed two ideas difficult for the Jews to grasp, but of deep importance to God's plan: all nations would be called to know and love God, and redemption would come about through the suffering of the innocent Servant of Yahweh—a figure of Christ: **Read Isaiah 53, 3–7.**

After the exile, a remnant of Jews returned to Jerusalem and began to rebuild. They were chastened and strongly attached to the Law— the five books of Moses (or Torah) elaborated and explained by tradition—and convinced more than ever of their destiny as the chosen people. A total theocracy, with Yahweh as their sole ruler, they considered the high priest his representative and their leader.

In the fourth century B.C.E. they were conquered by the Greeks, persecuted, and became somewhat Hellenized. The Hebrew Scriptures were translated into the Greek Septuagint about 250 B.C.E. Then the Persians swept over Palestine, and finally in the century before Christ the Romans conquered the land and installed a puppet king, Herod.

The Old Testament ends with God's people longing for the Messianic Age to come, but there is confusion about it. Many looked for a new time of peace and great material prosperity. Others expected a great king, like David or Solomon, who would lead them to freedom and glory and establish once more the united kingdom of Israel.

Conscious of God's great deeds on their behalf over the centuries, they looked to his promises for the future. They were a small, almost obscure country on the fringe of a great empire. But they were a monotheistic stronghold in a world of polytheism, superstition, and rationalism, and their moral life was far above that of the rest of the Hellenistic world of the time.

We should note at this time the influential groups in Israel who were to play a role in Christ's life: Besides the powerful priestly class, there were the **Scribes** or **Lawyers,** the official interpreters of the Law, the most honored, influential group in the land. **The Pharisees,** formed to keep the people free of foreign domination, in Jesus' day were liberal in that they included laypeople and represented the common person. Some were sympathetic to Jesus, wanting to return to the spirit of the Law as he did, but others added numerous minute traditions to the Law and exaggerated its literal fulfillment rather than keeping its spirit. Jesus himself is called a "rabbi," that is, a Pharisee who had followers and who took part in their debates about the Law.

> *Gospel references to the "Scribes and Pharisees" as Jesus' enemies* should be seen in the light of the split, later in the first century C.E., between those Jews who believed in Jesus and those who did not. This led to an anti-Jewish polemic as these first Christians sought to establish their own identity vis-à-vis their fellow Jews (see chapter 8 regarding responsibility for the death of Christ).

The Sadducees were a proud, largely priestly group who represented the aristocracy and the moneyed class; along with the temple priesthood, they were dependent on the Romans for their wealth and power. More open to Gentile influences and holding only to the Torah, they did not, for instance, believe in the resurrection of the dead. Defenders of the status quo and of their own political power, the Sadducees and the temple priesthood would be Christ's strongest opponents.

The Essenes, the community of Qumran and the Dead Sea Scrolls, had denounced the temple priesthood and its supporters and withdrawn into the desert, to the shores of the Dead Sea, and lived a strict, monastic-like, community life in preparation for the coming of the Messiah and the Messianic Age (see chapter 11 regarding the Dead Sea Scrolls).

Last, there was the "remnant," the small number of people loyal to the Lord who were to be the start of the new Israel and the new covenant, the new people of God. Of no particular class or status, they tried to practice a purer, more perfect religion, in their hearts as well as externally. Mary, the mother of Christ, is their outstanding example. They are the "poor" of Israel, the "little ones" whose longing for the Savior is epitomized in this cry:

> But I am poor and needy; hasten to help me, O God! Thou art my help and my deliverer; O Lord, do not tarry! (Psalm 70, 5).

We can now sum up the main ideas of the Old Testament: God chooses the Israelites . . . makes a covenant with them, forming them into his people . . . speaking through human representatives who have his authority . . . and who guide the people in living the covenant and worshiping God by sacrifice . . . looking forward to the Messiah . . . who will usher in a Messianic Age of peace and prosperity.

IN THE LITURGY

The Psalms are the inspired religious hymns or poems of the Old Testament. The Church uses many of them in her liturgy, and priests recite many of them each day as the Church's official prayer. They make excellent and inspiring reading for anyone.

At Mass, immediately before reading the Gospel, the priest asks God to cleanse his heart and lips as he did Isaiah's, so that he may be prepared to announce his Word. In one of the official eucharistic prayers, at the heart of the Mass, we ask God to accept our sacrifice "as you accepted the offerings of your servant Abel, the just, the sacrifice of Abraham, our father, and that of your high priest, Melchisedech."

During the Advent season—which begins with the fourth Sunday before Christmas—we relive again each year the preparation for the coming of the Messiah. Passages from the prophet Isaiah are particularly set before us during this time.

DAILY LIVING: OUR FAITH EXPRESSED BY REVERENCE AND WORSHIP AND ITS RELATION TO THE JEWISH PEOPLE TODAY

Faith is the dominant role of God's people of the Old Testament from Abraham on. They are given very little to rely on, not even the assurance of a life after death, but are simply asked to have faith that God will bless them. And he did: far beyond their desire for lands and crops and offspring, he brought them to eternal happiness with himself.

When their faith would seem to be at its breaking point, God would intervene with some sign of his presence and love. Some miraculous event would take place, or a prophet would appear to encourage them. So, if we look closely, we can discern his action when we most need it in our lives.

Reverence for God was great among his people, so much so that they would not even pronounce his name. They had a great sense of awe in his presence. Abraham was seized with terror and felt himself dust and ashes before God; Moses and Elijah hid their faces in dread at his approach; Isaiah almost despaired; Daniel fell to the ground before God, his face pressed to the earth. Perhaps if we had a greater sense of reverence for God, we would be more aware of his presence in our lives.

God's people expressed their faith and gratitude for his help by worshiping him. They did this especially at the great moments in their history, by coming together as his people to worship him by sacrifice. So also today it is natural to show our gratitude for his action in our lives, and to do this not only as individuals but by worshiping together as his people.

The Mass, the way Catholics come together each Sunday to worship God, is a sacrifice and, as we will see, the "prolongation" of the perfect sacrifice of Christ. When we take part we try to give ourselves to God, in his special presence, to be united with him.

Finally, God's special regard for the Jewish people, so shabbily treated throughout history—and with unbelievable cruelty in the Holocaust—should lead us all to examine our consciences. Vatican Council II forcefully went on record against anti-Semitism:

> The Church, mindful of the patrimony she shares with the Jews and moved not by political reasons but by the Gospel's spiritual love, deplores hatred, persecutions, displays of anti-Semitism directed against Jews at any time and by anyone. . . . We cannot truly call on God, the Father of all, if we refuse to treat in a brotherly way any man (*Declaration on the Relationship of the Church to Non-Christian Religions,* no. 4).

Perhaps Pope John Paul II best summed it up when he visited the Nazi extermination camp of Auschwitz-Birkenau and openly wept as he knelt on the ground containing the remains of several million Jews, along with many Russians and Poles. He called it the "Calvary of the modern world," and said: "Auschwitz is a place everyone should visit and ask, 'What are the limits of hatred, what are the limits of destruction of man by man?'" He concluded: "The very people who received from God the commandment, 'Thou shalt not kill,' itself experienced in overwhelming measure what is meant by killing."

A mutually profitable dialogue has been progressing between Jewish and Roman Catholic scholars, a hopeful sign of a new era in world history. This dialogue goes on in many places and on every level: from Pope John Paul II's moving 1986 visit to Rome's main synagogue—a historical "first" for a pope—to local cooperation between parishes and synagogues. The Vatican's recognition of the State of Israel, the land sacred to the Jewish people, was also a great step forward—though obviously the rights of the Palestinian people must also be respected.

Noticeable progress in attitudes has emerged: Some Jews, for instance, consider Jesus as the last of the prophets. And Catholics in the official dialogue reached a consensus that there should no longer be attempts to convert Jews to Christianity (obviously some Jews may have long since lost contact with Judaism's own special heritage and mission, are cut off from their Jewish spiritual roots, and will come on their own to the Church seeking a meaning to life, a spiritual home).

The Jewish people still remain, in a very real sense, God's chosen, for God's covenant with them is irrevocable. "He does not repent of the gifts He makes nor of the calls He issues (cf. Romans 11, 28–29)" (*Declaration on the Relationship of the Church to Non-Christian Religions,* no. 4).

The Hebrew covenant is the foundation of the new covenant that, we will see, Christ will bring. The Hebrew Bible, the Christian Old Testament, is "old" only in the sense of being first, not as outdated or obsolete. It is inspired in its own right and not only as a precursor of the New Testament. It was a source of inspiration for Jesus, the New Testament writers, and later Christian writers, including those of today. (For more on the Jewish people, including their being blamed for the death of Christ and their role along with Christians today, see chapter 8.)

A practical, perhaps painful, note for those contemplating a Jewish-Catholic marriage: Despite the growing understanding spoken of above, there are, in many cases, deep problems that should be thoroughly and honestly gone into beforehand. These involve not only the couple's own feelings but also family religious traditions and especially the future religious upbringing of the couple's children. There should be much frank discussion, learning each other's basic traditions, consultation with clergy, and patient, sensitive, mature communication.

SOME SUGGESTIONS FOR . . .

DISCUSSION

Does the notion of worshiping God by sacrifice seem natural for humans, to show their feelings toward God? What limitations does this have?

From the role of the prophets in Israel, can you give a few reasons why such people are always needed, including today? Have you personally experienced someone who forcefully reminded you of your duty—and of God's unceasing love seeking you?

From the Jewish people's experience of exile and return, can you recall times in your own life when difficulty or tragedy might have brought you back to God?

Someone once said that the particular glory as well as burden of Christians is their belief in the divinity of Christ, while that of the Jewish people is that they have been chosen by God. Can you comment on this?

On Israel's yearly Day of Atonement (Yom Kippur), the sins of the people were symbolically placed on a goat, which was then driven into the desert. Can you discern our sinful tendency to "scapegoat," to blame others, such as the Jewish people, for things we ourselves are guilty of, especially our tendency toward envy?

FURTHER READING

- *Yeshua,* Swidler (Sheed & Ward, 1988)—An insightful little book on the Jewish Jesus in his Jewish context, by a well-known Christian theologian.
- *The Prophetic Imagination,* Brueggemann (Fortress Press, 1978)—This relates Old Testament themes to modern life and spirituality; it is little in size but large and powerful in content.
- *The Anguish of the Jews,* Flannery (Paulist Press, 1985)—Revised and updated, this is a classic history of anti-Semitism through the centuries up to our day.

- *An Interrupted Life: The Diaries of Etty Hillesum, 1941–1943,*
  Pomerans, trans. (Pantheon Books, 1983)—This is a truly remarkable, moving, and quietly powerful personal record of the spiritual
  growth of a bright, young Jewish woman in Holland during the Holocaust years.

For more reading on Jewish-Christian relations, including some sensitive issues and practical helps, see "Further Reading" in chapter 8.

6

Christ Comes Among Us

How do we know about Jesus Christ? What was so unique about his life? Who did he claim to be? Why was he not accepted more widely? What relevance has his teaching for me today?

THE COMING OF JESUS CHRIST

We saw that the Jewish world of the first century was looking for the coming of the Messianic Age—a king, a kingdom that would fulfill the prophecies and bring God's blessings once again to his people. The New Testament tells of the life, death, resurrection, and teachings of Jesus Christ, in whom, for Christians, these hopes were transformed and fulfilled.

An incident that took place during the first days of the Christian Church is recorded in the Acts of the Apostles: **Read Acts 3, 1–10.** This story of a man cured instantly "in the name of Jesus Christ of Nazareth" is typical of Christianity from the beginning. Jesus Christ of Nazareth was the inspiration and the power of Christianity from its inception. He is probably the best-known person in the history of the world. Who was he, and what do we really know about him?

The New Testament is the principal source for the life and teachings of Jesus Christ, although he is mentioned briefly in a number of ancient writings. This second part of the Bible consists of twenty-seven books: the four gospels—a series of incidents, teachings, sayings, and so on of Jesus arranged in story form; the Acts of the Apostles—some incidents in the life of the early Christian Church; the epistles—letters written by Christ's apostles or their followers to early Christian communities; and Revelation, or the Apocalypse—a highly symbolic writing about the early Church and the final events of history.

The New Testament gives a substantially accurate outline of Christ's life and teachings, but not a scientific, detailed biography. There is as much evidence for the authenticity of the main events and sayings contained in the New Testament story of Jesus as there is, for example, of Julius Caesar, or any other ancient historical figure. But the authors give only a framework, the substance of what Christ said and did. They were not writing biographies of Christ as people write biographies today.

The New Testament is the record of the early Church's growth in faith and understanding of who and what Jesus Christ is. The authors tell the story of Christ's saving deeds as seen through the eyes of believers writing for believers. Their concern is to show not only an event but its inner religious meaning. They are not greatly concerned about when or where a thing happened, the details of what happened, the exact words Christ used, and so on. They show a gradual growth in understanding of who Christ was and of his revelation. To bring out the inner religious meaning of the events of Christ's life, they sometimes arrange details according to Old Testament concepts and often express themselves in the imaginative language of their Semitic background.

To guide us in our interpretation of the New Testament, then, we use tradition, his Church's understanding of Christ's teachings. Since the New Testament came from the early Christian community, it is best interpreted in the light of the community's beliefs. This is found particularly in the other writings of Christ's early followers that have come down to us.

Since the New Testament is a record of faith, the reader must have faith—or at least be open to the possibility of faith—if she or he is to derive full benefit from it. The skeptic, the one whose mind is closed against the possibility of a divine coming in Christ, will get little profit from it.

The four gospels, particularly, tell of Jesus' life and teachings. They are attributed to Matthew, Mark, Luke, and John. They are really four different accounts of the single "gospel," that is, the "good news" that God has come and saved humankind, climaxing his mighty deeds of the Old Testament. This good news was first announced by the preaching of the apostles and then gradually took on written form in the Christian Church.

The gospel authors take excerpts from Jesus' life and teachings and arrange and interpret them for the particular needs of their audience. Matthew writes particularly to show that Jesus is the promised Messiah; Mark's is the oldest and shortest gospel and is the basis for much of Matthew and Luke; Luke's is the most complete gospel and shows particularly a very human and universal Jesus; John's is the most symbolic of the gospels and was written to show that Jesus is the eternal Son of God who revealed himself through many "signs."

There is practically nothing known about the early life of Jesus, until he begins to preach publicly. The gospel writers are concerned primarily with his public teachings, his message through them to the world. But since the whole of the gospels was written to tell us something, we will consider briefly the story of Jesus' early years.

The life of Jesus begins with the story of the angel coming to Mary, which brings out the divine origin of Jesus: Read Luke 1, 26-38. Luke tells us in this account that God somehow communicated to Mary that she was to be the mother of the Savior, and she consented. She then, by the power of the Holy Spirit, conceived Jesus Christ. The Church celebrates this event as the feast of the Annunciation, March 25.

These initial chapters of Luke and Matthew are the Jewish style of writing, in which the sacred Christian mysteries are illustrated by prophetic Old Testament situations. Here the angel's greeting alludes to the prophecy of Zephaniah (3, 14-20) in which God expresses his love for the virgin "Daughter of Zion." Thus Mary symbolizes all that God loves in Israel. Mary is the new Ark of the Covenant, the place where God dwells, for she, too, is "overshadowed by the power of the Most High" (cf. Exodus 40, 35).

Mary, the mother of Jesus, conceived him and gave birth while remaining a virgin. Joseph was the husband of Mary and the foster-father of Jesus. This is traditional Christian teaching. Thus Luke emphasizes the virginal conception of Jesus by Mary's question to the angel: "How can this be, since I have no husband?" (1, 34). Matthew tells how Joseph's doubts upon seeing Mary pregnant were settled by a revelation that the conception was miraculous (1, 18-25).

As with every teaching about Mary, her virginity is a statement about Jesus first—that while he is truly a man, he is unique, his origin is in God, he is one with God from the moment of his conception—and about Mary only secondarily, that is, that God does marvels through humble human instruments (in Luke 1, 46–55, Mary herself beautifully proclaims this).

The Church taught Jesus' virginal conception and birth from her first creeds, and while little was said about Mary for the first two centuries, Christian writings from c. 200 C.E. on almost universally attest to Mary's perpetual virginity. Belief in Mary's virginity became an adjunct to the core Christian dogmas of Christ's divine origin as well as his true humanness, over against early heresies that denied one or the other.

Some Scripture scholars today contend that Jesus had actual brothers and sisters, that the Greek term *adelphos* used in the gospels clearly means brothers and not cousins, that the New Testament has another word for cousin—and that this opinion, though conflicting with the prevailing one holding to Mary's perpetual virginity, was held by several early Christian Church Fathers. Yet highly reputed Scripture scholar John Meier, for example, concludes that none of these arguments can produce absolute certitude in a matter for which there is so little evidence.

Today many Scripture scholars and theologians see a fuller meaning to Mary's virginity. It is more than her physical inviolability. It also has the broader, symbolic, universal meaning of her profound attitude of total openness to God alone, her total commitment to him, to doing his will before anyone or anything else—and in this each of us, virginal or not, can imitate her.

Mary the Virgin also symbolizes God's relation with his "bride," Israel (cf. Ezekiel 16, 1–63; Hosea 1, 2–9). And, as we will see (chapter 23), Mary is a figure of the New Testament Church, and her virginity is a prophetic sign of the Church's ideal purity and total dedication to Christ. She is the model Christian, completely given only to God.

Note that this teaching, the virginal conception and birth of Jesus, should not be confused with Mary's immaculate conception, her personal freedom from sin (cf. chapter 7).

Luke continues the story by telling us that Mary went to visit her cousin, Elizabeth, the mother of John the Baptist: "And when Elizabeth heard the greeting of Mary, the babe leaped in her womb. And Elizabeth was filled with the Holy Spirit, and she exclaimed with a loud cry,

'Blessed are you among women and blessed is the fruit of your womb! And why is this granted me, that the mother of my Lord should come to me?'" (Luke 1, 41–43).

This greeting of Elizabeth concludes the first part of the prayer, the "Hail Mary." Mary is the last and noblest of the long line of Israel's "poor," the humble ones who will be the start of the new Israel. Mary's answer to Elizabeth, as Luke presents it, is a mosaic of Old Testament texts expressing joy at what God has done through her. The Church uses these verses in its traditional blessing of a mother and her newborn child: "My soul magnifies the Lord, and my spirit rejoices in God, my Savior; for he has regarded the low state of his handmaid . . . " (cf. Luke 1, 46–55).

Luke continues with the oft-told story of the birth of Jesus: Read Luke 2, 1–7.

Christmas Day, December 25, is the day on which we celebrate the birth of Jesus. It is a holyday on which all Catholics attend Mass to rejoice at this great event. Fourth-century Christians chose this date to replace a pagan feast celebrating the winter solstice. Also, Jesus was actually born about 7 B.C.E.—our present calendar, which dates years from the birth of Christ, took the wrong year as a starting point.

By placing Jesus' birth in Bethlehem, Luke and Matthew make the point that he was the Messiah, since this was David's home and the Messiah would be of David's lineage. Jesus' birthplace was probably Nazareth, but this should not turn us off to the rich symbolism and profound meaning of the first Christmas story.

Jesus' birth in poor circumstances is a lesson to us in humility and detachment from riches. The first to greet him were God's faithful poor, Mary, Joseph, and the shepherds from the neighboring hills. Luke tells how an angel announced Jesus' birth to the shepherds and invited them to be his first worshipers; he concludes with the song that has been immortalized in Christian worship:

> And suddenly there was with the angel a multitude of the heavenly host praising God and saying, "Glory to God in the highest heaven, and on earth peace among those whom he favors!" (Luke 2, 13–14).

The gospels tell of other early events of Jesus' life. These stories are meant to show that Jesus is the expected Messiah-king and that he is more than human.

His presentation in the temple forty days after his birth (cf. Luke 2, 22–39) is celebrated each year on February 2, and it was also called the feast of the Purification of Mary. Since Christ was hailed in this incident as the "light of revelation to the Gentiles," on this day in all Catholic churches the candles used in divine services are blessed—hence the popular name "Candlemas Day."

The coming of the Magi, celebrated as the feast of the Epiphany, portrays the coming of the first Gentiles to worship Jesus and the flight of the Holy Family into Egypt to escape Herod's persecution (Matthew, chapter 2).

> Matthew, to show that Jesus is the new Moses, the new leader of God's people, parallels the coming of each in the first two chapters: Rulers and their courts tremble at the announcement of their births; Herod consults his scribes as Pharaoh did his astrologers; both tyrants decree the murder of children, from which both heroes escape; and both saviors, persecuted and away from their people, receive a heavenly message to return.

Jesus' early years are summed up by Luke: He tells us how the child Jesus had been lost by his parents in Jerusalem when he was twelve. They found him in the temple in deep discussion with the teachers of the Law, who "were amazed at his understanding and his answers." When Mary reprimanded him, his response shows an awareness of his mission: "Did you not know that I must be in my Father's house?" Then he grew up, obediently, in simple, humble surroundings:

> Then he went down with them and came to Nazareth, and was obedient to them. His mother treasured all these things in her heart. And Jesus increased in wisdom and in years, and in divine and human favor (Luke 2, 51–52).

Years pass, and then comes John the Baptist, the last of the prophets, preaching repentance and conversion to prepare the way for Jesus. John developed as a strict ascetic in the desert, and one day appeared, a striking figure, proclaiming, "Repent, for the kingdom of heaven is at hand" (Matthew 3, 2).

John the Baptist asked people to be changed interiorly, to repent of their sins and be converted, to turn fully toward God. His "baptism" was a sign of this, a primitive forerunner of the Christian sacrament of baptism. When the people wanted to acclaim him the Messiah, he told them he was only preparing the way: "After me comes he who is mightier than I, the thong of whose sandals I am not worthy to stoop down and untie" (Mark 1, 7).

Jesus comes to John and asks to be baptized, and then prepares for his public life by a forty-day fast in the desert. Jesus asked for baptism to connect John's mission with what he would soon begin himself. His desert ordeal, climaxed by severe temptations from the devil, parallels the forty years the Israelites wandered in the desert and is the model of our practice of penance during the forty days of Lent (cf. Mark 1, 9–14; Matthew 3, 13–4, 11).

Jesus starts his mission in the harsh desert, as Israel had, to show that he is the beginning of God's new people. He is to be the "new Israel," the one who takes on himself all the aspirations and inadequacies of God's people and begins a new, transformed people. In the desert he also faces God in stark loneliness, emptiness, fear, and the temptation to discouragement and rebellion—and thus purified he begins his mission or public life.

Jesus' public life is the two or three years that he spent preaching, teaching, and working miracles, leading up to his suffering and death. He became known as a great preacher, a reader of hearts, and a wonder-worker:

> And he went about all Galilee, teaching in their synagogues and preaching the gospel of the kingdom and healing every disease and every infirmity among the people. So his fame spread throughout all Syria, and they brought him all the sick, those afflicted with various disease and pains, demoniacs, epileptics, and paralytics, and he healed them. And great crowds followed him from Galilee and the Decapolis and Jerusalem and Judea and from beyond the Jordan (Matthew 4, 23–25).

THE KINGDOM OF GOD IS HERE!

The central theme of Jesus' preaching is the good news of the kingdom of God: "Jesus came into Galilee, preaching the gospel of the kingdom of God, and saying, 'The time is fulfilled, and the kingdom of God is at hand. Repent and believe in the gospel'" (Mark 1, 14–15).

Jesus' announcement of the kingdom was what the Jewish people had been anticipating for hundreds of years. We have seen how they were awaiting this new, wonderful Messianic Age of great blessings. Christ now revealed that it was coming about. This was the best possible news they could hear—and thus it is called the gospel, the good news.

But when Jesus revealed that his kingdom was an interior, spiritual one, only a comparative few accepted him. These were the small remnant, the poor ones whose hearts were truly open to God's teaching and rule. We saw how most people expected a great political king, or one who would bring many material blessings, or who would perfectly observe the Law—but Jesus asked an interior change in oneself to belong to his kingdom.

The kingdom of God is his loving rule, his reign over us, and our submission to him. When we believe in him and do his will, we belong to his kingdom. God's reign or kingdom is his guiding presence, his grace-presence, within us; to submit to his loving guidance is to belong to the kingdom.

To be a part of God's kingdom, Jesus said, we must undergo an interior conversion. We must have a change of heart, repenting of our sins, determined to begin a new life: "Repent and believe in the gospel"—here Jesus was fulfilling what John the Baptist had announced. Then in the beautiful and famous "Sermon on the Mount" he tells us how to live this conversion in order to be a part of his kingdom (cf. Matthew, chapters 5–7). He begins with the eight beatitudes, the way to true happiness (the word *blessed* means "happy"): **Read Matthew 5, 3-12.**

Jesus usually taught by parables, simple, everyday little stories. But the stories are often puzzling, go against common sense, contradict accepted attitudes. Jesus' listeners would suddenly realize they were being challenged to complete the stories in their own lives, to look at things in a new way, to change their lives—and thus become part of his kingdom.

For example, what laborers are given a full day's pay for an hour's work (Matthew 20, 1–6)? Or who would awaken a neighbor at midnight, seeking bread (Luke 11, 5–8)? Or who expects to be punished for not using even the smallest God-given gift (Matthew 25, 14–30)?

The parables were later added to and modified; thus they can have several levels of meaning (see "Further Reading," page 81).

Jesus began preaching his kingdom by proclaiming he was fulfilling what was prophesied centuries before by Isaiah: he had come to help the poor, the sick, the oppressed: **Read Luke 4, 16–21.**

Jesus scandalized even his followers by associating women with himself as ones chosen for his kingdom. Though his time and culture severely restricted women's roles, Jesus welcomed women as his followers and even learned from them. In a moving vignette, a Canaanite woman, for example, helps persuade him to broaden his mission (cf. Matthew 15, 22–28). And his disciples are taken aback by his freedom in associating with women—the story of the Samaritan woman in John 4, 5–42, is an example.

In this kingdom the poor, the humble, the oppressed, the "little people" are the happy ones—a complete reversal of the world's usual standards whereby the rich and powerful are the favored ones. Anyone who has experienced injustice and looked to God for a better life knows what Jesus was talking about.

A new commandment, love, is the one important rule in this kingdom. We have seen that the Jews, as well as Jesus, lived by the Law, particularly the commandments. Now Jesus summed up the whole Law in what would be the one law of his kingdom: "A new commandment I give to you, that you love one another; even as I have loved you, that you also love one another" (John 13, 34).

We will live in this new kingdom forever. Those who follow Jesus and become part of his kingdom will be raised up from death: "Whoever sees the Son and believes in him, shall have everlasting life, and I will raise him up on the last day" (John 6, 40). This was indeed tremendous news to the Jews who did not have the well-developed belief in a personal, happy afterlife of some of their neighboring cultures. The place of the dead was generally considered one of stillness, darkness, and total helplessness: it was only after the exile that they began to look to God to remember and reward in the next life those who had been faithful to him in this life.

Now on earth, those who follow Jesus pray and work to extend God's kingdom of love increasingly to all people. One day in heaven the kingdom will be completed—God's love will rule over us all—and we will see creation in all its glory and understand the "why" of suffering and injustice. During our present life we pray as Jesus taught us: "Thy kingdom come, thy will be done on earth as it is in heaven."

Jesus chose apostles to help spread his kingdom. They were the beginning of his Church: "And he appointed twelve that they might be with him and that he might send them forth to preach" (Mark 3, 14). Inspired by Jesus, they would try to make themselves and all people submissive to God's love. He gave them "the keys of the kingdom," the power to guide people to his truth and love.

THE PROMISED MESSIAH—AND HIS REJECTION

"I am the way and the truth and the life. No one comes to the Father but by me" (John 14, 6).

The early Christians, reflecting on Jesus' teachings and the meaning of his life, came to look on him as the perfect king, priest, and prophet. This summed up his earthly mission. As the "way" Jesus is our king, the perfect king predicted in the Old Testament, now come to begin an eternal spiritual kingdom. As the "truth" Jesus is the perfect prophet or teacher looked for in the Old Testament, come to give us the fullness of God's truth. As the "life" Jesus is, as we shall see, the perfect priest who sacrificed himself for us.

> There is the very human story of Jesus' encounter with the Samaritan woman who had had five husbands and was then living with another man. Jesus reveals her past to her, and taken aback, she tries to change the subject by defending her Samaritan worship. When she refers to the coming Messiah whom the Samaritans thought of as a great prophet to come, Jesus tells her simply, "I who speak with you am he" (John 4, 5–42).

The early Christians realized that Jesus was the Messiah, but in a new, fuller, spiritual sense. We saw that the Jewish people expected the Messiah to be a great worldly leader, the inaugurator of a new age of peace and prosperity. Jesus' followers came to see, however, that he called for an interior, spiritual conversion, that he came to establish a kingdom over the hearts of individuals, not to rule over a people. He was bringing messianic blessings that were eternal, beyond his people's fondest dreams. But only those who are willing to hear the truth can know of this: **Read John 18, 33-37.**

Jesus' followers saw him as relating himself to the mysterious "Son of Man" who would one day come on the clouds of heaven (Daniel 7,

13–14). (In Ezekiel this term simply means "man.") As he was on trial for his life, "the high priest began to ask him, 'Art thou the Christ, the Son of the Blessed One?' And Jesus said to him, 'I am. And you shall see the Son of Man sitting at the right hand of the Power and coming with the clouds of heaven' " (Mark 14, 61–62).

He shocked his followers by speaking of himself as a humiliated and suffering Son of Man, the "suffering servant" who had been predicted (Isaiah 52, 13–53, 12).

> And he began to teach them that the Son of Man must suffer many things and be rejected by the elders and chief priests and scribes, and be killed, and after three days rise again. And he said this plainly. And Peter, taking him aside, began to rebuke him (Mark 8, 31–32).

Many who had heard him were skeptical, but he offered proof of his divine mission by working miracles, fulfilling the messianic prophecies in a new, fuller sense, and making prophecies of his own. In particular, he predicted that he would return alive after his death; so astounding was this that only a chosen few later grasped it: **Read John 2, 18–22.**

Jesus stressed the original purpose and meaning of the old Law, in opposition to those who were concerned only with formalism and legalism, and summed it up by his perfect law of love. "Do not think that I have come to destroy the Law or the Prophets," he says in Matthew. "I have come not to destroy but to fulfill" (5, 17). He did this as a prophet with unique authority about the Law, one who "spoke with authority" (Mark 1, 22). He allied himself with those reformers who stressed that the Law was for life, emphasizing the parts of it that were grounded in love and castigating those who emphasized mere outward observances. He said that what God wants is not numerous religious observances and practices but love, mercy, justice, and honesty.

Most of the people did not accept Jesus, but a small number did. They were to be the beginning of his Church. The crowds who had been drawn to him by his miracles largely deserted him when he refused the role of a worldly Messiah who would bring immediate peace and prosperity. Because he loved all people without exception, most people rejected him. Matthew quotes him as wryly commenting:

> For John came neither eating nor drinking, and they say, "He has a demon"; the Son of Man came eating and drinking, and they say, "Behold, a

glutton and a drunkard, a friend of tax collectors and sinners!" (Matthew 11, 18–19).

Stung by Jesus' fearless preaching, some of the leaders of the people decided he would have to die. As his influence over the people grew, the "temple establishment"—the Sadducees, the temple priesthood, and Pontius Pilate, the Roman governor—saw his popularity as a threat to Roman power and their own influence. Despite his holiness and miracles, they decided that for the good of the people he would have to be eliminated. Like many who suppress freedom movements today, they became very much concerned with public safety and order. They then approached Judas, Jesus' traitorous apostle, and made a deal to seize his master for what a cheap suit of clothes would cost today.

After a triumphal entry into Jerusalem on Sunday, Jesus began the last week of his life, called by Christians "Holy Week." On Holy Thursday he ate his last supper with his apostles. He then went out into the garden of Gethsemane to pray, and there, with Judas' help, he was seized by his enemies.

A farcical trial was held, and Jesus was condemned to death. He was taken first before the Jewish high priest and then before Pontius Pilate, who alone had the power of life and death. He was then condemned to death.

Mocked and beaten and scourged, Jesus carried his cross to Calvary, and there he was crucified. After three hours on the cross, he died. It was the first "Good Friday." To his followers, this looked like the end of all their hopes.

But on Easter Sunday morning Jesus came back alive again as he had predicted he would. For forty days he appeared to his followers, and then finally disappeared from the earth at his Ascension. His followers returned to Jerusalem, somewhat encouraged, to await the coming of the Holy Spirit, as he had told them.

IN THE LITURGY

The "liturgical year" is the way in which we relive each year the great events of Christ's life by a series of feasts. It is centered around the two great Christian feasts of Christmas and Easter.

The Mass, our great act of worship, is centered on Christ. As the Scriptures are read, we should remind ourselves that Christ is speaking to us. The last reading, the gospel, gives us his words and teachings directly. Later, in chapters 14 and 15, the Mass will be gone into in detail.

The rosary is a devotion meaningful to some Catholics, during which one meditates on the important events—or mysteries—in the life of Christ as experienced by Mary. One does this while "fingering" the beads of the rosary. Many cultures have beads that one fingers as an aid to prayer and tranquillity.

There are fifteen mysteries divided into three sets of five each. During each meditation, a decade (one "Our Father" and ten "Hail Marys") is said. The repetition of the "Hail Marys" can serve as an aid to meditation, a sort of "mantra" that holds one's attention on God, while one's imagination dwells on the scene of the mystery and its meaning and one's fingers are occupied with the beads.

The five joyful mysteries concern early events of Christ's life: The Annunciation to Mary (Luke 1, 26–38), her Visitation to her cousin, Elizabeth (Luke 1, 39–56), the Birth of Christ (2, 1–20), his Presentation in the temple (Luke 1, 22–40), and Mary and Joseph's finding him in the temple (Luke 2, 41–52).

DAILY LIVING: THE LIFE OF HIS KINGDOM IS LOVE

Jesus taught us above all to love God and our neighbor: Love is the cornerstone of his teaching. It was so important in his eyes that he exhorted us to love even our enemies—a teaching that is revolutionary still today: **Read Matthew 5, 43–48.**

He lived all his teachings, but particularly that of love. He proved his love by dying for us, and as he was dying he prayed for his enemies: "Father, forgive them, for they do not know what they are doing" (Luke 23, 34).

Each one of us, in some small way, can imitate Christ's love. Christ showed his love in many ways during his life. In our life there is usually some one aspect of love, some virtue, that we particularly need. We might consider what one characteristic—or more—we need especially.

Jesus loved God humbly, perfectly submissive to his will. This desire to do the Father's will was so outstanding that he could say, "I always do the things that are pleasing to him" (John 8, 29). Even in terrible anguish, contemplating his coming sufferings and death, he prayed: "Father, if it is possible, let this cup pass away from me; yet, not as I will but as you will" (Matthew 26, 39).

Jesus taught us that we learn how to love by prayer. He taught us to pray by his constant example. He frequently spent the whole night in prayer; he began all his important actions with prayer; he prayed especially in suffering and crisis (cf. Luke 6, 12; John, chapter 17; Matthew 26, 36–44; Luke 23, 34 and 46). He particularly taught us **humble prayer** in the parable of the Pharisee and the publican (cf. Luke 18, 9–14).

Jesus had courage in doing the Father's will, and in speaking the truth, no matter what people thought or what it cost him (cf. Matthew 15, 12–14).

Jesus showed a special love for the sick, the poor, women, sinners, and those despised by others—the social outcasts, those who hadn't "made it" in society (cf. Luke 7, 1–7; John 9, 1–38; Luke 7, 36–50).

He taught us to love our neighbor, regardless of his or her race, sex, or social status, particularly in the parable of the Good Samaritan (cf. Luke 10, 30–37).

He taught us pointedly to forgive those who injure us, or else God will not forgive our misdeeds, in the parable of the unmerciful servant (cf. Matthew, 8, 21–35).

Jesus' whole life exemplified a detachment from wealth and human possessions. We have seen his humble birth and background. During his public life he showed a special love for the poor, and he had no home and few possessions of his own. One day he remarked, "The foxes have dens, and the birds of the air have nests; but the Son of Man has nowhere to lay his head" (Matthew 8, 20). The ultimate foolishness of greed is shown in the parable of the rich man and Lazarus (cf. Luke 16, 19–31).

Jesus continually taught us that God will always forgive us, no matter what we have done, as long as we are truly sorry. The wonderful parable of the Prodigal Son illustrates God's love and mercy (cf. Luke 15, 11–32).

SOME SUGGESTIONS FOR . . .

DISCUSSION

If you could step back into history and be present at two events in Jesus' life, which would you choose?

What meaning do the events of Jesus' birth and early life have for you—particularly the first Christmas story?

What kind of reception do you think Jesus' preaching would receive in our culture today? Where and among whom would he be most welcome? What kind of reception do you honestly think you would give him?

What aspects of Jesus' teaching about his kingdom are most welcome and stirring for you? Which do you find most difficult to live by?

FURTHER READING

Note: We said that the basic source for the life of Christ is the New Testament, the second part of the Bible. Here, in the four gospels, are the records of Jesus' life, his words and actions as remembered and written down by his first followers. There are various translations of the Bible into English, and these are listed (with a few words of commentary about each) at the end of chapter 11, "The Great Book in Which We Meet God," along with other suggested books for studying the Bible. An excellent introduction to the New Testament, easily understandable, is Pheme Perkins's *Reading the New Testament: An Introduction,* second edition (Paulist Press, 1988). Listed below are some other resources:

•• *The Birth of the Messiah,* Brown (Doubleday, 1977)—America's best-known Catholic New Testament scholar discusses in detail the background, problems, and possibilities relating to Jesus' conception and birth. A two-hundred-page updating supplement was added in 1993. Another monumental study, •• *The Death of the Messiah* (Doubleday, 1994), is by the same author (see chapter 8, "Further Reading").

• *Jesus and His Jewish Parables,* Young (Paulist Press, 1988)—By situating Jesus' parables in their Jewish background, this pioneering book gives them a new richness and understanding for us today.

- *Jesus According to a Woman,* Wahlberg (Paulist Press, 1985)—Revised and expanded, this is an insightful portrait of Jesus from a woman's viewpoint. Excellent for both men and women.
- *The Infancy Narratives: How to Read the Nativity Stories of Jesus,* Scott (Catholic Update 1281, St. Anthony Messenger Press)—A very brief, excellent presentation of the differing views of Matthew and Luke.
- *Jesus: Self-Portrait by God,* Lyons (Paulist Press, 1995)—An excellent book for ordinary people, it uses Scripture and theology to make Jesus come alive.
- *The Four Gospels and the Jesus Tradition,* O'Grady (Paulist Press, 1989)—This book explores the "Jesus tradition" and shows how each church community associated with a particular gospel writer understood this tradition for their own community.
- *"He Is Risen!"* Humphrey (Paulist Press, 1995)—This innovative look at Mark's gospel invites us to look at its "story line" in order to appreciate its theological viewpoint.
- • *The Historical Jesus: The Life of a Mediterranean Jewish Peasant,* Crossan (HarperSanFrancisco, 1992)—A well-known Scripture scholar uses a variety of sources for this presentation of Jesus as a radical social revolutionary; the book begins with a reconstruction of the actual words of the historical Jesus as seen through the eyes of the "Jesus Seminar," an avant-garde group of scholars of which Crossan is a part.
- • *A Marginal Jew: Rethinking the Historical Jesus,* Meier (Doubleday, 1991, 3 vols.)—Another well-known Catholic Scripture scholar looks at Jesus, his background, and message. More middle-of-the-road than Crossan's, and more advanced than Brown's *The Birth of the Messiah* (page 81) and *The Death of the Messiah* (chapter 8, "Further Reading"), this monumental work also uses the latest sources available. Half of volume two is devoted to a careful, scholarly analysis of Jesus' miracles, which many today dismiss too quickly.
- *Jesus: A Gospel Portrait,* Senior (Paulist Press, 1992)—An easy-to-read picture of Jesus as presented in the gospels, by a respected biblical scholar and writer.

•• *The Good Wine,* Barnhart (Paulist Press, 1994)—Building on what could very well be the underlying "chiastic" literary structure of John's gospel, this classic by a very wise monk is replete with scriptural and spiritual insights for one willing to mine them.

• *Mark: The Good News Preached to the Romans,* Cunningham (Paulist Press, 1985)—An interesting, informative look at Mark's gospel from the perspective of its setting, a late-first-century Christian community in Rome, with reflections on its meaning for us today.

•• *What Are They Saying About Matthew?* Senior, and *What Are They Saying About Luke and Acts?* Karras (Paulist Press, 1983)—These two books are excellent updatings; Karras's book, particularly, is easy for anyone to read and profit from.

• *Praying by Hand: Rediscovering the Rosary as a Way of Prayer,* Pennington (HarperSanFrancisco, 1991)—A widely known monk-author builds on the use of strings of beads in various religions, gives the history of the rosary, and then provides reflections on each of its fifteen "mysteries" as well as other devotional possibilities for the rosary.

FURTHER VIEWING/LISTENING

The Four Gospels, Rohr (NCR cassettes)—Four very popular audio or VHS cassettes by a clear, informative, and challenging priest-educator.

Jesus of Nazareth, Zeffirelli (CBS Fox Video, 1977)—Available in three videocassettes, this is by far the best film of Jesus' life; though it takes a few liberties with scriptural accounts, it is generally accurate, sensitively done, and it has a superb cast. It is hard not to be moved by this film.

PERSONAL REFLECTION

Christ asked for a change of heart, a conversion, a rejection of one's sins, and a turning more fully toward him. I should get the inspiration and strength to do this if I meditate on his life each day, perhaps by reading at least a page of the New Testament, and then trying to apply it to my own life.

We suggest reading Luke's gospel since it is the most complete. A good book on the life of Christ can give a background to enrich this reading.

The great way Catholics believe they come into special contact with Christ is at Mass. By the power of God Christ becomes present among us, particularly under the appearance of bread and wine, and prolongs or re-presents his death and resurrection. He does this so we can all take part and offer ourselves to the Father with him. At holy communion especially we are united in a most intimate way with Christ under the appearance of bread and wine, and with one another. This, then, is our great expression of worship and love.

If I am seriously studying Catholicism I should experience the Mass for myself, each Sunday if possible. In preparation I might read beforehand the gospel for the coming Sunday. The first reading, mostly from the Jewish Scriptures, usually harmonizes with the third reading, the Gospel. The second reading is usually a letter from St. Paul read continuously each week, except for special times and feasts.

The Mass is explained in detail in the chapter 14 section, "Step by Step Through the Mass."

7

Christ Reveals to Us the Father, the Spirit, and Himself

What did Jesus tell us God is like? How can we have a meaningful contact with God? Can we be sure that Jesus Christ is divine and that his teaching is God's own?

It is natural to want to reveal ourselves to someone we truly love. We want that person to know as much as possible about us—to come to know our family, our friends, our daily life, our hopes and fears—and to accept us as we really are.

Jesus Christ gradually revealed to us his origin and background, his innermost life, and those with whom he shared it. He did this because he loves us and wants us to know about it.

"I am from him [God], and he has sent me" (John 7, 29). Jesus said this and meant it in its fullest, deepest sense. To understand Jesus Christ, we must try to penetrate the mystery of God's inner life. This he has opened to us. But this is not all.

Jesus Christ told us how we can ourselves share in God's own inner life, in the life of heaven itself, while here on earth. This, he said, is God's plan: that we should even now begin to share most intimately in his very life. To understand ourselves, then, our yearnings and fantastic capabilities, we study God's own life as Jesus revealed it.

OUR FATHER

In the Old Testament, God had revealed himself as one God, the Father of his people. Amid pagan polytheism many Jews had died for this truth. They came to think of God as a Father, from whom all things come, whose love was poured out on them, even when they turned from him: "Israel, says the Lord, is my first-born. . . . Israel in his boyhood, what love I bore him! It was I, none other, that guided those first steps of theirs, and took them in my arms, and healed, all unobserved, their injuries" (Hosea 11, 1–4).

Then gradually God came to be seen as the Father, in a special way, of the future king-Messiah: "I shall be to him a father, and he shall be to me a son" (2 Samuel 7, 14).

When Jesus came he spoke many times of God as a loving Father, his Father and ours. When he was twelve he was missing for three days; Mary and Joseph found him in the Temple and asked why he had left them. "Did you not know that I must be in my Father's house?" he replied. Like many a young person today, he was becoming aware of what his life's vocation was to be. He went back to Nazareth then, but his heart was increasingly with his heavenly Father.

When he began preaching, Jesus continually spoke of God not as a righteous or distant figure but as a loving Father who cares for all our needs: **Read Luke 12, 24–31.**

Jesus taught his followers to pray, "Our Father, who art in heaven, hallowed be thy name. . . . " They had asked him how to pray and he gave them this "Lord's Prayer" (Luke 11, 1–4). It would become the model for all Christian prayer. **Read Matthew 6, 9–13** for its full text.

For some today—usually women—"Our Father" is difficult to say because their human fathers have been absent or abusive. For these God as a loving Father becomes real only slowly and usually by experiencing the tender, enduring love of another, often a spouse.

Jesus was completely caught up in doing his Father's will. One day when his apostles realized that he needed food and begged him to eat, he said, "I have food to eat of which you do not know." They wondered at this and he explained, "My food is to do the will of him who sent me, to accomplish his work" (John 4, 31–34). When his enemies badgered him he told them, "I preach only what the Father has taught me. . . . I do always the things that are pleasing to him" (John 8, 28–29).

This total, selfless dedication to goodness has made Jesus history's most attractive figure.

THE HUMAN SON, ONE OF US

When present-day St. Petersburg was Leningrad in Soviet Russia, the Museum of the History of Religion (the "Museum of Atheism") had large displays devoted to the abuses of organized religion and its supposed incompatibility with the modern, scientific world. But in the whole building there was nothing about Christ, no derision of him, no attack on him.

In the larger art museums of the city there are many paintings of Christ by various masters—usually of the compassionate, very human Christ healing the sick or preaching to the poor—before which thousands of men, women, and children quietly pass. Even in the then supposedly atheistic state, Christ was a unique and respected figure.

Even for many today who say one can have no real contact with God, the figure of Christ, the "man for others," figures largely in their life and thought. They are attracted by him, and even as they debate who he was, they seek to imitate him.

In the first three gospels particularly, we see how very human Jesus Christ was. He led an uneventful life for thirty years and worked as a small-town carpenter. He gradually became more aware of his mission in life, and when he began to preach he suffered antagonism, insults, and the misunderstanding of his own friends and neighbors. On one occasion they even tried to kill him (Luke 4, 16–28). He was often hungry, thirsty, tired, with no home to call his own (Luke 4, 2; John 4, 6; Matthew 8, 20).

He was sometimes sad, and cried over the death of his friend Lazarus (John 11, 33–35). He could enjoy himself, too, and liked to see others enjoy themselves. His first recorded miracle was changing water into wine at a young couple's wedding reception (John 2, 1ff.); he often accepted dinner invitations from his friends (Luke 7, 36ff.); and he liked to be with little children, despite his followers' attempts to chase them away (Matthew 19, 13ff.).

He was acutely conscious of the difficulties, frustrations, uncertainties, and fears that all of us experience. Throughout his life he "increased in wisdom . . . " (Luke 2, 52). As his preaching continued he was constantly frustrated by the growing opposition of his enemies, the powerful leaders of the people. He realized that his preaching of conversion to the kingdom had failed, and that now he would have to suffer and die to bring salvation to his people. He saw that he was to be the suffering servant of God predicted by Isaiah (chapters 50–53), who was to die to bring others to God.

He was strongly tempted from the outset, drawn to sin as if he could fall—though he never did (Matthew 4, 1–11). His lifelong struggle to do his Father's will reached its climax in his agony before his death: "Father, if thou art willing, remove the cup from me; yet not my will but thine be done" (Luke 22, 42). And as he was dying, he cried out in anguish and darkness of soul, "My God, my God, why have you forsaken me?" (Matthew 27, 46).

But to his closest followers, Jesus was a paradox, a mystery. He was close to them, spent many hours instructing them to the point where they argued with him and almost took him for granted. But there was always something of a mystery about him. His personality was powerful, he spoke with a unique authority, but yet he was open, asked questions to learn what people thought of him (Matthew 16, 13), and was shaken by the death of a close friend (John 11, 33–36).

He worked wonders unlike anyone before: " 'Girl, I say to thee, arise.' And the [dead] girl rose up immediately" (Mark 5, 41–42). And yet he confessed that there were some things he did not know: "Of that day or hour [of Judgment] no one knows, neither the angels in heaven, nor the Son, but the Father only" (Mark 13, 32). He said, "All things that the Father has are mine" (John 16, 15), but on another occasion he said, "The Father is greater than I" (John 14, 28).

Gradually he was unfolding his innermost self . . .

THE DIVINE SON

Jesus' great revelation is that the God who is our Father has an only Son, also God, and that he is this divine Son of God. Others are sons and daughters of the loving Father—but Jesus is *the* Son. Gradually this unfolds in the gospels. Jesus says that he is so close to his Father that he alone knows and reveals him:

> "All things have been delivered to me by my Father; and no one knows the Son except the Father; nor does anyone know the Father except the Son, and anyone to whom the Son chooses to reveal him" (Matthew 11, 27).

Jesus calls his Father by the intimate term "Abba," which means something similar to "Daddy," "Dearest Father," or "My own dear father" (Mark 14, 36). This is a uniquely personal, intimate way of speaking about God; the term was used affectionately by children in Jewish family life. Jesus was experiencing the Father, God, as no one before or since—the Father is, somehow, uniquely, mysteriously but really *his own* Father.

This intimate, personal experience of the Father as his Father underlies everything Jesus says and does. He "identifies" totally with the Father, his Father, and lives to do only what he wills.

By showing God to be an always-loving Father, Jesus turned away from the image of God as a divine Patriarch who rules by power. Jesus did not come so much as God's power as his love seeking us. Thus he did not want any man to be called "Father" (Matthew 23, 9) when it implied male domination and lording it over others. That was the way the society of his day was structured—a patriarchy with power held by men at the top and few rights at the bottom. But for Jesus, we are all, rather, sisters and brothers—and mothers—to each other (cf. Luke 8, 20–21).

Some today find that while God as a loving Father is real to them, God as Mother is more meaningful still. Mystics like Julian of Norwich write beautifully and profoundly of experiencing God and also Jesus this way.

In the Jewish Scriptures, God is regularly spoken of as a Mother: "the God who gave you birth" (Deuteronomy 32, 18) is for Isaiah the one who "will cry out like a woman in labor . . . " (42, 14), and who says, "As one whom his mother comforts, so I will comfort you" (66, 13). In Psalm 22 God is a midwife: "It was you who took me from the womb; you kept me safe on my mother's breast. On you I was cast from my birth" (9–10). In the New Testament, Jesus, lamenting over what will befall Jerusalem, compares himself to a mother hen: "How often have I desired to gather your children together as a hen gathers her brood under her wings, and you were not willing" (Luke 13, 34).

The infancy stories of Matthew and Luke show the Church's belief that Jesus' origin was with God. At the start of his public preaching, after he was baptized, "heaven was opened, and the Holy Spirit descended upon him in bodily form as a dove, and a voice came from heaven, 'Thou art my beloved Son, in thee I am well pleased'" (Luke 3, 21–22). And in his last prayer, before his death, Jesus summed up his work as the Son of the Father: **Read John 17, 1–5.**

Jesus showed that he was more than human, by his evident holiness, his knowledge and superhuman insights, and his miracles. People began saying, "Never has man spoken as this man" (John 7, 46), and "Who, then, is this, that even the wind and the sea obey him?" (Mark 4, 40). Then one day he made the bold claim:

> "Abraham your father rejoiced that he was to see my day. He saw it and was glad." The Jews therefore said to him, "Thou art not yet fifty years old, and hast thou seen Abraham?" Jesus said to them, "Amen, amen, I say to you, before Abraham came to be, I am." They therefore took up stones to cast at him; but Jesus hid himself, and went out from the temple (John 8, 56–59).

John here tells us that Jesus is claiming the sacred name of God, "I am." His hearers understood his claim, since they wanted to stone him to death as punishment for blasphemy. He claimed to forgive sins, and his hearers concluded, "Who is this man who speaks blasphemies? Who can forgive sins but God only?" (Luke 5, 21). On another occasion he said openly, "My Father and I are one." His hearers again took up stones to cast at him, saying, "Thou, being a man, makest thyself God" (John 10, 33).

The gospels tell us that Jesus was a wonder-worker, who performed many miracles. They mention some forty miracles of all kinds, including three occasions on which he brought dead persons back to life. We do not know the details of his miracles, or how many he really performed—the gospels, we have seen, are records of faith and are not greatly concerned about historical details. But even the first-century Jewish historian Josephus and the anti-Christian pagan writers conceded that Christ was a wonder-worker. In John's gospel especially, Christ's miracles are called his "works," performed to prove his divine power:

> "Do you say of him whom the Father has made holy and sent into the world, 'Thou blasphemest,' because I said, 'I am the Son of God'? If I do not perform the works of my Father, do not believe me. But if I do perform them, and if you are not willing to believe me, believe the works, that you may know and believe that the Father is in me and I in the Father" (John 10, 36–38).

> *Miracles are seen today more as glimpses of an underlying order—of a more profound, divine level of reality—than as violations or suspensions of nature's laws.* Rather than interventions by God, they are occasions when those

CHRIST REVEALS TO US THE FATHER, THE SPIRIT, AND HIMSELF 91

who are open to them can see, briefly, God's constant, sustaining power in our universe. They are moments when, if we are so disposed, we can see beyond the surface of things to a higher order, a vaster, divine level of reality.

Only gradually, however, did it become clear who Jesus really was. The Jews for centuries had abhorred idolatry, the giving of divine honor to anyone or anything created. God had gradually become remote to them—even his name was too holy to be pronounced. So, though the people were awaiting a Messiah, they were totally unprepared for him to be divine. Then, too, Christ's mission on earth was to establish the kingdom of his Father among us, not to claim anything for himself. He shows his divinity more by his actions than by direct claims.

It is evident from the New Testament that there was a development in his followers' grasp of Jesus' divinity, that his apostles had no real understanding of this during his ministry. After the resurrection and the coming of the Holy Spirit they gradually came to understand—gradually, because they were not so much concerned with the abstract question of precisely who or what Jesus was as with the great things God had done for us through him. They were caught up in preaching the tremendous good news of our salvation by Jesus to eternal life, and with trying to convert everyone to share in this. But by the time of John's gospel and the epistle to the Hebrews, for instance, the realization of his divinity is expressed clearly (cf. John 1, 1; 20, 28; Hebrews 1, 8–9).

We should not be surprised that Jesus' full identity took a while to penetrate the understanding of his followers. We who so glibly call Jesus divine should try to realize how difficult it must have been for his first followers to come to understand this—that the man with whom they had so intimately associated had within himself the fullness of the infinite God. Their every instinct as monotheists was to reject as utterly blasphemous any implication that a human could in any way be divine. Only with the light of the Holy Spirit through the years after Pentecost did they begin to realize that this was so.

Then, too, Jesus really developed in the knowledge of himself and his mission. He "increased in wisdom and in years and in divine and human favor" (Luke 2, 52). What he always was and what he basically knew in the depths of his consciousness, that he was divine, he only gradually came to grasp in the context of his life situation. St. Paul says he "emptied himself " to become one of us—perhaps as if by a kind of divine amnesia he "forgot" he was divine and had to come to realize it again.

This is extraordinarily difficult for us who are only human to even begin to understand—how a human intellect could come to grasp the fact that one is a divine person—and ultimately it is a mystery beyond our understanding.

Perhaps as we know that we are spiritual beings, that we each have a soul, but we cannot directly conceive of or reflect on this aspect of ourselves, and as we only gradually come to realize through the experience of living what it means to become a human person—so Jesus only gradually became reflexively conscious of his divine personality, gradually came to know himself more and more deeply.

How much Christ's divinity "broke through" or was communicated to his human consciousness is currently the subject of much discussion. Many scholars today look at the scriptural evidence and think that while Jesus was always aware of a uniquely intimate relationship with his Father (God), he fully took hold of his divinity only at his resurrection, when he was filled with the Spirit and glorified.

In any event, one thing is becoming clearer today: Jesus is a more human figure, much more one of us, than many Christians, accustomed to thinking of him primarily as divine, had previously supposed.

The resurrection of Jesus, his return to life after his death, is the great testimony to his divinity. He is the only person in human history to have such striking testimony of his return to life. Not only the early Christians but billions of people through history have staked their belief on this.

The gospels go into detail to show that Jesus really died and came back alive again:

And as Jesus was going up to Jerusalem, he took the twelve disciples aside by themselves, and said to them, "Behold, we are going up to Jerusalem, and the Son of Man will be betrayed to the chief priests and the scribes; and they will condemn him to death, and will deliver him to the Gentiles to be mocked and scourged and crucified; and on the third day he will rise again" (Matthew 20, 17-19).

After the merciless scourging, Jesus had to carry his heavy cross through the city to the place of execution; the soldiers, fearing that he would die on the way, got someone to help him carry the cross (Matthew 27, 32).

After hanging on the cross for three hours, Jesus died. Soldiers examined Christ, saw that he was already dead, and pierced his heart with a spear. His body was placed in a new tomb, and a heavy stone was rolled across the opening to seal the tomb; Christ's enemies, remembering his prediction that he would rise on the third day, placed a guard of soldiers around the tomb (John 19, 31–37; Matthew 27, 62–66).

On Easter Sunday morning, some women followers of Christ arrived at the tomb and were amazed to find it empty; an angel told them that Christ had risen. Then Peter and John, hearing the news, ran to the tomb and also found it empty. Mary Magdalene, seeing the empty tomb, concluded his body had been stolen; when Christ appeared to her, she thought he was the gardener, but when he called her by name she realized it was him and ran to tell the others he was alive (Luke 24, 1–11; John 20, 1–18).

On Easter Sunday evening, Christ appeared to the apostles in a closed room. That same evening, Christ appeared to two of his followers on a road outside Jerusalem (Luke 24, 13–35). St. Paul says that at another time Christ appeared to more than five hundred people (1 Corinthians 15, 6). Apparitions of Christ are mentioned eleven times in all.

The accounts of the resurrection are inconsistent in details and chronology. This is natural since each account was written for a different audience in a different part of the early Church, and so each would stress things other accounts would not. They were written for believers, giving each author's view of the resurrection and not meant as proof in a modern sense. Also, the fact that Jesus was alive was so momentous that coordinating the stories seemed unimportant.

The resurrection stories can only inadequately describe the event. The concept of resurrection surpasses our understanding and even our imagination. It is about far more than a resuscitated corpse—it means that Jesus Christ, who was dead, is alive and glorified and filled with divine power. And, as we shall see, only those who have faith can believe it. Yet the stories, however much they fall short of the reality, can help us grasp something of the resurrection's meaning.

Christ's resurrection transformed his followers once they realized its meaning. Demoralized by Christ's death, they were not at all disposed to believe that he had risen from the grave. They tell us that when Christ did appear, they thought he was a ghost, and he had to eat something to convince them that he was truly alive (Luke 24, 36–43)—that the apostle Thomas would not believe until he could examine the wounds in Christ's body, then he exclaimed, "My Lord and my God!" (John 20, 24–29).

After Christ's several appearances, he ascended into heaven, and his followers awaited the coming of the Holy Spirit as he had instructed them. They had begun to believe, but they were still confused. Then the Spirit came, and the staggering fact now began to penetrate—it would take some years yet, but gradually they came to realize: God had come among them in Jesus Christ. The wonderful person with whom they had talked and eaten and toiled, who had led them and inspired them and who now was gone from them—this man had had within himself the full power of the divinity.

Convinced they were commissioned by Christ, they began to proclaim his resurrection and his message throughout the world. They had been commanded to "make disciples of all nations" (Matthew 28, 19). They called Christ "Lord" in the same way the Old Testament had spoken of God; he is God's power and wisdom (1 Corinthians 1, 24), the perfect reflection of his glory (Hebrews 1, 3). They worked miracles in his name, and they gladly died for him.

Belief in Christ's resurrection was, and is, the impetus behind the spread of Christianity. The early Christians never spoke of Christ as a dead hero but as one living in their midst. As the early Christian Church developed, this was its key teaching, and it has been so through the centuries. The belief of billions of Christians through history is summed up by St. Paul:

> And if Christ has not risen, vain is your faith, for you are still in your sins. Hence they also who have fallen asleep in Christ have perished. If with this life only in view we have had hope in Christ, we are of all men the most to be pitied. But as it is, Christ has risen from the dead, the first-fruits of those who have fallen asleep (1 Corinthians 15, 17–20).

> *It is important to remember what we assert, as Christians, when we say that Christ is risen.* We are saying that his complete humanity is glorified,

that it is perfect, unrestricted, unlimited, endowed with the fullness of divine power. We cannot conceptualize or even imagine a risen and glorified humanity. Thus when the resurrection narratives tell of Jesus appearing to his followers, being "seen" by them, "eating" with them, being "touched" by them, and so on, they are saying that his followers realized Jesus was truly alive and glorified. Such language was the only way Jesus' followers could get across their experience of him as alive and glorified.

This realization was a unique religious experience—to be a witness to Jesus' resurrection and be sent forth by him to tell about it made one an apostle. But we, too, by faith, "meet" the glorified Christ when we realize that he is alive and acting among us. Though not as uniquely spectacular as the experience of his first followers, it can be just as real and as transforming of our lives. Today many who are converted in adulthood to belief in the risen Christ testify to this, as do countless others who have experienced him in innumerable ways over the centuries.

We today experience Jesus personally, as we will see, in the eucharist and the other sacraments, in the Christian community at worship and at prayer, and in our own prayers and acts of faith and love toward others. The Jesus Christ we believe in and experience is the same person as the historical Jesus—or, as theology puts it, the Jesus of history is the same as the Christ of our faith. Our belief and experiencing does not depend on the latest historical-critical research—and it may be only gradual and shot through with doubt and difficulties. The first Christians who knew the historical Jesus only gradually came to realize that he was the Christ, the Messiah, and also, more staggeringly, God himself in human form.

John's gospel particularly gives the reflection of the late-first-century Christian Church about Christ when it calls him the Word of God who became a man. This gospel shows a maturing reflection about Christ's divinity-in-humanity. It continually points to his "works," his miracles, as signs that he is divine. It begins: "In the beginning was the Word, and the Word was with God, and the Word was God . . . and the Word was made flesh, and lived among us" (John 1, 1–14). The prophets had proclaimed God's Word, his message, as best they could—now the living Word, the perfect expression of God the Father, has come among us.

To believe in Christ's divinity one must have an open mind and a willingness to live his teachings—and the power of faith. Skeptics, those whose minds are closed to his teachings or to moral improvement, like Herod, Pontius Pilate, and the Pharisees, would have seen nothing had they been with the apostles when Christ appeared after his resurrection. Others may have open minds but lack the power of faith. (We shall consider this more fully in chapter 16 when we discuss faith.) St. Peter says,

> God raised him on the third day and caused him to be plainly seen, not by all the people, but by witnesses designated beforehand by God, that is, by us . . . (Acts 10, 40–41).

One should consider Christ's whole teaching before accepting or rejecting his divinity. Christ gradually reveals himself, usually through his message. As with Christ's first followers, it takes time to grasp the reality of who he is. If one is open to the truth and tries to live by what one discovers to be true, faith in Christ often comes as one ponders his teachings. The rest of this book concerns these teachings.

Jesus Christ is the perfect man, the "new Adam," the new head of the human race, the perfect lover of God and of us. He never sinned, nor did he ever turn aside from his Father's will. He is the only one in history who responded perfectly to God's outpouring love and who never faltered in his constant, all-embracing love for his fellow humans. St. Paul stumblingly grasps the reality of Jesus when he says that he is "the image of the invisible God, the firstborn of every creature. For in him were created all things in the heavens and on the earth, things visible and things invisible . . . " (Colossians 1, 15).

Divine and perfect though he is, Jesus Christ yet experienced all our human weaknesses and emotions. He "emptied himself" of his divinity, says St. Paul (Philippians 2, 7), and though he did not sin, he was tempted like any of us—but he loved so much that he never yielded. He experienced our joys and sorrows, our hopes and agonies. He struggled, as we must, to know the Father's will and to do it. He underwent all our difficulties, frustrations, uncertainties, and fears—and because of his total sensitivity he experienced these things more acutely than we ever could.

Jesus Christ, then, is both God and a man. This is the mystery of the incarnation, the fullness of God in human flesh. "The Word was made flesh and dwelt among us" (John 1, 14). Other cultures in their mythologies have had savior gods who came among humans, but no one dreamed that the infinite, unique, "totally Other" God would become one of us.

> By his incarnation, the Son of God has united himself in some fashion with every [person]. He worked with human hands, he thought with a human mind, acted by human choice and loved with a human heart. Born of the Virgin Mary, he has truly been made one of us, like us in all things except sin (*The Pastoral Constitution on the Church in the Modern World*, no. 22).

God became a human through Mary, his human mother, whom we call the Mother of God. We call her this because her son, Jesus, is God. Mary is a human being, infinitely below the Almighty. She was chosen to give Christ his human body, but obviously not his divinity or his human soul. But Mary is truly a mother—she is to Jesus all that any mother is to her son. Jesus is God the Son; the "I" or "ego" of Jesus is divine. Therefore, anything that Jesus has, he has as God. We can say that God had relatives, that God had a mother. The title "Mother of God" came to be used in early Christianity as a test of one's orthodox belief in Christ.

The "Hail Mary" is one of the most ancient prayers of the Church. The first part is Luke's portrayal of the angel's words to Mary at the moment of the incarnation, and also Elizabeth's greeting to her. The second is an ancient, popular petition.

"Hail, Mary, full of grace, the Lord is with thee; blessed art thou among women, and blessed is the fruit of thy womb, Jesus. Holy Mary, Mother of God, pray for us sinners, now and at the hour of our death. Amen."

Another ancient Christian belief is that Mary was conceived free from sin. This is Mary's immaculate conception, celebrated on December 8, a holyday in the United States on which Catholics take part in Mass to rejoice in the privilege Christ has given Mary, the model Christian.

> Mary's freedom from sin is something we should expect since she was chosen for the unique dignity of being God's human mother. Since Christ came to conquer evil, it is fitting that he should take his human body from a woman who was untainted with sin. Luke describes Mary's awe-filled realization: "He who is mighty has done great things for me, and holy is his name . . . " (Luke 1, 49).

This doctrine has often been a stumbling block to ecumenical relations with non-Catholic Christians, since there is no biblical evidence for it, and some of the early Church Fathers spoke of Mary's moral faults. Catholics consider it an example of a development of doctrine, not appearing clearly nor emphasized in Catholic life and teaching until the Middle Ages, and not defined until 1854.

A better way to view this is not so much as a personal privilege of Mary, but in its actual purpose: a part of the preparation for the coming of the Son of God into the world. It is actually, therefore, a statement about Christ. It was a privilege given to Mary for the sake of further sustaining the uniqueness of Jesus Christ. This, like everything else in her life, and indeed her very being, existed only for Jesus Christ.

Also, Mary is a symbol of the Church, and so this teaching can have a deeper meaning regarding the Church: Mary was preserved from sin, not through her own merit, but in anticipation of Christ's redemption—so the Church, though composed of sinful members, is also sinless in its nature, not through any human accomplishment, but by the power of Christ.

The meaning of the incarnation is that God loves us so much that he became one of us, to share his happiness with us. In our world, when a man loves a woman he wants to be with her, to share experiences, to make her happy. God loves us and comes among us, to share our experiences, to give us happiness beyond anything we can imagine. Perhaps this is why he became one of us, to convince us of this love and happiness. Otherwise we would never have believed our destiny.

THE HOLY SPIRIT

Christ spoke about the Spirit who would be sent by the Father and himself to complete his work. Sometimes called the Holy Ghost, Christ calls the Spirit the Paraclete or Advocate, that is, a Helper or Comforter. The Spirit is to help the apostles to at last understand Christ and his teachings:

"But the Advocate, the Holy Spirit, whom the Father will send in my name, he will teach you all things, and bring to your mind whatever I have said to you. . . . But when the Advocate has come, whom I will send you from the Father, the Spirit of Truth who proceeds from the Father, he will bear witness concerning me" (John 14, 26; 15, 26).

In the Old Testament the Spirit of God was thought of as a manifestation of the Father, his life-giving "breath" that takes possession of a person, renewing the person from within, making him or her responsive to God's Word. Thus the prophet Isaiah proclaims his mission: "The Lord has anointed me, on me his spirit has fallen" (61, 1). And Ezekiel beautifully proclaims the Lord's promise to his people: "I will give you a new heart, and breathe a new spirit into you; I will take away from your breasts those hearts that are hard as stone, and give you human hearts instead. I will make my spirit penetrate you, so that you will follow in the path of my law, and remember and carry out my decrees" (11, 19–20).

The Spirit worked within Jesus, a personal reality, guiding and inspiring him. At his baptism, "the Holy Spirit descended upon him in bodily form as a dove . . . " (Luke 3, 22). "Then Jesus was led by the Spirit about the desert" (Luke 4, 1) before beginning his mission. As he starts his mission, the Spirit gives him power: **Read Luke 4, 14–19.**

Near the end of his life Jesus told his followers that the Spirit would make his teachings clear to them: "It is expedient for you that I depart. For if I do not go, the Advocate will not come to you; but if I go, I will send him to you" (John 16, 7). After the Spirit came on Pentecost, Christ's disciples began to understand his teachings, among them the fact that the Father, Son, and Holy Spirit are one God.

The Holy Spirit is the successor of Jesus, who continues his work among us and within us. The Spirit continually moved the early Christian Church, and today is the source of God's life in the Church and in each Christian. The Spirit is the power that enables us to believe in Christ and live his teachings: "No one can say 'Jesus is Lord' except by the Holy Spirit," says Paul (1 Corinthians 12, 3). The Spirit is also our invincible power in the battle with sin and ignorance—though often we never suspect this presence, or suspecting it, we are afraid to open ourselves to it.

Reflecting on Christ's revelation, the Church slowly penetrated into the mystery of the Father, Son, and Holy Spirit. As Christianity developed, scholars and ordinary people alike tried to understand Christ better and his relationship to the Father and the Spirit. Guided by the Spirit, some facets of this mystery began to emerge and were proclaimed by the Church in several councils.

There is but one God, but in God there are three divine, completely equal Persons. This is the mystery of the Blessed Trinity. Each of the Three Persons is really distinct from the other Two. Each is wholly God, equal to the other Two. One did not come before the others. Yet there is only one God.

> *Traditional Catholic theology puts it this way:* the three divine Persons, distinct as Persons, possess the same single nature of God. This is based on the difference between the idea of "person" and that of "nature," taken originally from Greek philosophy and expanded by Christian thinkers: *person* tells *who* we are; *nature* tells *what* we are. Each of us, for example, is aware that she or he is a distinct person, different from everyone else. But each of us is also aware that she or he is human, has a human nature, and in this we are similar to everyone else. Each of us, then, is one person with one nature. It is quite possible—and this is the case with God—to have One who is Three Persons with one nature.

The Second Person of the Blessed Trinity, the Son, took on a human nature, became a real man, and lived and died among us as Jesus Christ. St. Paul tells us, "Christ Jesus, who though he was by nature God, did not consider being equal to God a thing to be clung to, but emptied himself, taking the nature of a slave and being born in human likeness" (Philippians 2, 5–7). This is the mystery of the incarnation.

> Jesus Christ, then, has two natures—a divine nature and a human nature. Jesus has his divine nature as God from eternity, together with the Father and the Holy Spirit. He took on a distinct human nature two thousand years ago.
>
> But Jesus is only one Person, God, the Son, who "uses" these two natures. With the power of his divine nature he acts as God; with the power of his human nature he acts as a man. But whenever Jesus did anything it was the one Person of God the Son who did it.

It is good to remember that the Blessed Trinity is a mystery. "The central mystery of the faith is the Trinity . . . the source of all the other mysteries" (*Catechism*, 234). We can know something about the Trinity, but in the final analysis very, very little.

Life is full of mysteries—the origin and destiny of the universe, what life itself is, why two people with the same genetic background and upbringing can turn out so differently—and so we need not be surprised that the inner life of God is the deepest of all mysteries. Also, whether or not one can believe in the Trinity depends not only on one's openness but on God's gift of faith.

Through history people continue to achieve new insights into God's existence and nature. God is ever leading us to a truer, more profound knowledge of himself and our relationship to him. What is proof of God for one person is not for another; what is widely accepted in one period of history may not be later. We believe the Church's insights are true. But they are only a few stumbling words about One who is immense, immeasurable, impenetrable love.

The work of any person's lifetime should be an endless quest for the infinite—to try to know, to understand a bit more, to make some sort of lasting contact with God. The tragedy is that people who give their lifetime to penetrating nature or organizing society never stop to reflect on the limitless God. If persevered in, no quest can be as rewarding. To this some of the greatest people of history and of our time testify.

The names of the Three Persons tell us something about them and their personal relationship to us. What one Person does for us the other Persons also do; yet each has a distinct role in God's plan. By grace we are joined to each in a distinct way:

The First Person is called the Father because this Person produces a Second Person, the Son. This First Person is spoken of as our creator; the word *God* usually refers to this Person. The First Person is the source from whom everything comes to us, and to whom our worship is ultimately directed. We address this Person when we pray the "Our Father"—the Lord's Prayer—and all the great prayers of Christian worship.

We have seen that because there is no gender in God, some today might better relate to this Person of origin, God our Parent, as Mother. What seems best for some is addressing God as our Father/Mother.

The Second Person is called the Son because he has his origin from the Father and receives the same divine nature from the Father. Similarly, a boy is called "son" because he has the same human nature as his father, received from his father. We saw that this Second Person is also called the "Word," the perfect expression of the Father.

Jesus Christ is the Son become human, our brother, through whom every grace comes to us and through whom we worship the Father. By being joined to Jesus Christ, we share in the very life of the Trinity—we somehow become sons and daughters in the Son. Our whole life is to be a gradual reproducing of his life in us. There is truly no limit to what we can do when united with him.

Though we pray to Christ, this prayer should lead us to pray *through* Christ and *with* Christ to the Father. We then share in Christ's perfect prayer to the Father. Our stumbling prayer becomes the prayer of Christ. This is the way the Church usually prays.

The Third Person is called the Holy Spirit and is produced by the love of the Father and Son for one another. So great is their love that it produces another Person, Love personified, the Holy Spirit; our word *spirit* is taken from a word meaning breath or sigh, a universal sign of life and love.

The Holy Spirit is the gift, the love, of the Father and Son to us—the one through whom we enter the life of the Trinity, who comes from Christ into us, and within us, unites us to Christ and the Father.

The Spirit is the one who is the source within us of our Christian prayer and worship. Our ability to pray is from the Spirit. When we pray, the Spirit prays within us, and gives form, meaning, power to our prayers. Thus we pray "in the Spirit" (cf. St. Paul's comforting Romans 8, 26).

The Spirit, for some theologians today, is seen as the "feminine" aspect of God. The Old Testament notion of "Wisdom," a personification of God communicating with us, is almost always a feminine figure. "Sophia," Wisdom in Greek, is also feminine. Thus Wisdom can be thought of as the feminine Spirit who infuses Jesus (who is called Wisdom incarnate) and us as well. The "motherly" Spirit acts in Jesus (and in us) not only as divine power and justice but as always-nurturing, intimately relating, unconditionally accepting Love, vulnerable but strong, gently guiding her children.

Some address the Three Persons as Creator, Redeemer or Savior, and Sanctifier, or in some similar way that makes use of their functions toward us. Through the centuries the Church's prayer life has been rich in its ways of addressing the Persons, together and individually, and we should use whatever has most meaning for us.

One of the great lessons we can derive from Christ's teaching about the Blessed Trinity is that God is not unlike us or separate from

us. Rather, God is Three Persons, a "family" who love one another with a joy and happiness we can only begin to imagine. Yet this is not all. God is not a family in which the Divine Persons are concerned only with themselves. The only way we know God is by the Persons relating to us, in Jesus Christ and the Spirit. We truly are "partners" with God, relating to and sharing in the very life of the Persons of God—and the way we, in turn, relate to one another comes out of this incredible intimacy we all have with them.

To summarize our relationship to the Three Persons:

Everything comes to us from the Father, through the Son-made-man, Jesus Christ, and we receive it by means of the Holy Spirit within us.

We, in turn, return our love to the Father, through and with his Son, Jesus Christ, and we do this by the power of the Holy Spirit within us: **Read Ephesians 5, 18-20.**

IN THE LITURGY

Almost every prayer and ceremony of the Church is done in the name of the Blessed Trinity. The Sign of the Cross and the Doxology are ancient prayers in their honor. We celebrate Trinity Sunday on the First Sunday after Pentecost each year.

At Mass, the Sign of the Cross is used several times from the beginning to the last blessing. The "Lord, have mercy on us . . ." asks their mercy; the "Glory to God in the highest," which follows, praises them. The Creed summarizes our belief in the Trinity.

Most other Mass prayers are addressed in the Church's ordinary way: to God the Father through the Son, in union with the Holy Spirit. The climax of the offering of our gift in every Mass is when the priest prays, "Through him [Christ], with him, and in him, in the unity of the Holy Spirit, all honor and glory is yours, Almighty Father, forever and ever"—and the whole congregation answers, "Amen!"

At Mass, we also affirm our belief in the incarnation. In the Creed, for instance, we profess that God the Son, the Word of God, "was made flesh . . . and became man." In the eucharistic prayer, at the heart of the Mass, we recount the fact that God's Son has become human in Jesus Christ.

DAILY LIVING: OUR DIGNITY AS BEARERS OF THE TRINITY AND SISTERS AND BROTHERS OF CHRIST

In revealing the Blessed Trinity to us, Christ showed us something of God's inner life and his amazing desire to be known to his creatures.

But this is not all. Christ said, "If anyone loves me, he will keep my word, and my Father will love him, and we will come to him and make our abode with him . . . " (John 14, 23). And speaking of the Holy Spirit, he said, "you shall know him, because he will dwell with you and be in you" (John 14, 17).

The Blessed Trinity dwells intimately within us. This is God's grace-presence. As long as we have grace, what we really have with us is this presence of God, united to us in the most intimate way possible. This is the "indwelling" of the Blessed Trinity.

This indwelling presence means that even now we are beginning the life of heaven. Anywhere, anytime—as long as we are not isolated by serious sin—we can communicate with the Trinity within us and be confident of their help.

By this indwelling presence we can come to know and experience the divine Persons. The Father, we realize, is *our* Father who loves us and shares his life with us. The Son is our brother, Jesus Christ, who is like us and communicates the Father's love to us and leads us to the Father. The Holy Spirit is most intimately within us, uniting us to Jesus, joining us to the Father—and to one another—through and with Jesus.

This indwelling presence means that we must respect our body and the bodies of others. St. Paul's words to his Corinthian converts who had been abusing their bodies might also be reminders to any of us:

> Or do you not know that your members are the temple of the Holy Spirit, who is in you, whom you have from God, and that you are not your own? For you have been bought at a great price. Glorify God and bear him in your body (1 Corinthians 6, 19–20).

We respect our own self as a person by realizing that we each are unique in all of creation and by developing our unique identity and sense of self-esteem. Each of us is known and loved by God within us in a most personal, understanding way. Thus, regardless of how others treat us, and regardless of our own weaknesses and needs, we are totally known and intimately loved by the only One who really matters, who holds the universe itself in existence.

This should give each of us, no matter how deprived, abused, or neglected, a deep sense of our dignity as a person of lasting worth, with unique powers and God-derived talents. Our concept of ourself as a person of limitless value, beauty, and lovableness should never depend on others' approval (even that of a special other).

Concretely, we respect ourself as a person by developing our talents, our unique giftedness. This means courage and imagination, the ability to rise above peer pressures, to avoid overindulgence in alcohol or smoking, the use of drugs, and the abuse of sex. Young people especially can be carried away by our overly permissive society, by an attitude of "everybody's doing it" (sometimes tacitly tolerated even by their parents, adults-in-years who are really children in emotional maturity).

We respect the dignity of others by treating them with true love and consideration. We should desire for all people everything that we seek for ourselves. We fail in this if we take advantage of or abuse anyone, for example, by unjustly overworking another, by discriminating against another because of his or her race, nationality, or age, by unjust anger, by hatred or bearing a grudge.

Sexism is also a way we fail to respect another's dignity. This is discriminating against another or denigrating another because of the person's sex. Usually directed against women, it can also affect men. In recent years many sexual stereotypes have been proven false, but people unfortunately tend to cling to them.

Sexual abuse and harassment are ways in which women (almost always the victims) are denigrated. The first is usually overt in its meanness and cruelty while the second can be more subtle. While our society is more aware of these evils today, it is estimated that one of three women in the United States will be sexually abused during her lifetime.

Rape is an obvious form of violence intended to denigrate women. Much pornography is also obviously sexually denigrating. Not as obvious are de facto unequal pay scales or withholding of promotions for comparable work, lack of adequate provisions for pre- and postnatal care, and so on.

Another reason for respecting ourself and others is because God's own Son became one of us, thereby teaching us that a human being is something wonderful indeed in God's eyes. He is the "first-born within a large family" (Romans 8, 29). In what better way could God bring home to us our tremendous dignity?

Because of the incarnation our earth is now especially sacred and worthy of our best efforts to care for it, to develop it properly, and to make it a better place for us all. Whether it is the combating of pollution, the preservation of the rain forests, or preserving the various species of plant and animal life—our planet is special because God's own Son chose to dwell in it.

God's Son remains among us, intimately involved with each of us—this we will see in the next chapter. He not only thought enough of us to become one of us, he remains totally, permanently involved with us. A modern writer puts it this way:

> In the Christian experience . . . God does not dip his finger into history; he totally immerses himself in it. When he visits the world he does not come slumming. He comes to stay (Dewart, *The Future of Belief*, p. 194).

SOME SUGGESTIONS FOR . . .

DISCUSSION

Which Person of the Trinity can you most easily relate to?

Can you see why alternative names for the Persons of the Trinity might be helpful, even necessary, for some believers?

"God is always taking us by surprise," someone has said. The fact that Jesus Christ is God become a human caused great problems for even his close followers, and they only very gradually came to accept it. How is this tremendous fact received today? How do you receive it? That is, what difference does it make in your life?

How, and when, is the living presence of Jesus most real for you?

Because of the indwelling Trinity we humans and our bodies are sacred, and because of the incarnation our earth and everything on it is also sacred. What is most necessary for you to respect the dignity of others? To respect your own dignity? The sacredness of our earth?

FURTHER READING

- *The Re-Creation of Eve,* Haughton (Templegate, 1985)—An insightful, revealing book about the women of the New Testament, including why they were forgotten, with an especially good chapter on "The Mother."
- •• *Jesus Risen,* O'Collins (Paulist Press, 1987)—A study of the resurrection in its various aspects, especially as seen by some modern theologians. In •• *Interpreting the Resurrection: Examining the Major Problems in the Stories of Jesus' Resurrection* (Paulist Press, 1989), the same scholar sheds new light on puzzling aspects of the stories of Jesus' appearances.
- *Introduction to New Testament Christology,* Brown (Paulist Press, 1994)—America's preeminent Catholic New Testament scholar reflects on how much Jesus himself knew, and how he—and then his followers—grew in knowledge of himself and his mission.
- •• *Sexism and God-Talk: Toward a Feminist Theology,* Ruether (Beacon Press, 1983)—In a well-written, balanced approach, a well-known Catholic feminist theologian discusses the implications of God as neither male nor female, and how our scriptural, liturgical, and doctrinal language has become unreflectively sexist.
- •• *Models of God: Theology for an Ecological, Nuclear Age,* McFague (Fortress, 1987)—Shows Jesus' message was inclusive of everyone and opposed to hierarchical structures, reflecting the God he came to reveal.
- •• *She Who Is: The Mystery of God in Feminist Theological Discourse,* Johnson (Crossroad, 1993)—A sweeping book on the way we conceptualize and speak about God and the Trinity and on the way we might, such as, for instance, Mother-Sophia, Jesus-Sophia, and Spirit-Sophia. Probably the best presentation to date of feminist theology.
- •• *God for Us: The Trinity and Christian Life,* LaCugna (HarperSanFrancisco, 1991)—Another sweeping, breakthrough book that looks at the historical development of the doctrine of the Trinity and then goes on to say that we know the Persons only as they relate to us, sharing their innermost life, in Christ and the Spirit.
- *An Experience Named Spirit,* Shea (Thomas More, 1983)—This popular, imaginative author here gives a very human yet profound account of the experiences that are the Spirit acting in our daily lives.

•• *The Divine Mother: A Trinitarian Theology of the Holy Spirit,* Gelpi (University Press of America, 1984)—A book that requires one's full attention, this is also full of rewarding theological and spiritual insights—a "breakthrough" work by an outstanding theologian and spiritual guide.

PERSONAL REFLECTION

The Blessed Trinity lives within us as long as we do not deliberately cut ourselves off from this grace-presence. The more I try to be aware of this presence during the day, the greater is my power of love, the easier it is to do good, and the greater will be my happiness and that of everyone with whom I come in contact.

The Blessed Trinity also lives within the bodies of others; an awareness of this will lead me to respect them.

I should set aside time, even just a few minutes each day, to communicate with the Trinity within, asking help to know what to do and to have the courage to do it.

8

Christ Saves Us by His Death and Resurrection

What is the ultimate reason that God came among us? What is the high point of human history? Why did Christ suffer and die? Is there any meaning to the suffering, humiliation, and frustration in our lives? Why are joy and hope natural to a committed Christian?

IN CHRIST WE DIED AND ROSE AGAIN

We have seen how God himself came among us in Jesus Christ. He told us of God's own innermost life, the Blessed Trinity, and how the divine Persons dwell intimately within us. He shared our human joys and afflictions and gave us a whole new way of life. He showed us by his own example how to live totally for God.

Jesus Christ, however, not only taught us how to attain heaven. More fundamentally, he made it possible for us. From Adam on, humankind had been cutting itself off from God by sin. Pride and selfishness had become imbedded in human nature. People were divided within themselves, from one another, and from God.

God's plan was to share his own life with us forever—and God's love is unwavering. He would save us from the predicament into which our sins had put us. We call God's actions toward humankind a "history of salvation." Its high point is the coming of the Savior.

God prepared our race for many years, from the first humans through the whole Old Testament period. He tried to attract humankind by being generous with us, giving his love in the measure that we could respond to it. Even when his chosen people violated their covenant with him again and again, he continued to reach out with his love and forgiveness. He worked slowly, by our standards, because he will never force people to come to him. Our love must always be given freely.

Humankind had become so sinful that it seemed that God's plan had failed, that the living God was dead—or at least missing. Widespread slavery, degradation of women, religious prostitution, human sacrifice, cruelty to the weak, average citizens taking their recreation watching other humans being torn apart—this was the world of two thousand years ago. But it was the "fullness of time" for which God had been preparing. Humankind had experienced the depths of sin. A faithful remnant acutely realized their need of a savior and longed for his coming. The Father then responded in an undreamed-of way.

God sent his own Son, Jesus Christ, to overcome the power of sin and fill us with his grace-presence. In his plan we are to grow in this gift of himself, this new life, until we are with him face-to-face forever in heaven. Jesus summed up his mission: "I came that they may have life, and have it abundantly" (John 10, 10). Those who knew that humankind needed a savior never dreamed it would be God's own Son.

Jesus could save us because he opened himself totally to the Father. He alone perfectly responded to the Father's will. "I seek not my own will, but the will of him who sent me" (John 5, 30). He was the perfect human who loved us so much that he remained untouched by the pride and selfishness around him. He is the "new Adam," the fresh starting point, the new and perfect head of our race. His obedience "made up for" the disobedience of Adam and of all of us. He showed us how to respond to love. He "emptied" himself, and the Father could then fill him with life and love for all humankind: **Read Philippians 2, 5-11.**

We must remember that each of us is in need of Christ as our Savior because each of us is a sinner. We are all born into the situation and environment of sin that we call original sin. We all need to be freed, raised up from our own prideful disobedience. We fall again and again into sin.

We need to be opened to God's love. We need someone to pick us up, to carry us beyond our sins to God.

What we could never do because of our sins, God did for us by becoming human in Jesus Christ. As a loving parent stoops to a helplessly crippled child and carries it along, so God accomplished for us what we could not do for ourselves.

Jesus Christ saved us by his death and resurrection. While every action of Christ's life helped to save us, his great central act of love was his death and resurrection. St. Paul says succinctly, "Jesus our Lord . . . was put to death for our trespasses and raised for our justification" (Romans 4, 25).

Christ's death and resurrection were able to help us because he united us to himself, so that we could share in what he did. In a mysterious and wonderful way we died and rose again with him. We know how love causes one to suffer with the beloved: parents suffer anguish at seeing their children in pain, a wife's sufferings cause her husband mental torments. Some people love enough to give up life itself for the one they love.

So Christ identified us with himself and died for our sins. Totally innocent himself, he yet gave himself totally for us. He is completely, unreservedly, the "man for others." He said, "No one has greater love than this, to lay down one's life for one's friends" (John 15, 13).

But Christ did even more. We alienated ourselves from him because of our sins, and yet he laid down his life for us and made us his friends. St. Paul exclaims:

> Why, one will hardly die for a righteous person—though perhaps for a good person one will dare even to die. But God shows his love for us in that while we were yet sinners Christ died for us (Romans 5, 7–9).

By dying for us Christ made up for our sins. When he was killed, he killed sin's ultimate power over us; when he was buried, the power of sin to keep us from eternal life was buried with him: **Read Romans 6, 4–11.**

Theology expresses in several ways what Christ did: He "redeemed" us, bought us back from our subjection to sin; "satisfied" for our sins, made "reparation" for them, that is, repaired the damage they had done; he brought about our "justification"; he "merited" grace for us; he "atoned" for our sins, made us "at one" again with God.

Jesus does not "appease" the divine "wrath" of a God outraged by our sins, nor does he "pay the price" to God for our sins. This view of a punishing God who demands even the death of his Son was widespread in popular Christian imagination and even in the liturgy until recently, spurred on by human tragedies that were seen as God's punishment. The fact is that Jesus, out of limitless love, offered to reunite us with God to save us from the alienation in which we put ourselves by our sins. He carried this out by his whole life of reconciliation, and when he saw that he might have to die violently for us, he accepted it as the only way to show us his, and God's, limitless love for us. He could, simply, do no more.

Feminist theologians, especially, today expose another distortion in this once-common view of a God who demands the death of his Son—that Jesus not only went to his death as a passive victim of violence but also "died like a man" in order to satisfy a God who sanctioned even this ultimate violence. But, in fact, this violence was unacceptable to God, for God overturned his Son's death by raising him from the dead. "God would always rather have us live for others than die for them," is the way one theologian sums it up.

By rising to new life Christ obtained for us the new life of God's grace-presence. Christ is now the head of a revitalized human race, the "firstborn of many brethren." He offers us this new life, a sharing in God's own life and Presence within us. If we accept it, it is the beginning of an unimaginable intimacy with him that will never end.

According to the Creed, Jesus "descended into hell" after his death and before his resurrection—he went not to the hell of the damned but through the "underworld," in Jewish tradition a shadowy state in which the dead awaited the final judgment. 1 Peter 3, 19, says that Jesus "preached to the spirits in prison"—in one tradition those who had lived since Adam and were awaiting salvation—freeing them and bringing them with him when he ascended into heaven. "Descending into hell" could also mean Jesus' being cut off from God, abandoned, powerless, the consequence of his decision to die the death of a sin-laden man.

Christ's death and resurrection is the great turning point in human history. An old world ended, and a whole new way of life, a new vision of reality, began. Now we can have a life of unimaginable love and intimacy with God himself.

THROUGH CHRIST'S PERFECT WORSHIP
WE CAN NOW REACH GOD

Through Christ's death and resurrection we can be sure of reaching God. People have always sought to contact God, to know if he is there, if he is interested. We wonder how we can reach him. As with people from primitive times, we want to be united with him, transformed, "taken up" into a new life with him. So it is that humans have always worshiped God, attempting to reach him particularly by offering him gifts in sacrifice. But people were only too aware of the inadequacy of their offerings.

Christ's death and resurrection was the one, perfect sacrifice by which people reached God. We have seen how God's people had worshiped him by sacrifices of animals and crops, offered by their priests. These sacrifices prepared the way for Christ's perfect sacrifice in which he offered his life as our gift to the Father.

> For if the sprinkling of defiled persons with the blood of goats and bulls and with the ashes of a heifer sanctified for the purification of the flesh, how much more shall the blood of Christ, who through the eternal Spirit offered himself without blemish to God, purify your conscience from dead works to serve the living God (Hebrews 9, 13-14).

Christ is our mediator, our perfect yet understanding priest. His obedience and love made his death the perfect sacrifice. He was the perfect "go-between." The Old Testament priests had offered sacrifices to God in the name of the people and had brought blessings from God. Christ offered his life to his Father and brought us the gift of eternal happiness. The priests of the old Law were imperfect men. Christ is the perfect human, yet one like us who understands our weaknesses. He is the greatest priest of all, our one perfect mediator: **Read Hebrews 5, 1-10.**

Christ's ascension into heaven completed his resurrection. His mission on earth was now totally fulfilled. He has returned to the Father and is glorified at his "right hand" in heaven.

Christ's glorification dramatically showed that the Father accepted his sacrifice and that we could now be united with God forever. To have meaning, a gift must be accepted by the one to whom it is given. In the Old Testament the death and burning of the sacrificial victim was meant to show God's acceptance of the gift, its transformation into something divine. Christ's resurrection and ascension strikingly showed that his gift of himself on our behalf was accepted by his Father.

THE NEW AND UNENDING COVENANT OF LOVE

Christ fulfilled beyond all expectation the passover of the Old Testament: he passed from death to life and from this world to the Father, bringing us all with him. God had passed over Egypt, saving his people from death and slavery, and the Israelites had passed over the waters of the Red Sea and the Jordan to become united with God in the Sinai covenant and the Promised Land. Whenever the Jews ate the annual paschal meal, they looked forward to a new passover, a new exodus to a new freedom and happiness.

Christ fulfilled this longing by making it possible for us to pass with him to eternal happiness. He is the "Lamb of God" (John 1, 29) sacrificed to save us all. "Christ, our paschal lamb, has been sacrificed," says St. Paul (1 Corinthians 5, 7): **Read John 8, 32-36.**

By dying and rising Jesus Christ brought us from slavery under sin to the perfect freedom of God's redeemed people. This is the new exodus, and Christ is the new Moses, leading us all to freedom and eternal happiness. If we join ourselves with him, our sins can no longer enslave us or prevent us from attaining true happiness.

Christ timed his passover to coincide with the annual commemoration of the first passover. He began his passage from death to life by eating the Jewish paschal meal, his last supper. As Moses had done, Christ gave his followers a ritual by which his passover would be commemorated for future generations. He said over the bread, "This is my body which is being given for you. Do this in remembrance of me"—and as he passed the last cup of wine, "This cup is the new covenant in my blood, which shall be shed for you" (cf. Matthew 26, 17-29).

Christ's ritual meal, however, would enable his followers through the centuries to rise above time and actually share in his very death and resurrection. This is the Mass, the great sacrifice and family meal of his Church.

By dying and rising for us, Jesus Christ began the new, perfect, eternal covenant. The ancient covenants of God with his people culminated in the old covenant of Mount Sinai. Moses had sealed this covenant by sprinkling the people with the blood of sacrificed animals; so now Christ shed his own blood in sacrifice to begin the new and unending covenant, the new testament. At the last supper before he died, he said, "This cup is the new covenant in my blood, which shall be shed for you" (Luke 22, 20; cf. Hebrews, chapters 8–10).

Under the old covenant, the blood of sacrificed animals was brought by the high priest into the Holy of Holies, the part of the tabernacle where God dwelt among his people. Now Christ offered his blood and entered God's dwelling place in heaven, bringing us with him, fulfilling humankind's yearning for union with God, which could only be hinted at before. "Christ . . . by a great and more perfect tabernacle, not made with hands, that is, not of this creation, neither by the blood of goats nor of calves, but by his own blood, entered once for all into the Holies" (Hebrews 9, 11–12).

By this new covenant God promises us a life after death of unending, unimaginable happiness, sharing his own life, living as he does. By the old covenant God gave his people land and temporal prosperity if they lived up to their agreement; they could not be sure of an unending life after death, much less know how to attain it. Now God is offering us himself forever. This is the most perfect gift of love possible, the closest personal relationship that we could have with him.

Our part of this covenant of love is simply to accept Jesus Christ and live by his teaching of love. So close, so personal is this relationship of love that God offers us that his own Son, Jesus Christ, is the living, walking, flesh-and-blood sign of it. Jesus Christ, in fact, *is* the new covenant. He unites in himself God and us. By believing in him we enter into this covenant. He, personally, is the great proof, the great sign that such a love relationship is for real. By accepting him we begin eternal life, God's grace-presence within us, here and now.

When we accept Christ and this new covenant we pledge ourselves to love. He showed us that this was a covenant of love in the best way he could, by dying for love of his Father and us, to unite us in love. If we make this new covenant, we must determine to love. As marriage is the covenant that seals the deep love relationship of a man and woman, so our covenant with God supposes that we have fallen in love, that we want to commit ourselves to a life of love with God and our fellow humans.

By his sufferings and death Jesus gave himself totally for others—for us. God "made Christ to be sin" (2 Corinthians 5, 21) for us—thus Paul tries to describe the sinless Christ's fearful experience of taking on our sins as if they were his own, of feeling totally cut off from his Father as he hung dying.

God let Jesus redeem us in this way so that God's love would be unmistakably plain to us. When we see his own Son humiliated and killed, we can begin to realize what it is for a God to love. It seems that in no other way could he have made clear to us his unfailing love—that in no other way would we have been convinced that we are always lovable in the eyes of the limitless God.

> In this is love, not that we loved God, but that he loved us and sent his Son to be the expiation for our sins . . . that those who believe in him may not perish, but may have life everlasting (John 3, 16; 1 John 4, 10).

This is how God establishes his kingdom, his rule of love over our hearts. Jesus came as a humble, loving prophet rather than as a powerful king. Where people might have expected a great display, Jesus made clear that he wanted to convert our hearts through love. This is always God's way: instead of compelling submission or awed adoration, he wants our freely given love.

Christ's death on the Cross shows strikingly the paradox of God's seeming powerlessness in our world, that is, he does not save us by means that seem effective but rather overcomes evil by his apparent defeat at its hands. This is the paradox of the Cross, and it is often evident in our lives. God does not intervene in our affairs with displays of power—but by his "absence" from our world he is prodding us to use our own resources to work with him to bring it to perfection.

Though truly present, close, and acting in our lives, God, like any good parent, wants to help us develop our own powers rather than doing things for us. Too often we depend on his intervention instead of ourselves becoming involved in the struggles of the "terrible everyday." We want God to play the indulgent Parent whom we can coax or cajole to do our bidding, while we only minimally help ourselves and our fellow humans.

Christ died for the sins of all of us, not merely because his fellow Jews wanted him killed. Though many of his own people rejected him, some accepted him, those who would begin his Church. The tragic history of blaming only the Jews had an early start:

When the early Christian community was writing about their leader who was executed by the Romans, they were living in the midst of a hostile Roman populace; they emphasized the collusion of a few Jewish leaders so as not to anger their Roman masters. After the destruction of Jerusalem and the Temple in the year 70 C.E.—which was taken as a sign of God's rejection of the Jews—a tragic enmity developed between those who followed Christ (still mostly Jews) and those Jews who did not. The beginnings of this are evident in the New Testament: Pilate is exculpated and the Jews are held increasingly guilty. Matthew especially, along with John, does this (in 27, 25, for instance, he has the Jewish throng cry out, "His blood be on us and our children").

The Fathers of the Church, the leaders of the developing Christian world, often expressed bitter sentiments against the "Christ-killers," and the Jews reacted by vilifying Christ. From the ghettos of the Middle Ages to the savagery of the Nazi "final solution" (all too frequently tolerated by Christians), we see how people can use even religion in a strange and distorted way. Blaming or scapegoating the Jews enabled Christians through the centuries to avoid facing the fact that we all, by our sins, are responsible for Christ's death. Spurred by the memory of the Nazi horrors, a new era is under way today in Jewish-Christian relations. Vatican Council II says emphatically:

What happened in his passion cannot be charged against all the Jews without distinction, those then alive, nor against the Jews of today. . . . The Jews should not be presented as rejected or accursed by God. . . . The

Church . . . decries hatred, persecutions, displays of anti-Semitism, directed against Jews at any time and by anyone (*Declaration on the Relationship of the Church to Non-Christian Religions,* no. 5).

Although Christians believe Jesus is the Messiah who has come and saved us, we also look forward to his second coming at the end of the world. As we will see in chapter 26, his work among us is not complete until this happens. Both Jews and Christians, then, look for the coming of the Messiah and messianic times, Jews for the first time, Christians for the second.

It is important to realize that both Christians and Jews have continued to develop in religious values, that one people has not eclipsed the other, nor has God abandoned either. For Christians to dwell only on Jesus as the Messiah who has already come can lead to a kind of triumphalism: it can dull our expectation of his future return, his second coming. We need to work together with all of humankind to bring about the future messianic times of peace, justice, and prosperity that are obviously—given the violence and injustice in today's world—not yet with us.

Catholics are asked to perform some act of penance each Friday as a gesture of grateful love. All American Catholics formerly abstained from eating meat each Friday, but now may voluntarily do this or some other act of penance of their own choosing (except for Ash Wednesday and the Fridays of Lent, which are still days of abstinence from meat). On Friday, the day Christ sacrificed his life for us, we make this small sacrifice to discipline ourselves and to overcome our sinful tendencies, that we might be more fully joined to him—and, not least of all, to be joined to the world's hungry and deprived.

The American Catholic bishops have made some other practical suggestions for Friday penance: doing voluntary work in hospitals, visiting the sick, serving the needs of the aged and the lonely, instructing the young in the Faith, participating as Christians in community affairs, and meeting our obligations to our families, our friends, our neighbors and our community, including our parishes, with a special zeal born of the desire to add the merit of penance to the other virtues exercised in good works born of living faith.

CHRIST IS IN GLORY AMONG US

Christ's resurrection is the key truth of our Christian faith. The first proclamation of the "good news," the pattern of the message that was to convert billions and change the world's history, stressed Christianity's basic and unique fact: Jesus Christ, who had been murdered, came alive from the grave by God's power and entered a perfect, glorified state: **Read Acts 2, 22-36.**

Christ's resurrection is the divine "seal of approval" on himself and his message, and it tells us that, joined to him, we, too, shall live on forever as he said. He delivered us from the fear of death and brought joy and hope to our lives: "I am the resurrection and the life; those who believe in me, even though they die, will live; and everyone who lives and believes in me shall never die" (John 11, 25-26).

The New Testament says that Christ appeared on earth for forty days after his resurrection to complete the training of his apostles and so that they could be absolutely sure that he was truly living among them. Forty is a Jewish "perfect number," one that recurs again and again in the Scriptures.

After his resurrection Jesus could exercise his lordship in a way he had not done before. By overcoming death, the ultimate frustration of all human efforts, he began the full exercise of his superhuman, divine power among us. His mission will be fulfilled only at the end of the world, when all evil powers have been overcome.

Jesus shares his victory with us, for now we, too, have the power to rise and be glorified forever. Christ has a glorified body, impervious to space, time, pain, and so on, perfect in every way. He promises that we, too, shall have such a body forever. "If the Spirit of him who raised Jesus from the dead dwells in you, then he who raised Jesus Christ from the dead will also bring to life your mortal bodies, because of his Spirit who dwells in you" (Romans 8, 11).

We must join ourselves to Christ and take part in his death and glorification to attain eternal life with God. Everyone who is saved is somehow joined to him, whether one realizes it or not. Christ is the one mediator for all. But some are called to join themselves to him more consciously, more fully.

We first join ourselves to Christ's death and glorification by faith and baptism. Baptism, we shall see, is the sacrament by whose ceremony we first take part in these great events. Sin dies within us and we rise from its water with the new life of God's grace-presence.

The Mass is the great way Christ himself prolongs for us his death and resurrection, so we can take part in it and thereby conquer our sins and receive his grace-presence. In each Mass Christ becomes present among us, and through a human priest presents for us his death and resurrection by means of signs or ceremonies. Taking part in the Mass is, we believe, the greatest way of sharing in Christ's love.

We call Jesus Christ the King of the universe, of angels, and of humans because all things belong to him as God and because as a human he redeemed us. The Church celebrates the Feast of Christ the King on the last Sunday after Pentecost. To the extent that he was humbled for us, now he is exalted: **Read Philippians 2, 8-11.**

What if there are rational beings on other planets, in other star systems—are they saved, able to attain heaven? There are many possibilities: they might be in an original innocence; they might be as yet unredeemed; they might also have been redeemed by Christ—God could have taken on other created natures besides our own. The possibilities are limitless. God can bring his creatures to happiness with himself in an infinite number of ways. What we do know is that he himself has come and brought us to himself forever.

Alice Meynell pictures what may be the scene when all creation is gathered in eternity:

O, be prepared, my soul!
To read the inconceivable, to scan
The million forms of God those stars unroll
When, in our turn, we show to them a Man.

"Christ in the Universe"

We are to be God's instruments for living in harmony with material creation, to preserve it and bring it to perfection. The material universe, also God's good creation, has become tainted by the sin of Adam and all of us. Now it "waits with eager longing" to become perfect, to also share in Christ's redemption. Every advance in protecting the material world in which we live and conserving its ecology carries out God's plan.

Jesus Christ is among us here and now, as fully as when he was visibly among people two thousand years ago. He is not in some "place" beyond outer space, but with us, within us, surrounding us with his love. Though invisible, his presence can be experienced by us whenever we open ourselves to him by faith and love. He yearns to bring us his love, to help us bring others, and the universe itself, to the perfection of love. We will see that the Church's whole reason for existing is to unite us with him.

At the end of the world he will appear visibly once more to judge, with a justice permeated by love, the whole human race. Then his work among us will be done. He will deliver us all in this kingdom of love to his Father forever.

Christ's work among us was to be completed by the Holy Spirit whom he would send. At his resurrection, Christ, filled with the Spirit, could now release the Spirit's full influence of love upon humankind. The Spirit would enable us to understand Christ's teachings and give us the courage to follow them: **Read The Acts of the Apostles 1, 4-8.**

IN THE LITURGY

In each Mass Christ is present, prolonging his sacrifice, his own death and resurrection, so we can make it our own. Each time we take part, we can offer perfect worship to God. We renew our covenant of love. We take a gigantic step, the greatest possible on this earth, toward our transformation into the divine, our union with God.

The prayers of the Mass emphasize that it is a re-presentation or prolonging for us of Christ's death and glorification:

At the consecration of each Mass we are particularly reminded of Christ's death, as the priest says separately over the bread and wine, "This is my body . . . this is the chalice of my blood." And immediately after the consecration, we are "calling to mind the blessed passion of the same Christ, your Son, our Lord, and also his resurrection from the grave and glorious ascension into heaven. . . ." Immediately before communion we call on Christ, the "Lamb of God," to have mercy on us.

The communion of each Mass particularly brings to mind Christ's resurrection: a meal gives life, and at communion we are united to the living Christ to share in his life of grace.

The Church offers all the great prayers of her liturgy to the Father through Christ, our mediator. The formula "through Christ our Lord" occurs again and again.

We relive annually the event of our salvation by the ceremonies of Holy Week, the most sacred time of the year:

On Passion (Palm) Sunday palm branches are blessed and distributed to the people and there is usually a procession as on the first Palm Sunday. During the Mass following, the gospel story of Christ's passion is read.

On Holy Thursday evening we celebrate the liturgy of the Lord's Supper. It commemorates Christ's great gift of himself to us in the eucharist, and his washing his disciples' feet as a sign that they should serve others in love. The celebrant may wash the feet of members of the parish community, or use some similar sign of service.

After the Holy Thursday service the tabernacle is empty and the altar bare; the eucharist is kept in a "repository" in another place. From now until the Easter Vigil we relive the time when Christ suffered and died and his dead body was in the tomb.

The service on Good Friday evening commemorates the death of Christ by means of readings, prayers, and the reading or singing of the passion, along with veneration of the cross and holy communion.

On Good Friday afternoon in many churches there are special services to commemorate the Three Hours during which Christ hung on the cross.

Easter Sunday, on which we commemorate Christ's resurrection, is the greatest feast of the Christian Church, and is celebrated at the Easter Vigil on Holy Saturday night: A new fire is lighted and blessed, to present Christ the "light of the world." From the fire we light the paschal candle, also representing Christ, and then the candles of the congregation. A hymn of triumph is chanted, followed by several Scripture readings telling the story of God's care for his people over the centuries. Baptismal water is blessed, and Christ's resurrection is symbolized by drawing the paschal candle from the "tomb" of the water.

There is usually the baptism of new converts, the heart of this service, at this point. In the ancient Church, the Easter Vigil was the great occasion for baptizing converts—and this is done again today for those who are not yet baptized as Christians. Having had their sins forgiven—

symbolically buried in the water—they rise from the water with Christ's new life of grace. Then all present renew their baptismal vows, once more committing themselves to live in and with Christ. The new converts are anointed with chrism, and finally, as the first Mass of Easter is celebrated (preferably about midnight), Christ reenacts in person his death and resurrection for us (we will see this in more detail in chapter 13).

Other Masses during the day on Easter continue the celebration of Christ's—and our—resurrection.

Each Sunday is a "little Easter." The reason Christians worship and Catholics take part in Mass on Sunday is to celebrate this great day of Christ's victory over sin and death. Sunday is the center of the Christian week.

From Easter to the Ascension, the Masses have a joyous theme. The paschal candle, representing Christ, is lighted at the main Masses.

The Ascension of Christ is celebrated on the seventh Sunday after Easter (it formerly was celebrated on Thursday forty days after Easter). Catholics attending Mass on this day commemorate Christ's triumphal ascent into heaven.

The "Sign of the Cross" is the way Catholics usually begin and end their prayers, from meal prayers to the great prayer of the Mass. It is an outward profession of one's belief, not only in the Blessed Trinity, but also in the suffering and death of Christ for us on the cross.

In popular devotion, the Stations of the Cross (Way of the Cross) are a series of usually fifteen pictures or crosses on the walls of Catholic churches. They commemorate the journey of Christ to Calvary, his death, burial, and resurrection. Their purpose is to help us realize God's astonishing love in saving us and to arouse sorrow for our sins that caused such suffering.

One can move from Station to Station while meditating on the scenes (all are mentioned in Scripture except the sixth, regarding Veronica, which is an ancient tradition). The Stations are most often said during Lent. There are booklets available with suggested meditations for each Station.

Devotion to the Sacred Heart of Jesus is for some a way of showing their love for Jesus Christ. The heart of Jesus, pierced for us (cf. John 19, 34), has become the symbol of his love for us and his mercy toward sinners.

The five sorrowful mysteries of the rosary commemorate Christ's sufferings and death, and the first two glorious mysteries, his resurrection and ascension.

The sorrowful mysteries are the Agony in the Garden (Luke 29, 39–53), the Scourging at the Pillar (Mark 15, 25), the Crowning with Thorns (John 19, 1–2), the Carrying of the Cross (Matthew 27, 31), and the Crucifixion (Luke 23, 33–49).

The glorious mysteries are the Resurrection (Luke 24, 1–11), the Ascension (Acts 1, 6–11), the Descent of the Holy Spirit on Pentecost (Acts 2, 1–47), the Assumption of Mary, and the Coronation of Mary. (The meaning of these latter two mysteries is explained in chapter 23.)

Finally, every Catholic church not only has many crosses throughout but also has a crucifix, or image of Christ on the cross, as a constant reminder of his death for us. It is also an old Catholic custom to have a crucifix in one's home, and some people carry or wear a cross or crucifix on their person.

DAILY LIVING:
OUR ATTITUDE TOWARD SIN AND SUFFERING

Christ chose his suffering and death freely to show us the seriousness of sin. He did not have to suffer and die, but he—God himself—went through this humiliation and anguish to free us from our sins, to make it possible for us to attain heaven. He thereby tried to convince us to do all in our power to avoid sin, since serious sin is the one thing that disrupts the universe and that might cut us off forever from God.

A genuine awareness of what Christ suffered should also make us keenly anxious to help others avoid sin—and perhaps cause alienation from God.

We can have some insights into the often agonizing mystery of why God allows us to suffer. We cannot understand fully the "why" of pain, but we can see something of its inevitability: perhaps if we were perfectly happy, possessing everything we want in this world, we might become smug, complacent, proud, and cease reaching out longingly for God and the life beyond, which is our true destiny. We might also cease working to-ward our "new earth" of universal love and peace (cf. 2 Peter 3, 13).

Often, when we are suffering God becomes close to us as never be-fore. Suffering can open us to God's caring, helping presence in a way nothing else can.

Then, too, God alone sees the whole picture. He asks us to trust him, much as a mother might tell her child who must undergo a painful opera-tion: "This is going to hurt, and you won't understand why—but trust me when I tell you that it will help you."

Also, if we are honest, we will recall times, perhaps many times, when we did not reap the bad consequences our actions deserved. Most of us, if at this moment we consider the justice done to us or not, would have to say that we have gotten as good or better than what justice would call for.

Instead of seeing God as somehow responsible for our suffering, we might honestly—if painfully—face our own clinging to passing things, which we must grow beyond if we are to attain our destiny—the total, unconditional love that God wants us to have forever. So much of our human misery is brought about by our inhumanity to one another, in-cluding acts of massive violence. Most of us realize how strongly we cling to passing things, to status, to power, to material things, to other persons, and even to spiritual feelings.

Our will, instead of surrendering itself to God's waiting love, struggles, holds itself aloof, clutches at these passing goods. Blaming God can be a cop-out, masking our clinging to unfulfilled desires and ambitions that may be child-ishly, even demandingly self-centered. Usually it is only slowly and painfully that we submit to what is humanly incomprehensible, the unconditional love that is God. Very often, with one's struggling "leap" of humble surrender, there comes not an explanation but a profound sense of understanding, ac-ceptance, and deep peace.

Then, too, many who truly believe in an eternity of love and happiness come to see the sufferings of this life, terrible as they may be now, as only a brief instant by comparison—like a painful injection that takes but a moment, in return for which we have unending health.

Christ as God coming among us and suffering for us gives us a glimpse of a profound mystery: God is always with us in our sufferings,

mysteriously but actually enduring our pain with us. The concept of a God who suffers with us is hard to grasp—it seems at odds with our belief in an all-powerful, transcendent God. But Christ in his suffering gave us a glimpse of how God is totally one with us, now, today, always, in our uncertainties and pain as well as our joys.

Process theology offers us this view of God: God is our "cojourneyer," totally involved out of limitless love with us, subject, as any of us, to people and events. He is not "perfect" in the sense of being immutable, self-sufficient, and in splendid isolation, but rather is totally involved with us. He sees what is ultimately best for us and lovingly tries to draw us to choose it, to lure us to love. But, somewhat like a human parent of a maturing child, he must await people's free choices—he does not see ahead of time what they will choose, nor can he step in to prevent their choosing evil—and he suffers with us the consequences of these choices.

So, far from sending us suffering or even allowing it, God is also pained by its effects. Though he knows the eventual outcome of his creation, the ultimate triumph of love, he goes through with us every anxious, painful step of bringing it about.

An imminent God who suffers with us daily—and yet is the transcendent Creator and Sustainer of all that is—is terribly hard for us to grasp and is, ultimately, a mystery. Yet Christ's revelation of God as being one with us in all we do should be, for most of us, a great comfort and support as we journey through life.

Ultimately, the profoundly painful question of why innocent people suffer such undeserved, often unremitting pain will be fully answered only after death. It would be callously foolish to pretend we have a complete answer to this now. But, in the meantime, Christ's example strikingly shows us how suffering can bring about great good here below.

Christ showed us that suffering has great power to spread love in the world, to bring ourselves and others to unending happiness. God could have saved the world from sin in any way he chose, but he let his only Son be fully human, and undergo death at the hands of his fellow humans, to bring it about. He thereby taught us that our sufferings, frustrations, and humiliations can have great power for good—how much we will realize only in eternity.

The follower of Christ, then, while not seeking out suffering, knows she or he must suffer with Christ. Jesus said, "He who does not carry his cross and follow me cannot be my disciple" (Luke 14, 27). And Peter says, "Unto this, indeed, you have been called, because Christ has suffered for you, leaving you an example, that you may follow in his steps" (1 Peter 2, 21). There is simply no way for a Christian to avoid this part of our life's journey.

When suffering comes, we should unite it with Christ's sufferings, asking him to help us bear it and profit from it. Besides spreading love in the world, suffering can teach us humility, patience, tolerance, and our utter dependence on God. Many of us learn in no other way. St. Paul put it: "I die daily . . . with Christ I am nailed to the cross" (1 Corinthians 15, 31; Galatians 2, 20).

The Christian must continually die with Christ to rise with him—disciplining oneself, controlling one's sinful instincts, that the new life of grace might grow in one. "And they who belong to Christ have crucified their flesh with its passions and desires" (Galatians 5, 24). This is mortification—we die in order to live: **Read Matthew 16, 24-26.**

As Christ's sufferings led to his triumphant glorification, so our sufferings will someday end in the eternal joy and peace we call heaven. A transition from death to life—a passing through suffering to attain joy—is the way God's plan is carried out in history. The Israelites underwent the slavery of Egypt and then passed on to freedom. Christ's suffering and death had to precede his resurrection and glory: **Read Acts 26, 22-23.**

Our lives consist of innumerable "dyings" and "risings" by which we are like Christ. Vatican Council II sums up our human situation:

> On earth, as yet pilgrims in a strange land, tracing in trial and oppression the paths he trod, we are made one with his sufferings, as the body is one with the head—suffering with him, that we may be glorified with him (Romans 8, 17) (*Constitution on the Church*, no. 8).

Hope and a deep joy and peace, then, are natural to true followers of Christ. Beyond any Pollyanna-like optimism, we know with a profound, deeply peaceful, usually unexplainable conviction that our present sufferings will one day end in the joy of heaven with our glorified Savior.

SOME SUGGESTIONS FOR . . .

DISCUSSION

Can you appreciate humankind's need of a savior?

"Christ's death and resurrection shows us what it is for a God to love—God could simply do no more." What does Christ's death and resurrection mean to you personally? How might it help your view of yourself as limitlessly loved by a limitless God?

While not seeking failure or suffering and death, Christ came to see that he had to accept these to carry out his life's mission. Can you see the difference between masochism, or fatalism, and suffering, perhaps even dying, for another?

In view of Christ's death and resurrection, how might the suffering of so many innocent people become, if not understandable, at least more acceptable? How might it make the suffering and perhaps the death of someone close to you more acceptable?

Have you—or someone you know—ever experienced new life and growth coming out of failure and suffering? How would faith help?

Can you see how a Christian is basically a person of hope, joy, and deep peace?

FURTHER READING

- *Jesus Through the Centuries,* Pelikan (Harper & Row, 1985)—Subtitled "His Place in the History of Culture," this excellent book looks at Jesus through the various titles he has been given throughout history.

- *How to Read the Passion Narratives of Jesus,* Brown (Catholic Update 0484, St. Anthony Messenger Press)—A very brief but very informative presentation of the different evangelists' views.

- *The Challenge of Jesus,* Shea (Thomas More Press, 1984)—An excellent little book—practical, inspiring, easy to read—on the effect Jesus can and should have in our daily life.

- • *The Death of the Messiah: From Gethsemane to the Grave,* Brown (Doubleday, 1994)—Subtitled "A Commentary on the Passion Narratives in the Four Gospels," this monumental, two-volume work by an outstanding biblical scholar is unexcelled regarding the death of

Jesus. Fair-minded as well as scholarly, Fr. Brown gives a wealth of detail—and the reader may be left with the eerie feeling that this was just how it was.

•• *Who Killed Jesus?* Crossan (HarperSanFrancisco, 1995)—Subtitled "The Roots of Anti-Semitism in the Gospel Story of the Death of Jesus," this controversial, perhaps upsetting work sees a single original Passion Narrative composed to meet early Church needs, including the exoneration of Pilate and the guilt of the Jews. It also suggests the radical view that there may have been no trial or burial of Jesus because he wasn't considered worthy of it, so closely was he identified with the poor and outcasts of society.

• *What Are They Saying About Christian-Jewish Relations?* Pawlikowski (Paulist Press, 1980)—A fine little book with a chapter on "The Deicide Charge and New Testament Antisemitism."

• *Faith Without Prejudice: Rebuilding Christian Attitudes Toward Judaism,* Fisher (Crossroad, 1993)—Revised and expanded, this is, first, a clear, concise treatment of the history of Jewish-Christian relations; then it gives excellent, practical help for integrating Jewish and Christian feasts and devotions, an evaluation of the content of religious texts, official Catholic documents regarding Jewish-Catholic relations, and detailed suggestions for further reading. A "must" for anyone interested in Jewish-Christian relations today.

• *Catholic-Jewish Relations: We've Come a Long Way!* McGarry (St. Anthony Messenger Press, Catholic Update 0491)—A very brief but excellent sketch of the history of these relations up to the present, with comments on a few particularly sensitive questions.

• *The Coming of the Cosmic Christ,* Fox (Harper & Row, 1988)—A sweeping synthesis of the reemergence of wisdom, the feminine, creativity, mysticism, and Mother Earth; if occasionally enthusiasm overrides scholarship, this is nonetheless insightful and immensely hopeful.

• *The Way of the Cross: A Lenten Devotion for Our Times,* Wintz (St. Anthony Messenger Press, Catholic Update, February 1988)—A brief, very good little folder for those wanting to make the Way of the Cross (the Stations), this can be used either with a leader or alone.

FURTHER VIEWING/LISTENING

- *Don't Tell Me to Suffer Patiently!,* Rohr (NCR audiocassette, 70 mins.)—A very wise, very popular priest/writer/retreat master looks at the mystery of suffering as seen in the innocent Job, discerning that spiritual depth and intimacy with God may sometimes be more important than relief.

PERSONAL REFLECTION

Each time I look at a cross or crucifix, I realize that God loved me enough to die for me. That God should become a human, should suffer and die—that he should put himself in a position where the selfishness and cruelty of people could touch him, that he should ever bother with humankind at all—is a mystery—and the only possible answer is his love. "By this we know his love, that he laid down his life for us . . ." (1 John 3, 16).

To be united with God by love, to have his grace-presence growing within me, is the most important thing in life. At this moment I am either united with him or separated from him by unforgiven serious sin. The ultimate tragedy would be to go through life cut off from God's great love by an attitude of unrepentance.

An act of kindness or self-discipline on Friday can show my love for Christ on the day he died and help free me from the self-enslavement of my sins. This Sunday I might worship God with Christ at Mass, thanking him for his death and resurrection on our behalf, and seeking to be more a part of it.

9

Christ Sends the Holy Spirit to Form His Church

What provision did Jesus Christ make for his teaching, his work among us, to be carried on through the centuries? What special characteristics did Christ's Church have from the beginning? What is the real, inner meaning and purpose of Christ's Church?

THE SPIRIT FORMS GOD'S NEW PEOPLE

Read Acts 2, 1–4. On Pentecost, Christ sent the Spirit, as he had promised, to complete his work. Christ had told his followers to await the coming of the Holy Spirit, who would give them power to carry his teaching "even to the very ends of the earth" (Acts 1, 8). He had promised "when the Spirit of truth comes, he will guide you into all the truth" (John 16, 13). In one of his appearances after his resurrection, he had "breathed" on some of them, giving them the Spirit (John 20, 22–23). Now, on Pentecost, the time of the Holy Spirit began—the Spirit was strikingly manifested to all his followers.

With the coming of the Spirit, Christ's followers went forth as God's new people. As God had chosen the twelve tribes of Israel in the Old Testament, so Christ chose the twelve apostles. As God had come down upon Mount Sinai to make Israel his people amid a storm, lightning, and earthquake, so now on Pentecost the Spirit came amid fire and a roaring wind to send Christ's followers forth as God's new people.

As God had begun his people of the Old Testament by making a covenant with them at Sinai, so Christ began the new People of God, his Church, by the covenant made in his death and resurrection. He had shed his blood on Calvary to establish the new covenant, as the old had once been sealed by the blood of animals on Sinai. The Church of the New Testament, then, "came forth from the side of the dying Christ." But only with the coming of the Spirit were Christ's followers aware of what he had done and of who they were.

Christ's followers are the new People of God, the Church of the New Testament. " 'The Church' is the People that God gathers in the whole world," says the *Catechism* (752). God had chosen the Israelites and made them his church: he gathered them together, gave them his teaching, made a covenant with them, and lived in their midst. When God became human and dwelt among us as Jesus Christ, he also chose for himself a people, a Church.

The People of God is the moving symbol chosen by Vatican Council II to describe the Church from its beginning until today. In the next chapter we will discuss the Council, the greatest Church gathering in the twentieth century—but here we are concerned with its chosen image for the Church: "Like a pilgrim in a foreign land, it [God's new People] presses forward amid the persecutions of the world, and with the consolations of God . . . " (*Constitution on the Church*, nos. 8 and 9).

The Church as God's "pilgrim people" has particular meaning for many today who see themselves on a journey through this life to their destined eternal home. This is not an escapist rejection of the world—the Church very much embraces the world—but in this present life we have not yet arrived at the Kingdom for which we were ultimately created.

The twelve apostles were its first and leading members, the remnant that would grow mightily. As God had dwelt among the Israelites, so Christ now lives among us in his Church. Christ said, "I have come not to abolish . . . but to fulfill" (Matthew 5, 17). God's plan is consistent. The early Christians were reminded:

You are a chosen race, a royal priesthood, a holy nation, God's own people, that you may declare the wonderful deeds of him who called you out of darkness into his marvelous light. Once you were no people, but now you are God's people; once you had not received mercy, but now you have received mercy (1 Peter 2, 9–10).

The Spirit, symbolized by the unbridled, mighty wind, means power and freedom for Christ's followers. As ancient Israel had been freed from Egyptian slavery and made God's free people, so the Spirit now brings freedom to Christ's followers. No longer need we be slaves to sin, held back from happiness by sin. Nor need we continue to live in fear, under oppression from the world's injustices. The Spirit brings us the power to be truly free, to strive effectively for the happiness due us here and for unending happiness hereafter.

THE COMMUNITY OF THE SPIRIT

The Spirit enabled the apostles finally to understand Christ's teachings and courageously to go and spread them. Before the Spirit came they had been huddled together, weak, fearful, and confused. Now they began to realize that Christ, who had chosen them, was truly divine. They grasped the meaning of his teachings and became eloquent and courageous witnesses.

They were led by Peter, whose Pentecost sermon proclaimed Christ as the divine Messiah (cf. Acts 2, 12–36). He assured his hearers that the apostles were not drunk but filled with the fervor of the Spirit as the prophet Joel had foretold, "I will pour out my Spirit upon all flesh. . . . " He told them that they had killed their Messiah, and then boldly concluded:

> This Jesus God raised up, and of that we are all witnesses. Being therefore exalted at the right hand of God, and having received from the Father the promise of the Holy Spirit, he has poured out this which you see and hear. . . . Let all the house of Israel therefore know assuredly that God has made both Lord and Christ this Jesus whom you crucified (Acts 2, 32–36).

The Spirit constantly guided Christ's first followers. The Acts of the Apostles, a sort of brief history of the first Christians, shows the Spirit acting again and again, and Paul's epistles mention the Spirit several hundred times. The Spirit is present at their meetings, guiding their decisions: "It has seemed good to the Holy Spirit and to us . . . " (Acts 15, 28). The Spirit guides the activities of the apostles: "And while Peter was pondering the vision, the Spirit said to him . . . " (Acts 10, 19). On occasion, this presence deeply stirs them:

> And when they had prayed, the place where they had gathered together was shaken, and they were all filled with the Holy Spirit, and spoke the word of God with boldness. . . . And with great power the apostles gave their testimony to the resurrection of the Lord Jesus, and great grace was upon them all (Acts 4, 31–33).

This community formed by the Spirit had several very noticeable characteristics. These are given in the Acts of the Apostles, in its picture of the Jerusalem community of Christians.

The community was above all united in love. Christ had made clear that this was to be the outstanding characteristic of his followers:

> "A new commandment I give to you, that you love one another. By this all men will know that you are my disciples, if you have love for one another" (John 13, 34–35).

They practiced love to the extent of sharing all things in common (Acts 2, 44–45; 4, 32–35). As the Church grew this was replaced by a more practical but equally generous spirit of helpfulness to one another—such a spirit that a pagan contemporary said of them, "See how they love one another."

They were under the authority of the Twelve, with Peter as their leader (Acts 1, 13; 6, 1ff.). We shall see this more fully in the next chapter.

They preached constantly the good news that God had come and saved us in Christ (Acts 2, 14ff.; 3, 12ff.).

They admitted new members to their community by baptism, which had to be preceded by an interior conversion, a true change of heart:

> Now when they heard this [Peter's Pentecost sermon] they were cut to the heart, and said to Peter and the rest of the apostles, "Brethren, what shall we do?" And Peter said to them, "Repent, and be baptized, every

one of you, in the name of Jesus Christ for the forgiveness of your sins; and you shall receive the gift of the Holy Spirit" (Acts 2, 37–38).

They celebrated together the eucharistic "breaking of the bread," the primitive Mass, as Christ had told them to. It was by this particularly that they felt united with Christ and one another (Acts 2, 42; 20, 11).

The Spirit fills and guides Christ's Church today so that it has these same characteristics. The Spirit is in the Church as a whole, and in each member, giving understanding, power, love, and freedom. The Spirit will be with Christ's Church "forever . . . [as] the Spirit of truth" (John 14, 16–17).

A UNIFIED, UNIVERSAL COMMUNITY

Christ's followers were to be particularly united, as God's people had always been. One of the great concerns of the Old Testament was that God's people should always be united. When Israel was split, it was regarded as an intolerable situation that would someday be healed by God. Christ refers constantly to the unity his Church should have. "There shall be one flock and one shepherd" (John 10, 16). It is one vineyard, one tree, one building, one bride, one vine. Christ stressed this unity particularly the night before he died, when he prayed several times that his followers would be one, so that people would believe his teachings: **Read John 17, 20–23.**

We would expect Christ's Church to be united, in order to avoid confusion and needless disputes, to better spread his teachings and love throughout the world, to give a confused world some certainty about eternal happiness.

The unity of the first Christians was an evident, visible thing. They were united in love, under the authority of the apostles, sharing the same basic doctrines and the same worship that made them one. St. Paul rebuked some who began dividing into factions: "Has Christ been divided up?" (1 Corinthians 1, 13; 12, 25). Speaking of their common worship, he said:

> The bread which we break, is it not a participation in the body of Christ? Because there is one loaf, we who are many are one body, for we all partake of the same loaf (1 Corinthians 10, 16–17).

On another occasion St. Paul gave his converts the ideal for Christians: **Read Ephesians 4, 1-6.**

Perfect unity is the ideal, never quite achieved but always to be striven for. Christ's apostles argued among themselves. The first Christians at Jerusalem tended to form two factions, the "Hellenists" and the "Hebrews." Soon, as the Church's mission became clearer, a better unity was achieved, but disputes still arose, so that St. Paul wrote from trying experience (words that could be repeated in any period since):

> I appeal to you, brethren, by the name of our Lord Jesus Christ, that all of you agree and that there be no dissensions among you, but that you be united in the same mind and the same judgment (1 Corinthians 1, 10).

The *Catechism* says that the Church is like a sacrament—"a sign and instrument . . . of communion with God and of unity among all [humankind] . . . " (775). In chapter 12 we will see more about the sacraments, the Church's "signs" among us that actually do what they signify. The Church as a sacrament is a sign of God's presence among us, as well as a sign of unity amid diversity—and, as we will see, it helps bring about that oneness with God and unity among ourselves.

Catholics consider their Church to be particularly united. Everywhere among every social group, it has the same basic teachings, the same basic moral code, the same authority that all basically acknowledge, and the same ritual of Mass and sacraments. It has always had a basic, visible unity of structure throughout its history. This unity was especially evident in Vatican Council II: twenty-seven hundred bishops representing at the time over half a billion Catholics, meeting together and often disagreeing, but all concerned for unity in essential doctrines and morality.

Catholics also must work to heal the disunity of Christians for which they are partly to blame. The unity for which Christ prayed, the Christian ideal, is closer today than for centuries. But it is still a long way from reality. The weakness and sinfulness of Christians have caused our divisions. Striving to love more will bring us together.

Christ expanded the old Law by making his Church catholic, that is, universal or all-inclusive. He would give all sorts of human beings the opportunity to become members of his new People, whatever their race or social position: "Go into all the world and preach the gospel to the whole creation" (Mark 16, 15). "Go therefore and make disciples of all nations . . . " (Matthew 28, 19).

Peter on Pentecost announced that anyone, Jew or Gentile, could now be saved through Christ. Inspired by the Spirit, he quoted the prophet Joel:

> And it shall come to pass on the last days, says the Lord, that I will pour forth my Spirit upon all flesh. . . . And it shall come to pass that whoever calls upon the name of the Lord shall be saved (Acts 2, 17, 21; Joel 2, 28).

But it took some years for this idea of catholicity to penetrate the thinking of the early Christians. Imbued as they had been with the notion that God's people meant only the Jews, they made no attempt to convert the Gentiles. Then Peter was given a special vision that prompted him to baptize the first Gentile convert, Cornelius. He explained his action by saying, "'God has shown me that I shall not call any man common or unclean. . . . ' While Peter was still speaking these words, the Holy Spirit came upon all who were listening to his message. And the faithful of the circumcision . . . were amazed because on the Gentiles also the grace of the Holy Spirit had been poured forth . . . " (cf. Acts, chapters 10 and 11).

St. Paul, the great "apostle of the Gentiles," was personally chosen by Christ to spread his teaching to all humankind. He had been Saul, a fanatical Pharisee, hater of Christians, and was one day on his way to Damascus to take as prisoners the Christians there. The story of his conversion is one of the most striking of all literature: **Read Acts 9, 3-22.**

He then took his Roman name, Paul, and directed his restless zeal to preaching Christ throughout the Roman Empire, to Gentiles as well as Jews. Harried, misunderstood, driven by the Spirit, he traveled unceasingly, spreading the gospel until his death in Rome as a martyr. Most of his epistles (letters written to young Christian communities) have come down to us; they constitute about half of the New Testament. Paul's own description of what he endured makes it easy to understand why he is the model of all Christian missionaries: **Read 2 Corinthians 11, 23 to 12, 9.**

This missionary aspect of Christ's Church—that it is to be preached to all humankind, as a way of love possible for everyone— came to be one of its distinguishing characteristics. This was in contrast to other sects of the ancient world. The label "catholic" was as well known as, and synonymous with, the title "Christian." Paul could say, finally, "I thank my God through Jesus Christ for all of you, because your faith is proclaimed in all the world" (Romans 1,8). Very soon the Church came to include all types of people, from every level of society, to the astonishment of the pagan world.

Throughout history Christians have tried to spread Christ's teachings to all humankind, at the cost of much suffering and a great sacrifice of human lives. Sometimes nationalism, forced conversions, or a lack of appreciation of native religious insights has weakened their witness. But in the great majority of cases they have been impelled by love and preached love above all else. Along with Christianity they spread civilization, peace, and progress.

The enormous achievements of missionaries in Africa, for example, came to the world's attention with Pope John Paul II's overwhelming welcome by millions when he first visited there. One American newsmagazine commented: "Africans are still surprised and touched by the willingness of missionaries to struggle in the hinterlands, helping to dig wells, teaching reading and writing, bringing life-giving sacks of grain during periods of famine, risking their lives trying to cure the sick" (*Time,* May 12, 1980).

> *In many places the missionaries were also, in a very real sense, converted as well.* One Maryknoll nun said, "I went to China with love and got much love back." It has usually been a happy exchange of helpfulness and caring love, and it continues to be such.

Catholics find their Church to be particularly catholic. It is for them a universal home, a place for anyone. It has often been remarked that every type of person, whatever his or her intelligence, background, race, or social position, can find satisfaction in Catholicism. Sometimes its very catholicity, its multiplicity of ways to God, confuses those looking at it from without. But of its many practices, a few are essential, many more are optional. There is a basic unity and certitude and yet "something for everybody."

> Each individual part contributes through its special gifts to the good of the other parts and of the whole Church. Through the common sharing of gifts

and through the common effort to attain fullness in unity, the whole and each of the parts receive increase (*Constitution on the Church,* no. 13).

True catholicity, however, is an ideal, as yet unrealized, toward which we strive. The Church continually seeks to be more "whole," to learn from all, so that it can more truly be "all things to all people" (1 Corinthians 9, 22). "The Church must somehow find expression in all languages, all historical situations, in all the personalities who will ever come into human history" (*Constitution on the Church in the Modern World*).

UNION WITH CHRIST AMONG US

Two people in love want to be with each other. United, they give each other love, strength, encouragement. Sometimes they can be united only by thought, at a distance, and then they long to be together physically.

Christ remains invisibly but really among us, in order to be united with us in the closest possible intimacy. Though he saved us two thousand years ago, his love impels him to remain with us now, personally drawing us to the Father and eternal happiness.

It is by being united with Christ that we learn his teachings and receive his grace. Glorified, invisible among us, he is the source of all the helps by which we attain heaven.

St. Paul calls Christ's risen body a "spiritual body" that is "lifegiving" (1 Corinthians 15, 44–45). By Christ's "body" St. Paul means the person of Christ himself, body, soul, and divinity. He gives us from himself the new life of grace. This new life with Christ is invisible but real: "your life is hidden with Christ in God" (Colossians 3, 3). Our life is truly a life in Christ—we are "incorporated" into him. We can say with St. Paul, "I live, now not I, but Christ lives in me" (Galatians 2, 20).

This is what the Church really is: Christ among us, working through his Spirit, uniting us to himself and to one another in order to bring us to his Father. Christ is more involved now in human affairs, in our lives, than he was during his visible life on earth. Now glorified and all-powerful, he works among us through the Spirit. The Church is simply Christ reaching us through his Spirit with his teachings and grace-presence—and the way we return with him to the Father.

The Church, then, is Christ and all those who are united with him in the Spirit. It is Christ extended through space and time, joining us to himself, the "fullness of him" (Ephesians 1, 23). "By communicating his Spirit, Christ made his . . . [followers], called together from all nations, mystically the components of his own body" (Vatican Council II).

Christ gave many descriptions of the way we are united to him and one another in his Church. The New Testament gives some ninety different images of the Church—all attempting to describe the mysterious and wonderful reality of Christ among us and one with us. Here are some of them:

The Church is *the bride,* and Christ is its loving bridegroom (Matthew 9, 15; Ephesians 5, 26ff.). For many this is a particularly striking image.

It is a *"little flock"* of which he is the shepherd; "I am the good shepherd, and I know my own and my own know me, as the Father knows me and I know the Father; and I lay down my life for the sheep" (John 10, 14–15).

It is the field, the *vineyard* cultivated by God. Christ says, "I am the vine, you are the branches . . . apart from me you can do nothing" (John 15, 1ff.).

It is *God's building.* Christ is the rejected stone that became the cornerstone (Matthew 21, 42). It is built on the foundation of the apostles (1 Corinthians 3, 11) and of Peter (Matthew 16, 18). We are to be "living stones" built into it (1 Peter 2, 5).

It is *our mother* meant to give us understanding, tender love, and guidance (Galatians 4, 26).

It is *an exile* journeying on earth as in a foreign land (2 Corinthians 5, 6; Colossians 3, 1–4).

It is the place where the kingdom of God is particularly found, "the germ and beginning of the kingdom on earth . . . [which] strains toward the completed kingdom" (Vatican Council II).

It is *God's family* (Ephesians 2, 19). Our Father gives us his own life, and brings us into the loving life of the Trinity. The members of this family love one another and are dependent on one another. Each is important, each has something to contribute to the others; the weak members are given more honor, as a handicapped child might be the center of a family.

It is made up of sinners as well as good people, a "field" with weeds and wheat growing together (Matthew 13).

To express the union of Christ with his Church, St. Paul often called it Christ's body, of which Christ is the head. "Christ is the head of his body, the Church" (Colossians 1, 18). The head was considered by the ancients the dominant part, controlling and giving life to the rest of the body. Christ the head leads us and gives us his life of grace. The Holy Spirit can be called its soul. The soul gives unity to a body, and so the Holy Spirit is the invisible unifier of the Church, joining the members to one another and to Christ the head, inspiring every good action in the members of the body.

All the members, as parts of the body, are united with one another as well as with Christ the head. Each member is important and what one does affects the others: Read 1 Corinthians 12, 12-27. As our physical body has millions of tiny cells, all working together and contributing to the life of the whole body, so the Church has millions of members helping one another spiritually. If one part of our physical body is sick or in pain, other parts often feel poorly; so if a few members of the Church are "sick" in sin, they hurt not only themselves but others as well. And as the healthy parts of our body come to the assistance of a sick part, so the members of the Church by their prayers and good works can aid those who are in sin.

As each part of our physical body has a particular function, so each member of the Church has a particular role in bringing grace and holiness to the rest. "For just as in one body we have many members, yet all the members have not the same function, so we, though many, are one body in Christ" (Romans 12, 4–5). Some humble, "hidden" member may be helping the others far more effectively than those in positions of prominence.

Our physical body grows and adds new cells; so the Church strives to grow in love and add new members. "[We] grow up in all things in him who is the head, Christ. For from him the whole body . . . derives its increases to the building up of itself in love" (Ephesians 4, 16).

Through the members of his Church particularly, Christ teaches us how to attain heaven and gives us his grace. He teaches us by using certain members to whom he has given the power to teach. He enables us to work with him in spreading his grace-presence to ourselves and others. "And the eye cannot say to the hand, 'I do not need your help'; nor again the head to the feet, 'I have no need of you . . . '" (1 Corinthians 12, 21). God's plan, therefore, is that we "gain" Christ's grace for one another, helping others attain heaven, and others helping us. Paul deeply realized this:

> I rejoice now in the sufferings I bear for your sake; and what is lacking of the sufferings of Christ I fill up in my flesh for his body, which is the Church . . . (Colossians 1, 24).

We work with Christ by praying for others, offering our work and sufferings for them, and as we shall see, by taking part in his sacraments. There are people whom Christ's love will not help as it might, people who will suffer needlessly unless we help them.

Because we are all joined together, the power of our love knows no bounds. We saw how each child is born into a situation of sin—an inheritance and environment of selfishness, pride, dishonesty, hatred, and so on, that we call original sin, and that has been snowballing since the first sin. Each child, in turn, will influence others as he or she grows by the evil that he or she does, adding to the accumulating sin of the world. But good also snowballs. Whenever we do an act of kindness, or act justly, patiently, and honestly when tempted to do otherwise, this adds to the accumulating good and love in the world—and since our redemption by Christ this has a new power to affect people eternally. Often we can see this in practice: we do a kindness to someone, and that person is moved by our consideration to be kind to another, and so on.

We are never alone or without help in Christ's body. Even if it seems that we haven't a friend in the world, Christ is always helping us, and countless other members—including people we will not know until the next life—are working with him to help us. At this very moment someone on the other side of the world may be praying or suffering, and Christ may be using his or her love to help us attain the peace and joy of heaven.

IN THE LITURGY

At Mass during the eucharistic prayer we pray for the Church, for its guidance, peace, and unity throughout the world.

In the Prayer of the Faithful and particularly during the eucharistic prayer, we pray for all the types of people within the Church: the clergy and laity, the living and dead, and "us sinners" that we might be united with the saints.

Before communion we pray that Christ will give his Church peace and unity. At the handshake or embrace of peace we show our desire to be united with one another. Communion, which is the body of Christ, as we shall see, both symbolizes and brings about the unity of Christ's Church.

DAILY LIVING: LOVING OUR FELLOW MEMBERS OF CHRIST AND ALL PEOPLE

So close is the union of Christ with the members of his Church that what we do to them, we do to him. This was brought home to Saul on the road to Damascus as he was on his way to persecute the early Christians—Christ said, "Saul, Saul, why do you persecute me?" (Acts 22, 7). Christ himself tells pointedly how he will judge us one day: **Read Matthew 25, 34-40.**

Since we are joined with one another in Christ's body, what we do to another we also do to ourselves. When we hurt another, we hurt ourselves, making it harder for both of us to achieve happiness. "For no one ever hates his own body, but he nourishes and tenderly cares for it, just as Christ does for the Church . . . " (Ephesians 5, 29).

Love, therefore, is the test of being a Christian. It is the Spirit that must infuse anyone who claims to be a Christian—and it is the Spirit who is Love within us. We must love others just as we would Christ, and as we love ourselves.

Christians should witness to love by loving their fellow members of the Church in a special way. Because Christians should be conscious of their union in Christ, people today should be able to say of us as of the first Christians, "See how they love one another!" We should work and pray especially for full Christian unity, that all Christians will one day show the united, universal love for which Christ prayed.

But we should treat all people as we would Christ himself, with love. Mother Teresa says she sees Christ in everyone she helps—and she helps everyone. Christ died for all people, not just Christians. Non-Christians are often called "hidden" members of Christ's body. They often show a great deal of love in their lives, sometimes far more than Christians, and they thus reveal they have more of Christ within themselves. Often, too, they are deeply in need of Christ's love and will experience it only from us.

The true Christian, then, treats everyone with love, regardless of race, class, nationality, sex, politics, religion, or social status. In our daily actions, at work, at home, or at school, we try to avoid anger, and particularly deliberate injustices or seeking of revenge—just as we would avoid injuring Christ himself. In our speech, we are careful of calumny or detraction—no easy feat, often, in our highly competitive, individualistic society. A person who needs a friend or an "assist," or a homeless person needing help, reminds the Christian of St. Paul's classic "Who is weak, and I am not weak?" (2 Corinthians 11, 29).

The true Christian is mindful of today's particular test of love— one's attitude toward those who are different in race or nationality. Any refusal to work with, give equal opportunity to, live alongside of, or associate with someone because of his or her race or nationality is a rejection of Christ himself. Attitudes of discrimination can be deep and subtle—we tend to enhance our own sense of self-worth by feelings of superiority toward others, especially those who are different. We may indeed be gifted beyond some others who are different, but this can easily lead to stereotyping "them" as deficient when compared to "us."

A good self-test is to **Read Luke 18, 10–14,** and ask what group or groups we thank God we are not like.

The true Christian is honest in dealing with others. In dealing with others, Christians are dealing with Christ himself. Cheating, lying, or any form of dishonesty is unworthy of a member of Christ. "Therefore, putting away falsehood, let all of us speak the truth to our neighbors, for we are members one of another" (Ephesians 4, 25).

The *Catechism* reminds us that it is the responsibility of the media to tell the truth, that their information should be at the service of the common good and should not be based on sensationalism or "values not in tune with the Gospel" (2493–96).

Finally, the true Christian respects his or her body and the bodies of others, by temperance and sexual self-control. Our bodies are united to Christ. When we abuse them, we abuse Christ himself: **Read 1 Corinthians 6, 15–18.**

SOME SUGGESTIONS FOR . . .

DISCUSSION

Can you visualize the coming of the Spirit to Christ's first followers, and their transformation because of it? Have you ever had, in a small way, a similar experience?

Does it make sense to expect—and work for—a worldwide unity among Christ's followers? What might you find difficult about being one with some members of the Church? What might they find difficult about you?

What image or description of the way we are united with Christ and one another in the Church most appeals to you?

Can you see how the Church, in its true, inner reality—and occasionally in its outer, visible aspect—can be said to be Christ among us?

What for you would be an honest, no-nonsense test of Christian love? Of your Christian love?

PERSONAL REFLECTION

Christ lives in my fellow human beings, even the most lowly and despicable. He thinks enough of them to die for them and to live now in a most intimate union with them. Trying to see Christ in all people, especially those who seem most unlike him, is reaching out for a great reality.

I might perform an act of kindness, if possible, toward someone different from me: someone retarded; one of another race who needs help in obtaining decent housing or a good job; one of another religious belief that I have difficulty understanding, or of another political persuasion with whom I have clashed.

10

Those Who Serve as Our Guides

What is the origin of the pope and bishops of the Church? How can a human be infallible? What place does authority have in religion?

CHRIST CHOOSES THE APOSTLES AND PETER

God's way has been to come to us through other human beings. While each person must find him in his or her own heart, God gives us his love and help most often through others. He uses other people to draw us to himself. We realize his presence to the extent that we are loved by others and give love to others.

In the Old Testament God always taught his people and led them through those specially chosen by him—the patriarchs, kings, priests, and prophets. This is the pattern of God's plan. Christ also chose humans to spread his teachings and his grace.

Christ chose the twelve apostles as leaders, among God's new People, to give his teachings and grace to humankind. They were the leaders of the faithful remnant who began spreading God's kingdom among men and women. An apostle is a witness of the resurrection sent by Christ to testify to this. More than twelve were apostles, but the Twelve were the nucleus mentioned in all the gospels; as Israel's twelve sons had founded the twelve tribes, so the twelve apostles would lead the new Israel, Christ's Church.

Most of the twelve apostles were simple Galilean fishermen. One, Matthew, was a tax-collector. Another, Judas, betrayed Christ; after he killed himself, Matthias was chosen in his place. The greatest apostle, Paul, not one of the Twelve, was a persecutor of Christ's Church whom Christ converted on the road to Damascus. Christ's choice of Simon Peter, the leader of the apostles, his brother Andrew, and Matthew, is related by Luke: **Read Luke 5, 1-11 and 27-28.**

While on this earth Jesus Christ traveled only through the small country of Palestine and spoke to comparatively few people. He was concerned with bringing God's kingdom among us rather than setting up an organization. The Twelve and the others he chose would work out the best way of carrying his teaching to others, guided by the Spirit. Luke tells how he set the Twelve apart after a night of prayer: **Read Luke 6, 12-16.**

The apostles were to carry on Christ's own work as prophet, priest, and king. They were to teach all humankind, as prophets of the new law of love:

> "He who receives you, receives me; and he who receives me, receives him who sent me. He who receives a prophet because he is a prophet, shall receive a prophet's reward; and he who receives a just man because he is a just man, shall receive a just man's reward" (Matthew 10, 40–41). And Jesus drew near and spoke to them saying, "All power in heaven and on earth has been given to me. Go, therefore, and make disciples of all nations, baptizing them in the name of the Father, and of the Son, and of the Holy Spirit, teaching them to observe all that I have commanded you; and behold, I am with you all days, even unto the consummation of the world" (Matthew 28, 18–20).

They were to teach with Christ's own authority, to share in his kingly power: "He who hears you, hears me; and he who rejects you, rejects me; and he who rejects me, rejects him who sent me" (Luke 10, 6). "Whatever you bind on earth shall be bound in heaven, and whatever you loose on earth shall be loosed in heaven" (Matthew 18, 18).

They would continue Christ's priestly work of offering worship to the Father and giving his grace to people. They were to be his instruments, as when he told them to forgive sins: "As the Father has sent me, even so I send you. . . . Receive the Holy Spirit. If you forgive the sins of any, they are forgiven . . . " (John 20, 21–23). He would use them to make himself present in a special way and commemorate his death: "This is my body . . . this cup is the new covenant in my blood. Do this, as often as you drink it, in remembrance of me." Of this St. Paul comments, "For as often as you eat this bread and drink the cup, you proclaim the Lord's death until he comes" (1 Corinthians 11, 23–26).

When the Spirit came upon the Christian community at Pentecost, they went forth under the leadership of the apostles to spread Christ's teachings. Before Pentecost they were confused and frightened; afterward, though still imperfect humans who could quarrel among themselves, they taught clearly and fearlessly. The community "devoted themselves to the apostles' teaching . . . " (Acts 2, 42). After Samaria had been evangelized, "the apostles who were at Jerusalem sent there Peter and John . . . " (Acts 8, 14). Also Paul, who, though chosen personally by Christ to be an apostle, wanted to be united to and recognized by the apostolic group of Jerusalem (Galatians 1).

The apostles taught with a clear authority. When a dispute arose, the apostles met in Jerusalem and issued a decree that began "the Holy Spirit and we have decided . . . " (Acts 15, 28); they knew they could speak with the authority of the Spirit. John wrote of himself and the other apostles: "We are of God. He who knows God listens to us. He who is not of God does not listen to us. By this we know the Spirit of truth and the spirit of error" (1 John 4, 6; 2 John 1, 10).

The apostle Paul forcefully reminded his converts of his authority when he wrote about a faction that opposed him: **Read Galatians 1, 6–9.**

Finally, whenever people join together to accomplish anything there is usually one person in charge. A nation has a president; a city, its mayor; a business firm, its president or chairman of the board. In the Old Testament God was represented among his people by some leader, a patriarch, king, or high priest. So, too, Christ chose one man as the leader of his followers. This would assure unity, that all might work together to spread his teachings.

Christ chose Simon Peter as the leader of the twelve apostles. A reading of the gospels shows clearly that Peter was the leader of the group—he is mentioned six times as often as any other, is listed first, and is the one who speaks for the others. Three of the gospels tell us how Christ singled out Peter and gave him a special authority over the others. These testimonies come from different parts of the Church and this despite the fact that all knew he had denied Christ. John and Luke describe

Christ's first meeting with him at which he changed his name from Simon, son of John, to Peter, which means "rock" in the language spoken by Christ (John 1, 42; Luke 6, 14).

Matthew describes Christ's choice of Peter as leader in this incident: **Read Matthew 16, 13-19.**

A rock is strong, permanent, the base that holds a structure together; to the Jews of Christ's time *the* rock was Mount Zion, which according to legend shut off the underworld and therefore provided protection against the devil's powers. The keys given Peter symbolize authority, power (cf. Isaiah 22, 22; Revelation 1, 18). To bind and loose means a lawmaking power.

Luke describes Christ at the last supper telling Peter to strengthen the other apostles, and this despite the fact that Peter will deny him: "When you have turned again, strengthen your brethren" (Luke 21, 32). John portrays Christ after his resurrection making Peter the shepherd or leader over his flock, his followers: **Read John 21, 15-17.**

Christ had often referred to himself as a good shepherd and his followers as his flock (cf. John 10, 11ff.; Luke 15, 1-7; Luke 12, 32; Matthew 10, 16; Acts 20, 28). Later, others came to be called shepherds or pastors (1 Peter 5, 1-3). To "feed" expresses teaching, ruling; the triple repetition means a solemn, binding affirmation, like a modern oath.

Peter went eventually to Rome where his position as leader of the early Christian Church was passed on to his successors, the bishops of Rome. Peter's prominence is evident in the early Church, yet not as one endowed with supreme jurisdiction over the others. All the apostles had been commissioned by Christ and evidently felt little need to refer to Peter. They spread the faith largely independent of one another. Peter went to Rome—where the Church was already established—because it was the center of the civilized world, and he was martyred there. As time went on and the Church grew throughout the world, the unifying authority of Peter's successors grew with it, and they became recognized as the leaders of the Christian Church and were eventually called popes.

Peter's leadership was based especially on his being the first of the twelve apostles to witness the resurrection (Luke 24, 34). He also presided over

Matthias's election, worked the first miracle, was the first to preach the gospel, received the first pagan convert, and regularly spoke for the other apostles. Yet Peter is also pictured as consulting the others and being sent out by them. Paul, on starting his ministry, visited Jerusalem to speak to Peter (Galatians 1, 18); when Paul later "opposed him to his face" because of his vacillating conduct, the description of the incident (Galatians 2, 11) shows not only Paul's determined opposition but also Peter's special position. Thus Peter's leadership, while evident, is nothing like the authority the popes would exercise several centuries later.

THE COLLEGE OF BISHOPS

We have seen how Christ left behind a community, under leaders he had chosen, to carry on his teaching and loving service to humankind. Throughout history any great leader—religious, political, social reformer—attracts followers who want to carry on his or her insights, work, and teachings. The leader gives birth to an "organization," small at first, that grows and develops after he or she has died. We saw how the Christian Church began with the small community of Christ's first followers after the Holy Spirit came upon them at Pentecost—and how they began to organize and spread Christ's teachings, bit by bit, throughout the known world.

Most people, at one time or another, see organizations and institutions as a somewhat regrettable necessity of human life. Most of us undoubtedly wish there were fewer organizations and institutions with which we had to deal. Organizations have a way of developing bureaucracies, rules, and red tape, and it seems that more and more people are needed to run them. Yet we also know that as human beings we need organizations and institutions.

No idea or insight—good or bad—can be passed on and be effective among us humans without some sort of organization. "Large" insights, ones that affect many people at a basic level, that originate with some great leader, tend to grow and develop, be somewhat changed, and spawn disagreements among their adherents. For example, insights of Freud in psychology, of Einstein in physics, of our "founding fathers" about democratic government, developed, grew, gave birth to further insights, and have inevitably led to conflicting notions of what is true and best in the particular field. Jesus' insights into the whole meaning of life itself, despite his clear provision for unity and peace among his followers, have resulted in all sorts of interpretations of what he meant, how best to apply his teachings today, and so on. This is our fallible human way, even with the noblest of ideas.

So, in the matter of religion, of people's relationship with God, and of living out their life according to its most basic meaning, people naturally tend to come together, to organize. Though religion is always very personal, people join together to share, to develop and spread their insights—particularly if they have been inspired by a truly great vision of their founder.

And if the founder is divine and has taught uniquely insightful, profoundly inspiring and revolutionary ideas about love, service, and what is of ultimate importance in life—as Jesus Christ did—his followers form a community, organize, share, study, and even give their lives in the hope of serving and renewing all humankind, of one day making all people brothers and sisters in love.

And just as with a team, an idea of human service, or government, any movement that is going to be lastingly effective needs people to take the lead in organizing it and guiding the group to most effectively carry out its renewing mission to humankind so as to provide a unity among those inspired by the idea. There is, then, a natural need for guidance, organization, and authority in religion, as in all of life.

From the early years of the Church there has been a hierarchy, that is, different degrees of authority: bishops, priests, deacons. Bishops have the full power of the apostles, priests some of the powers, and deacons lesser powers. As in the Church of the Old Testament, and as in any organization, so there are various offices in Christ's Church.

The organization of the early Church, however, was formed only gradually. Jesus left behind no detailed organizational blueprint, and scholars disagree regarding the extent to which he foresaw the future of the Church; some point out that though Jesus was divine, his human knowledge was truly human and hence limited. In any event, the Spirit sent by Christ, as well as Christ himself, would guide the Church's organization and development until the end of time.

In the very early Church there were two general types of organization, one hierarchical and the other "charismatic." Luke pictures Paul appointing presbyter-bishops in the communities where he worked (Acts 14, 23; 20, 17), and Paul in Philippians 1, 1, mentions bishops in the church he had founded there. On the other hand, the church at Corinth had no evident hierarchical leader but people with different charisms or gifts; what soon prevailed, however, was the hierarchical form. (At the end of the first century, for instance, a letter of Clement of Rome to Corinth shows bishops leading the church there.)

In John's writings the early "Johannine" communities did not have an authoritative or hierarchical structure, but they considered the Paraclete, the Holy Spirit, as their sole authoritative Teacher. Later this group split, and the majority who held to the preexisting divinity of Jesus came to accept the need of authoritative presbyter-bishops to preserve the true teaching regarding Jesus' full divinity and full humanity.

What emerges universally by the end of the second century is a "monarchical" episcopate: the bishop presides as the head of the local church and the priests form a "college" around him, assisting him. Thus Ignatius, the influential bishop of Antioch, writes c. 110 C.E.: "You must all follow the lead of the bishops as Jesus Christ followed that of the Father; follow the presbyterium [college of priests] as you would the apostles; and reverence those in the diaconate as you would a commandment from God. . . . Let no one do anything touching the Church apart from the bishop. . . . Where the bishop appears, there let the people be, just as where Jesus Christ is, there is the Catholic Church" (*Letter to the Smyrnaeans,* 8; cf. also *Constitution on the Church,* no. 20).

A bishop is the leader of the local Church or diocese, its spiritual father and center of unity. Each diocese is the Church in miniature: each is a family under the bishop's fatherly guidance; as in any family, the talents of the members of the diocese are to be used for the good of all; each must contribute what he or she can.

A common early method of selecting bishops was election by the local congregation. Soon local choices had to be approved by the more important "metropolitan" bishops or archbishops, in the West by the bishop of Rome—this usually to safeguard the episcopacy from unfit men. Since the early Middle Ages bishops have been selected by the pope, usually upon recommendation of the other bishops of the area. Often the pope only acceded to the choice of the local bishops. Civil rulers often had—and some today still have—a voice in selecting bishops, frequently with unfortunate results (as in the struggles with Communist governments over this in recent years).

Today there is discussion of again giving the local People of God, perhaps through select clergy and laity, a voice in choosing their bishop. It is only in recent years that Rome has had the final say in choosing bishops, as it has today. As democratic processes spread throughout the world and as the Church's people are becoming better informed and educated, the Church might once again become open to the Spirit's guidance in this way.

The "College of Bishops" is considered the successor of the group of apostles. In the very early Church various groups or ministries were called successors to the apostles, but by the third century the bishops alone were considered such. Also, although bishops are today appointed by the pope, they are not his agents, nor do they get their authority from him. It is as a member of the group of bishops, the successor of the group of apostles commissioned by Christ, that the bishop has authority.

Each bishop also has a responsibility toward the whole Church. The apostles and their delegates worked jointly for the conversion of the whole world, and the early bishops showed great charity even to distant churches. This responsibility of the bishops, obscured for a time, was stressed again by Vatican Council II:

> Each of them . . . is to be solicitous for the whole Church . . . to instruct the faithful in love for the whole mystical body of Christ, especially for its poor and sorrowing members and for those who are suffering persecution . . . and to supply to the missions both workers and also spiritual and material aid, and . . . to gladly extend their fraternal aid to other churches, especially to neighboring and more needy dioceses . . . (*Constitution on the Church*, no. 23).

The bishop, by the laying on of hands, shares some of his powers and duties with priests and deacons. Just as Moses was helped by many elders when he led the Israelites through the desert, as a priesthood always existed in Israel, as Christ chose other disciples besides the twelve leaders, so, too, the bishop is helped particularly by his priests and by deacons. They assist in worshiping God and bringing his grace-presence and teaching to people.

THE PAPACY

The bishop of Rome, the pope, is Peter's successor among the bishops and the visible leader of Christ's Church on earth. Later we shall see how the pope is chosen.

The title "pope" means "father of fathers" and was once used for the heads of all important dioceses; it came to be used solely for the Roman bishop in the eleventh century. The popes have rejected other titles, such as "universal bishop," that might seem to derogate from the position of their brother bishops. "Pontiff," which has been sometimes used, comes from Imperial Rome and means "bridge-builder" or priest connecting God and humans.

The preeminent authority of the Roman Church was recognized from the early centuries by most of the Christian world. Ancient Christian documents tell us that the Roman Church was the only one that claimed such a primacy over the others, particularly in the West, as the center of unity and settler of disputes. It was the only one recognized as universal leader, at least to some extent, by the Christian world in general. It consistently upheld what came to be recognized as orthodox Christian teaching.

As the Christian Church developed, the great dioceses became leaders of their areas and centers of unity. In the East these were Alexandria, Antioch, Constantinople, and Jerusalem. Their bishops were called metropolitans, archbishops, or patriarchs. The other bishops became to some extent limited; for example, the metropolitan had to consent to their election. Rome, the only apostolic patriarchate in the West, thus developed as the unifying center and leader of Italy and the West.

Its actions showed that Rome increasingly considered itself preeminent throughout the whole Christian Church. Near the end of the first century, for instance, Clement, Peter's third successor, settled a dispute at Corinth in Greece. Irenaeus of Lyons near the end of the second century expressed the growing conviction that it was necessary to be united to the Roman Church to have the true teaching of the apostles: "the superior pre-eminence of that Church is such that every Church—I mean the faithful of any country whatsoever—necessarily agrees with her, that is, every Church in any country in which the apostolic tradition has been preserved without interruption"

(*Adv. Haer.*, III, 3.2). Increasingly, Rome came to be considered the center of Christian unity and its teaching the test of orthodoxy; some accused of heresy, for instance, felt obliged to explain their teachings to the bishop of Rome.

However, during the first four centuries recourse to Rome by the Eastern Churches particularly was rare. It became more frequent from the fifth century on when the strong leadership of the papacy as we know it began to take form; thus the bishops assembled for the Council of Chalcedon in 451 stated their acceptance of the view of the current pope, Leo: "Peter has spoken through Leo."

It was natural that Rome should develop as the leader of the Christian world. The Roman empire's traditions of stability, law and order, practical justice and discipline, its penchant for institutionalism, and its conservative regard for tradition—all these worked to make the Church of Rome the stabilizing influence and center of unity of a developing Christendom. Particularly after the barbarian invasions, it became evident that the Roman Church was the only one that could effectively reform and reorganize the often scandal-ridden, weakened local churches. Catholics see in this developing authority of the Roman Church an evolution planned by God to give a center of unity and certainty to his Church as it grew.

Jesus Christ himself working through his Spirit is the real leader of the Church; the pope is called his vicar or visible representative. Christ is the true rock, the one shepherd, and all human authority only represents him and is his instrument. The hierarchy of human leaders is necessary, but it is only temporary until Christ comes again in glory.

The college of bishops under the leadership of the pope has the authority of governing Christ's Church. The pope has supreme power, but when he uses it he acts on behalf of the whole college of bishops; the episcopal college has full power, but the "keys" to the use of the power are in the hands of the head of the college, Peter's successor, so that it can never be used against his will.

This authority can be used in several ways. The bishops can exercise their supreme power in union with their head, the pope, as in an ecumenical council like Vatican Council II. Or the bishops can teach or act in union with the pope while remaining dispersed throughout the world; this way of teaching has never been very developed, but with today's swift means of communication it might well be. Or again, the pope himself can teach or legislate for the whole Church, speaking for all bishops, but not dependent upon the consent of the Church or of the bishops, though he does consult the Church and particularly the bishops before he speaks.

Vatican Council II thus sums up the governing authority of the Church:

> Just as in the gospel . . . St. Peter and the other apostles constitute one apostolic college, so in a similar way the Roman Pontiff, the successor of St. Peter, and the bishops, the successors of the apostles, are joined together [carrying on] the very ancient practice whereby bishops . . . in all parts of the world are in communion with one another and with the Bishop of Rome in a bond of unity, charity and peace. In virtue of his office . . . as vicar of Christ and pastor of the whole Church, the Roman Pontiff has full, supreme and universal power over the Church. And he is always free to exercise this power. The order of bishops, which succeeds to the College of Apostles . . . is also the subject of supreme and full power over the universal Church, together with its head, the Roman Pontiff, and never without this head. This power can only be exercised with the consent of the Roman Pontiff . . . (*Constitution on the Church*, no. 22).

> *There is discussion today regarding the limits and overlapping of the authority of the pope vis-à-vis that of the bishops.* For instance, the authority of the various national episcopal conferences, envisioned by Vatican Council II, is still vague and in need of development in order that many matters now referred to Rome might better be settled on a national level.

An ecumenical council, a gathering of the bishops of the world in union with the pope, best shows this "collegiality" or coresponsibility of the bishops and pope for teaching and guiding the Church. Such a council is to be called by the pope, presided over by him or his delegates, and its decrees approved by him.

> *Councils have undergone a historical development.* Some early councils were convoked by the emperors and presided over by them or their representatives, though the papal delegates had positions of honor and the popes' pre-

vious attitudes guided the orthodox course of most councils; conciliar decrees were often promulgated by the councils on their own authority, receiving papal approbation later. For a council to be truly ecumenical, then, it must have been representative of the bishops of the whole Church, and its decrees at least eventually accepted by the pope.

Today many wish to have future councils or their equivalent open to lay participation, pointing out that a council should truly represent the Church. The Church itself is the "council" called together by God, comprising the whole people of God. As many levels as possible should be present at these gatherings, pope, hierarchy, priests, religious, and people of all sorts: married, unmarried, scientists, laborers, and so on. Early and medieval councils had lay participation and future councils may once again.

Vatican Council II was held from 1962 to 1965, with approximately twenty-five hundred bishops in attendance. It was the major event in the Church's history in the twentieth century. It was the twenty-first ecumenical council of the Church (by the reckoning of most authorities). Only the bishops voted, but much influence for its decrees came from the Church's leading theologians, non-Catholic observer-delegates, and laypeople and religious who were also invited to give their views.

A "synod" of bishops meets with the pope, usually every three years, to help him guide the Church. Most of these bishops are elected by national bishops' conferences around the world, and their smaller number enables them to function as a kind of consultative "senate" within the Church. Commissions of bishops from all over the world have been carrying out the teachings of Vatican Council II; they meet regularly with clerical and lay experts in various fields.

To help the pope in the day-by-day governance of the Church there is a "curia," various congregations or groups of cardinals, bishops, priests, and laypeople. As scholars and administrators, they study and advise the pope in matters of doctrine, morality, seminary formation, marriage, liturgy, ecumenical relations with other churches, and so on. They can issue decrees or instructions in matters pertaining to their field, subject to the pope's approval. Some act as the pope's (and the Vatican State's) representatives with the various governments of the world.

There are also theologians or scholars in the Church. They specialize in various fields, such as Scripture, doctrine, morality, church governance, and others. They research, reflect on, and work at expressing various aspects of the Church's teachings and the experience of Christians in living out those teachings. They advise and work with the pope and the bishops, contributing the expertise of their scholarship and reflection. They try to discern the ways in which the Spirit is acting in the Church, its future possibilities, and the ways it can profit from other fields of knowledge (and vice versa). They have a vital role as teachers in the Church.

Theologians often represent different approaches to more fully understanding and developing the core truths Christ gave his Church; thus there are different theologies within the mainstream of Catholic tradition. Theologians also on occasion might dissent from a noninfallible teaching of the pope and/or bishops. This is not a dissent from the latter's right and duty to teach, but from the factual grounds on which a teaching is based or the way it applies to a particular cultural or historical situation. Though this can sometimes be confusing to some people, it can make for a "creative tension" that, especially in a time of transition like our own, can ultimately be healthy for the whole Church. Some time ago, representatives of the American bishops and of mainstream American Catholic theologians arrived at guidelines delineating each one's areas of responsibility, as well as some procedures for dealing with public dissent.

The Magisterium refers to the teaching power in the Church. It is vested in the pope and bishops as the official teachers in the Church; thus when the term *magisterium* is used it refers to the pope and bishops exercising their role as teachers. Theologians also contribute to the magisterium when fulfilling their role described above. The people of the Church contribute to it as well, using their particular charisms or gifts.

The Church should not be thought of as having two clearly distinct levels, one only teaching or giving, and the other only learning or receiving—this Vatican Council II makes clear. The laity and the clergy outside the hierarchy also are gifted to give, teach, and contribute in special ways. (We will see more about this later, especially in chapter 22.)

THE GIFTS OF ALL TO SERVE ALL

Christ showed his followers how to use their authority by being the servants of others. He gave himself totally in serving others, even to dying for them. He told his apostles: "You know that the rulers of the Gentiles lord it over them, and their great men exercise authority over them. It shall not be so among you; but whoever would be great among you must be your servant, and whoever would be first among you must be your slave; even as the Son of Man came not to be served but to serve . . . " (Matthew 20, 25-28).

Just before he died, Jesus dramatically showed Peter and the other apostles by washing their feet that their authority should be humble service (this ceremony is reenacted in the Holy Thursday liturgy each year by the pope and by many bishops): **Read John 13, 2-16.**

Christ's followers realized they were to serve not only God but others. They served God by serving others. Paul constantly calls himself a "slave" who does not want to "lord it over" others. "Be servants of one another," he says (Galatians 5, 13). Peter exhorts the elders to "tend the flock . . . not as domineering over those in your charge but being examples of the flock" (1 Peter 5, 2). The usual New Testament word for authority, used again and again, is *diakonia,* service or ministry.

Some, the hierarchy, are to be leaders in service. They lead in order to unify, structure, and organize the service of all, so that it can be truly communal and effective; they are chosen to be mediators, priests, instruments in a special way. Their service is to be given in a more intense manner—sometimes as a model to their flock by dying for them, as their master did and many have done through history.

The pope is called "the servant of the servants of God." He is the "shepherd" who leads, but he leads only in order to take care of the Church, to serve it, and perhaps to die for it. The Caesars killed thirty of the first popes, almost one after another. Many others have suffered much, as they bore the burdens of Christianity's leading figure (Pope John Paul II was shot in an assassination attempt in 1981).

Unfortunately, popes and bishops have not always remembered their duty of service. Particularly in medieval times, they were more often worldly lords than spiritual leaders serving their people. Much of this was historically inevitable as European civilization developed, but great evils came to the Church because Christ's representatives ruled in an autocratic manner.

Recent popes and bishops have been much more conscious of this duty of service. Vatican Council II says of the bishops' mission: "That duty, which the Lord committed to the shepherds of his people, is a true service, which in sacred literature is significantly called 'diakonia' or ministry" (*Constitution on the Church*, no. 24).

The Church is a living community of people with different gifts or "charisms" for the service of all: Read 1 Corinthians 12, 4–11.

Vatican Council II has stressed these gifts of the Spirit once again: "The Spirit . . . equips and directs the Church with various hierarchical and charismatic gifts. . . . Among these gifts the grace of the apostles is pre-eminent . . . [but] he distributes special graces among the faithful of every rank. . . . These charisms, whether they be the more outstanding or the more simple and widely diffused, are to be received with thanksgiving and consolation, for they are perfectly suited to and useful for the needs of the Church" (*Constitution on the Church*, nos. 4, 7, 12).

Each member of the Church, clergy and laity, has something to contribute. We have seen how each member of Christ's body has a vital function, how the Spirit dwells in each member. Some of the extraordinary gifts St. Paul mentions above existed primarily in apostolic times, to help the Church get underway. But many exist today in modern form, together with other gifts particularly suited to our present needs.

Each must try to use his or her gifts. Some are called to be leaders, administrators, or organizers, while others have gifts for taking care of the "little ones," the poor, sick, and disabled. Some excel in teaching, others in works of charity, art, or Christian witness. One is gifted in speaking out boldly, another tempers our works by prudent observations, and still another does day-to-day tasks extraordinarily well.

The greatest gifts are those of loving, not those of authority. Christ makes clear that we will one day be judged on our works of charity, not on our status (Matthew 25, 31ff.). St. Paul says, "Love never ends; as for prophecy, it will pass away; as for tongues, they will cease; as for knowledge, it will pass away" (1 Corinthians 13, 8). The most notable member of the Church is a woman, Christ's mother Mary, who never exercised any hierarchical function. Ultimately, only holiness matters.

The leaders of the Church must try to be aware of, judge, and use the gifts of all. Much of what is best in the Church has been initiated by the Spirit among the laity and priests, reaching the attention of the bishops only later. The bishops' role is to engage in a continual dialogue with the people, trying to be open to the Spirit who often speaks through their gifts. "Judgment as to their genuineness and proper use belongs to those who are appointed leaders in the Church, to whose special competence it belongs, not indeed to extinguish the Spirit, but to test all things and hold fast to that which is good" (*Constitution on the Church,* no. 12; 1 Thessalonians 5, 12; 19, 21).

The Church, then, exists to serve God and the world. Its organization, which will one day pass away, exists only that it might better serve by witnessing to truth and love. It must imitate its founder in service particularly to the "little ones," the poor, sick, and ignorant, and in trying to further the good in all people.

THE GIFT OF INFALLIBILITY

We would expect that Christ would give his followers some guidance when they set out to spread his teachings. Even the most brilliant people can disagree or be mistaken, and Christ's followers were to communicate God's own special revelation of truth. To be sure people would get his message, and to avoid confusion, Christ gave his Church infallibility.

Infallibility means Christ's guidance of the Church through the Holy Spirit so that it cannot make a mistake in teaching his message. We saw how Matthew shows Christ telling the apostles as a group, and Peter as an individual: "Whatever you bind on earth shall be bound in heaven, and whatever you loose on earth shall be loosed in heaven" (16, 19; 18, 18). Sending them out to teach, he says, "He who hears you, hears me . . . " (Luke 10, 16). Before leaving his followers Christ told them that he would be with them "always, to the close of the age" (Matthew 28, 19). He promised them also that the Father would give "another Counselor, to be with you forever, the Spirit of truth . . . "

(John 14, 16–17). The apostles knew that they had the authority to speak for God himself, as we saw; Paul thus speaks of "the Church of the living God, the pillar and bulwark of the truth" (1 Timothy 3, 15).

Infallibility is expressed by the belief of the people of the Church who are in union with the pope and bishops. When the people as a whole believe a doctrine, it must be true. "The entire body of the faithful, anointed as they are by the Holy One . . . cannot err in matters of belief" (*Constitution on the Church,* no. 12).

There is a "sense of the faithful," what the people of the Church in fact believe. It is expressed, as we will see shortly, by whether or not they "receive" a teaching.

The people sometimes express the faith better than their leaders. Cardinal Newman has shown, for instance, that during the fourth century it was the belief of the people that was largely responsible for keeping the true Christian doctrine about the nature of Christ's divinity, while the bishops were either silent or divided (cf. Newman, *On Consulting the Faithful in Matters of Doctrine*).

Christ's infallible guidance also passed on from Peter and the apostles to the popes and bishops. It was inevitable that disagreements and confusion would creep in among Christians, particularly as they got further from the time of Christ. Therefore the successors of the apostles and Peter would have an ever-greater need of an infallible guidance.

Infallibility is expressed by the bishops as a group, as a college. As the successors of the apostles they use the charism when teaching or protecting Christ's revelation concerning belief or morality. Sometimes they teach "solemnly," in an extraordinary way, gathered in an ecumenical council together with the pope. Usually they exercise "ordinary infallibility," that is, they separately teach the same doctrine throughout the world.

Infallibility is expressed by the pope when teaching "ex cathedra," that is, under these conditions: when he teaches as the visible head of the Church, to all Catholics, on a matter of religion or morality, intending to use his full authority and give an unchangeable decision. Infallibility refers only to the pope's power or charism of correctly teaching Christ's revelation to humankind under these specific conditions. In be-

lief or morality, in science, politics, and so on, and sometimes in noninfallible teaching regarding faith and morals, the pope can be wrong. He can
sin, and make mistakes—and many have—in governing the Church.

> By this power the pope does not give new revelation but rather serves and
> protects the revelation Christ has given us. It is no guarantee of his personal
> faith, good judgment, or prudence. It is rather a testimony to his, and our,
> human weakness that needs this guidance.
>
> The pope does not need the consent of the Church in the sense of a vote
> taken by, for example, an ecumenical council, but he does require the
> Church's consent in the sense that what he teaches must be consistent with
> the actual faith of the whole Church.

A teaching must be "received" by the whole Church, a traditional
concept that has come to the fore since Vatican Council II. While the
Church's people do not, of course, vote on a teaching, they must make
teachings their own, by a kind of consensus, indicating that they regard
them as accurate expressions of Catholic belief.

In 1950, for example, when Pope Pius XII was going to proclaim with
solemn infallibility the doctrine of Mary's assumption, he questioned the
bishops of the world regarding what they, and their theologians, were
teaching on the matter as well as what the belief of their people was. He
was not asking advice on what to believe, but rather, he was trying to discern what in fact they actually believed.

> *For a teaching to be infallible,* almost all theologians hold, it must not only be
> taught by the pope but also by a consensus of the bishops teaching through-
> out the world; it must be a matter of "public revelation," that is, contained in
> Scripture and tradition; and, as said above, the teaching must be received by
> the people of the Church.
>
> Individual popes (and the *curia*, or those who assist the pope in govern-
> ing the Church) as well as local groups of bishops have proclaimed matters as
> infallible—or its historical equivalent—that did not meet these criteria. Pro-
> claiming any teaching as infallible, unchangeable, irreformable, and so on
> does not mean it is free from the need for later revision. In 1995, when a cur-
> ial congregation said that it was infallible teaching that women could not be

ordained priests, its statement did not meet these criteria—as was noted at the time by theologians throughout the world, as well as by some bishops.

Another way of saying this is that the Church's ordinary magisterium (or teaching power) gives expression to an authentic teaching when it is (1) taught by the pope and a consensus of bishops teaching throughout the world, (2) taught by a consensus of theologians, and (3) received by the Church's people.

In using this power the pope is the "mouthpiece" of the Church. He speaks on behalf of all the bishops and the believing people. He does not act arbitrarily, pulling teachings out of the air. He rather expresses more clearly a teaching already within the life of the Church; assisted by the Holy Spirit, he can clarify or bring out further implications in what the Church has been believing.

Infallible teachings about God's revelation (dogmas) are the Church's basic, unchanging beliefs. Catholics see a sign of God's guidance in the Church's use of infallibility over the centuries, for the popes and councils have never contradicted the solemn infallible teaching of other popes and councils. Considering the evident weaknesses of some popes and bishops of history, their corrupt lives, the pressures upon them, and the fact that some personally held erroneous beliefs, such consistency in infallible teaching is seen to be truly extraordinary.

There is a development of doctrine in the Church, however, a deepening understanding and clearer expression of the doctrines revealed to the apostles. Though the Church's basic teachings are unalterable and can never be negated, their formulation can change, grow, and develop to express the truth more fully. As one entering a darkened room gradually makes out the shapes of the furniture, or as a film being developed gradually becomes clearer, so the Church's teachings develop. The Church might be compared to a flowerbox in which many seeds—God's revelation to humankind—have been planted; some are now blossoming, others are partly grown, and others have only just begun to appear—so the Church's teachings are in various stages of development.

A dogma is proclaimed solemnly only when there seems a need to do so, and after long study, reflection, and sometimes debate. The dogma of papal infallibility itself was not proclaimed solemnly until the year 1870, at Vatican

Council I, although it can be seen emerging in the Church through the centuries as part of the developing concept of papal authority.

Actually, the Church's infallible teachings, while giving us a basic measure of certainty in our service of God, say very little. By its infallibility the Church does not claim to possess the whole truth of God and his relationship to humankind but only what we humans are able to see of his revelation at this particular point in history. Any teachings (or all of them together), while true, do not claim to express the whole truth.

St. Paul put it: "Now we see in a mirror, dimly, but then face to face. Now I know in part; then I shall understand fully, even as I have been fully understood" (1 Corinthians 13, 12).

For those concerned over the concept of infallibility as expressed by papal pronouncements, seeing in this an insurmountable barrier to Christian unity, it should be remembered that only one such infallible pronouncement has been made since the definition of papal infallibility in 1870, that is, the assumption of Mary, declared in 1950 (after the then Pope Pius XII had consulted all the world's bishops about their belief and that of the people of their dioceses, down through the centuries). Though the assumption is not found in Scripture—along with Mary's immaculate conception—when properly understood it may not be that much of a problem for other Christians, as we will see in chapter 23.

Infallible teachings are being seen today as more than statements of literal truths (thus the renowned psychoanalyst Carl Jung rejoiced at the proclamation of Mary's assumption, seeing its more profound, symbolic, universal meaning).

The tenor of Vatican Council II, of recent popes, and of almost all theological thinking today is to avoid making any further solemnly defined infallible pronouncements, but rather to go deeper into the truths we already know, to probe their fuller meaning, and to express them in concepts understandable to our modern world.

The renowned Irish writer and dramatist George Bernard Shaw—certainly one of organized religion's most biting critics—observed in the preface of *Saint Joan:* "Compared with our infallible democracies, our infallible judges, and our infallible parliaments, the pope is on his knees in the dust confessing his ignorance before the throne of God. . . . "

Teachings must also be seen in their historical setting, that is, in the light of the time and circumstances in which they were formulated. The substance of what is taught must be distinguished from the formulation used to communicate it. Phrasing that was relatively clear in a particular historical time and cultural setting might not express the teaching as clearly to people in today's world, especially to those in a largely different cultural situation.

For example, theologians today have been trying to express the dogma of the true humanness of Christ in a clearer, more relevant way, while also holding to his true Godness or divinity. The sharing of authority in the Church, the concept of ordination, the meaning of ministry, the role of women, Christ's teaching on marriage—as well as other matters—are being reexamined in the context of our modern, post–Vatican II world.

Catholics also follow the guidance of the pope and their bishops in religious matters when they are not teaching infallibly. These are set down in the great majority of the Church's laws. Some have greater authority than others. They can and do change, according to circumstances and the needs of the times. They are given especially in encyclical letters—which have the most authority—and also in instructions, decrees, catechisms, and so on. Ecumenical councils have, in part, dealt with many noninfallible or disciplinary concerns.

It is obvious that the Church must have these, too, just as a city must have health regulations, parking laws, and so on, which good citizens normally obey. To have unity instead of confusion—so that all may benefit from the common wisdom—we have this authority to which Catholics give their free allegiance.

Among the Church's teachings, then, some are more important and meaningful than others. The Church's basic teachings about the nature of God, Christ, our salvation by Christ, the Bible, baptism, and the eucharist are a far greater part of an educated Catholic's life than, for instance, truths about Mary and the saints, the nature of purgatory, or papal infallibility. "In Catholic doctrine their exists an order or 'hierarchy' of truths, since they vary in their relation to the foundation of the Christian faith" (*Decree on Ecumenism*, no. 11).

IN THE LITURGY

Pentecost Sunday, fifty days after Easter, is the feast on which we commemorate the coming of the Holy Spirit on the apostles. It is often called the birthday of the Church.

At Mass in the beginning of one of the eucharistic prayers we offer our gifts "in the first place . . . for your holy Catholic Church throughout the whole world . . . together with your servant our pope, with our bishop, and with all who faithfully teach the Catholic apostolic faith." Since these men are God's special instruments, they need special help.

Then we recall the fellowship we have with "your holy apostles and martyrs, Peter and Paul, Andrew . . . Linus, Cletus, Clement [the first successors of Peter] . . . "—reminding us that this is the same Mass in the same Church as that of the apostles and Peter.

A **"novena"** is nine days of public or private prayer in preparation for some feast. This practice comes from the nine days the apostles prepared, after Christ's ascension, for the coming of the Holy Spirit at Pentecost.

DAILY LIVING: OUR ATTITUDE TOWARD AUTHORITY

To the Catholic believer an infallible authority is natural and what one would expect from God. If God has come among us to teach us a way to himself, we would expect him to provide us with a certain amount of surety in knowing his teachings. In human affairs, we always try to come as close as we can to an infallible truth—if we have a disease, we want a doctor who knows as much as possible about curing it—and it is obviously much more important to have at least a minimum of truth about God and eternal happiness.

An infallible authority, far from limiting our freedom, can give us greater freedom. Christ says of his teaching, "You will know the truth, and the truth will make you free" (John 8, 32). Knowing the truth about anything frees us from ignorance, doubt, insecurity—if we know our watch is correct, we are freed from uncertainty about the time. The more truths science discovers about humankind and the universe, the greater freedom we can have from disease and other calamities. In somewhat the same way, a Catholic, guided by the infallible authority of the Church, can have a basic freedom from ignorance and error in this most important area of life.

Obedience to authority is natural, too, in less important, noninfallible matters. All day long we obey authorities, sometimes reluctantly, but seeing the necessity for it—conforming to parking laws, paying taxes, obeying those we love or those over us at work and school. We realize that we are free to disobey, but then we must face the consequences. We realize, too, that we must live with the weakness and inequalities of any human authority.

> *There may be situations in which a Catholic cannot agree with some authoritative, noninfallible teaching* (e.g., the present papal teaching on birth control or the ordination of women, or that of the pope and American bishops regarding nuclear weapons or economic policy). One cannot reconcile the teaching with one's grasp of the total gospel preached by the Church.
>
> *There can be a responsible, informed dissent—a well-founded "loyal dissent"*—as opposed to an immature selfishness or uninformed stubbornness. One might ask oneself: Have I tried to be informed about the Church's position on an issue and the reasons behind it? Has there been prayerful reflection on the matter? Have I tried to eliminate selfish motives?
>
> In all of this, one's conscience must be one's ultimate guide. One tries to inform one's conscience, but following it, even when it is objectively erroneous, is always the bottom line.
>
> Obviously, too, while all dissent is serious, an inability to accept, for example, the divinity of Christ, his presence in the Church and the eucharist, is more serious and alienating than, for example, problems with the Marian doctrines, papal infallibility, or teachings on sexual or social morality.
>
> Church historians note that dissent became an acceptable position for large numbers of Catholics after "Humanae Vitae," the 1968 papal encyclical outlawing contraception. At the time, the American bishops proposed these conditions for public dissent: serious and well-founded reasons, no intention to question or impugn the Church's teaching authority, and the avoidance of scandal. Today the Church is still struggling to reach a consensus regarding such expressions of dissent. Excommunication, depriving one of access to the eucharist until one ceases one's dissent, is hardly ever used today—it is seen as not only opposed to the open spirit of Vatican Council II but is usually impractical and unenforceable as well.

Dissent has always existed in the Church, and our media age, plus Vatican Council II's emphasis on the primacy of conscience, makes its public expression a fact of life. Yet dissent should never be taken lightly; and especially in our highly individualistic society much dissent stems from a simple unwillingness to live the gospel message. But other, well-founded dissent must be taken seriously—especially when it is backed by a solid body of theological opinion and is held by a large body of otherwise faithful and conscientious Catholics. Several matters that are now Catholic teaching were once considered dissent from previously accepted teaching (e.g., Vatican Council II's teaching on religious liberty and the primacy of conscience).

One's attitude toward religious authority is conditioned by one's lifelong relationships to other authorities. One who has experienced little loving authority in his or her personal life might have continual problems relating to a Church that speaks with authority. Another might have a personal need for constant approval of an authority, and so might be overly dependent on structured religious guidance. Between these two immature extremes people vary in their need for or independence of religious authority.

Ex-Catholics frequently are such because they have been poorly treated by churchly authorities, in many cases compounding ill treatment or neglect in their childhood homes. They can be poor advertisements for the Church, especially in the eyes of those who may be thinking of joining it, but underlying their alienation are often unsatisfactory, perhaps painful relationships with these significant authorities in their lives. Many of these—some statistics say half—return to the Church when they are older and able to share their stories (and their feelings of anger, guilt, and so on) with churchpeople and others who are understanding and accepting.

Catholics should give free obedience to the Church's authority. They hopefully try to be open, ready to learn, to make the teaching their own. They know the bishops are gifted by the Spirit to pass on Christ's saving truth, and they try to obey as intelligently and authentically as they can.

But this obedience is not just an immature rule-keeping, obeying minimal laws that make a person's decisions for one, as children might do. Rather it is an openness to guidance in making decisions oneself, guided by one's conscience, a readiness to apply to oneself the general principles of authority, especially Christ's supreme law of love—and above all, an openness to discerning the Spirit acting in one's life.

SOME SUGGESTIONS FOR . . .

DISCUSSION

What advantages might Christ have foreseen in choosing a center of authority and unity in the Church? What disadvantages?

Can you understand the basic meaning and limits of infallibility, and how the people of the Church, as well as the pope and bishops, share in it?

Can you see how some teachings are more important than others, even among those that are infallible? How there is a development of teachings in the Church?

How did Christ live out, by the concrete example of his own life and death, his ideal of authority as service to others? Do you know of any examples of this today? What makes living this out difficult?

Can you see how one's attitude toward authority might include, at times, responsible dissent? How one's attitude might also verge on irresponsible individualism? How one's informed conscience should discern the difference and must always be one's ultimate guide?

FURTHER READING

- • *Authority and Leadership in the Church: Past Directions and Future Possibilities,* Rausch (M. Glazier, 1989)—A clearly written, balanced, and hopeful book with an ecumenical slant that concisely reflects current theological thinking.
- • *The Beginnings of the Church,* Cwiekowski (Paulist Press, 1988)—An excellent middle-of-the-road treatment of the origin and early years of the Church, reflecting the findings of recent scholarly research.
- • *Witnesses to the Faith,* Gaillardetz (Paulist Press, 1992)—Discusses the development of the ordinary magisterium, or teaching authority of the bishops, in the light of contemporary theology, and proposes a Church-communion under the guidance of the Spirit rather than a centralized, hierarchical dominance.

- *Priest and Bishop, Biblical Reflections,* Brown (Paulist Press, 1970)— A brief, excellent study by an outstanding biblical scholar about the biblical background of the priesthood and the hierarchy of the Church.
- *The Churches the Apostles Left Behind* (Paulist Press, 1974)—This is also by Raymond Brown, and it superbly studies the diversity of seven different early church-communities.
- *Faithful Dissent,* Curran (Sheed & Ward, 1989)—A careful study by a respected moral theologian of his controversy with the Vatican over the legitimacy of theological and practical dissent.
- • *Dissent in the Church: Readings in Moral Theology,* No. 6, ed. Curran and McCormick (Paulist Press, 1988)—An excellent, comprehensive collection of authors giving different views of dissent and its meaning today.
- *Your Conscience and Church Teaching,* Lohkomp (Catholic Update no. 122, St. Anthony Messenger Press)—A very brief, excellent treatment designed to resolve conflicts.
- *Why Be Catholic?* O'Malley (Crossroad, 1993)—Refreshingly frank, this discusses some of the basic aspects of Catholic belief, warts and all, through the centuries. Thoroughly enjoyable as well as informative.
- • *The Roots of the Catholic Tradition,* Rausch (M. Glazier, 1986)— Using the Bible and Church history, this book treats some of the main elements of the Catholic tradition and shows how this tradition is developing today.
- *Documents of Vatican II,* ed. Flannery (Eerdmans Publishing, 1984)—This New Revised Edition of the Council documents includes significant documents implementing the work of Vatican II; a new translation, with a valuable Appendix and Index, this is an excellent sourcebook in one paperback volume.
- *Vatican II: More Postconciliar Documents,* ed. Flannery (Eerdmans, 1982)—A further selection of significant documents implementing the work of the Council; in one paperback volume, this is another good sourcebook.
- • *The Code of Canon Law: A Text and Commentary,* eds. Coriden, Green, Heintschel (Paulist Press, 1985)—This is the English text of

the 1983 revision of the Church's laws, done in the light of Vatican II, with an excellent commentary; commissioned by the American Canon Law Society.

•• *Creative Fidelity,* Sullivan (Paulist Press, 1996)—This author, perhaps the leading American theological expert on the Church's authority structures, discusses a mature and "creative" faithfulness to the Church's teachings—including a look at the proper role of infallibility.

• *Catechism of the Catholic Church* (U.S. Catholic Conference, 1994)—The English translation of the latest compendium of Catholic teaching. This is also available in a more compact edition by Doubleday.

• *Introducing the Catechism of the Catholic Church,* ed. Marthaler (Paulist Press, 1994)—Some of America's leading theologians discuss the *Catechism's* strengths and weaknesses—a "must" for using it intelligently.

Also, see the "Further Reading" section of chapter 24.

FURTHER VIEWING/LISTENING

Two Views of the Church: American and Roman, McBrien (Paulist Press)—An excellent audiocassette on the differences in the way U.S. Catholics and Vatican officials view the nature, purpose, and inner workings of the Church.

PERSONAL REFLECTION

The Apostles' Creed is the most ancient Christian profession of faith, having come to us from shortly after the time of the apostles. It is twelve brief statements taken from Scripture and arranged so one can easily remember them. In the early days of the Church, especially during times of persecution, Christians held this profession as sacred—they lived by it and many gave their lives for it. Down through the centuries it has been our simplest, most fundamental expression of what we believe and try to live by.

Today a child being raised as a Catholic—or an adult becoming a convert to Catholic Christianity—learns this as his or her most basic expression of belief. It is an excellent prayer to say frequently as a reminder and renewal of one's commitment to belief in today's wobbly world:

I believe in God, the Father almighty
   Creator of heaven and earth.
I believe in Jesus Christ, his only Son, our Lord,
   He was conceived by the power of the Holy Spirit,
   and born of the Virgin Mary,
   He suffered under Pontius Pilate,
   was crucified, died, and was buried.
   He descended to the dead;
   On the third day he arose again.
   He ascended into heaven,
   and is seated at the right hand of the Father;
   He will come again to judge the living and the dead.
I believe in the Holy Spirit,
   the holy catholic Church,
   the communion of saints,
   the forgiveness of sins,
   the resurrection of the body,
   and the life everlasting. Amen.

In previous chapters we treated most of what is professed in this creed. Later we will discuss, in detail, judgment, the communion of saints, the forgiveness of sins, the resurrection of the body, and life everlasting.

When people who desire to become Catholic are received into the Catholic Church, they say this creed together from memory, when they have become sufficiently familiar with its meaning and with trying to live it out in their lives. As we will see, this creed and/or the Nicene Creed, usually said each Sunday at Mass, is a part of the Rite of Christian Initiation of Adults (chapter 13).

11

The Great Book in Which
We Meet God

Why is the Bible a special book? How can one better understand the Bible? How can one be helped by reading the Bible?

THE BIBLE, GOD'S WORD AND OURS, TOO

We have seen how God revealed himself and his plan to humankind through the people and events of the Old Testament, and then he finally revealed himself fully in Jesus Christ. God's revelation to us culminated in the teachings of Jesus Christ as set down in the New Testament. We saw that over the centuries the Church has been developing new insights into his teachings, and he is himself continually among us, revealing himself to his followers in a number of ways. But the basic source of what we know about God and Jesus Christ, the Church's great contact by which all other claims to contact with God are tested, is the revelation given us in the Bible.

The teachings of Christianity and of the Catholic Church have their basis in the Bible. This was dramatically demonstrated at Vatican Council II when, each day, the book of gospels was solemnly placed before the assembled bishops at the start of their deliberations. Near the close of its last session the Council thus summed up the Church's dependence on the Bible:

All the preaching of the Church must be nourished and regulated by Sacred Scripture. For in the Sacred Books, the Father who is in heaven meets his children with great love and speaks with them; and the force and the power in the Word of God is so great that it stands as the support and the energy of the Church, the strength of faith for her . . . [children], the food of the soul, and the pure and everlasting source of spiritual life (*Constitution on Divine Revelation,* no. 21).

The Bible is called the "Word" of God because through it God communicates himself, expresses himself, to us. As we communicate ourselves to others through our words, so by the Bible God communicates himself to us.

The Second Person of the Trinity is the almighty Word, the perfect expression of the Father. The Bible is God's created Word. He expresses himself through it by guiding the human authors. The Word-made-flesh, Jesus Christ, and the Word-that-is-the-Bible are mysteriously and intimately connected: Today's theology speaks of the "sacramentality" of the Bible because through it we are offered a special opportunity to encounter God in Jesus Christ. This is brought about by the Bible's direct contact with the human intellect, imagination, and emotions. In some ways it can excel the encounter with God that comes through the sacraments because it might offer more substance to people.

The Bible is inspired by God, that is, he guided the human authors so that they wrote what he wanted. Even though the human authors sometimes may not have been aware of his guidance, nevertheless they set down in their writings what he wanted them to. Thus we read it as the world's most sacred and special book.

The Bible is also the work of humans who expressed their own thoughts as they wrote in their own way. The human authors were not merely passive instruments of God, but wrote freely, using the language and style of their time and culture to communicate their message in the way that seemed most appropriate to them. The writers were like us, sinful, subject to error, and unable to grasp the fullness of God's revelation.

The prophet Jeremiah shows an awareness of his human limitations by opening his book thus: "The words of Jeremiah . . . to whom the word of the Lord came" (Jeremiah 1, 1-2). Luke in his prologue (1, 1-4) wrote: "Inasmuch as many have undertaken to compile a narrative of the things . . . it seemed good to me also . . . to write an orderly account. . . . " Thus the Scripture is the words of humans seeking to express the word of God that had come to them.

The Bible gives the inspired record of God's revelation from the time when the revelation was originally given. God guided his Church to put together the Bible because he wanted us to have his teachings in the actual form in which they were first given—when the great, "breakthrough" events of our salvation were still fresh in people's minds—so that down through the centuries we might draw inspiration from them.

A person might set down in a diary an account of some great event in his or her life soon after it took place, and then years later upon rereading it, be deeply stirred. Reading the words of the Bible makes God's great actions seem very close to us—and helps us realize that he is just as truly acting in our lives today.

The Bible is a special type of literature, and its books must be understood as God and the human authors intended. It contains many different kinds of writing, or literary forms, each of which presents the truth but in its own way—such as poetry, parables, hyperbole, metaphors, satire, and so on. "Since God speaks in Sacred Scripture through humans in human fashion, the interpreter of Sacred Scripture, in order to see clearly what God wanted to communicate to us, should carefully investigate what meaning the sacred writers really intended, and what God wanted to manifest by means of their words" (*Constitution on Divine Revelation*, no. 12).

The *Catechism* also says that in order to read the Bible correctly, we must take into account the conditions of the biblical authors' time and culture and "the modes of feeling, speaking and narrating then current" (110). It reiterates what the Council said about being attentive to the whole of Sacred Scripture—including not taking things out of context—and, as we will see, reading it "within the living tradition of the whole Church . . . [where] it is written principally in the Church's heart rather than in documents and records . . . " (113).

The purpose of the Bible and its style of writing has already been discussed. See "The Source of Our Story" in chapter 2. To understand particularly the literary style of the New Testament, see "The Coming of Jesus Christ" in chapter 6.

The reliability of the historical setting of the books of the Bible, once challenged by critics, has been confirmed again and again by modern archeological findings. Just as Christian scholars have come to see the importance of understanding the literary forms of the biblical books, so the discoveries of modern archeology have confirmed the Bible's antiquity and the authenticity of the historical setting in which its events took place.

In 1947, the "greatest manuscript discovery of modern times" occurred in the finding of the first of a collection of ancient scrolls in a cave near the Dead Sea. Since then, ten additional caves within a radius of a few miles of Qumran have yielded more material. To date there have been found the remains of some eight hundred manuscripts, consisting of about a dozen complete scrolls and thousands of fragments dating from the third century B.C.E. to the early Christian decades. About a fourth of the material comprises copies of the Hebrew Scriptures, including a well-preserved scroll of Isaiah and manuscripts representing every Old Testament book except Esther. Of the deuterocanonical books, fragments of Tobit, Sirach, and the Letter of Jeremiah were found. These ancient writings were used by the Essenes, thought by most scholars to have been a separatist Jewish sect living in a monastic community at Qumran. (A recent proposal that the Qumran ruins were a Roman villa or military fortress has been rejected by most scholars.) The other writings of this priceless discovery consisted of commentaries on various books of the Old Testament, the theology of the sect, and the organization of the community and their disciplines. There are over four hundred documents being translated by various scholars and still to be assembled and published.

For a timely, informative history of the scrolls and their discovery, see *Responses to 101 Questions on the Dead Sea Scrolls* by Fitzmeyer (Paulist Press, 1992).

In 1945, discoveries were made at Nag Hammadi in Egypt of many early Christian writings, mostly by Gnostic Christians—among them the Gospel of

Thomas, of Philip, of Mary (Magdalene), and other writings giving sayings and incidents of Jesus' life from a gnostic point of view. These give us much information on the development of early Christianity, and especially of this cultlike group, which died out after the second century. The gnostics are so-called from their claim to a secret self-knowledge ("gnosis") that enabled them to become divine as, they believed, Jesus had done. Some writings express a beautiful, mystic, inner spirit, but many gnostics also rejected the body as evil—since it was material—and sexual intercourse as a turning of one's spirit into a slave of one's body (which may account, in part, for their dying out so quickly).

More recently discovered and already famous are the Ebla tablets, found in northern Syria. The milieu of the culture that produced these writings has many similarities to the world of the Bible. Important cities of the Old Testament are mentioned, and there appear to be parallels in family and clan names, reflecting a period just prior to the patriarchal period.

Many other discoveries of manuscripts and papyri in the Middle East have been, and are, shedding further light on biblical times. Biblical archeology, a relatively new scientific discipline, is continually expanding our knowledge of the background and meaning of the biblical texts. Some recent exciting discoveries include the first reference outside the Bible to King David; a small inscribed ivory pomegranate identified as the only known relic from Solomon's temple; a boat recovered from the bottom of the Sea of Galilee dating back to the time of Christ; an ossuary (a stone box in which a deceased person's bones were placed a year after death) of the high priest Caiaphas, who presided at the trial of Jesus.

None of the original manuscripts of the Old or New Testament books remain today, but our copies are more ancient and numerous than any other books of that period. Our earliest copy of Horace, for instance, is dated 900 years after his death; of Plato, almost 1,300 years. But we have a complete copy of the gospels dated 250 years after its writing, an almost-complete copy dated 100 years earlier, plus fragments from the second century. Compared to the few dozen ancient copies we possess of the best-preserved classics, we have a few thousand of the Scriptures. Also, in other early Christian writers we find thousands of biblical quotations and citations, from the New Testament particularly, all testifying to its authenticity.

Because the biblical authors did not write a scientific detailed history in our modern sense, some critics have said that we cannot arrive at a true picture of the historical Christ. They say that what we have in the New Testament particularly are only testimonies of the writers' faith, fragmentary and mythological accounts. However, a conclusive majority of Christian scholars, while agreeing that the faith of the Christian community shaped the writing of the New Testament and that it does use some mythology, nevertheless hold firmly that at the basis of the gospel accounts is a real person, Jesus Christ, who said and did certain definite things.

One writer puts it: "Faith in Christ is not a spontaneous creation, a satellite which never had a launching pad." The evangelists wrote within the early Christian community, amid either eyewitnesses or those who had intimately known eyewitnesses. There is no explaining the faith and influence of these Christians unless the Christ portrayed in the gospels is real. Otherwise no one would believe in such a totally unique character, preaching such a doctrine: perfect and yet very human, claiming to be the unique revelation of God among humans, assuming absolute authority over the sacred Law of Judaism, demanding that people change their lives for him even to loving one's enemies and dying for him, finally going to his death and appearing alive again as proof of his teaching.

Unless this portrayal is real, there is no logical reason why Christians should ever have believed in him or have convinced so many others of his teachings. There is no other explanation of his great impact and following.

THE BIBLE'S ORIGIN AND DEVELOPMENT

The Scriptures used by the apostles and the primitive Christian Church was a Greek translation of the Old Testament called the Septuagint. This translation had been originally made of the then-existing writings of the Old Testament in the third century B.C.E. at Alexandria in Egypt for the Jews of the diaspora (those living in foreign lands away from Palestine and the temple). Certain other sacred writings were added to this original Greek translation in the next century and a half (some Psalms, Daniel, Esther, Tobias, Judith, Wisdom, Sirach, Baruch, and 1 and 2 Maccabees). When the Christian Church expanded beyond Palestine and began to evangelize the Hellenistic world, this Greek Bible was used with great enthusiasm. It became the Bible of the Church during its first generation.

The New Testament canon, the Christian writings considered the inspired Word of God, was slow in developing. At first the early Christians were not concerned with providing written records for posterity because they believed that Christ's second coming would occur in their immediate lifetime. With this in mind, missionary efforts were primarily directed toward preaching the oral gospel. Not until the death of most of the first-generation Christians—the apostles and others who were actual witnesses of Christ's public ministry, passion, and resurrection—did a concern arise to preserve the gospel for future generations.

With the last half of the first century Christian literature began to develop. Some of these writings would eventually make up the New Testament. St. Paul's first letter to the Thessalonians is the earliest of all New Testament writings to reach us in its original form. It was written from Corinth about 50 C.E. Paul followed this with additional letters to various and scattered groups that he had converted to Christianity. His letters were written for the practical purpose of encouraging, instructing, and admonishing these far-flung churches. The earliest gospel that we have in its original form is Mark, written some time before 70 C.E.

From this point on there was a great increase in Christian writings. The other extant gospels were written within a decade or two. Many other writings were highly regarded by local churches, such as the Epistle of Clement, the Didache, Gospel of Thomas, Shepherd of Hermas, and so on. But it was almost unanimously held that the writings that had some apostolic origin were to be placed in a special category. During the third century our present New Testament books came to be basically accepted by the Christian world, though some books were not widely used.

There is a development in Christian theology among the books of the New Testament. From its earliest book, Paul's first epistle to the Thessalonians, to the second epistle of Peter, the last to be written, there is an evident development in the Church's understanding of Christ and his teachings. Under the influence of the Holy Spirit, Christ's first followers were coming to understand and set down in words what God had done in Christ.

The canon, or Church-accepted list of books of the Old and New Testaments, was established by the end of the fourth century for all practical purposes. Certain early Church "Fathers," scholarly and sometimes holy churchmen who were often bishops, particularly influenced the selection of the books that would constitute the New Testament. More and more these twenty-seven books were used by the Church, and the other writings fell into comparative disuse.

> Clement of Alexandria (150–215 C.E.), Eusebius (d.c. 340 C.E.), and Jerome (d.c. 420 C.E.) were some of these Church Fathers. Athanasius in 367 C.E. issued a list of twenty-seven books, which is the same as our present New Testament; this was accepted as canonical by the synods of Hippo (393) and Carthage (397, 419). About this time Pope Damasus I commissioned Jerome to translate the Septuagint and the canonical Christian writings from Greek to Latin, the spoken language of the Roman empire. This translation is known as the Vulgate and was used as the Church's official version until recently.

In the Old Testament, Catholic Bibles have seven more books than most non-Catholic versions, called the Apocrypha or deuterocanonical books. There is no substantial difference in the New Testament. Though some early Christian writers had reservations about seven Old Testament books, scholars today agree that they were generally accepted and used throughout the Christian Church from the beginning. The books are Tobias, Judith, Wisdom, Sirach (Ecclesiasticus), Baruch, 1 and 2 Maccabees, and parts of Daniel and Esther.

The difference of opinion about the books is an ancient one:

> The Jews at the time of Christ had no fixed list of books. The theory that the Greek Septuagint, translated and used by the Jews of the diaspora, had a fixed canon that was eventually adopted by the early Christian Church is questioned today. The great codices of the Septuagint—Vaticanus, Sinaiticus, and Alexandrinus—that should bear witness to this supposedly fixed collection are in disagreement. The same situation existed among the Palestinian Jews and is attested to by the fact that the Essenes of the Dead Sea included some of the deuterocanonical books in their collection of Scripture. It is generally believed that the rabbinical schools of Palestine, because of the growing controversy with early Christianity and the development of Christian writings being used as Scripture, did establish a canon in the late second century—although there are echoes in rabbinical literature well into the third century of individuals questioning the status of some of the writings.

The Jewish historian Josephus alludes to a rabbinical tradition that Ezra closed the canon of the Bible; this tradition, which is in fact unfounded, is probably an attack on the Septuagint. Another rabbinical tradition attributes the delineation of the canon to a synod at Jamnia in Palestine about 100 C.E., but there is little reliable information on the activities of this synod.

At the time of the Reformation, Martin Luther made a translation of the Bible using the Palestinian canon as the basis for his Old Testament—thus eliminating Judith, Tobias, Wisdom, Sirach, Baruch, 1 and 2 Maccabees, and parts of Daniel and Esther. These books were placed in an appendix to the Old Testament. He also rejected Jude, Hebrews, James, and Revelation from the New Testament. The other Reformation churches, however, did not dispute the New Testament canon, and Lutherans returned to the traditional New Testament listings in the seventeenth century. By the end of the nineteenth century most Bibles published by non-Catholic sources did not include the disputed seven books of the Old Testament.

In 1546, the Catholic bishops at the Counter-Reformation Council of Trent declared that the seventy-three books that had been used to that time by the Christian Church were canonical and the inspired Word of God.

"The quarrels over the authority of the Apocrypha are now largely matters of the past. A generation that has witnessed the discovery of the Dead Sea Scrolls will probably agree with Hastings' *Dictionary of the Bible* that 'modern historical interest . . . is putting the Apocrypha in their true place as significant documents of a most important era in religious history'"** (Preface of Thos. Nelson & Sons RSV Apocrypha).

Most of the best recent versions of non-Catholic Bibles are available in editions with the apocryphal books. To quote prominent Protestant biblical scholar E. Jacob: "These books do not appear to be a roadblock but rather a bridge between the two testaments. Certain doctrines such as the resurrection of the dead, angelology, and the concept of retribution, have assumed in the apocryphal [deuterocanonical] literature the aspect under which they materialize in the New Testament. To not include them is to run the risk of removing a precious link in the web that constitutes the unity of revelation."

Catholics and Protestants are now working together to produce common Bibles, especially in the minor languages of the mission fields, and these Bibles contain the apocryphal (deuterocanonical) books.

The Catholic Church, within whose influence the Bible was formed, has always reverenced it, and today especially the Church urges her people to read it daily. The Bible has always been the basis of the Church's teachings and of her liturgy. Its use was not as widespread in past centuries as today, mostly because people generally could not read and understand it. Before the Reformation there were translations of the Bible into almost every modern language and many in Latin, which was understood by most educated people.

The Church, particularly in post-Reformation times, banned certain translations of the Bible because they were considered to have distorted some passages or to teach erroneous doctrines. Because of this defensive mentality, the post-Reformation Church placed too little emphasis on the Bible, and sometimes discouraged private Bible reading altogether.

Today there is a great biblical revival in the Church, and the Bible has become the great force for Christian unity. Christian scholars of all faiths are working together on the ancient biblical manuscripts, sharing their discoveries with one another. They are in almost unanimous agreement on the Bible's translation, and the more biblical studies progress the closer they draw together on its meaning.

The King James version, known for its classic English, came to be called the Authorized Version of the English people. For two and a half centuries it remained unchallenged. In 1870 a revised version was made in which something like thirty-six thousand corrections were entered; other revisions have been published since.

In America the most widely used edition today is the Revised Standard Version, recently redone as the New Revised Standard Version (NRSV). The **Oxford Annotated Edition** with Apocrypha has excellent footnotes, maps, and supplementary information. Both of these Bibles are available in Roman Catholic editions, that is, with Apocrypha. The **HarperCollins Study Bible** is a very recent, excellent edition.

The New American Bible, first completed in 1970, was the first translation of the entire Bible from the original language into English under Catholic auspices. Authorized for the "Lectionary," the Scripture readings used in the Mass, it has become the most widely used Bible by American Roman Catholics. It is in modern English, and some editions have excellent footnotes. A new translation of the New Testament with inclusive language and other significant changes has been available since 1986. **The Catholic Study Bible** is a 1990 edition that has been called the best Bible to date for use in Bible study by individuals and groups.

The Jerusalem Bible, first translated by English Roman Catholic scholars in 1966 and thoroughly redone as the New Jerusalem Bible, is another modern English text with a wealth of explanatory notes and other supplementary information as well as excellent marginal cross-references to other parts of the Bible.

The **New English Bible,** authorized by the Church of Scotland and other British churches, was completed in 1970. It is exceptionally effective in its use of modern English and its continuity with older versions. A 1989–90 revision is now available as the **Revised English Bible.** Another very fine translation in modern English is the **J. B. Phillips New Testament.**

Good News for Modern Man, the New Testament of Today's English Bible, was published by the American Bible Society in 1966 and has become the best-selling book ever produced. A companion volume of the Old Testament was produced in 1976, and this complete Bible is called the **Good News Bible.** Since 1979 an edition with the Apocrypha has been available, and today it is widely used by all faiths.

In recent years Bible scholarship has been bringing together people of all faiths in cooperative ventures. An example of this is the scholarly **Anchor Bible** being published with an extensive commentary, one book at a time. It is being translated by the most renowned Scripture experts of Judaism, Protestantism, Catholicism, and Orthodoxy.

THE CHURCH'S TRADITION INTERPRETS THE BIBLE

Christ did not leave his followers a religion in the sense of a "package" of clear, well-defined truths. His teaching was to be completed by the Holy Spirit and undergo development in the course of centuries. While he gave us the fullness of God's revelation, much was yet implicit, unable to be grasped by the ones to whom it was given—and today much is unable to be grasped by us. To help each age understand Christ's teachings, his Church must adapt their expression to the mentality of that time. The teachings remain basically the same, but we progressively see into them more fully, more relevantly. The Holy Spirit guides each generation to add its own understanding to them.

Nor did the apostles sit down and write a handbook of the Christian faith. Their religion was still "finding itself," growing in an understanding of its true mission—sometimes through painful controversy, as in the battle over the "Judaizers" who would have kept Christianity an aspect of the Jewish faith. These were the problems of the humans who tried to carry on after Christ. They were inspired by the Spirit but still remained very human.

The primitive Church developed through the oral teachings of the apostles and others who were the witnesses to the great events of Christ's life. The Christian writings that later made up the New Testament were comparatively slow in developing, so that in the first decades of Christianity the faith was based solely upon oral apostolic traditions. In fact the people based their faith almost entirely on the preaching Church until near the end of the second century. The basic elements of the faith were being revealed during the full period of the apostolic age. Only slowly did the Church arrive at a definite creed in the sense of a clearly defined set of truths.

An example of the development of revelation can be seen in the formula for baptism. In the earliest oral proclamation as recorded in the sermons of the book of Acts, the apostles stated that one must be "baptized in the name of Jesus Christ" (Acts 2, 38; 8, 16). As a deeper understanding of the faith was revealed to them, they baptized "in the name of the Father, and of the Son, and of the Holy Spirit" (Matthew 28, 19).

Christian traditions were expressed in both oral and written form. St. Paul wrote to the Church in Thessalonica, "So then, brethren, stand firm and hold to the traditions which you were taught by us, either by word of mouth or by letter" (2 Thessalonians 2, 15). Christianity did not simply become a religion of a book. The Church often asserted apostolic sanction for traditions and usages that could not be traced to apostolic writings.

The Bible came from the living Church—the Old Testament from the living community of God's people, Israel, and the New Testament from the apostolic community that Christ founded, his Church, the new Israel. The books accepted as part of the New Testament, particularly, had to be orthodox, to match the belief of the Church. For every accepted book, the Church rejected a similar one. God's truths are revealed to us in the Bible, but to understand them in their fullness, they must be seen along with the tradition of the Church from which they first came.

Tradition is the way Christ's Church understands and lives his teachings. It is not merely the quaint customs of the Church, things like our practice of shaking hands upon meeting a friend. It is the way Christ's teachings were and are lived by his Church.

Tradition comes from many things: the Church's creeds, the records of the Church's worship and liturgical practices, the writings of scholars and Church leaders, the decrees of popes and councils, the prayers of the Church's people, and so on.

> The Church pays particular attention to the tradition that comes from the ancient Church, from those who were closest to Christ. This is called "apostolic tradition." It is found in the early records of the Church's worship, the writings of the early Church "Fathers," ancient Christian inscriptions, paintings, and so on—anything that tells us what Christians believed and did from the time of the apostles.

Tradition is also continuing and developing today. It is the way the Church here and now understands and lives Christ's teaching. It is going on now, in the writings of scholars, the decrees of Church authorities, the practices of the liturgy, and the Christian practices and devotions of the people. Since Christ and his Spirit guide the Church, they are continually forming this tradition.

Tradition, then, is the way in which the teachings of the Bible are understood and put into living application in the Church. The teachings of the Church, contained in the Bible, are interpreted for us by the Church's tradition. To understand Christ's teachings we look both to the Bible for the "Word" and to tradition for the "Spirit" in the interpretation of sacred Scripture. It is something like looking at a house from the outside and from the inside—in either case you are looking at the whole house, but both points of view are necessary to grasp it fully.

While the Bible contains God's original revelation, the Bible cannot be understood alone. The Church's living tradition is necessary to understand it. Sometimes all that it gives us is a hint of a particular teaching, and while some of its teachings are explicit, others are only implicit. To try to interpret the Bible without the aid of Christian tradition would be like trying to interpret the American Constitution while ignoring the other writings of the Founding Fathers, the constitutional interpretations of the courts, commentaries of legal scholars, and so on.

None of the biblical authors had any idea of writing a book that would of itself give us all of God's revelation. John wrote the last and longest gospel and says at the end of it: "There are, however, many other things that Jesus did; but if every one of these should be written, not even the world itself, I think, could hold the books that would have to be written" (John 21, 25). St. Paul says, "Hold the teachings that you have learned, whether by word or by letter of ours" (2 Thessalonians 2, 15). We saw that Christianity was in existence almost two hundred years before the biblical writings were known throughout the Christian world, and even after this the books were accepted and passed on under the aegis of the Church's authority.

So we cannot arbitrarily use biblical texts to "prove" a teaching apart from the Church's tradition. Through the centuries people have tried to "prove" almost everything by quoting biblical texts without regard for the living tradition of the Church. We recognize that each individual cannot be given his or her own copy of the American Constitution to interpret and live as he or she sees fit; so we cannot understand and live the teachings of the Bible without the traditions of the Church.

God's revelation, then, is something that is happening to God's people today, as well as what the Church has possessed from the beginning. In the events of their daily lives, Christians should be making personal contact with Christ revealing himself to them. They should experience this especially when they gather together for the liturgy, as we shall see, or when they pray, or when they encounter God in some deed of kindness, justice, fortitude, and so on. For the committed believer, everything that happens is divine.

AN OUTLINE OF THE BIBLE

The Old Testament tells the story of God's revelation of himself and of his plan leading up to the coming of Christ. It contains forty-six

books, written by various authors over a period of many centuries. (The older, alternate titles of the books are shown in parentheses. The books are arranged in the order of their appearance.)

THE PENTATEUCH: THE FIRST FIVE BOOKS

Genesis, Exodus, Leviticus, Numbers, and Deuteronomy—also called the Law (Torah)

This begins with a primitive history of humankind presented in a mythological setting. It continues with God's choice of his people, given in a historical setting. Its high point is the making of the old covenant. It also contains religious legislation covering the way of life of God's chosen people. Once thought to be the writings of Moses, it is seen by scholars today as the work of a redactor (or final editor) who edited oral and written traditions into its present form in the fifth century B.C.E.

THE HISTORICAL NARRATIVES

Joshua (Josue), Judges, Ruth, 1 Samuel (1 Kings), 2 Samuel (2 Kings), 1 Kings (3 Kings), 2 Kings (4 Kings), 1 Chronicles (1 Paralipomenon), 2 Chronicles (2 Paralipomenon), Ezra (1 Esdras), Nehemiah (2 Esdras), Tobit (Tobias), Judith, and Esther

These books give a general history of Israel. They tell us of the conquest of the Promised Land, Canaan, the development of the kingdom of Israel as an ancient world power under the reign of Kings David and Solomon, and the divided kingdoms of Israel and Judah, the destruction of these kingdoms, followed by the captivity in Babylon, and finally the return and attempt to rebuild Jerusalem and the temple to their former glory. Tobit, Judith, and Esther are colorful oriental tales of fictitious characters cast in a historical setting. They give us authentic descriptions of the customs and culture of that time.

WISDOM LITERATURE AND POETRY

Job, Psalms, Proverbs, Ecclesiastes (Qoheleth), Song of Solomon (Canticle of Canticles), Wisdom, and Sirach (Ecclesiasticus)

Historically these books have been classified as the seven "sapiential books," or collections of wisdom sayings, though they contain poetry, prayer, liturgy, and love songs as well.

THE WRITTEN PROPHETS

Isaiah (Isaias), Jeremiah (Jeremias), Lamentations, Baruch, Ezekiel (Ezechiel), Daniel, Hosea (Osee), Joel, Amos, Obadiah (Abdias), Jonah (Jonas), Micah (Micheas), Nahum, Habakkuk (Habacuc), Zephaniah (Sophonias), Haggai (Aggeus), and Zechariah (Zacharias)

These men of God are unique not only among the people of ancient times but in the entire literary history of the world. Their office was not filled by human choice but by God. Occasionally and rarely predictors of the future, their main concern was the current situation among God's people. They were a comparative handful of extraordinary preachers who dramatically exhorted, inspired, and tried to reform God's people at times of great crisis.

THE HISTORICAL BRIDGE TO THE NEW TESTAMENT

1 and 2 Maccabees (Machabees)
This is the saga of the period in Israel's life from 166 to 37 B.C.E.

THE NEW TESTAMENT

The New Testament gives the early Christian Church's view of Christ's life and teachings. It contains twenty-seven books, written between 50 C.E., and the early years of the second century C.E.

The four gospels, as we saw, are arranged as rough outlines of Christ's life and teachings. Each has its particular viewpoint, audience, and purpose. The first three, called the synoptic gospels, closely resemble one another: Both Matthew and Luke show that they got much material from Mark, the earliest gospel, and some material from another collection of Jesus' sayings, which is now lost (designated as "Q," from the German word *quelle,* meaning "source"). In addition certain traditions only available to each writer were included. Originally the gospels were anonymous writings; it was sometime in the second century that the Church named them.

Matthew portrays Christ as the promised Messiah of Old Testament prophecy. This is most apparent in his particular infancy narrative. Christ is also the new Moses who in the Sermon on the Mount urges a more radical obedience to the Law, while rejecting authoritarian legalism and commanding that we love even our enemies (5, 43–48).

The Church is seen as a unique structure apart from Judaism, from which it came. The writer presents the earliest regulations governing the life of the new community. He also shows Peter in a distinctive role as "the rock" (16, 18–19). Its dramatic conclusion contains a universal message in which the risen Lord commands his followers to "make disciples of all the nations" (28, 29).

Matthew was written about 90 C.E. in or around Antioch in Syria, from where the mission to the Gentiles began. Most scholars doubt its authorship by Matthew the tax collector and apostle. A growing consensus says the author was a converted rabbi or someone highly educated in rabbinical lore.

Mark is the earliest and shortest gospel; it is the primary source of information about the life and teachings of Jesus. It is made up of a collection of separate units of oral traditions used by teachers and preachers, edited and arranged in their present form by the author.

Mark begins with Jesus' baptism by John the Baptist. The first half gradually reveals the mystery of Jesus' messiahship and is highlighted by Peter's confession, "You are the Messiah!" (8, 29). The last half reveals the mystery of the suffering Son of Man. Written for Christians who were suffering persecution, this gospel is saying that Jesus, in his suffering, is indeed God's son.

Mark was written before 70 C.E., the date of the destruction of the temple, in a prominent Church center, probably Rome. It gained wide acceptance and was copied and circulated throughout the early Christian world.

Luke, identified by second-century Christians as a physician and follower of Paul, shows special concern for the poor and the outcasts, women and children, Samaritans and Gentiles. In his particular infancy narrative, Mary, the mother of Jesus, and Elizabeth, the mother of John the Baptist, are central figures. He also has the narrative of the child Jesus in the temple.

Only Luke has the raising of the widow's son at Nain (7, 11–17), the Mary and Martha conversation (10, 38–42), and the visit to the home of Zacchaeus (19, 1–10). Some of the best-known parables appear only in Luke: the Good Samaritan (10, 29–37), the lost coin (15, 8–10), the Prodigal Son (15, 11–31), the rich man and Lazarus (16, 19–31), and the Pharisee and the publican (18, 9–14).

Luke was written c. 80–85 (C.E.) in Achaia or Rome, for a Gentile audience. It is the first part of a two-volume work, the second being the Acts of the Apostles.

John's gospel has a very different way of presenting the life of Jesus. He tells no parables; he heals no lepers; he does not institute the eucharist on the night of his betrayal. The eucharist theme is tied into the feeling of the five thousand: "If you do not eat the flesh of the Son of Man and drink his blood, you have no life in you" (6, 53).

Theologically, John is the most advanced gospel—it shows the mature faith of the Church in the divine Jesus—and it is the most lofty, the most filled with symbolism. In the prologue, Jesus' divine Sonship as the Word of God is revealed. There are seven miracles, which are seven "signs" attesting to his divinity. There are a number of theological discourses and debates with his opponents over his claim to divine Sonship. Jesus is presented as the "I AM" (8, 24, 27; 13, 19), clearly referring back to the "I AM" of Moses' God of the burning bush (Exodus 3, 14). Jesus says he is the bread of life, the light of the world, the good shepherd, the resurrection and the life, and the true vine.

At chapter 12, Jesus ends his public ministry to be with his apostles. Chapters 13 through 16 are his great "priestly" discourses, the core of which is his command to them to love one another, "as I have loved you." This is followed by the passion narrative, with the author's particular additions.

Probably written just before 100 C.E. in Ephesus in Asia Minor by an unknown author, it reflects a community based on a sacramental life, especially baptism and the eucharist. Most think that the gospel we have today has been edited several times. But some recent scholars think that John was composed by a single author using a complex "chiastic" literary structure like that of some other ancient writers.

The Acts of the Apostles, also written by Luke, begins where the gospel ends, with the ascension of Jesus. The descent of the Holy Spirit follows. The author then presents his version of the expansion of Christianity from Jerusalem to Rome. In the early chapters he presents the struggle of the primitive Christian community to free itself from the Law and Judaism.

The last half of Acts presents the three missionary journeys of Paul. The author composes sermons that he attributes to Paul and others, giving us insights into the early apostolic preaching.

The fourteen epistles attributed to St. Paul are letters written to early Christian communities or to individuals. They are letters of instruction, guidance, and admonition, written to strengthen the faith of the early con-verts and to put down errors. They were either dictated by Paul himself or were written by his followers from the teachings he gave them. In their pages is a summary of Christian theology as presented by the great apostle of the Gentiles. The reader should notice how Paul's inspired insights de-velop in these, how they grow in their perception of Jesus as the eternal Son of God, and how they expand upon the relatively simple sayings and stories of Jesus given especially in the first three gospels. As with the au-thor of John, much of Paul's knowledge comes from his own mystical ex-periences of his Lord.

Paul was almost single-handedly responsible for the wide dissemi-nation of Christ's teachings into the vast Gentile world. Jesus consid-ered himself sent primarily to the Jews; Paul began with them, but spent most of his life among the Gentiles. His epistles deal with many fundamen-tal aspects of Christian belief and practice that the gospel writers do not.

The letters written by Paul himself include Romans, 1 and 2 Corinthians, Galatians, 1 Thessalonians, Philippians, and Philemon. Paul's authorship of Hebrews is universally rejected among critical scholars, along with the "pas-toral" epistles (1 and 2 Timothy, and Titus). Most question the Pauline au-thorship of Ephesians and 2 Thessalonians, and many that of Colossians; however, there is no doubt that these last letters were written in the spirit of Paul's theology.

The seven "catholic" epistles are letters addressed to the Church in general, one of James, two of Peter, three of John, and one of Jude. Attrib-uted to these apostles and reflecting their thought, these letters were writ-ten by their followers.

Revelation, or the Apocalypse, gives a series of figurative visions using the symbolism of Jewish apocalyptic writing, in which God strik-ingly intervenes to save his people. Writing around 95 C.E. during a Roman persecution in which many Christians died as martyrs, its author saw no earthly solution to the Christians' plight except God's interven-tion, and this he predicts in a series of dramatic images. Today, as regu-larly throughout history, this book is seen by some as a literal scenario of the "end time" through which, they usually believe, we are now passing. But while we know that Jesus will return, his words are clear: "As for the exact day or hour, no one knows it, neither the angels in heaven nor the Son but the Father only" (Matthew 24, 36).

IN THE LITURGY

The Bible forms the basis of our worship. Most of the prayers of the Mass, the sacraments, the daily prayer of priests and religious, are composed of prayers from Scripture.

The best way to receive God's Word is when the Scriptures are read to us at Mass. The first part of the Mass is called the Liturgy of the Word because it gives us God's Word, especially in the Scripture readings and the homily or sermon, which should be based on these. It is then that God addresses his Word to his people. At Mount Sinai, the chosen people assembled to hear God's Word read to them; they then agreed to his Word and a covenant was established by sacrifice. God's people assembled today at Mass likewise listen first to his Word, and then show their acceptance by taking part in the renewal of Christ's perfect new covenant sacrifice.

Sacred Scripture, then, is at the heart of the Mass. Just as we receive Christ in the sacraments, so also we receive Christ in the "Word." The Lectionary, or book of Scripture readings used at Mass, provides a varied reading of the Bible by arranging the texts in a three-year cycle.

There are three Scripture readings in the Sunday Mass (and two on weekdays). The first is from the Old Testament and is chosen for its relationship to the gospel, thus stressing the unity of the Old and the New Testaments. The second reading consists of semicontinuous passages from the letters of Paul and James. The gospel, the final reading, follows the theme of the liturgical season.

DAILY LIVING: THE BIBLE IN OUR LIFE

Before attending Mass on Sunday, we might meditatively read over— and reflect on—the three Scripture readings described above.

When we meditatively read the Bible and try to apply its words to our lives, God communicates with us. He helps us to know what to do and have the courage to do it. The Bible's words are addressed to us as much as to the people among whom it was written. The deeds related in the Bible are meant to show us that God is continually present among his people, that he acts to help us here and now as he once helped them.

The Bible's power in one man's life is illustrated by this real-life story: Raised as a midwest minister's son, a young man was accustomed to daily Bible reading in the home, but with adulthood and financial succcess he abandoned any practice of the Christian faith. Then a crisis caused the breakup of his marriage and he gradually turned again to reading his deceased father's Bible. Eventually he was converted to Catholicism, and now, years later, he leads an outstanding group of lay ministers, conducts seminary classes, and is in constant demand for his penetrating talks on the Bible.

SOME SUGGESTIONS FOR . . .

FURTHER READING

BIBLE STUDY AIDS

Many people become discouraged in their attempts at Bible reading because they are using an older version in which the style and language are obsolete and difficult to follow. Thus it is important to look over the newer versions of the Bible. A number of these are listed above. In addition, there are other study aids available.

A Bible dictionary offers facts and data about persons, places, ideas, words, and themes from the Bible. It provides pertinent information from other sources dealing with history, geography, archeology, and language studies that can further illuminate one's Bible study.

Recommended are McKenzie's *Dictionary of the Bible* and *Harper's Bible Dictionary.* A scholarly yet succinct work is Léon-Dufour's *Dictionary of the New Testament.*

A Bible atlas contains maps of important historical periods in Bible history, with a commentary on the events occurring in those eras. Among the many good ones are *The Oxford Bible Atlas* and Grollenberg's *Atlas of the Bible.*

A concordance lists alphabetically all the words that are found in the Bible. This helps one find particular Bible verses and also helps locate material topically. Some good concordances are Nelson's *Complete Concordance of the New American Bible,* and those of Cruden, Young, and Strong.

A commentary provides an explanation of the Bible passages book by book and verse by verse. It illuminates difficult and obscure passages and gives an interpretation of the meaning. Among the best available today in one volume are the *New Jerome Biblical Commentary* (1990), a thorough revision of the popular 1968 work, and *Harper's Bible Commentary,* an excellent recent work. *A New Catholic Commentary on Scripture* and *The Collegeville Bible Commentary* are both excellent and recent.

The *New Jerome Bible Handbook* (Liturgical Press, 1993) is very good for high school students and other new readers of the Bible.

Also valuable are *A Commentary on the Gospel of Matthew* and *A Commentary on the Gospel of John,* both by Kirk and Obach, and *A Commentary on the Gospel of Mark,* Keegan (Paulist Press, 1979–80, 1981).

Among the excellent **general introductions** to the Bible are *The Bible Makes Sense,* Bruggemann (Westminster, 1985).

For **Bible study groups** there are some fine books available, including *Spiritual Growth* (Revised), Jungerman (Paulist Press, 1984) and *A Guide to Reading the Bible,* a four-pamphlet set issued by ACTA Publications.

Share the Word (Paulist National Evangelization Association) is a very popular, bimonthly commentary on the Sunday, daily, and feastday lectionary readings. The *Little Rock Scripture Study Program* (Liturgical Press) and *Scripture from Scratch* (St. Anthony Messenger Press) are excellent and very popular today, combining print and video materials.

Computerized Bible study is now available, allowing quick access to large amounts of information. Bible texts can be examined while working simultaneously with atlases, commentaries, various translations, and dictionaries. New programs are being made available that make a study of the Scriptures much easier and give access to sources that most people would never have had previously.

Among the excellent Bible software packages available are the following: the *New American Bible with Revised New Testament* (Anno Domini, Ann Arbor, MI) with footnotes and cross references, lectionary readings, and topic verse lists. Also recommended are the *New Oxford Annotated Bible with Apocrypha: Electronic Edition* and the *New Revised Standard*

Version. The *Anchor Bible Dictionary* (Anchor Dell) and other Bible study aids in a Catholic collection will be available soon. The *Bible on Disc for Catholics* (Liguori Faithware,) is available in the Revised Standard Version. New programs are constantly being produced.

DISCUSSION

Can you understand how Christ's teachings spread and how the Bible enjoyed a natural and gradual development?

Does it seem natural to you that God's revelation should be continuing today in our lives?

What parts or books of the Bible are the most meaningful to you?

PERSONAL REFLECTION

We should all read a bit of the Bible each day, asking the Holy Spirit to open our mind as we do so. Below are suggested readings, with a prayerful response to each. As I read one of the suggested sections, I should ask myself, "What is God saying to me here?"

When temptations are great, read Matthew 4, 1–11; James 1. Pray Psalm 139 (140).

If you have fallen into serious sin, read Luke 7, 36–50; 1 John 1 or 2. Pray Psalm 50 (51). Then express your sorrow as perfectly as you can to God whom you love.

When you need strength to overcome your weakness, read Romans 8; Ephesians 6, 10–24. Pray Psalm 31 (32).

If you need reassurance, read 1 John 3. Pray Psalm 26 (27) or 90 (91).

When you are lonely, read John 14. Pray Psalm 22 (23).

If you are facing a crisis read Colossians 1 or 1 Peter 1. Pray Psalm 15 (16) or 120 (121).

When ill or in pain, read 2 Corinthians 1 or 4 or 12, 1–10, or James 5. Pray Psalm 40 (41).

If you fear death, read John 11 or 20 or 2 Corinthians 5, or Revelation (Apocalypse) 14, 12–13. Pray Psalm 85 (86).

When you are in grief, read Wisdom 3, 1–9, or 1 Corinthians 15 or 1 Thessalonians 4, 13–18, or Revelation 21 or 22. Pray Psalm 102 (103) or 115 (116).

When following the crowd seems easier than following God, read 2 Corinthians 6. Pray Psalm 36 (37).

12

The Great Signs in Which
We Meet God

Can we reach God by our worship? How can we experience God's presence in our lives? Why are people moved by religious ceremonies?

THE SACRED LITURGY, CHRIST'S SIGNS OF LOVE

We have just studied the Bible, which tells us of God's great works among his people in times past. Now we will take up the sacred liturgy, in which God is present and acting among us today. We can meditate on the Bible, but far better, we can actually relive its great events ourselves by taking part in the ceremonies of the liturgy.

To understand the sacred liturgy, we must have some appreciation of the meaning of love. Love is not only the basic concept of Christianity but indeed of all human existence. We cannot be happy, even in this life, unless we are loved and can give love. Love means giving ourselves to the one we love, in order to be united with our beloved, to bring our beloved happiness.

Christianity is simply a love affair between God and us. God first gave himself to us, and we respond by giving ourselves to him. Through this intimate, mutual giving, we attain union with God and happiness forever.

God draws us to himself by giving us his teaching and his grace. He teaches us how to come to him and he gives us his own presence, grace, to raise us to himself.

We give ourselves to God by worshiping him. We saw that this is our basic, most natural attitude before God—to honor him, to try to make contact, to ask his help.

It is by being united with Christ that we worship God and receive his grace and teaching. We saw that Christ is our Savior and Mediator, risen and living among us in his Church, acting through his Spirit. God gives himself to us to the extent that we are united with Christ, and we can give ourselves to God only in and through Christ. Many do not know Christ, but are united to him as "anonymous Christians."

The believer, united to Christ, can meet God as an individual, worshiping him alone and receiving his grace and truth. We might do this in the prayer of our own heart, in the silence of our own room, or in the stillness of a forest. Or we can meet God in our fellow humans—by an act of kindness or courage or honesty—worshiping God by this and being more filled with his presence.

Christians, however, can unite themselves with the worship of the whole Church—meeting God in the sacred liturgy. No longer do they approach God merely as individuals. Now they are united in a special way to Jesus Christ and to all the members of his Church. Their poor pleadings become those of Jesus Christ himself and of everyone in the Church expressing his or her love.

The sacred liturgy is the "signs"—or better, the "symbols"—by which Christ and his Church worship God and are filled with his grace-presence. In the liturgy we use ceremonies that symbolize our feelings toward God and one another, and we thereby express our love together, as a community of God's people. They are signs that express not only our love but also our needs, hopes, and gratefulness.

By a sign we mean something visible, some action, that expresses our inner feelings, especially our love. A kiss is a visible sign of love, which is something spiritual, invisible. A handshake is a sign of friendship. Because we are human, it is natural and necessary for us to express our love for God, and be assured of his love, by means of visible signs—as a child spontaneously hugs a parent, as a caring husband shows affection for his wife.

Symbols are signs that point to the inexpressible, the vastly "more," and help bring about the presence of what they point to. Making love, by two people committed to each other, is a symbol that not only says they love but makes their love present, deepens it, and elicits a mutual response of further love. The couple is caught up in something far greater than they can express. So it is with the symbols of the liturgy: we are not only expressing but making present the mystery of God, Limitless Love—and we are being caught up in this Love, growing in an inexpressible love relationship.

Rituals, symbolic ceremonies, and signs are part of our daily lives. We use symbolic ceremonies, rites, or rituals to celebrate, to express, and to bring home to ourselves the meaning of the significant events of life: for example, celebrations at our work for promotions and retirement, rites of initiation, graduation from school, a couple's marriage commitment, a nation's annual ceremonies commemorating the great persons and events of its history.

Christ is present in a special way in the sacred liturgy, acting on our behalf, joining us to himself. His worship becomes ours. We receive grace as part of him. We no longer appear alone and inadequate before God our Father, for now Christ is pleading for us. We are behind him, in a sense, in his shadow. He is our High Priest, "able at all times to save those who come to God through him, since he lives always to make intercession for them" (Hebrews 7, 25). To take part in the liturgy, Christians receive a "character," a special power joining them to Christ so they can share in his work as priest and mediator.

When we take part in the liturgy, our worship has a great, new power to help others as well as ourselves. The worship of the whole Church now becomes ours. We pray with the power of the whole Church behind us, knowing we are joined by countless others—something like an ambassador speaking with the country behind him or her.

> The *Catechism of the Catholic Church* points out that the word liturgy originally meant a public work or some service done in the name of and on behalf of the people. In Christian tradition it means the participation of the people of God—the Church—in the "work" of Christ as he continues humankind's salvation. In the New Testament the word means not only worshiping God but also proclaiming the gospel and performing works of active charity. The liturgy, then, is a service of God and of our neighbor in the image of Christ who came to serve his Father and us (1069–70).

The liturgy is the worship of the whole Church and comes from the Church. It is the Church's official, "public" worship. To have liturgy, with all its power, requires more than assembling a group of Christians to pray together; although Christ would surely be in their midst, yet his presence in the liturgy is more. The Church determines what is liturgy, for the liturgy belongs to all of us, to the whole Church. It has a sacredness, a power transcending any individual or group. This is why it must be guided by the spirit and rules of the Church.

In the liturgy we "ritualize" or "symbolize" the great events of Jesus' life, bring them into the present, and powerfully link them with what we go through in our daily lives. The many "dyings" and "risings" of our daily lives, the experiences of hurt, pain, and confusion, as well as those of joy, hope, and love—those that are small and those that change our lives—all these we join with the same events in Jesus' life, and above all with his dying and rising for us. The power of his death and resurrection gives meaning to our "deaths" and "resurrections" and gives us strength to persevere and grow in faith, hope, and love. The liturgy vividly reminds us of what God-made-human went through for us, and it contains his powerful grace-presence, his own strength, confidence, and love, so that we can cope and can grow spiritually when we go through these things every day.

Vatican Council II further summed up how the liturgy shows what Christ is and what his Church is: "She is both human and divine, visible and yet invisibly equipped, eager to act and yet intent on contemplation, present in this world and yet not at home in it. . . . In her the human is directed and subordinated to the divine, the visible to the invisible, action to contemplation, and this present world to that city yet to come which we seek" (*Constitution on the Sacred Liturgy,* no. 2).

When we take part in the liturgy we are plunged into the past and are also living in the future. Mysteriously the liturgy brings together past, present, and future. Time, relative even to us, cannot restrict God. By the ceremonies of the liturgy time is "stretched out" for us. Christ conveys to us here and now the actions by which he saved us two thousand years ago—and by these same signs we are actually beginning now our life in eternity, the future "heavenly liturgy," the worship and love that will absorb us forever. Of all the moments of our life, then, we are the most in contact with God, the most "in eternity," when we are taking part in the liturgy.

The liturgy, then, is the great way in which we are taught about Jesus' work—and also are caught up into its mystery, the mystery of God himself among us (*Catechism*, 1075). From the visible we move into the invisible, learning about it and also being drawn into it. Through the symbols and ceremonies, we not only learn about what God does among us, we are made a part of his work and his presence among us.

Through the liturgy Christ prolongs through the centuries his death and resurrection, his great acts of love for us, so we can share in them. Through the ceremonies and feasts of the liturgy we live "in Christ," actually taking part in these great events of his life. We continually die with him to sin and rise with him to the new life of grace, offering perfect worship with him and growing more and more in love.

The liturgy is, then, the great way in which Christ speaks to us now and tells us of his love, not only by the words of Scripture but by actions or signs of his love. As a couple in love dwell on each other's words and gestures, even those that appear to others the most ordinary, so to the Christian in love with God the words and ceremonies of the liturgy convey God's own personal and tender love. As God in the Old Testament reassured and strengthened his people assembled together at Mount Sinai, for example, and as Christ spoke so lovingly and intimately to his followers at the last supper, so today he speaks to us, tells us of his love by his Word given to us in the liturgy. And more than this, God through his Son is communicating his love to us in each ceremony of the liturgy—each is meant to be a sign of himself and his love reaching out for us—and each has a meaning for the Christian truly in love with him.

The rites and ceremonies of the liturgy must express our inner love. Without a sincere attempt to love, the ceremonies are valueless, empty signs. Christ stresses that we must adore God "in spirit and truth." He continually condemned the Pharisees, the "whited sepulchres," "hypocrites," whose lives were a mere external observance of rituals that lacked inner meaning and sincerity.

In order that the liturgy may be able to produce its full effects, it is necessary that the faithful come to it with proper dispositions, that their minds should be attuned to their voices, and that they should cooperate with divine grace, lest they receive it in vain (*Constitution on the Sacred Liturgy*, no. II).

The Mass and the seven sacraments are the great ceremonies of the liturgy. We prepare for them by the "little things" of the liturgy, the sacramentals.

THE SACRAMENTALS—REACHING OUT FOR CHRIST

Little children were brought to him then that he might lay his hands on them and pray; but the disciples rebuked them. But Jesus said to them, "Let the little children be, and do not hinder them from coming to me, for of such is the kingdom of heaven." And when he had laid his hands on them, he departed from that place (Matthew 19, 13–15).

Just as Christ himself did during his life on earth, so today his Church calls down his blessing on us at different times in our lives. The story of creation concludes, "God saw that all he had made was very good." The Church asks God to bless not only us but many of the ordinary things of life, so that they might lead us to him.

A sacramental is the Church's prayer asking Christ's blessing on someone or something, or it is an object that is thereby "blessed." The Church's prayer asking Christ's blessing is usually given by a priest; however, parents can bless their children, people ask God's blessing on their food, or they can bless themselves with the Sign of the Cross. Some blessings are given to dedicate a thing to a sacred use.

Some of the more common sacramentals: the Sign of the Cross, blessed candles, blessed pictures, statues, medals, scapulars, holy water, the rosary, the Stations of the Cross, Benediction of the Blessed Sacrament, the Divine Office.

Statues, pictures, and so on, are not prayed to as having power of themselves; rather they remind us of God's presence. God commanded the Jews long ago: "Make two cherubim of beaten gold . . . which you shall then place on top of the ark" (Exodus 25, 18–20). Christian art from the early centuries has used images of Christ and the saints to stimulate devotion.

Some sacramentals are given on certain days during the year: Candles are blessed and distributed on Candlemas Day, February 2; throats are blessed on St. Blaise Day, February 3; on Ash Wednesday, blessed ashes are placed on our foreheads; palms are distributed on Palm (Passion) Sunday; fields may be blessed on August 5. Other blessings are given at any time, such as, the blessing of a mother before or after childbirth.

A sacramental is a reminder, but it is also something more: it is a special way of putting ourselves in Christ's presence, asking his help and blessing. The woman who reached out for Christ acted as we might in using a sacramental: **Read Luke 8, 40-48.**

When we use a sacramental with faith and devotion, we reach out for Christ— and somehow, the entire Church joins with us. We can be sure that he will help us in some way. When a mother receives the Church's blessing on herself and her newborn child, she comes into Christ's presence, asking his blessing on herself and her baby. Having our automobile blessed, with a determination to drive carefully, is asking Christ to drive with us and protect us.

We should use the sacramentals reverently but also avoid superstition. What we derive from them depends on God's will, the Church's prayer, and our own faith and devotion. We must be careful not to look on them as magical, producing effects automatically. If we use them with a living faith, they are wonderful ways to make us aware of God's presence in our everyday lives, in everyone and everything around us.

The sacramentals are particularly meant to prepare us for the sacraments, which are the all-important signs by which we come into a most intimate grace-giving contact with Christ. The sacramentals are the less-important signs by which we reach out for Christ. They prepare us for our meeting with Christ in the sacraments by stirring our faith and devotion, and they prolong the effect of the sacraments in our lives.

When becoming a Catholic Christian, one is signed with the Sign of the Cross, anointed with oil, clothed with a white robe, and given a lighted candle—these and other sacramentals prepare us for and help prolong the meaning of one's baptism and/or reception into the Church.

CHRIST'S SEVEN SACRAMENTS—
OUR GREAT, INTIMATE CONTACTS WITH HIM

After relating Christ's healing of the woman with a hemorrhage, Luke continues with the incident of the dying twelve-year-old daughter of Jairus: **Read Luke 8, 49-56.**

While visibly present on earth, Christ often used physical actions, his own ceremonies, as instruments of his divine power. In this incident he gives life by calling out to the girl, taking her hand, raising her up.

Christ also communicates the divine life of grace through ceremonies or signs. Just as his human body was the instrument of his divinity two thousand years ago, so today he uses the human members of his body, the Church, to give us the life of grace through these ceremonies. These are the all-important signs of the liturgy, the seven sacraments.

A sacrament is a sacred sign of worship by which we come into intimate personal contact with Christ and receive his grace—a ceremony in which we meet Christ most intimately and receive his grace— and by which we join with Christ particularly in his great action of dying and rising.

> By these meetings with Christ we are joined most intimately with the whole Trinity. It is the Spirit within us that unites us with Christ in the sacraments, and they join us ultimately with the Father. Our love relationship with each Person is deepened by each sacrament.

Christ gave us the sacraments two thousand years ago. He instituted them, that is, he provided that his grace would be given especially by some suitable signs. These he left mostly to his Church to determine.

Christ gives us the sacraments here and now. Through them we come into intimate, personal contact with him giving us grace—each is a "sacramental meeting" or "encounter" with him, like the meeting on the road to Emmaus: **Read Luke 24, 15-32.**

When we take part in a sacrament, Christ's presence is also concealed, but he is there, affecting us intimately by his love. We on earth cannot yet bear to look upon Christ glorified in heaven—but in each sacrament he is with us, using this ceremony to reach out to us, taking hold of us as one in love embraces the beloved, as a mother embraces her child. We know that sometimes a single contact with one we love, even a glance or smile, can greatly affect and even change our life—so Christ in his sacrament can totally renew us.

Christ uses human beings within his Church, usually bishops and priests, to give us his sacraments. But the person who gives the sacrament is only Christ's instrument; Christ himself communicates his grace to us through the words and actions. The goodness or badness of the human instrument makes no difference as far as our receiving grace is concerned. We are always assured of contact with Christ, of deepening God's grace-presence within us.

Christ is the "sacrament" of God. We have seen that a sacrament is something visible that conveys a spiritual reality. In Christ's humanity we meet visibly, palpably, the invisible God. And Christ in his humanity is called the fundamental, "primordial," or "root" sacrament because the other sacraments have meaning only in and from him—as a root is the source out of which a vine lives and flourishes.

So, too, his Church is the "sacrament" of Christ. In Christ's visible Church we make contact with Christ invisibly among us. And Christ is the root by which the Church lives—or, as the moon, which has no light of its own, reflects the light of sun, so the Church exists to reflect Christ. And only when it reflects Christ is it genuinely the Church.

We should note that all of creation is "sacramental" in that everything and everyone is permeated by God's grace—nature, other people, other creatures are all signs that can convey to us God's love and goodness. Everything and everyone can truly be sacramental in this broad sense. The seven sacraments especially are conveyers of God's grace for Christians and hence can be said to be sacramental in a stricter, more focused sense.

The seven sacraments are "signs" in this way: when the visible ceremony takes place, Christ brings about an invisible spiritual change within us. Every sign or ceremony conveys an idea, but it does not actually produce an internal change—a handshake conveys the idea of friendship, but it does not make two people friends. The sign of a sacrament, however, not only tells us about the spiritual change taking place within us—Christ uses it to actually produce that change. A sacrament gives the grace it signifies. In baptism, for instance, as the priest pours the water and says the words, Christ is bringing about an invisible change in us—we are receiving grace and being freed from sin.

Christ gives us these visible signs so that when we go through them, we can be sure we have been in contact with him and have received his grace. The ceremony assures us that he is there. Just as it is not enough for a child merely to know of his or her mother's love but needs her actual embrace, just as a husband and wife need to show their love by signs of affection, so we need these sacramental signs of Christ's presence and love.

A sacrament, if entered into with faith and love, always affects us interiorly, always gives us grace. It is Christ's powerful gesture of love, causing us to respond, as a firm handshake compels a firm grip in return. Christ always gives us grace unless we deliberately block him. But the sacraments are not magic. One might block Christ's grace by receiving certain of them, such as confirmation, holy orders, or marriage, in serious sin; if the sin is later forgiven, Christ then can give us his grace.

> *The sacraments intensify our faith and our love for God and our fellow human beings as well as help make our sufferings bearable and meaningful.* They unite us to the humiliated and glorified Christ. They do not eliminate suffering from our lives, but they help us bear it. They deepen our Christian joy and assure us of our ultimate resurrection with Christ.

Each sacrament, then, makes us more like Christ, assimilates us to him so that his thoughts and words and actions become ours—or rather, ours become his. The more we share in his sacramental life, the more we are transformed, drawn to him. Through the sacraments we gradually acquire his love, his sensitivity for others, his zeal and passion for justice, his compassion for the sick and "little ones," his single-mindedness in doing his Father's will.

The sign or ceremony of each sacrament teaches us about its special effect upon us. While all the sacraments increase God's presence within us, Christ does something special for us in each. The ceremonies are sometimes difficult to understand today, but originally they were taken from the people's ordinary life and given a religious meaning.

> *The basic rites, while particularly meaningful to the people of the Bible, are fundamental human symbols found in almost every culture,* such as washing

with water, placing hands on another's head, eating a symbolic meal together, anointing with oil. Obviously some symbols that came from a simpler pastoral society, or from among people accustomed to court ceremonial, may not be as meaningful to an urban, democratic, technological culture like ours. Yet most will appeal to our sense of mystery, rooted as they are in centuries of tradition, of humankind's reaching out for the beyond, for God.

It takes much patient and prayerful effort to develop signs that keep our link with the past and yet are meaningful in the present. The Vatican Council has given a basic norm for this: "The rites should be distinguished by a noble simplicity; they should be short, clear, and unencumbered by useless repetitions; they should be within the people's powers of comprehension, and normally should not require explanation" (*Constitution on the Sacred Liturgy*, no. 34).

A sacrament does not "take place" only at the moment the core sign or ceremony is performed, but it is also a process that begins before and continues after the sign is given. Though the core sign or ceremony is the sacrament's necessary and most important part, it is not, of itself, the totality of the sacrament.

In the baptism of an infant, for instance, the Christian lives of the parents leading up to the pouring of the water and their lives with the child afterward are all part of the sacrament and determine how effective it will be. Or, with marriage, the developing covenant-commitment of the couple before pronouncing their vows is part of the sacrament, just as in their continuing covenanted life together afterward they are, in a very real sense, continuing to marry each other.

Christ left his Church to be the guardian and giver of his sacraments—to choose the signs that best express the grace he gives through the particular sacrament (except for the eucharist and probably baptism, whose signs seem to have come directly from Christ himself). The essential signs of some sacraments, then, have changed in the Church's usage over the centuries.

The power to give a sacrament is communicated to those especially chosen by Christ's Church in the sacrament of holy orders. A person must be empowered by this sacrament—a special laying on of hands—in order to communicate Christ's grace sacramentally to others (except for baptism, confirmation, and marriage).

The sacraments, though, should be seen as actions of the whole church community in which all share rather than as simply being given or conferred by a single celebrant to a passive recipient. Thus this book talks about people "taking part" in the sacraments rather than "receiving" them. In the new rituals of the sacraments it is envisioned that those present in the church community also share in the sacramental celebrations, such as crossing and laying hands on the one being baptized and confirmed, laypeople administering the eucharist, a couple marrying each other, all present laying on hands in the anointing of the sick, and so on.

Christ uses the sacraments to build up his Church community. In each community sacrament Christ unites us in a particular way with the other members of the Church, so that we can help and be helped by them. Each one strengthens the bonds of community in a particular way.

Baptism joins us to Christ's body, his Church. Confirmation makes us adult Christians, specially empowering us to help spread Christ's body. The eucharist unites us most intimately not only with Christ but with the other members of his Church. Reconciliation (penance) gives us the forgiveness of the mystical body and is a reconciliation with Christ and all whom we have offended by our sins. The anointing of the sick either restores us to the Church on earth or it prepares us to enter the Church in heaven. Holy orders and marriage provide for the continuation of Christ's Church on earth.

A sacrament is a sign of our worshiping love. Our part is vital in this meeting with Christ. When we take part in a sacrament, we express our faith, love, and worship. The greater our faith and love, the more sincere our worship, the more Christ can fill us with his grace-presence.

Therefore, we should prepare well to meet Christ in each sacrament. We must come to it with the proper intention, with sorrow for our sins, with faith and love. A sacrament is not a mechanical "thing," or something magical, that gives us grace automatically without any contribution on our part. It is a meeting in which we must respond to Christ reaching out for us. As we would prepare ourselves for any special meeting with one we love, so the better we prepare the more we will receive from our meetings with Christ in the sacraments.

To help us prepare and to bring out its full meaning, each sacrament has some lesser signs, or sacramentals, along with its essential

sign. The ceremony by which each sacrament is given, including the prayers and sacramentals connected with it, is called the "rite" of the sacrament.

Christ's help for us in the sacraments is intensified or weakened by our everyday actions, and vice versa. The more we consciously try to get strength from the sacraments, the more they help us to use countless other daily opportunities to grow in grace—much as a mother derives strength to deal with a crisis in her teenager's life from the memory of the joy her child brought when he or she came into her life. A sacrament is a powerful beginning—comparable to a first meeting with someone we admire—whose purpose is to impel us to a more Christian life moment by moment.

The sacraments are the great ways in which Christ encounters us and gives us his grace, but he also uses many other ways. Like a stone thrown into a pond, making ripples that spread out in continuous circles, so grace flows from Christ's Church to humankind: the inner, distinct circles are the sacraments, beyond these are the less clearly defined sacramentals, and still further from the center are the other good actions of people.

One might experience God more intensely and receive grace more fully outside the sacraments, but normally they are the great moments at which Christ meets us and helps us on our way to heaven. A man and woman in love, separated for several months, finally come together again—their meeting is a special moment of sharing in love, to which our encounter with God in the sacraments is comparable.

Christ gives us the sacraments, then, to help us at the important moments of life. People have always surrounded the great moments of life with sacred symbols and ceremonies. Christ uses these occasions to give us his saving grace: birth, growth to maturity, our daily need for nourishment, moral failure, marriage, serious illness and death, a need of human help to reach God—these are the pivotal points of our lives on earth and at these Christ stands with his sacraments.

These are the seven sacraments, and briefly, what Christ does through each:

Baptism joins us to Christ and his Church, gives us grace, and takes away all sin.

Confirmation makes us adult witnesses for Christ.

The Holy Eucharist is Christ himself coming to us under the appearance of bread and wine.

Reconciliation or *Penance* Christ uses to forgive us our sins after baptism and to reconcile us to his Church.

The Anointing of the Sick Christ uses to strengthen us in serious illness.

Holy Orders is the way Christ ordains bishops, priests, and deacons for his Church.

Marriage is the way Christ unites a Christian man and woman in a lifelong union.

Among the sacraments, baptism and the eucharist are the most important. Baptism begins in us the Christian life, and the eucharist is our main source of strength along the way.

WORD AND SACRAMENT

To sum up: The great means by which God gives himself to us are the Bible and the liturgy—"Word and Sacrament." Each is a special meeting with Christ and the Trinity. God uses them above all else to give us his grace and teaching. Together they form the Christian's way to God.

There has always been an intimate connection between the Word of God and the worship of God. The books of the Bible, both Old and New Testaments, came from the community's liturgy in the sense that the scriptural narratives, hymns, and prayers were either meant to be used at worship or they came from the actual worship services of God's people. Even the New Testament epistles or letters were intended to be read when the Christian community assembled for the liturgy (cf. 1 Thessalonians 5, 27).

The Bible gives us God's teaching and at the same time prepares us to receive his grace in the sacraments. Christ speaks to us through the Scriptures, arousing faith in us, leading us to respond by the sacraments. The better prepared we are by the Scriptures, the better is our worship and the more of God's grace-presence the sacraments bring us.

It is in the liturgy, on the other hand, that we best hear, understand, and respond to God's Word given in the Bible. The ceremonies of the liturgy not only teach us in a living way the sacred events of the Bible, they also enable us actually to take part in them here and now. Our reading of the Bible is meant to lead to the sacraments in which our most powerful and most lasting bond with Christ and our fellow Christians is established.

DAILY LIVING: SIGNS OF GOD'S PRESENCE

If we believe in God, in Christ, we should have some signs of this in our home. Many people find that they need some reminder of God's presence, particularly since our lives today are becoming so secularized.

We might, in our home, have a cross or crucifix, a Bible placed where we will read it, or perhaps a picture or statue that appeals to us and will inspire us. There is much good religious art available today, whatever our personal taste.

We should also take advantage of what the Church has to visibly remind us of God's presence. Anyone, including one who is not Catholic, can receive the sacramentals of the Church. If used with sincere faith, they can help anyone to be aware of God's presence.

SOME SUGGESTIONS FOR . . .

DISCUSSION

Signs and gestures of our feelings are an intimate part of life. Liturgy, the Church's ceremonies or symbolic signs, is at the heart of Catholic Christianity. How meaningful to you is the use of such signs or symbols?

What, for a Catholic, is special about our worship in the liturgy? Can you understand how, though some Catholics might get more out of it than others, it is an essential part of being a Catholic?

If one should expect an appreciation of these symbolic ceremonies to take time, how might one further enhance one's sharing in them?

What sacramentals seem to have particular meaning for you?

If sacraments always bring about what they signify, how can we distinguish a sacrament from magic? How should one enter into taking part in a sacrament, to get the most out of it?

FURTHER READING

- •• *Sacramental Theology, A General Introduction,* Osborne (Paulist Press, 1988)—An excellent, clearly laid out, general introduction to all aspects of the sacraments, especially good for one who wants an overview and updating.

- • *The Book of Sacramental Basics,* Guzie (Paulist Press, 1981)—This popular author here gives us a modern understanding of the sacraments as humans celebrating their common experience of God's care for us in Christ; this book is concise, readable, and insightful.

- • *Sacramental Guidelines: A Companion to the New Catechism for Religious Educators,* Osborne (Paulist Press, 1995)—A fine writer and highly respected theologian gives help to religious education teachers regarding "defined teaching" on the sacraments, what can be changed, and what is theologically still unresolved.

- •• *Women at Worship: Interpretations of North American Diversity,* eds. Proctor-Smith and Walton (Westminster-Knox, 1993)—Describes what is shared and what is diverse as women theologians look at the sacramental rites, language, celebrants, and so on from a new perspective.

- • *Sacraments and Sacramentality,* Cooke (Twenty-Third Publications, 1994)—A fine theologian and clear writer takes a fresh, in-depth look at these core concepts by which we express our faith; this book is well worth reading.

- • *A New Look at the Sacraments,* Bausch (Twenty-Third Publications, 1983)—An excellent overview, informative, practical, inspiring.

- •• *Christ, The Sacrament of the Encounter with God,* Schillebeeckx (Sheed & Ward, 1963)—Still a theological classic for those who want a thorough understanding of the notion of sacrament: it shows how Christ is the sacrament of God and the Church is the sacrament of Christ, as well as the reality and depth of the Church's seven sacraments.

PERSONAL REFLECTION

Each time I look at an inspiring cross or crucifix, or a moving work of religious art, I can be reminded of God's presence in my daily life.

If I am alert to them, there are many other signs of God's presence around me: the beauty of a landscape, a sunset, the laughter of a child, the peaceful countenances of an old couple, the eager joy of young lovers, the infinite patience of a face worn with suffering, the quiet dignity of many who are poor, and many others.

13

Christ Unites Us to Himself and to One Another by Baptism

Why is baptism so important? What is the meaning of the ceremony of baptism? What is meant by saying that a person is converted? What of most of the human race who are not baptized as Christians?

WHAT CHRIST DOES FOR US IN BAPTISM

We saw how God uses the signs of the sacred liturgy, particularly the sacraments, to come into our lives today. By entering into these signs we meet Christ most intimately and go with him to the Father. These are the great meetings by which we are filled with his grace-presence.

The first of these great signs is baptism. Here Christ unites us with himself in a new, deeper way, to live more truly and fully with him. Somehow, mysteriously, we now go with Christ through the great actions of his life, particularly his death and resurrection. We begin journeying with him to the Father. We will suffer and die with him, and one day we shall rise with him to our real, full life after death.

Baptism is the sacrament in which Christ joins us to himself as a member of his Church. Baptism is often called a "christening," expressing how we are made one with Christ, a completely new person. St. Paul tells how baptism unites us to Christ, so that we are "in" him as in a garment:

For all you have been baptized into Christ, have put on Christ. There is neither Jew nor Greek; there is neither slave nor freeman; there is neither male
nor female. For you are all one in Christ Jesus (Galatians 3, 27-28).

Scripture tells us how baptism is to be given. Matthew attributes to
Christ himself this ancient formula:

Jesus . . . said, "All power in heaven and on earth has been given to me. Go,
therefore, and make disciples of all nations, baptizing them in the name of the
Father, and of the Son, and of the Holy Spirit . . . " (Matthew 28, 17-19).

**The sign or ceremony of baptism is to pour water on the person's
forehead—or immerse the person in water—while saying the words, "I
baptize you in the name of the Father, and of the Son, and of the Holy
Spirit."** To "baptize" means to wash with, to immerse in water. The water
is ordinarily poured on the person's forehead, but the norm for adults is
to do it by immersion, as it was usually done in the early centuries—and
which more fully brings out what it does, as we will see shortly. Sprinkling
on the forehead is also done, especially by Eastern Christians.

**By baptism, Christ initiates us into his Church, joins us to his
body, the Christian community.** He thereby gives us the ability to take
part fully in the other sacraments. "For in one Spirit," says St. Paul, "we
were all baptized into one body, whether Jews or Gentiles, whether slaves
or free" (1 Corinthians 12, 13).

**In baptism the new Christian is pledged to the Christian commu-
nity and the community in turn pledges itself to that person.** It is the
entrance into the Christian family with a pledging of love and service on
both sides. The new Christian now will seek God particularly within this
Church community, and the community promises its love, prayers, and
help. Just as belonging to a natural family is far better than being an orphan, so being a part of the Christian family can give love and support one
would not have on one's own. The growing and recommended custom of
baptizing at the Sunday eucharist brings out well this mutual pledge of
love and service.

**Baptism gives the new life of grace to the one who does not have it:
Read John 3, 1-6.**

The new birth of which Christ speaks is baptism; the new life it gives us is sanctifying grace, God's living and loving presence within us.

By baptism Christ forgives us all our sins. If we are truly converted, we make a fresh start, we begin living a new life with and in Christ. "If anyone is in Christ, he is a new creation" (2 Corinthians 5, 17). All our sins are totally made up for; it is as if we had never sinned. When Peter on Pentecost preached the gospel to its first hearers, they were "cut to the heart" and asked, "Brethren, what shall we do?" He replied:

> Repent, and be baptized, every one of you, in the name of Jesus Christ for the forgiveness of your sins; and you shall receive the gift of the Holy Spirit (Acts 2, 37–38).

Christ frees us from sin and gives us grace in baptism by joining us to himself in his own death and resurrection. We saw that his death and resurrection was the great action by which he freed us from the power of sin to keep us from heaven, and by which he obtained for our whole race the new life of God's grace-presence. By baptism we first unite ourselves to Christ's death and resurrection. St. Paul explains: **Read Romans 6, 3–11.**

Sin's power "dies" within us and is "buried" as we go under the water, and we rise to a new life of grace as we come up out of the water. We are thus united with Christ's death, which overcame sin, and to his resurrection, which brought us the new life of grace. The ordinary ancient way of baptizing fully expresses this: the person is immersed or "buried" in water and then drawn out of it.

The ceremony of baptism fulfills in a perfect way the deliverance to life and freedom that was begun in the Old Testament. God's people were saved by the waters of the Red Sea from Pharaoh's army and given a new life of freedom. Christ leads us through the waters of baptism to free us from sin and death and give us the new and eternal life of grace. Baptism is our Christian passover, our own personal exodus.

> The use of water to overcome death and slavery and give new life is often foreshadowed. Water has always been a symbol both of death and of life; the ancient Hebrews feared the waters of the sea, and yet as a desert people they knew that water also meant life.

By baptism one is drawn into the new covenant. Under the old covenant God was present among his people in the Ark of the Covenant, which they brought with them through the desert and later enshrined in the temple at Jerusalem. Now, under the new covenant, God lives within each of his people, most intimately, and they in him. He is himself the new promised land; instead of a geographical territory, he gives us himself—and for all eternity.

Baptism, then, is the sign of our true, interior life, God's grace-presence within us. Now we are publicly (and consciously, if old enough) pledged to live with an awareness of this presence within us: the Persons of God are within us, transforming us, giving a new meaning and power to everything we do. Mysteriously, wonderfully, we are joined in a particular and intimate way to each of the Three Persons. Within us, surrounding us, filling us, guiding and loving us, the Trinity draws us into their own life. This is the "indwelling" of the Blessed Trinity—it is heaven already begun within us.

> "Grace" is simply our relationship to the divine Persons, the "state," the life situation in which the Persons come to us, live with us, and love us. By this we have a special relationship to each of the Persons. Now that we have penetrated further into God's plan, and have seen something of the actions of the divine Persons in human history, we might reread the part of chapter 7 dealing with our personal relationship to each Person. This should now have a deeper meaning.

Like any personal love relationship that fulfills, elevates, and transforms, so grace makes us more and more like God. A deep friendship, the love of a man and a woman—these raise and fulfill one's personality wonderfully. We become fuller persons ourselves, even as we take on more of the characteristics of our friend or loved one. So here we are raised to the very level of God, transformed more and more into him. "It is no longer I who live, but Christ who lives in me" (Galatians 2, 20).

This is the "kingdom of God" that Christ preached: God's grace-presence within us. To have God's grace-presence within us is to belong to the kingdom, to submit to his loving guidance from within. When we believe in him and try to do his will, we belong to this kingdom. We might recall what Christ said about this kingdom: the poor, the humble, the oppressed are the happy ones, and the one law in the kingdom is that of love. The kingdom is not yet completed—we must suffer and work for its fulfillment, that God's grace-presence will fill all people—and so we pray "thy kingdom come, thy will be done on earth as it is in heaven."

To help us live the Christian life, Christ gives us special powers: the virtues. The virtues are powers or attitudes within us: faith, hope, and charity. They are explained in detail in chapter 16. Christ also promises us all the day-by-day helps, the "actual grace" necessary to live as his followers. A person's Christianity may never develop, through no fault of his or her own; Christ guides him or her through life nevertheless, giving more than sufficient help to attain heaven.

At baptism the Christian receives the power to share in Christ's own work as priest, prophet, and king. This is the "priesthood of the laity," the power to offer Mass fully with Christ and take part in the other sacraments, to act as a mediator in prayer and other ways. It is a prophetic and kingly power in that we now openly witness to the faith, hope, and love within us—to the kingdom of God, God's grace-presence within us.

WHO CAN BE BAPTIZED?

For those who know about and believe in Christ's teaching, baptism with water is the necessary first step to eternal happiness. This has been the Church's belief from the beginning, seen especially in Christ's words to Nicodemus, "Unless a man be born again of water and the Spirit, he cannot enter the kingdom of God" (John 3, 5). It is evident again and again in the epistles, the Acts of the Apostles, and other early Christian writings.

Therefore we baptize infants so they can begin growing in the life of grace within the Christian community. Though adult baptism was the rule in the first Christian centuries, infant baptism—a whole family, for instance, being baptized together—was practiced almost from the beginning.

Infants being baptized should not be looked upon as if they were somehow interiorly evil, needing to be washed "clean" or "purified" by the waters of the sacrament. Rather, they are good and beautiful in God's eyes, and certainly free of moral fault. But they share the inherent human weakness that we call original sin and experience what it is to be unloved, beginning in the womb, and will be unloving in return. Baptism sets up a new relationship by giving infants a new orientation, pointing them in the direction of God through Christ and the Church; now the vision of God and a new, perfect world is before them. Baptism is thus a new birth, to eternal life, and a new creation, for by it one shares in the vision of a new universe. Now it is up to the parents of those baptized—and the whole local Christian community—to help develop their part in this new universe.

The *Catechism* reiterates the importance of infant baptism, even if the parents are not immediately prepared to profess their own faith. Baptism is not merely a sign of faith but a cause of faith and thus is not normally denied an infant without good reason. This is discussed further on. Also, infants are baptized into the faith of the whole Church, and it is the Church—not solely the child's parents—that is responsible for proffering an education in its beliefs.

Regarding what happens to unbaptized infants, we have no clear teaching of Christ or doctrine of the Church. Some older theologians thought that they went to "limbo," which they regarded as a state of perfect, unending "natural" happiness, but much less than the happiness of heaven. However, most by far today think that such an infant would attain heaven. They simply say that God accepts each of us (though we can reject him by living in a state of serious sin); our conscious response to his love is secondary, and certainly not necessary for these innocent little ones. The *Catechism* says that the Church can only "entrust them to . . . the great mercy of God who desires that all . . . should be saved" (1261). The renewed process of Christian initiation and the possible deferral of baptism (discussed further on) should do away with this notion once and for all.

Unbaptized older children who have reached the age of reason (about age seven) and desire baptism should have a grasp of Catholic Christianity consonant with their age and ability and must express, as freely and as informed as possible, a desire for baptism. It is envisioned that older children go through the steps of Christian initiation, discussed later in this chapter, adapted to their age and ability.

A priest or deacon usually gives baptism. However, in cases of necessity or danger of death anyone can baptize, even one who is not a

Christian. Such people, of course, must baptize correctly and have the intention of giving Christian baptism.

At baptism we have sponsors or godparents—a Catholic man and woman chosen to help their godchild live his or her Catholic faith fully. One sponsor is sufficient, of either sex, and this is usually the case with adult converts. A sponsor should be a practicing Catholic, at least sixteen years of age, and someone other than one's parents. Also, besides the Catholic sponsor, one may have a non-Catholic Christian "witness" to the baptism.

It is a privilege to be a baptismal sponsor, and that privilege involves a sacred duty. It is a ministry in the Church for which preparation is normally necessary. Sponsors should be active, mature Catholics who realize that they must keep in touch with their godchild, and help the young person grow in the faith. Sponsors often honestly realize that they themselves need more mature study in order to be "updated" in their knowledge and practice of their faith. The priest arranging the baptism may help them to do this.

Sponsors for adult converts take part with their godchildren in each step of the process of Christian initiation, as we will see. This can be a wonderful experience of growing together into a mature faith.

Parents should choose as a sponsor someone who will be in regular contact with the child and help him or her grow into Christian maturity—not just a relative who will have little contact with the growing child.

The parents, and if possible the godparents, of infants (or young children) are expected to have some instruction on the meaning of baptism, its lifelong implications and the obligations they are undertaking. Ideally done in a discussion setting with other couples, this can be not only informative but strengthening of a family's life—perhaps a chance to "clear the air" of unreal assumptions and sometimes an occasion for needed healing.

Since one becomes a new person interiorly at baptism, one may take a new name, that of a saint, or a name signifying a "Christian mentality." The saint chosen becomes one's patron, a lifelong model to follow as he or she imitated Christ. St. Paul said, "Be imitators of me, as I am of Christ" (1 Corinthians 4, 16). An adult convert usually takes this additional patron's name (and together with those already baptized may also take a confirmation name when entering the Church).

We should learn something about our patron saint in order to better imitate him or her. Our patron in turn is vitally interested in us and helps us attain heaven, as will be explained later.

Infants are usually baptized in the parish of their parents; adult converts are generally baptized where they take instructions. Converts are baptized when the one instructing them judges them ready, ideally when the process of Christian initiation has sufficiently prepared them.

Baptism usually takes place within the Mass, immediately after the prayer of the faithful—the assembled community can welcome and pledge its support to its new members. When celebrated apart from Mass, other prayers and minor ceremonies or sacramentals constitute part of the rite.

An infant is usually baptized within a few weeks after birth. But the infant's parents (and sponsors) should be knowledgeable about and freely committed to the child's Catholic Christian upbringing. Thus the infant's baptism may have to wait until they are sufficiently ready for this mature, free commitment—and this, as said above, involves instruction, reflection, and discussion on their part.

Sometimes, too, baptism is delayed until the child is older, and then it can be combined with confirmation and the eucharist as part of Christian initiation.

A priest may have to refuse to baptize someone if he judges that the person (usually an infant) will probably not lead an active Catholic life. There may be no indication—no well-founded hope—that an infant of nonpracticing Catholic parents has much chance of learning about Catholicism, as a viable adult faith, from his or her parents' example. Baptism is the beginning of a new way of life, not just a formality of family tradition, nor insurance against "limbo," nor a sort of magic inoculation of godliness that somehow takes effect despite a child's lack of religious upbringing.

There are, however, couples who, though they do little or nothing formally "Catholic" (no longer take part in Mass, for instance), still regard themselves as Catholic and wish their child to be baptized. It might be illusory, even hypocritical, to baptize their baby, since the child has little chance of being taught about or of living a Catholic Christian life. Yet the practice of the Church has never been to declare such parents cut off from membership in the Church. Though they do not currently practice Catholicism, that is, are not actively participating in a church community, yet the Church's teachings—and God's grace-presence—may be operating in their lives of overall moral goodness, private prayerfulness, and a real, if passive, belief in God and Jesus Christ. Also, a good test of what parents really believe, of their basic aspirations, is often what they want for their children, not what they presently (often regretfully) have not been able to find meaningful for themselves. Thus an infant in danger of death can always be baptized.

A couple should have a frank, imaginative talk with a priest or churchperson, and afterward they may want to update themselves on the Church's teachings, including the part they will play in their child's religious upbringing (and particularly the more active role of the Catholic partner in an interfaith marriage). Then baptism might be given the child.

The couple in this situation usually rethinks deeply (and hopefully discusses together) their own life-values and the place of God and religion in their own lives. Frequently they find after a course of study updating them on their faith, that they can recommit themselves to a now more mature and growth-producing practice of their religion in a compatible parish church-community.

Confirmation is meant to be joined to baptism—together with the eucharist, these are the sacraments of initiation into the life of Christ and the Church community. In the early Church, confirmation was celebrated along with baptism, as a completion of baptism. When infant baptism became common, confirmation gradually became a separate sacrament. We will consider confirmation more fully in chapter 17.

When an adult is baptized today, confirmation is celebrated immediately afterward, as in the early Church, and then one receives the eucharist for the first time—thus completing one's initiation into the life of Christ and the Church community.

If one who was baptized a Christian wants to become a Catholic, he or she would not be baptized again, unless there was genuine doubt about the validity of the previous baptism. Most baptisms of other Christian churches are accepted as valid by the Catholic Church. One previously baptized as a Christian should obtain a certificate of this baptism, so that the information can be entered on the records of the Catholic Church.

The already baptized Christian who wishes to become a Catholic makes a Profession of Faith, a statement of his or her belief in the teachings of the Catholic Church, and then receives the sacraments of confirmation and the eucharist. But before becoming a Catholic Christian, one must be converted. . . .

CONVERSION

The Acts of the Apostles tells how the deacon Philip one day met an official of the Queen of Ethiopia and told him the good news about Christ, as they were driving along the road from Jerusalem. They came to a stream, and the official said, "See, here is water; what is there to prevent my being baptized?" Philip said, "If you believe with all your heart, you may." And the official answered: "I believe that Jesus Christ is the Son of God." Then they stopped the chariot and went down into the water where Philip baptized him (cf. Acts, 8, 26–39).

Of course, the whole incident is condensed (when it was written, around the end of the first century, the much more lengthy process of Christian initiation had been developing for some time). But it tells us very succinctly what conversion is all about: One has to believe "with all [one's] heart." So anyone wanting to be baptized and/or converted to Catholic Christianity must not only accept intellectually the teachings of the Church, believing them to be true, but must also be determined to live up to those teachings as best he or she can. Peter's Pentecost sermon expresses it similarly: "You must reform [convert, turn around your life, have a change of mind and heart] and be baptized . . . " (Acts 2, 38). St. Paul, too, reminds his converts "how we entered among you, and how you turned to God from idols, to serve the living and true God" (1 Thessalonians 1, 9).

A conversion, therefore, is a total "turning" toward Christ and a new way of life. We accept the Church's teachings as true and, repenting of our sins, are determined to live a good Christian life. It is a total interior change of mind and heart. With all our heart we turn away from our sins, toward Christ and his Church. We make a total commitment of ourselves to Christ. We may have sincerely tried to serve God before, but now we are determined to do so to the full extent of our new and fuller knowledge of the truth.

Conversion means a firm determination, but not a certainty, that one will never sin again. Perhaps converts are realistically fearful, even quite certain, that they will fall again into their old sins, but they commit themselves nevertheless, trusting in God to help them and pick them up should they fall.

The power to be converted is given by God and is often called the "gift of faith." It presupposes our own sincere efforts, as we shall see. But it is God who first attracts us, motivates us, "calls" us by a loving invitation that is usually gradual but nonetheless persistent to turn completely to himself.

To express their conversion, adult converts to Catholicism make a Profession or Act of Faith. They solemnly read this profession before a priest and, ideally, the assembled Christian community, affirming their acceptance of the Church's basic teachings and their commitment to live by them. If one cannot make one's profession before the community, there is present at least one witness or "sponsor" (usually an adult who can help the new Catholic adjust to his or her faith and live it out most fully). If the new convert is to be baptized, this profession is done immediately before baptism, as part of the Rite of Christian Initiation.

Vatican Council II provided a way for one who is converting—baptized or not—to become a Catholic Christian. It is the Rite of Christian Initiation of Adults. . . .

THE CHRISTIAN INITIATION OF ADULTS

The Rite of Christian Initiation of Adults (or RCIA), the process by which adult converts are received into full communion with the Catholic Church, is an updated version of the way the early Christians became followers of Jesus Christ. The process of initiation developed gradually, until by the mid–second century it extended in some places over a period of years.

In those early days, becoming a Christian meant not only going against many customs of the pagan world, but it might also be a commitment to death (Nero began persecuting Christians in the 60s C.E.). The rite of initiation, therefore, was more than an outward formality: it was a series of steps by which the aspirant gradually came not only to understand Christ's teachings but to live them—and perhaps die for them—as part of a committed Christian community.

Those preparing to be baptized as Christians were—and are— called "catechumens," and they form the "catechumenate," a group within the Church undergoing Christian initiation. The catechumenate died out around the sixth century, when those becoming new Christians were mostly children, but it was revived by Vatican Council II. Today, though the odds are against one's actually dying for becoming a Christian, in many places in the world people are suffering and dying for espousing Christian principles. And to live as a committed Catholic Christian in our own highly individualistic, materialistic society can frequently be as demanding as it was two thousand years ago. The catechumenate is meant to form mature Christians who have experienced learning and living in an actively believing, worshiping community.

The Rite of Christian Initiation takes place in stages, each expressing a further development or deepening of one's faith-commitment. Since arriving at a mature grasp of the Catholic Christian faith takes time, potential converts are immersed in a step-by-step, learning-and-living experience. During all this time God is marvelously working within them, deepening their faith, hope, and love, and further uniting them with Christ and the many people who make up his Body, the Church.

Catechumenate sessions usually begin each year in the fall, culminate in the Easter Vigil, and continue into late spring (with less-frequent gatherings often continuing in the fall). How much time each person spends in the catechumenate is an individual matter, but a year or two is normal. Some may already know and be living Catholicism as fully as most Catholics, and they may not need all the stages; others may know something of Christianity but need more knowledge and an experience of Catholicism's beliefs and practices; yet others may be inquiring into a formal religion for the first time in their lives.

During this period the catechumens are on a journey, within themselves, with those sharing the catechumenate with them, and above all

with God himself, in search of his will for them—and of their own willingness to commit themselves totally to him. As a community journeying together, the growing mutual support and caring of those sharing the
catechumenate experience can become strikingly evident.

**The local church-community each year renews its own faith and
commitment to live it,** as it supports the catechumens by its prayers and
takes part in the rituals of initiation. Some members of the community
will be with them all along the way, perhaps as sponsors, others at different times along the way—some sharing their knowledge and faith experiences, others their hospitality, culinary or artistic skills, and so on.

The first step toward initiation is a period of inquiry (or the precat-
echumenate). This is a series of sessions for those who are interested but
are making no commitment to the Church (though some may have already decided to join). Here they get an overview of Catholic Christianity,
its teachings and practices.

Inquirers usually discuss prayer, understanding the Mass, and how to do
Scripture reading; they are encouraged to perform acts of service toward others. They begin to experience being part of a church-community and hopefully will begin attending Mass regularly. Honest questioning should take
place, not only with the priest or whoever is conducting the inquiry sessions,
but with all who are involved. People may share their personal stories of how
God has acted in their lives—but the inquirer should always feel free to just
sit and listen.

*The inquirer then decides whether to go on to the next stage, the catechu-
menate proper,* often after consulting the priest or whoever is conducting the
sessions. Some inquirers may want to take time out for further reflection,
prayer, reading, and so on. Some may not be able to accept basic Catholic
teachings about Jesus or about the role of the Church. An inquirer might ask
himself or herself: Can I accept what I have heard so far? Do I want to know
more about Jesus Christ and the Catholic Church? Do I want to continue to
share my journey with others—at this time, with this community?

One should never feel pressured to go on to a further stage, for this is a
most intimate matter between oneself and God (who may or may not be leading one to Catholic Christianity). Every priest understands this and will respect each person's desires. Family members and friends, too, should and

probably will have a like respect. Some of the most loving and selfless people in history have been "inquirers" all their lives.

The next stage, the catechumenate proper, consists of further instruction and living as a Catholic Christian. It is designed for those who wish to continue toward full membership in the Catholic Church—either they have, at this point, decided to join the Catholic Church or they are very seriously considering it. Thus catechumens are "believing learners."

Catechumens not only deepen their knowledge of Catholic Christianity but they pray over and meditate on what they are learning—and, most important, they try to live day-by-day lives of caring love toward others. They also experience more fully being part of a believing, caring community: catechists or "guides"—and especially one's sponsor—share their knowledge, insights, and support. Often weighty problems of belief and/or living one's faith are best dealt with over coffee or a meal.

This stage begins with a ceremony of acceptance or welcoming into the Church community, normally on the first Sunday of Advent. They express their belief and willingness to live as Catholic Christians. They are signed with the cross, the central symbol of their life from now on. They are presented with a Bible (or a Lectionary, the Scripture readings used at Mass), to show that God's Word is to be the source of their further learning and moral growth. From now on they should read and ponder beforehand each Sunday's Scripture readings.

From here on only those who have never been baptized are called "catechumens," while those who have already been baptized in another Christian faith are called "candidates." The Rite of Initiation, originally the way for unbaptized adults to become Christians, is today also generally used as the way for those who have already been baptized as Christians—but are no longer active members of another Christian church—to become Catholics. They are candidates preparing not for baptism but for confirmation and the eucharist, as distinct from the not-yet-baptized catechumens.

The catechumens and candidates follow the ancient custom of leaving Mass after the Liturgy of the Word—symbolically showing that they are undergoing more preparation before sharing fully in the community's eucharistic meal. Instead of "breaking bread" in the eucharist they gather and further "break open" the Word of Scripture, usually using that Sunday's Scripture readings as the basis for discussion, learning, and growth.

The catechumens and candidates are given—or may choose—a sponsor: someone to accompany them during the remainder of the catechumenate and help them, out of their own experience, to grow in faith and love. One's sponsor should be compatible, caring, and a committed Catholic. Often a member of the parish community serves as sponsor: he or she has usually undergone special training and can help integrate the catechumen more easily into the parish community. At the next stage the catechumen's sponsor may also become his or her sponsor or godparent for baptism, or someone else may be chosen by the catechumen—or sometimes both may accompany the catechumen.

The catechumens are prayed over at certain times and are anointed with the oil of catechumens (symbolizing the strength they will need from God as they continue on). They are enrolled in the Catechumenate Register. Catechumens and candidates are considered Catholics, but in the learning stage; they may be married as members of the Church and receive a Christian burial.

As the end of the catechumenate nears, the catechumens and candidates must discern whether to enter the next stage, to become a Catholic Christian. Each might ask: Can I accept what I have learned, at least the Church's basic teachings? Do I want to know Jesus better, to live his life more deeply? Do I want to continue to live as a Catholic Christian? Do I feel at home in this community? Is it the kind of community I would want to be part of? Do I feel at home at Mass? Or do I want more time, to learn, pray, attend Mass, and so on before deciding (perhaps even despite a loved one's expectations)?

It might be helpful here to read in chapter 24 the section entitled, "Whether or Not to Join the Church."

Some may want to wait and continue next year, some may wait for several years before continuing, and some will never continue—but they are far better persons for their seeking, for what they have received and what they have given.

In making this decision one should seek the help of the priest or whoever is conducting the sessions, of the catechists or guides, as well as one's sponsor. The one conducting the sessions usually sees each person individually, to assure himself or herself that the person is prepared and is being called by God to become a Catholic Christian.

The next stage is that of election or choice, which culminates in baptism and/or reception into the Catholic Church. Meant to take place during the Lenten season, this begins with the Rite of Election and Enrollment on the First Sunday of Lent.

This is a recognition that those who have completed the Catechumenate have been chosen or called by God to become full members of the Catholic Church. The catechumens and the candidates first gather with the parish community. Having been affirmed by their godparents and sponsors, they symbolically step forward; the catechumens are enrolled in the Book of the Elect. The community prays for them all and then sends them forth, with their godparents and sponsors, to the bishop.

They assemble, if possible, at the cathedral with other catechumens and candidates from throughout the diocese for the Rite of Election and Call to Continuing Conversion: After hearing the testimony of the catechists, godparents, and sponsors that they are prepared, the bishop first receives the catechumens among the elect and then welcomes the candidates for full membership in the Church. He instructs both catechumens and candidates regarding what they are undertaking and, if he is able, meets and welcomes each personally.

Lent becomes a time of spiritual deepening or enlightenment for the elect—of prayer, quiet recollection, openness, and meditation more than study. They fast as best they can, and each usually has a Lenten "practice"—something concrete one chooses to help one be more fully converted. They also usually take part in a retreat day or weekend, to deepen their self-knowledge and preparation.

On the third, fourth, and fifth Sundays of Lent, the elect gather for the rite of "Scrutinies"—not a questioning about faith but a deepening discernment of what is weak and what is strong within—and as much of the local community as possible takes part. There are the Presentations of the Creed and of the Lord's Prayer, the "symbols" or expressions of what we as Christians believe and how Christ taught us to pray.

On Holy Saturday morning, the elect gather and recite the Creed, have their ears and mouth symbolically opened by the Ephphetha rite, and formally choose their baptismal and/or confirmation name. Holy Saturday should be a day of retreat, of rest, fasting, and prayerful meditation on what they are undertaking that evening.

Then, at the Easter Vigil, the elect take part in the ancient Sacraments of Initiation. Their long period of preparation is completed and now before the whole congregation they become Catholic Christians:

After the initial ceremonies, they reject sin and affirm the Creed as their Profession of Faith. Then they are baptized—cleansed from sin, they rise from the water with the new life of grace—and they receive a white garment and lighted candle as signs of this new life. Then they are confirmed with the oil of chrism and are told to witness for their new faith. Finally they take part fully for the first time in the meal of the holy eucharist—the culmination of their initiation and Christ's greatest act of love, in which they can now share as often as they wish.

The final stage of initiation, "mystagogia," (or "learning the mysteries") takes place during the whole post-Easter season. The neophytes (or new converts) deepen their Catholic Christian commitment—by further instruction, by meditating on what they have undertaken, by grateful acts of kindness or charity, and by trying to develop a particular way of ministering within the community. The local Christian community, in turn, helps them find the particular ministry in which they can best use their particular gifts. They should particularly try to deepen their spiritual life, their experiencing of God in their life. They are still on a journey, a lifelong one toward God and eternal life.

The RCIA may differ from diocese to diocese and from parish to parish in the way it is done. There are numerous options for rituals to best bring out their meanings, and their use may vary according to the people of a particular parish, the experience of its RCIA team, and so on.

It might not always be possible or necessary to do all the stages of initiation as envisioned, since individuals and groups vary. Stages may be shortened, lengthened, or combined—or some converts will best be received into the Church at a time other than the Easter Vigil. Some places where people are already deeply Christian receive them at Epiphany, Easter, and/or Pentecost. But the full rite, with sufficient time given each stage in order, and climaxing in the Easter Vigil, is the ideal.

It is important to remember that a baptized Christian who enters the Catholic Church is already a member of the Body of Christ, and therefore does not have to go through the whole process of Christian initiation. But many Christians are such in name only: they need all the steps of initiation (except baptism), since they are coming as mature adults to a Christian community for the first time. Others have a good knowledge of Christianity, have been living it for years, and need less instruction and formation. Most want to go through as much of the catechumenate as possible, not only to thoroughly learn about Catholic Christianity, but to experience living it as part of a believing community, with all its customs, rituals, and opportunities for spiritual growth.

Also one who has been baptized as a Catholic, but never raised as such, might well want to go through the whole process except baptism. It can be a wonderful experience in gradually learning and living what one missed out on, or was not prepared for, earlier. Obviously, each person's situation should be discussed with the priest or whoever is conducting the sessions and worked out to their mutual satisfaction.

The Christian Initiation of Children is for children receiving baptism when they are older (usually about seven years) along with confirmation and first eucharist. As said earlier, their free, informed consent and desire for these sacraments is necessary—then it is envisioned that they go through as many of the steps of Christian initiation as may be possible and suitable for them.

IN THE LITURGY

The Church's creeds summarize its basic beliefs and attempt to state succinctly what is seen, at a particular time in history, to be God's revelation. We saw the Apostles' Creed, the basic, earliest expression of Christian belief, in chapter 10.

The Nicene Creed is the other key creed of the Catholic Christian faith. It is usually said at Mass on Sundays and major feasts, and may be said by converts as their Profession of Faith upon entering the Church. It gives the Church's basic teachings as stated by the Council of Nicea (325 C.E.) and the First Council of Constantinople (381 C.E.):

We believe in one God, the Father, the Almighty,
    maker of heaven and earth, of all that is seen and unseen.

We believe in one Lord, Jesus Christ, the only Son of God,
    eternally begotten of the Father,
    God from God, Light from Light, true God from true God,
    begotten, not made, one in Being with the Father.
    Through him all things were made.
    For us and for our salvation he came down from heaven;
    by the power of the Holy Spirit
    he was born of the Virgin Mary and became man [human].
    For our sake he was crucified under Pontius Pilate;
    he suffered, died, and was buried.
    On the third day he rose again in fulfillment of the Scriptures;
    he ascended into heaven, and is seated at the right hand of the Father.
    He will come again in glory to judge the living and the dead,
    and his kingdom will have no end.
We believe in the Holy Spirit, the Lord, the giver of life,
    who proceeds from the Father and the Son.
    With the Father and the Son he is worshiped and glorified.
    He has spoken through the prophets.
    We believe in one holy catholic and apostolic Church.
    We acknowledge one baptism for the forgiveness of sins.
    We look for the resurrection of the dead,
    and the life of the world to come. Amen.

The use of holy water, particularly when making the Sign of the Cross upon entering or leaving church, is a reminder of the water of our baptism: as it cleansed us originally from sin, so now it reminds us to live free of sin. Holy water is ordinary water blessed by a priest with the prayer of the Church that whoever uses it reverently will remain cleansed from sin.

THE MAJORITY WHO ARE NOT BAPTIZED

There are other ways of being united to God besides baptism. Most of the human race has never heard of or cannot believe in Christ or baptism. And as the world population increases, Christians become a proportionally smaller percentage of it. The Christian life begun by baptism is becoming more and more the privilege and responsibility of a relatively smaller number. Most of humankind is united with God in other ways.

An adult who believes in God and basically desires to do his will, and who has sorrow for his or her sins out of love of God, has God's grace-presence by this sincere desire. His or her sins would be forgiven. This is called "baptism of desire." So, too, a potential convert would receive grace if he or she desired to receive baptism and had sorrow for his or her sins out of love of God; if such a person died before baptism, he or she would attain heaven. Also an unbaptized person who dies for his or her belief in God or some Christian teaching—though the person may not recognize it as Christian—is said to be "baptized" in his or her own blood and thereby receives grace and salvation.

People come to God in this way through other, non-Christian religions. They would not normally have available the fullness of helps that Christ gives to his Church. Since he is "the way, the truth, and the life," the privilege and responsibility of being fully and consciously united with him belongs to Christians. But God is present among these others, as Vatican Council II points out:

> The Catholic Church rejects nothing that is true and holy in these religions. She regards with sincere reverence those ways of conduct and of life, those precepts and teachings which, though differing in many aspects from the ones she holds and sets forth, nonetheless often reflect a ray of that Truth which enlightens all [people] (*Constitution on the Church in the Modern World,* no. 2).

So, too, one who cannot believe in a personal God but is committed to following one's conscience receives God's grace-presence. The basic orientation of one's life would be to some ideal outside oneself, such as the good of humankind or the welfare of those one loves. In seeking this, one is unknowingly seeking God—and God comes to such a one.

> Some who sincerely seek truth oppose Christ and his Church, by harassment or even open persecution. Perhaps they have encountered believers whose behavior is blatantly un-Christian and who, as Vatican Council II says, "conceal rather than reveal the authentic face of God and religion." Perhaps they see glaring deficiencies in the Church's institutional practices. God lives

within many of these unbelievers, though they may oppose him or those who try to work for him.

But these other ways of being united in God's grace-presence do not normally produce the full, deep union that begins by Christian baptism. Baptized Christians who try to live out their baptismal commitment can know more of the basic truths about God, humankind, the universe, and life's purpose. They have the power to love and serve others more effectively, share in a special way in Christ's priesthood, and be more conscious of God's Presence in our world—in worshipful prayer, in our fellow human beings. With the Christian community's continuing help, committed baptized Christians can see opportunities for growing in love and union with God and others where they might otherwise miss them.

A person who knows about and believes in the sacrament of baptism must receive it, with all its privileges and responsibilities. Otherwise the person would be untrue to his or her conscience, and such a person should realize that he or she will have to answer for this, not only to himself or herself but to God. It would be tragic to refuse Christ when he invites us personally, as he did his first disciples, "Come, follow me . . . " (Mark 1, 17; Matthew 9,9).

Yet baptism is only the beginning. Its power can be frustrated by an un-Christian upbringing or environment, by a lack of sufficient love in one's life, or by a deliberate rejection of baptism's consequences. Some Christians live as if they were inoculated by their baptism against true Christianity—they have long since convinced themselves that they are living as Christians, but their smugly sinful lives are hardened against Christ's message. Conversely, some who are not baptized may, by their sincere and open lives, grow more fully in God's presence and spread far more love in the world.

Some words should be said here about "born-again" Christians. These comprise a broad spectrum of people. They have in common a usually sudden, often unexpected experience of being "saved" or "accepted" by Jesus, to whom, in turn, they commit themselves wholeheartedly as their personal Savior (or in some similarly expressed way). Those who have had this conversion experience seem to fall into two general types (with many shades in between):

The first group has had a genuine experience of conversion, and as a result their lives are changed: faith, hope, and Christian love have begun to shape their lives, perhaps for the first time, perhaps as a profound reconversion to the faith in which they were baptized but which had been dormant, unlived, for years. Most of these conversion experiences take place in the context of an evangelical or conservatively oriented Christian church, which usually stresses a simple experiencing of Jesus and God that more intellectually oriented, socially liberal Christians may find hard to understand. Conservative Christians generally place more emphasis on living out traditional Christian values (expressed best for them in the Ten Commandments) than on changing society's structures to promote justice, peace, and equality—though many also seek these, they are more concerned about the erosion of family life, sexual immorality, and the hedonism of much of our society.

They also generally place special emphasis on "bearing witness," on publicly professing and zealously spreading their belief in Christian "basics." They have a deep regard for and love of the Bible as God's Word. Yet they don't take every word literally. While they accept much of modern biblical scholarship, they also tend to look to the Bible mostly for guidance—a book to be lived by daily rather than one to be overly analyzed. Sometimes conservatively oriented Catholics find much in common with these, for instance, in some charismatic Christian groups.

The other type of "born-again" Christian is the one that Catholics in general find hard to accept. Without judging the genuineness of these people's conversion experience (obviously something only God can and should do), it is especially their basic attitude toward the Bible and social issues that Catholics (as well as "main-line" Protestants) object to. These are often contrary to the Church's teaching, especially as expressed by Vatican Council II, recent popes, the American bishops, and lay groups within the Catholic Church.

These people are more "fundamentalist" than conservative: they take Scripture literally, regarding its every word as inerrant, and allow for no symbolism, mythology, and so on. Thus they reject modern Scripture scholarship, Protestant or Catholic, and emphasize the Old Testament's traditional strictness of the Law and Commandments more than Christ's forgiving, all-embracing love. They display a narrow, unshakable certitude about the truth of their beliefs and in the sinfulness and even damnation of those who violate their norms and refuse to "repent"—and they seem driven to impose their beliefs on others. Usually little concerned with the poor and deprived, especially of other nations (except insofar as they can convert them), they seem overly concerned with combating "godlessness," "tolerance," and "humanism." Their stance on issues of social justice, peace, disarmament, and so on also seems totally opposite of Catholic teaching.

DAILY LIVING:
RENEWING OUR BAPTISMAL CONVERSION

We have seen that baptism does not give us faith permanently, nor "magically" enable us to live a truly Christian life. We must continue to grow and to cooperate with what God is continuing within us. Believers must continually be open to the Spirit as they practice their faith, expecting difficulties, doubts, and failures in their attempts to live and love as a Christian should—as well as in the attempts of churchpeople to communicate Christ to them.

They realize that, especially in today's rapidly changing world, they must be continual learners, trying to assimilate the Church's new insights into ancient truths, and to be involved with whatever loving causes they can—and particularly to develop a life of prayer and appreciation of the eucharistic Christ. Thus, in growing and developing a truly adult faith, there gradually comes a more intimate relationship with Christ and a realization of God's continual, loving Presence . . . even in the midst of adversity and wrenching pain.

Thus a Christian's life is one of continual conversion—or periodic reconversions. Christians may fail in their baptismal commitment—perhaps again and again—and may fall into a state of serious sin. But when they are sorry, they renew their commitment (and perhaps take part in the sacrament of reconciliation). They humbly ask God's help and begin again. If they are truly wise, they know that God's love is endless as it continually draws them on. The great St. Paul, as close to Christ as he was, movingly expressed his own continuing weaknesses: **Read 2 Corinthians 12, 7-10.**

SOME SUGGESTIONS FOR . . .

DISCUSSION

What, for you, is the significance of baptism?

Can you see the need for a true, adult-level conversion—and has it been happening in your life? How have others been part of this—or not been a part of this—for you?

Looking back on your life's journey, can you see how and where God has been leading you? Is it to enter more fully into the Catholic faith?

How can people grow spiritually as they share in the steps of Christian initiation? If you have been taking part in it, how have you grown?

What, at this point, do you find hard to accept about the Catholic faith? How would you advise someone to deal with this same difficulty?

FURTHER READING

- • *The Christian Sacraments of Initiation: Baptism, Confirmation, Eucharist,* Osborne (Paulist Press, 1987)—A good presentation of the biblical, historical, and theological backgrounds of these sacraments in reference to today's use.
- • *Confessions,* St. Augustine—There are many editions of this classic autobiography (the first ever in Western literature) and personal conversion story of one of the Church's greatest saints; this profoundly moving story of his struggle with God and himself should be "must" reading for anyone.
- •• *Full Christianity,* Chilson (Paulist Press, 1985)—This is an insightful, comprehensive book meant to help Catholic Christians, especially, answer the questions often put to them by fundamentalist, born-again Christians.
- • *Fundamentalism: A Catholic Perspective,* O'Meara (Paulist Press, 1990)—A brief but incisive look at the extreme conservatism that is fundamentalism as it exists inside and outside the Catholic Church, its causes and psychology, and how to deal with it.
- •• *RCIA, The Rite of Christian Initiation, study ed.,* USCC (Liturgical Press, 1988)—The official ritual for use in the United States (a.k.a. the White Book).

Note also this book's appendix on using this book with the RCIA. There are many excellent resources available for using the RCIA. These are a few:

- *The RCIA, Transforming the Church: A Resource for Pastoral Implementation,* Morris (Paulist Press, 1989)—A good book that combines an explanation of the rite with possibilities for using it, plus other resources.

- *Breaking Open the Word of God: Resources for Using the Lectionary for Catechesis in the RCIA, Cycle A, B, or C,* Hinman-Powell and Sinwell (Paulist Press, 1986–88)—Three fine books for weekly catechumenate meetings; used imaginatively and selectively, these are excellent resources. Completing these three, by the same authors, is
   • *Ninety Days: Resources for Lent and Eastertime in the RCIA* (Paulist Press, 1989).

- *Guide for Sponsors,* third ed., Lewinski (Liturgy Training Publications, Chicago, 1993)—Excellent for sponsors, by a pioneer in the field.

- *How to Form a Catechumenate Team,* Hinman-Powell (Liturgy Training Publications, 1986)—This gets excellent marks from those experienced in forming such teams in parishes.

- *Step by Step We'll Make This Journey,* ed. Lumas—This is a 1990 presentation of the RCIA adapted to blacks, done by a fine team of those associated with the National Black Sisters' Conference.

- *Experiencing Mystagogy, The Sacred Pause of Easter,* Baumbach (Paulist Press, 1995)—A fine companion on the journey of faith for those newly baptized and/or received into the Church.

- *Experience the Mystery: Pastoral Possibilities for Christian Mystagogy,* Regan (Liturgical Press, 1994)—Concisely written, this very good book gives the history of mystagogy as the experiencing of God, its eclipse in the Church in recent centuries, and its many possibilities in the worldwide Church today.

- *A Catechumen's Lectionary,* ed. Hamma (Paulist Press, 1993)—A basic book of liturgical readings for catechumens and candidates, with helpful suggestions for praying with them and putting them into practice.

FURTHER VIEWING/LISTENING

Becoming an RCIA Sponsor, Hamma, Fisher, and Dunning (Paulist Press)—A videocassette in three parts that gets high marks from sponsors.

PERSONAL REFLECTION

God's special Presence or closeness, received in baptism, or by the sincere desire to do what God wants, is the only important thing in life. It is God himself, intimately within me, the beginning of heaven while here on earth. I should resolve to do all in my power to avoid sin, particularly habitual serious sinning that robs me of God's love and cuts me off from others.

14

Our Worship Together: The Mass

What is the meaning of the Mass? Why go to Mass at all? Why is the Mass the greatest thing in this life? Why is it arranged the way it is? How can we derive real value and help from the Mass?

WHY WE GATHER TOGETHER TO WORSHIP

We saw that worship is an expression of what God is worth to us—our deepest feelings of reverence, need, and gratitude—and our confidence that we are uniquely loved, worth very much to him. Worship is our trusting "yes"—however difficult, even painfully given at times—to the Mystery of caring Love we call God. And it is a "yes" to the whole wonderful mystery of our own life, its joys and sorrows, its peaks and pits, its loves and its times of crushing rejection.

We saw, too, that worship means joining others to express and share together our feelings of reverence and need toward God, and our feelings of caring and need for one another. As human beings, as people needing people, we find it as natural to worship together as it is to eat together, to work together, to live together. "No man is an island," as the poet John Donne put it, and we surely cannot find God only in isolation; it is too easy to come up with a magnified version of our own ego. We need others' experiences, insights, encouragement, and honest proddings—just as they need ours.

As Christians we are not ashamed to acknowledge that we need one another, that we need to gather together in church as we go on our particular journeys through life. One doesn't consider Weight Watchers a failed organization because those who gather for its meetings are overweight—nor deride Alcoholics Anonymous because those it brings together have drinking problems. So we gather together in worship to learn how to love and support one another, how to best and most caringly cocreate a "new earth" in space and time as we make our way toward heaven.

> *To get anything out of going to worship together, we obviously need a mature, realistic patience and openness.* We must make sure we are doing our part, if we are to be aware that God is there and doing his part. Each liturgy will touch, be truly meaningful to, only so many people; worshiping together is not something magical, a quick fix of inspiration for all present. We need to remind ourselves that someone (perhaps many others) will receive help—that if this week's worship does not come home to us, perhaps next week's will. And perhaps during the week we will help bring this about by preparing: by lovingness toward others, by honest moments of private reflection.

CHRIST GATHERS US TO SHARE IN HIS GREATEST ACTION

We have seen God's love for us and his desire to be with us. He came among us in Jesus Christ. He lives among us today in his Church. He reaches out to us through the sacraments: baptism, by which he unites us to himself, and confirmation by which he sends us his Spirit.

Wonderful though it is that God should come among us, more wonderful yet is the destiny he has prepared for us. He wants to raise us to himself, to the very level of divinity, to know and love him most intimately in unending happiness.

Humankind had rejected the grace that made this possible, but Christ came and redeemed us, making it possible once more. This, our salvation by Christ, was the greatest act of his life and the central event of all history. By it people could attain union with God, face-to-face, forever.

Yet in order to profit by this great act of Christ's love, we must unite ourselves freely to it. We must make it our own. We must somehow take part in Christ's life, but especially in his death and resurrection in order to attain the perfect union of love with him that is heaven. This is because he loves us and wants us to be with him, freely and most intimately.

It is natural to want to share in the things that happen to those we love, and particularly in the great events of their lives and their intense moments of joy or suffering. A husband wants to be by the bedside of his critically ill wife, parents want to take part in their child's graduation, friends take part in one another's weddings, and so on.

Jesus Christ in his love has made it possible for us to share in what happened to him. We can read a biography of a great leader and be caught up by his or her spirit, courage, and example. In a way, we can pass over into the lives of such people and to some small extent share their great experiences. Jesus has made much more than this possible for us. We can actually relive his life, mysteriously but really. We try to imitate Jesus, but even more we can actually go through—with him—what he did. His actions, his way of experiencing things, gradually become our own. So St. Paul, perhaps his greatest follower, says: "I have been crucified with Christ. It is no longer I who live, but Christ who lives in me . . . " (Galatians 2, 20).

Above all, Jesus Christ wants us to take part with him in his death and resurrection so that our own "dyings" and "risings" can be a part of his—and his a part of ours. He wants us especially to enter into these great events of his earthly existence so that he can come with his power and love into the "pits" and the "peaks" of our life—our daily deaths and resurrections, our plunges into pain and our small triumphs. He wants us to share his own "passage," his own experience of death and new life, his going back to the Father and unending happiness. He wants to catch us up into himself, so that what we go through will be part of what he went through and so that our sufferings and joys will have sense and meaning and be filled for us with his own loving power.

We saw how Christ unites us for the first time to his death and resurrection at baptism. After baptism, each sacrament unites us in a special way to Jesus Christ as he saves us. But the greatest partaking possible is by the sacrament of the holy eucharist.

The holy eucharist is Jesus Christ living among us under the appearance of bread and wine. When the priest at Mass says the eucharistic prayer over the bread and wine (at the heart of which are Christ's words, "This is my body . . . This is the chalice of my blood . . . "), where there were before only bread and wine there is now the living Jesus Christ. This is the sacrament of the holy eucharist. By the power of Christ working through the priest as he leads the people in the eucharistic prayer, the bread and wine, though still appearing to be bread and wine, are now Christ, present and acting among us in a special, powerful way.

This might sound strange indeed to some and is open to misunderstanding. When we say that the bread and wine "become Christ" we are not saying that bread and wine are Christ, nor are we practicing some form of cannibalism when we take this in communion. What we mean is that the bread and wine are a sign of Christ present, here and now, in a special way—not in a mere physical way, as if condensed into a wafer. Somehow his presence has "taken over" the bread and wine, so that, for us who believe, it is no longer merely bread that is present, but Christ himself.

The "how" of Christ becoming present has traditionally been called "transubstantiation," that is, the substance of the bread and wine is changed into the body and blood of Christ, although the appearance and characteristics (or "accidents") remain those of bread and wine. Some modern theologians find other ways to better explain what is, ultimately, a mystery (cf. chapter 15, the section entitled "Christ Among Us in the Eucharist").

Jesus Christ lives among us in the holy eucharist for a purpose—to make present for us his death and resurrection so that we can take part. This is the Mass. Jesus said, "This is my body given up [to death] for you. . . . This cup is the new covenant in my blood" (1 Corinthians 11, 24–25). Christ's death and resurrection, his going to the Father, is made present in this ritual so that Christians till the end of time can take part in them, gradually going with him to the Father. The Mass is the great way we are drawn to God and our great source of strength for the journey to him.

There are various ways in which we can take part in a great historical event, for example, a stirring gathering for human rights or for peace. We might have heard of it, we might see a film of it on TV, or we might have actually been a part of it. The more we enter into it and the more we are involved in it, the more we will get out of it and the more it will mean to us and affect our actions toward others.

At Mass, we are not only present at Jesus Christ's actual death and resurrection, prolonged through time and space. We also really take part in them to the extent we want to. Christ's death and resurrection are here; we are present at them, but they are hidden—they are present here under the ritual signs of bread and wine. The more these signs mean to us and the more we consciously join our daily "dyings" and "risings" with the great struggle of Christ's death and resurrection, then the more we actually are part of them, the more our life and our pain become meaningful, the more hope we have, the more love we will spread in the world, and the closer we come to eternal life and oneness with God himself.

THIS IS OUR COVENANT MEAL

The night before he died Christ gave us the great way of continually sharing in his death and resurrection—by means of a meal, the last supper: Read 1 Corinthians 11, 23-29. To understand this incident we recall that this meal was the passover meal, eaten yearly to commemorate the salvation of God's people from slavery and death, and the old covenant of Mount Sinai. Whenever the Jews ate this meal they looked forward to a new passover to come, a new salvation, a new exodus to a new freedom. Our redemption was Christ's great new passover, from death to life, from this world to the Father—and he began it by eating this paschal meal, his last supper. He gave this paschal meal a new power and new meaning. He made it the way his followers could actually share in his passover, in his death and resurrection.

By the words, "This is my body given up for you. . . . This cup is the new covenant in my blood," Jesus Christ mysteriously but really made himself present where before there were only bread and wine. Thus Jesus Christ gave us the sacrament of the holy eucharist. The bread and wine, though still appearing to be bread and wine, were now Jesus Christ present in a new and wonderful way. And it was the whole living Christ present under the appearance of bread, not only his body, and the whole living Christ present under the appearance of wine. In the language Jesus spoke, "body" and "blood" could signify not just part of a person but the total, living self.

But above all, Jesus was presenting before his apostles his death and resurrection, which would take place the next day, and which

would begin his new covenant. The bread was his body that would, he said, be "given up" in death for us all. The cup was his blood that would be shed to establish his new covenant. By these words he made present at the last supper, mysteriously but really, his bloody death and his resurrection. It was a living preview of what would happen the next day, Good Friday, and on Easter Sunday morning.

This meal by which Christ began his passover also began the events by which he made his new, perfect covenant. "This cup is the new covenant in my blood," he said. As he and his apostles ate the meal that commemorated the old covenant, he was looking forward to the new covenant that he would shortly begin. Then as Moses had once sealed the old covenant by sacrifice and the sprinkling of animals' blood, Christ shed his blood in sacrifice on Good Friday to begin the new covenant. As the greatest event of the Old Testament had been celebrated by a meal, so Christ made his meal the occasion of celebrating the greatest event of his life and of all history.

Then Christ gave his apostles the power to do what he had done, to make present his death and resurrection after changing the bread and wine into himself: "Do this in remembrance of me," he said (Luke 22, 19; 1 Corinthians 11, 25), thus giving his followers the power to somehow extend or continue his death and resurrection down through history. Each time this took place, his passover, his covenant would be renewed again. Every other action of history is bounded by limitations of space and time except this.

Every priest by his ordination receives the power of making Christ present and re-presenting his death and resurrection. This power has been passed on in the Church by the sacrament of ordination, holy orders. By giving this power to his first followers, his Church, Christ provided that down through the centuries we could continually take part in the great events of our salvation—and by so doing, continually renew our personal covenant with him.

. . . AND OUR PERFECT SACRIFICE

One way of understanding the Mass is to recall that the great events of life are celebrated by giving gifts or presents—as on birthdays, weddings, anniversaries. Giving gifts is as old as humankind and as widespread. Our gift can express many things: love, praise, thanks, repentance, and it can implicitly ask for something. A gift stands for the giver—accepting a gift often means acceptance of the one who gives it, as when a girl accepts a ring from a boy. A gift, then, particularly expresses our desire to be united in love with the one to whom it is given.

From ancient times, we have seen, people have offered gifts in sacrifice to God (or their concept of God). They have done this to show their feelings toward him and their desire to be united with him. We saw in the Old Testament sacrifices how God helped his people express their feelings toward him, guiding them to offer their gifts to him.

Sacrifice means offering a gift through a priest, changing it in some way, and sometimes eating of it. People would take some gift that represented themselves and offer it to God by means of their representative, a priest. He would change or transform the gift to signify that they were giving it to God, that it no longer belonged to them—often he would kill a living gift or victim—and then he might burn it to further show God's acceptance and possession of it. Sometimes there would be a meal or banquet, a communion, to further signify their union with God by eating of what was now divine.

Something was lacking even in the Old Testament sacrifices. His people never had a suitable gift for an infinite God, nor did they have a worthy priest to represent them; then, too, these sacrifices often left them unable to feel as closely united to God as they wished.

If I were hungry, I should not tell you, for mine are the world and its fullness. Do I eat the flesh of strong bulls, or is the blood of goats my drink? (Psalm 49, 12–13).

When humankind was ready, Jesus Christ offered the perfect sacrifice by his death and resurrection. He was the perfect gift and the perfect priest making this offering. The best gift, after all, is that of a living person, as when a couple give themselves to one another in marriage—and Christ is the divine Son giving himself to the Father. By his death he gave himself to his Father; his resurrection and ascension showed that the Father accepted his gift.

Christ left us the power to offer this same perfect gift, himself, to continually share in his death and resurrection by the holy eucharist.

Christ went beyond humankind's greatest expectations and gave us the holy eucharist, the concrete sign of his living presence, so we can continually join ourselves to him in his perfect sacrifice. Now, at last, we can adequately express ourselves to God: Christ, totally one with us, can perfectly express our hopes, fears, pain, and thankfulness.

Thus Christ's priesthood is passed on in his Church: At first Christ's followers thought of the eucharist only as the meal by which he was again present among them, reliving for them his life, death, and resurrection. Then gradually his death and resurrection came to be seen as the perfect sacrifice, and the apostles came to be considered the first priests of the New Testament—as Aaron and his sons were the first priests of the Old Testament. And as the powers of a special priesthood were passed on in Israel, so the powers of Christ's priesthood came to be passed on by ordination to those he chose through his Church.

Every Christian also shares in Christ's priesthood and in this offering of himself, which is his death and resurrection prolonged. We have seen how, by baptism and confirmation, each Christian receives this power of the lay priesthood. In the eucharist, the ordained priests of the Church act as Christ's instruments making him present. Then the whole Christian congregation uses its priestly powers to offer him, and themselves with him, to the Father.

The Mass, then, is the renewal of Christ's sacrifice, of his passover and new covenant, by him and us, his Church. At each Mass Christ becomes present; he prolongs and renews his sacrifice so we can be a part of it, so we can pass with him through this world to eternity, and with him continually renew our own covenant.

Christ is present among us at Mass with the same intention or desire to give himself for us, but now he shows this by the separate signs of bread and wine. Instead of undergoing a bloody death, he now expresses his giving of himself ritually with bread and wine. In our own actions, it is our inner intention, our sincere willingness to do something, that really matters—there is a great difference between a person giving up his or her life voluntarily and being forced to die. Christ is present among us at Mass with the same inner intention, the same desire to be sacrificed for us that he had on Calvary two thousand years ago. But now instead of hanging on the cross, he expresses it by the separate signs of bread and wine.

It is somewhat as if our war dead could came back alive on Veteran's Day, inspired by the same interior willingness to give their lives, and went through a pageant reenacting the way they died, that we might now unite our feelings with theirs. "Do this for a remembrance of me," said Christ—the Mass is a living remembrance, a living memorial that brings the past into the present.

At Mass Christ does not suffer or die again. Rather he re-presents, prolongs, continues, renews his great moment of sacrifice down through the centuries so that we can be a part of it. There are millions of Masses, but only one sacrifice of Christ. If we at Mass were to close our eyes it would be the same as if Christ's followers on Calvary closed theirs; the same great action is taking place before us and we are able to be an intimate part of it.

Through the Mass Christ does many things for us. Above all, he enables us to offer perfect worship and be perfectly united with God. The people of the Old Testament strove to bring this about but never could. Now at Mass we are joined with Christ as he appears before his Father and ours. The Father no longer sees the poor actions of mere humans—you and me with our sins and weaknesses—but only the gift that God himself cannot resist.

If our eyes could see what is really happening at any Mass, we would see Christ at the altar and among us, leading us and drawing us all into himself. Then, with him, we would ascend to the Father's presence. We would also see the Holy Spirit within each of us, uniting us, inspiring our offering. We would see the Father giving us in return his Son, Jesus Christ, the best gift God can give mortal beings, and we would see ourselves being drawn into an indescribable union with divinity.

THE MASS IS GOD'S WORD, OUR GIFT, AND HIS GIFT

When giving a gift, there is conversation, some sort of preparation to bring out its meaning and significance. We do not merely thrust our gift at its recipient. Particularly if it is a noteworthy gift, there is conversation and ceremony with it. When a national hero is presented with the Medal of Honor there are speeches, music, and so on. So, too, we prepare to offer our gift in sacrifice to God by conversation with him, by listening to his Word, and by ceremony.

God had called his people together at Mount Sinai to hear his Word and respond to it by sacrifice (cf. Exodus 24, 7–8). This assembly of the Israelites established the old covenant, making them his people. This "assembly of Yahweh" is the same as the New Testament word for "Church." The basic meaning of a Church, then, is this: God's people assembled by him to hear his Word and respond to it by sacrifice.

After Christ's ascension his followers assembled to receive his teaching from the apostles and offer the eucharistic sacrifice. This is the Church of the New Testament. The eucharistic meal, called the "breaking of the bread," and the teaching that went with it would gradually develop into the pattern of worship that would be the Mass.

> And they devoted themselves to the apostles' teaching and fellowship, to the breaking of bread and the prayers (Acts 2, 42). On the first day of the week, when they were gathered together to break bread, Paul talked with them, intending to depart on the morrow; and he prolonged his speech until midnight. . . . And when Paul had gone up and had broken bread and eaten, he conversed with them a long while, until daybreak, and so departed (Acts 20, 7, 11).

Many Scripture scholars see in chapter 6 of John's gospel an excerpt from an early Christian liturgical service; the "beloved disciple" himself may have conducted primitive services in this way. Verses 35–50 give the doctrine or teaching, and verses 51–58 the eucharistic part of the service. This, then, is the pattern: the Word of God followed by the eucharist.

The Mass, then, is the assembly of God's new people, his Church, called together by him to hear his Word and to take part in his perfect sacrifice. When we come together for Mass we are not only going to church—we are making ourselves a Church. The Mass welds us into one people as we renew our common covenant, offer our gift, and share our meal that is Christ. It is by the Mass that the Church is continually renewed in what it is.

The Mass as the meal that renews Christ's sacrifice can be compared to the meal when a family comes together. First, the family gathers;

they talk to one another, learning the events of one another's lives. The table is set and the food is prepared. Then the family prays together over their food, offering thanks to God for all he has given them. Finally, they eat together, taking part in the food and in one another's companionship.

So, too, at Mass we first come together and prepare ourselves, cleansing ourselves of sin, speaking with God, and learning from him the great events of our salvation. Then we prepare our food, the bread and wine. We then join in the great eucharistic prayer of thanksgiving to God over our food, which is now Christ his Son. Finally, we take part together in our meal of holy communion, nourishing ourselves on Christ and joined with one another in the companionship of our Christian family love.

STEP BY STEP THROUGH THE MASS

The arrangement of the Mass expresses the fact that it is an exchange of love.

God gives to us—his Word, the Scripture readings:

The Mass begins with the Entrance Rite or introduction. The ministers of the Mass process in while a song introduces the theme of the Mass. The priest greets us and then leads us in recalling our sins, asking God's pardon so that we may worthily worship him. We sing or say the Gloria, a hymn of praise (except during Advent and Lent). Then the priest's opening prayer invites us to pray; the response, "Amen" ("So be it") concludes every prayer and expresses our acceptance and affirmation.

The first main part of the Mass is the Liturgy of the Word, the Scripture readings. We have assembled together as God's people and have prepared ourselves by prayer. Now God addresses his Word to us. Later we will respond to his Word by our sacrifice. This, we have seen, was the way God's people worshiped in the Old Testament and the way Christ's first followers continued to worship. Christ himself had followed this pattern when he prepared his apostles by his last discourse (John, chapters 13–17), and then went forth to his death and resurrection. The first Christians originally adopted this part from the Jewish synagogue service of prayers, readings, and commentary.

Faith is stirred and we are enlightened and made open and receptive for Christ by the Scripture readings and the preaching that follows. Before our gifts of bread and wine are changed into Christ, our hearts must be changed, opened, by this instruction. On Sunday there are three readings:

The first reading is usually from the Old Testament and harmonizes with the gospel. It is followed by a psalm reflecting themes in the readings.

The second reading is from one of the New Testament epistles (or Acts or Revelation) and is a cycle independent of the other readings, so that outside of special times and feasts the letters are read continuously from week to week.

Then, after the Alleluia ("Praise God"), the third reading is from one of the gospels. These readings are chosen according to a three-year cycle on Sundays (a two-year cycle on weekdays). Then, in the homily (sermon) Christ addresses his message to us through the priest who represents him. We should remember that it takes time to understand the Scriptures, and that Christ always has something for us in the homily, however poorly packaged it sometimes may be.

We then respond to God's Word on Sundays and major feasts by professing our faith, saying together the Nicene Creed. Then, in the Prayers of the Faithful, we pray for all those who need help and for the things we, the Church, and the world particularly need.

Then we give to God—our sacrifice-offering of thanksgiving, Christ, and ourselves with him:

The second main part of the Mass is the Liturgy of the Eucharist (or the Liturgy of Sacrifice). Here we prepare our gifts, they are transformed into Christ, and through him and with him we offer ourselves in thanksgiving to the Father. The Father, in return, gives us the same perfect gift, Jesus Christ, who unites us to himself and to one another.

We begin with the Offertory Rite during which we prepare our gifts, the bread and wine, and unite ourselves to them. We unite ourselves and all we wish to pray for with these gifts, so that later when they have become Christ we will be united with him in his offering to the Father. The gifts are brought up to the altar in an offertory procession. The collection, to support the upkeep and ministries of the parish, is taken up and brought forward as part of our gifts.

The drops of water mixed with the wine, originally done to dilute or "cut" the wine, symbolize Christ's humanity and divinity, and his Church's unity with him. The washing of hands symbolizes our desire to be cleansed of sinfulness.

With the preface we begin the great eucharistic prayer (or canon), during which Christ's presence transforms our gifts, and we offer ourselves with him in this great prayer of thanksgiving to the Father. This is the heart of the Mass, its most solemn part. We call this the eucharistic prayer, that is, a prayer of remembrance and thanksgiving. We remember the great love God has shown us by his actions for us, and we are particularly grateful for what he has done for us in Jesus Christ. We then give him the best possible thanks by offering him Jesus Christ, his Son, and ourselves with him.

> The term "eucharist" comes from the prayer of thanksgiving said by the Jewish people at the end of a meal, gratefully recounting and "blessing" God for his creation and for his mighty deeds for his people over the centuries. So Christ at the last supper "took bread and when he had given thanks he broke it and gave it to them . . . " (Luke 22, 19). During the eucharistic prayer we remember everyone and everything, joining all creation in our thankful worship.

The preface is a kind of dialogue between priest and people inviting all to praise and thank God. It ends with our singing or saying the "Holy, holy, holy, . . . " taken from Isaiah's awe-filled experience of God (Isaiah 6, 3). After thanking the Father for Christ, the priest asks him, in a prayer called the "epiclesis," to send the Holy Spirit to transform our gifts into Christ's body and blood.

Then there is the Institution Rite, the core of which are Jesus' words said over the bread and wine: "This is my body which will be given up for you. . . . This is the cup of my blood, the blood of the new and everlasting covenant. . . . Do this in remembrance of me." This is called the "consecration." The words bring home to us how our gifts are being transformed into Jesus Christ himself in this eucharist, and how he is making present his death for us. The words said over the bread remind us that it is his body "given up" to death that is before us; in a moment the bread will be broken to further bring home to us his death. The words said over the wine tell us that it is Jesus shedding his blood for us who is before us, dying in order to begin his new covenant-commitment of unending love and life for us.

The separate signs of bread and wine bring home to us how his blood was drained from his body as he hung dying for us on the cross. He is present among us with the same willingness to die for us as on Calvary two thousand years ago, but now he shows his total, unending love by these separate signs of "consecrated" bread and wine. His powerful presence here gives us the strength to go through the "dyings" necessary in our daily life as a Christian—to increasingly let go of the things that can keep us from him—in order to "rise" to a new aliveness, a new lovingness with him.

Then the priest sums up the Christian memory of Christ's saving acts for us, his death and resurrection, now marvelously before us in "this life-giving bread, this saving cup." Called the "anamnesis," this "remembrance" meant, in Christ's culture, not only to recall something but to enter into it and bring its power into the present—so, now, in our remembering, we actually enter into Jesus' sacrifice with all its power to help and save us.

The priest then calls on the Holy Spirit to unite us as we share in Christ's body and blood. Then we pray for those in the Church on earth who need our prayers and for those among us who have died, and we ask to be united with those who have already attained heaven.

Our eucharistic prayer culminates in the offering of ourselves and of all creation with Christ to the Father. Christ has taken our poor gifts and transformed them into himself. Now, joined with him, everything we are and have is offered in a great thanksgiving gift. This prayer climaxes with the offering to God of our gifts and ourselves "through him [Christ], with him, and in him" and concludes with the great "Amen" by the whole congregation.

Finally, God gives to us—his Word, the eucharistic Christ:

Our gift has been offered in sacrifice, and now we prepare for our sacrificial meal, holy communion, God's gift to us. God now shows us strikingly that he has accepted our gift, that we are truly united with him. He comes to us himself in the form of food—something of which people in times past would not even dream. This is the greatest gift he could give us. He unites each of us to himself in the most intimate way possible, through Christ his Son. Christ comes to us in this sign of food to bring home to us that he is our spiritual strength and nourishment.

We begin the Communion Rite by saying or singing together the prayer that Christ himself taught us, the Lord's Prayer, or "Our Father." Then the priest prays for freedom from sin and anxiety "as we wait in joyful hope for the coming of our Savior, Jesus Christ."

With the prayer for peace we give the handshake or embrace of peace to one another. This is an outward sign of the peace and unity in which we are trying to grow as a Christian community.

Then there is the breaking of the bread, which tells us how Christ's body was "broken" for us as he died for us. At the last supper his followers shared the same loaf to symbolize their oneness with and in him. (The early Church called the eucharistic service the "breaking of the bread.") The priest breaks a particle off the sacred bread and drops it in the chalice or cup to symbolize our unity through this eucharist (in the ancient Church a particle from the sacred bread used at the bishop's Mass was sometimes taken to the other churches and dropped in the chalice as a sign of the Church's unity).

The congregation sings or says the "Lamb of God" ("Agnus Dei" in Latin), a threefold plea to Jesus as he was called by John the Baptist, that taking part in his passover meal may bring us God's mercy and peace.

Now Jesus unites himself with each of us in holy communion. First the priest and then the people take part in communion. Though Christ is present under either form, bread or wine, taking part under both forms most fully expresses our meal of union with Christ and is today the norm (though those who wish to take part under only one form must be respected).

Holy communion is our great and joyous meal of love, unity, and thanksgiving. People have always expressed their happiness, friendship, thanksgiving, and particularly their unity by having a meal together. We have seen that the joining of two parties in a covenant was often celebrated by a meal together; today a couple often has a wedding meal to celebrate their lifelong covenant of love. We have seen that Israel celebrated its union with God through the old covenant by the passover meal, which also looked forward to a new, more perfect union. Now we have a far more intimate and perfect union with God in this sacrificial meal of the new covenant. But this is not all Christ does:

The cup of blessing which we bless, is it not a participation in the blood of Christ? The bread which we break, is it not a participation in the body of Christ? Because there is one loaf, we who are many are one body, for we all partake of the same loaf. Consider the practice of Israel; are not those who eat the sacrifices partners in the altar? (1 Corinthians 10, 16–18).

Christ through holy communion also unites us with one another, making us "one body," one Church. Just as many grains make one bread, so we, by eating the eucharist, become one. Eating together draws people together, especially when celebrating a great event, as Christmas or Thanksgiving dinner, a wedding breakfast, or a banquet. A family meal is normally the center of its life together.

Christ chose this custom of eating together to draw his followers together, to unite us not only with himself but with one another. Holy communion, then, is the great banquet of God's family, his Church, by which the members are drawn together in love. We are so truly united with one another that St. Augustine could say, "You are the body of Christ, and when you receive the body of Christ you receive yourselves." Singing together when taking part in communion particularly emphasizes our unity.

The communion meal is the part of the Mass that particularly reminds us of Christ's resurrection. A meal symbolizes life—we must eat to live. This eucharistic meal not only symbolizes but gives us Christ resurrected, living again, communicating to us his own life of grace.

Christ usually appeared after his resurrection during meals and ate with his followers. The authentic witnesses of the resurrection, says Peter, are those "who were chosen by God as witnesses, who ate and drank with him after he rose from the dead" (Acts 10, 41). When Christ appeared to two of his followers on the road to Emmaus, they did not realize who it was until "he took the bread and blessed it, and broke it, and gave it to them. And their eyes were opened and they recognized him . . . " (Luke 24, 30–31). After his ascension Christ's followers felt that he was living in their midst especially when they gathered for the eucharistic meal, and they looked for his second coming one day at this event.

The Dismissal Rite follows after communion: the Mass concludes with prayers of thanksgiving, the final blessing, and a closing hymn.

Strengthened and united with Christ and one another, we are now sent back into our daily lives to live the life of Christ.

This, then, is the Mass—the wonderful way in which Christ continually joins us to the great actions by which he saved us, the greatest event of human history. Now we can take part in them most intimately, continually drawing strength from them for our journey to the Father. We who take part in Mass today are as truly a part of Christ's greatest deeds as if we were his followers standing on Calvary, and in some respects we can join in even more intimately. This privilege is ours as Christians—for many, it is their privilege every day.

DAILY LIVING: THE MASS AND OUR DAILY LIFE

All the actions of a Catholic's daily life should lead up to the Mass and flow from it. When we take part in the Mass, we unite ourselves with Christ and through him we reach out and are drawn to God. This act of worship is certainly the most significant and important action of the day and of the week.

At Mass we personally renew our covenant with God for that week. The more we prepare for it, and try to remember and prolong it in our daily life, the more truly Christian—Christ-filled—our life will be.

Our offering at Mass must be interior and sincere. Christ sacrifices himself at Mass by his interior desire to give himself for us. The more we unite ourselves interiorly, by our own sincere desire, to Christ's offering— the more we offer something that is really of ourselves—the more effect the Mass will have on our daily lives.

An excellent way to prepare for Mass is by reading over beforehand in one's Bible the Scripture readings for that day and then briefly and prayerfully reflecting on them. Most weekly parish bulletins now print the Scripture readings for the coming week.

SOME SUGGESTIONS FOR . . .

DISCUSSION

Can you understand Jesus' leaving us the eucharist as a way of being united with him and one another through the centuries?

Does the notion of the Mass as a meal have meaning for you? As a sacrifice affecting us today?

Can you understand why the Mass is arranged the way it is? What part of it has a special appeal for you?

How, in your opinion, could one get more out of the Mass?

PERSONAL REFLECTION

Each Mass is a renewal of my covenant with God. He pledges himself to give me eternal and unimaginable happiness, if I will only be faithful this little while here on earth. I should take every occasion I can to renew my covenant with him, to open myself in sincere acceptance of his love. The Mass is the great way in which I can do this.

15

The Eucharist in Christ's Church Today

How and why has the Mass developed and changed? How are Christians drawing closer in their worship? How can one get more out of the Mass? Or take a special role in it? Why are the Sundays and feasts arranged the way they are?

HOW THE MASS DEVELOPED

The Mass at first was a simple service that took place after a meal, as at the last supper. The meal was the "agape" and the eucharistic service was called the "breaking of the bread" or the "Lord's supper." In Jerusalem the first Christians continued to attend the temple together, but then "breaking bread in their homes, they partook of food with glad and generous hearts" (Acts 2, 46). We read of Paul's visit to Troas: "On the first day of the week, when we were gathered together to break bread, Paul talked with them . . . " (Acts 20, 7ff.).

Soon, however, abuses crept in, and gradually the eucharistic service was separated from the agape-meal: Read 1 Corinthians 11, 17-22. When the eucharistic meal became a separate service and gradually took on a regular form, it was begun by the reading of the Word of God and prayers. The Christians at first had continued taking part in the Jewish service of prayer and instruction in the temple or synagogue; now this became a part of their own service in their homes. We saw how the gospels came from the narratives, prayers, and hymns used at worship, and the epistles were written to be read at the assembly's worship.

An early Christian writer has left us the first full description of a Christian Mass celebration, about the year 150 at Rome:

> And on that day which is called after the sun, all who are in the towns and in the country gather together for a communal celebration. And then the memoirs of the apostles or the writings of the prophets are read, as long as time permits. After the reader has finished his task, the one presiding gives an address, urgently admonishing his hearers to practice these beautiful teachings in their lives. Then all stand up together and recite prayers. After the end of the prayers . . . the bread and wine mixed with water are brought, and the president offers up prayers and thanksgivings, as much as in him lies. The people chime in with an Amen. Then takes place the distribution, to all attending, of the things over which the thanksgiving has been spoken, and the deacons bring a portion to the absent. [He had previously remarked, "This food itself is known amongst us as the eucharist. No one may partake of it unless he is convinced of the truth of our teachings and is cleansed in the bath of baptism. . . . "] Besides, those who are well-to-do give whatever they will. What is gathered is deposited with the one presiding, who therewith helps orphans and widows . . . (Justin Martyr, *First Apology*, c. 67).

As time passed, other prayers were added, but the pattern of worship was this: God's Word, the eucharistic offering of thanks, and the eucharistic meal. The key actions were central, done in comparative simplicity; everyone stood closely about and had an active part in the ceremonies, which were in the people's language. By the third century, the simple meal aspect had disappeared, and the pattern became reading of the Word, the eucharistic prayer of thanksgiving, and communion.

Gradually, after the persecutions ended, the Mass became more complicated, acquired many forms and elaborate rites, and became distant from the people. The Arian heresy, which denied the divinity of Christ, became widespread; to stress Christ's divine presence, altars gradually were moved away from the people, the priest turned his back on the people and alone said the eucharistic prayers, communion railings went up to separate the sanctuary from the people, at which they knelt to receive the consecrated bread from the priest who alone could touch it, and prayers expressing our unworthiness became common in the Mass. By the early Middle Ages, many court ceremonies had become incorporated into Christian worship in an attempt to make it more solemn: genuflections, bowing, kissing, incensing, and so on. Also, to weld together the various conquered tribes, the Franks had imposed on them the Latin language and liturgy, which was less and less understood by the people.

By the high Middle Ages the Mass had become largely separated from the people and was the business almost exclusively of the clergy, who often did little more than say "their" Mass, which was felt to have an almost automatic value. The great cathedrals of Europe reflect the devotion of the people but also their growing distance from the mysteries of worship. Communion became less and less frequent and was taken increasingly under only one form. The sacrifice aspect of the Mass was overstressed. Private devotional practices multiplied, especially those to the saints, and people began to turn to superstition; relics were sold and stolen. The clergy in many places became smug and corrupt in their status. Then the inevitable happened—the Reformation took place. Luther's first demands included the reform of the clergy and Mass in the vernacular.

The Church reacted at the reform Council of Trent by curbing the abuses that had crept into its worship as well as other aspects of its life. However, in the Church's view the reformers had gone too far in setting aside the separate, hierarchical priesthood and the sacrificial aspect of the Mass. Its Counter-Reformation, though, swung the pendulum too far—it "froze" the ceremonies of the Mass, the use of Latin, the stylized role of the priest, and the silent and nonscriptural participation (or nonparticipation) of the people.

With the beginning of the twentieth century, however, a healthy counteraction began: Under Pope Pius X the Church began gradually moving toward restoring the Mass to its early, ideal form. But the progress was sporadic and only among a comparative few. Few had any idea of the great reform that would shortly take place.

The 1963 Constitution on the Sacred Liturgy of Vatican Council II was the culmination of the work of those who were trying to make our worship more meaningful. It has been called by many, non-

Catholics as well as Catholics, the most revolutionary and far-reaching document of its kind in the Church's history. Some of its main points are the following:

> People should be able to easily understand the rites and take part in them fully, actively, and "as befits a community." The rites should have a "noble simplicity," and be short, clear, unencumbered by useless repetitions, and normally should not require much explanation. The people should take part by means of acclamations, responses, and songs, as well as by actions.

> There is to be more reading from holy Scripture, and it is to be more varied and suitable—and the ministry of preaching is to be fulfilled with exactitude and fidelity. The use of the mother tongue may be "of great advantage," and, avoiding a "rigid uniformity," elements from the traditions and cultures of individual peoples might be made part of divine worship.

The liturgical reforms of the Council, seen thirty-plus years later, have had an immense effect in making the Mass-mystery meaningful to almost all. But it will always be a challenge to meet the diverse needs of different congregations and cultural backgrounds. There are those for whom the use of the vernacular, for instance, lessened their sense of mystery, or for whom participating "as befits a community" will never come easily—but the great majority of Catholics have welcomed the reforms and grown spiritually in countless ways because of them.

> The liturgical authorities in Rome have the final decision about when and what major changes should take place so as to keep a certain uniformity throughout the worldwide, changing Church. National bishops' conferences work to integrate local customs into the Mass, aided by "input" from the laity. Today, the new norms, used with sensitive imagination, allow the Mass to be a genuinely God-filled experience, suitable to our modern needs.

The ceremonies and language of the Mass may differ from place to place, according to the Church's different "rites" or liturgies. There are eight different rites, most as ancient or more so than the Latin, especially among the churches deriving from the Middle East. But the essential actions of the Mass are the same throughout the worldwide Church. A Latin Rite Catholic would derive a good deal of profit from taking part in an Eastern Rite Mass.

The Mass throughout most of the Western Church is in the Latin Rite, but the Latin language has been replaced by the vernacular so all can better take part. Latin was retained for centuries as a reminder of the antiquity and universal sameness of the Mass; today, however, it is seen that universal unity does not depend on uniformity of language and ceremonies. For those who wish, Latin masses are still available.

The vestments worn by the priest at Mass remind us of the antiquity of the Mass, and also that Christ is present working through the priest. In a sense the vestments "hide" the priest, bringing home to us that he stands at the altar as Christ's instrument. They came originally from the ordinary clothes worn in the early centuries when the Mass began. There is a long white garment called the "alb" (from *albus*, Latin for "white"), which both men and women wore at home. Over this goes the "chasuble" ("little house" in Latin), which was worn in public. Finally, since the early Middle Ages the priest has worn a "stole," a long piece of cloth draped around his neck, when administering the sacraments.

The setting, solemnity, and music of the Mass can vary greatly. In a "sung Mass," usually celebrated on special occasions, the priest-celebrant may be assisted by a deacon or acolyte. Incense is often used—a symbol of our prayers rising, pleasing to God, and of the respect due things or people considered holy. Parts of the Mass may be sung or chanted by the priest, with a choir and/or congregation responding. The singing, chanting, and special prayers can vary a good deal from place to place.

Mass is sometimes "concelebrated," that is, a group of priests may take part with the presiding celebrant, sharing in the prayers and readings and all exercising their power to consecrate. This brings out strikingly the unity of the priesthood, particularly in its great role of celebrating the eucharist.

Today there are often different types of Masses for different groups, with the prayers and readings adapted to the particular group—such as for school children, teenagers, college students, office workers, those in the inner city, suburbanites, professional people, and so on—besides being adapted to the occasion on which the Mass is celebrated.

In recent years there have been many developments in the use of music at Mass, as well as liturgical dance, as ways of praying. Popular folk music has been deeply stirring, especially for the young. More and more good religious music is available today, and most parishes have a blend of various kinds of music—including Latin hymns and chants that have a perennial meaning for most Catholics. Though still novel in most places, liturgical dance—seen as far back as David dancing before the Ark of the Covenant—is becoming more widely used and appreciated.

> *The ceremonial and musical setting of the Mass has also developed for different national and racial groups within the Church.* Hispanics, African-Americans, Native Americans, and so on have developed liturgies that express what is best out of their cultural backgrounds.
>
> *A close sense of participation and oneness is often best attained when Mass is celebrated among smaller groups,* whether in church, in someone's home, on retreat and perhaps camping weekends, for parish groups, for people with a common ministry, and so on. There can be, for instance, a discussion of the homily with all adding their insights, as well as meaningful music, symbolic little ceremonies, and so on.

THE MASS AND CHRISTIAN UNITY

Since the worship of God is the greatest thing we can do on this earth, the way we worship is vitally important. When giving someone a present, we try to find out what will please that person, how we can best express our love by our gift. God in his love helps our worship by showing us how best to do it. As he once guided the Israelites in their worship (cf. Exodus, Leviticus), so now he guides our worship through his Church. Through Christ he gave us the best way we could possibly worship him, the eucharistic service, which developed in the Church as the Mass. This is why many Christians, including Catholics, have been particular about worshiping with other church groups.

However, worship among separated Christians can express the unity we have and also powerfully ask God to unite us further. The Vatican Council here opened new doors: "In certain special circumstances, such as in prayer services for unity and during ecumenical gatherings, it is allowable, indeed desirable that Catholics should join in prayer with their separated brethren" (*Decree on Ecumenism,* no. 8). Nothing is as effective as praying together to make us experience the unity we have and to make us yearn for further unity.

Sharing in communion between Catholics and other Christians is normally not allowed, since such sharing has always been considered the fullest expression of Christian unity—and we are as yet disunited on some important teachings. However, there may be circumstances in which the grace to be gained by such a practice would outweigh any wrong impression of a premature unity, and it might be appropriate—the eucharist could be a means of unity as well as a sign of it.

This is not "open communion," in which any baptized Christian would be invited to communion any time in the Catholic Church; this is not permitted, for the reasons given above. Nor is this "intercommunion," in which mutual eucharistic sharing takes place between Catholics and other Churches that have preserved "the substance" of the eucharist.

Sharing in communion is allowed on particular occasions when individual non-Catholic Christians freely and spontaneously "request" it in the Catholic Church. The non-Catholic Christian might experience a serious spiritual need for communion, have the same fundamental belief in the eucharist as Catholics, lead a genuinely Christian life, and not be forbidden by his or her own Church from taking part. Obvious occasions on which this might happen are an interfaith marriage, an anniversary, a first solemn communion, and so on. Also, the local bishop may issue guidelines for his priests regarding sharing in the eucharist in situations such as this.

Often this central, symbolic sacredness of the eucharist and the rules surrounding it are difficult for non-Catholic Christians of good will to understand—and for many Catholic Christians as well. The restrictions should be seen not as a denigration of the status of other Christians but (as with Orthodox Christians) as a way of affirming our particular expression of rootedness in Christ's continual Presence in the midst of a swiftly changing world. Being unable to communicate together should make Christians work all the harder for ecumenical understanding and cooperation, to bring about the day when they can do so.

In the Catholic view the full sacramental sign of unity and grace comes about only through the instrumentality of a priest at Mass. Yet when the eucharist is celebrated in another Church, there is present in some way the reality of the eucharistic mystery; despite the possible lack of valid priestly orders that express the unity of the Church, there is yet some real presence of Christ in these "other eucharists." A devout non-Catholic receiving the eucharist in his or her church might have more of the reality of the eucharist than a lukewarm Catholic (*Decree on Ecumenism*, no. 22).

The official dialogues between Roman Catholic and Anglican theologians, and also between Catholic and Lutheran theologians, have produced statements saying, in effect, that their churches are in substantial agreement in their teaching on the eucharist and recommending that steps be taken by Church leaders toward intercommunion.

Christians who truly desire to be united with Christ and their fellow Christians by communion, and who have sorrow for their sins and love in their hearts, are really united in love with Christ and the rest of the Church when they take part in communion in their own particular church. Perhaps, then, one great thing that all Christians can do to bring about unity among themselves is to take part in communion in their own churches whenever they can.

Many today, particularly those who are younger, feel that if they can live and work together as Christians, they should also, at least on occasion, worship and take part in communion together—and they simply take part in communion together when an occasion seems to warrant it. Some note the near-total agreement regarding the eucharist arrived at by their churches' theologians. For others, the theological issues that so divided their elders seem to be of no great importance, while the need to express their Christian unity and love in worship seems to be a movement of the Spirit.

Christians today have been drawing closer and closer in their forms of worship. Vatican Council II stressed things dear to non-Catholic Christians: Christ's presence among the people at worship, their full participation, the Word of God read and preached upon, an openness to spontaneity and change in worship, and so on. Protestant Christians, on the other hand, are stressing more and more things that Catholics consider vital, particularly the inclusion of the eucharistic prayer and communion as a regular part of the liturgy and belief in the presence in some way of Christ's unique sacrifice in the eucharistic act.

CHRIST AMONG US AT MASS

When Christ becomes present among us in the eucharist, it is not as if he were coming among his followers for the first time. Christ is already present in the hearts of his people by faith, grace, and love, when they come together to take part in the Mass.

At Mass Christ is among us in several ways. He is in the signs of the eucharist prolonging his sacrifice and uniting us with himself in his passage to the Father; this great action, we have seen, is what the Mass basically is. But Christ is also present in the priest who represents him and who leads the people in worship. He is present speaking to us and opening our hearts through the Scripture readings and homily. And he is present in the communion meal by which he comes to us as food.

Christ is present also in the Christian community as it worships. He is in the midst of his brothers and sisters, the Christian people, worshiping the Father in and through them. He is in each and all, inspiring their love of one another and of the whole human family. "Where two or three are gathered together in my name, there am I in the midst of them" (Matthew 18, 20; cf. *Constitution on the Sacred Liturgy,* no. 7).

The presence of Christ in these various ways should make us realize why the Mass is so important. Christ loves us so much that he uses all these ways to communicate himself to us, to become united with us, to strengthen us, and to give us his love. "Christ is present from the first word to the last, from one wall of the church to the other," says one theologian.

Christ is with us at Mass in all these ways above all to unite us, the Christian community, as one body. He unites us to his sacrifice, presides through the priest, speaks to us in the Scriptures, comes to us as food—all in order that we might be truly united in love, that we might become one body with him and with one another. It is at Mass above all that we are united. It is at Mass that we best show our unity. And it is at Mass that we become the presence of Christ in the world.

At Mass we are continually becoming a Church. We have seen that the Church is not a static "thing," but the growing, developing way we are united to Christ and one another. It is basically a love relationship, and like any such relationship it must express itself, continually growing and developing. The Mass is the great way the Church grows. Here the Church is continually renewed, cemented, strengthened. Here it worships, grows in love, and receives God's love and teaching.

Were Mass no longer celebrated, the Church would cease to exist. A good gauge of the spiritual health of the Church is the participation of the people in the Mass. Historically, those who have attacked the Church have almost always begun by prohibiting the Mass. "It's the Mass that matters" is an old adage that sums up its place in the Church.

THE CHRISTIAN PEOPLE AT MASS

In the liturgy we pray and sing together because, though many, we are one—and we want to become one. The liturgy should bring about a great awareness of one another—that we need one another and are helped by one another, in worship as in life. We are joined together as we offer our common gift and receive God's gift to us. We join our incompleteness to that of others, and together, as a worshiping family, we most perfectly express our stumbling attempts at union with divinity.

The Mass, then, is not only the best sign of our unity—it also is the great cause of our unity, particularly when we partake together of our great family meal, the "Lord's Supper" (1 Corinthians 10, 17). During the week we are scattered in our homes, factories, schools, and offices. At Mass we come together for the great banquet that makes us one. The more closely we take part in it the more we will appreciate and love our fellow Christians. Christ is here among us in the closest possible way, joining us with himself and one another.

The Mass is our great weekly Christian social event, the family worship of God's people gathered together with Christ. The priest who leads the people never prays in his own name or for himself alone, and the congregation's prayers are also for one another: "The Lord be with you. . . . Let us pray. . . . Let us give thanks to God. . . . " The frequent "Amen" of the whole congregation perfectly expresses their unity in love and offering.

Particularly at Mass God's new chosen people use the power of their "royal priesthood." By their baptism, and again by confirmation, they share in the priesthood of the laity, able to offer perfect worship to

God for themselves and others and to bring his graces to the world. They do not claim to be holier than others, but they know Christ is in their midst, using them in a special way, poor instruments though they may be, to spread his love to others. What was said of the Israelites in the Old Testament is now said in the fullest sense of the Christians of the New Testament: **Read 1 Peter 2, 4–10.**

The Mass is meant to bring out the true unity in catholicity of the Church. All races, classes, and social strata should be one in this worship. When we gather together for Mass we should heed St. James's reminder to the first Christians not to look down on those who have less: **Read James 2, 1–4.**

"The eucharist commits us to the poor," says the *Catechism* (1397), and it goes on: "To receive in truth the Body and Blood of Christ given up for us, we must recognize Christ in the poorest, his brethren." It quotes St. John Chrysostom: "You dishonor this table when you do not judge worthy of sharing your food someone judged worthy to take part in this [eucharistic meal]."

Since the Mass is a family worshiping and eating together, each member has a part to play. Christ is among us, invisibly present as our real head and leader. The bishop is his visible representative who guides our worship so that it is truly a part of the liturgy of the whole Church. The ordained priest is Christ's representative who leads the people at this particular Mass; through his words Christ becomes present in the eucharist, and then he leads us all in offering Christ and ourselves to the Father.

The people's part is to respond to God's Word, to unite themselves to the offering of Christ, and to join in the banquet of holy communion. They express their part by praying and singing together, by contributing in some way to the offering, by responding to the great prayers of offering, and above all by taking part together in the eucharist.

Some of the people, called to special ministries, have special roles at Mass: Proclaiming the Scripture readings (except the gospel) and commenting on their setting; assisting the priest as acolytes (girls are now allowed to act as these); organizing and directing the music; acting as lay ministers of the eucharist by helping to distribute communion at Mass, as well as bringing it to the sick in their homes, hospitals, and so on, and conducting communion services when no priest is available; giving catechetical instruction to children (or adults undergoing Christian initiation) in the Word that is the Bible. These people are commissioned by the bishop for their ministries.

Other people also minister in ways for which they are gifted, some as choir members, some preparing banners or flowers or otherwise making the church a beautiful, reverent place in which to worship, some welcoming people at Mass, some baby-sitting, and in many other ways.

> *It takes time to appreciate the liturgy fully, to feel at ease in community worship, and to participate actively.* The Mass prayers will be led by priests at varying speeds; the Mass becomes so much a part of a priest that it reflects his temperament and background. Some congregations respond with more uniformity and seeming devotion than others. Distractions occur constantly. To adjust to the great reality behind all this takes time and patience.

> *We should remember, too,* that while the Mass is primarily a social and sharing event, there are times when we want to—and should—pray in our own way during it, expressing our most personal feelings toward God, our deep longings, particular needs, our secret fears and joys—or just being quiet in his presence. There are periods of silence in the Mass to allow this, and it is important that they be respected.

Catholics are expected to take part in Mass each Sunday and also on the holydays throughout the year. Only a Catholic with a poor understanding of the meaning of the Mass would take these responsibilities lightly, especially that of Sunday Mass. Of course, important work, sickness in the family, and such events excuse one from taking part—though one could join in the Mass prayers at home, or meditatively read the Scripture readings for that Sunday, or take part on another day. Also, the Sunday or holyday Mass may be anticipated on the previous evening to make it more available for those taking part.

The holydays in the United States are six: Christmas (Dec. 25), the feast of Mary Mother of God (Jan. 1), the Ascension of the Lord (the seventh Sunday after Easter), the Assumption of Mary (Aug. 15), All Saints (Nov. 1), and the Immaculate Conception of Mary (Dec. 8).

> *We can offer our Mass for anyone, living or dead, or for any good intention. Naturally we derive from the Mass what we bring to it.* The more faith and

love in our worship, the more it will unite us with God and help others. The prayers of the liturgy are not just external ceremonies but actions into which we must enter with our minds and hearts.

The priest, too, offers Mass for a particular intention, and people may make an offering, not to pay for the Mass, but to help support the priest and his good works. Every Mass, however, benefits the whole Church and each member. In the early Church the people brought the things necessary for the Mass-meal, for the support of the priest, the poor, and so on, but today the collection fulfills this function.

When no priest is available to celebrate Mass, a eucharistic minister may conduct a communion service: after introductory prayers he or she reads the day's Scripture and gives a commentary on it; then after a preparatory prayer and/or the Lord's Prayer, gives communion.

With the increasingly critical shortage of priests today, such services are becoming more common. But they obviously are not meant to be a lasting substitute for the Mass.

The eucharist and the Mass, then, are the center of the Catholic faith. The other sacraments converge on this. Baptism and confirmation lead up to it and are ideally given at a Mass so that the whole community can take part; penance and the anointing of the sick prepare one for it, and the anointing is ideally done at Mass, so that the whole congregation can join in praying for their ill members; holy orders are given at Mass; and a Catholic couple usually take part in a nuptial Mass when they are united in marriage. After death one's body is brought to the church for a Mass of Christian Burial.

So, then, nothing else has meaning or power except in relation to the eucharist and the Mass. This was brought out at Vatican Council II when each day's session began with a Mass in which all the assembled bishops took part.

Each day Mass is celebrated, normally, in every Catholic parish. It can be a source of daily graces to that whole neighborhood, not in some magical way, but as a special presence of Christ among us radiating his love to all who take part and to all in the vicinity who (believers or not) are in need of his love and help. The Mass, too, can be the center of a priest's day, from which he regularly draws strength for his other activities. Many Catholics take part in Mass on weekdays, and some come daily to draw help from it for their daily lives.

RELIVING CHRIST'S LIFE THROUGH THE LITURGICAL YEAR

Since Christ's life and sacrifice are such a tremendous, infinite reality, we cannot grasp them all at once. It takes time to grasp and be changed by them. The Church in the liturgy presents Christ's life and sacrifice in parts, so that we can live them out event by event.

The liturgical year is the way we relive each of the great events of Christ's life. It is the way the Church each year teaches us these events by living them again, through a cycle of seasons and feasts. It begins with the First Sunday of Advent (the fourth Sunday before Christmas) and ends with the feast of Christ the King.

Each Mass has an ordinary or unchanging part as well as a proper or changing part that varies according to the liturgical year. Some of the proper or changing prayers may be said or chanted together by the people: the entrance antiphon, the gradual (or tract or alleluia), the offertory antiphon, and the communion antiphon. The lay lector reads the Old Testament excerpt and the epistle for that day, and the priest or deacon reads the gospel. The priest reads the collect, the prayer over the gifts, and the prayer after communion.

Through the events of the liturgical year we actually relive, with Christ, the events of his life, death, and resurrection. People attend a movie or a play or watch a TV presentation that reenacts the events in the life of a great person. During the liturgical year we reenact the events of Christ's life—but unlike a person portrayed in a movie, Christ is actually present in each Mass, and we not only watch, we actually take part in the great events of his life. He is present in a special way at each feast, communicating something special to us each time.

Throughout the liturgical year the Church brings before us God's Word, the Bible. A three-year cycle of Sunday Scripture readings (a two-year cycle on weekdays) brings before us all the significant parts of the Bible, and the most significant for our salvation recur each year.

The liturgical year is the cycle of events called the Proper of the Seasons: the two central feasts, and the two seasons built around them, are Christmas and Easter. The Scripture readings, prayers, and music are "proper" to the season. Each feast has a season of preparation, the central feast itself with its minor feasts, and a continuation or prolongation of the spirit of the feast:

1. THE CHRISTMAS SEASON—Theme: The Coming of Jesus Christ, the Incarnation

Preparation during Advent: The Church year begins in late November or early December with these four Sundays before Christmas (purple vestments). Through prayer, reflection, and self-discipline we prepare ourselves for the coming of Christ—the Scripture readings are mainly from the prophets who foresaw the Messiah. We also look forward to his second coming—the Scripture continues this theme from November.

Celebration—Christmas, December 25: We rejoice that God has come among us and that we have been born with him into the new, eternal life of grace (white or gold vestments).

The lesser feasts that follow are: *Holy Family Sunday* (between Christmas and January 1); the *Octave* (a celebration eight days after) of Christmas and the Feast of *Mary, Mother of God* on January 1—also a day to pray for world peace—and a holyday for U.S. Catholics; the *Epiphany* on January 6 (or on the Sunday between January 2 and 8) on which we celebrate the call of the Gentiles to follow Christ.

Continuation—Sundays in Ordinary Time, leading up to Lent (green vestments)—We continue celebrating the coming of Jesus Christ, with the *Baptism of the Lord* (the Sunday after January 6) and the beginning of his ministry among us with his first miracle at Cana.

Note that during the Sundays of Ordinary Time we read through one of the four gospels, roughly in sequence, using the three-year cycle to bring before us the words and actions of Jesus' life and ministry: Cycle A is Matthew, Cycle B is Mark (with some of John), and Cycle C is Luke (C is read in years divisible by three, such as 1998): John's gospel is mostly reserved for the seasons of Lent and Easter.

2. THE EASTER SEASON—Theme: Christ's Death and New Life—Our Salvation

Preparation during Lent, the forty days (excluding Sundays) from Ash Wednesday until Easter (purple vestments). Through this time of special prayer, fasting, and voluntary self-discipline, we do penance for our sins, trying to "die" to selfishness, greed, and self-indulgence—and we prepare to "rise" to a new commitment of our life to Christ at Easter with those being baptized. Forty signifies a sufficiently long period of time—so Christ was tempted in the wilderness for forty days, as Israel had wandered in the desert for forty years. The gospel readings focus on repentance and rebirth. For the Elect, the third, fourth, and fifth Sundays are from Cycle A, and they center on baptismal symbolism from John's gospel—something the whole community seeking rebirth and recommitment can also enter into.

The last Sunday of Lent is *Passion Sunday (Palm Sunday),* and we enter Holy Week, the most sacred time of the year. During Holy Week we reenact in the liturgy the sufferings and death of Christ, taking part in them as much as possible, so that we can bear our sufferings and put aside our sins, which are the cause of suffering.

The Easter Triduum—Holy Thursday, Good Friday, and Holy Saturday eve—celebrates the great events of our salvation, with special services each day. It is the climax of the Church year and of human history. These three days are Christ's Pasch, his passing over from death to new life for himself and us.

Note that Easter is the first Sunday after the first full moon of the spring equinox (March 21–22). Its date determines the number of Ordinary Time Sundays before Lent begins and also the end of the Easter season (and thus the number of Ordinary Time Sundays after Easter). The date is reckoned by the Jewish lunar calendar rather than the later Roman solar calendar, the basis of our calendars today.

The Celebration of the Triumphal Resurrection of Jesus Christ at Easter is the greatest feast of the Church and the basis of our faith; it begins with the Easter Vigil service on Holy Saturday night and climaxes with the first Mass of Easter. We have seen that it is the time for converts to be baptized and/or received into the Church.

The two feasts following upon Easter are the *Ascension of Christ,* celebrated in the United States on the seventh Sunday after Easter, and *Pentecost,* fifty days after Easter (white or gold vestments, except for the red of Pentecost). On Pentecost, considered the third great feast of the Church year, we conclude the celebration of Easter with the coming of the Holy Spirit, the "birthday of the Church," the sending forth of the community that would spread Christ's teaching and love through the ages. The Sunday after Pentecost is Trinity Sunday, celebrating the mystery that is our uniquely Christian belief about God. The next Sunday (in the United States) is the feast of *the Body and Blood of Christ,* celebrating his eucharistic Presence.

Continuation of Ordinary Time, leading up to Advent: Now we return to the weekly cycle of gospel readings begun before Lent. This is twenty-four to twenty-eight weeks, through summer and fall (green vestments). During these months we follow the words and actions of Christ, seeking to grow in faith and love. As this season draws to an end in November, the readings concern the consummation of history and the coming of Christ's kingdom in glory. The season, and the liturgical year, concludes with the Sunday celebrating the feast of *Christ the King* as the Lord of creation. Then we begin over again with the Advent Season, our preparation for Christmas.

There is also the Proper of the Saints, the liturgical cycle of lesser importance. In using this we derive inspiration, creativity, and strength from the example of the saints, the outstanding personages of the Church. Often, the date is the day of the saint's death, his or her "birthday" into eternal life. The Proper of the Mass changes on that day, according to the particular saint; a "Common" is a Proper for a particular type of saint and may be used for a number of similar saints. By bringing before our minds these different saints, the Church wants to teach us that we can imitate Christ's suffering and glorification as they did.

There are ranks of feasts in the Church's liturgy, the most important taking precedence. Sometimes a lesser feast is commemorated by adding some of its prayers to the Proper used that day. Any missal gives the rank of feasts and includes a calendar telling what Proper is to be used on a particular day.

The Liturgy of the Hours (or the Divine Office) is the daily prayer of the Church by which we follow Christ's example and exhortation to "pray," "ask," "seek" during each day (cf. Matthew 5, 44; Mark 13, 33; Luke 6, 28; John 14, 13ff). It helps us enter into and prolongs the spirit of the Mass. As Christ prayed regularly through the day (and night), so does his Church. The Office (or Divine Work in Latin) is composed mainly of psalms, other Scripture readings, hymns, prayers, and readings from the Church's tradition. It is arranged according to the liturgical year and divided into various "hours" or periods of prayer. Chanted in choir by monks and other religious, usually contemplatives, as much as possible is read by priests as their daily prayer.

Today a growing number of laypeople are saying part of this as their prayer. It comes in four volumes, but a one-volume version called *Christian Prayer* is available. People find that saying it (or as much as they can) in the morning and evening gives meaning, strength, and tranquillity to their often very difficult workdays.

CHRIST AMONG US IN THE EUCHARIST

Christ's presence among us in the eucharist has been a central teaching of the Christian faith from the beginning. We have seen that through bread and wine Christ becomes present in the eucharistic celebration under this form of food. His presence remains as long as the form or appearance of bread and wine remains. But his presence has a purpose—to gradually, and literally, change us into himself.

Theologians today stress a dynamic or existentialist view of Christ's presence in the eucharist, that he is present with a purpose. He is not just a passive presence in the host, but rather he is present doing something to the Christian communicant, meeting him or her person to person, bringing life and love. And only one who meets Christ in the eucharist with faith and love derives something from this.

There can be degrees of one person's presence to another: one might vaguely notice a person across the street, or pass close to the person, or engage in a deep conversation, and so on—the more one gives of oneself, the greater is the communication of oneself to another in understanding and love. In the eucharist Christ comes to us in the fullest possible expression and communication of his love. The more we try to be aware of him and what he is doing for us, the more we try to give ourselves to him as we meet him in communion, the more intimate will be our union with him, the greater will be the love and grace we will receive, and the more we will be transformed into him by this experience.

Another way of looking at this is to see the eucharistic meal as a sign through which we meet Christ and by which he expresses or "signifies" his love for us. A woman might best express herself and her feelings by playing a violin for us; we would more fully "meet" her by listening to her play than by merely having her present. As the violin is an extension of the violinist, so the consecrated bread and wine are an extension of Christ through which we meet him most fully and are changed by him. Sharing in food expresses refreshment, strength, and a sharing in love—so Christ expresses these things to us, in an infinitely greater way, through the eucharistic food. Through this food Christ expresses himself and his love for us in the most intimate way possible. The more we try to express our love as we take part in communion, the greater our love will grow through it.

We need not take part in the sacrament of reconciliation, or confession, before taking part in holy communion—unless we are in a situation of being alienated from God and the community by serious sinfulness. To take part in communion before confessing one's alienated state of serious sin, and being reconciled, would be an act of fundamental hypocrisy: we would be publicly proclaiming our unity with the rest of the Church by taking part in this sacrament of unity while all the time realizing that we are cut off from them by our unrepentant sinfulness.

But the great majority of Catholics would not be in a state of unrepentant sinfulness, and therefore they should not deprive themselves of Christ's strength and love in the eucharist. It is food for sinners who have need of it, and not just for the perfect. We will see that the purpose of the sacrament of reconciliation (penance or "confession") is particularly to restore us to loving union with the "whole Christ," with Jesus and with our fellow humans.

It might happen that a person who is conscious of being in a state of serious alienation would find it necessary to take part in communion—it might, for instance, be seriously embarrassing or hurtful to another not to—and one would not have the opportunity for confession. In this case sorrow should be expressed out of whatever love one can muster, and then there should be no hesitation about taking part. (One should, of course, intend to confess when reasonably possible.) Jesus' desire would surely be for us to come to him and to share in this healing sacrament.

Before "first communion" (or First Solemn Communion) the sacrament of penance should be available to a child, but, as with adults, there is no obligation for children to confess unless they are in serious sin—and most question the ability of a young child to be in a situation of serious sin. Yet there can be value for a child to be aware of his or her faults in a setting not of guilt and punishment but of accepting love and forgiveness. Thus young children are normally introduced to this sacrament through communal penitential rites, and then gradually accustomed to individual confession, as we shall see in chapter 19.

We are asked to fast before taking part in holy communion, to help us prepare for it. We normally do not eat or drink for one hour before communion (water or medicine, however, may be taken at any time). Just as one would not spoil one's appetite by eating before a special meal, so we sharpen our spiritual appetite for Christ by this bit of self-discipline.

Catholics of the Latin Rite sometimes take part in communion under the appearance of bread only. This became customary in the late Middle Ages when the meal aspect of the Mass was being largely overlooked. Today it may be more feasible to take part under one form, especially where large city congregations are involved; the whole living Christ is present either under the appearance of bread or that of wine, so it is only necessary to take part under one form. Also, one might take part in communion under the appearance of wine alone, for a serious reason (such as an illness).

However, the norm for Latin Rite Catholics today is to take part in communion under both the form of bread and the form of wine. Vatican Council II revived this because it brings out more fully our sharing in the eucharistic meal as Christ instituted it. The Eastern Rites of Catholicism have always communicated under both forms. Yet, as the Council says, it has no wish to impose a "rigid uniformity," and some people for personal reasons prefer communicating under only one form.

The custom has grown today of taking communion in one's hand. This is the way communion was received throughout most of the Church's history. For many this practice is a visible, reverent expression of their desire to feed themselves, as spiritually adult Christians, on the body of Christ. Others today wish to have the host of bread placed on their tongue by the priest;

their lifelong expression of reverent love in this way is a beautiful thing that should claim our respect.

A Catholic's "Easter duty" means that he or she must take part in communion once a year, normally during the Easter season, that is, from the First Sunday of Lent until Pentecost Sunday. Otherwise, while still a Catholic, one would not be considered practicing because one has refused to take part in the greatest thing the Church offers—the help toward which all the other helps of one's religion are directed. Christ said, "Truly, truly, I say to you, unless you eat the flesh of the Son of Man and drink his blood, you have no life in you . . . " (John 6, 53).

A good Catholic should take part in communion at least weekly—normally at Sunday Mass, our great Christian family meal. Unfortunately some, from faulty training or timidity, hold back from the eucharist when they could easily take part. They realize they are unworthy, but they should remember what Christ said: "Those who are well have no need of a physician, but those who are sick" (Luke 5, 3). Not to take part in communion is to expect God to accept our gift while refusing his gift.

What Christ does for us in holy communion is shown by this sacrament's sign: he comes to us in the form of a meal, of food. As we must eat to maintain life, to grow, and to remain strong, so this food is the great means of growing in the life of grace. A preview of this food was the manna by which God kept the Israelites alive in the desert; Christ refers to this and then tells us that he himself will be the food that sustains the infinitely greater and eternal life of grace: **Read Exodus 16, 4-21.**

Read John 6, 47-59. Christ in the eucharist, then, is our "living bread," our greatest way of growing in God's grace-presence, his life within us. As a good meal can have an immediate effect of contentment and satisfaction, so we may sometimes experience a certain spiritual peace and strength after taking part in communion. As food builds energy and strength for the future, so Christ here strengthens us for further temptations. As we are sometimes hungrier, perhaps from hard work, than at other times, so we sometimes need more spiritual strength and should receive Christ more often.

Food must be taken frequently; so our spiritual growth requires frequent reception of the eucharist. Paradoxically, this food satisfies but also increases our hunger: the more we receive Christ, the more we inevitably hunger for God.

Our eucharistic meal is above all our greatest way of being united to one another in the Church. The more we eat together with our family and friends, the more we get to know and understand one another, the stronger our love should grow. So, too, with this meal. Its greatest effect is the unity of all of us, Christ's body, his Church.

By frequently taking part in the eucharist we are gradually transformed into Christ. We share the very life and personality of the risen Christ. We gradually shed our weaknesses and assume something of his own strength. His outlook, his reactions bit by bit become ours. Because we have here a real contact with Christ's risen body, this sacrament is the most effective way of keeping our bodily passions under control; many Christians can testify that it is for them the best way of remedying abuses of sex, drinking, anger, and so on.

The more of ourselves we put into celebrating the Mass and partaking of the eucharist, the more we will derive from it. Christ is present in the priest and in the people, as we read and listen, preach and sing, and as we offer the great eucharistic prayer of thanks. The better we try to do these things, the more consciously we join ourselves to him, the more we will receive from our union with him in holy communion. The eucharist can be the most intimate, personal, and meaningful union with Christ possible—if we prepare for it and generously give ourselves to him. He gives us himself totally. The rest is up to us.

The eucharist is the greatest way to grow in the Christian life. Each time we take part in the eucharist we repledge ourselves to our baptismal commitment to Christ. The eucharist is the greatest way we grow in faith, hope, and love, the greatest source of light and strength for our prayer, and the surest way to grow in appreciation of the world around us.

Through the eucharist we are already beginning the life of heaven. We are on our way to the final resurrection and our eternal glorification with the Father. Heaven is often referred to in Scripture as a banquet, a wedding feast. Now, through this food that is Christ, we are already beginning to take part in it.

Christ's presence in the eucharist in the tabernacle of every Catholic church is a way in which God today dwells among his people

with special closeness. This is why our churches are open daily, why people often drop in for a "visit" to share their joys and sorrows with Christ or just to talk things over. We saw how God was present among the Israelites, invisibly hovering over the Ark of the Covenant in his tabernacle or tent in the desert. Today we have God become human in our midst. "And my tabernacle shall be with them and I will be their God, and they shall be my people" (Ezekiel 37, 27).

Because of this presence of Christ, upon entering their churches Catholics sometimes genuflect (go down on the right knee) or bow their heads as an act of adoration before entering the pew. Also, the candle kept burning day and night near the tabernacle signifies this eucharistic presence of Christ in our midst.

We honor Christ in the holy eucharist in many ways. On Holy Thursday each year we celebrate with special liturgical services the great feast of Christ's institution of the holy eucharist at the last supper. On the Sunday after Trinity Sunday we celebrate the feast of the Body and Blood of Christ.

The "Forty Hours Devotion" is a special service of honor and reparation to Christ in the eucharist, which is held in many Catholic parishes each year; by special Masses, processions, prayers, and preaching we pay him homage. This devotion commemorates the forty hours during which Christ's body was in the tomb before Easter Sunday. During this time, the host is exposed in the monstrance on the altar.

The service of Benediction ("Blessing") consists of putting a large host in a gold monstrance; it is then put on the altar for all to adore, hymns of praise are sung, and the host is incensed; then the priest blesses the people by making the Sign of the Cross over them with the monstrance containing the host.

The vigil lights or votive candles that one sometimes sees in churches are there to "keep watch" with Christ in place of the people who must be elsewhere. They represent our desire to be with him.

DAILY LIVING: ONE BREAD MAKES US ONE BODY (1 CORINTHIANS 10, 17)

On the occasion of the first eucharist Christ said, "By this everyone will know that you are my disciples, if you have love for one another" (John 13, 35). The great thing we should get from the eucharist is a greater love—not only of God but of our neighbor. We prepare best for Mass by attempting to practice some kindness or forgiveness in our daily life—and we best prolong the Mass in our daily life by this same concrete love.

Sincerely and actively taking part in the Mass should make us dynamic, socially minded Christians. If we are sharing in the Mass as we should, we will become aware of how we are joined with God's family throughout the world. Those who cry for social justice, who are discriminated against, the underprivileged of our cities, the poor of all nations, the billions who will never hear of Christ and his love—these needs become ours.

People sometimes remark on Christians who worship on Sunday but live unChristian lives the rest of the week. All too often this is so. Sometimes it is the result of a wrong emphasis in one's religious upbringing, a stressing of external obligations to the neglect of the inner spirit. However, we should remember Christ's warning not to judge, "that you be not judged." Sometimes seemingly immoral people are struggling against tremendous odds of background, deprivation, strong passions—and at least they manage to worship God and reach out for his help. They might be much worse without Mass.

Also, some cheat themselves of much of Christ's help by not taking part in communion when they attend Mass. They realize their unworthiness, but forget Christ's loving mercy and his desire to come and be their strength. Then, too, those who do communicate regularly may show no striking improvement in their lives, but might be undergoing a gradual, almost imperceptible growth in holiness.

The way many people come to desire union with Christ's Church is by taking part in the Mass. The disciples at Emmaus recognized Christ only in the "breaking of the bread"; they then realized why their hearts were burning within them. So, too, many today come to recognize Christ in his Church and want to be an active part of it by regularly taking part in the Mass.

SOME SUGGESTIONS FOR . . .

DISCUSSION

Can you understand how the Mass developed and why changes have been taking place in recent years—changes that most have welcomed but some at times find hard to accept?

Can you appreciate the fact that the Mass and the eucharist are the center of the Catholic faith? Can you understand why this is our great way of having Christ among us?

What part of the liturgical year most appeals to you? What season or part would you like to better appreciate?

What part of the Mass means the most to you? How might one better appreciate the Scripture readings and the homily?

Does Catholic belief in the "Real Presence" of Christ in the eucharist have a significant meaning for you?

How do you think you might deepen your appreciation of the Mass and bring from it more love into your daily life?

FURTHER READING

- *An Important Office of Immense Love: A Handbook for Eucharistic Ministers,* Champlin (Paulist Press, 1981)—A fine relatively brief "must" for all concerned with their special role as ministers of the eucharist.

- *To Dance with God: Family Ritual and Community Celebration,* Nelson (Paulist Press, 1995)—A wonderfully creative book that shows how to use ritual and celebration throughout the church year by combining rites with folk customs.

- *Footprints on the Mountain: Preaching and Teaching the Sunday Readings,* Faley (Paulist Press, 1995)—A complete, practical scriptural guide to the lectionary that includes background on all three Sunday cycles and applications for daily life.

- *St. Joseph Daily Missal* (2 vols., Catholic Book Publishing, 1975)—A complete daily missal of all the Mass prayers and readings for each day; handy for those who prefer a book of "permanence" rather than the seasonal and disposable booklets in the pews of many parishes.

PERSONAL REFLECTION

A **"communion of desire"** can be made by one who cannot take part sacramentally in the eucharistic meal. One does this simply by telling Christ that one believes in his presence in the eucharist, is sorry for one's sins, and desires to be united with him. This can deepen one's intimate union with Christ and one's neighbor.

If I cannot be united with Christ sacramentally, I might resolve to do so by desire at Mass this Sunday.

I might also drop into some Catholic church during the week to make a "visit" with Christ in his eucharistic presence—perhaps just sitting there quietly, thinking, and talking things over with him.

16

The Inner Life of a Christian

How can one obtain faith, and why do some people have more faith than others? What sums up the whole of Christ's teaching? How can one get help from prayer?

We have seen how baptism is the climax of one's conversion and the beginning of a totally new life. God lives his own life within us—we share in his life. To live and grow in this life he gives us new powers.

The virtues are attitudes, powers, relationships that we have as a result of God's presence within us. The virtues help us to look at things differently, to act differently, to relate differently to others—to conform ourselves to Christ's way of thinking and acting. They are sometimes called habits, since they make it easier for us to act as Christians should.

The three fundamental virtues of a Christian are faith, hope, and charity or love. They make it easier for us to give ourselves to God, to trust him, and to love him and our neighbor. Those who are not Christians may also have these powers as a result of God's grace-presence within them, but the Christian should be more aware of them, better able to grow in them, and thereby witness to Christ's life within.

These virtues are meant to grow stronger by our developing them, as any attitude or relationship should between those in love. The virtues are not static "things" but living ways in which we express the grace-life within us. Every time, for instance, that we express our faith by our words and actions, the attitude of faith grows within us and makes easier our next act of faith.

FAITH—ACCEPTANCE AND COMMITMENT

Faith is our saying "yes" to God as he reveals himself to us. It is our response to Christ—he invites us and faith is our acceptance of his invitation. It is something lasting—an attitude, a relationship to God by which we can open ourselves to him.

Faith is the power, the ability to say "I believe" to God in whatever he teaches and to commit ourselves to live by his teachings. When people generally speak of "faith" they mean accepting something on the word of someone else. Daily we make countless acts of this sort of faith: that the food we eat is nourishing and not poisoned, that the car we drive is safe, and so on. We do not test these things for ourselves; we take another's word. By the virtue of faith we take God's word for something we cannot prove for ourselves.

There are several aspects or steps to a person's faith: first, faith is a personal contact with Christ, an intimate "meeting" or "encounter" with him. This usually happens gradually, and one's awareness of it is vague, unrecognized. Perhaps one will never recognize it explicitly. But the experience is real, profound, and bit by bit we are changed by it. Through Christ we gradually come into contact with the other two Persons of the Trinity, the Father and the Holy Spirit.

Then, by faith we believe that what God tells us is true not because we see the evidence for ourselves but simply because we realize that God is telling us. We are certain that it is true, even though we cannot fully understand it. Yet, knowing with a certain degree of clarity that God has spoken is one thing; faith is something further. . . .

Faith is ultimately a commitment, a free choice by which we give ourselves to Christ and begin living a whole new way of life. It is a free and deeply personal decision to abandon ourselves to the living God. We are converted, we turn fully toward him, a changed person.

Faith is perhaps best looked at as a dynamic relationship, a living and continual encounter between God and us, by which we continually grow in knowledge of him and his will for us and commit ourselves to live by this.

We have great need of faith because it is the basis of our life with God. Without it we cannot accept God's teachings, nor can we commit ourselves to live by them. Our minds are obviously limited especially when faced with the mysteries of the infinite God, and our wills are weak.

Faith is like a microscope enabling us to see God's design in the smallest things—though by faith we do not see clearly, but rather "in a mirror dimly, but then [in heaven] face to face" (1 Corinthians 13, 12). It can be compared, also, to a powerful magnet that draws us to God.

There are degrees of this faith-relationship. One person might be able to believe only in God, another might be able to accept the divinity of Jesus Christ, and yet another might perceive the role of the Church—with all sorts of degrees in between.

One might have some faith before being baptized, responding to what she or he can accept of the truth. Upon becoming a Christian—and particularly upon becoming a Catholic—one's faith is broadened, deepened. One is able to accept more of Christ's teachings and to commit oneself to living them more fully. He or she is now a conscious, contributing member of God's people and has the Catholic Christian community's help to grow in faith.

The faith necessary to be a Catholic Christian—the "gift of faith"—is the ability to believe God in whatever he teaches us through his Church and to commit ourselves to live by those teachings. It is our response to what we now see is the fullness of God's revelation to us. We see that this is much more than we have believed before, and we are determined to live by this new knowledge. We realize that we previously held many good things, but now we see that we are getting more. We feel, somehow, that God wants us to embrace this teaching and way of life. We feel that our spiritual "home" is now in the Catholic Church.

The Church is called a "community of faith" because our common faith-commitment is what basically binds us together. It brings us together on Sunday to worship and share in the eucharist, and it is what undergirds our daily attempts to live as Christians. It is what makes us cling together in times of difficulty or persecution, and it is what distinguishes us from any other group of people trying to do good in the world.

If we have faith, we will show it by a life of love, by good works. "In Christ Jesus," Paul says, the only thing that avails is "faith working through love" (Galatians 5, 6). The faith that would not result in works of love would be counterfeit, spurious, a hypocritical delusion on the part of the "believer": **Read James 2, 14–18.**

This faith needs to prove its fruitfulness by penetrating the believer's entire life . . . and by activating him toward justice and love, especially regarding the needy (*Constitution on the Church in the Modern World*, no. 21).

Faith is not an assurance that we are already "saved" regardless of our actions. If our faith is genuine, good works will follow—but one can always fall away from faith. "I chastise my body," says Paul, "and bring it into subjection, lest perhaps after preaching to others I myself should be rejected" (1 Corinthians 9, 27; cf. 1 Corinthians 10, 12; 13, 2; Philippians 2, 12; James 2, 14–26). On the other hand, we cannot "work" ourselves to heaven; God's gift of grace is necessary, initially and continually, that we might freely cooperate with him, that we might have the encounter of faith.

Some "unbelievers" show that they have more faith than some who profess Christianity. Their works of mercy and their exemplary lives prove this. Often they put to shame their Christian neighbors. They live according to their conscience, responding to God's call, but without an explicit awareness of it. However, moral goodness is not always a sign of a sincere faith; it might come at least in part from a self-justifying pride.

On the other hand many believers reveal their weak faith by constantly failing in charity. They may attend Church services and keep most of the Church's "rules," but in times of testing they act primarily out of self-interest or they "follow the crowd." They might, for instance, oppose minorities in their neighborhood, object to needed aid for the underprivileged, or adopt as their major goal in life the achieving of a certain material status.

HOW ONE COMES TO FAITH

The way faith comes to an adult is a mysterious, individual, and awesome process. One must be careful here of preconceptions, of assuming that God would or would not act in a particular way. Both the one who is seeking a possible faith and the one who seeks to lead him or her to faith must hold themselves open to the infinitely free action of the Spirit.

Faith, we know, is a free gift of God that we cannot earn by ourselves. It is God who enables us to have the attitude of faith toward him. Others may help to bring one to faith, but only because God wills to use them for this. "For by grace you have been saved through faith; and this is not your own doing, it is the gift of God—not because of works, lest any-one should boast" (Ephesians 2, 8–9).

But we can and must do our part to obtain faith by humbly pray-ing to know the truth and for the ability to live by it. St. Paul assures us that God "desires everyone to be saved and to come to the knowledge of the truth" (1 Timothy 2, 4). St. Mark's gospel tells the story of the father who brought his boy possessed with convulsions to Jesus and asked, "'If you can do anything, have pity on us and help us.' And Jesus said to him, 'If you can! All things are possible to him who believes.' At once the father of the boy cried out, and said with tears, 'I believe; help my unbelief!'" (Mark 9, 21–23). Jesus then cured the boy, showing us that a sincere plea for faith will not go unanswered.

"Ask and you shall receive," said Christ—and humility is vitally necessary: "Truly, I say to you, whoever does not receive the kingdom of God like a child shall not enter it" (Luke 18, 17). "I thank thee, Father, Lord of heaven and earth, that thou hast hidden these things from the wise and proud and re-vealed them to babes" (Matthew 11, 25).

We must also study, sincerely and open-mindedly seeking the truth. In Christ's words, "Seek and you shall find." We must use our minds and be always open to truth wherever it may be found. Some have preconceived notions, prejudices that blind them.

Christ refused to work miracles in his own town of Nazareth, for the people there had the unshakable idea that he was nothing more than a carpenter. Herod was convinced that Christ was merely a great magician; no matter what miracle Christ worked, Herod would only be confirmed in his opinion; so Christ scornfully "made no answer" to his questioning (Luke 23, 6–9).

To obtain faith we must live up to what we already believe. People often cannot see the truth of the Church's teachings because they are clinging to habits of sin. The blatantly immoral Herod, Pontius Pilate, and the other hypocritical leaders of Christ's time are examples of this. We must live up to what we see of God's will in order to grasp more: "Anyone who desires to do his will will know whether the teaching is from God . . . " (John 7, 17).

We can reject the faith that God is offering us, perhaps because we are proud and unwilling to seek it sincerely, perhaps because we are unwilling to live as we know we should. God always respects our free will and never forces himself upon us.

An adult comes to faith in the Church usually gradually and often painfully. It means facing oneself honestly, critically, perhaps breaking old habits, overcoming the fear that one cannot live one's new life. Like Christ, one struggles to do the Father's will. And like him, one must die—not physically, but interiorly and often as painfully—in order to live the new life of faith.

Our coming to faith might be like that of the Samaritan woman who met Christ, was upset and embarrassed by him, gradually accepted him, and ended by bringing others to him: **Read John 4, 1-30.**

Faith is a risk, a "leap." The evidence is never so clear that one is forced to believe. A natural explanation can always be given for any divine intervention. To believe is to take a risk—it is the risk, really, of giving oneself to another in total love. The truly convinced believer is willing to risk all that he or she is sure of, even life itself, for a new life of love with Christ.

Elements of doubt always remain to plague one, and so there is conflict, a struggle over this choice: On the one hand there is the attraction of Christ and the unseen life he promises. On the other, the visible reality and concrete allurements of life here and now.

Some expect a "sign," a special experience of good feeling to assure them of God's presence. But usually God does not work this way. Often he prepares one for faith by allowing one to feel a great need, a discontent, an irritation, a helplessness. Slowly, by humble prayer, by study, and by trying to live a good life, we will usually experience faith—when we are ready for it and can appreciate it.

Often the example of those who have given all for their belief helps to persuade the sincere seeker—those who give their lives to serve others, truly dedicated and unselfish missionaries, those who are living a day-by-day martyrdom with a self-centered and perhaps neurotic marriage partner, those who do not marry in order to better serve others, or those who commit themselves to working among the poor and uneducated.

Many have been helped in their search for faith by reading the experiences of others who sought and found faith. There are available a number of interesting biographies and reflections of converts and other seekers of the truth, many in paperback editions.

Often believing friends or loved ones can be a great help in arriving at faith. By their love, prayer, and exemplary lives they win God's grace for the seeker and show how to believe. They can make God's love real for the one who is seeking, sometimes making up for an earlier lack of love that had made God seem remote, unreal. If there is any way to overcome deeply rooted erroneous notions or previous unpleasant experiences, it is through close contact with a genuine believer, cleric or layperson.

DOUBTING, GROWING, RETURNING TO FAITH

The extent of one's faith is influenced by the circumstances of one's life, besides God's gift and one's own free response. Faith comes to anyone who is baptized, yet its growth is affected by one's background, love relationships, education, and so on. It may always remain stunted, through no fault of one's own. God only expects us to respond to the extent that we are able.

Faith is not something that is possessed once and for all, but rather it must be constantly renewed. It is a personal relationship that must continually grow, or else it weakens, perhaps dies. It is each instant a free gift of God for which we must continually ask.

We grow in faith by praying for a stronger faith, by publicly expressing our beliefs when opportunities arise, and particularly by trying to live according to our beliefs. Faith is not a flight from a sinful world, nor a sentiment to be kept within our hearts. If it remains only interior, it will die within us. The true Christian realizes that he or she must freely and openly express his or her beliefs to others, hoping to bring them as well to a further faith, to love a bit more.

The Christian's commitment of faith is strengthened or weakened by whether or not he or she lives the Christian life of love. The immoral, uncharitable Christian will soon find that he or she cannot accept many things in the belief he or she professes.

The believer must continue to learn more about his or her beliefs, particularly in our age of rapid change, new knowledge, and consequent confusion. Learning more not only deepens our own faith but enables us to communicate it to others. The humble and realistic Christian knows that she or he cannot be constantly concerned with material things and this-worldly knowledge, however good, and yet expect the unseen world of faith to mean much.

We should note that faith is different from accepting, or not accepting, a series of beliefs. A believer may have problems with some of the Church's beliefs and still have faith. In chapter 10, we discussed the need of seeing beliefs in context, the relative importance of the Church's teachings (the "hierarchy" of beliefs), and how one might in good conscience dissent from certain beliefs.

Uncertainty and doubt will always coexist with our faith. Faith is not knowledge that frees us from the proddings of doubt. Faith rather gives a certain deep direction, a meaning, illumination, and purposefulness to our life. God will never overwhelm us with proofs that will force us to believe, since he can be known only by a free, personal surrender. An unbeliever can always give a logical, rational explanation for any of God's actions in history. This is because God loves us—he seeks to persuade rather than compel our assent.

The believer bred in the Christian faith must often painfully discard the uncomplicated faith of childhood and adolescence and form a new, adult, simpler, deeper, more mature and realistic belief. This means for many a "crisis of faith"—usually in the late teens or early twenties, though it can come earlier or later—often involving a rejection of many of the Church's "rules" and structures.

Believers for the first time may face a challenge to what they have always accepted. They see now that they must be personally involved in and committed to living what they profess. They examine their beliefs critically, testing their power and relevance in their lives. They see the weaknesses of the Church, the mediocrity of many Christians, and the dedication of many unbelievers. They may find the Church's moral code difficult to live with and they may wonder if it is not largely unrealistic.

They must now distinguish the core of Christian belief from what is peripheral, the teachings of Christ from the weak human instruments who propose them, and the Christian faith as it really is from what they may have been taught.

Mature persons will realize their own weakness and their critical need of guidance during such periods of massive doubt. They will realize that they must now study their faith on an adult level, that they cannot solve the problems of a sophisticated adulthood with an adolescent's knowledge of religion. They will also face their own moral weaknesses and realize that they are open to the promptings of pride and sensuality and the enticements of material success. They will humbly pray "help my unbelief!" (Mark 9, 23). Finally, hopefully, they will emerge from this period of crisis recommitted to a new, mature, and realistic Christian faith.

IN THE LITURGY

The Church provides many opportunities for publicly renewing our commitment of faith. The choice of faith made at baptism is reaffirmed by us whenever we take part in any of the sacraments, but particularly in confirmation and at Mass. A renewal of baptismal promises is part of the Easter Vigil service, the high point of the Church's yearly liturgy. Taking part in a parish renewal, a retreat, or cursillo are other ways of renewing one's faith.

HOPE—A CONFIDENT EXPECTATION

Following from faith is the virtue of hope, an attitude of confident expectation or trust in God, joined to a deep yearning for him. Christian hope is not "hope" as we use the word in our everyday speech. It is not just wishing or yearning for something. It is, rather, based on what we have already experienced, what we have already had a "taste" of (however small)—that God is real, totally loving toward us and faithful to his promises. It is a confident looking-forward, an expectation or yearning for what we know is to come fully. Sometimes this confident knowing is subject to periods of confusion and even doubt, as with faith, but it remains deep within us.

God gives us this power. It is a deep desire for God and for the consummation of his plan that all people will be united in perfect love with him and with one another, without any more strife, injustice, or pain. But hope is also confidence that his plan will come about fully—and that God will give us all the help necessary to do our part to attain our eternal destiny and that of all humankind. It is also the day-by-day confidence that he will take care of all our needs and will never abandon us for an instant.

By our attitude of hope we put our lives into his hands, confident that he will forgive our sins and will turn even misfortune and suffering to humankind's eternal advantage. Paul describes the effects of hope in his own life when he says, "Now may the God of hope fill you with joy and peace in believing . . . " (Romans 15, 13).

Despair and presumption are the two attitudes by which people reject God's gift of hope. Despair is a loss of hope in God's mercy, the depressing conviction that one is rejected by God or that God is not interested in us. It is the most tragic of attitudes because it forgets that God has revealed himself to be above all else a God of merciful love, willing to undergo a humiliating death to convince us that he cares for each of us.

Presumptuous people, on the other hand, count on obtaining heaven while doing little or nothing to overcome their sins. They might consider God a sort of benign "Force" or "Power" who always "understands" their unrepentant wrongdoing. Such people act like spoiled children and must sooner or later mature and face not only themselves but the living God.

We especially need hope in today's world because of the tensions and insecurity, the crimes, wars, and suffering of the innocent we see in our lives—as well as the ongoing threat of nuclear disasters. To avoid discouragement or bitterness, to realize that good will come from the evil about us, we need the joyful trust that is hope. "Cast all your anxiety upon him, because he cares for you" (1 Peter 5, 7).

The way to grow in hope is to pray for it and confidently and expectantly to live according to our beliefs. We should pray for this attitude of confidence in God especially during times of temptation, when depressed, in mental or physical suffering. St. Paul suffered as few of us will, but he wrote from his imprisonment:

No one took my part; all deserted me. May it not be charged against them! But the Lord stood by me and gave me strength to proclaim the Word fully, that all the Gentiles might hear it. So I was rescued from the lion's mouth. The Lord will rescue me from every evil and save me for his heavenly kingdom. To him be the glory forever and ever. Amen (2 Timothy 4, 16–18).

LOVE—THE ONE THING NECESSARY

The central point in Christ's teaching, the topic to which he returned again and again, is love. No religion or philosophy before or since has taught love as Christ did. Though he derived it from his Jewish background, he made it his core teaching. Only Christianity presents a transcendent, all-powerful God who is yet so loving as to become one of us, is disgraced and dies for us, and sums up his whole teaching in love: **Read Matthew 22, 34–40.**

> Again he said: "I give you a new commandment, that you love one another. Just as I have loved you, you also should love one another. By this everyone will know that you are my disciples, if you have love for one another" (John 13, 34–35).

The greatest virtue, then, is charity, or love: the power given us by God to love him above all things and to love our neighbors as ourselves. "So faith, hope, love abide, these three; but the greatest of these is love" (1 Corinthians 13, 13). Love is not merely an emotion or feeling; it is not only physical or sexual; it is primarily spiritual, something that comes from God himself. "God *is* love," says St. John. The more of him we have in our life, the more we truly love—and the more we have of true love in our life, the more of him we possess.

Love is concern for another's happiness. Consider human love: when we are truly in love, we are primarily concerned with making another happy. It is the very opposite of selfish concern for oneself. We want to please our beloved in every way possible.

When we love, we want to be united with the one we love. We gladly give ourselves, seeking to be united with our beloved. The more we give ourselves, the more we fulfill ourselves—this is the paradox of love. We give ourselves in order to make the one we love happy. That one's happiness, in turn, brings us the greatest happiness.

By the virtue of love we give ourselves to God and our neighbor, to make them happy. We are primarily concerned with what God wants and the happiness of our neighbor. We give ourselves to God, either directly or through our neighbor, in order to be united with her. And in this, paradoxically, we fulfill ourselves and attain limitless, eternal happiness.

God has shown us how to love by loving us first and totally. He has given us everything we have, our life, our talents, our destiny. Above all he has given us himself—the root meaning of "charity" is the total gift of oneself. When humankind was unfaithful to him, he became one of us and died to prove his love for us. "In this is love, not that we loved God but that he loved us and sent his Son to be the expiation for our sins" (1 John 4, 10).

Though he has no need of us whatever, he yet gives us a share in his own life. He is constantly concerned with our happiness and wants us to be united with himself. His love knows no limits, for he is willing to forgive us again and again.

We love God above all things by making him the center of our life, by trying to please him in everything we do. As a man would love the one woman who really matters to him, and she him, so we should try to love God. We will think of him each morning, offering ourselves to him. We are united with him especially by worshiping him, showing our love before others, celebrating it at special times. We respect his name, as a man would tolerate no one speaking disrespectfully of the woman he loves.

We want to know more about him, his desire, his friends, his innermost life, as a young man and woman falling in love take joy in discovering more and more about each other; the Bible particularly tells us about him. We know that love is tested, not in the initial glow of romance but in the long hours of suffering, and so we are willing to bear the cross with him. As the center of our life, God will always come first: our family, friends, work, recreation should never cause us to do anything that would lead us away from him. We should be able to face him honestly each night, ask his pardon for any selfishness, and quietly, peacefully renew our profession of love.

If we truly love God, we will also love our neighbor, our fellow human beings. It is impossible to love God and not love our neighbor. "Beloved, if God so loves us, we also ought to love one another. . . . Those who say 'I love God' and hate their brother and sisters are liars" (1 John 4, 20). Everyone else has been created by God for heaven, just as we are; they have the same dignity, are redeemed by Christ, and have God living within them.

Every person is our neighbor, whatever his or her race, color, background, belief, or talents. Christ made this clear in the famous parable of the Good Samaritan: **Read Luke 10, 29-37.**

We should note that this story, Christ's great example of love of neighbor, concerns love between people of different racial and religious backgrounds. Christ's fellow Jews looked on the Samaritans as an inferior breed and as heretics. Christ told the Samaritan woman that "salvation is from the Jews," but he significantly chooses a Samaritan as his great example of brotherly love.

Not only racism but any form of prejudice or discrimination is a rejection of Christian love: If we avoid or look down on another because of his or her background, lack of social position, or past moral failings, Christ makes clear how we will be judged at the end—as we treated our "least" brethren. **Read Matthew 25, 35–40.**

We also fail to love our neighbor by not respecting him or her: by anger, by jealousy or envy of another's good fortune, and particularly by hatred or desiring revenge. If we love our neighbor, we will also respect the other's right to the truth and to a good name, avoiding lying, calumny, and detraction; we have no right to repeat something detrimental to another, even if true, unless necessary for a higher good.

If we love our neighbor, it shows habitually in what we call the moral virtues. These are four aspects of our love of others, and they include prudence, by which we form a right judgment as to what to do or not to do; justice, by which we give all people what is due them as God's children; fortitude, courageously facing opposition to our Christian ideals; and temperance, controlling our passions so as to use them more fully to truly love.

True love means that we respect the one we love, especially in the use of the power of sex. If we truly love one another, we do not ever want to treat another person as a "thing," as the outlet for our passions. True love cannot be forced, as for example a man demanding that a woman give in to him. Nor can love be bought, as a woman might confusedly try to do in giving herself to a man. Even a couple deeply in love, who experience how naturally sexual intimacies can express their love, must realize that a true and mature love requires discipline and sacrifice.

The love of our enemies, as difficult for us today as when Christ first proposed it, is the test of a truly committed follower of Christ. Sometimes we may have to defend ourselves or others against our enemies, but always and only to the extent that we must, never using immoral means, and always ready to forgive without exacting vengeance. Christ said simply that if almighty God puts up with their sins, so should we: **Read Matthew 5, 43–48.**

Christ as he hung dying at the hands of his enemies gave us a strong hint as to why we should forgive those who have hurt us: "Father, forgive them; for they know not what they do" (Luke 23, 34). People rarely, if ever, hurt us with full deliberation—and even then they may think their action is for our good. Usually people bring to their actions all sorts of personality traits, pressures, and drives from their background and daily environment. Only if we were fully aware of these could we judge them—and God alone knows all that is within us, driving us on. So Christ says, "Judge not, that you be not judged" (Matthew 7, 1).

> *A famous modern poet/monk/mystic gives this insight about love:* "All life is love. . . . Men love, whether they know it or not, and never cease loving. . . . Love is. All else is not, because in the same measure in which things partake of being, they partake of love. All that is not love, is not. . . . The conflicts which beset our world are not caused by the absence of love, but by a love which refuses to acknowledge itself as such, a love which has become ill because it fails to recognize its true nature and has lost sight of its object. . . . Cruelty is misdirected love, and hate is frustrated love. . . . " (Thomas Merton's introduction to Ernesto Cardenal's *Love*).

Last, but certainly not least, we must love ourselves. Christ implied this when he told us to "love your neighbor as you love *yourself*." True self-love, as opposed to narcissistic self-centeredness, is a virtue to be cultivated. It means several things: accepting yourself, your whole self, good and bad (as God actually does), "liking yourself," and realizing that, despite your failings, you have rights and abilities to contribute to others and to the world (whatever your IQ, personality, looks, and so on). It means not being afraid of being alone, enjoying your own company, and not needing continual social "strokes" or the constant approval of others. Finally, it is gradually developing a sense of self-worth and self-respect, an ever-growing sense of your own identity and of your ability to have intimate, enduring relationships.

CHRISTIAN PRAYER:
TOUCHING THE MYSTERY, THE PRESENCE

By prayer we communicate with God, open ourselves to him, find out his will for us and obtain the strength to live as we should. In the first chapter we saw the vital necessity of praying. We can never know God or ourselves unless we pray. In its daily necessity prayer can be compared to eating: sometimes it is enjoyable, sometimes not; it is more enjoyable for some than for others, but a daily necessity for everyone; as physical nourishment is more pleasurable if prepared well, so will our prayer be if we prepare by reading and reflection.

The prayer of a Christian has a new meaning and new power. The Christian knows that any prayer is joined to Christ's prayer. She or he knows that Christ's prayer is already answered, that it can never fail to bring about good. The more we are consciously united in prayer to Christ, the more God can communicate himself to us and spread love in the world.

A Christian's prayer is especially powerful when she or he is united with Christ's whole body in the prayers of the liturgy. Whenever one unites with other believers in prayer, Christ promises his special help: "Where two or three are gathered in my name, there am I in the midst of them" (Matthew 18, 20). But the private individual prayer of a Christian also has special power.

Prayer is the great way in which God allows us to work with him in saving ourselves and others, in spreading love in the world. We do not pray to ask God for something he does not know we need; nor is prayer a cringing before a whimsical deity, coaxing him into giving what we want; nor is it something we give to God, "bargaining" with him, that he might proportionately help us in return. Rather it is our small but real contribution to the love that runs the universe. God wills that we shall obtain certain things for ourselves and others if we do our part, contribute our love, by expressing our reliance on him in prayer. He treats us like adults, with dignity and even reverence, giving us a part in the working out of our salvation.

The most important moments of our life are the moments of prayer—and someday we may come to see this. We can learn more in one second of pure prayer than in all the books ever written. We can accomplish more by one fervent moment of prayer than we might otherwise in a lifetime of effort. "The man of prayer is a worker of miracles" (Léon Bloy).

In the heart of Manhattan there is a convent of contemplative nuns whose lives are devoted to praying and doing penance for that vast city. Unnoticed, this little group of women has a sublime and joyous faith that God is using it to bring his love to others. In almost every metropolitan center of the world a group like this lives a life of prayer and self-discipline to open the hearts of the rest of us to God's love.

Some critics of religion, often people who themselves were once religious, dismiss prayer as useless, usually because it has not "worked" for them at some critical time in their lives. It is hard to accept that Someone out there is paying attention to you if you sorely needed an answer, a bit of meaning to help make sense of it all, and nothing came. So attempts at prayer may be dismissed as useless escapes at best and harmful superstitions at worst. Better, it would seem, to do something about life than sit and pray about it.

But prayer becomes a hunger. For those who regularly, daily, spend time in prayer, life would be empty and meaningless without it. They may know that they need to pray lest they be worse than they are—to keep from turning aside from good and lapsing into profound evil, or to restore the balance of things when they have submitted to evil. They are also drawn to pray as by a hunger because there they encounter Someone, an intimate, unfailing Presence who is limitlessly understanding, accepting, always-supporting Love.

Some who dismiss prayer seem to consider reality to be limited to what they, personally, are able to experience. They apparently know nothing of what pray-ers experience: the place of refuge where one must also be utterly honest, the hours of confusion and anguish, of trying to find one's way, of crying out in the night and wrestling with one's own demons—and above all with the Divine—and the unexpected insights, the solutions, that suddenly appear—and the profound, indescribable joy and peace that come, often when least expected.

When we pray we try to make contact with God, become aware of him, open ourselves to his love and his desires for us. We can never become aware of his will for us unless we pause to pray. This is our basic human need—to give ourselves to the will of the Father, who, after all, knows what is best for us. So underlying our every prayer must be Christ's prayer: "My Father . . . not as I will, but as thou wilt" (Matthew 26, 39).

How does prayer for others "work"? This question puts us before a great mystery, so we cannot analyze prayer in a mechanistic way. But we can say this: When we pray for others, our love reaches out to them through God—when we speak to him about them, his all-powerful love is joined to our poor, stumbling love, and now our joint love enfolds them. Our prayer for others also changes us, so that we are more open and loving toward those others and toward God.

We should not pray to God, however, to do what we should do ourselves. Sometimes, instead of asking him to help someone or remedy some situation, we should be doing something about it ourselves. Our prayer should thank him for making us such wonderful and capable human beings, who can do such great things in partnership with him, and a plea that we might use our talents in the best way possible. At times, however, our weakness overwhelms us and we can only beg for his all-powerful help.

It is often hard to pray, and we must discipline ourselves to do it. Our sins keep us from prayer and disturb us when we do pray. In praying we must learn humble, loving adoration before our infinite God; pride resists this, telling us to rely on our own efforts. Our minds are usually undisciplined, at least in trying to contact the Infinite, and so distractions are natural. We must quietly "focus" our divided psyches and gradually open them to pay attention to what God is doing in us. Prayer usually does not develop spontaneously but is learned by persevering practice.

Christ tells us how to pray: first, confidently and perseveringly. We must remind ourselves that God always answers, in some way, every sincere prayer. Christ's parable is plain: **Read Luke 18, 1-7.**

We must be humble and reverent as we pray. We are sinners putting ourselves in the presence of the infinite God. Moses took off his shoes to approach the burning bush; and the Church uses Jacob's cry to describe a house of prayer: "Terrible is this place!" We sign ourselves and take holy water to remind ourselves that we are coming into God's presence to pray. We might kneel when we pray, an ancient, spontaneous attitude of reverence. We realize our sinfulness, but we are like children who know they are loved and trust in their father's forgiveness: **Read Luke 18, 10-14.**

Christ also reminds us that our prayer should be simple and sincere—the best prayers are usually those in our own words. "And in praying do not heap up empty phrases as the Gentiles do, for they think that they will be heard for their many words" (Matthew 6, 7). We may say just a few simple, stumbling words—reaching out to make contact, to realize his presence.

Perhaps we will form no words—this is meditation. "The mind seeks to understand the why and how of . . . life" (*Catechism,* 2705–8), the things that happen every day as well as the big, overall picture. We sit quietly in God's presence, perhaps pondering, reflecting, or just being there in openness and attentiveness to God—"Be still, and know that I am God" (Psalm 46, 10). We are opening ourselves to the Lord to "discover the movements that stir the heart," to discern what God wants us to do, and to find the strength to do it. We may use a "mantra," a word or phrase that arises in our mind over and over again.

We will get more out of our prayer/meditation if we prepare for it by reading spiritual books, especially the Bible. It is only natural that prayer will be difficult if we put no spiritual substance into our minds. "Meditative reading" is an excellent way of doing this: reading a bit, thinking over what we have read, then perhaps speaking to God whatever comes to mind—or just saying nothing. Or we might ponder "the great book of creation" (*Catechism,* 2705), God's wonders revealed in nature's order and beauty.

> *There are many methods of meditation, including those using the spiritual insights and techniques of the great traditions of the East.* Zen Buddhism and the various yogas (roughly, disciplines) have been of great help to many in their attempts at meditation. These can bring a quieting of one's body, mind, and spirit, a clarity, a unity and "centeredness," a deep openness to one's inner self, and a "letting go" of one's ego-centered reasoning and "false" self.

Contemplation or contemplative prayer is the silent, inner prayer in which our attention is fixed on God or on Jesus. The *Catechism* quotes St. Teresa as calling it "a close sharing between friends; . . . taking time frequently to be alone with him who we know loves us" (2709). It is a gift or grace from God. One sits before him in poverty, faith, surrender, and utter humility—a poor sinner who yet knows she or he is loved and who wants to respond by loving even more. An intense prayer, it often brings tears. But it is deeply peaceful and at times profoundly joyous. It "illumines the eyes of our heart"—we see everything "in the light of Jesus' truth and his compassion for everyone" (2712–15). It is "silent love," and at times for some may be like fire: "Words in this kind of prayer are not speeches; they are like kindling that feeds the fire of love" (2717).

It is often good to have a spiritual guide (or "director"), usually a priest or religious, though it might be a gifted layperson—someone to whom we can talk freely about our personal spiritual life, our life of prayer, who seems to understand us, and who can make suggestions for our further growth. Sometimes members of a prayer group can also give one another some profitable spiritual direction.

The Church's pattern for prayer is an ancient one: to God the Father, through Jesus Christ, in union with the Holy Spirit within us. We are children, weak but loved, coming before our all-powerful Father. We try to unite ourselves with Christ, our Brother—he is there leading us to the Father—and we realize that it is the Spirit within us who is actually praying, who gives form, power, and meaning to our prayers—so we try to hold ourselves open to the Spirit.

The Church often prays by prepared formulas, which are meant to help us. These are most often prayers that have helped billions of people throughout Christian history, and so they might be helpful to us as well. Sometimes it is hard to become used to praying in set words, especially when the prayer is gone through rapidly. Anything done over and over tends to become hurried, but we should remember that the attention of the will is what is important, the attempt to make contact with God—just as a couple in love may talk for hours and later are unable to tell what they discussed.

We should pray often—several times a day if possible. Prayer should become a habit but not a routine. We read how Christ many times "withdrew . . . and prayed" (Luke 5, 16; Matthew 14, 23; Mark 6, 46), and sometimes he spent the night in prayer. Our prayers need not be lengthy, as long as we try to have some sense of "making contact." Nor should we feel obliged to say a particular formula of prayer that is no longer meaningful. God may just want us to be quiet with him.

When beginning to pray, it is best to find a quiet place, then breathe deeply, slowly, in and out, until we feel our body "letting go."

Some good times to pray are in the morning upon arising and in the evening before retiring; when in special need of help, as in times of temptation, confusion, or before making an important decision; also, before meals—it is often hard for a family, for instance, to gather and then pause to pray, but it can come to mean much, especially if those who want to can express themselves in their own words, however briefly.

The *Catechism* describes obstacles to prayer as mostly of three kinds:

Distractions: Ranging from insignificant little matters to major preoccupations, these can invade the mind when we sit down to pray, at times like ceaseless chatter. But "to set out hunting down distractions would be to fall into their trap" (2729). Rather, we should quietly "turn back to our heart," gently returning to the One who we want to prefer before all else, especially as we pray.

Dryness: Our heart seems separated from God "with no taste for thoughts, memories and feelings, even spiritual ones" (2731).

Many times we will get nothing out of our attempts to pray. Everyone who seriously tries to reach God experiences this. Our prayer has no fervor: it seems to be cold, mechanical repetition. Often God himself seems to have disappeared, and we may even wonder whether he exists at all. We should expect this: God seems "gone" from us, perhaps so that we realize how much we need him, so that we will reach out for him all the more, and especially because we are not truly open to what he is trying to say to us. Also, God wants us to mature spiritually, to grow in "naked faith." We are sharing in Christ's desolation, in this worst of his sufferings—and as with him, this is the very time when we are accomplishing the most to spread love in the world.

Depression: We may be too physically tired or psychologically weary to pray as we want to. But this is different: while not clinical depression, it is a sadness or lassitude due to "lax ascetical practice . . . [or] carelessness of heart" (2733). We don't want to give up certain things or practices or people, and the realization that we should do so depresses us. Or perhaps we are just weary of the whole spiritual effort.

We should pray for everyone and anyone—for all humankind, especially those close to us, those for whom we have a responsibility, those who need it the most, sinners, those for whom God is not real, and for our enemies. Our prayer can also embrace all creatures, including those who may be on other planets, that they, too, will attain their destiny with God. Our prayer truly has no limits.

Often the greatest help we can give someone is to pray for him or her. A disabled person may need help in standing and we reach out, and help the person up, or someone may be in pain or sorrow, and we comfort him or her with words of sympathy—or we extend the love-power of our prayer and we help the person as much and perhaps more.

We should remember that worship is our highest form of prayer— adoring, praising, thanking God for his goodness, instead of constantly asking for help. The great "practitioners of prayer," the saints and mystics, prayed mostly by pouring out their gratitude, admiration, and awe before the Lord.

DAILY LIVING: LOVE IN OUR LIFE

Our life with God, with his grace-presence within us, gives us fantastic new powers. By the virtues we can live the very life of Christ—the life of heaven already is a part of us. The whole purpose of our life is to grow in grace and the virtues, especially in love.

To be a successful Christian there is only one thing we have to do: love. Faith is meant to end in love, and the whole purpose of prayer is to make us love more. Conversely, if a Christian does not truly love, his or her Christianity is in vain. We might profess our beliefs and keep all the Church's rules, but unless we honestly love it is all a sham.

We cannot prove our love of God except by loving our fellow humans. Jesus Christ loved God precisely by loving his fellow men and women. In his act of dying he loved God perfectly, by loving us to the extent of giving his life for us.

We cannot love everyone at once. But perhaps we could try to commit ourselves to one other person who is unlike us in some way, someone to whom we normally would not be attracted but who needs our help, and whom circumstances have brought into our life. At the very least we can try to be aware of someone in our life who is in need of love, whom we can consistently treat with kindness: someone insecure, or hypersensitive, or narrow and unimaginative, or perhaps one who is moody or melancholy—someone whom we can say is experiencing life as "the least of my brethren" (Matthew 26, 40).

SOME SUGGESTIONS FOR . . .

DISCUSSION

Have you experienced why coming to faith, and growing in faith, can be difficult and frustrating as well as deeply joyous and peaceful?

Can you see how accepting a set of beliefs is part of faith, but also different from it?

Someone has said that hope is our greatest need today—if you agree, why?

What particular demand involved in loving some neighbor do you personally find the most difficult?

Have you ever prayed from the very depths of your being, perhaps in great need, confusion, or pain? How could such a prayer open you to God and his desires for you?

What setting—preparation, posture, and so on—do you find most helpful for your prayer? Can you just let yourself be quiet and enjoy God's presence?

What do you personally find most helpful in combating racist attitudes that are often inbuilt from our earliest years?

FURTHER READING

- *The Kingdom Within,* Sanford (Harper & Row, 1987)—A new, expanded revision of a very popular book relating what Jesus says to our interior life.
- *Women at the Well: Feminist Perspectives in Spiritual Direction,* Fischer (Paulist Press, 1988)—A truly fine book on spirituality and spiritual direction that gives as many new insights to men as to women.
- *Addiction and Grace,* May (HarperSanFrancisco, 1991)—An excellent book by a psychiatrist and popular, profound spiritual author on the various, often unrecognized addictions confronting us today.
- *Sadhana: A Way to God,* DeMello (Institute of Jesuit Resources, 1978) —A popular, insightful work combining East-West ways to go. •*Song of the Bird* (Doubleday Image, 1984) is another book by this recently deceased bright spirit. • *The Way to Love* (Doubleday, 1992). This is the most recently published of this popular author's works.

- *Chaos or Creation: Spirituality in Mid-Life,* Carroll and Dyckman (Paulist Press, 1986)—A small but "packed" book drawing on different psychological models to help one deal with midlife spiritual problems.
- *Becoming Adult, Becoming Christian,* Fowler (Harper & Row, 1984)—This book by a pioneer in the field summarizes years of work with the "stages" many encounter as they mature in years and belief.
- *Pathways of Prayer,* Wintz (Catholic Update 0381, St. Anthony Messenger Press)—A very brief, excellent summary of various ways of praying.
- *Mystical Theology: The Science of Love,* Johnston (HarperSan Francisco, 1995)—A very popular, very wise spiritual writer and retreat giver bridges East and West, past and present, in this discussion of experiencing God in our world today.
- *Julian of Norwich: Showings,* eds. Colledge, Walsh, LeClercq (Paulist Press, 1978)—One of the greatest English mystics gives her insightful, witty, and wonderful perceptions of God as Mother, creation, the Church, and other matters. Also, • *Meditations with Julian of Norwich,* Doyle (Bear & Co., 1983) is a small, beautifully arranged book of her insights with two excellent forewords.
- *30 Days with a Great Spiritual Teacher,* Chilson and Kirvan (Ave Maria Press, 1995)—A series of insightful little books by two men of wide experience for a do-it-yourself retreat; available to date are Julian of Norwich, the Psalms, and Meister Eckhardt.
- *Gratefulness, the Heart of Prayer,* Steindl-Rast (Paulist Press, 1984)—A contemplative monk uses a basic attitude of gratefulness to incisively reflect on the many aspects of the spiritual life.
- *Ordinary People as Monks and Mystics,* Sinetar (Paulist Press, 1986)—This book is by an organizational psychologist with a good spiritual grounding, and it looks at how ordinary people find fulfillment in a solitary lifestyle. Also available as two audiocassettes titled *Everyday People as Monks and Mystics.*
- *Thomas Merton: Spiritual Master,* ed. Cunningham (Paulist Press)—A one-volume anthology of the spiritual writings of the man whose works have had an immense impact on American Catholic spirituality. • *Run to the Mountain* (HarperSanFrancisco, 1995) and • *Enter-*

ing the Silence (HarperSanFrancisco, 1995) are the first two volumes of *The Journals of Thomas Merton,* a seven-volume series of his personal diaries, which could not be published until twenty-five years after his death. The first gives the story of his early life and vocation; the second, his reflections on the beginning of his life as a monk and writer.

- *Quest for the Grail,* Rohr (Crossroad, 1994)—In this book, the very popular author and retreat director reflects on male spirituality.
- *Spiritual Friend,* Edwards (Paulist Press, 1979)—An excellent, practical guide for anyone searching for the "special friendship" of support one Christian can give another—an imaginative approach to spiritual direction.
- *Stories of Faith,* Shea (Thomas More Press, 1980)—An imaginative, beautiful, down-to-earth book on discovering the meaning of our own life's story, our experience of relating to the mystery of God and the meaning of church, and how we can relive Jesus' story for ourselves.
- *The Other Side of Silence,* Kelsey (Paulist Press, 1976)—A fine, comprehensive study of religious experience by a seasoned psychologist. It includes helpful, practical, concrete "ways to go" in the last chapter.
- *Daily We Touch Him,* Pennington (Doubleday, 1977)—A simple, practical book on praying and religious experience; very popular.
- *Christian Life Patterns,* Whitehead and Whitehead (Doubleday, 1982)—A husband and wife, theologian and psychologist, skillfully treat many aspects of maturing and adulthood.
- *Zen Mind, Beginner's Mind,* Shunryu Suzuki (Weatherhill, 1981)—For those drawn to this way of meditating, here is a concise, excellent introduction to the Soto way of Zen Buddhism by a revered teacher.

FURTHER VIEWING/LISTENING

Twelve Steps Spirituality, Rohr (Paulist Press)—In this 90-minute audiotape, a very popular priest-author describes twelve-step spirituality as a way of life full of mystery, awe, and miracles.

Guidance in Prayer from Three Women Mystics: Julian of Norwich, Teresa of Avila, Therese of Lisieux, Margaret Dorgan (NCR audio, 7 cassettes, 7 hours)—A wise Carmelite nun shows how three great women mystics prayed and familiarizes the listener with their lives and thought.

Learning Solitary Prayer, Sr. Jose Hobday (NCR audio, 34 minutes)—Some practical ways to improve one's prayer in a setting of stillness and solitude, by a very popular retreat-giver.

Spiritual Hunger: Choosing Your Joy, Meadow (NCR audio, 59 minutes)—An insightful psychologist and spiritual writer discusses St. John of the Cross and the Buddha on the dangers of attachment and how to overcome it.

PERSONAL REFLECTION

I should treat at least one other person with true Christian love. I might reread the story of the Good Samaritan (Luke 10, 29–37) and then pray that I might honestly put it into practice in the next few days.

17

Our Christian Presence in the World

What of Christians who are concerned only with getting themselves to heaven? What practical things can one do to show concern for others? What can the average Christian do now about the glaring injustices in our world? What can one do to bring about peace in our world? What does the sacrament of confirmation do for us?

OUR CHRISTIAN PRESENCE OF SERVICE

A self-centered Christian is no Christian at all. We cannot attain heaven alone. Following Christ, our God who came to share what he had with us, Christians try to share their faith and love with others. Millions today are without any strong religious or moral convictions. Millions more suffer from a gross lack of love and concern, in conditions of hunger, destitution, and hopelessness. The need of countless people for something to believe in, or a faith to give meaning to their lives, or for someone to show a bit of caring concern over their poverty and powerlessness is painfully evident to anyone who looks honestly at our world. **Now read Christ's way: John 13, 1–12.**

A Christian is a serving person, a ministering person, one who bears witness to her or his belief by loving words and actions. This is "evangelization," sharing Christ's good news with all, in its truest sense. The original apostles had a unique role as witnesses of the resurrection and sharers in Christ's personal love. They were sent forth to serve their fellow human beings by sharing their belief and their love. Each Christian today is also chosen by Christ to speak about him in his name and love others as truly parts of him. In this loving service it is the Holy Spirit, the Spirit of Christ, who works within one, using one in a special way.

The particular sign of a follower of Christ is concern for those who are poor, neglected, underprivileged, and discriminated against. Thus the Church's "preferential option" is for the poor—it must care for these above all others. Jesus simply said, "As long as you did it for one of these, the least of my brethren, you did it for me" (Matthew 25, 40). He identified himself with those who are the "least." A true follower of his, therefore, will see something of him, however obscured at times, in the poor and deprived: **Read, and ponder, Matthew 25, 31ff.**

Groups, formal and informal, work in the Church today in many forms of Christian service or ministry. Teaching, caring for the elderly and the disabled, helping the poor in various ways, "consciousness-raising," helping those who are not able to cope or receive what is legally and rightfully theirs, improving the quality of a neighborhood, working for decent housing, acting politically and lobbying for those unable to help themselves, feeding and housing the homeless, nursing services for the sick, child care, aiding children and adults with disabilities, and so on—these are just a few of the works that groups in the Church are undertaking today (see also in chapter 22 the section, "God's Gifted People").

Some groups train laypeople for service in foreign countries, some work among those in need here at home, and some do both. These "lay missionaries" may be either married or single, and they usually volunteer to serve for a year or two (though some serve for life). Examples of groups are the Grail, the Glenmary Lay Volunteers, the Jesuit Volunteer Corps and International Volunteers, the Maryknoll Associate Lay Missioner Program, the Lay Mission Helpers Association, the Latin American Mission Program, the Missionaries of Charity, the Catholic Worker Houses of Hospitality, Covenant Houses, the St. Vincent de Paul Society (established in most U.S. parishes), and Catholic Relief Services (the U.S. bishops' overseas funding and support agency). Also see "Further Reading" at the end of this chapter.

THE DIGNITY AND SACREDNESS OF EACH HUMAN LIFE

A basic teaching of the Church is that of an individual's right to life, including the right to live with dignity and with a just share of the material necessities for a dignified life. Though sometimes observed more in the breach than in practice (e.g., the Wars of Religion, the Crusades, and the Inquisition), the Church and churchpeople most often emerge as the champions of this most fundamental human right when history is considered as a whole. Today, particularly, Christians are becoming more and more conscious of this right. It is hard to ignore the fact that millions are being deprived of their right to live, and to live in freedom, justice, dignity, and peace.

> *Blatant examples of deprivation abound in our culture,* usually ignored by people until they are forced to become involved. Many old people live in near-ghetto conditions, often hungry and housebound by fear. Most mental institutions still have little corrective therapy and often use unnecessarily incapacitating drugs to control patients' behavior. And many mentally ill or minimally functioning people are homeless—having been deinstitutionalized without anywhere near adequate supervisory care. Also, our overcrowded youth detention and adult prison systems make only minimal efforts at rehabilitation, despite proven successes with tens of thousands—especially with youthful offenders.

Most of the developed nations of the world—as well as many not as technologically advanced—have abolished capital punishment without any reservations. *The Catechism of the Catholic Church* acknowledges the traditional right of the state to punish wrongdoers, including "in cases of extreme gravity [when it is necessary to defend society] the death penalty." But it goes on to ask that the state limit itself to "bloodless means" of punishment, which "better correspond to the concrete conditions of the common good and . . . the dignity of the human person" (2266, 2267).

In addition to Pope John Paul II, the U.S. Conference of Catholic Bishops has several times gone on record against capital punishment. In the words of Archbishop John Quinn, "Capital punishment, like the crime for which it is imposed, only serves to cheapen human life, and further perpetuates a 'chain of violence'—a life for a life—as the means of guiding and protecting our society."

Despite the expressed will of the great majority of Americans for effective control of handguns, as shown in poll after poll, the "gun lobby" continues to defeat every national effort toward this. The American bishops have for years been asking for effective legislation for national controls on the use of handguns. In Christ's plain words to Peter, who used his sword to defend Christ from seizure by his enemies and eventual death: "He who lives by the sword will perish by the sword" (Matthew 26, 51–53).

In the area of genetic research, developments are coming faster than almost anyone could predict, confronting us with many moral dilemmas and decisions. We must be courageous and dedicated in working to solve problems of infertility, as well as those of genetic defects that cause abnormal children. But many scientists, as well as others, realize that we must also have the farsighted courage to proceed with care and caution where human subjects and human life are concerned. The ultimate question here is the total good-over-evil of this for humankind as a whole and for generations yet unborn.

Experimentation on human beings is morally allowable only if it avoids disproportionate physical and psychological risks and has the informed consent of the subject or those who legitimately speak for that person (*Catechism,* 2295). The same avoidance of undue risk and informed consent should also be present for organ transplants (2296).

Regarding the bringing about of human life outside the womb, that is, the producing of babies by "in vitro" fertilization, a 1987 Vatican Instruction points out that this is a wrongful manipulation of the human person at inception and can have long-range results harmful to our basic values. Donor fertilization, too, is wrong, as are the use of surrogate mothers and embryo freezing—in these, besides the manipulation of the incipient human person, the introduction of a third party's sperm or ovum violates the exclusivity of the marriage covenant and can have harmful psychological and social results (as is evident from recent legal actions). However, regarding fertilization with the husband's sperm and embryo transplant, many moralists see this as defensible—and Cardinal Bernardin of Chicago noted that a couple might in conscience regard this, subjectively, as moral.

The patenting and marketing of new life forms, including marketing for financial profit of human genetic material—our own life-technology left in the hands of profit-making corporations—is of concern to many, scientists, religionists, and humanists alike. Future genetic-engineering can mean replacing defective genes that produce abnormalities—an evidently laudable, promising prospect. But it could also mean the attempted production of flawless or "perfect" human beings (positive eugenics). Pressing questions arise here: Once we begin selectively breeding human children, where will we stop? What constitutes the most desirable human being? Who decides this? And what happens to the unfit, the undesirable, who are costly to maintain?

Euthanasia, the direct killing of sick or disabled people, is wrong because it deprives them of their right to life. This is different from needlessly prolonging people's lives by using extraordinary means to keep them alive, or sustaining them in a persistent vegetative state through artificial nutrition. Allowing such people to die only makes sense, especially if death is seen not as the end of life but as the door to an everlasting afterlife. But allowing people to die is one thing; encouraging them to die is another. To pressure old, chronically ill, poor, or disabled people to "get out of the way" is clearly wrong and un-Christian.

Pope John Paul II, in his 1995 encyclical "The Gospel of Life" (Evangelium Vitae), exposes the current "culture of death" and the "network of complicity" behind it: the desire for comfort, along with a distaste for limits, that provokes irritation with the baby—or infirm old person—who compromises our time and material lifestyle; the notion of unrestricted freedom, the desire to "have it all" for oneself that promotes and even legalizes the killing of "inconvenient" infants, older people, and the chronically sick or disabled. Asking us to have the courage to look truth in the eye, the pope recalls the biblical story of Cain and Abel: Cain, confronted by God after he has killed his brother Abel, retorts, "Am I my brother's keeper?" The answer, the pope says, is "Yes"—we are linked in a common command to respect all of life, since all of it is a sacred gift from the Creator.

Abortion is wrong because it takes away an innocent infant's right to life. Albeit a developing life, the embryo, and later the fetus, is the product from conception of a *human* couple, both of whom have *human* genetic structures—and thus is a human life.

The unborn infant has a right to life, as does any human person, no matter what age or in what condition. If we take innocent human life in the womb because this is judged to be for the good of others—even for the child's good—there is logically nothing to prevent society from one day doing away with anyone judged to be useless, incapacitated, a burden on society, or simply unwanted.

Abortion is an immensely complicated and highly charged issue today, among Catholics as well as others, and these few words, it is realized, can only scratch the surface.

The Church from its beginning has condemned abortion. In the ancient pagan world it was almost alone in this, and with a few vacillations, it has opposed abortion through the centuries as direct killing of an innocent person and therefore a serious sin. "Indirect" abortions have been allowed, that is, those that save the life of a mother with a cancerous uterus or an ectopic pregnancy. Further, while official Church teaching still holds that a human life is present from the moment of conception (*Catechism*, 2270 ff.), theologians would allow this procedure up to fourteen days, or implantation, after which it is settled whether there will be one or more human beings—the preembryo, they agree, is not a person. They reason that, since most fertilized eggs do not implant, to hold otherwise would be to contend that most human beings live and die with no one ever knowing about it—an evident absurdity.

Currently there also is discussion among some theologians regarding genetic individualization, spoken of above, vis-à-vis developmental individualization or integration of the central nervous system. The question is not whether abortion is moral—it is not—but what constitutes a human being, that is, at what point is a human being present. In all this, finally, there is general agreement that there must be regard for the mother and her well-being as well as for that of the child. And there is agreement that the Church needs to listen more to women, who are the ones primarily involved in this matter.

There is a sad irony about the current number of abortions in the United States, which has one of the highest abortion rates of any developed country. Though theologians agree that laws absolutely prohibiting abortion would be unenforceable in our pluralistic society, and therefore would not be good laws, at the other extreme is the fact that one out of five couples in the United

States is unable to have a child when they are ready and the child is wanted—which means that the demand for infants and even older children for adoption is far greater than the children available. So, while millions of people are living through the very painful realization that children are indeed God's most precious gift—a gift that they might never have—at the same time many very much wanted children are being aborted.

In recent years a "consistent ethic" of life has evolved in Church teaching, as this chapter tries to show, which holds all human life sacred—from its beginning in the womb to that of the poorest among us, a criminal convicted of a capital crime, or a "useless" old person nearing death.

"Birthright" and other groups offer free counseling, pregnancy testing, financial help, and other services to women to help them realize that there are alternatives to abortion. While especially needed by women who are young, unwed, poor, and of racial minorities, these services are available to all. A woman (or a couple) in the often agonizing dilemma of whether or not to have an abortion should talk to someone who shares their basic values. There *are* understanding, balanced, and competent people wanting to help.

Finally, our society must do more to help women who are de facto driven to abortion—to offer effective financial support to needy mothers not only during pregnancy but afterward, as well as better child care and educational opportunities for teenagers and women with children. Poverty, lack of education, lack of healthy recreational alternatives to sexual promiscuity, and similar inhibiting factors make a mockery of saying that aborting or not is simply an individual matter of a woman's free choice. Abortion is plainly a social problem that involves all of our society, and on this almost everyone, pro-life or pro-choice, can agree.

It is also worth noting, in view of the heatedness that frequently accompanies discussions of abortion, that there are points on which moderates of both sides can agree without compromising their principles—see "Further Reading."

OUR CHRISTIAN COMMITMENT TO JUSTICE

Our respect for the dignity of others and our Christian love are most basically proven by our sense of justice, our willingness to share with

those in need. To be treated with justice or fairness is something we desire and need from childhood. Our heavenly Father has given his human children enough resources—natural resources, and those of human talent and ingenuity—for all his children on earth to have a just share of what is necessary for a dignified human life: a sufficient diet, a decent place to live, humane working conditions and a just wage, the education of one's children, and sufficient leisure.

Our planet's resources can easily give these basic necessities for a dignified human life to every person on earth—and to many more besides. This has been shown by numerous studies. The basic problem is distribution. A relative few are the "haves," while most by far are the "have-nots." Most of us in the United States—and in Western Europe, Japan, the OPEC countries—not only have what we need for a dignified human life but have far more than we need. At the same time, the majority of our fellow humans lack proper nourishment, decent housing, sufficient clothing, productive work, and even minimally adequate education. "Some people are needy because other people are greedy"—thus eight-year-old Marc one day summed up this world situation.

In the United States itself today, thirty-seven million people live below the poverty level. Fifteen percent, urban and rural, suffer from some serious form of malnutrition. One-fourth of our children are born into poverty. More than five million U.S. children are hungry at any given time. A third of our senior citizens must go without some necessities to pay their bills each month. Yet the upper and upper-middle class of our society, taken together, throw away as garbage enough edible food to feed all our deprived people adequately—as well as tens of millions of hungry people in the third world.

Despite some advances, the gap continues to widen between the well-off of our society and the very poor, the truly helpless—mostly blacks, unskilled whites, Hispanics, Native American Indians, and children (especially black children), many from single-parent households headed by women. While 1 percent of the U.S. population has 40 percent of our country's wealth, the approximately 25 million poor Americans—relatively unskilled or unable to work, sick (many mentally ill), elderly, and homeless—often live each day hungry and chronically ill.

Besides the malnutrition weakening them mentally and physically, their housing conditions are filthy, their education and health care far below average, and neglect, fear, and often utter loneliness are what they face each day. The temptation to escape into drugs or alcohol is constantly with them (most young black men, for instance, have no role models and little chance for either adequate education or a steady job). And many adults of whatever race or background simply have no hope.

Christian social justice works to change unjust "structures" and institutions of society—as well as individuals—to conform to Christ's teachings on simple justice and love. It works to overcome the "institutionalized greed" of many corporations and conglomerates, the excessive profits that accrue to a small minority—those who have more and more, while most of the world's people have less and less—and who feel little or no obligation to share with those in need. Christian social justice upholds the right of workers to organize to be paid a just wage and have decent working conditions. It also works to eradicate the corrupt practices of some labor unions and their officials.

Christian social justice also tries to stop the exploitation of the poor that often accompanies the development of less-developed countries, where corrupt local officials, financed by a wealthy few, work hand in glove with the military (usually), assuring stability for investments at the expense of the basic human rights of their own people: **Read Luke 16, 19–31.**

Wealth is not wrong in itself, but it can easily be a detriment to following Christ and a continual temptation to pride, arrogance, greed, political corruption, and injustice. Jesus permitted no one to follow him without that person giving his or her accumulated wealth to the poor (cf. Mark 10, 17–22), and he said that it is "easier for a camel to get through the eye of a needle than for a rich man to enter the kingdom of heaven" (Mark 10, 25). His parable of the rich man and Lazarus, given above, clearly says that those who indulge their affluence, while giving token "crumbs" to the poor, will simply not attain salvation. The early Christian Church took him seriously and practiced a communal sharing of their possessions (cf. Acts, chapters 2, 3, 4; 2 Corinthians 8 and 9).

Catholic social teaching regarding justice was enunciated by Vatican Council II in making clear what everyone has a right to: "There

must be made available to all everything necessary for leading a truly human life, such as food, clothing and shelter, the right to freely choose a state of life and to found a family, the right to education, to employment, to a good reputation, to respect, to be informed, to be able to act in accord with the upright norms of one's own conscience, to protection of privacy, and to rightful freedom in religious matters also" (*Constitution on the Church in the Modern World*, no. 26).

The Council spoke further regarding the traditionally affirmed right to private property, and it addressed those who think it is sufficient to occasionally give a bit of charity after all their other needs and wants have been satisfied:

"Persons should regard their lawful possessions not merely as their own but also as common property. . . . The right to have a share of earthly goods sufficient for oneself and one's family belongs to everyone. . . . People are obliged to come to the relief of the poor, and to do so not merely out of their superfluous goods. If a person is in extreme necessity, such a one has the right to take from the riches of others what he or she needs. . . . This Council urges all . . . to remember the [early Christian] saying: 'Feed those dying of hunger, because if you have not fed them you have killed them' " (*Constitution on the Church in the Modern World*, no. 69).

Pope Paul VI's 1967 encyclical, "On the Development of Peoples," concerned the widening gap between the "have" and "have-not" nations of the world. It spelled out practical norms for worldwide social action and for anyone seriously wanting to live as a Christian in today's world.

The central message of the encyclical is a call for social and economic justice on a global scale. The pope summed up what is most inimical in the intrinsic greed-orientation of much of our economic thinking: "The baseless theory which considers profit the key motive for economic progress, competition as the supreme law of economics, and private ownership of the means of production as an absolute right that has no limits and carries no corresponding social responsibilities. This has led to dictatorships and the international imperialism of money."

Calling development "another word for peace," Pope Paul challenged our well-fed complacency with some practical tests of our Christianity and human-

ity: "Let each . . . examine his conscience. . . . Is he prepared to support out of his own pocket works and undertakings organized in favor of the most destitute? Is he ready to pay higher taxes so that the public authorities can intensify their efforts in favor of development? Is he ready to pay higher prices for imported goods so that the producer may be more justly rewarded? . . . When so many people are hungry, when so many families suffer from destitution, . . . when so many schools, hospitals and homes worthy of the name remain to be built, all public or private squandering of wealth, all expenditure prompted by motives of national or personal ostentation, every exhausting armaments race, becomes an intolerable scandal."

Pope John Paul II's 1988 encyclical, "On Social Concerns," continues and updates the teaching of Vatican Council II and Pope Paul VI: Read again Matthew 25, 31-46. The pope's message is based on the plain words of Christ. The pope stresses human "solidarity," including solidarity with the earth, and says that "the goods of creation are meant for all" and must be distributed fairly, especially to those in need. As rich individuals have an obligation in justice to the poor, so are rich nations obliged to help poorer ones—as in the parable of Lazarus and the rich man. **Read Luke 16, 19-31.**

In this encyclical (as in his earlier "Redeemer of Man") he criticizes both Marxist collectivism and capitalist consumerism for exalting materialism, undermining the dignity of the individual and his or her rights, and for considering private ownership an absolute right—and he calls the East-West confrontation and the cost of the arms race a terrible burden laid on the world's poor. Nor does he spare the Church: it could be obligatory, he says, to sell superfluous church ornaments and costly furnishings to help the poor.

In a 1981 encyclical, "On Human Work," Pope John Paul II wrote that human labor was part of God's plan, and that workers and their work must never be subordinated to productivity, by either capitalism or collectivism, nor to capital and property. Asking, as always, for an equitable worldwide distribution of goods, he said that all have a right to "humanizing" work, called labor unions an opportunity for a wider solidarity of all who work, and said we must overcome dehumanizing corporate and class "egoism"—in short, work is for humans, not humans for work.

In his encyclical "The Hundredth Year" (1991), Pope John Paul II further reaffirms that Catholic social teaching is an essential part of the Christian message. Issued on the centenary of Leo XIII's first papal encyclical on labor, "On New Things," this encyclical—while saying that the Church has no specific programs to propose—restates the Church's "preferential option for the poor." It stresses the dignity of each human person, the right of governments to interfere on behalf of those in need, and the right of workers to social security, pensions, health insurance, and compensation for accidents. The pope criticizes the "domination of things over people" and the "idolatry of the market," as well as the idea that a business exists solely to make a profit. He also says that the state must provide for "natural and human environments which cannot be safeguarded simply by market forces."

The Catechism of the Catholic Church also condemns economic and political systems that reduce persons to nothing more than a means of profit (2424) and opposes the excesses of both communism and capitalism (2425). It says further that the goods of creation are destined for the whole human race (2402), that this fact takes primacy over the right to private property (2403), and that rich nations have a grave moral responsibility to help those nations who are unable to develop or attain liberation by themselves—especially if the prosperity of the wealthy nations has come from resources that have not been paid for fairly (2438–40). It quotes what many today would consider an outrageous statement by St. John Chrysostom: "Not to enable the poor to share in our goods is to steal from them and deprive them of life. The goods we possess are not ours, but theirs" (2446).

Applying the teaching of the council and popes to the United States, the American bishops' 1987 pastoral letter, "Economic Justice for All," deals with Catholic social teaching and the U.S. economy. As with their 1983 letter, "The Challenge of Peace," all segments of the American and especially the Catholic community, in large numbers, contributed to this letter. It builds on several basic principles:

—*Every economic decision and institution must be judged by whether or not it protects the dignity of the human person,* and this dignity can be realized only in community: "love thy neighbor" requires a commitment not just to individuals but to the common good, the good of all.

—*All people have a right to participate in and contribute to the economic life of society,* and all members of society have a special obligation to the poor and vulnerable. Thus no one is justified in keeping for his or her exclusive use what he or she does not need when others lack necessities.

—*Human rights include economic rights, that is, a right to life, food, clothing, shelter, rest, medical care, education, and employment.* Individuals as well as the institutions of our society—business, industry, government, and so on—have a moral responsibility to secure and protect these rights for each person.

The bishops ask all Americans, especially Catholics, to study and reflect on their letter, pray about it, and then reach out personally to the hungry and homeless, the poor, powerless, and vulnerable—and to become informed, active citizens "using your voices and vote to speak for the voiceless, to defend the poor and vulnerable and to advance the common good."

Some question the bishops' right to speak on economics, since they are not economists. But economic behavior has ethical aspects, as does science, politics, and so on. Moral principles "cannot be left at the level of appealing generalities." One's conscience may lead one to disagree, but one must at least honestly reflect—in the light of the vast numbers of deprived in our midst today—on what the bishops are saying.

The bishops continue to urge the rejection of limits on welfare for the poor, the underprivileged, immigrants, and especially children. Realizing that many in our country want to drastically cut aid to those least able to afford it, the bishops compare themselves to headlights on a car. They are not the motor, nor the driver—they do not make or enforce the laws, nor do they want to—but they are prophetically trying to show where our country is headed when it penalizes those who are least fortunate among us. They see ahead a basically un-Christian society and reject as plainly contrary to the words and actions of Christ the notion that depriving needful people of benefits will "shock" them into caring for themselves.

They also continue to ask for comprehensive health care for everyone: "This right," they say, "flows from the sanctity of human life and the dignity that belongs to all human persons who are made in the image of God" (Statement of Nov. 15, 1995).

A significant movement in the Church for social justice, particularly in Latin America, has been based on "liberation theology," or the theology of the oppressed. As is well known, there is poverty, exploitation, and political oppression in many nations of Central and South America. Tens of millions suffer from poverty, malnutrition, and political oppression, while a very small number (usually of the traditionally wealthy families) control the economy and live luxuriously, allied often with ruthless military leaders who pay lip service to democracy.

The Latin American bishops' conference at Medellin in 1968 confronted this problem, and the great majority spoke out in a now-famous statement signaling that the Church would henceforth be the main champion for social change in Latin America. The bishops said simply that Christians and their churches cannot be silent, ignore their share of responsibility for change, or remain inactive. As a result, many bishops, clergy, and laity have confronted governments and institutions that oppress and dehumanize the poor and destroy whole native cultures; there have been many incidents of bishops, priests, and laypeople being imprisoned, tortured, killed, or simply "disappearing."

The third Latin American bishops' conference at Puebla, Mexico, in 1979 and the fourth in 1992 reaffirmed this commitment to labor for the material betterment of their oppressed people, as well as for their spiritual needs. Following the lead of Pope John Paul II, who opened the 1979 conference, the bishops noted the dangers of both a simplistic Marxist solution to their countries' social problems (e.g., the inevitability of class struggle and violence) and the even more present danger of exploitative capitalism—particularly multinational corporations (many controlled by U.S.-dominated corporate conglomerates), who are aligned with the oppressing elite of their own countries, that is, the military, greedy landholders, and exploitative industrialists.

Recently, liberation theologians have stressed peacemaking and nonviolence as the way to achieve justice for the oppressed. They have been more nuanced and critical not only of violence—which brings its own injustices—but toward "dependence theory," which says that underdeveloped nations are simply being kept that way to support the development of more advanced capitalist countries. But they also continue to point to the "institutionalized violence" of extreme class differences as a sinful social fact in much of Latin America.

Laypeople, particularly, have been wonderfully and courageously active in movements for social reform in Latin America, as well as numerous bishops, priests, and religious. "Conscientization" is the amazing phenomenon of largely uneducated and impoverished peasants coming gradually to realize their human (and divine) dignity and their right to demand a more just share of what they produce.

Long established in several Latin American countries are "Christian base communities" (which today exist in many parts of the world): small groups of laypeople, clergy, and religious meet together regularly to pray, reflect (in the light of the Scriptures) on their experience of trying to live dignified Christian lives amid impoverishment and unjust working conditions, and then act on their conclusions. Many still must meet secretly, risking imprisonment, torture, and death.

Small Christian communities or groups, through which people overcome the anonymity of large parish congregations, are growing rapidly today. People gather in support of one another for various purposes: to pray, to study and reflect, to do works of justice, to prepare for the sacraments, to help those in need, to assist those who are new to or returning to the Church, and so on. These groups have a variety of purposes and structures. Many are associated with parishes but some are not. Whatever their purpose and structure, they all consist of people "being Church" to one another.

OUR CHRISTIAN COMMITMENT TO PEACE

Where there is no justice, there is violence—or, put another way, "Peace is the fruit of justice," as St. Augustine perceived centuries ago. If people live in conditions of injustice, violence will inevitably result. This was the meaning of Mother Teresa of Calcutta's receiving the Nobel Peace Prize for 1979. Why give a nun, who has spent most of her life working among the poorest of the world's poor, this most distinguished award for peace? In her own words, "Greed is the greatest obstacle to peace in the world today—greed for power, for money, and for fame." So the fact of injustice, that some people are needy because other people are greedy, is the greatest obstacle to peace in the world.

The Christian ideal is clearly set down in Christ's words and in the example of his own life. We must use only peaceful, nonviolent means to achieve the purpose of his gospel, a just and loving world as a prelude to an eternity of peace, love, and joy. Remember Christ's uncompromising words to St. Peter, after Peter uses his sword to defend Christ against seizure by his enemies and eventual death: "Put your sword back into its place, for all who take up the sword will perish by the sword" (Matthew 26, 51–53). Then Christ set the example for his followers through the centuries, allowing himself to be unjustly scourged, mocked, and put to death.

There are those who point out that this is an imperfect world, that violence is permitted as a last resort in a just war or just revolution against a tyrannical government. They point out that there would today be no United States of America unless a war had been used against injustice, or that Hitler, for instance, could have conquered the world unless force had been used to stop him. This does indeed pose a dilemma for most Christians, and thus the "just war" theory has evolved over the centuries.

The traditional conditions under which a just war may be fought are (1) there is a just cause; (2) every possible peaceful way of settling the conflict has been taken; (3) the war is declared by a legitimate authority; (4) the means used to fight the war will not do more harm than the purpose sought in going to war—this is called "proportionality"; and (5) there is no direct killing of non-combatants (sometimes a relatively small number of civilians might be killed "indirectly," that is, their deaths are not directly intended as a means of, or part of, a strategy of stopping the enemy)—this is called "discrimination," that is, discriminating between civilian and military targets. These last two conditions, proportionality and discrimination, are what modern war especially violates—and what makes nuclear war unthinkable.

Thus Pope John XXIII said succinctly in his 1963 encyclical "Peace on Earth": "In an age such as ours which prides itself on its atomic energy, it is contrary to reason to hold that war is now a suitable way to restore rights which have been violated."

Certain means of warfare are plainly immoral. The fact that so-called Christian nations have used them in the past is all the more reason for plainly repudiating them now. Some are the attempted destruction of entire cities or of extensive areas along with their population; indiscriminate bombing of populated areas; bombing or terrorist tactics aimed at civilians to weaken the morale of the enemy; torture of prisoners; use of chemical or biological weapons excluded by international agreement; indiscriminate use of napalm; acts of reprisal against prisoners of war or civilians; depriving large numbers of the civilian population of food through crop destruction; demands of unconditional surrender that kill reasonable hopes of a negotiated settlement; and the use of nuclear weapons designed to include the destruction of civilian populations. If an enemy uses these or other immoral means, it gives us no right to retaliate in kind. The test of a Christian is one's willingness to act as a Christian when others do not.

The Christian ideal and purpose are obviously the elimination of all warfare, the way of Jesus and his closest followers, as we have said. In modern times, the Church's position has been evolving—particularly since Pope John XXIII's encyclical "Peace on Earth" (1963)—from a kind of opposition to but pained acceptance of the inevitability of war (and the just war position) to one of continual condemnation of the arms race and nuclear proliferation, a constant encouragement of every effort to negotiate arms reduction, and a vindication of the rights of conscientious objectors and Christian pacifists.

> *In 1965, Vatican Council II said this about war and the arms race:* "Any act of war aimed indiscriminately at the destruction of entire cities or extensive areas along with their population is a crime against God and man himself. It merits unequivocal and unhesitating condemnation. . . . The arms race is an utterly treacherous trap for humanity, and one which injures the poor to an intolerable degree. . . . It is our clear duty, then, to strain every muscle as we work for the time when all war can be completely outlawed by international consent . . . " (*The Church in the Modern World,* no. 81).

The U.S. bishops' 1983 pastoral letter dealt with "The Challenge of Peace" at a time of "supreme crisis"—the then growing possibility of nuclear warfare. This widely acclaimed letter was the result of an unprecedented process by which hundreds of thousands of people from all walks of life contributed their views. It reiterates the moral norms of the just war tradition, plus those of Vatican Council II and recent popes:

While every nation has the right and duty to defend itself against unjust aggression, offensive war of any kind is not morally justifiable. The intentional killing of innocent civilians or noncombatants is always wrong (discrimination); and no defensive response, even to an unjust attack, can violate the principle of proportionality.

The bishops then applied these norms to nuclear weapons, not only ruling out their use for civilian targets and indiscriminate retaliatory bombing, but saying that nonnuclear attacks by another nation must be resisted by other than nuclear means, and that a no-first-use policy should be adopted as soon as possible. They said further that a nuclear-deterrence policy is acceptable only on a strictly conditional, temporary basis, that arms control and disarmament through negotiations must be pursued, and they gave their support to "immediate, bilateral, verifiable agreements to halt the testing, production and deployment of new nuclear weapons systems."

They then strongly urged that the United States promote political and economic policies aimed at the needs of the world's poor, stating unequivocally that there can be peace only if social injustices are eradicated. They restated Vatican Council II's description of the arms race as "an utterly treacherous trap for humanity, and one which injures the poor to an intolerable degree." Quite simply, the several trillion and more dollars spent on arms in the last decade could feed, clothe, house, educate, and provide jobs for our own and the world's poor many times over.

The bishops have continued to point out that the United States is the world's largest supplier of arms, and they echo Pope John Paul II, who called those who look to continuing to profit by arms contracting "merchants of death."

The bishops have also tried to sketch out a theory of just sanctions, like the historical theory of a just war, in a 1993 letter following up what was said above.

The bishops challenge us not just to avoid war but to build peace. "A whole new outlook is needed," says Pope John Paul II. *This is Christian hope,* the confident expectation that we *can* have world peace and disarmament. God's caring love ceaselessly prods us. If we do our part, we will find solutions that now seem impossible. We need to pray daily for peace and for the openness of world leaders to God's guidance.

Some feel called to be conscientious objectors and "public authorities should make equitable provision for them" (Catechism, 2311). They deserve the support of the Christian community, and they, in turn, should support that community in some other way. Others feel called to public demonstration and perhaps to nonviolent civil disobedience for peace and against arms proliferation, and these people also deserve the support of the Christian community. The American bishops have long called (unsuccessfully) for a recognition of the principle of selective conscientious objection—people who, for instance, would have fought against Hitler or in defense of the fifty states found it hard to justify our continued presence in Vietnam. Of course, the true pacifist, Christian or not, believes that it is morally wrong to fight in any war.

Others opt for following their consciences as part of the armed forces, and they, too, deserve our support. "If they carry out their duty honorably, they truly contribute to the common good of the nation and the maintenance of peace" (Catechism, 2310).

CHRIST SENDS US THE HOLY SPIRIT IN CONFIRMATION

At baptism we were united to Christ and born into the life of grace. We came forth as children of God from the "womb" of baptismal water. Yet, as we know from everyday life, children must become adults. They must be concerned for others, more sharing, more responsible. So, too, Christ through his Church enables us to mark our adult responsibility for sharing our beliefs and values with others. This is the sacrament of confirmation.

Confirmation is the sacrament in which Christ gives the Holy Spirit to continue and complete our baptismal commitment, especially our bearing witness for our faith. We saw earlier that, as part of Christian initiation, confirmation is given after baptism and before taking part in the eucharist. What we have received and pledged ourselves to in baptism—especially its "missionary" dimension of bearing witness—is ratified, sealed, or "confirmed" by our taking part in this sacrament.

In the early Church, confirmation was given with baptism, as part of the rite of baptism—followed by the eucharist, this was Christian initiation and was presided over by the bishop. When infant baptisms increased and also the number of rural parishes, it became difficult for the bishop to get to all the baptismal celebrations. Gradually, in order for the bishop to come to those who had been baptized, confirmation in the West became separated from baptism. By the eleventh century in the West, confirmation as a separate sacrament administered by the bishop was a general practice. In the twentieth century it came to be associated with a child's maturing and was given about the age of puberty. In the East, however, it has continued to be given to infants with baptism (and the eucharist) by the officiating priest.

The Rite of Christian Initiation, as we have seen, envisions children receiving confirmation when they are baptized—followed by first eucharist—as part of the same rite. The children would go through the steps of the RCIA according to their ability and readiness, and these sacraments of initiation would then be received together at the Easter Vigil. Done usually when children are at the age of reason (at about seven years) or a bit beyond, this presupposes close parental participation and a free desire on the children's part. Then, hopefully, there would be a late-teens recommitment of the young people to their faith, preceded by a retreat or other preparation.

In many places today, however, confirmation is given in the late teens, also after a period of preparation. The young almost-adults are required to formally say "yes" or "no" to a more mature recommitment to their baptismal faith before receiving confirmation. Hopefully, they will recognize that God is calling them to be part of a loving community of faith, and they will freely declare their desire to follow Christ and live out their life's mission as Christians. Some may decide not to be confirmed, but whatever their choice, it will be a more mature one.

When confirmation is given in this way, separately from baptism, the fact that it is a continuation of baptism is brought out by the baptismal promises that all participating say together. Those who were baptized as infants thus recommitment themselves on their own to what was pledged for them at their baptism.

At confirmation Christ sends the Holy Spirit in a fuller outpouring of his indwelling presence. At baptism we received by grace the presence of the Trinity within us. Now we receive a great increase of

God's grace-presence, and particularly an increase of the presence of the Holy Spirit.

Confirmation leads the Christian to a deeper life of the Spirit within. Prayer and meditation are ways in which this life of the Spirit manifests itself in the life of a Christian. The whole "spiritual" life is rooted in the Holy Spirit, who dwells in the believer and who directs and guides each person who is attentive to that presence within. Preparation for receiving the sacrament of confirmation focuses on the qualities of the spiritual part of life so that we can come to experience the peace and joy of that rich inner life that flows from the coming of the Holy Spirit.

The Holy Spirit is especially associated with maturely and courageously "bearing witness" to our beliefs and moral convictions. The Spirit often moved the Old Testament prophets to bear witness. Luke points out how the Spirit inspired those associated with Christ's coming: Mary, Elizabeth, Zachary, Simeon (chapters 1 and 2).

Christ himself is given the Spirit by his Father. When he goes forth to preach the gospel, the Spirit inspires him:

> Now . . . when Jesus also had been baptized and was praying, heaven was opened, and the Holy Spirit descended upon him in bodily form, as a dove. . . . And Jesus, full of the Holy Spirit, returned from the Jordan, and was led by the Spirit for forty days in the wilderness . . . (Luke 3, 21–22 and 4, 1).
>
> And Jesus returned in the power of the Spirit into Galilee; and a report concerning him went out through all the surrounding country. And he taught in their synagogues, being glorified by all. And he came to Nazareth . . . and he went to the synagogue . . . on the sabbath day. And he stood up to read . . . the book of the prophet Isaiah. . . . "The Spirit of the Lord is upon me, because he has anointed me to preach good news to the poor . . . " (Luke 4, 14–18).

Christ promised to his Church the Holy Spirit that he had received from the Father. When Christ sent his apostles to carry on his mission, he predicted that they would be persecuted, but that the Spirit would sustain them and speak through them (Matthew 10, 16–22). Further, he told the apostles that "the Spirit of truth" would be with them forever (John 14, 16). After his resurrection the Spirit came in fullness to Christ. Then, about to leave his apostles, Christ gave them the great promise:

But you shall receive power when the Holy Spirit has come upon you, and you shall be my witness in Jerusalem and in all Judea and Samaria, and to the ends of the earth (Acts 1, 8).

We have seen how Christ fulfilled his promise and sent the Holy Spirit on Pentecost, transforming the fearful and confused apostles into courageous and eloquent witnesses. Amid a violent wind and tongues of fire, they "were all filled with the Holy Spirit" (Acts 2, 4). On another occasion after this "they were all filled with the Holy Spirit and spoke the Word of God with boldness" (Acts 4, 31). Threatened by the authorities, they answered, "We cannot but speak of what we have seen and heard. . . . We must obey God rather than any human authority" (Acts 4, 20; 5, 29). Scourged by the authorities, "they departed from the presence of the council, rejoicing that they were counted worthy to suffer dishonor for the name [of Jesus]. And every day in the temple and at home they did not cease teaching and preaching Jesus as the Christ" (Acts 4, 41–42).

The incident of Stephen, the Church's first martyr, is typical. Courageously professing his faith in Christ, he underwent death by stoning, "being full of the Holy Spirit" (Acts 7, 55). We read of the activity of the Holy Spirit, especially during the first three centuries, a time of almost continuous persecution and courageous witnessing. Today, too, there are many who are strengthened by the Holy Spirit as they suffer and die for their convictions, especially for justice and freedom for the world's deprived and oppressed people.

At our confirmation the Holy Spirit comes to us, deepening our power to maturely understand and profess our faith. As at baptism the mystery of Christ's passing from death to life becomes visible in our life, so by the ceremony of confirmation we can envision the event of Pentecost happening to us.

The apostles gave others the Holy Spirit by the ordinary ancient way of imposing hands on them. From time immemorial the laying on of hands has been connected with the gift of the Spirit among God's people. It was only natural, then, for the apostles to also use this: **Read Acts 8, 14–17.**

The sign or ceremony of confirmation is the imposition of the bishop's hands and anointing of the forehead with chrism. This ceremony gradually developed over the centuries as the essential part of the sacrament, best expressing the interior coming of the Spirit with power and strength. The bishop and priests present lay their hands on those to be confirmed. Then the bishop anoints the forehead of each with the oil of chrism, and says, "N., receive the seal of the Holy Spirit, the gift of the Father."

Oil is a sign of mission, of a giving out of joyful abundance. It cleanses and limbers, soothes and heals, and gives strength and health (*Catechism,* 1293-94). We are thus empowered to share our faith and moral principles with others, to be strong, adaptable, and resilient in living out the Christian life. This oil, the oil of chrism, also symbolizes our fuller sharing in Christ's priesthood—blessed by the bishop on Holy Thursday, it will be used when ordaining a priest. Chrism and the word Christ have the same root, that is, one who is anointed for a special mission or role.

By confirmation we share particularly in the prophetic work of Christ—teaching and bearing witness as he did—so we should have confidence when we speak of our religious convictions. The Holy Spirit illumines our minds, so that we may better understand and explain the things of God. The Spirit deepens our faith so that we can more clearly and intelligently tell of it to others. Whether we realize it or not, however poor our words seem, we have something of Christ's own power and forcefulness in our witnessing: **Read Matthew 10, 19-20; 1 Corinthians 2, 9-13.**

In today's Church many laypeople are outstandingly using their prophetic gifts. While the prophetic function of teaching truth belongs in the strict sense to the official teachers in the Church, it belongs as well to the whole Church and particularly to those gifted with this charism. A modern theologian has written perceptively, "Prophecy within the Church is a remedy against corruption on all levels. There are times when the officers of the Church fail to speak as they ought; those who utter the authentic voice of the Church in such moments are prophets. There are times when the hierarchy itself needs to be redeemed from corruption; those who rebuke it are prophets. Prophecy in such times of need can be either speech or action [and it] is not found in any one class or level in the Church" (McKenzie, *Authority in the Church,* Doubleday Image, 1971, p. 134).

By confirmation we share more fully in Christ's priestly powers, deriving more from the Mass and sacraments. We are changed interiorly, and this change is called the "character" of confirmation. By our baptismal character we received the power to take part in the Mass and other sacraments; by confirmation's character we further, more maturely take part in them.

By confirmation the Holy Spirit inspires us to help develop the society in which we live. It is the social sacrament. It makes us more aware of our opportunities and responsibilities as members of society.

The seven gifts of the Holy Spirit, received by everyone at confirmation (Isaiah 11, 2-3), are a fuller outpouring of what we received at baptism. The Spirit moves us by them, like sails on a boat, to the extent that we are open. They are wisdom, understanding, counsel, fortitude or courage, knowledge, reverence or piety, and awesome wonder or "fear" of the Lord.

Each person has special gifts that can—and should—be used for the good of all, for the whole Church. We spoke of these earlier in chapter 9: the Spirit inspires our efforts, unifies them, and makes them truly effective. "Now there are varieties of gifts, but the same Spirit . . . varieties of service . . . for the common good" (1 Corinthians 12, 4–7).

St. Paul describes the special gifts evident among the first Christians: **Read 1 Corinthians 12, 8-11.** We will see in chapter 20 that some today have gifts of healing, and so on. Though most today are not gifted in such clearly noticeable ways, there are quiet, everyday miracles of love—the healing of battered egos, those knowledgeable in little but very needed ways, the older and mature who often speak with tongues of true wisdom. If we pay attention, we can discern giftedness all about us.

In response to Vatican Council II, which stressed the vital need of laypeople taking part in Church affairs, diocesan and parish councils of clergy and laity have been set up in most places. In this way the clergy and laity consult regularly with one another and with the bishop, and the gifts and talents of all can be used for the good of the parish, the diocese, and in the nation and world as well (see also chapter 22).

We take part in confirmation only once because it has a permanent effect on us (like baptism). By this "character," as said above, we are changed interiorly for life, with new powers and social responsibilities.

The local bishop determines the age and other qualifications for confirmation; he consults with the national bishops' guidelines, and pastors, religious, and laypeople engaged in catechetical ministries.

Adults being initiated into the Catholic Church as converts are confirmed along with their baptism and/or reception into the Church as part of the full Rite of Christian Initiation. Already baptized Christians, of course, would not be rebaptized; after their profession of faith they would be confirmed—an especially mature commitment and fuller reception of the Spirit—and for the first time partake fully of the eucharist, the great sacrament that makes us one Body.

If those who have already received confirmation in a Protestant Church desire to become Catholics, they would take part in the Catholic sacrament of confirmation at their reception into the Catholic Church.

Confirmation normally takes place within the Mass, with as much of the whole parish community as possible taking part. As the now fully initiated Christians commit themselves to be part of the worship and life of their church community, so the community pledges them its support along the rest of life's way.

Those being confirmed in a parish might take part in this sacrament along with the catechumens and candidates who are being baptized and/or received into the Church at the Easter Vigil.

We use the name of a saint at confirmation. We may use our baptismal name, or we may take an additional name, perhaps that of a favorite saint, as another patron and model to bring us closer to Christ. If we take an additional name, we should choose someone whose life inspires us in a committed and courageous way.

There is a sponsor (or sponsors) at confirmation, representing the commitment to one's spiritual growth of the whole Church community. Having one's baptismal sponsor is usually preferable, though one may choose someone else. If one does choose another sponsor, that person should be a practicing Catholic, at least sixteen years of age, of either sex, and, most important, a person who will help one develop in a maturing, adult faith. Sometimes when a group is confirmed, a man and woman will sponsor the whole group; they symbolize the whole parish community.

DAILY LIVING: BEING OPEN TO THE
SPIRIT, PEACEFUL AND PRODDING

The Spirit is the one who, in the practical situations of life, inspires our choices, our willingness, our sensitivity, our acting—if we but allow this. The Spirit moves us to see how we should best plan for and react to the events of our life and prompts us toward what is best to do in times of trouble, pain, and confusion. The Spirit stirs within us the grace of continual conversion, of understanding, and of compassion, and gives us mature, unselfish sensitivity and the courage to act as we know we should.

Pope John XXIII, the old man who brought new life to the Catholic Church, said that our day is a "new Pentecost," and he called our times the age of the Holy Spirit. Many today are becoming more open to the Spirit, moving toward a sensitive, sharing, adult faith—and away from a self-centered and childishly narrow and threatened view of life.

An adult, loving faith will help us see honestly the pressing needs of our time and inspire us to do something about them. They are summed up in this chapter: the need of each human person to have his or her dignity respected and the right of each to live in conditions of justice and basic human decency, sharing the earth's goods.

Mother Teresa of Calcutta says simply that we who think ourselves fortunate are in fact the unfortunate ones. We who have so many material things are so often driven by them to aggression, overcompetitiveness, overachievement, "me-ness," insensitivity, and just plain greed. But we also have so much more potential to act effectively, to use our cocreativity and technology, our comparative wealth and abilities, to bring justice and peace to our own country and to the world.

Pope John Paul II challenged us from a Brazil slum: "Look around you a bit. Does it not hurt your heart? Do you not feel stings of conscience for your surplus and your abundance?" Some are looking around and acting in truly effective ways:

Instead of opting out of the political process, many are asking for accountability from their elected representatives, informing themselves about candidates' voting records and the Christian and human rights issues involved, and are joining together with others to see that their votes make a difference. Some are becoming aware of the power of consumer boycotts: they persevere, are willing to sacrifice their time and personal interests for a more just, more loving society, and are making a difference. Every diocese has social justice and peace groups that welcome any help or interest, however small. Often people in business and politics are not aware of what they can do to correct injustices and help make a better world; many dioceses and parishes are conducting study and discussion sessions in which different viewpoints are heard and practical conscience-decisions are arrived at.

Most of us live lives relatively unaffected by the others among us who simply cannot fend for themselves. These are not only the homeless and those who need the continual help of welfare, but the working poor, those on marginal incomes, those left behind by downsizing, or who find themselves redundancies along the electronic highway—and those of other cultures who will never have a chance to attain what we take for granted. It is as if we humans are from two planets, and those less fortunate occasionally visit us, staying mostly on the fringes of our lives. While we recognize that there are some among us who would prefer to live off the rest of us, there are far more who honestly need help along life's journey, who for very good reasons are simply unable to cope.

The *Catechism* quotes St. Catherine of Siena, a medieval mystic and very wise lady, to the effect that God distributes strengths or "virtues" diversely. He does not give all of them to each person but some to one and some to others. In this way, she says, we need one another—we will appreciate one another and practice charity to one another (1937). Those of us who are gifted in a material way, with talents very useful in an advanced, technological society, need to appreciate those who are not, who have other things to offer our human family. Often, unfortunately, it is only when one is seriously set back materially—and is deeply needful—that one comes to recognized the less obvious, often overlooked giftedness of others.

Perhaps the hardest thing of all is to boycott our own inbuilt tendency toward "consumerism," toward succumbing to the temptation that we must have the latest and/or the best. Our technology (which has done so much good) can subtly take over our lives. We can let machines and their products become our masters and overlook the things that cost little or nothing. Or we can become compulsive shoppers, often to allay our insecurities.

> There is the inexpensive gift that says "I love you" better than an expensive adult toy—the simple beauties of nature, of making do without gadgetry, the small, creative joys of making things ourselves, of working together—and giving the money we save to those in need. Best of all, we can give some of our time—however little—to sharing ourselves with someone who needs a bit more faith, hope, and love.

SOME SUGGESTIONS FOR . . .

DISCUSSION

Can you see a priority among human rights, such as that the right to the food and basic goods needed for a decent life has precedence over the right to private property and to surplus profits?

Can you see why Catholic teaching on the dignity and sacredness of human life has been called a "seamless garment" (after the robe Christ wore at his crucifixion), that all life is sacred or no life is sacred?

What do you think of "tithing," not necessarily in the biblical sense of setting aside 10 percent of one's income, but regularly giving a portion of your money and/or time for those in need?

While avoiding Marxist oversimplification, can you see a connection between greed and war and social unrest—or between the selfishness of the "haves" and the sometimes violent behavior of the "have-nots"?

How might you try to live out, in your own life, Christ's and the Church's "option for the poor"?

How might one do something, however small, to concretely help the growing number of those who have less and less?

Do you see a concrete way in which to make a contribution toward world peace and disarmament?

If you are in a large parish, how might you make it more personal and effective in helping others, by being part of a small community?

How might the Holy Spirit be prodding you to be a more sharing person?

FURTHER READING

- *Pacem in Terris (Peace on Earth),* Pope John XXIII (Paulist Press)—The late, great pope's "breakthrough" encyclical of 1963 says simply that there can be no world peace without world justice; this encyclical, together with his • *Mater et Magistra (Mother and Teacher),* Pope Paul VI's • *Populorum Progressio (On the Development of Peoples),* and Pope John Paul II's • *Laborem Exercens (On Human Work)* and • *Sollicitudo Rei Socialis (On Social Concerns)* are the five basic papal writings of our time on peace, social justice, and the arms race.
- *Economic Justice for All: Catholic Social Teaching and the U.S. Economy* (USCC, 1987)—This is the U.S. Bishops' Pastoral Letter that forthrightly applies biblical and traditional Catholic social teaching to our society today. *For All the People,* Hug (USCC) is a good summary of the letter together with a study text on implementing it. Also, Catholic Update 0187 (St. Anthony Messenger Press) is a condensed version of the letter.
- *The Challenge of Peace: God's Promise and Our Response* (USCC, 1983)—This is the breakthrough U.S. Bishops' Pastoral Letter on nuclear weapons and the arms race, which had a great impact in the United States as well as abroad; included in this are a summary and footnotes for further discussion. The *Summary, The Challenge of Peace* (USCC) may be obtained separately—and Catholic Update 0883 (St. Anthony Messenger Press) is a highly condensed version. Spanish-English texts of both these pastoral letters are available from the USCC.
- *How Should We Think About the Poor?* Untener (St. Anthony Messenger Press, Catholic Update 792)—In this very brief but wonderfully incisive presentation, a bishop who has long been dedicated to the poor discusses some problems in dealing with them and how we might easily adjust our attitude toward them.
- *Hunger for Justice: The Politics of Food and Faith,* Nelson (Orbis, 1980)—An objective, comprehensive view of this worldwide tragedy, its urgency, and what the ordinary person can do about it; a study guide, "Living for Justice," can be had with it.
- *Bread for the World,* Simon (Paulist Press, 1984)—This is a revision of the award-winning classic on this subject.

- *Narrowing the Gap* (Catholic Relief Services)—This brief booklet is a factual, excellent updating of the world situation on hunger, poverty, and development.
- *Something Beautiful for God,* Muggeridge (Doubleday Image Book, 1977)—This is the original work on Mother Teresa of Calcutta, the saintly nun and Nobel Prize winner who has captured the hearts of the world by her work among the poorest of the poor.
- • *Health and Medicine in the Catholic Tradition,* McCormick (Crossroad, 1984)—One of America's leading moral theologians discusses issues of sexual, medical, and family morality.
- • *Corrective Vision: Explorations in Moral Theology,* McCormick (Sheed & Ward, 1994)—In another excellent work, American Catholicism's premier bioethicist discusses his own search for truth regarding several bioethical issues, the role of the Church (which is not always honest with itself), and the problems and possibilities in this area today. Chapter 15, "Abortion: The Unexplored Middle Ground," gives twenty starting points for a reasonable and unheated discussion of this issue in our pluralistic society.
- *Euthanasia: Moral and Pastoral Perspectives,* Gula (Paulist Press, 1994)—In this compact book, a theologian and popular teacher discusses different aspects of this issue clearly and compassionately.
- • *Bioethics,* ed. Shannon (Paulist Press, 1993)—The fourth edition of this widely used, comprehensive presentation of basic writings on the key ethical questions in this field.
- • *Consistent Ethic of Life,* Bernardin, ed. Fuechtmann (Sheed & Ward, 1988)—This sets forth the position of consistency across a broad range of "life" issues, with response papers from different perspectives.
- • *Abortion and Catholicism: The American Debate,* ed. Jung and Shannon (Crossroad, 1988)—These articles give a cross section of the Catholic community on this issue, from theologians and Church leaders to politicians and editors.

Also, the Bishop's Committee for Pro-Life Activities has many good publications on human life issues. Feminists for Life, Justlife, and the Seamless Garment Network are groups that promote a consistent-ethic-of-life position.

Network (806 Rhode Island Ave., Washington, D.C. 20018) is a group that distributes information nationally about books, activities, and so on concerning issues of justice and peace.

The Common Ground Network for Life and Choice consists of women on all "sides" of the abortion debate who join in discussion groups to seek an alternative to what has often been angry rhetoric. Getting to know one another's views without sacrificing their own principles, they cooperate on such matters as helping women to stay out of abortion clinics in the first place.

- *The Gift of Life (Donum Vitae)*—The 1987 Vatican document on "reproductive technologies," its substance is referred to in the text above.
- *Catholic Women and Abortion: Stories of Healing,* ed. King (Sheed & Ward, 1994)—Catholic women who have experienced the aftershock of an abortion tell their stories as part of their healing and realize they are not alone.
- *Putting Children and Families First: A Challenge for Our Church, Nation and World* (USCC, 1992)—Frank, moving statement by the U.S. bishops detailing the dire conditions under which many children, poor and vulnerable, live in our country, and what we are challenged to do about it.
- • *Fulness of Faith: The Public Significance of Theology,* Himes and Himes (Paulist Press, 1993)—A superb synthesis of key aspects of the Church's social teaching, from human rights to abortion to the environment to patriotism, and other issues as well.
- • *One Hundred Years of Catholic Social Thought: Celebration and Challenge,* Coleman (Orbis, 1991)—A collection of the most significant Church writings regarding social teachings issued over the past century—an excellent representative selection.
- *What We've Seen and Heard* (St. Anthony Messenger Press)—This is the Black Bishops' of the U.S. 1984 Pastoral Letter on Evangelization that encourages blacks to evangelize themselves by drawing on their own spirituality, culture, and religious sense.
- *The Church and Racism: Towards a More Fraternal Society,* Vatican Commission on Justice and Peace (USCC, 1989)—Only forty pages but this is a frank, excellent history and summary of racism worldwide and the Church's efforts to confront it.

•• *A Theology of Liberation,* Gutierrez (Orbis, 1986)—This is the second edition of the pioneering work on Latin American liberation theology by the respected Peruvian theologian.

• *Cry of the People,* Lernoux (Doubleday, 1982)—Factual and well written by a highly respected writer, this is a moving account of oppression in Latin America.

For sample writings by feminist theologians of different cultures concerning "liberation" issues, see "Further Reading" in chapter 22.

• *The Response: Lay Volunteer Mission Opportunities* (International Liaison, USCC)—A continually updated directory of the many groups in which one can serve in the United States and abroad, giving concrete details about each.

• *The Second Wave,* Deck (Paulist Press, 1989)—A fine book on the Church's ministry with Hispanics in the United States, including pastoral issues and the growing formation of "base communities" among Hispanics in this country.

• *Naming and Claiming Our Resources,* ed. Lumas (The National Black Sister's Conference, 1989)—This is a periodic updating of an excellent resource for those ministering in black communities.

• *The History of Black Catholics in the U.S.,* Davis (Crossroad, 1995)— The sweeping, often surprising history of black Catholicism in the United States is laid out in this excellent, easily readable book.

• *The Holy Spirit—Yesterday and Today,* Wintz (St. Anthony Messenger Press, Catholic Update 0580)—A succinct, quite good presentation of how the Holy Spirit has acted in our Judeo-Christian history and still acts in the Church today.

• *Nurturing Young Catholics: A Guide for Confirmation Sponsors (and Other Caring Adults),* Moore (Paulist Press, 1995)—Written by the author of CHOICE, the country's most popular Confirmation program, this is a "how to" book for any adult who is helping a teen grow in the faith.

FURTHER VIEWING/LISTENING

Mother Teresa of Calcutta—A wonderful film about the life, work, and the community founded by this saintly nun.

For All the People—An excellent video on the Bishops' Economic Pastoral, this can be used with the summary mentioned on page 337.

El Norte—A moving, authentically done film about a brother and sister fleeing from Guatemala to the United States after their parents are killed.

Romero—An excellent movie about the archbishop of San Salvador and his journey from coward to champion of the poor to death at the hands of a right-wing death squad—produced by a priest friend of this author who wouldn't give up until he was able to tell this powerful story.

Dead Man Walking—A superb movie whose plot mainly concerns capital punishment, this is based on a book by a real-life nun/prison chaplain whose ministry to death-row inmates broadened to include the families of their victims.

Raising a Faith-Filled Child in a Consumer Society (Paulist Press, Fisher Productions)—This twenty-five-minute video gives practical, realistic guidance for helping children develop self-worth and true spiritual values in a materialistic society.

Beyond the News: Racism (NCR videocassette)—A six-part video with study guide, this presents experts in various fields sharing their insights about racism and what might be done about it.

PERSONAL REFLECTION

Two out of every five people in the United States—two out of four in our world—are steadily becoming poorer and less able to "catch-up" to the others, who are just as steadily doing better. If I am a Christian, I have two fundamental choices: simple honesty says that I must choose to either commit myself to those who are going down, and who desperately need to start going up, or to identify primarily with those going up, whose overriding concern is themselves and their wants and who let others fend for themselves. God reads my heart and knows my choice.

If I am in doubt about it, I can read Luke 16, 10–14 ("mammon" means money, possessions). A test might be whether I am willing to concretely commit some time and/or some financial contributions to the poor on a regular basis, to extend myself and help a particular person better "make it," to risk speaking my convictions before others of status, and so on.

18

Sin and What It Can Do to Us

What is sin? How does it affect us? Why do we sin? How can we overcome our sins? Everyone at one time or another asks oneself these things. To understand sin we must try to appreciate God's love, which it rejects.

SIN IN OUR LIFE

Read Luke 19, 41–44. The gospel picture of Christ weeping over Jerusalem is striking. He loved this city and its people, but he foresaw that despite his warnings the city would be utterly destroyed. It was, in 70 C.E., with the slaughter of a million people. Here is strikingly shown the effect of sin, of rejecting God's love.

We are the most fortunate beings in creation, for we are loved by the limitless God. He has given us life, an eternal destiny with him, and has himself come to save us. By baptism, we become his specially adopted children. In return, we should constantly desire to please him and to respond to his love. Yet often we do not. We sin against him and against our fellow humans whom he also loves.

Sin is a rejection of God's love, a refusal of an opportunity to accept his love and pass it on to others. All day long he gives us opportunities to respond to his love by our love—sin is a knowing neglect of these. It is as if God says, "Here is an opportunity to spread love in the world, to grow yourself in love and happiness"—and we refuse, we reject his loving guidance. Ultimately sin is a personal rebuff to our loving Father, to Christ our Brother and Savior, to the Spirit who is love within us. Incredibly, the infinite God is concerned with our rejection of this love. Christ tells us, also, "as you did it to one of these, the least of my brethren, you did it to me" (Matthew 25, 40).

People are often fearful of facing their sins, of honestly acknowledging their sinfulness. Christ longs to help them if only they would humbly turn to him. His entire life and teaching divides people into two classes: those who admit they are sinners—and these he goes out of his way to forgive, again and again—and those who refuse to acknowledge their sins—and these he castigates, "Woe to you, scribes and Pharisees, hypocrites. . . . "

Sin is immaturity; it distorts our personality and leads to ultimate frustration. By sinning, we yield to selfish, primitive urges. We refuse to recognize our personal relationship with God, our dependence on him, and we form an unreal concept of ourselves, making ourselves and our desires the supreme guide for our actions. Ironically, when we reject God's love, we spurn the one thing that can perfect our own personality and fulfill our aspirations.

Sin, then, is a failure to fulfill ourselves, to grow, to develop, to realize our potential. We fail to fulfill our capacity for good, for love, for lasting self-achievement in this particular situation. We miss a chance to achieve what we could: **Read Genesis 3, 1-5.**

Sin can be social, as well as individual, built into our society and its institutions. It can exist in greedy capitalism as well as in socialist systems that deny God and exploit the individual.

The seven deadly or capital sins are not so much sins as tendencies or "drives" within us that lead to sin. At bottom they are distortions of love or misplaced love; love, as we have seen, sums up the whole Christian life.

Pride is excessive love of self, the tendency to make oneself God. It rejects the love that would bring us out of our egotistical little worlds, into union with God and others; it is, ultimately, the source of all sin. *Covetousness or envy* is fear that someone else may have something we do not; our pride is offended because they outdo us. *Anger*, while sometimes proper and necessary—Jesus was angry (cf. Matthew 21, 10–16)—ultimately stems from wounded pride or a sense of inferiority. *Sloth*, or laziness, is neglecting to do what we should or could; it is a tendency to give up, often because we lack sufficient self-esteem to try to achieve. *Greed,* which leads us to excessively seek money or possessions, is so pervasive in our consumerist society that it is often made a virtue; we tend to judge ourselves and others by what we—or they—have, rather than what we are. *Gluttony* is a tendency to excess in food or drink or any substance; it can lead to addiction, a large problem in our society—we seek fulfillment by "bingeing," a vicious, unsatisfying cycle. *Lust* is a tendency to divorce sex from love, to use another as an object instead of treating the other as a lovable person; lust can be a fear of intimacy, of the commitment it calls for.

We should remember, incidentally, that thoughts or desires can be sinful, as well as actions or neglecting to do something we should. Christ says, "Whoever looks with lust at a woman has already committed adultery with her in his heart" (Matthew 5, 28). Sinful, too, would be a desire to harm or have revenge on someone. People also sin by neglect— parents, for example, who neglect to guide their children, those who have no concern for the poor, who deliberately refuse to worship the God they know they should.

One who continually and deliberately indulges in the same sin finds it harder and harder to stop and gradually becomes the slave of sin. Bit by bit one can blind oneself to God's truth and deafen oneself to the promptings of grace. One's sin becomes a habit, a vice. Scripture says of such: "For what the true proverb says has happened to them—a dog returns to his vomit, and a sow even after washing wallows in the filth" (2 Peter 2, 22).

JUDGING THE SERIOUSNESS OF SIN

Read Matthew 26, 20–24. Some sins are obviously worse than others. We recognize the terrible malice of Judas's betrayal of Christ. So, too, hatred of another is worse than an impatient word, and embezzling millions is more serious than stealing a few dollars. Some sins more deeply reject God.

As in human love there are slight offenses—a man might be carelessly late in picking up his fiancée. Or the offense can be a more serious rejection of her love—he might begin dating another woman behind her back. Ultimately, the love relationship might be destroyed altogether.

Because of the fact of our human weakness and sinfulness, and our tendency to become discouraged at keeping moral laws, there developed over the centuries in Catholic theology the legally based notions of mortal and venial sin. Inadequate as is this categorizing of sin, these notions can yet provide us with some basis for making realistic judgments about our moral faults.

A mortal sin is a fundamental rejection of God's love. By it we drive his grace-presence from us. "Mortal" means "death-dealing"—this sin kills God's life and love within us. "Then desire when it has conceived gives birth to sin; and sin when it is full-grown brings forth death. . . . All wrongdoing is sin, but there is sin which is not mortal" (James 1, 15; 1 John 5, 16).

For us to sin mortally, our offense must be seriously wrong, we must fully realize it is seriously wrong, and we must fully want to choose our way over God's. In sinning mortally we make a basic choice of our own way over God's, and we are willing to repudiate our friendship with God over this choice. We thus want this thing or person more than we want God. Such a choice must engage one's whole person to the depths of one's being.

Not all serious wrongs are mortal sins. Many people do seriously wrong things without fully realizing they are such, such as the millions who have had little or no education regarding Christ's moral teachings, the many nominal Catholics who do not sufficiently know their religion, or some converts before studying Catholicism. Some do seriously wrong things but do not fully want to do them; people often act under pressing mental strain or from deeply rooted bad habits. Most would rarely, if ever, make a fundamental and lasting choice of their way over God's.

Mortal sin, then, is a fundamental choice of oneself over God that engages us to the depths of our being. Rather than thinking of mortal sin as a particular action, we should see it as a fundamental option, an attitude, a state of living contrary to God, that we knowingly and deliberately choose.

Some might conclude that it is impossible to choose to live in mortal sin—to fully and deliberately reject God's will for us—so that even serious sins need not be taken too seriously. But mortal sin is an attitude that is built up by continual sinning. Each sinful act turns us further from God and hardens us in our growing attitude of rejection. Therefore each must be taken seriously. Otherwise we may become so hardened, bit by bit, that we will not recognize the point of ultimate rejection.

Mortal sin, which is a fundamental option for oneself and against God and others, is the ultimate evil of anyone's life. One whose basic commitment or life orientation is toward oneself to the exclusion of God and/or others is choosing to cut himself or herself off from God's love. While in this state or attitude, one is paralyzing the power of one's own actions for good. God's love—actual graces—still surrounds one, but one is interiorly rejecting God's (and other's) attempts to reach one. Like an anorexic, one is spiritually starving oneself.

The vast majority of sins are less serious rejections of God's love, called venial ("more easily forgiven") sins. The offense is not serious, or the person does not fully know or fully want to do a serious wrong. A venial sin weakens our love for God and our neighbor. It is like a spiritual sickness or wound that hurts but does not kill or lessen God's grace-presence within us. A venial sin can be lesser or greater, as a sickness can, according as we realize its evil more clearly or consent more willingly.

Even our less serious sins should not be taken lightly. Deliberate, continual venial sin, like a virus, can leave us prey to the deadly infection of mortal sin. People who try only to avoid mortal sin and are unconcerned about venial sins have a relationship with God like that of a married couple who, though living together, argue ceaselessly. Their love is weak and stunted.

Each person must follow his or her own conscience in judging whether an action is sinful and how serious it might be. One's personality, moral awareness, and other circumstances surrounding one's sinful acts have a bearing on their seriousness. One's conscience usually considers these things. Our conscience, however, is influenced by many things—environment, passion, lack of knowledge—so that we obviously need guidance in forming a true conscience about sin.

Christ through his Church helps us form a true conscience, to best express our love and arrive at heaven. Like anyone in love, we want to know how best to express our love and how to avoid anything that might disrupt our love. We can look at the Church's moral teachings like a road map and set of directions given us for an auto trip; some may seem negative, restrictive, warning us to avoid certain things—but only to bring us and our fellow travelers more easily and safely to our destination.

Christ's Church points out some actions that are normally considered seriously wrong. Long study by the teachers of the Church and the basic moral norms of Christian believers over the centuries, reflecting on Christ's teaching given in the Scriptures, show that these things—or, better, attitudes—most often are serious rejections of God's love:

> Deliberately refusing to worship the God one believes in; blasphemy; hating, or seriously injuring the reputation of, another; refusing to help someone in serious need; adultery, or sexual intercourse outside of a marriage commitment; serious scandal; stealing, cheating, lying, or making unjust profits; drunkenness or drug abuse (note that alcoholism is considered a disease); racial, religious, and sexual discrimination when these do serious harm; lustful or hateful thoughts that are deliberately prolonged and fully wanted; seriously neglecting one's duties to family, job, country, to helping the world's poor, underprivileged, and so on.

Those who judge themselves to be in a state of mortal sin must confess their sinfulness and be reconciled to Christ and the Church before they can take part in the eucharist. It would be a living lie to proclaim our union with Christ and our brethren by taking part in communion if all the while we were cut off from them by an unrepentant attitude of serious sin. The purpose of the sacrament of penance or reconciliation is to reconcile us to our brothers and sisters in the Church, as well as to God.

God will forgive any sin again and again—even the most serious— as long as we are truly sorry. "If your sins be like scarlet, they shall be made white as snow; and if they be red as crimson, they shall be white as wool" (Isaiah 1, 18). We shall see that Christ has given us the sacrament of penance within his Church, by which he forgives our sins.

God never punishes us for our sins—rather we do that ourselves. Perhaps others afflict us or we "punish" ourselves for our misdeeds, but punishment does not come as a kind of retaliation from God.

When we hurt someone we deeply love, feelings of regret and remorse can dog us, even though our beloved has forgiven us. This is a dim comparison of how we can feel once we truly realize God's limitless, unconditional love, and the hurt and sorrow we can cause him by our sins. *Our* remorse in the face of such Love is itself our punishment. Most of us, however, raised with the concept of a just God who must punish evildoers, wrongfully judge that God acts as we would. We cannot shake the idea that God intervenes and disciplines us when we do wrong. But in previous chapters we have seen Christ's revelation of God, the unconditionally loving Father who treats us not as children to be punished but as responsible adults to be drawn by limitless love.

Sometimes unconscious or semiconscious emotional drives carry people toward sin, inhibiting free will and reducing responsibility. Many compulsively reach out for what they can get here and now. Though their action is objectively sinful, they may have little or no guilt in God's eyes. St. Paul experienced this: "I do not understand my own actions. For I do not do what I want, but I do the very thing I hate. . . . So then it is no longer I that do it, but sin which dwells within me. . . . I can will what is right but I cannot do it. For I do not do the good I want, but the evil I do not want is what I do" (Romans 8, 15–19).

Some people have an overdeveloped sense of sin. They are scrupulous— judging things to be sins that are not, exaggerating their guilt, constantly fearful of offending God, hounded by guilt feelings. This is an emotional problem, in need of counseling and often professional treatment. From childhood such people have never been loved properly, so they find it hard to believe in God's love and mercy. Usually they can grasp the fact of God's love only through others who accept and love them.

Many people today, however, have an underdeveloped sense of sin: they do not consider things to be sinful that actually are. Some may not be subjectively guilty before God, but they injure their fellow humans and hinder the spread of God's love in the world. Some are guilty of insincerely preferring to remain in ignorance rather than trying to find God's will. The saints who loved God most perfectly had a most profound awareness of their sinfulness.

THE CONCEPT OF HELL

"If thy hand is an occasion of sin to thee, cut it off! . . . And if thy eye is an occasion of sin to thee, pluck it out! It is better for thee to enter the kingdom of God with one eye, than, having two eyes, to be cast into hellfire" (cf. Mark 9, 24–48)—these harsh words on the lips of the usually gentle, merciful Christ emphasize the Church's teaching on hell.

Hell, in Christian tradition, is the state of those who die totally turned away from God, in which they continue to reject him forever, deprived of all love and happiness. The concept of an eternal, personal punishment after death took many centuries to develop. Israel had no complete notion of this. Perhaps it came when humankind was ready and might better appreciate what totally rejecting God's love could mean. In any event, Christ's words above are colored by Jewish apocalyptic thought, which used strong, dramatic images to depict God's intervening to rescue his people and separate the good from the wicked. Thus Matthew has Christ speaking of a place "where the worm dies not" and "the fire is not quenched" (Matthew 13, 26ff.; 25, 41ff.; cf. 2 Thessalonians 1, 7–9). But, reflecting on these words, and spurred by an early opinion (of Origen) that hell was not eternal, the Church came to teach an eternal hell as a possibility after death.

We know next to nothing about hell, but reflecting on its concept, its greatest suffering may be the realization that one has forever cut oneself off from God, for whom one longs with one's whole being. Christ's words seem not so much of bodily punishment as of rejection, eternal isolation: "Then he will say to those on his left hand, 'Depart from me, accursed ones, into the everlasting fire . . . ' " (Matthew 25, 41). One might reach out to God with one's whole being and at the same time must reject God, for one has chosen oneself over God.

A person might now glimpse hell, in a sense, if the person deliberately cuts him- or herself off from God by continually living in a state of serious sin, clinging to some sinful situation while fully realizing that he or she is choosing it over God. Then if God had been at all real in the person's life, he or she would not able to communicate with God any longer. Prayer would become an impossible situation. The person wants God, needs him, but cannot reach him—and the torment of this state might be something like the beginning of hell.

If hell is alienation, it is complete alienation. One would be eternally alone. There is no sympathy, no sense of companionship, only emptiness and hatred—of oneself, of the other damned, of all creation, of God. One ceaselessly turns within oneself, finding only oneself. One fully realizes that one has re-jected the good God.

Some wonder how a merciful God could send anyone to hell eternally. It would seem that, if anyone is in hell, he or she has chosen it, and God only re-spects the free choice. One who has made oneself totally the center of one's world, who refuses to love anything beyond and greater than oneself, could not be happy in heaven, for heaven is giving totally in love and being loved. God would not force such a one to love, since love cannot be forced. At death one would have for all eternity what one wanted—oneself and only oneself—and this would be hell.

Some theologians today say that a person who would choose to love only him- or herself, and is thereby totally isolated, is in a situation in which no one can exist. Thus the person is choosing to not-be, that is, self-annihilation, to cease to exist.

We should not fear hell in a morbid way, nor make this fear the mo-tive for living a Christian life. Jesus continually shows us a God who is love, mercy, compassion, and who draws us to love in return. "God who wishes everyone to be saved" assures us over and over again, through Jesus, that he loves us and gives us a superabundance of graces, chances, warnings, and proddings to accept his love. His whole revelation of him-self as a loving God makes it clear that no one will go to hell except one who, with full awareness, fundamentally and permanently rejects God with his or her total being.

Significantly, while the Church proclaims a large number of saints to have attained heaven, it has never declared anyone damned. In Catholic teaching, heaven is a fact, while hell is only a possibility. Guilt-ridden peo-ple, particularly, perhaps with an image from childhood of a stern, pun-ishing God—and/or who cannot forgive themselves for past sins—should put aside thoughts of hell and try to learn of God's love.

Even the very possibility of hell should make us realize how much we crave to be united with God. There must be good reason for God's bringing the concept of hell to our attention. Perhaps even its possibility, of what it could mean to totally reject God, will make us realize how terri-ble is any separation from him by sin. For those who truly love, the thought of losing their beloved, however remote, will spur them on to greater appreciation and love.

Theology has no complete answer as to how, or even whether, anyone might be damned forever. Many theologians, and ordinary people as well, feel that no one is damned; they cannot conceive of a person choosing with full knowledge and deliberation to be cut off from God forever. They question how one with only limited knowledge can make an eternal, limitless choice. Or, put another way, how can a finite being, in a finite lifetime, merit infinite punishment? Nor can these people conceive of the loving God they experience letting one cut oneself off from him forever.

There also has been an ongoing view among some Catholic theologians that even the damned will be saved at the end of the world (universalism)—that only this is compatible with God's revelation of himself as compassionate and forgiving and one who urges us to always forgive.

Some believe they make their hell here on earth, through their alienation from God, others, and even themselves. In any event, two things come out of God's revelation—his loving will is that we all be with him forever, and there is a state of hell for any who reject him. How to reconcile these is a mystery we cannot resolve. This we can be sure of: if any are damned, it is through their own, fully free, most fundamental choice—and God's love surrounds each of us with countless helps toward heaven.

MAKING UP FOR SIN

Read Luke 7, 36-50. The penitent prostitute fell at Christ's feet, bathed them with her tears, and anointed them with the most expensive ointments. She tried to show her gratitude for Christ's forgiveness of her sins by making up for them in this touching way. So our love should impel us to do something to make up for the sins God forgives us.

When God forgives us, he forgives thoroughly and asks nothing in return. He is not like a judge imposing a sentence for a crime. He "blots out" our sins, "forgets" them, "hurls them into the sea." When the Scriptures picture him threatening punishment for sin, it is a way of saying that his people are bringing punishment on themselves—"Salvation is mine, O Israel, destruction is thy own": **Read Psalm 103, 8-14.**

Though God does not demand that we make up for our sins, there is a necessity within ourselves to do so, to rebuild the love between us. When a person has offended someone he or she truly loves—

and especially when the person realizes the beloved is so much more loving than him- or herself—the person cannot be happy until he or she has made up for the offenses.

We make up for our sins by uniting ourselves to Christ, who has made up for them. We particularly join ourselves to Christ's great act of healing love, his death and resurrection. By this we simply express our sincere willingness to let ourselves again be loved by him.

United with Christ, we can make up for our sins in many ways: by acts of worship, particularly the Mass, by the sacraments, deep sorrow in confession, prayer, offering up our sufferings, doing "penance" for our sins by any good action, and by helping our fellow humans whom we have hurt.

An "indulgence" has reference to a practice that began in the early Church: the bishop would lessen a sinner's public penance if a martyr would offer his or her sufferings to help make up for the penitent's sins. Gradually the Church declared that certain prayers or good works could gain an "indulgence," usually stated as the equivalent of a certain period of penance in the early Church. With the very long penances of the medieval Church, indulgences became a practical necessity to make them livable; with the token penances of recent times, this is no longer the case. Indulgences were never considered "automatic" ways of making up for sin—one had to be in the state of grace and sorry for one's sins to gain them, and their effectiveness ultimately depended on God and one's own faith and love—but they were greatly abused and even sold by some medieval preachers, occasioning Luther's original and rightful protest.

Today indulgences are seen as of minor importance in Catholicism. At Vatican Council II, new, more meaningful interpretations of indulgences were proposed, but the question was not declared upon. The whole practice has been simplified by new regulations—but the relevance of indulgences to modern Christians is highly questionable. In practice, indulgences can be viewed simply as the Church's recommendation of a particular prayer or good work.

If at our death we have not yet made up for our sins, traditional Catholic teaching is that we must make up for them in the next life, by passing through the state called purgatory. Our love may still be too weak for us to be taken up into God's all-consuming love. In the view of some, this is our shattering meeting with God in the experience of death. We shall see this in more detail in the last chapter.

IN THE LITURGY

The Mass prayers several times remind us of our sinfulness: the opening confession of our sins, the Lord's Prayer, the "Lamb of God, have mercy on us," and so on.

Besides the use of the sacrament of penance, the Church sets aside certain seasons to particularly make up for our sins: Advent, Lent, and in popular devotion the "First Fridays."

DAILY LIVING: OVERCOMING SIN

Read Matthew 4, 1-11. At the beginning of Christ's public life, the devil was there to tempt him—to an empty display of power by turning stones to bread, to challenge his Father's providence by hurling himself from the temple, to throw in his lot with the devil and thereby receive power over the whole world. He was tempted as each of us is, continually, but far more excruciatingly.

So strong was this initial temptation of Christ that "angels came and ministered to him." During the agony before his death, Luke tells us, he underwent a bloody sweat. On the cross he cried out from a terrible sense of abandonment: "My God, my God, why have you forsaken me?"

Temptations—attractions or enticements to sin—are inevitable. God permits us to have these not that we might sin but that by overcoming them we might be strengthened spiritually. Soldiers are toughened by obstacle courses, cars are tested on rough roads—not to weaken them, but to make them stronger. Temptations also humble us, making us realize how much we need God's help. When St. Paul complained of a constant temptation, Christ told him, "My grace is sufficient for you, for my power is made perfect in weakness" (2 Corinthians 12, 9): **Read 1 Peter 5, 8-10.**

We are attracted to sin by the pleasures of the material world, the weakness of our own flesh, and the influence of the devil. We must recognize our weakness: inclined by original sin, we are further weakened by our past personal sins. We may also be trying to compensate for a lack of love in our life; God may not be very real, and sinful human loves are.

The devil—the demonic—the mysterious power of evil among us, exploits these weaknesses. Many sinful acts do bring a certain happiness. But eventually sin leaves only a deep uneasiness within us. We may try to ignore the "still, small voice" of conscience, or attempt to drown it out, but it persists.

When we are tempted, a good rule is to pray quickly for help, and then calmly turn our attention to doing something else that engages us. God is always there, giving us the strength to overcome temptation. "God is faithful and he will not let you be tempted beyond your strength, but with the temptation will also provide the way to escape that you may be able to endure it" (1 Corinthians 10, 13).

Even when we fall into sinful acts again and again, God's grace is always there to save us from sinning with full deliberation, inspiring us to start over continually—perhaps until our deathbed.

To overcome sin, we obviously must avoid situations that might normally lead to sin. It is only common sense that we must avoid situations—and/or people—where past experience tells us we will probably commit serious sin. Psychology shows us how, in certain situations, emotions and passions can overwhelm our reason and our will—and to put ourselves in these situations without sufficient reason is already to sin.

The mature Christian, however, concentrates on doing good, rather than merely avoiding sin. If one flies from New York to Chicago, looking forward to seeing someone one loves, what motivates one's travel is the positive desire to be in Chicago, not merely an urge to leave New York. So we should desire to show our love for God and our neighbors in our actions, instead of merely trying to avoid hurting them.

The life of a Christian should be a personal, free, loving response to God's love—doing good out of love, not because we feel forced to. In Exodus, before God lists the commandments that his people are to observe, he reminds them of how he has shown his love for them. "I, the Lord, am your God, who brought you out of the land of Egypt, that place of slavery . . . " (Exodus 20, 2). Realizing how much God has loved us, even to dying for us, we spontaneously want to please him, like anyone in love.

We should never become discouraged about overcoming even the worst habit of sin. It was not Judas's betrayal of Christ that ruined him, but his despair: **Read Matthew 27, 3–5.**

Here we see the one lasting tragedy of sin—the conviction that it is no use trying any longer. God does not ask that we succeed, but only that we sincerely try. It may take years, even a lifetime of struggle, but God's grace will always sustain our efforts.

Often the hardest battle is the initial decision to renounce one's sin, to start over—and often over and over again. Countless people over the past fifteen hundred years have echoed St. Augustine's classic description of the clinging power of sin:

> The very toys of toys, the vanities of vanities, my old mistresses, still held me; they plucked my fleshy garment, and whispered softly, "Do you cast me off? And from this moment shall we no more be with thee forever?" . . . I hesitated to break away and shake myself free from them, and to lean over to where I was called. A violent habit said to me, "Thinkest thou, that thou canst live without them?" (*Confessions,* Bk. 8).

Our sins can be turned to profit. Through sorrow and repentance, the experience of sinning can teach us much: humility, our weakness and need of God's helping grace, understanding and tolerance of others, gratitude for God's love, which receives us back again and again.

SOME SUGGESTIONS FOR . . .

DISCUSSION

From your own experience, why do you think people are reluctant to face their sins and try to do something about them?

What do you think of the doctrine of hell—and the fact that the Church has never said that anyone is in this state, while it has said that many canonized saints are in heaven?

Is the notion of social sin, especially as we discussed it in the last chapter, real to you? If so, in what way?

Alcoholics Anonymous, though seeing alcoholism basically as a disease, requires that one make a searching moral inventory and then admit whatever wrong one has done, to God, to oneself, and to another human being. Many alcoholics testify that God's presence becomes real, or more real, during the twelve steps they share with others on their journey of recovery. Can you see why the admission and renunciation of one's sinful habits or addictions—and seeking help in overcoming them—is so necessary?

What do you find most effective for dealing with the particular temptation that most often besets you?

Someone has said that if a person prays regularly, he or she will either stop sinning—even if only for a time—or will stop praying. Have you experienced this?

FURTHER READING

- *A Contemporary Social Spirituality,* Meehan (Orbis, 1982)—This fine book brings a keen pastoral touch to a variety of subjects concerning the often forgotten social side of sin.

- *A New View of Sin,* Maguire (St. Anthony Messenger Press, Catholic Update 081)—A very brief but very well done presentation that goes beyond individual sin to look at today's social sin and our "four failures" regarding it.

- *Guilt—A Tool for Christian Growth,* Wintz (St. Anthony Messenger Press, Catholic Update 0286)—This brief but incisive presentation by a priest-psychologist discusses healthy versus neurotic guilt, guilt feelings, guilt trips, and how to grow out of unhealthy guilt.

- *Recovering Catholics: What to Do When Religion Comes Between You and God,* Larsen and Parnegg (HarperSanFrancisco, 1992)—Two experienced addiction counselors, one a former priest, discuss breaking away from an unhealthy, codependent relationship with God and the Church, and how to establish a more mature, more deeply spiritual relationship.

- *Dare We Hope "That All Men be Saved"?* vonBalthasar (Ignatius Press, 1988)—A prominent Catholic theologian, recently deceased, here advances the case that not only are all saved but that we should hope and pray for this outcome.

- *Bound to Forgive,* Jenco (Ave Maria Press, 1995)—Written by a priest who was a hostage in Lebanon for eight years, this very moving book tells what it means to live with a Christian attitude of forgiveness and reconciliation in the most trying circumstances.

FURTHER VIEWING/LISTENING

Good Goats, Linn (Paulist Press)—This forty-minute video tackles, with thought-provoking images, tough questions of hell, sin, and vengeance, and then leads viewers to transformation and healing.

Obsessions: The Empty Tyranny, May (NCR, four audiocassettes)— Here an insightful psychiatrist and spiritual writer combines the wisdom and insights of contemplatives with contemporary neurology to give help on our journey to inner freedom.

PERSONAL REFLECTION

Since Adam and Eve, sin has weakened our whole race and brought the fearfulness of death, endless pain, and inhumanity to our world. Serious sin can cut me off from God and turn me against my fellow human beings. I should meditate frequently on how God has shown his love for me in my life and consider what I can do to show my love for him—and others—in return. Such thoughts are the best way to defeat temptations to sin.

Before retiring I might examine my conscience, concluding with an expression of sincere sorrow and a firm resolution to turn away from at least any serious sin.

The Jesus Prayer—"Lord Jesus Christ, Son of God, be merciful to me, a sinner"—comes from Eastern Christianity and has had wide power with people everywhere as a kind of mantra. I might try saying it regularly, or perhaps simply the last part.

19

The Christian's Continuing Conversion

What can we do when we have sinned, and we also know that we will surely sin again? How can we be helped by confessing to a priest? What does a Catholic do in confession?

OUR NEED OF CONTINUAL CONVERSION

Read Luke 15, 1–24. Christ recognized that the life of the average Christian would be a humiliating process of falling and rising and falling again—of sinning and continual reconversion. By this parable of the sinful son's return, Christ brings home to us God's immense love and joy at our return from sin. We plunge into sin, like going down into the grave, but Christ is always there to raise us up again. All God asks is that we sincerely continue to try, to be converted again, and never despair.

"Then Peter came up to him and said, 'Lord, how often shall my brother sin against me, and I forgive him? Up to seven times?'" (Matthew 18, 21). In Peter's question "seven times" means an indefinite number. Christ's answer is even more emphatic: "seventy times seven"—that is, we should never cease to forgive. Why? Because God never ceases to forgive us.

GOD WANTS TO FORGIVE OUR SINS

The assurance of forgiveness and reconciliation is a vital part of love. Couples in love often experience the wonder of mutual forgiveness after an argument; in fact, some of the deepest moments of love come after making up. On the other hand, a refusal to forgive can be a terrible thing. A memorable news story told of a woman on her death-bed refusing to forgive her unfaithful husband, though he knelt tearfully beside her begging forgiveness. Ancient peoples often thought that the gods would not forgive the offenses of humans, and throughout history people have considered themselves damned by an implacable deity or rejected by a blind, unfeeling fate.

Many sincere people today, realizing their moral failings, feel that they ought to do something about them. They know that they have been selfish, insincere, immoderate, and have hurt others, even those they love. They vaguely wish for a chance to acknowledge their guilt, to be assured of understanding and forgiveness, and for the strength to make a "fresh start." They may not realize it, but they are looking for God's forgiveness, for his understanding acceptance, and an assurance of his help to do better.

God has revealed himself to be, above all, understanding, merciful, and always forgiving. Centuries ago his inspired psalmist proclaimed, "Not according to our sins does he deal with us, nor does he requite us according to our crimes." The prophet Hosea, from the example of his own life, portrays God as a husband who loves his wife and forgives her even when she degrades herself by prostitution. The book of Jonah describes in a delightfully human way how this prophet was scandalized because God did not destroy the sinful Ninevites but allowed them to repent.

Micah says God "delights in mercy . . . he will put away our iniquities, and he will cast all our sins into the bottom of the sea" (7, 18–19). And the Lord bade Ezekiel to answer the sinful Israelites:

> You people say, "Our crimes and our sins weigh us down; we are rotting because of them. How can we survive?" Answer them: "As I live, says the Lord God, I swear I take no pleasure in the death of the wicked, but that the wicked turn from their ways and live . . . " (Ezekiel 33, 10–11).

Read Luke 7, 36-50. Christ above all revealed God's merciful, forgiving love, by associating with sinners, and particularly by forgiving their sins. He welcomed this sinful woman who came weeping to him in Simon's house, and silenced his host's objections: "'Her sins, many as they are, shall be forgiven her, because she has loved much.' And he said to her, 'Thy sins are forgiven.'" He often proclaimed that he was sent particularly to sinners, the "lost sheep." He scandalized the influential leaders of his people by his continual association with sinners.

Read Luke 5, 18–26. As an assurance that he could forgive sins, Christ cured the paralytic, "that you may know that the Son of Man has power on earth to forgive sins. . . . I say to thee, arise, take up thy pallet and go to thy house." This same assurance of forgiveness and reconciliation can be ours today when we submit ourselves to his merciful forgiveness.

CHRIST FORGIVES AND RECONCILES THROUGH HIS CHURCH

Christ continues to forgive and reconcile us today through his Church. The New Testament describes how Christ told his followers to forgive sins in his name. John pictures him on Easter Sunday night telling them, "If you forgive the sins of any, they are forgiven, if you retain the sins of any, they are retained" (20, 19–23). Earlier, in Matthew, Christ says, "Whatever you bind on earth shall be bound in heaven, and whatever you loose on earth shall be loosed in heaven" (16, 19; 18, 18).

Our sins are forgiven, and we are reconciled by baptism and particularly by the eucharist. Baptism forgives all our sins, even the most serious, and we become fully one with the Church and all who constitute it. The other sacraments also forgive less serious sin. But the eucharist is especially a ritual of forgiveness and reconciliation:

> *We begin Mass by asking pardon for our sins* and by asking God three times for mercy; we pray in the Lord's Prayer that God will forgive us as we forgive others, and we exchange the sign of peace to show our desire for reconciliation with one another; then, before communion, we ask Christ to have mercy on us and again express our sinful unworthiness; and at communion we are united in a great act of reconciliation not only with Jesus but with one another.

But sometimes we are conscious of especially serious sin that alienates us not only from God but from our fellow Christians—or it is a time when we have a special need or desire to be reconciled with God and others. . . .

Penance, or reconciliation, is the special sacrament by which Christ forgives our sins and reconciles us to our fellow Christians. Its sign or ceremony is the sinner's showing sorrow by acknowledging his or her sins and the priest's words of forgiveness and reconciliation. When a priest is ordained, he receives the power of giving Christ's own assurance of reconciliation and forgiveness.

One is reconciled by the priest, the representative of the Church, because one has offended the whole Church by one's sins, and one comes to be reconciled to one's fellow Christians. Sin, we have seen, is essentially selfish and alienating. Even our secret sins deprive our fellow Christians of love, and serious sin may cut us off from them. So the ceremony that restores our full love union with them has its communal aspect: our confession of sins may be private, but we appear in church, before our fellow Christians and the priest as their representative, to acknowledge that our sins have affected them as well as us and that we wish to be reconciled to them as well as to God.

The *Catechism,* discussing how our sins affect our brothers and sisters in the Christian—and human—community, says simply, "Reconciliation with the Church is inseparable from reconciliation with God" (1445).

An acknowledgment of one's guilt before others has usually been the first step in receiving God's forgiveness. Those who came for forgiveness to John the Baptist, Christ's precursor, "were baptized by him in the river Jordan, confessing their sins" (Matthew 3, 6). Over and over again sinners came to Christ himself, acknowledged their sinfulness, and received his forgiveness. When Paul preached Christ at Ephesus, "many also of those who were now believers, came, confessing and divulging their practices" (Acts 19, 18). And St. James exhorts, "Confess, therefore, your sins to one another, and pray for one another, that you may be saved" (James 5, 16).

We can acknowledge our guilt, ask forgiveness, and be reconciled either privately—also called confession—or publicly, in a penitential service. If we come to a priest privately, it is usually in a confessional room, where we acknowledge or confess our sins and then receive forgiveness and reconciliation. But, as said above, the priest is the representative of the Christian community, and we come realizing that our sins have upset our relationship to other members of the community as well as to God. If we take part in a public penitential service, while we confess privately, we show before all that we are sinners and that we seek their forgiveness as well as God's.

Note that the word penance, the name of this sacrament of reconciliation, also means the way we show our sorrow by trying to "make up" to God and the community for our sins.

From the early centuries of Christianity, the Church has had a rite of reconciliation by which sins were forgiven. Most people were forgiven their ordinary sins by participating in the eucharist: after asking for forgiveness together in a prayer before communion, taking part in the eucharist was a perfect sign of their reconciliation. But the problem soon arose of those whose sins were very serious and publicly known, and a rite of reconciliation for these came into being: They were excluded from the eucharist, sat in a special place in the congregation, wore penitential clothes, asked for the prayers of the congregation, and so on. After a long period of rigorous public penance, the penitents were forgiven and reconciled to the assembled community and admitted to the eucharist, usually by the bishop.

Eventually the severe penances led to most Christians avoiding the penitential process. Then, in the sixth and seventh centuries, Irish monk-missionaries introduced into Europe a form of private penance in which different offenses had appropriate penances, listed in manuals or "penitentials"; after performing one's penance, one was readmitted to the eucharist. Gradually private confession became more common. For a while public penance was done for public, notorious sins, and private penance was allowed for secret sins. Then, because of the still severe penances in the penitential books, penitents were reconciled before they performed the penances—and finally the penances were made milder, usually the recitation of certain prayers.

Read Luke 22, 54–62. In each act of penance, the one we really come to meet is Christ. Though he is invisible, we encounter his look of love, and like Peter after his denial, we are penetrated by sorrow for our sins. Then through the assuring words of the priest we know that Christ is forgiving us. There is the silent and wonderful realization that he joyfully welcomes us back as he did Peter: "When they had finished break-fast, Jesus said to Simon Peter, 'Simon, son of John, do you love me more than these?' He said to him, 'Yes, Lord, you know that I love you.' He said to him, 'Feed my lambs'" (John 21, 15).

In this sacrament of reconciliation Jesus Christ heals us spiritually, restoring God's grace-presence if we have lost it by mortal sin, and strengthening us to avoid future sins. Of course, this depends on how sorry we are and how determined we are to avoid sin in the future. Besides bringing home to us our sinfulness, this sacrament should make us aware of not only our need of God's constant help but that he is always with us, eager to give his help whatever our past and whatever our present situation.

Private reconciliation or confession has advantages: A trained, experienced, and compassionate priest can help us face our sinfulness without equivocation, but also without discouragement over any habits of sin we might have. He can give positive suggestions to help us do better in the future—or at least be patient with ourselves and our efforts—and to open ourselves more fully to the Spirit who is trying to guide us. Some priests are particularly gifted at extending God's healing in this sacrament.

It is often said that the need to confess one's wrongdoings is natural. There can be psychological benefits in confessing, though these should not be exaggerated. Confession can relieve the natural sense of guilt that follows upon sin and might decrease some neurotic guilt feelings. While the function of the confessor and the therapist should not be confused—the former deals with conscious guilt, the latter with often unconscious, neurotic guilt—they can overlap, and a priest with training and sensitivity can help one as a whole person deal with the evil in one's life.

Confession can give one a sense of being personally open and accountable to God. One expresses one's personal sorrow for the sins that are one's personal responsibility—as well as one's particular need of God's help. One rarely lays oneself as open, and as humbly, in the course of one's life. Though Catholics confess privately less often than formerly, many can testify that when they do it can be a penetrating spiritual experience.

To safeguard this sacrament no priest is ever allowed to reveal, directly or indirectly, anything he has heard in confession. It is a remarkable fact of history how few instances there have been of the violation of this confessional "seal," despite priests' human weakness, persecution, and so on.

SORROW, THE ONE THING NECESSARY

Read Luke 18, 9-14. Our Lord's parable is a glimpse into the life of the Pharisee and publican. Undoubtedly there were many times when their real-life counterparts played out this scene—the Pharisee proudly enumerating his good works, while the publican could only acknowledge sorrowfully that he was a sinner—yet it was the publican who merited God's loving approbation.

When we ask God's forgiveness, the first and most important thing we must have is sorrow or contrition—as in any breach of human love. Without true sorrow there can be no forgiveness, and any ceremony of reconciliation would be a mockery.

True sorrow need not be felt. It is basically the will to be sorry. A feeling of sadness, tears, and so on is an emotional reaction that may accompany some people's sorrow, but sorrow is essentially one's willing or wanting to be sorry.

The test of true sorrow is our determination not to sin again. We must be determined to avoid at least all serious sins and the situations that lead to them, to seek more help from prayer, the sacraments, and so on.

We should try to be sorry primarily because of our love for God. We call this "perfect" sorrow. We may have other motives as well, but we are sorry most of all because we have offended one who is so good, who deserves all our love—simply because we want to love him and know that he loves us.

When we are sorry primarily because of love, our sins are forgiven immediately, and God's grace-presence is restored if we have lost it. This is the way most people's sins are forgiven. So if we realize that we are in a state of serious sin, we should try to express our sorrow out of love as soon as possible.

For a Catholic this perfect sorrow includes a determination to take part in the sacrament of penance as soon as normally possible. One realizes that one's sin has offended the whole Church, that one is alienated, and must therefore come to be reconciled.

Those who are sure they are in a state of serious alienation should be reconciled before taking part in holy communion. It would be a living lie to take part in this greatest sign of our unity while yet cut off from one's fellow Christians by a state of serious sin.

But otherwise we need not confess before taking part in holy communion. We need do so only if we are sure of being in the state of serious, alienating sin. If normally conscientious Catholics doubt whether they are in serious sin, they can simply express their sorrow out of love of God and then take part in the eucharist without confessing.

We might be sorry primarily because of what our sins have done to us—a wholesome fear of losing heaven and going to hell, a sorrow because of the punishment we are inflicting on ourselves by our sin. This relatively selfish sorrow is sometimes the most one can arouse.

Though we should try to be sorry from a motive of love when confessing, this less perfect sorrow is sufficient to obtain forgiveness. The sacramental grace Christ gives us makes up for our deficient sorrow and raises it to a perfect sorrow. This is a great advantage of penance—a sinner who could arouse only imperfect sorrow could still be assured of forgiveness because of his or her special meeting with the merciful Christ in this sacrament.

THE RITE OF RECONCILIATION

There are three ways in which one may be reconciled: privately, by coming alone to the priest in a confessional room; publicly, by taking part in a group celebration of penance; and finally, in extraordinary circumstances, there may be a general absolution for the community without confession. The first is the older, once normal way. The second includes individual confession and absolution.

The rite for private reconciliation of one person is usually done in a confessional room or reconciliation room, where the priest and penitent sit comfortably face-to-face—or, should the penitent wish to remain anonymous, he or she confesses through a "screen."

The rite of reconciliation or confession should first be prepared for. Before entering the confessional room we should examine our conscience. We ask the Holy Spirit particularly to help us be sensitive to our state of sinfulness and to be truly sorry. Then we run through in our mind our Christian duties, considering particularly any sinful attitudes we may have acquired, especially our *particular* weakness. We might consider some of the things mentioned in chapter 25 of this book, "Living Daily the Christian Life." One who has any sort of sensitive Christian conscience is usually quite aware of his or her main sinful attitudes and need not review every possible sin.

We should note particularly any seriously sinful attitudes and how often we give in to these in our daily lives—any action or neglect that deeply alienates us from God and from others. The purpose of this sacrament is especially to assure us of forgiveness for these and to effect our reconciliation to the Christian community. Most people who come to this sacrament are aware of a less serious or venial state of sin—one that injures our relationships of love rather than destroying them. This sacrament gives us a chance to acknowledge and talk about these less serious sinful attitudes.

The rite for the reconciliation of an individual begins with a welcome by the priest, and if you, the penitent, are unknown to the priest, you might indicate your state in life, the time of your last confession, and your age.

Then you or the priest, or both together, may read an appropriate passage from Scripture, particularly one relating to conversion, God's mercy, love, and forgiveness.

You then confess your sins and sinful attitudes to the priest. This best takes the form of a dialogue between you and the priest, in which you "talk a bit" about your sins, why you think you have done them, what could be done to correct them, and so on. To be particularly avoided is the "grocery list" type of confession in which you recite every possible fault you can think of, with no attempt at assessing your really basic sinful attitude(s) and what you can do about these. The priest, for his part, will, hopefully, sensitively assist you, perhaps questioning you, trying to discover your expectations, fears, and hopes. The priest should sense, and usually does, when you want to talk about something and when you wish to say very little.

Then the priest asks you to do some "penance" as a sign of your sorrow and your renewed way of life. This penance should correspond to the seriousness and nature of your sins. It might be the saying of some prayer, an act of charity or self-denial—or perhaps to ask the forgiveness of a person you have hurt. Sometimes the priest may ask you to suggest a penance of your own choosing—or the two of you might discuss this together. The penance, of course, is only a token, a small start on what should be a renewed Christian way of life.

Next you pray for God's pardon, perhaps by some formalized prayer, perhaps in your own words. On occasion, you and the priest might pray together.

Then the priest extends his hand(s) over your head and says the formula of absolution (forgiveness and reconciliation). The essential words of this are: "I absolve you from your sins in the name of the Father and of the Son and of the Holy Spirit." In this the priest acts as God's instrument, himself sinful, but the one chosen to thus reconcile the penitent.

There is often a short final prayer, perhaps said together, and the priest bids you in your newly renewed state to go in peace. It is, indeed, as if you are a new person, anxious to obey the Lord's command: "Go, now, and sin no more."

Then there is the rite of reconciliation for a group of penitents, usually called a penance service or a communal penance service. This has become popular today in many places and brings out the fact that we are a community of sinners, that our sins affect one another, and that we are willing to forgive and be reconciled to one another.

The rite may begin with a hymn, then prayers, then usually a Scripture reading (or more than one reading), followed by a homily designed to help the community better enter into the reconciliation and mutual forgiveness. There may be a period for each to examine silently his or her conscience, and the priest may have suggestions to guide them.

As said above for private confession, we should run over in our mind our sinful attitudes, noting particularly those that seriously affect our relationship with God and others, and then consider what, in a practical way, we can do to change. Then all may join in a prayer asking forgiveness and reconciliation—often the Lord's Prayer is said together.

Then those who wish to confess their sins go to the priest of their choice (there are usually several priests present for this), and they usually mention some particular sin or sinful attitude for which they are particularly sorry. All serious or mortal sins must be confessed. The priest then gives a suitable penance, and says over each penitent the form of absolution, acting as God's instrument in reconciling him or her.

There may be a closing prayer or hymn, and then all leave, renewed and reconciled, to try to live out more perfectly their Christian way of life.

Finally there is the rite of reconciliation for a group, with a "general" absolution said by the priest over the group. This is the same as the reconciliation ceremony for a group described above, with the exception that there is no individual confession, and the priest says the words of forgiveness and reconciliation over the whole group.

An act of penance is proposed by the priest for all, and they also say together some prayer indicating their sorrow for their sins and their intention to improve in the future.

This form is used only in a situation of extreme necessity, such as when there is a large number of people and an insufficient number of priests present to properly hear the sins of each and give individual absolution. The American bishops' current guidelines allow this form if the people present could not otherwise confess within a month. Also, those conscious of being in a state of serious sin, alienated from God and the community, should confess this state of sin individually to a priest when they reasonably can.

Private reconciliation, or "confession," is usually available in the average Catholic parish each Saturday, before major holydays, and so on. One should check one's local parish schedule. A person wanting to confess to a particular priest should contact him privately.

How often one should come to be reconciled depends on one's individual need. There are special circumstances and special times. One might have committed some upsetting sin or series of sins and want to express sorrow and be reconciled; one might feel a particular need for Christ's special help to do something about some sinful attitude; one might feel the need to again recommit oneself to a fervent Christian life; or there might be a special occasion for which one wishes to prepare by confession and reconciliation: a birthday, anniversary, special feast, or some other important event in one's life.

Many people come for reconciliation and forgiveness during Advent, and particularly during Lent, the Church's time of penance.

Most today are making use of private confession much less frequently than formerly. Some may attend communal penitential services regularly, and some are making their private confessions much more meaningfully when they do come. They confess privately perhaps once or twice yearly, but it is often a deeply renewing experience, during which they examine themselves extensively and show a profound intention of changing their life.

A person who feels sure of being in a state of mortal sin should, of course, be reconciled as soon as possible, so he or she can return to the eucharist with a clear conscience. If such a one did not go to the eucharist for a year, he or she would no longer be considered a practicing Catholic.

To get the most out of each confessional-encounter with Christ, we should prepare well, but not indulge in anxious soul searching. We should try to arouse in ourselves a deep, true sorrow for our sins, realizing the sufferings they have caused God who loves us infinitely, and how they have hurt our fellow humans who so need our help. On the other hand, we should not try to ferret out each and every sin—serious attitudes of sin will usually come to mind immediately. Nor should we waste time in useless regrets, but rather make a confident, thoughtful resolution to avoid whatever might lead to future sin.

Many find it helpful to confess regularly to the same priest, a "confessor," often one's spiritual director. One should try to find an understanding priest with whom one thinks one can be comfortable as well as challenged, helped to grow spiritually. One should be able to unfold, over time, one's spiritual state and anything relevant: habitual sins, doubts, fears, pains, hopes, one's family life or job situation—anything for which Christ's peace and healing help are needed.

DAILY LIVING: DOING PENANCE FOR OUR SINS

The test of our sincere desire to recommit ourselves is our willingness to "do penance" for our sins—by the sacraments, prayer, works of love, and self-discipline. If we are truly sorry for offending a loved one, we go out of our way to be kind to that one in the future. We try, in this way, to repair the damage to our relationship. St. Paul unequivocally states his need of bodily penance: "I chastise my body and bring it into subjection, lest perhaps after preaching to others I myself should be rejected" (1 Corinthians 9, 27).

Since the penance given us is usually only a token atonement for our sins, simple justice and love will impel us to do more, especially if we have sinned seriously.

A particular way of doing penance is to fast and abstain. Fasting means eating less at mealtime (our two lesser meals combined should not exceed our main meal) and not eating between meals; abstinence is refraining from eating meat. In the United States, Ash Wednesday and Good Friday are days of fast and abstinence for those from eighteen to fifty-nine years of age; these two days and the Fridays of Lent are also days of abstinence for those fourteen and over. Many people realize their need of voluntarily fasting on occasion, particularly during Lent.

> *Today a growing number of people fast and abstain, and some have only water and juice, often on a Friday,* to be one with the poor and deprived worldwide. The money saved is often given to some work of charity, justice, or peace.

Catechumens often fast in preparation for their baptism and/or reception into the Church. As well as disciplining the body, fasting can purify or clarify one's thoughts, allowing one to focus and be open to God's action.

The best way of doing penance, of course, is to perform some act of charity or kindness to another. We cannot make up to Christ, for he has totally forgiven and forgotten our sin, but we can make up to him in other people who need our love and kindness—often almost desperately. A kind word, a bit of sincere interest, a favor done for someone, even just patiently listening to someone—these can often go a long, long way.

To summarize, the one great lesson for us all is that we should never become discouraged about our sins. We may fall into sin again and again, and there seems no way of stopping. We are harassed by past falls, and perhaps our present situation demands of us heroism of which we are incapable. We are tempted to despair, to turn from God, saying like Peter, "Depart from me, for I am a sinful man, O Lord!" But God's purpose in all this is to make us nakedly face our weakness, our nothingness, our total dependence on him.

The only possible solution, then, is to flee to God in a supreme act of trust, to tell him that we are so sure of his love that we dare to come to him even as unfaithful as we are, that we know he loves even our worst weakness. We accept our sinful selves and throw ourselves on his love, determined to keep trying, though we may never cease falling—we know that at every moment, including our last, we can always return home to him. He is our Father who will always be waiting.

SOME SUGGESTIONS FOR . . .

DISCUSSION

How have you experienced, in your own life, forgiveness and reconciliation?

Can you understand the need of accountability to and reconciliation with the Church community, as well as God, for our sins?

Does falling back into sin, even over and over, necessarily mean one is not truly sorry? What is a test of one's true sorrow for one's sins?

What is most appealing to you about expressing your sinfulness, confessing, and being reconciled? What is most difficult?

How, for you, might "doing penance" help restore your love?

FURTHER READING

- *Signs of Reconciliation and Conversion: The Sacrament of Penance for Our Times,* Hellwig (Michael Glazier, 1983)—A well-written book by a well-known theologian, this gives many helpful insights into this sacrament.

PERSONAL REFLECTION

The only thing that ultimately matters in life is to have God's grace-presence within us, to grow in his love.

A brief daily examination of my conscience, and a sincere expression of sorrow and recommitment to Christ by a specific resolution, can be the most realistic thing I do all day.

If I am truly penetrated by sorrow I will want to do something— preferably some act of love or kindness—to make up for the harm of my sins.

20

When Illness or Disability Comes to a Christian

Why is there so much sickness in the world, and what purpose can it serve? What of those who are disabled, perhaps for life? What help does God gives us in sickness or in disability? How can one have a more profoundly Christian and growth-ful attitude toward sickness and disability?

THE POWER OF SICKNESS OVER US

Read John 9, 1–3. Sickness, particularly when serious and disabling, is often regarded as evidence that God is not really loving and forgiving after all. Many people cannot understand why a good God would allow sickness in his universe, particularly the sufferings of the innocent, and because of this they sometimes reject the existence of a personal and loving God.

Public opinion in Israel in Christ's time—and of many people since—held that sickness and disability always comes upon us because of our sins. It is God's way of punishing us. Job's friends remonstrated with him because of his afflictions, and Christ's disciples spontaneously asked whether the blind man's condition was due to his sin or that of his parents. Christ rejected this overly simple solution. We might bring suffering on ourselves by some sins, such as intemperance or stubborn pride—but the good can also suffer, as exemplified above all by Christ himself.

Sickness shows the influence of the power of evil in the world. In the gospels the cure of diabolic possession and of disease were considered the same—defeats for Satan, for the demonic in the world.

When our body is weak we can be tempted to despair or unbelief. Satan's influence always appears, not in vitality and joy and peace, but in misery, boredom, and pain. Sickness, therefore, should be looked on like any temptation—it can be an occasion for growing in love, but it is basically bad and to be avoided as far as possible. Every cure of sickness is a setback for the power of evil. A Christian should not be passively resigned to sickness or disability but should do all he or she reasonably can to be cured, or to overcome limitations imposed by one's disability.

Sickness, however, might also lead us back to God, to discerning what is important in our life. The *Catechism* points out that, while illness can lead to anguish, self-absorption, and at times even to despair, it can also make us more mature and open us to God. It can make us realize "what is not essential so [we] . . . can turn toward that which is" (1501). Sometimes it is only when we are weakened, perhaps near-helpless, that we open ourselves to God and his help—to surrendering our way to his, to realizing other possibilities that he might have in mind for us.

CHRIST'S POWER OVER SICKNESS

Read Luke 7, 20-23. Christ's life was unceasingly devoted to curing the sick. Such cures were to be a sign to the Jews of the Messianic Age, and Christ pointed to his cures as proof of his divine mission: "Go and report to John what you have heard and seen: the blind see, the lame walk, the lepers are cleansed, the deaf hear, the dead rise. . . . " By his touch or by a simple command, he performed all sorts of healings.

Christ sent out his apostles with power to heal the sick and disabled: "He gave them power and authority over all demons, with the power to heal diseases. And he sent them to proclaim the kingdom of God and to heal . . . " (Luke 9, 1-2). These cures were done in two ways: the apostles laid on hands, and they "anointed many sick persons with oil, and healed them" (Mark 6, 13). Among the Christians of the first few centuries, particularly, special powers of healing appeared quite often.

Above all, Christ conquered the power of sickness over us, so that we can now use it to bring ourselves and others to heaven. Most of the sick he did not cure, and he did not abolish sickness, death, or drudgery. But far more important, these can now be united with his sacrifice to accomplish great good. We can overcome Satan in the very misery of sickness.

THE ANOINTING OF THE SICK

From the beginning Christ's followers used the power he had given them over sickness, anointing the sick with oil to heal the body and forgive sins: Read James 5, 13–16. This ceremony is the basis for today's sacrament of anointing. Christ's followers were to "pray over" the sick person after "anointing [the person] with oil" and this would "raise up" the sufferer and forgive his or her sins. This was a ceremony distinct from the miraculous gift of healing that some possessed.

In the sacrament of the anointing of the sick, Christ uses the anointing and prayers of the priest to give comfort and strength to the soul and sometimes to the body of one seriously ill. We meet Christ here to receive his healing comfort, strength, and pardon. Anyone who is seriously ill, mentally or physically, may take part in it—or one who is weak from old age.

The rite of anointing the sick today is this: the priest prays over the sick person, lays hands on him or her, and then anoints the forehead and hands with oil, saying, "Through this holy anointing may the Lord in his love and mercy help you with the grace of the Holy Spirit. Amen. May the Lord who frees you from sin save you and raise you up. Amen."

The full ceremony of anointing is designed to comfort and inspire: the priest blesses with holy water the one to be anointed; together they pray that God will have mercy and forgive our sins; comforting passages from Scripture are read, after which the priest may give a short exhortation; then all join in a litany asking for God's healing and his help for those who care for the sick. Then follow the laying on of hands and the anointing with oil. A prayer follows, and then all join in the Lord's Prayer. Communion may be given, and the service concludes with a final blessing.

Ideally the ceremony is celebrated before the whole community, preferably at the Sunday eucharist, so that the prayers of all might aid the sick in their midst. The oil used, incidentally, is a special oil of the sick blessed by the bishop at the chrism Mass on Holy Thursday.

Usually, however, the sacrament is celebrated privately. But when done outside of Mass, the sacrament of reconciliation may be celebrated beforehand so the anointing itself may be more public, with others taking part.

In this sacrament Christ's power may help to heal the sick—if it is for their good and they have sufficient faith—and it always strengthens and comforts them to bear their illness. The oil signifies what it produces—a soothing, comforting healing—in the way that we might use sunburn oil or certain liniments. The sick person may be healed to the extent that God sees it is for his or her spiritual good; and also, as one gospel of anointing says, "It shall be done in answer to your faith." But more important it gives one peace, strength to offer up this illness, to put aside fear and bitterness and entrust oneself to God.

> *By this anointing Christ forgives the sick person's sins if he or she cannot confess but is interiorly sorry*—as when unconscious or unable to respond. If one is able, however, one makes one's confession, since this is the particular sacrament of forgiveness and reconciliation.

This sacrament is the prayer of the Church-family, represented by the priest, that the sick person will soon return to his or her place among them as they worship and work together. It assures one of the healing love of Christ and one's fellow Christians. It should help one have the will to live, to be back with one's friends who miss one, joined with them again in the eucharist. The priest prays, "In your mercy give him health . . . that he may once more be able to take up his work . . . and give him back to your holy Church, with all that is needed for his welfare."

But if the sickness is our last, this sacrament will help us toward the great family of heaven. It should never be delayed—otherwise we may be deprived of the strength, resignation, and purifying love Christ wishes to give through it. It helps us die as a totally committed Christian. It gives us the prayers of our friends, joined with Christ, making easier our passage into eternity.

This is primarily Christ's sacrament for the healing of sickness, more than a help for the dying, and should be given as soon as possible in any serious illness—so that Christ's loving grace can help our attitude and determination to get well, which is so often, as any doctor can testify, the determining factor as to whether people recover or not. Like all the sacraments, the more faith and love we can put into it, the more benefit we will receive from it. Though it has a special power to help the dying, it is primarily Christ's rite of healing, meant to help us overcome and profit from our illness or disability.

> Holy viaticum is meant to be the sacrament of the dying. Thus people should take part in it as soon as they are deemed to be in any close danger of death. To wait until people are dying—and are most likely unconscious or sedated—before calling a priest is to deprive them of their last eucharistic meal, the divine food for their journey into eternity. Even if one is not in immediate danger of dying, the priest should be called so that the person can more consciously and more fully benefit from it.

Anyone can take part in this sacrament who is sick or disabled from mental or physical illness, old age, or accident. A person may be anointed before surgery. The elderly and those weakened in health may be anointed even if no dangerous illness is present. Those who have lost consciousness or the use of their reason should be anointed if, when they were in possession of their faculties, they would have asked for it. Children should be anointed if they have sufficient use of their reason to be comforted by it. This sacrament may also be repeated during the same illness if the sick person's condition becomes more serious. Non-Catholics may also be given this sacrament if they request it and have some grasp of its meaning.

The ideal setting for this sacrament is when it is given to the sick at the parish Mass. Those who are ill or disabled gather before the priest, and he lays his hands on them, while the congregation prays silently for their recovery. Then the priest anoints each with oil. There are other prayers, songs, and Scripture readings to show that the community cares for those who are sick among them and wishes them to be restored to the health that God wants us all to have.

Through this sacrament, then, Christ gives us the power not only to overcome the evil in our sickness but to grow spiritually, to reflect on and make up for our past sins, and often to reflect on the course of our life and the things that are ultimately important. It can give us new insight, new quiet strength to overcome sin's power now and in the future.

Some Christians have a special "charism" or gift for healing those who are sick. While some of these are priests or nuns, most are laypeople. The use of this gift is not meant to supplant needed medical care but to supplement it. The attitude of sick persons, as said above, is usually crucial as to whether or not they recover. If certain individuals can help induce an attitude of faith in God and a desire to be well in order to better and longer serve the needs of others, then their "healing" power can be a true gift in the Church today, as it was among the first Christians.

Today at charismatic prayer meetings and healing services people use the gifts they have been given not only for healing but for speaking in tongues, interpretation of tongues, prophecy and its interpretation, and so on: **Read 1 Corinthians 12, 8-11.** The "charismatic renewal" moved many thousands to become better Christians, and in recent years it has broadened its outlook to also trying to build a better society. Charismatics usually experience a "baptism" of the Spirit, a sensible religious experience that—though not intended to replace the sacraments—has often deepened them spiritually.

In each parish community, there should be a ministry to the sick, a caring for their needs, of which the priest's anointing is only a part. Christians increasingly seem inclined to take responsibility for the sick among them today, whether or not they are personally acquainted with those who are ill. The appreciation of those who are ill can often astound us. Those who are old or in rest or convalescent homes are particularly grateful for even the slightest attention given to them.

DAILY LIVING: OUR ATTITUDE TOWARD SICKNESS AND DISABILITY

Read 2 Corinthians 12, 7-10. Our sickness or disability when "offered up" makes us more like Christ. When St. Paul complained of his sickness, the "messenger of Satan," Christ reminded him, "My strength is made perfect in your weakness." We should try to overcome sickness, but when it must come, our attitude should be more than mere resignation. Our sickness should be looked upon as an opportunity for Christ to gradually take over our life.

"We bear at all times in our body the sufferings of the death of Jesus, that the life of Jesus also may be manifested in our body." Suffering like him and with him, we die to selfish egotism, become aware of our utter need for the Father's help, and are also made more understanding toward the weaknesses of others.

Sickness can be a power given to us to spread love in the world, to help others toward heaven, to make up for their sins, and to open them to God's love. Realizing this, Paul could say: "I rejoice now in the sufferings I bear for your sake; and what is lacking of the sufferings of Christ, I fill up in my flesh for his body which is the Church" (Colossians 1, 24).

Our suffering, then, can be united with Christ's suffering and is far from useless or a total waste. When it comes to us and we try to unite it with Christ's suffering, it can be a powerful way of helping others. We can offer our sufferings for someone and help them as surely as if we picked them up when they had fallen. It often takes strong faith to realize this, but many people who are ill or disabled do so marvelously.

A great opportunity for genuine Christian living is to help others in their illnesses, caring for them, visiting them, consoling them and their families. The sick are especially in need of our loving attention, and few people are more appreciative. Christ assures us, "As long as you did it for one of these, the least of my brethren, you did it for me" (Matthew 25, 40).

A particular need of our time is to recognize the human and Christian dignity of disabled people. Influenced by our culture's idealizing of youth and beauty, we can view the physically and emotionally handicapped as difficult to deal with, and we tend to avoid them in our daily lives. Perhaps we are uncomfortable in their presence because of our inability to perceive the simple dignity and spiritual depth that often lie beneath their "different" appearance.

An especially pressing need today is sincere interest in the mentally ill. So often we avoid emotionally disturbed people, when what they need is a bit of friendship, someone to be concerned about them. Love is the best therapy, and one we can all give.

SOME SUGGESTIONS FOR . . .

DISCUSSION

Has serious illness or disability ever left you feeling helpless and abandoned, perhaps even cut off from God? How, on the other hand, might it have opened you to God and brought you closer to him?

Does it make sense that many people still tend to shy away from one who is disabled or retarded or challenged in some way—and especially from one who is mentally unable to fully cope? How might your own attitude be more enlightened?

If you have witnessed or taken part in this sacrament of anointing, what effect did it have on you? On the one(s) anointed?

St. Paul thought of his sufferings as being able to "complete what is lacking in Christ's sufferings for his body, the Church." What value or power might someone who is ill have to contribute to the other members of the Church, as well as her or his fellow humans? Have you ever had occasion to experience this?

Do you know anyone who has a genuine charism or gift of healing—perhaps physically, perhaps in other ways?

FURTHER READING

- *And You Visited Me: Sacramental Ministry to the Sick and Dying,* Gusmer (Liturgical Press, 1984)—This is a good commentary on the *Rites of Anointing and Viaticum,* revised to include parts from other rituals and some newly composed texts.
- *Healing of Memories,* Linn and Linn (Paulist Press, 1975)—This small book is on how prayer, especially charismatic prayer, and confession can help one's inner healing.
- *Healing the Eight Stages of Life,* Linn, Fabricant, Linn (Paulist Press, 1988)—Following Erickson's eight stages of life, this shows us how to heal ourselves and share it with others. Also in three two-hour videocassettes.

- *Expect a Miracle: The Miraculous Things that Happen to Ordinary People,* Wakefield (HarperSanFrancisco, 1995)—Starting with the miracles in his own life, this well-known author gives many examples of miracles in the everyday lives of others.
- *Dreams and Healing: A Succinct and Lively Interpretation of Dreams,* Sanford (Paulist Press, 1978)—A popular book by an Episcopal priest-psychologist and widely read author.

FURTHER VIEWING/LISTENING

Prayer Course for Healing Life's Hurts, Lynn and Fabricant (Paulist Press)—Twenty-four thirty-minute sessions on six two-hour videocassettes that can be used with the book of the same name from Paulist Press. Also, *Praying with Another for Healing,* from the same source, is twelve thirty-minute sessions on three two-hour videocassettes on this way of using Scripture and prayer that has been helpful for many.

PERSONAL REFLECTION

Christ accomplished the greatest deed of history, our salvation, through suffering. Offering up my sufferings and frustrations with his may be the greatest thing I accomplish in my life. Christ lives particularly in those who are sick. I might visit someone who is ill, mentally or physically, or one neglected or isolated because of a disability.

21

Christ Joins a Man and Woman in Marriage

What is unique about Christian marriage? How can one have a happy marriage? How can one best raise a Christian family? What about divorce? Planning a family? Can mixed-religion marriages work?

WHY MARRIAGE?

God originated marriage as the basic way of giving and growing in love and together attaining salvation. He created us in such a way that we would find happiness in one another. We are not meant to live in isolation but to find and fulfill ourselves through the love of others. The figurative story of Genesis conveys how close was the union of the first husband and wife: **Read Genesis 2, 18 and 21-25.**

Marriage is God's way of joining a man and woman in love and fidelity and of bringing new human persons into existence. Genesis pictures God saying to the first couple, "Be fruitful and multiply, and fill the earth and subdue it . . . " (1, 28). Through the union of marriage, God's human creatures come to be, grow in knowledge and love, and eventually attain perfect union with him forever. Marriage is thus a continuing, living sign of God's love for humankind.

A loving family, then, is God's purpose in originating marriage and should be the reason a couple marry. Love and fidelity are part of but are not the fullness of the ideal of marital love. Neither is the desire for children sufficient, unless the couple have a true and mature love for each other. The loving fidelity and the cocreation of children obviously take time to achieve—and sometimes both cannot be achieved. What is important is that the couple desire both these ideals, see how they go together, and do their best, then, to attain a loving family.

Throughout the history of his dealings with humankind, God shows his regard for the marriage union. Though the language is patriarchal—women considered men's inferior and possession—the nuptial theme is woven throughout Scripture: Israel is God's spouse, pledged God's unending love by the covenant-bond, and even when unfaithful is taken back by God again and again.

Marriage is a covenant, monogamous and permanent. Vatican Council II goes beyond seeing marriage as a contract and speaks of it rather as a covenant of love. Two people pledge themselves to each other for life. Polygamy, polyandry, divorce, and remarriage—all appear as exceptional in the biblical presentation of God's desires for marriage: "A man cleaves to his wife and they become as one flesh" (Genesis 2, 24).

> Throughout most of history, marriages have been arranged by the family or society in which the couple lived, the bride especially having little to say about it. In recent times, since prospective partners are better educated and presumably more capable, the commitment to each other in our society is made by the couple themselves. Thus their great responsibility is to prepare themselves well; the choice is ultimately theirs alone.

WHAT IS CHRISTIAN MARRIAGE?

It is significant that Christ's first miracle was performed—before he was ready to begin his ministry, it seems—to help a young couple on their wedding day: **Read John 2, 1-11.**

Christ made marriage a sacrament in that he gave it a new meaning, a new power, and new beauty. Though he left it to his Church to develop over the centuries—it was finally infallibly declared a sacrament in the sixteenth century—he yet made it one of the great ways of encountering him and receiving abundantly his grace and help. When two people take each other in marriage, they are uniting themselves not only to each other but to Christ. Further, by this they become a living microcosm of Christ's love-union with his Church. Their relationship is *the* example, in miniature, of Christ's bond with his Church.

St. Paul uses the patriarchal imagery of his day and culture (when wives were considered their husband's property) to express this as beautifully as he could: the husband should love his wife and even die for her as Christ, our Savior, did for us; and the wife should love her husband as we are to love Christ: **Now read Ephesians 5, 21-33.**

Marriage is the sacrament by which Christ joins a Christian man and woman in a grace-giving, lifelong union of mutual growth and creativity. Any two baptized people capable of marriage, when they freely take each other in marriage, thereby give the sacrament of marriage to each other. Even when one of the parties is not baptized as a Christian, Christ comes to join them by his sacramental presence, "invited" formally by the Christian partner—and hopefully, too, by the non-Christian who would at least want to bring Christ's ideal of love into the marriage.

> *Christ joins the couple together and guarantees them all the love and help they need to make their union a success*—provided they do their part, using their intelligence to prepare well and seeking assistance not only for difficulties in their life together but for positive growth. This help is always waiting for them from God, their third partner. But, like any true lover, God will never force himself upon them. They must open themselves to his guidance by their prayer, their intimacies and sharing, worshiping together, and seeing themselves in their children.

Marriage is in a special way a sacrament of the Church-community, the "whole Christ" uniting the couple by their communal love and pledging the couple their lifelong support. The couple, in turn, pledge themselves to the community, to help it grow, particularly by the new life and creativity they will bring to it. This is why the sacrament of marriage is celebrated before the Church-community—ideally with the couple and the community taking part together in the eucharist, the greatest sign and builder of union we have on the earth. Also, this is why there are two witnesses to the marriage: they are the very minimum of the community taking part in the sacrament with the couple.

The couple give the sacrament of marriage to each other in what is probably the most important exercise of their priesthood. As the ordained priest is Christ's instrument in bringing about the eucharist or in giving Christ's forgiveness in confession, so the husband gives this sacrament to his wife, and she to him. The priest or deacon acts as the official witness of the Church to their union and brings to the marriage the Church's blessing.

The power of Christ's action in this sacrament comes fully when the couple are joined by their mutual "I do." His grace continues to strengthen them each day and hour of their married life as they continue to give this sacrament to each other. Each sacrifice, each act of love, each bit of work for their common good is used by Christ to communicate more of his love. As they give themselves more and more to each other, he can give himself more fully to them.

The sign, the core ceremony, of the sacrament of marriage is the couple's exchange of vows, but it is also a process that begins before and continues afterward throughout their life together. Their covenant-commitment of marriage begins in their developing relationship and continues throughout their life together as, in a very real sense, they continue to marry each other. The ceremony, then, is not something magical that assures the success of their life together; it is only as effective as their mature preparation beforehand and their working at it throughout their life together afterward.

Christian marriage is not only a goal in itself but the way in which a couple will attain their ultimate goal of eternal life. This is their vocation, their call from God, the state by which they will attain heaven; it is the most important part of God's plan for their salvation. As a couple work at their marriage, they grow in love of God as well as each other.

A Christian marriage is a sign to the world of Christ's presence among us. Marriage partners accept the responsibility not only for their own salvation but for that of their mate and for each member of their family. The family, in turn, is responsible for showing the world that total and enduring love is possible in this life. In this way the Christian couple take on at marriage a lifelong commitment to be ministers of Christ's love in the world.

Permanence is of the very nature of Christian marriage. As said above, each Christian marriage is a miniature of Christ's union with his

Church. Just as there is no divorce between Christ and his Church, so there should be none between a Christian husband and wife. "Is Christ divided?" says St. Paul. This is the Christian ideal and challenge: a lifelong commitment, requiring one's best efforts for years—which emphasizes the need for care in choosing one's partner.

> *Few couples marry foreseeing that their union probably will not work. But remaining together is no easy task in our society today,* which often offers only minimal support of permanent commitments. More and more children of divorced parents are marrying—and almost all couples have numbers of divorced friends—and to many couples, however determined to succeed they were at their marriage's beginning, when crises come, failure can subtly but strongly seem almost inevitable for them as well.
>
> Marriage needs to be a truly permanent commitment—to give oneself fully to the other, without the undermining possibility that one will leave when the going gets rough (and in almost every marriage at times it gets very rough indeed). There needs to be a commitment to "work through" the crises together as well as to enjoy the happy times. People are free to enter into this covenant or not, but once decided, the choice should be for life. The marriage vow, "all the days of my life," should mean just that, or it should not be given until it does.

The Catholic Church teaches that there can be no divorce and remarriage for Christians. This teaching developed gradually over the centuries as the Church tried to discern Christ's mind in this matter. The *Catechism of the Catholic Church* recognizes that this is a hard teaching, but it says that Christ gives couples the strength and grace to live out their marriage, to take up their crosses and live out marriage's original indissoluble meaning (1614–15).

Read Matthew 19, 3-11. In this passage Christ is evidently changing the Mosaic law that allowed divorce and remarriage. Scripture scholars today see him here liberating women, who under Mosaic law could be "put away" by a man, but not vice-versa; the reasons were debated, but Christ is clearly distancing himself from this patriarchal tradition.

> *Some also see Christ here issuing a challenge or invitation* to those who would follow him regarding what their attitude must be—but not a specific rule of

conduct—like his saying that one must tear out one's eye or cut off one's hand if necessary to avoid lethal sin (Mark 9, 43–49), or give up one's wealth and follow him in poverty (Mark 10, 17–22), or be willing to give up father, mother, spouse, and children (Mark 10, 28–32).

Though debated by some, the phrase "except for unchastity" (v. 9) is taken by many Catholic scholars today to mean the legal uncleanness of marrying within the degrees of kinship forbidden by Jewish law (cf. 1 Corinthians 5, 1). Such a marriage would not be a real and valid marriage, and therefore one could separate and remarry. There is no exception mentioned in the earlier version of Mark (10, 2–12), in Luke (16, 18), or by St. Paul (1 Corinthians 7, 10–11 and 39).

It should be noted, then, that Jesus is laying down the basic principle of Christian married life when he excludes divorce—but he is not specifying the exact marital laws that would be appropriate for his followers in attempting to carry out that principle in practice.

Some couples must face the agony of divorce—they realize they are destroying themselves and perhaps their children and have no alternative but to separate and begin a new life. Particularly today, in our unstable society, this is often the decision—painful but courageous—that many people will have to make.

Separation and divorce without remarriage are allowed by the Church for a serious reason. Catholics may go through the formality of a civil divorce or separation to settle custody of children, property, support, and so on—but not remarry in the Church. They can still take part in the eucharist. And if they do remarry, for example in a civil ceremony, they are not excommunicated (as was once the case in the United States).

Divorce and remarriage are also not allowed in the Eastern Churches united with Rome, but they were allowed by the Eastern Churches during the ten centuries that these churches (now overwhelmingly Orthodox) were in union with Rome. Vindicating reasons were "moral deaths," such as long separation, incurable disease, or adultery; and remarried persons had to undergo a period of penance before they would be admitted to the sacraments. There are also instances of this in the Western Church.

The Eastern Orthodox Churches today continue this tradition of allowing divorce and remarriage for serious reasons, although a second or third marriage is not considered sacramental.

Some bishops at Vatican Council II and some prominent canon lawyers and bishops today, as well as many married couples, have been urging that the Church reconsider its position on remarriage in cases of desertion, where the bond of love and therefore the marriage is "dead." At the 1980 Synod of Bishops, which discussed the family, some cardinals and bishops again called for a restudy of the Eastern practice.

To many in the Church, it seems inhuman to require that divorced people, except for some few exceptions, remain unmarried for the rest of their lives. However, the Church sincerely believes that for the common good of all humankind it must clearly teach the permanence of marriage as a real demand, as something quite possible and not merely an unattainable ideal. This is especially so today, when society often encourages people to enter marriage too lightly and separate too quickly.

But for most divorced Catholics who worked hard to preserve their marriages, and who sincerely want to practice their faith, this teaching can pose a painful dilemma. Estimates say a third to a half of all married Catholics in the United States will divorce or permanently separate. Many give up the practice of religion altogether, while a minority join other churches that recognize a second marriage as valid. A relatively small number remain single, while most remarry "outside" the Catholic Church.

Today, however, there are some possibilities that should be seriously considered by divorced and/or remarried couples who wish to fully practice their Catholic faith. It should be noted, parenthetically, that Catholics who are divorced, even those remarried "outside" the Church, are not excommunicated. Today, broadened annulment requirements enable many to remarry with the blessing of the Church, as we will see shortly.

It should be noted that, as far as Catholic teaching is concerned, the marriages of non-Catholics are real marriages and are valid until death (on condition, obviously, that they were free to marry—not married before, and so on—and did so freely and legally, intending to enter a permanent union). Obviously the Church cannot judge the conscience before God of a divorced and remarried person, Catholic or non-Catholic.

The Church may dissolve a valid marriage when one (or both) of the parties is not baptized as a Christian. This practice dates from the early Church (Paul mentions it in 1 Corinthians 7, 12–15—hence the name "Pauline Privilege" given to some of these cases), and it is predicated upon one of the parties sincerely wanting to become a Catholic and marry a Catholic. This second marriage is allowed because of the advantage to the partners and their children of Christians being married to other Christians rather than to persons who do not share their faith. Much investigation is usually required for this, and hence a priest should be consulted early in the relationship if one thinks this may apply to his or her situation.

An annulment is a declaration that, in the eyes of the Church, no marriage bond existed in the first place. It says nothing about the legal or social status of the marriage, that children born of the marriage are illegitimate, and so on. An annulment might be given if:

The partners never intended to enter a permanent union or intended absolutely never to have any children; if there was "fraud," that is, deception that, if known, would have caused the innocent party not to marry (such as sterility, homosexuality, a previous marriage, a criminal past, and so on); if one were seriously lacking in discretionary judgment about the nature and obligations of Christian marriage (such as immaturity, impairment by alcoholism or drug abuse, inability to be independent of one's parents, marrying only to legitimize a child, and so on); if there were psychological causes that could prevent the particular couple from relating in a permanent partnership—or for other causes that might affect one's capacity to consent to and fulfill the obligations of marriage; and if a Catholic were to marry without the Church's permission before a judge or non-Catholic minister—but note that remarriage in the Catholic Church is not allowed unless the natural responsibility of caring for the former spouse and/or children is being met. Also, the annulment process will not begin unless one has already obtained a civil divorce or separation.

Today annulments may be given for a wider number of reasons than ever before, as should be evident from what was said above—particularly with regard to medical or psychological problems that existed from the beginning but came to the surface perhaps years later. Therefore persons whose marriages have permanently broken up should not hesitate to talk to a priest about their situation—an annulment might be possible in their case.

For others, not able to be remarried in the Church, unofficial or private "solutions" are proposed by theologians for those who deeply desire to again take part in the eucharist.

One possibility is the "internal forum" solution: One's conscience tells one that a first marriage was invalid, but for various reasons (including near-insurmountable personal difficulty) one cannot get a Church annulment. One repents of any moral fault on one's part, no public scandal would be caused, and a second union is stable and proving to be a good relationship morally and spiritually. A priest in a situation of confessional confidentiality might verify that such a person could again take part in the eucharist. Some theologians would allow this even if the first marriage was likely a valid one but is "dead," that is, irretrievably broken. Though this is not officially recognized, theologians proposing it point to the pastoral practice of the Church through the centuries allowing truly repentant people to return to the sacraments.

The German bishops recently issued a letter advising their priests to allow some divorced and remarried Catholics to receive communion even if their first marriage was not annulled by the Church. If a person is convinced that the first marriage was not valid, "the Church and the parishioners should accept this decision," the letter said.

It is wise to consult a priest or trained layperson before judging whether or not someone's marriage—including one's own—is valid and permanent in the eyes of the Catholic Church. An understanding priest, religious, or layperson can be a great help to those puzzled over their marriage situation. Though greatly simplified today, the Church's marriage laws can be complicated—but very often help can be given a couple when it seems nothing could be done. Marriage is society's basic institution, and all sorts of possible situations can arise.

The Church has its own system of marriage courts, staffed by trained, sensitive priests, deacons, religious, and laypeople to investigate and judge these situations. Usually the process is not as long or difficult as many imagine, and often it can in fact be a "healing" one for all involved. The Church's investigation is always confidential, and in most countries (including the United States) it has no legal effect, so one should not hesitate in seeking advice regarding this.

In many places today, divorced Catholic groups offer the support and understanding so often desperately needed by a divorced person—and these groups often counteract deep feelings of failure, guilt, and insecurity. Often these people give moving, personal testimony to their need of another marital relationship that hopefully will be successful.

BEFORE MARRIAGE

Today a married couple must undergo many confusing, painful stresses on their relationship. The American Catholic divorce rate is almost as high as the average—between one out of two or three will divorce or separate. Thus it is vitally important that couples be sufficiently prepared, by reexamining and deepening their commitments to their religious beliefs, their maturity, and their ability to relate for life to each other, to raise children, and to mesh this with their career/job plans. With the great majority of married women working outside the home at least part-time—and many full-time for most of the marriage—there are inevitable stresses, misunderstandings, and confusion over roles.

A couple should be mature—ready and able to assume the responsibilities of married life, the daily struggles as well as the joys, and the financial and social obligations that will come.

A couple should pray each day for a happy marriage and frequently take part in communion, asking for God's insights and blessings upon their union. "God is love," says St. John, and the more of God they have in their union, the more genuine love there will be.

A wise couple will seek out some sort of premarital instruction or counseling, to prepare them for this greatest venture of their lives. They should particularly examine their religious convictions, especially if they are entering an interfaith marriage—this is often the most open time of their lives—and in most places today competent adult religious instruction or discussion is available.

Many places have a series of lectures or discussions to prepare couples regarding the different aspects of marriage: spiritual, psychological, sexual, financial, and so on. Some places have premarriage "encounters" in which a group of people spend a weekend together in prayer and practical preparation for their marriage. Most U.S. dioceses require a four- to six-month period before marriage for sufficient preparation, especially for younger couples.

> *A couple should be mature enough to seek counseling if there is some continuing, upsetting difficulty that they are not resolving:* deep, ongoing disagreements among themselves; ongoing disputes regarding either person's family;

deep religious or moral conflicts; doubts about financial capabilities—or anything that is causing continual worry.

True and lasting intimacy can only be had between two people who are firm in their own sense of identity (a "comfortableness" with oneself and a mature sense of one's self-worth). Countless marriages end in divorce because the partners enter this relationship of intimacy to find out who they really are—in effect, each one using the other to try to get a secure sense of one's identity, one's true needs, abilities, and limitations. It is primarily saying, "I *need* you," rather than, "I *want* you."

In their developing relationship, a mature couple grow to respect each partner's individuality. They try to learn about each other—likes and dislikes, hopes and fears, strengths and weaknesses—then they try to encourage and foster what is best in the other without trying to fundamentally change the other. When one partner has convictions and personality traits quite different from—and even opposed to—the other's, they may find it hard to acknowledge these differences as being compatible with their deeply felt love.

They respect and show mature love for each other, as well, in the difficult and beautiful area of sex. They realize that sex is a powerful thing, reflective of their deepest attitudes toward each other, and it is the power that produces new human life. In this matter, particularly, the wise couple respect each other's wishes and ideals.

Premarital chastity has been the Christian norm through the centuries not because sexual intercourse is something "dirty" but because it is the symbol and expression of a permanent union, of a lifelong commitment to one's partner.

Some men and women run from a real-life, permanent commitment to one involving "true love"; they flit from one affair to another, trying to convince themselves that they are involved in loving—or seeking a true, lifelong love—but actually they are avoiding truly deep and mature human relationships. They usually have experienced some rejection in their own childhood attempts to love, and ever after they have been fearful deep within themselves of being ultimately rejected, and so they never give themselves totally. The bottom line is that they cannot really conceive of themselves as truly lovable—as one who could be intimately known and yet deeply cared for by someone else day after day and year after year.

However, there are those who are capable of loving maturely, who are truly in love and intend to enter a permanent union, and who therefore want to express their love, meaningfully and totally, by intercourse. Here, too, premarital chastity is the Church's norm because the public, lifelong communal commitment of the marriage ceremony has not yet been made. God, who surely is already present in the relationship, comes in this ceremony in a special and fuller way, as the couple make their commitment public before the Christian community and the world. In this ceremony they pledge themselves to this community, and to the world, no longer as two, but as one—and this permanently. They are announcing publicly that they belong solely to each other—they are now celebrating this with the community of those who know and love them most. The community, in turn, pledges them its support and strength for the rest of their lives.

By the marriage ceremony, then, the couple express and celebrate publicly the commitment they have made to give and accept each other totally for life, taking on all the day-to-day consequences with no longer any possibility of its ending. It expresses their total covenant commitment and their receiving of God's special blessing and peace.

The act of intercourse is the fullest possible physical expression of the couple's total giving to each other. The Christian teaching, then, is that it should take place when there has been the public, total, and final commitment of one to the other in the marriage ceremony. The partners save, in a sense, their wedding gift to each other—this fullest expression of their love. Many couples have found by experience that it is deeply worth waiting until marriage before engaging in sexual intercourse because it makes the marriage that much more special.

Some couples feel that they have a deep, mature, and permanent commitment to one another before the marriage ceremony—and often it has its consummation in the sexual union—and in the judgment of the couples this is not wrong. Their commitment draws them to a fuller expression of their love. Priests who are counseling couples, when they present the Church's teaching regarding this, also realize that this teaching will be difficult for some couples to accept. Each couple, in dialogue with God, will have to do what they are capable of. Discipline is always necessary, and the realization that there will always be difficulty in attaining the values present in sexual restraint. Yet individuals and their moral capacities do differ; while there are objective moral norms to guide us, not everyone can follow these equally.

Sex can be a beautiful experience; it can express and deepen the growing together of a couple, the developing, expanding, and deepening that are what life is all about. Accepting one's sexuality—being regarded fully as a woman or a man—can be a wonderful experience. It implies commitment and growth together, not something passing or merely fulfilling of one's physical or emotional needs. It means there must be love—enduring, growing daily, experiencing together the grime as well as the glory—in other words, a permanent commitment to each other.

Usually living together sexually is a stumbling, questing experience in which two people seek to discover each other—as well as themselves. The couple should bear in mind that this is a powerful thing that brings them together; if it comes to be regarded lightly (as can happen easily in our society), they will have destroyed the meaning of one of the most beautiful and fulfilling experiences in life.

Sinfulness enters into sexuality when one uses it to take advantage of another, or uses another for one's own selfish ends, as an object of one's lust, hostility, or the need to build one's own ego. This exploitation of another through sex is the root meaning of the "adultery" forbidden by the commandment of Judaism and by Christ himself.

There can also be a sinful *mutual* exploitation by a couple engaging in sexual actions; they might use each other as objects, to simply gratify their passions, escaping from life's responsibilities in each other's arms, seizing this passing sexual pleasure without reference to the future. They may indulge in the immature and sinful "luxury of suspended commitment." This is a great temptation in today's rapidly changing world.

One thing is certain: A fully authentic act of sexual intercourse will be expressive of a love that is totally self-giving, a lasting, exclusive commitment.

The love of a couple, if it is genuine, will be expansive. It will not only stay within themselves but reach out to others. The couple will see beauty everywhere, especially in other people. They will find themselves more concerned with others, more understanding, tolerant, sympathetic. They will want to share their happiness with all.

The couple realize that they are still part of the human family and have relationships to others of love, friendship, concern. Their own love should help, should deepen their bonds with others—and in turn, by the mysterious chemistry of charity, their love will be deepened by these other human involvements.

The deep sharing and intimacy of love can involve risks for the couple, but the risks, if the love is genuine, are worth it. A test might be this: Does their relationship make them turn out toward others in understanding and concern—even though they may at times fail—or does their relationship cause them primarily to turn in on themselves, feel sorry for themselves, be disturbed, not at peace, or resentful of others?

HOW TO GET MARRIED

A Catholic is normally married before a priest or deacon and two witnesses. Marriage is a sacrament of the Catholic Church. Just as other important religious actions are celebrated by Catholics in the presence of the Catholic community, with a clergy representative presiding—for example, confession or holy communion—so is marriage normally solemnized this way. Also, with the bishop's approval, a nun or layperson may be delegated to preside—as the community's representative—if no priest or deacon is available in the area.

> *For good reason the bishop may allow an interfaith couple to be married before a non-Catholic minister.* This might be more deeply meaningful to a couple, or at least to the family of the non-Catholic. In some cases a couple may wish a priest to be present also and offer some prayers or a blessing after the minister has officiated at the exchange of vows. Each couple should work this out for themselves, respecting each other's religious sensibilities.

These are some of the things necessary for a valid marriage in the Catholic Church: A man and woman must be of age, never before validly married (unless one's previous spouse has died), capable of sexual intercourse, freely intending to live together until death and to raise a family (if possible for them), not closely related by blood or marriage, and otherwise legally capable of marrying. The Church, incidentally, sees no obstacle to marriage in the fact that prospective partners are of different races.

What was mentioned above covers most of the impediments or "blocks" that the Church has set up to safeguard marriage. The most common of these are grave fear or violence, deception, a lack of sufficient age or maturity, a close blood or marriage relationship, a previous marriage by either party, lack of intention to live together and have children, certain mental or physical defects, and the common impediment of one party not being a Catholic. When there is sufficient reason to do so, the bishop may grant a dispensation that nullifies certain impediments.

To arrange for a marriage, the couple should see a priest in the parish of the bride or groom at least several months before their intended marriage, to fill out the necessary papers and to take part in whatever instruction he judges necessary. In the case of an interfaith marriage, the couple should see a priest in the parish of the Catholic party, and they should allow an additional month or two for instructions.

The "banns" of marriage were formerly announced on the three Sundays before the marriage, so that all the church community might take part, in the respective parishes of the bride and groom. Today the premarital questionnaires and other preparation replace the banns.

Catholic marriage is normally celebrated at a nuptial mass, although a couple can be married outside of Mass. (The nuptial Mass is briefly described in the section "In the Liturgy" on page 410.) The bishop can permit marriage in a "suitable place" other than a parish church. Interfaith marriages may also take place at a nuptial Mass if the couple so desire; also, if so desired, in a suitable place other than a parish church.

There should normally be two Catholic witnesses to the marriage, but one may have a non-Catholic as best man or maid of honor. Other attendants may also be non-Catholic.

CREATIVE, RESPONSIBLE MARRIED LOVE

True married love shares in the love of God for us, the love of Christ for his Church. By the total giving of one's self to another, asking nothing in return, the married couple participate in the nature of God, which is love. And likewise, both receive the tremendous support that comes with having their love accepted by their spouse. One can abandon oneself in complete trust to the other. Christ's example of love is his death, his abandonment of self, and his resurrection. For the married couple, sexual intercourse is the highest expression of total, unselfish, trusting love, of the abandonment of giving the other one's body, intellect, and spirit.

Like the love of God for us, true married love is meant to be creative. As the resurrection followed Christ's death, so new life follows the gift of selves between married couples. This life is shown in a deeper love between the couple themselves and the more encompassing love that they extend beyond themselves to include others. The unique extension of total love expressed by sexual intercourse—the living symbol and embodiment of their love—is another human being, their child.

A couple's sexual expression of their love, therefore, is a wonderful privilege given them by God. The married man and woman celebrate each other's beauty and goodness, with truly creative interaction, sharing intimate knowledge of each other. "With my body I thee worship" runs the mutual pledge in the form used by English Catholics. In an earlier period in the Church, the priest would often bless the wedding bed of the newly married couple; it is for them a sacred place where they find God in each other. There is a call to complete trust in the hands of the other. The body of each is sacrament: "This is my body, which is for you."

Sexual intimacy is a profound communication of one partner to the other, sometimes revealing God himself. Some testify to this: in the heights of sexual union, they may soar beyond themselves and experience a sense of "otherness" that can only be God. Some, on occasion, compare this to experiences of mystics in prayer—"out of" themselves, surpassingly beautiful, indescribable.

This can also be vastly revealing of oneself, and therefore cries out for a fully open and honest commitment. This profound discovery of God and each other in sexual intimacy, this most beautiful experience, means that it must never be abused, but must be used with deep consideration, foresight, and honesty as God meant it from the beginning.

Sexual intimacy is meant to be used according to reason and God's plan. Humans alone can use this power according to judgments of mind and will, as well as instinctual attraction, simply because its use has such deep and lasting effects. This power can be compared to a beautiful lake formed above a dam: properly channeled, the water provides life and beauty, but if uncontrolled, havoc and hurt will follow.

Because this is such a complex power, reflecting the depths of a person's being, it takes time for a couple to adjust sexually to each other. A mistaken modern notion is that sexual compatibility can be achieved almost immediately, or that its near-perfect "performance" is necessary to the success of a marriage. There will be intercourse of the mind and heart between a couple a hundred times more often than that of the body. Each couple has special communications—words, touches, even looks—that can be as meaningful as the act of intercourse, and sometimes more so.

The deliberate abuse of one's sexual powers is seriously wrong and can often contribute to the destruction of a couple's happiness, if not their marriage. Adultery, manipulatively refusing intercourse to one's partner, and sometimes masturbation are ways by which people abuse their sexual powers.

Adultery (sexual intercourse with someone other than one's marriage partner) is a perversion of the basic meaning of the act of intercourse. It makes of this fullest sexual expression not a giving of oneself to fulfill one's covenant of love but rather a means of self-gratification, or a confused seeking of intimacy and love elsewhere. Adulterous relationships are signs that something is seriously wrong in the marriage and that help should be sought by the couple.

Also it is a sign of something seriously wrong in the marriage when one partner continually has problems with sexual intimacies that are reasonably desired by the other. The act of sex is an expression of mutual love, of union, of total giving. At times one partner may not feel up to it and should not be afraid to say so, and the other partner should be responsive and understanding. One should not expect perfection from oneself and the other. However, when sex is continually used as a weapon, a reward for good behavior, or a way of manipulating one's partner, the marriage is in trouble. In these situations, the couple should be honest about their feelings, and together they should seek competent help.

Obviously there will be times when love requires that partners restrain themselves or put up with some manipulative use of sex that vents frustration from other areas of life. Often a person's temporary impotency or frigidity—or inability to fully enter into what the other desires—directly reflects one's feelings of impotency or unfulfillment in areas one cannot control, such as some period of change or crisis in one's life, one's work, and so on. Wise, mature partners are sensitive to and usually become accustomed to each other's feelings, needs, and abilities.

Homosexuality, too, has been considered through the centuries as a perversion of the natural order of the sexes—a teaching reaffirmed by the Vatican in 1975 and 1987 and in the *Catechism,* which calls such sexual relationships "intrinsically flawed" (2357)—and often as a threat to human society. Modern studies and pastoral experience, however, show that there are types and degrees of homosexuality, some evidently morally culpable and some not, and that many homosexual people have made outstanding contributions to human society.

The sin in a homosexual relationship, as with all sexuality, comes when it is a stunting process, a lustful or mutually narcissistic escape from the responsibility of human growth. Most confessors today would urge their actively homosexual penitents to do what is possible for them, to realize their human dignity and talents, to avoid self-castigation on the one hand and lust on the other, and never to lose hope for deep and stable friendships, consider themselves pariahs, or give up the eucharist because of this.

Anyone who has worked with pastoral sensitivity among homosexual and bisexual people knows of the self-hatred and contempt, loneliness, and fear of disclosure that have haunted so many of them. Their sad history of abuse and discrimination is fortunately changing. The American Catholic bishops in their statements have discerningly recognized several things:

There is nothing evil or wrong in being homosexual. Most homosexual people do not will to become such. But there is a wrongness attached to homosexual "acts." Further, confessors should not insist that homosexual people seek psychiatric treatment when it is clear that their sexual orientation is "fixed" or irreversible. Homosexuals are urged to practice sexual abstinence—and as with anyone, self-control; they need deep and stable friendships among both heterosexuals and other homosexuals (the same need for human intimacy we all have, and a necessity for mature growth as a person, psychologically as well as spiritually).

Also, the bishops state, homosexual people have the same human and civil rights as anyone, including the right to jobs for which they are qualified. Finally, the bishops encourage homosexuals to be active members of their local church communities.

Today more has become known about homosexuality, and continual theological reflection is being done in light of our broadening knowledge. Many Scripture scholars, for instance, say that some passages thought to be clear, strong condemnations of homosexuality may refer primarily to other offenses —Genesis 19, 4–11, for instance, regarding the sin for which blindness struck the men of Sodom (hence "sodomy") may be a violation of the sacred duty of hospitality. Thus, too, with passages that give explicit condemnations of homosexual practices (Leviticus 18, 22 and 20, 13; Romans 1, 27; 1 Corinthians 6, 9–10, and 1 Timothy 1, 9–10)—the point of the condemnations may not be the perversity of the act but the religious unfaithfulness manifested by the act. And this unfaithfulness as a rejection of one's basic option for God and others rather than for oneself alone—that is, as a sin cutting oneself off from God— would be as rare among homosexuals as among anyone.

Thus some seemingly strong scriptural condemnations (often grist for fundamentalist preachers) may have a further, deeper meaning. A homosexual Christian today should take comfort in knowing that our biblical tradition is not as unsparingly condemnatory as was heretofore supposed.

The aim of most gay people, like that of most heterosexuals, is a committed, stable, lasting relationship with another. The theological problem has been with homosexual acts. Traditional Church teaching says that such acts are always sinful in themselves—thus the *Catechism of the Catholic Church:* "Homosexual persons are called to chastity" (2359). An opposite opinion says that such acts are morally neutral, that their goodness or badness depends on the genuine intrapersonal love, or lack of it, in the relationship. A larger, "mediating" group of theologians, while holding that the ideal meaning of human sexual relationships is in terms of male and female, considers homosexual acts in the context of a loving relationship that is striving for permanency to be objectively morally good.

It seems clear that there are "true" homosexuals, that is, those who are comfortable within themselves regarding their basic gay orientation. And there are those who are not, who may have had homosexual encounters— even over a period of years—but who are still unsure of their basic sexual orientation. Whether actually bisexual or not, many people like this have been helped by competent counseling.

Finally, as Christians we know that each gay and lesbian person is an individual of dignity and lovableness, and as with anyone, has particular talents and gifts to contribute to the Christian community and the world. Especially among Christians, homosexual people should find sensitivity, appreciation, caring, and opportunities for mutual growth. The Vatican's declarations on this subject and the *Catechism of the Catholic Church* (2358) call on us to treat gays with compassion and understanding and to avoid unjust discrimination against them. Thus, to see AIDS, for example, as some sort of curse sent by God on gays is totally un-Christian.

Masturbation also has been considered wrong through the centuries as a perversion of the sexual act, which by its nature is social, meant to be generative and expressive of love, and not solitary. This is reaffirmed in the *Catechism of the Catholic Church* (2352). Priests and others who counsel regarding this today find that masturbation is often described as a satisfying release from tension, frustration, loneliness, and so on, and it is an almost inevitable experience of adolescents as well as a regular one for many adults—and contemporary studies bear this out. The *Catechism* also speaks of circumstances that lessen or even extenuate moral culpability.

Habitual, compulsive masturbation in adulthood might also be a sign of a deeper problem that requires attention. The sin here is in using this as an escape, a stunting of one's interpersonal growth. One should avoid worrying over masturbation as a great, serious wrong but not take it too lightly, with little or no attempt at personal discipline.

Parents should have "human and Christian responsibility" in the raising of their family (*The Church in the Modern World,* no. 50). Procreation involves not only having but also raising children. God does not demand that a couple have as many children as possible. Parents must return to God mature Christian adults, not babies. Responsible parenthood goes on for years and demands the best talents, the fullest response a couple are able to give. Each couple must look conscientiously at themselves and at the generosity of their life service—and generosity is not always measured in numbers, though the sacrifice of couples who have raised large families and the wholesome love evident in many of them is beyond question a wonderful thing.

How many children a couple should have and when is something that only they in dialogue with God and each other can determine. This is usually not easy to decide. Some couples need to plan their family more than others, and for many it can become a positive obligation. Couples differ greatly—some have difficulty raising a few children while others can successfully raise many. Capabilities, temperament, financial circumstances, health, and ability to live up to the Christian ideal can vary a good deal. Vatican Council II says: "Let them thoughtfully take into account both their own welfare and that of their children, those already born and those which the future will bring. For this they need to reckon with both the material and the spiritual conditions of the times, as well as of their state in life . . . [and] they should consult the interests of the family group, of temporal society, and of the Church herself. The parents themselves should ultimately make this judgment in the sight of God" (*Church in the Modern World,* no. 50).

Natural family planning is approved by the Church. It is considered natural, and therefore morally unobjectionable, since nothing mechanical (condoms, diaphragms, intrauterine devices [IUDs]), nothing chemical (the "pill," "Norplant") or "artificial," is used to prevent conception. Direct sterilization—at present America's most-used method of birth control—is considered unnatural because it deprives a person of his or her ability to reproduce, one of the two purposes of marriage.

Contraceptive birth control as a means of preventing the generation of children has been considered wrong in the Church's teaching. The Church has held to this through the centuries because of its regard for marriage and the sacredness of human life, including the way in which it is brought about. One of the great purposes of the sex act is to bring into existence new human beings who will live forever; to interfere with this act unnaturally is to prevent life in an act meant to give life. Further, artificial birth control can frustrate the total physical self-surrender that is vital to married love. Pope Pius XI, Pius XII, Paul VI, and John Paul II have all condemned contraceptive birth control.

However, as is generally known, there has been much discussion within the Church about this question. Many point out today that a consideration of what is "natural" involves not only the physical sex act but its meaning to the human persons involved and the total context in which it is done (the family the couple already have, their physical, mental, and material capabilities, the society in which they live, and so on); as with any action, the circumstances and purposes of the sex act must be considered in determining its morality. The intentions of some couples seem to be purely selfish, while others are trying their best to live a truly Christian marriage. Further, while their conscience is always their ultimate guide, they must also consider the objective standards of morality given them by the Church.

In recent years our understanding of human problems has increased rapidly. New social conditions, cultural outlooks, and pressures are now upon us. Most women in our culture, for instance, must work outside the home, and the cost of raising and educating children is often prohibitive. Instead of society's needing more children, as in times past, overpopulation is becoming a critical problem. Our understanding of human nature and of marriage is developing as articulate Catholic laypeople, particularly, give their views.

In this matter, as in anything, the Church has not spoken the final word, and a development of its teaching is quite possible in the future. The large majority of theologians agree that no question of infallibility is involved (see chapter 10 regarding the conditions necessary for an infallible teaching). The traditional teaching was questioned on the floor of Vatican Council II by leading cardinals and bishops, and a commission appointed by Popes John XXIII and Paul VI of bishops, theologians, doctors, psychologists, demographers, married couples, and others recommended by a ratio of four to one that the Church liberalize its teaching on contraception.

Pope Paul VI in July 1968 supported the minority on the commission and reaffirmed the traditional ban on contraception in his encyclical *Humanae Vitae* (Concerning Human Life). In addition to the reasons given above, the commission minority expressed concern that changing Church teaching in this matter would put in question the Church's authority to teach in moral matters. But soon after the encyclical five hundred American theologians—in concert with many throughout the world—asserted that for grave reasons Catholics may follow their consciences on this matter even though the pope had spoken. Also, many national bishops' conferences, while affirming the pope's right to speak authoritatively in this matter, also recognized the difficulties in conscience for couples trying to adhere to his teaching, and said that these couples may follow their informed consciences.

The large majority of Catholic couples have been unable to square this teaching with their consciences. Priest-sociologist Andrew Greeley estimates that nine out of ten Catholic couples practice contraception at some time during their childbearing years. These couples may be respectful of the Church's duty to teach in moral matters, are trying to live good Christian married lives, and are willing to practice self-denial. They have tried to inform their consciences as best they can, and feel that for serious physical, financial, or psychological reasons they cannot use periodic abstinence. Their consciences tell them that another child at this time would cause great damage to their marital love, and perhaps to the children they already have—and, for some, contraception presents itself as the only alternative to a possible abortion, obviously a far greater evil.

As we have seen, it is a clear teaching that, while erroneous decisions might be made in following one's conscience, one who has tried to inform one's conscience as best one can must then follow it.

In all this, mature couples know that much sacrifice is often needed in living out their vocation of creative intimacy, that they must often choose between a kind of creeping self-indulgence—with expectations of almost instant gratification—and the Christian ideal of patient, persevering, sharing, disciplined love. They know that a lasting, deep intimacy comes about only if children are appreciated and valued. The inability of one out of five couples in the United States to have a child when they are ready and a child is wanted should make them aware that they do not have ultimate control over human life—and that children are indeed God's most precious gift.

CHRISTIAN FAMILY LIFE DAY BY DAY

A Christian marriage is a public expression of a deep, personal, and spiritual commitment—much more than a license from society or an agreement to live together. It is a lifelong commitment of two persons to merge their two lives into one. It is an awesome commitment and an awesome responsibility—possible only because of God's help.

God is the third partner in every successful marriage. A Christian couple pray regularly for their marriage and for their family. Many spend some "quiet time," or solitude, periodically, in prayerful reflection before God, considering the course of their life and marriage, as well as the needs and wants of their partner. Then, on occasion, they spontaneously share what has come to each in solitude with God. Some may set aside a time regularly to share their solitudes. Some very happy couples pray together regularly or read and reflect on some of the Scriptures with each other.

Success in marriage requires much more than a romantic feeling of loving and being loved. True marital love consists of a fundamental choice made from the depth of one's being, a decision to give oneself totally and unconditionally to one's partner, and a living out of this when the glow of romance goes.

A Christian marriage is a commitment of a man and woman to learn to love ever more perfectly. It is a promise to grow in love, including a pledge to cooperate actively in providing nourishment to the budding relationship. Marriage is not an "end" but rather a "means"—and thus only the beginning of an ever-deepening love relationship that will require a great deal of effort, patience, and grace. It requires a strong, total commitment to the basic marriage commitment—and to its permanence. When times of conflict arise, this "commitment to the commitment" can provide the determination necessary to refuse to abandon a troubled marriage and to work together through the difficult times toward a more rewarding marriage relationship.

Christian marriage is also a commitment to life—to becoming fully alive. A mature Christian marriage provides a secure setting in which the partners have the time and freedom to become more truly themselves, more creative, more productive, more nourished by the spouse's love and support, and more mature. Guided and strengthened by one's faith, marital love thrives in an atmosphere of freedom and trust, where each is allowed and encouraged to grow, individually and together. In the absence of this, the marriage commitment can become a stifling bond that hinders rather than aids the partners' development and that can eventually suffocate the love relationship.

The partners, then, should be free to develop their own interests, while at the same time being sensitive to their mutual need to share common interests and goals. It is vitally important that basic long-range goals be similar and that each one's expectations be discussed honestly and regularly, so that the partners are working in the same direction, rather than one or both being (often silently) frustrated, confused, and resentful.

A mature Christian married couple will realize that they are an integral part of the human community that surrounds them in their daily living. They reach out in love to others who come into their lives, as much as is practicable, rather than becoming selfishly absorbed in only their own happiness. They develop relationships of love, friendship, and concern with those around them, according to each one's ability to do so. These relationships can contribute to the growth of the couple, individually and jointly.

Each partner most often has some personal friendships that the other does not share. Even cross-sexual friendships need not be a threat to fidelity; they can contribute to a deeper appreciation of one's partner and to a growth in fidelity unpoisoned by possessiveness and jealousy. One's mature sense of "territoriality" will tell one if one's partner is overdoing this, and it should be discussed frankly, or advice should be sought from a counselor.

Mature couples realize that there will be inevitable stresses and conflicts because of the changing nature of marriage and family life today. With most married women working full- or part-time there may be "role reversal" problems—insecurity, identity-confusion, feelings that one's partner "does not understand," and often serious communication breakdowns. Partners must try to appreciate the other's viewpoint, vital interests, and needs, and keep trying to communicate.

Partners in a successful marriage learn to develop a sensitive imaginativeness and spontaneity. They make every effort to be aware of the little things that especially bring joy and pleasure to their spouse; one of them may be better at this, by nature and temperament, than the other. They express the often unpredictable excitement of real loving, discovering new depths and resources within each other. A good spouse is like the Holy Spirit, peaceful but also prodding (that we might be our best self). Often this requires a conscious effort to plan for special times together, away from the kids, and so on.

The sexual expression of their love is usually each person's most precious gift to his or her beloved. Each should be sensitive to the partner's needs and desires and try to approach their love-making in a spirit of loving cooperation, imagination, creativity, discovery, and fun. The sexual act is meant—and is used—by God to be literally love-making, that is, to bring about new, deepening, more binding bonds of love between each other and with God himself.

Good communication is an absolutely essential ingredient of a successful marriage. If the partners are able to express themselves freely, and if each has learned to really listen to what the other is trying to say, almost any problem that arises can eventually be resolved. Truly honest communication can be delightfully satisfying, and painfully disrupting, with many variations in between. But for real knowledge and true understanding of one's partner, honest communication is absolutely necessary.

To maintain open and intimate emotional contact, it is essential to share verbally one's honest likes and dislikes, compliments and complaints, hopes and fears—though perhaps not as the first thing in the morning, or immediately after coming home from work. Partners who continually avoid the discomfort and often anger that honest interchanges can bring usually wind up with a superficial, frustrating, unfulfilling relationship—a mere living together for social acceptance, personal security, or occasional sexual strokes, instead of a deep, truly sharing, truly mature Christian union.

Financial difficulties are the most common cause of many marital problems. Some people allow themselves to be slowly and subtly enslaved by an ever-increasing desire for material things, for the comforts and status that money can bring, by a feeling that they should have what neighbors, relatives, business associates, and friends have. One day they may find that they have all the material things they want, but have no marriage. In their struggle to have, they have forgotten how to be—how to love. Many couples suddenly find that spending more than they can afford—the so-easy use of credit cards, for instance—causes much anxiety and affects every area of their marriage.

A couple must be truly wise to resist the bombardment of modern advertising (especially from television) that makes luxuries seem like necessities, the badgerings from their children, and the temptation to give material gifts as a substitute for one's time or one's self. Often the pressure (and/or inner psychic need) to succeed, and the constant competitiveness that is endemic to our society, can make one a quasi—or full-blown—workaholic, and perhaps one day the wealthiest person in divorce court.

Disagreement over having, and especially over the raising of, children is another large problem. Here, as in all areas, wise partners must continually communicate, openly and sensitively, sharing their most honest feelings and opinions, in order to achieve a unified method of parenting—firm but always flexible. Methods of child-raising will vary from family to family, and degrees of firmness or permissiveness differ, but good guidance and many good books on the subject are available. See "Further Reading."

WHAT OF INTERFAITH MARRIAGES?

The Catholic Church, like most other faiths, wants marriage partners to be of the same religion, but it allows interfaith marriages because of the circumstances of our society. A couple who disagree on the basic points of religion usually cannot expect to have the perfect union and total sharing of interests and ideals that those of the same religion should have. Serious differences often arise over prayer, church attendance, the children's education, and so on. Religion is often pushed into the background because it is a point of conflict, and both parties and their children can end up with no religion.

However, some interfaith marriages have a greater chance of succeeding than others. There is, first of all, a crucial distinction between a marriage of two Christians, one of whom is a Roman Catholic, and a marriage of a Christian to one who is not. Further, if a couple are compatible in other things, well adjusted, and mature, their interfaith marriage obviously has a better chance of succeeding than one in which there are other major differences as well. If both can genuinely agree on the religious upbringing of the children, they have far more in their favor than if one only reluctantly agrees to raise the children in another faith. If each has a thorough understanding of the other's religious belief, the chances for a successful marriage are greater.

The Catholic in an interfaith marriage is asked to promise "to do all in my power to share the faith I have received with our children by having them baptized and reared as Catholics." This simply means that Catholics will do all that, according to their grasp of and degree of faith, they feel is necessary and feasible for the children's religious upbringing. What is able to be done by one parent in one marriage may not be possible for another in another marriage. The couple must respect each other's conscience and religious sensibilities. A Catholic upbringing means a pledging of the child to this Christian community in baptism and the other sacraments; it does not necessarily mean attending Catholic schooling, nor that other religious beliefs should not be taught, but that the child's basic orientation is Catholic. It is a choice made for the child, as parents will do in many areas they consider important; later in life the child may wish, in good conscience, to change her or his religious commitment.

The Church asks this promise because it honestly believes it can present children with the truth that God gives us in Christ and that any good Catholic would want her or his children to share that faith. All responsible parents want their children to have the best training and upbringing possible; in this most important area of all, our relationship with God and attainment of heaven, the Catholic parent normally wants her or his child to have all the help she or he has in attaining salvation.

A problem that might arise is that the partners may not be able to agree on the religious upbringing of their children. Couples should definitely discuss this before marriage. Sometimes the inability of a couple to agree beforehand on this is a sign, however painful it is to face, that their marriage might not work out. They may simply be too far apart on what, for each, is a fundamental conviction in their lives. They may need the maturity and courage to break off their relationship. One person may "give in" to the other, but as the children arrive and grow, there may develop a smoldering resentment that can destroy or paralyze the marriage. Couples who must maturely face the need of breaking off a relationship should realize that the experience has not been a total loss, that each has received much from the other, that they both have matured toward even better future relationships—however remote this may seem at the time.

It seems, however, that today the religious question can usually be resolved by the couple, particularly if they are in agreement on other aspects of their future relationship. But occasionally a deep disagreement over religion by the couple is a telltale clue that there are other fundamental incompatibilities that they are unaware of or are ignoring. Sometimes it is in reality a signal that there is already under way a "power struggle" for dominance in the relationship. Here, of course, perceptive and unhurried premarital counseling is needed.

The Church's attitude toward interfaith marriages has changed in recent times, from grudging approval to giving as much help as possible to the union. The nuptial Mass and blessing may be used to celebrate interfaith marriages, if the couple so desire. The couple may ask a minister to say some prayers and give a blessing and exhortation to the couple after the Catholic wedding ceremony. Also the local bishop may allow the couple to have a non-Catholic minister perform the whole marriage ceremony, with or without a priest present, if there is some good reason for doing so.

If the non-Catholic partner is a Christian, the couple may get permission to take part in communion together; sharing in the eucharist, as said earlier, is a help toward a closer unity as well as a sign of oneness.

With intelligent cooperation and the help of God, an interfaith marriage can enjoy a good deal of success—and sometimes have more of God's love than one between those who have the same faith but are lukewarm in their practice of it and their love. The couple must respect each other's beliefs and should try to discuss their religious convictions frankly and with a sincere desire to learn.

In many cases, especially after adequate previous instruction, the points of agreement will be found to far outweigh those of disagreement. Above all, religious discussion and practices should never be pushed into the background simply because of differences.

The common religious beliefs of a couple should be sought out and emphasized, particularly in raising their family. Both partners should take an active part in the religious upbringing of the children, for each has insights, ideals, and practices to communicate; a situation should never develop where one party feels "left out." Although the children are being raised basically in one belief, the convictions of the other partner should also be honestly and tactfully presented.

Some further suggestions: If both parents believe in God, they can pray together and with the children—prayers of any faith, or those "made up" by the parents or children. The Bible can usually be a common source of religious inspiration, stories, and teachings for the children in which both parents can

take part. Teachings and stories about God, his love for us, our moral obligations, and so on are things in which both can share.

If both parents are Christians, they can share even more: they pray to the
same Triune God, profess their faith in the same Apostles' Creed, take their
teachings from the Bible, believe in Christ as Savior, acknowledge their
Christian unity by baptism, know the importance of the eucharist and of forgiveness of sin, share basically the same moral code, celebrate the same feasts,
and often follow the same liturgical cycle of Scripture readings.

IN THE LITURGY

**The Catholic marriage ceremony takes place after the gospel of the
nuptial Mass.** The priest usually gives the couple an instruction on
marriage. Then the bridegroom and bride exchange vows. The wedding
rings are blessed and exchanged by the couple. The priest asks God's
blessing upon the couple, and the Mass continues: the couple offer themselves through Christ, with Christ, and in Christ to the Father; after the
Lord's Prayer the priest reads over them the nuptial blessing; at communion they are joined in the most intimate way possible with Christ and
through Christ with each other. After communion there is a final blessing,
and they go forth as husband and wife.

Couples now plan their wedding service to reflect themselves and
the role of their families, friends, and the Christian community closest to
them. They choose meaningful Scripture readings and prayers and can
write their own wedding vows (including, of course, the essential element
of a lifelong commitment of fidelity). They can include family and friends
in the readings, prayers, and other little ceremonials that they will talk
over with the priest as they plan their marriage. The service should be
a joyous, personal, and shared event of culminated love. See "Further
Reading" for books and booklets to help the couple prepare spiritually,
and in other ways, for their ceremony.

**The Feast of the Holy Family—Jesus and his human family, Mary
and Joseph—is celebrated on the Sunday after Christmas.** The great
feast of the Incarnation, Christmas, is immediately followed by this feast,
thus proclaiming that God himself came among us as part of a very ordi-

nary human family—and was nourished and loved, and grew in wisdom and learning, in his human family, just as any of us.

> Parishes may have a renewal of marriage vows on this day. A Christ-conscious parish will be sensitive to all its married members on this day: those who are living out their marriage vows in pain, those who are separated or divorced, and those who are remarried.

DAILY LIVING: RENEWING ONE'S MARRIAGE

Every married couple eventually needs to take a fresh look at their relationship, and taking part in a marriage encounter, or a couples' retreat, can be a wonderfully helpful way of doing this. Of course, much depends on who is conducting it, but at a marriage encounter, for instance, a number of couples come together, and guided by an expert team consisting mostly of other couples, each husband and wife "encounter" each other for a weekend of honest, insightful, and inspiring mutual growth. A couples' retreat can also be an excellent way for a couple to grow together, usually in a less structured format.

SOME SUGGESTIONS FOR . . .

DISCUSSION

What do you perceive as unique about a Christian marriage?

What expectations do you think a couple should have when entering into a Christian marriage? What expectations should they not have? What might be done to prevent an unsuccessful marriage?

What alternatives are there for those who are divorced and remarried and who want to take part in the eucharist?

What elements should be part of a truly Christian attitude toward gay people?

What, concretely, do you—and your partner—consider essential ingredients for a successful marriage? Is one of these a willingness to seek counseling when some serious problem between you cannot be resolved?

What do you think are some of the liabilities and possibilities of an interfaith marriage?

What are the most important aspects of a truly Christian family, in your experience?

FURTHER READING

- *Beginning Your Marriage,* Thomas and Thomas (ACTA Publications, Chicago, 1994)—Recently revised and in its eighth edition, this is a very popular book that has been widely used for marriage preparation. Also available in a Spanish edition.
- *Perspectives on Marriage* (ACTA Publications, Chicago, 1992)—This popular workbook for marriage preparation, recently revised, is available in a Catholic Wedding Ceremony Edition (also in Spanish) and an Ecumenical Edition for mixed-religion marriages. A Leader's Guide is also available for the Catholic editions.
- *Can Your Marriage Be a Friendship?* McDonald and McDonald (Paulist Press, 1996)—A practical, popularly written book that shows how to develop one's marriage into, of all things, a friendship.
- *Creating a Marriage,* Greteman (Paulist Press, 1995)—This is an inspirational yet practical book that shows how to integrate the stages of individual life development into the stages of marriage.
- *Marrying Well: Stages on the Journey of Christian Marriage,* Whitehead and Whitehead (Doubleday, 1983)—One of the most complete books on Christian marriage and family life, this is practical and inspiring; it is well worth buying to read together and ponder over.
- *The First Two Years of Marriage,* Hart and Hart (Paulist Press, 1983)—This is an insightful and practical little book about the most critical period in any marriage; it should be "must" reading for every couple. Also available in video.
- •• *What Is Marriage? Marriage in the Catholic Church,* Mackin (Paulist Press, 1982), *Divorce & Remarriage: Marriage in the Catholic Church* (1984), and *The Marital Sacrament* (1989)—These three excellent volumes are a monumental study of the history, theology, and practices relating to marriage and divorce.
- •• *Contraception: A History of Its Treatment by Catholic Theologians and Canonists,* Noonan (Harvard University Press, 1985)—Here the consultant to the papal birth control commission, a legal historian, ethicist, and judge, argues that as the Church's teaching on usury and

organ transplantation changed from outright rejection to acceptance, so it might regarding contraception.

- *Sexuality and Catholicism,* Fox (Braziller, 1995)—This frank, insightful book by an editor who thoroughly knows American Catholicism discusses all the areas of conflict regarding sexuality within the Church.
- *Why You Can Disagree and Remain a Faithful Catholic,* Kaufman (Meyer Stone, 1989)—A well-researched book by a monk-theologian on birth control, divorce and remarriage, and intercommunion.
- *Annulment: Your Chance to Remarry Within the Catholic Church,* Zwack (Harper & Row, 1983)—A practicing Catholic and attorney wrote this encouraging, informative little book as a beginning step for the many couples who could seek annulments but do not.
- *A Woman's Healing Song: Prayers of Consolation for the Separated and Divorced,* Hide (Twenty-third Publications, 1993)—This sensitive, insightful little book offers prayerful ways for women to transform the pain of divorce or separation into spiritual growth.
- *The Many Faces of AIDS* (NCCB, 1988)—This gives the generally very good, concrete guidelines of the American bishops on AIDS education.
- *Building Bridges: Gay and Lesbian Reality and the Catholic Church,* Nugent and Gramick (Twenty-third Publications, 1992)—Coauthored by a priest and a nun who have written much about the Church and homosexuality, this insightfully discusses fears and myths about gay and lesbian people, what they have to offer the Church, and vice versa.
- *"New Ways Ministry"* has several publications, and also audiovisual cassettes dealing with various aspects of homosexuality (many as NCR Credence Cassettes—*Ministry and Homosexual People,* Gramick and Nugent, is an especially fine help in ministering to gay people). Mutual support groups help homosexual persons deal with problems of supposed rejection by God and very real rejection by others, self-doubt, and so on. *Dignity* is the best known of these, and many dioceses and parishes have their own groups.
- *The Federation of Parents and Friends of Lesbians and Gays* (PFLAG) is a group that helps parents relate to their homosexual children.

FURTHER LISTENING

A Letter to a Friend with AIDS, Gallagher (NCR audio, 75 minutes)—A priest with much experience and compassion speaks simply and strongly to those facing death from AIDS.

Homophobia: Acknowledging a Prejudice, Nugent and Gramick (NCR, 2 hours)—An unacknowledged fear of gay people is a problem for some who are straight—this cassette by two experts in the field can bring light and a healing of such attitudes.

PERSONAL REFLECTION

Christ promises a couple all the graces they need to make their marriage a success—but he will never force himself upon them. The couple must come and receive these graces, especially by acts of mutual love and caring, by prayer and taking part in the Church's worship and sacraments. In the sacrament of reconciliation the couple should focus on overcoming the faults that interfere with their union and their role as parents; when taking part in communion they should particularly ask to grow in love for each other and their children. Each of us should pray daily for our own marriage and/or for those close to us who are experiencing problems and pain in their relationships.

22

The Family that Is the Church

How can the Church be a meaningful community of love in today's world? What place do laypeople have in the Church? Why are priests and nuns particular groups within the Church, and what are their basic functions? What emerging role do women have in the Church? What is the role of the bishop?

GOD'S GIFTED PEOPLE

The Church is a family in which all the members should love and serve one another and all people. We are "one body and one Spirit." We have "one Lord, one faith, one baptism: one God and Father of all, who is above all and throughout all, and in us all" (Ephesians 4, 4–6). What affects one, affects the others. We must love one another and work together for the good of all. Christ tells us clearly, "By this everyone will know that you are my disciples, if you have love for one another" (John 13, 35).

Our Christian family love extends to all people, for all have God as their Father and Christ as their brother. Race, creed, color, sex, age, talents, or social status should make no difference. Christ reminds us again, "As you did it to one of the least of these my brethren, you did it to me" (Matthew 25, 40).

No one is essentially holier or better than anyone else in the Church. Christ said to all his followers, "You therefore, must be perfect, as your heavenly Father is perfect" (Matthew 5, 48). The Church today emphasizes his words: "All the faithful of Christ, of whatever rank or status, are called to the fullness of the Christian life and to the perfection of charity . . . " (*Constitution on the Church*, no. 40). Some seek this holiness as priests, others as nuns or brothers, others in the married state, and yet others in the single state.

Everyone in the Church, clergy and laity, is to share in its work, each using his or her particular gifts. We have seen how all the members of the Church have particular charisms, or gifts of the Spirit, to be used for the good of all.

> Let it be recognized that all the faithful, clerical and lay, possess a lawful freedom of inquiry and of thought, and the freedom to express their minds humbly and courageously about those matters in which they enjoy competence (*The Church in the Modern World*, no. 62).

We have seen that every Christian shares in Christ's priesthood and is a special mediator between God and humankind. All Christians by the power of baptism, and again by confirmation, can offer Christ at Mass in a special, powerful way, and can bring down grace upon humankind by their prayer and partaking of the sacraments: **Reread 1 Peter 2, 9–10.**

Every Christian also teaches and bears witness to his or her faith as one specially chosen by Christ. "Christ . . . continually fulfills his prophetic office . . . not only through the hierarchy who teach in his name and with his authority, but also through the laity whom . . . he made his witness and instructed by an understanding of the faith . . . and the grace of the Word . . . " (*Constitution on the Church*, no. 35). All persons have the understanding, power, and grace to be instruments of the Spirit in their own way, and all should ask the Spirit to help them find and fulfill their roles.

Today, many new possibilities for all people to serve or minister are clearly set forth as part of the regular "structure" of the Church, along with their rights and duties as part of the Christian community. They are trained, usually for a few years, judged suitable, and commissioned by the bishop (and also are to receive adequate financial compensation).

PRIESTS, GOD'S INSTRUMENTS AT THE SERVICE OF PEOPLE

Humans have always had need of mediators, those who can give assurance, particularly from the witness of their own lives, that they are "in touch" with the beyond. They are those who struggle as anyone does, but they show by their example, by the inspiration, learning, discipline, and service of their lives that they know of a power beyond. People want the testimony of someone they can trust, particularly if that person is learned, not prejudiced or narrow, in touch with human realities, and concerned about them. People seem to intuit the divine presence behind one's words, that one is the instrument, however poor and stumbling, of this power.

There have always been priests among us, mediators between God and humankind. Ancient pagan tribes had priests to offer sacrifice. In Israel as in other societies the oldest member, or patriarch, of the family or tribe offered sacrifice and acted as mediator between God and his people. Then Aaron and his sons were chosen as priests, to offer sacrifice; they were to be made "holy to the Lord," specially consecrated, clothed in sacred vestments, and anointed with oil: **Read Exodus 40, 12-15.**

Jesus Christ is the one priest of the new covenant, the great and only necessary mediator between God and us. He offered himself in sacrifice, shedding his own blood, to seal the new covenant for all time.

> The former priests were many in number, because they were prevented by death from continuing in office; but he holds his priesthood permanently, because he continues forever. Consequently, he is able for all time to save those who draw near to God through him, since he always lives to make intercession for them. . . . He has no need . . . to offer sacrifice daily, first for his own sins and then for those of the people; he did this once for all when he offered up himself (Hebrews 5, 23-27).

Christ chose the apostles to carry on his work. They would come to be looked on as his first priests. He sent them out to preach the kingdom of God, to exhort the people to conversion, to cast out devils, and heal the sick (cf. Mark 6, 7-13). At the last supper he gave them what would come to be the central priestly power of continuing his eucharistic meal: "Do this in remembrance of me" (cf. 1 Corinthians 11, 23-26). He also gave them the power of forgiving sins (Matthew 18, 18; John 20, 21-23).

Thus though there is no evidence the apostles were "ordained" priests by Christ—nor that they "ordained" others in turn—they were chosen by him to do essentially what ordained priests would later do. In the New Testament the word *priest* is used almost exclusively of the Jewish priesthood; it is applied to Christ in the Epistle to the Hebrews, and to the whole Christian people who are called a "royal priesthood" (1 Peter 2, 5 and 9). We have seen (in chapter 14) that the concept of the eucharist as a sacrifice developed only gradually. We don't know who presided at the early eucharistic meals. In some places in the early "house churches" there is good evidence that women did.

From the beginning in the Church certain ones were chosen, by laying on of hands and prayer, to minister to the spiritual needs of the community. In the account of the Seven who would serve at table (undoubtedly often the Lord's supper or eucharist) and who later preached and baptized, we read, "These they set before the apostles, and they prayed and laid their hands upon them" (Acts 6, 1-6).

We have seen (chapter 10) that the organization of the early Church was formed only gradually—Christ left it to his followers to work out—and that New Testament terms did not necessarily mean what they have come to mean. But the terms "presbyter" (elder) and "bishop" refer to those who had some power of presiding over the local churches (Acts 14, 23; 20-28, etc.). The empowerment of Timothy as chosen by Paul to lead a local church is thus set forth: "Do not neglect the gift you have, which was given you by prophetic utterance when the elders laid their hands upon you. . . . I remind you to rekindle the gift of God that is within you through the laying on of my hands . . . " (1 Timothy 4, 14; 2 Timothy 6).

While the New Testament stresses the pastoral work of bishops, Christian tradition shows that early on they also presided over the eucharistic sacrifice-meal. Clement of Rome writes near the end of the first century: "It will be no small sin for us if we eject men who have irreproachably and piously offered the sacrifices proper to the episcopate" (Epistle to the Corinthians 42, 44). These sacrifices are "the bread and the cup," the eucharistic sacrifice. In an early-third-century Roman liturgy, the newly ordained bishop consecrated the bread and chalice and then addressed God with the remembrance prayer, or "anamnesis": "Doing therefore the anamnesis of his death and resurrection, we offer to thee the bread and the cup, making eucharist to thee because thou hast bidden us to stand before thee and minister as priests to thee" (*Apostolic Tradition of Hippolytus* 4, 11).

From the first century there has been a hierarchy of orders in the Church—bishops, priests, and deacons. For the first eight centuries the rite of ordination to these offices was an imposition of the bishop's hands and an invocation of the Holy Spirit. In the Middle Ages the rite was expanded to include an anointing of the hands, bestowal of chalice and paten, and so on. In 1947 Pope Pius XII declared the essential part of the rite to be the laying on of hands and the words invoking the Holy Spirit.

The earliest detailed rite is given in the *Apostolic Tradition of Hippolytus* referred to above, a Roman bishop's book compiled about 215 C.E. In this we find the hierarchy of bishops, presbyters, and deacons, each ordained by a laying on of hands. There are other, lesser offices, but these are merely appointed, not ordained by a laying on of hands. The bishop is chosen by all the people and is ordained by the imposition of hands of his fellow bishops alone; the presbyter is ordained by an imposition of the bishop's hands with "the presbyters also touching him."

Men become priests today by the sacrament of holy orders—the laying on of the bishop's hands and prayer. Through this sacrament Christ changes one interiorly, giving one the powers of the priesthood, a great increase of his grace-presence, and a promise of all the actual graces and helps he needs to carry out his priesthood.

Holy orders are received only once, like baptism and confirmation. By it one is given an interior "character," a permanent change. Even if one stops practicing the priesthood, or is released from his priestly vows, one is still an ordained priest, established for all time in this permanent function for God and for people.

There are different orders or degrees in the priesthood:

A bishop has the fullness of Christ's priesthood. He is a successor of the apostles in that he carries on what they received from Christ himself. In the name of the Church he acts as Christ's instrument in giving all the sacraments. He is the only one who can administer holy orders and is normally the one to give confirmation.

A priest has the power of presiding at Mass, leading the people, making Christ present, and re-presenting Christ's sacrifice. He also acts in the name of the Church as Christ's instrument in giving the sacraments (except holy orders), in preaching and teaching, and in asking God's blessing upon people and things. Only he can give penance, the sacrament of reconciliation.

A deacon's ministry is to baptize, distribute communion, read the Scriptures and preach, preside at marriages and funerals, give sacramentals, and give himself to works of charity and administration; these works are done to the extent the local bishop sees fit. A deacon is also ordained by a bishop. A permanent diaconate was revived by Vatican Council II and includes married men "of more mature age" as well as celibate younger men.

Also, today nonordained people who are gifted with various ministries work with the priests and deacons in the service of the people, caring for the people according to their particular gifts, or charisms, and suitability. In the 1983 revision of the Church's laws, these laypeople are envisioned as holding a wide variety of offices and performing many functions of service.

Many of these ministries were spoken of earlier. The local bishop determines their nature, the qualifications necessary, and so on. Others arise more informally, as in local parish settings where laypeople have been doing marvelous things in various ministries. It should be noted, incidentally, that acolytes and lectors at Mass, when permanently installed, can be men only; but when installed liturgical ministers are not available, any layperson can perform their functions.

A *monsignor* (as the term is used in America) is a priest who receives this honorary title from the pope, at the request of his bishop, because of some outstanding work he has done or some position of importance he holds.

"Priests, as co-workers with their bishops, have as their primary duty the proclamation of the gospel of God to all. In this way they fulfill the Lord's command: 'Go into the whole world and preach the gospel to every creature' (Mark 16, 15)" (*Decree on the Ministry and Life of Priests,* no. 4). Preaching the Word leads to faith, to conversion, to holiness. To take part profitably in the Mass we should listen openly to this preaching, allowing our hearts to be converted. God speaks even through the dullest homilies; his Word always does something to us if we but let it.

The celebration of the eucharist, the Mass, is the high point of a priest's work, "the source and the apex of the whole work of preaching the gospel. . . . The other sacraments, as well as every ministry of the Church . . . are linked with the holy eucharist and are directed toward it . . . [as] the very heartbeat of the congregation of the faithful over which the priest presides" (*Decree on the Ministry and Life of Priests,* no. 5).

Priests are chosen from among God's people to serve the people. They are first of all Christians, and then priests. They live a special life in order that they may be better instruments of Christ in serving the whole Church. They are not necessarily holier, nor of a higher class in the Church's structure; whatever authority they have, or respect they are given, comes to them only because they visibly represent Christ—as deference to an ambassador is meant for the country he or she represents. Laypeople may often be gifted by God to accomplish far more for the Church and the world.

Vatican Council II says that while priests are "set apart" among God's people, "this is so, not that they may be separated from his people or from any [person], but that they may be totally dedicated to the work for which the Lord has raised them up. They cannot be ministers of Christ unless they are witnesses and dispensers of a life other than this earthly one. But they cannot be of service to [people] if they remain strangers to the life and conditions of [people]" (*The Ministry and Life of Priests,* no. 3).

Today in the Church there is stress on the priesthood of service, on the ministering as well as the cultic priesthood. The modern priest sees that he follows one who "came not to be served, but to serve" (Mark 10, 45), and who gave a striking example of service by washing the feet of his first priests, the apostles, when he "ordained" them at the last supper.

Priests also have different charisms or gifts for different works. One is talented at a certain type of work, while another may be a failure at it. In today's age of specialization, particularly, it is almost impossible for priests to be "all things to all people"—and yet this is required of many, especially parish priests. Catholic people, however, are usually wonderfully understanding of the inadequacies of their priests.

To become a priest one studies and prepares from four to five years after completing college. Usually he does his graduate work in theology, Scripture studies, and pastoral practice in a seminary with other candidates for the priesthood. He must not only have the continuing and free desire to be a priest but must be judged suitable (by his bishop or religious superior) in learning, character, psychological maturity, and health.

Priests of the Latin Rite bind themselves to celibacy, not to marry. This custom began to grow from the fourth century and was made a general law of the Western Church in the twelfth century. Priests of the Eastern Rites may marry, usually before the diaconate. The basic reason for celibacy is so that the priest might better be a living sign or witness to the reality of Christ among us. In giving up the fundamental and deepest human love relationship, marriage, the priest expresses his total attachment to the divine. He is staking all on the reality of God among us. The loneliness that is his gives him a kinship with all who are alone or who are neglected in their pain, and it can propel him into a deep intimacy with Christ. Christ alone is at the core of his being, and no one else. "Priests are lonely," says Pope John Paul II, "so that others might not be lonely."

The celibate priest can often have a greater independence, be more totally at the service of others. St. Paul expresses it: "The unmarried man is anxious about the affairs of the Lord, how to please the Lord; but the married man is anxious about worldly affairs, how to please his wife, and his interests are divided" (1 Corinthians 7, 32–34).

Scripture scholars today, however, see St. Paul's recommendation of celibacy, as well as that of Christ himself, as part of their message to prepare for the end of the world, which evidently seemed quite near; to marry and attempt to raise a family would distract one from readying oneself for this apocalyptic event. The next generation of Christians, realizing the end was not coming soon, softened this message—as in the later epistles attributed to Paul. Celibacy also was associated with an ancient "ritual purity" required of one offering sacrifice to God.

Most in the Church today recognize that there is no necessary connection, historically or pastorally, between the priesthood and celibacy. Pope Paul VI in his encyclical reaffirming celibacy allowed for further study of the question. Most today recognize that among priests, as among all Christians, there are different charisms. Some are called to work and witness as celibates, others as married. Many feel that good men are being eliminated from the priesthood because of celibacy while the near-worldwide shortage of priests is steadily worsening. Among Eastern Rite Catholics and Orthodox Christians both forms of the priestly life have always been recognized. Countless Protestant ministers have effectively served the Lord and their people while married, while celibacy is also practiced among them by individuals and small groups. Also married Episcopalian priests have been ordained to the Roman Catholic priesthood in recent years. Most who advocate optional celibacy in the priesthood do not wish to abolish celibacy but to make it a freer choice. In the Church of the future, many predict, religious communities will be celibate, while diocesan priests will embrace either state of life.

There are two general types of priests: diocesan or secular, and religious. While the work of the priesthood is basically the same, these two general types of priests have developed over the centuries to better carry out this work. The diocesan priest works under the bishop of a particular diocese, is bound by the law of celibacy (not to marry, in the Latin Rite), and provides for his own support from a small salary, offerings, and so on. The average parish priest is a diocesan priest, though these may also specialize in particular works. Bishops are usually chosen from among these.

Religious priests belong to a religious community and take vows or solemn promises: poverty (in some way restricting their ownership of things), celibacy or chastity, and obedience to their religious superior whom they usually elect. Each religious community has a particular spirit and work and strives to have a "common life," praying and working together as a group and ready to move from diocese to diocese or to other countries to carry out their particular priestly work.

Priests are human instruments of Christ, often sinful and defective, and in need of the support and prayers of the people. Eleven of the first twelve priests deserted Christ, their leader denied him, and one of them betrayed him—so we should expect to find weaknesses among his priests today. People often do not realize how much their priests need the constant support of their prayers. Recent revelations of the sexual abuse of children, though involving only a very small number of priests, show how low priests can fall—and the need of psychosexual maturity in those who hold this office. No one realizes his inadequacies, limitations, and sinfulness more than a priest. St. Paul expresses every priest's feelings when he writes: **Read 1 Corinthians 1, 26-31.**

Vatican Council II also poignantly expresses the mind of every priest and committed layperson: "The ministers of the Church and even, at times, the faithful themselves feel like strangers in the world, anxiously looking for appropriate ways and words with which to communicate with it. . . . The modern obstacles which block faith, the seeming sterility of their past labors, and the bitter loneliness they experience can lead them to the danger of becoming depressed in spirit. . . . Priests should remember that in performing their tasks they are never alone . . . " (*Decree on the Ministry and Life of Priests,* no. 22).

Christ, then, shows himself among us today in a particular way in his priests. One of Christ's first and greatest priests, St. Paul, describes all priests when he says, "We are ambassadors for Christ, God making his appeal through us" (1 Corinthians 5, 20). Through the priesthood Christ makes himself available to all in a special, organized, human way. The priesthood witnesses to God's loving reality among us by serving all people everywhere—making God's love real to people as best we poor humans can.

The *Catechism* expresses the priestly ideal: to become better servants and lovers of God's people. It quotes St. John Vianney, the nineteenth-century pastor of the little French town of Ars, who worked and prayed almost without sleeping while living as a strict ascetic—and whose funeral brought crowds from all over France: "The priesthood," he said, "is the love of the heart of Jesus" (1589). There are few professions today besides the priesthood in which one can do as much, or as little, for others.

The priest is there at the high points and critical moments of people's lives: when people come before God in worship, when they come to express repentance, at the moment of their lifelong commitment in marriage, in sickness, and when they are facing the conclusion of it all in death—and with advice and guidance in many little ways along the path of life.

Every priest also has insights, like that of the fictional Pope Kiril I, in Morris West's novel *The Shoes of the Fisherman:* "Once more I have been brought to see vividly that the real battleground of the Church is not in politics or in diplomacy or finance or material extension. It is the secret landscape of the individual spirit. To enter into this hidden place the pastor needs tact and understanding, and the very particular grace bestowed by the sacrament of holy orders. . . . "

The great priest-paleontologist Teilhard de Chardin expressed his priestly vocation in this way: "To the full extent of my power, because I am a priest, I wish from now on to be the first to become conscious of all that the world loves, pursues and suffers; I want to be the first to seek, to sympathize and to suffer; the first to unfold and sacrifice myself . . . to become more widely human and more nobly of the earth than any of the world's servants."

Today it is increasingly seen that the Church is a community in which different people have different gifts, all of which are necessary and important. The once-clear division between priestly leaders and people whose role was mainly to follow has been disappearing. We realize that each member has something to contribute, and often the contribution of a layperson in a particular matter is more vital than that of a priest or religious. We see that the Spirit speaks and acts through all, particularly where "two or three are gathered together" as a group in Christ's name. Sometimes the special way of dress, titles, separate living facilities, and so on that are generally part of a priest's lifestyle need not be necessary to the priest's role in the community, and sometimes may in fact be a hindrance in his work.

One way of viewing the priesthood in the community is to see the priest as the one who particularly shows forth, and brings about, the unity and order of the community—and this especially when he leads the community in liturgy. Though others may have gifts that are more important to a particular community, the priest is the unifier and the one who assures that gifts of all are recognized and used effectively.

Some today also see the priesthood as an office within the community to which one is called by God either for life or for a time—though the role of the priest and the inner "character" of ordination would seem to call for a lifetime commitment, as has been the Church's tradition.

THE ROLE OF RELIGIOUS

The religious life is that by which priests, nuns, or brothers join together in a particular religious community, with a particular spirit and "rule," or way of life, to do particular works in the Church. Religious life is found in all the world religions, in Islam, Buddhism, Hinduism, among Catholics and Orthodox Christians, and it is a small but growing movement in Protestant Christianity. In the Catholic Church there are several hundred religious communities—or "institutes"—each with its particular spirit and functions.

"Religious," that is, men and women in religious communities, have a "common life." They usually live together, have some daily pattern of prayer and work, and to a greater or lesser extent share what they own with one another.

Most communities have some distinctive "habit" or garb worn by the members; this might be thought of as a sort of uniform signifying their profession. Most religious habits have been modified today, and some religious wear ordinary clothing, perhaps with a crucifix, cross, and so on. Some religious exercise their ministry in regular jobs or professions, and may live alone, with laypeople, and so on; these gather regularly for prayer, study, and spiritual renewal.

Religious take vows, or solemn promises, of poverty, chastity, and obedience. By these they seek more fully to imitate Christ and serve the Christian community.

By poverty they restrict their ownership of things and depend for their support upon their religious community; this detachment from material things enables them to give themselves more fully to God and to others. By chastity they give up intimate sexual relationships in order to give themselves fully to the services of all the Christian community. Obedience puts them at the service of the Christian community in that they better use their talents in the cooperative effort of all. In some newer religious groups, the members write their own expressions of dedication that retain the essence of the three vows.

These vows do not mean that religious are in a state of life higher than that of the other people of the Church, nor that they are holier.

Rather they join together with others in the stable life of a religious community, and bind themselves by vows, to better attain the perfection to which all Christians are called, and by their lives to be "a sign that can and ought to attract all the members of the Church to an effective and prompt fulfillment of the duties of their Christian vocation" (*Constitution on the Church,* no. 45). They are living reminders to all Christians that Christ is now among us and that shortly we will be with him forever.

A nun or "sister" is a woman who belongs to a particular religious community. Nuns serve the Church and the world as educators, doing hospital and social work, by working in the missions, in the business world, in the sciences, and so on. Some live in relatively secluded contemplative communities, as models of total dedication and detachment (see below).

A brother is a man who lives the religious life in a state other than the priesthood. As with nuns, some brothers are teachers; others do hospital, social, or missionary work, or any work for which they are needed and suitable. Some, too, are in contemplative communities.

"Contemplative" communities focus mainly on the worship of God and union with him through prayer. They live relatively secluded, simple lives of prayer and detachment, doing a minimum of outside work to sustain themselves. They might be compared to unnoticed but vitally necessary power plants—they bring God's grace and love into all our lives by their prayer and penance. Many of these contemplative communities share their insights and wisdom with those who come to their "guest houses" for retreats or other spiritual guidance.

To become a nun or brother, as in becoming a priest, one must have a desire for this life, undertake several years of study and training, and be judged suitable in character, learning, and health. After taking temporary vows (or solemn promises) for several years, perpetual vows are taken committing one for life to this vocation.

All religious communities today have updated themselves, adapting to the principles of Vatican II and to changing modern conditions. The process of change, often painful and stress-filled, has gone forward amazingly. Some smaller, less-structured groups are emerging, focused on better using the talents of individual members. Most older communities, in adapting to the

Church's changing needs, are also better utilizing their members' particular gifts—spurred in part by a decline in new members. Many communities, however, in finding new opportunities for service, are also attracting new members who are often older and more mature.

Religious and priests might be compared to signposts—standing somewhat apart, often lonely, but at the service of people as they point the way to God; others may pass them on the way to holiness, but without them the others would have a much harder time finding their way.

There are also laypeople—married or single—who belong to these communities and who commit themselves to living the gospel's values in their everyday jobs or professions and in their family life; they follow a "rule" of prayer, meeting regularly, and so on. They are called "associates," "comembers," and "oblates," among others. Some, in "secular institutes," vow or consecrate themselves to a relatively structured way of life. Some, in the traditional "Third Orders," are attached to older religious communities; today many are becoming more autonomous, though still as part of the same "family" in their spirit and purpose.

OUR BISHOP AND OUR DIOCESE

A bishop has the highest degree of holy orders, the greatest share in Christ's priesthood. We have seen (chapter 10) that the bishops came to occupy the same place in the Church as the apostles chosen by Christ—that they are ordained by the laying on of hands of another bishop (usually three bishops take part)—and that bishops are chosen by the pope usually upon the recommendation of the other bishops of the area, and, finally, that many today favor the practice of giving the local clergy and laity once again a voice in the selection of their bishops.

The bishops of the Church are responsible for the welfare of the whole Church. Their responsibility for teaching all parts of the Church is at present exercised through elected representative-bishops who, usually triannually, meet to advise the pope in a World Synod (see chapter 10). Each bishop should also be concerned to provide material help and personnel for deprived parts of the Church.

There are also national and regional conferences of bishops with responsibility for their own country or region. These episcopal conferences, as envisioned by Vatican Council II, teach authoritatively for their part of the Church. In the United States, the National Conference of Catholic Bishops (NCCB) fulfills this function.

The bishop is the leader of the local church or diocese—in a sense, its spiritual father. If the diocese is large, he may be assisted by auxiliary bishops. Dioceses are grouped into provinces centered around an archdiocese (usually the largest diocese of the area) presided over by an archbishop. Each bishop in his diocese is independent, subject only to the pope and in some matters to the national conference of bishops

A **"cardinal"** is a bishop who is the leader of a particularly large archdiocese or who has some high administrative position in the Church. This is essentially an honorary title, dating from the Middle Ages. The cardinals come together when a pope dies to elect a new one, chosen for the last several centuries from their own number—in this they are the successors of the ancient clergy of Rome who from the earliest days came together to elect their bishop, who was therefore the pope. The pope chooses the members of the "college of cardinals," which in recent years has been made a more international and representative group. Some have speculated as to the future status of this group; their function of advising the pope and setting Church policy, and perhaps the election of the pope, may at some future time be taken over by or shared with the synod of bishops.

The bishop is the chief preacher and teacher of his diocese, its chief priest and pastor. He should make Christ's doctrine relevant to the needs of the time, bring forth holiness in people, and should himself give an example of holiness "in charity, humility and simplicity of life." The liturgy celebrated with the bishop is the high point of the worship of the diocese (*Decree on the Pastoral Office of Bishops,* nos. 12, 13, 16).

"In exercising his office of father and pastor, a bishop should stand in the midst of his people as one who serves." A bishop is not above the Church, nor is the Church his private domain. He is to be a servant of the people of God, in imitation of the servant of all, Jesus. He should know his people and they should know him. He should "so gather and mold the whole family of the flock that everyone, conscious of his own duties, may live and work in the communion of love" (*Decree on the Pastoral Office of Bishops,* no. 16).

The people of a diocese, in turn, should assist and work with their bishop in whatever way they can. The people realize that bishops are only human, that in fact the twelve apostles themselves could even betray, deny, and desert Christ. They know, too, that only so much can be expected of some bishops in today's rapidly changing world. They realize that their bishop is given a special gift to guide them. They should remember particularly that he is in need of their prayers because of his special responsibilities.

The priests and people of a diocese should be in continual communication with their bishop. Vatican Council II spoke of their "active cooperation." The bishop needs them as much as they do him—and they should offer their particular gifts for the service of the diocese, realizing that the Spirit also acts through them. How to use their gifts is up to the bishop, and every bishop has clergy and laypeople to advise him in this.

All the people of the diocese are to share in the work of the diocese. The bishop is required to seek the advice and guidance of his people in leading the diocese, according to the revised (1983) Church laws. He is required to have a *presbyteral (or priests') council,* and a *finance council;* in important matters these must be consulted, and in some cases must give their consent, before the bishop can act. The local bishop now has more autonomy, and he decides how these councils are to be chosen. However, participation, consultation, and attempting to arrive at a consensus are to be hallmarks of these, as well as of the other groups recommended for each diocese:

> *The diocesan pastoral council* consists of clergy and laity who truly represent the makeup of the diocese, and it meets at least once a year. *The diocesan synod (or "conference," or "convention")* has wider representation—which may include non-Catholic observers—and a broader agenda; it meets less often and might be seen as analogous to a political party's national convention in reflecting desired guidelines, and so on. Finally, an *episcopal council,* or bishop's "cabinet," meets regularly.
>
> *Also, "due process,"* that is, an individual's right to have a fair hearing and judgment (analogous to our secular legal system) is now recognized in Church law; the guidelines for the United States have been set up by the NCCB.

Dioceses are divided into parishes, each of which has a pastor and possibly assistant or associate pastors. The pastor and priests are to serve the people of the parish, teaching and working with them, leading them in liturgy and in lives of practical charity. The people cooperate with them, contributing whatever talents they can. All are necessary that all may profit. There is usually some parish ministry or organization of which one can be an active part; if not, there often is one in a neighboring parish—or one can find his or her place in a diocesan or informal inter-parochial group.

Today, much of a parish's ministry is taken care of by laypeople. As we have seen with the diocese, so with the local parish: the new Church laws make participation and consultation part of its structure.

There are many pastoral and administrative ministries for which laypeople are gifted: catechetical ministries, social concerns and the care of the poor, counseling of various kinds, finances, marriage programs, and others. And where there is no priest available the pastoral care or leadership may be given by the bishop to a layperson or a religious—and/or to a pastoral team of people with different gifts.

Where the above-mentioned structures of sharing are functioning effectively, getting them under way was usually a difficult process. Gradually clergy and laypeople came to know and trust not only one another but the democratic process and the Presence of the Holy Spirit; this can require much patience, openness, mutual respect, and charity. But countless parishes have found that it does work. Where structures of communication and consultation are not yet fully or adequately set up, laypeople should write their bishop, so the bishop can more easily get to know their views. Credibility gaps between the bishop and his people, or between the pastor and his people, or among the people themselves—as well as "blind spots" on certain issues—are part of a Church made up of humans. We must except these, and expect as well to work with charity, prayer, and perseverance to overcome them. Christ is always there among his people, and eventually even the most difficult situations can usually be worked out (cf. Matthew 18, 20).

The parish, with the church as its center, is the place where the Christian people gain strength and go forth continually into the world to witness to Christ. From the local Christian community grace goes forth into the whole neighborhood—and the more truly Christian they are, the more their influence will radiate to everyone, to the whole world.

The parish priest is the living sign of the unity-in-service of all those who are part of the community.

However, in today's increasingly urban, mobile society, large city parishes particularly are less able to produce a real sense of community among the people within their boundaries. Different solutions are being tried, including special services for specialized groups.

Pastoral teams are becoming more common in today's parishes. Consisting of priest(s), perhaps a deacon, and religious and laypeople, all share in decision making as well as exercising their various ministries. Some work full-time, some part-time, and many work in several parishes.

Today many people seek out parishes other than their own where the style of worship and activities are compatible with their religious needs. While we might wish that every parish could be "all things to all people," it is evidently not possible in this age of change and fragmentation.

Mutual aid among parishes of a diocese—and of the world—should be practiced more and more, with the wealthier in terms of money, talent, and stable population helping the less well off. Interparochial structures are also being used more today, particularly for effective religious education, social action, and so on.

THE EMERGING ROLE OF WOMEN IN THE CHURCH

Today an increasing number of women are emerging into new, more equal, and more creative roles in the Church, as in all of society. There is no doubt that, despite the dignity given women in Christianity (in part due to the cult of the Virgin Mary), women have often been exploited and reduced to an inferior status by some male celibates who, though usually unconsciously, have often been de facto antifeminist and even misogynist. This has been changing. Today's sexual revolution, quietly in preparation for centuries, has been fully with us—especially during the past few decades—and is probably the most far-reaching in history.

The ideal Christian (and human) community, toward which the Church is committed to strive, was simply stated by St. Paul almost two thousand years ago: "There is neither Jew nor Greek, there is neither slave nor free, there is neither male nor female, for you are all one in

Christ Jesus" (Galatians 3, 28). Vatican Council II explicates this for us today:

> Where they have not yet won it, women claim for themselves an equity with men before the law and in fact ... [and] every type of discrimination, whether social or cultural, whether based on sex, race, color, social situation, language, or religion is to be overcome and eradicated as contrary to God's intent (*The Church in the Modern World,* nos. 9 and 29).

Official Church attitudes toward women have been steadily changing in recent years. As with much of society, these attitudes have developed from seeing women's role primarily in marriage—subject to men and belonging in the home—to recognizing their contributions and "intrinsic" equality in all areas of society. Church statements in recent years have been calling for a recognition of this equality, as well as for an elimination of the evils associated with discrimination against women.

Pope John Paul II said in 1995: "There is an urgent need to achieve real equality in every area: equal pay for equal work, protection for working mothers, fairness in career advancements, equality of spouses with regard to family rights and the recognition of everything that is part of the rights and duties of citizens in a democratic state." Condemning atrocities against women, such as rape, he said developed societies have been "corrupted by a culture of hedonistic permissiveness which aggravates tendencies to aggressive male behavior." Further, "the great process of women's liberation . . . has been substantially a positive one . . . a journey [that] must go on . . . [including] an effective and intelligent campaign for the promotion of women, concentrating on all area of women's life and beginning with a universal recognition of the dignity of women" (Preparation for the 1995 Beijing World Conference on Women).

Women, however, have traditionally been excluded from the Church's officially designated ministries—but this is changing. The American bishops, for instance, in a 1995 statement envision all Church offices except the priesthood being open to women.

The priesthood has been limited to men from its beginning. In view of the low social status of women in ancient Israel, it is not surprising that they were not among the Twelve chosen by Christ. However, as we have seen, there is no evidence of Christ ordaining anyone a priest in the later sense of presiding at the eucharistic sacrifice. Women were prominent among Jesus' followers—and Mary Magdalene, sent by Jesus to tell the apostles after he appeared to her, was thus called "the apostle to the apostles." Women were active in the early Christian ministry, and some probably presided at "house church" liturgies. There is no doubt that they acted as deacons. Women and men shared equally in the essential function of discipleship in the early Johannine community, and the same equality existed in the early Corinthian church.

Women's prominent role in Christian ministry died out around the turn of the second century, but influential women continue to appear, especially as spiritual directors and founders of religious communities.

In medieval times, influential abbesses often took an active part in local and ecumenical Church councils. Women like St. Teresa of Avila and St. Catherine of Siena had decisive influences on the course of Church history. During the nineteenth and the early twentieth century women religious helped powerfully in shaping the growing American Church, as typified by St. Elizabeth Ann Seton, the first native-born U.S. citizen canonized a saint.

The Church's traditional restriction of ordination to men has been restated by Pope Paul VI and Pope John Paul II as well as the Catechism of the Catholic Church *(1577).* The core of the papal teaching is that it is the will of Christ that only men be ordained—that he did not call women to be part of the Twelve—as well as being the constant practice of the Church. A 1976 Roman decree also says that a priest celebrating the eucharist acts "in the person of Christ"; since Christ was a man, women lack a "natural resemblance" to Christ. A 1995 Vatican statement further declared the restriction of ordination to men to be infallible teaching—but most theologians writing about this today say that no question of infallibility is involved (see chapter 10 regarding the criteria for papal infallibility).

Many theologians do not find the theological reasons against the ordination of women convincing. They do not see masculinity as intrinsic to the theology of the priesthood. Some ask, logically, if a female priest cannot represent the male Christ, how could the male Christ redeem females? A papal biblical commission found that there are no conclusive scriptural arguments either for or against women's ordination—as said above, there is no evidence of Christ ordaining anyone, male or female, a priest in the later sense of presiding at the eucharistic sacrifice.

A majority of American Catholics of both sexes favors women's ordi-nation—as is also the case in most Western European countries—and the percentage of those supporting it is steadily increasing. This, of course, should not be seen as taking a popular vote on what teachings are to be be-lieved but as an indication of a shift in the "sense of the faithful," what the people of the Church in fact believe, what they "receive" or accept as authen-tic teaching (as was discussed in chapter 10). An accelerated process of theo-logical development in this area has been under way since Vatican Council II. There are precedents for such a "dramatic" development in belief in a rela-tively short time: the Church's teaching on lending money at interest, for ex-ample, changed from condemnation to acceptance in the course of thirty years.

Seen in worldwide perspective, the movement favoring women's ordina-tion is strongest in the United States, Canada, and Western Europe. In places like Latin America, though this movement is growing, the focus is more on simple survival, on women's equality in marriage, and their freedom from sex-ual exploitation and domestic violence. The Orthodox Christian Churches still strongly oppose the ordination of women, and thus the movement toward unity with the Orthodox—something especially dear to Pope John Paul II—is in conflict with it. But many feel that social, cultural, and educational differ-ences in the universal Church should be taken into account when discussing the role of women in the Church—which brings us to the more immediate possibility of women as deacons:

Regarding the ordination of women as deacons, something generally ac-knowledged to have existed in the early Church, several European bishops' conferences, as well as unofficial groups of bishops in the United States, Canada, and elsewhere, have asked that steps be taken toward this. Women would thus receive the sacrament of holy orders and minister as do men in the permanent diaconate, preaching, baptizing, confirming, and presiding at marriages.

Some women—as well as men—see the concept of ministry, rather than or-dination, to be more in keeping with the mind of Christ and the practice of the early Church, that is, all Christians using their gifts or charisms as equals in the service of the community. Some regard being ordained to the priesthood as a perpetuation of male clericalism. In all this, a basic problem is that lead-ership offices and power in the Church come through priestly ordination, so that a woman's position and ministry continues to be secondary to that of an ordained male priest. A growing number of Catholics, then, men as well as women, view the denial to women of any participation in the sacrament of holy orders as a sign of their de facto inequality in the Church.

Also, though there has been a dramatic increase in the number of women obtaining degrees in theology, people today are increasingly deprived of regular eucharistic celebrations because of a lack of priests. Understandably, then, there is much pain, division, and anger over this issue. Patience, openness, honest dialogue, and a willingness to listen to all levels of the Church—which Vatican Council II so strongly espoused—are needed as never before.

Meanwhile women are creatively developing their own models of ministry. They have been contributing their insights and strengths on pastoral teams, administering parishes lacking priests, in diocesan administrative posts, as hospital and prison chaplains, and so on. They are increasingly the articulators not only of family values but of business and professional ethical norms and defenders of the victims of our highly competitive, often macho society. The U.S. bishops, rejecting sexism in all its aspects, have urged that more top jobs in the Church be filled with women; with a small change in the Church law requiring cardinals to be bishops, women could be named as cardinals.

Women have also been growing in numbers and importance as competent, innovative theologians and Scripture scholars. Feminist theology, once a novelty, is more and more a given in Catholic academia, and women today routinely teach those in training to be priests and bishops.

Today there are feminine "theologies," reflecting different cultural and individual viewpoints, rather than one single women's view on issues. But there are some common notes: Women theologians, for instance, reject a notion of "complementarity," which holds that the qualities of leadership, strength, and so on are male while more passive qualities like acceptance and caring are considered female. They stress qualities like mutuality, that humans are interdependent and affective rather than primarily rational and autonomous—and that we humans have the right to control our own bodies and to be free of exploitation and violence.

Women also read Scripture and Church history with a more discerning or "suspicious" eye because these were usually written by men who, however unwittingly, often ignored or distorted the role of women. Pope John Paul II recently acknowledged that by focusing on extraordinary or catastrophic human events, "the history that results is almost exclusively that of the things men have accomplished. . . . It would be opportune to rewrite history in a less unilateral way" (Preparation for the 1995 Beijing U.N. World Conference on Women, Catholic News Service).

IN THE LITURGY

At Mass in the Prayer of the Faithful we pray particularly for those who are associated with us in the Church—for those who are sick, deceased, or in any need, as well as for our bishop, priests, and religious. During the eucharistic prayer of the Mass we pray for all the types of people in the Church, clergy and lay, living and dead, and ask the intercession of those who have gone on ahead of us into eternity.

DAILY LIVING: THE MATTER OF VOCATION

People are gifted and inspired by God to live a particular form of life. This is their vocation. Most are called to be in the married state, others are called to be priests or religious, and yet others are attracted to remain in the single life. An indication of one's vocation is an attraction to that particular state plus the capability of living it. All persons should ask for guidance in choosing or in living the vocation that they feel God wants them to have.

We should also recognize the single life—aside from the priesthood or religious life—as a true vocation, and one that can be fruitful and joyful. Some can be single involuntarily, or have a divided mind about marriage, and their lives might be filled with sadness and frustration. Some are thrust into the role of a single parent. Among those who are single, many are fulfilled in their single state, try to center their lives on others, and often show great creativity in helping people and the world in general. Some of the best people in the Church are living this sort of life.

If one's son or daughter feels an attraction to the priesthood or religious life, he or she should be encouraged to follow this up freely and intelligently. Good counseling about this is available today, and no seminary or religious community wants to carry along those who would be misfits in such a life. Increasingly, this choice is being made when young people are more mature, usually well into adulthood, and thus they are more likely to find it is their particular vocation.

SOME SUGGESTIONS FOR . . .

DISCUSSION

How is your parish—and your diocese—fulfilling its role as a family or community in which all use their particular gifts? Can you give a few concrete ways in which this might be done better?

Do you know someone in your parish or diocese who is specially gifted in helping others? From your own life experience, how might you be gifted to help others in the Church?

"Clericalism" means, roughly, those who are ordained expecting special treatment and deference, but the term can also apply to others who are ministering, including clergy of other denominations. Though the large majority of clergy do not practice this, some on occasion do. What kind of experiences have you had with priests and other churchpeople? Can you see the importance of distinguishing between the messenger and the message? What do you look for most in someone who is ministering in the Church?

What particular problems can you see for priests today, including celibacy? For nuns and brothers? For others who are ministering in the Church? What graces and opportunities might outweigh these problems?

Do you see ways in which the role of women in the Church has been changing, often dramatically?

Can you see reasons for the Church's traditional restriction of the priesthood to men? Can you see reasons for its teaching in this matter to develop or change?

FURTHER READING

- *Theology of Ministry,* O'Meara (Paulist Press, 1983)—This is an excellent book on the history, nature, and function of ministry in the Church; it should be read by all involved in any sort of ministry.
- • *Priesthood: A History of the Ordained Ministry in the Roman Catholic Church,* Osborne (Paulist Press, 1988)—An excellent, comprehensive study of the sources, including controversies, views of the Re-

formers, and pertinent documents, and including a brief treatment of the ordination of women.

- *Ministry,* McBrien (HarperCollins, 1987)—By the author of *Catholicism,* this is a small but fine book on the evolution of ministry, the qualities ministers need, and ministerial spirituality.

•• *Lay Ministry in the Roman Catholic Church: Its History and Theology,* Osborne (Paulist Press, 1993)—A well-written, comprehensive look at lay ministry by a highly regarded, pastorally sensitive theologian.

•• *The Church with a Human Face: New and Expanded Theology of Ministry,* Schillebeeckx (Crossroad, 1987)—One of the Church's best-known theologians, an architect of Vatican Council II, discusses ministry and the priesthood in the light of history and future possibilities.

•• *In Memory of Her,* Schüssler-Fiorenza (Crossroad, 1984)—Subtitled "A Feminist Theological Reconstruction of Christian Origins," this pioneering, scholarly, but readable book is an excellent presentation of a basic but until now overlooked view.

•• *Transforming Grace: Christian Tradition and Women's Experience,* Carr (Harper & Row, 1988)—Showing how one can be both a Christian and a feminist, this book is an excellent, systematic presentation of the contributions of feminist theology in our culture.

- *New Catholic Women: A Contemporary Challenge to Traditional Religious Authority,* Weaver (HarperCollins, 1996)—An updating of a fine book that puts in historical perspective the role of women today within a Church that "they wish neither to desert or destroy, but rather to transform." An excellent, concise history of Catholic feminism.

•• *Sexism and God Talk,* Ruether (Beacon Press, 1983)—This is a perceptive treatment of how unconsciously sexist our theological, liturgical, and other religious concepts and language have been through the centuries; the author, a pioneering Catholic feminist theologian, takes a relatively reconciling, middle-ground approach.

•• *She Who Is: The Mystery of God in Feminist Theological Discourse,* Johnson (Crossroad, 1992)—A sweeping book on the way we conceptualize and speak about God, this is probably the best presentation to date of contemporary mainstream Christian feminist theology.

•• *Feminist Theology from the Third World,* ed. King (Orbis, 1994)—A broad sampling of writings showing the diversity as well as the depth of feminist theology as it is developing in the third world.

•• *Freeing Theology: The Essentials of Theology in Feminist Perspective,* LaCugna (HarperSanFrancisco, 1993)—An excellent overview for one who wants to understand the broad scope of mainstream feminist theological concerns.

• *Apostolic Letter on Ordination and Women,* Pope John Paul II (USCC, 1994)—This reaffirms the Church's traditional teaching restricting ordination to men (and a similar 1977 Vatican Declaration). The core of this papal letter is given above.

• *Like Bread, Their Voices Rise! Global Women Challenge the Church* (Ave Maria Press, 1994)—On the basis of 1,200 questionnaires and interviews given to women on four continents, this nun and former missionary concludes that despite their diversity Catholic women everywhere are increasingly challenging their place in the Church today.

• *What Paul Really Said About Women,* Bristow (Harper & Row, 1988)—Short and easy to read, this book puts the seemingly derogatory statements of Paul in perspective.

• *Autumn Gospel: Women in the Second Half of Life,* Fischer (Paulist Press, 1995)—This wonderfully done book uses stories, experiences, and research to explore the spiritual dimensions of women's middle and late years in a variety of traditions and cultures.

• *Creating Small Faith Communities: A Plan for Restructuring the Parish and Renewing Catholic Life,* Baranowski (St. Anthony Messenger Press, 1988)—A pastor's practical steps for creating small, sharing groups within the parish. A highly praised book.

• *The Community of the Beloved Disciple,* Brown (Paulist Press, 1979)—An outstanding Johannine scholar shows how all were equal in this early Christian community.

PERSONAL REFLECTION

God has given each of us particular talents—gifts to help carry out his plan. I might ask myself how well I am using the gifts I have—particularly in working with others in the Church family, or with other people of good will.

23

The Greater Family
to Which We Belong

Why do Catholics pray to saints? Why is such honor particularly paid to Mary, the mother of Christ? Is prayer to Mary or the saints essential for a Catholic? Can these and other dedicated Christians help us to lead better lives?

THE SAINTS: OUR MODELS AND INTERCESSORS

To be a Christian is to realize that we are joined with one another on the way to heaven. One does not go alone, as if sealed by oneself in a sort of space capsule. We must help and be helped by others. Unfortunately, the religion of some is narrowly individualistic, a "God-and-me" relationship. The Church, however, is a family in which we are concerned for one another: "If one member suffers, all suffer together; if one member is honored, all rejoice together" (1 Corinthians 12, 26).

    Besides our Church family on earth, we belong to a larger family of God, the Communion of Saints. We are united with those who have gone before us—those in heaven and in the preparatory state of purgatory (these latter we will discuss in the last chapter). We call this the Communion of Saints, that is, the union of all who share in the life of Christ, whether on earth or in the next world; this is why the early Christians used the term "saint" for one another. Later the word came to mean primarily a person in heaven.

From the beginning Christians have believed that our love and help for one another could extend beyond death (except, of course, to the damned). Early inscriptions, as in the Roman catacombs, show that some of the first Christians prayed for those who had died, and also asked their prayers. Those who had died were still part of the Christian family, loving and being loved, only temporarily hidden from the sight of those yet here below.

We honor and imitate the saints—those in heaven—as we would anyone we love, particularly if he or she is outstanding. The saints are the outstanding members of our Christian family, our Christian heroes. They are the truly great lovers of history. Each one shows some particular aspect of Christ, and in imitating them we are trying to imitate Christ; thus St. Paul could tell his converts, "I urge you then, be imitators of me" (1 Corinthians 4, 16).

There are saints from every class, every occupation, with every type of temperament and background. They show us how Christ can be imitated in anyone's life, including our own. As we tend to follow models in medicine, business, science, homemaking, and so on, so here. Statues, pictures, relics (things that belonged to the saint) are reminders of them and their holiness; such things have no power of themselves, and to believe such would be superstition.

The Church is careful about who is declared a saint. For the past several centuries candidates have had to undergo the long process of "canonization," a scrupulous investigation for many years of every aspect of their lives—including, until 1983, the scrutiny of a "devil's advocate" whose sworn duty it was to try to disprove their holiness—and usually the requirement of miracles (cures with no known physical or psychic explanation) through their intercession. Despite this, several thousands have been canonized for their heroic sanctity, declared to be with God in heaven.

In earlier centuries saints often became such through popular acclamation or continued veneration. During those more credulous times some were venerated as saints about whom little or nothing was known, and others have been shown by modern research to have little claim to our veneration. Historical researchers have been at work in the recent past systematically and painstakingly separating fact from fiction about the saints. No claim is made that the canonized saints are more than a tiny fraction of those who are with God in heaven. They are simply the ones that God has brought to our attention in the Church, to spur us on to imitate them. Undoubtedly there are other and holier people in heaven, but the saints are proof that holiness and heaven are attainable, that it *can* be done, and they show us how to do it amid the same circumstances of life as our own. The great Swedish Lutheran Bishop Söderblom put it precisely: "The saints make clear to us that God lives."

We ask the saints to pray for us, as we might ask someone here on earth for his or her prayers. Since we are all one family, if we are attracted to certain saints and ask for their help, their love can help us as it might have if we had known them on earth. This is only natural; if love and interest toward our neighbor sums up the way we should live on earth, we would not expect that those in heaven would suddenly forget us here on earth and have no more interest in us.

For those not used to asking others to pray for them, this practice will seem especially strange. Sometimes Catholics are little help when they speak of "praying to Saint So-and-So"—actually a prayer can end only with God, and to believe differently would be idolatry; we should rather speak of asking a saint to pray with us, or for us, to Christ and the Father. The Church's liturgy always asks the saints to pray for us through Christ to the Father.

A patron saint is chosen for an infant at baptism, and if the baptized later wishes, at confirmation. This should be someone with whom we can feel particularly close—in modern terms, a role model. Most churches are named in honor of saints, and there are patrons for various professions, trades, and so on, usually because of some connection that the saint had with that work.

Devotion to the saints, while optional, is one of the practices of Catholicism that often helps people in their faith and prayer life. As was pointed out at Vatican Council II, some 90 percent of the saints venerated by the Church until that time came from the three major Latin countries of Europe. In the history of Catholicism there has been a good deal of exaggeration in the veneration of the saints; abuses regarding this were reprimanded by the Council, and significantly at the particular behest of the Latin American bishops. Today, people of many cultures and more laypeople—with whom the average person can more easily identify—are being canonized as saints. Also, the number of saints' feast days in the Church's worldwide liturgy has been sharply reduced. Many saints have a local cultural symbolism quite meaningful to the people of a country or an area, and their feast days are times of celebration for everyone.

Reading a well-written, modern life of a saint—or one of the good collections now available—can be a great help and spur to the better practice of one's own faith, especially when we feel the need of understanding support from one who has "been there."

GOD'S MOTHER AND OURS

We particularly honor Mary, the mother of Christ, because of her role in God's plan of salvation as the one closer to Jesus than anyone. It was he who chose her for the great honor of being Jesus' human mother. Mary's whole role is to show forth Christ, and the teachings regarding her ultimately show forth some aspect of him. If she were the mother of a great, holy man, we would have some reason for honoring her but not for paying her the honor we do—but if one believes that her Son is divine, then it is only natural to honor her greatly. The fact that she is the Mother of God is the basis of our veneration of her.

Mary is God's masterpiece. To honor her is to honor God who made her what she is. Luke depicts her saying this: "For behold, henceforth all generations will call me blessed, for he who is mighty has done great things for me . . . " (Luke 1, 48–49). If we are sincere in our praise of an artist, for example, we will praise his or her paintings without hesitation. Mary is God's creature, infinitely distant from him, as are any of us—but she is unique among us in that she was totally centered on God.

Mary shows what God could do with any of us, if we but fully opened ourselves to him. She gave herself wholly to doing God's will—this was the purpose of her Son's mission and therefore of his life. We read how she continually "kept all these things in her heart" (Luke 2, 51; cf. Luke 2, 34). She pondered God's will with utter openness, even when it made no sense, and she became wise in following it.

One day a woman cried out to Christ, "Blessed is the womb that bore you, and the breasts that you sucked!" His answer shows the real source of Mary's holiness: "Blessed rather are those who hear the word of God and keep it!"

Because of Mary's great role she was conceived without sin, remained sinless throughout her life, and was perpetually a virgin. We have seen the continuous belief of the Church in Mary's lifelong sinlessness and virginity. These privileges of Mary, however, should not obscure the fact that she was totally human, tempted like any of us, sometimes lacking in understanding of her Son's mission and pained by it (Luke 2, 48–49). But she clung to God's will in great faith, as we must often do.

We believe in Mary's assumption, that "she was taken into heaven body and soul at the end of her earthly life." Here again Mary imitated her Son who was "taken to heaven" when his work was finished. What happened to her is meant to encourage the rest of us who are also merely human. As she was taken to heaven and glorified, we have the assurance that one day we also will be. She was taken in a special way because it was not fitting that the body from which the Son of God had taken his human body should undergo corruption.

Mary's assumption is celebrated on August 15 as a holyday in the United States. The assumption was declared solemnly to be an infallible teaching of the Church in 1950, but belief in it goes back to the early Church; a tomb of Mary was venerated, but there were no relics of her body, as there were of the apostles and other early Christian heroes; when Christian writers and the liturgy became concerned with Mary's assumption in the sixth and seventh centuries, it was accepted throughout the Church.

But what does the assumption literally mean? Here popular imagery and art, and the use of symbolic language, can obscure what is meant. We certainly should not think of Mary's being "taken up" through the clouds and earth's atmosphere to some "place" in outer space. It simply means that Mary upon "leaving this earth" was in the state we call "heaven"—that she went the way we will all go, but in some extraordinary, undefined way, more lovingly, more strikingly. Mary, like Christ himself, has disappeared from physical contact with us, and is with God, but in a real sense she is also among us and present to us. She is thus seen as the "first among Christians," the model for all followers of Christ. What we all look forward to one day, our total transformation in God, happened to her in the most loving way possible for a human.

Viewed positively, Mary's assumption strikingly points out that it was a woman who was most intimately associated with God-come-among-us, even to the end of her life. The assumption can thus be seen as the Church's way of proclaiming the extraordinary dignity and holiness of a woman—something sorely needed today as women strive for the recognition of their equal rights and dignity with men.

We give special place to Mary's intercession and sometimes consider her our spiritual "mother." Scripture shows her interceding with Christ for a young couple on their wedding day, and despite his seeming reluctance he worked his first miracle to fulfill her request (cf. John 2, 1–11). Many of the early Church Fathers saw a special significance in Christ's giving his mother to John as he was dying on the cross—she was to be a mother to all his followers, by her love and tenderness bringing them to him, as she had once brought him to the world (cf. John 19, 26–27). So many today, as through the centuries, ask her intercession.

Mary's intercession must not be misunderstood. Vatican Council II told us: "There is but one mediator as we know from the words of the apostle, 'for there is one God and one mediator of God and [humankind], the man Christ Jesus, who gave himself as redemption for all' (1 Timothy 2, 5–6). The maternal duty of Mary toward [us] in no way obscures or diminishes this unique mediation of Christ, but rather shows his power. For all the salvific influence of the Blessed Virgin on [humankind] originates . . . from . . . Christ. It rests on his mediation, depends entirely on it and draws all its power from it. In no way does it impede, but rather does it foster the immediate union of the faithful with Christ" (*Constitution on the Church,* no. 60).

How, then, can we speak of Mary's intercession or mediation? The more perfectly our will is aligned with God's, the more we ask for whatever he wants to give humankind, the more grace and love we can have a share in spreading in the world. Thus St. Paul said, "I complete what is lacking in Christ's afflictions for the sake of his body, that is, the Church . . . " (Colossians 1, 24).

Mary's will was perfectly open to God's will. She cooperated with Christ's work of salvation as fully as she knew how, more fully than anyone before or since. Not only did she give him birth and lovingly raise him, she watched the progress of his preaching, his final rejection, and then as he hung dying she freely and painfully offered him back to the Father. Her faith and obedience to God's will were total. In heaven now, she continues to totally desire God's will, asking for whatever he wills to give to us still on earth.

It is in this light that we must understand such terms as "spiritual mother," "mediatrix," "co-redemptrix," and "Queen." By her special closeness to Christ and openness to God's will she does for all what the rest of us do for some. She leads us in our intercession and mediation.

MARY, FIRST AMONG CHRISTIANS

Mary is the model Christian, the preeminent member of the Church. She is a model for us all, particularly in her faith and love. At Pentecost she is the always-faithful disciple of her Son, around whom the apostles and others gathered as they await the Holy Spirit (Acts 1, 13–14). She is not noted in Scripture for any great deeds except "pondering in her heart," being totally committed to God's will. She is the "fully redeemed one"—she shows how Christ's saving power can transform the entire personal existence of a humble being—and in this she can give us all hope.

Mary is also the image and model of the Church itself. She is unique in that no other person has the Church so fully concentrated in him- or herself. From the early Christian centuries the same titles are again and again given to Mary and to the Church: for instance, both are referred to as the Woman who is the enemy of the serpent (Genesis 3, 15), as the Virgin Mother, the Bride of Christ, the great sign that appeared in heaven (Revelation 12), and as the "New Eve" who undid the damage of the first by her cooperation with Christ, the New Adam.

Mary was the embodiment of the church of the Old Testament, the "daughter of Zion" who personified the people of the promise (cf. Isaiah 66, 7ff.). She was the climax of the Old Covenant, the one who was perfectly faithful, who alone could fully welcome the Messiah and be the dwelling of God among men.

From what Mary is, the Church sees what it should become: by her virginity Mary shows the total dedication to God and to Christ that the Church, too, must have. As Mary, the Church must be the "handmaid of the Lord" in her trusting faith and love and service. As Mary was the Mother of Christ, so the Church is the mother of Christians—we often speak of "Mother Church." Mary particularly shows the patience, gentleness, and understanding the Church must have to balance its organizational and legalistic aspects.

Mary is particularly the model of our worship. We could say she is in the first pew, leading us by her example, directing us to her Son and our Brother as together we worship the Father. "But standing by the cross of Jesus were his mother . . . " (John 19, 25)—as she was there on the first Good Friday, so she above all will help us to sacrifice ourselves totally with him at each Mass. Her whole life and purpose are simply to bring us to him.

Mary's influence in the history of the Church has been great. At first little attention was paid to Mary because of the necessary concern with who and what Jesus Christ was. Then she came to the fore particularly as the "Mother of God," a title that was meant to safeguard the true nature of Christ. The medieval veneration of the virgin-mother did much to give women a dignity that was unthought of in the ancient world.

The devotion of the rosary has had a tremendous influence in helping hundreds of millions of Christians to pray. Among Orthodox Christians an even greater regard for Mary has developed than among Catholics. The shrines of Mary have also had a great influence, particularly places like Lourdes in southern France where each year several million people come to strengthen their faith in the supernatural—or Guadalupe in Mexico City or Czestochowa in Poland, which has been the center of that nation's resistance to political and religious oppression. Medjugorje in the former Yugoslavia has also been attracting many in recent years.

There have been, and are, exaggerations in the honor paid to Mary. Some, particularly among the less educated, have tended to regard her in isolation from the Church, as one who grants favors in her own right; perhaps much of this is inevitable, particularly among those for whom Christ is more divine than human, who would therefore turn to another whom they could more easily think of as human like themselves.

As we have seen (chapter 15), when Christ's divinity was overstressed in the medieval liturgy, devotion to Mary and the saints developed in order to bridge the gap with the divine. Also some prayers and devotions, even of recent times, have been exaggerated, or could easily be misunderstood. On the other hand, we should not expect the language of poetry and popular piety to be theologically exact. An Anglican priest writes of this: "Prayer should always be theological, but not nervously so. Always to be stopping short in praises of the Virgin lest we might overstep the bounds of exact truth is like the man who is terrified lest he might say something extravagant about his mother. A good mother would not mind if he did; still less, . . . would a good father overhearing" (*Ways of Worship,* WCC).

Today many non-Catholics recognize the rightful place of Mary in the Christian Church, just as Catholics recognize a periodic overemphasis on her role. Many theologians in Protestantism are urging that a proper honor be paid to Mary and the saints as a way of bringing us closer to Christ.

IN THE LITURGY

At Mass we commemorate Mary and the saints during the eucharistic prayers, asking their intercession, that we may be admitted to their eternal fellowship. The various feasts of Mary and the saints during the year are meant to spur us on to imitate Christ's passion and glorification as they did.

The rosary is the devotion by which we meditate on Christ's life and ask Mary to bring us closer to him. During the months of May and October devotions to Mary are held in some places.

DAILY LIVING: THE SPUR OF SANCTITY

The example of what others have done can often spur us on to do good. Considering how others have overcome their weaknesses can help us to overcome self-pity and do something concrete about our faults. Sometimes, when we realize what others have suffered for God and their fellow humans, we can be very ashamed of our complaints.

We should read the life of some dedicated Christian, some saint, or some truly committed person—Christian or not.

In asking the help of those who have gone before us, we need not be concerned only with the Christian saints. Perhaps we might feel a kinship with other outstanding and dedicated people of our own era who are in the next life, such as the great Indian leader Gandhi, Dag Hammarskjöld, or some friend or relative whom we greatly admired during life.

There are many kinds of saints, today as in times past, both canonized and unrecognized. Some years ago twenty-two young men were canonized as saints and martyrs of the Church in Uganda. They were lay catechists, tortured and killed by a fanatical anti-Christian king because they would not renounce their new faith.

During World War II, Fr. Maximilian Kolbe, a Polish Franciscan priest, volunteered to die in another man's place at the infamous Auschwitz death camp; he was declared a saint in 1982, an example of how one person's sacrificial love overcame modern barbarity. A current candidate for canonization, Fr. Titus Brandsma, was a Dutch priest who defied the Nazi occupation authorities and saved many of their intended victims; imprisoned, he was sent to Dachau for leading prayers among the prisoners and was there beaten to death.

More recently there were four American churchwomen, three nuns and a lay volunteer, who were raped and killed by a death squad in El Salvador—and also Archbishop Oscar Romero of San Salvador, who would not be silenced and was finally shot to death while saying Mass. Then six Jesuit priests, along with their housekeeper and her daughter, were "executed" in that city by a death squad. These are some of the best-known cases, but in Latin America many thousands have been killed for trying to obtain a decent life for the poor.

Many today remember Dorothy Day, a Catholic laywoman who had an immense influence on the U.S. Church as well as our whole society. She was the founder of the Catholic Worker "Houses of Hospitality" for the poor and a lifelong pacifist as well as an activist for social justice, and her funeral was attended by all segments of the American Church, including many members of the hierarchy whose consciences she regularly prodded. A devout, almost strict Catholic, she may never be formally canonized (which would be just fine with her), partly because she was regularly jailed for her public protests against injustices and nuclear armaments. But she lives on in the minds and hearts of numerous people who care about the poor and seek justice and peace.

There are also those who are, unnoticed, living daily lives of heroic sanctity, like the slum mother abandoned by her husband who works twelve hours daily to keep together her family of three children; the possibility of giving up, of turning her children over to the welfare authorities, never occurs to her. She has a face worn beyond her years, but her tough, bright spirit shines through.

SOME SUGGESTIONS FOR . . .

DISCUSSION

Does it seem logical that our love for one another should extend beyond the grave?

Does the notion of Mary as the model Christian have meaning for you?

Is there some outstanding person now dead, Christian or non-Christian, for whom you feel a particular attachment and whose example is of help to you?

FURTHER READING

- *Saint Watching*, McGinley (Thomas More, 1982)—A wonderful look at some saints by a modern Catholic poet.
- *What Are Saints?* Martindale (M. Glazier, 1989)—A new, revised edition of a book that covers a wide variety of saints, both popular and unknown.
- *God's Fool*, Green (Harper & Row, 1988)—A beautifully told, factual story of the man said to be the most like Christ, St. Francis of Assisi.
- *Miryam of Nazareth, Woman of Strength and Wisdom*, Johnson (Ave Maria Press, 1984)—A book of beautifully insightful "ponderings" by Jesus' Mother, Mary, on her place among Israel's great women, in Jesus' life, and in the infant Church.
- *Miracles of Mary*, Durham (HarperSanFranciso, 1995)—A journalist tells the story of the many apparitions of Mary and the miracles connected with them across the centuries.
- *Two Sisters in the Spirit: Therese of Lisieux and Elizabeth of the Trinity*, Balthasar (Ignatius Press, 1992)—A well-known theologian tells the story of two Carmelite mystics, the first canonized a very popular saint and the second about to be canonized.
- *365 Saints*, Koenig-Bricker (HarperSanFrancisco, 1995)—Subtitled "Your Daily Guide to the Wisdom and Wonder of Their Lives," this

delightful book offers a year full of meditations and practical suggestions for imitating the saints.

- *Elizabeth Seton,* Hindeman (Srena Lettres, 1976)—This is a very simple and moving biography of our first native-born American saint, a woman who followed her conscience and changed the Church in America.
- *Harvester of Souls,* Langon (Our Sunday Visitor, 1976)—This is a very good biography of the saint and bishop John Neumann, called "the father of American parochial schools."
- *A Woman Wrapped in Silence,* Lynch (Paulist Press, 1968)—A beautiful work, in blank verse, expanding the scriptural passages concerning Mary; this is an older classic that once again has become popular.
- *The Word Remains: A Life of Oscar Romero,* Brockman (Orbis, 1982)—The factual, moving story of the Archbishop of San Salvador, who persistently preached peace with justice until he was martyred in 1980.
- *Spiritual Pilgrims: Carl Jung and Teresa of Avila,* Welch (Paulist Press, 1982)—This interesting book looks at the psychological and spiritual journey of the great Spanish mystic St. Teresa of Avila through the concepts and imagery of Jungian psychology.
- *A Woman in Love,* LeJoly (Ave Maria Press, 1993)—This is an updated version of the life and work of Mother Teresa of Calcutta.

FURTHER VIEWING/LISTENING

Therese of Lisieux, Dorgan (NCR audiocassette, 50 minutes)—An explanation of the simple but profound piety of one of the most popular and appealing saints of recent times.

The Spirit of St. Francis, Rohr (NCR, 2 audiocassettes, 2 hours)—This is by the popular writer and retreat master who knows and loves and delights in the spirit and tradition of Francis of Assisi.

PERSONAL REFLECTION

I might try asking for the help of someone I believe is now with God in heaven. Perhaps it will help me to better imitate Christ.

24

Christ's Church in the World Today

What does Christ's Church have to offer the world today? How does one know whether or not to join the Church? What of the scandals and weaknesses within the Church? What of the scandal of disunity among Christians?

CHRIST'S CHURCH IS DIVINE

Vatican Council II "yearns to explain" to all people the Church's work in the world today. The Church is at the service of humankind, particularly to make all people brothers and sisters. "Inspired by no earthly ambition, the Church seeks but a solitary goal: to carry forward the work of Christ . . . [who] entered this world to give witness to the truth, to rescue and not to sit in judgment, to serve and not to be served" (*The Church in the Modern World,* nos. 2 and 3).

Christ's Church is himself and us—divine and holy, and yet human and imperfect. We have seen how Christ is among us in the Church, uniting us with himself, using human instruments to bring us to heaven. He teaches us with authority and certainty through the pope and bishops. He communicates his grace primarily and publicly through those the Church chooses as his instruments.

The Church is divine and holy because she has Christ as her head, is guided by the Holy Spirit, and has all the helps necessary for us to

live a holy life. Obviously not all Christians are holy, but the Church has all the means to make them so. These we have seen: the Mass and the sacraments; the great ways we meet Christ at the critical moments of life, and by which we can be certain of making contact with God; and all sorts of devotions and sacramentals to bring God into our daily life. The Church's laws provide that we perform regular acts of worship and reparation for our sins. It has many groups to help us, and millions of people whose lives are totally dedicated to God and others.

The Church has produced thousands of saints, extraordinarily holy people. It is hard to find any group in history that compares with them. The Anglican author Evelyn Underhill says in her classic work *Mysticism* that it is a historical fact that mysticism is at its best in Christianity and that the greatest mystics have been the Catholic saints.

The Church through its history has worked to take care of the poor, uneducated, and underprivileged, laying the foundation for the education and philanthropy of our Western civilization and influencing other cultures as well. The hospitals, old age homes, orphanages, schools, and so on that have become a part of our way of life were originally sponsored by the Church. The Church civilized and Christianized the pagans, and while forced conversions were at times all too common, it nonetheless brought to the world a new respect for women, marriage, and virginity. It led in taking care of the poor, the sick, and the aged, all the while continually upholding the dignity of the individual person.

Today many have noted that the Catholic Church has a particularly universal appeal while yet maintaining a striking unity—that it seems to have more to offer for more people of diverse cultures and social classes. In this it is trying to earn its title of "catholic."

The survival and influence of the Church after almost twenty centuries of opposition and persecution and scandal seem to many Catholics to show that it is uniquely guided by God. The Church began with a dozen simple men—one a traitor, another a perjurer, and the rest cowards—and the wildly improbable story that a man put to death by his own people as a criminal was God himself. They started out preaching a way of life that challenged almost every standard of the world around them. Christ had predicted, "They have persecuted me; they will persecute you also . . . " (John 15, 20). And so they were. First they were persecuted by some leaders of the Jews, their own people; then under the Roman emperors the Church endured three centuries of persistent harassment, torture, imprisonment, and death.

The official attitude was, *Non licet esse vos!*—"It is not permitted you to exist!" The Roman emperor Diocletian confidently built himself a column bearing the inscription: "To Diocletian, who destroyed the very name Christian." Yet the Church did not change its principles in the face of this. Unlike other kingdoms and empires of history, the early Church spread simply by sanctity and suffering.

Scarcely had the Church gained recognition in the Empire when there came the barbarian invasions and the gradual collapse of civilization. The Church converted and civilized the barbarians and became the center of stability and learning, the heart of Western civilization in the Middle Ages. But then scandals, quarrels, and apostasies disrupted it from within. Often those within the Church who paid it lip-service— Catholic princes, its own officials—were its greatest enemies because of their greed and corruption. And in the Crusades and Inquisition it became the persecutor of others.

By all human rules, the Church should have died many times. There were scandals even in the highest places—Dante put two popes in his Inferno. Then came the Reformation, which rent the Church, the "Enlightenment" with its rejection of religion (and vice versa), the age of reason, and the modern "isms." There has been no period, except briefly in the Middle Ages, when the Church was in tune with the prevailing intellectual atmosphere. Yet today those who considered the Church backward and dying are themselves dead and largely forgotten, and the Church continues to influence hundreds of millions.

The Church has been persecuted in almost every modern nation. It has survived Nazism, and Communism had been until recently waging against it a relentless war of suppression, wherever possible closing churches and schools, harassing, imprisoning, and killing believers who spoke out for human rights or too vigorously practiced their faith. Pope John Paul II lived most of his adult life first under the Nazi tyranny in Poland and then for thirty-five years in a constant war of nerves with a Communist state that wanted to eliminate Christianity altogether (this is nothing new to the Poles who have had to fight for their Christian beliefs and identity for a thousand years). In Latin America today, the entrenched upper class aligned with greedy economic imperialists are daily trying to destroy or negate the Church's influence because it is often the only effective defense of the poor and oppressed.

Catholics conclude that in their Church Jesus Christ makes available to them in a unique way his truth and grace. The Church can trace itself back to Christ and the apostles, under the authority of the pope and bishops, with the same basic teachings of the apostles. It is united throughout the world in its basic doctrines, fundamental moral principles, and liturgy, with the same authority guiding all. It embraces all types of people, of every race, nation, and social class. Its countless people who are sincerely striving for holiness, and its survival and influence for nearly two thousand years, show it to have a unique role in the world. For Catholics, then, it is the Church founded by Jesus Christ to give a special fullness of his teaching and grace to the world.

What many Catholics see as "special" for them about their Church is its extraordinary unity-in-catholicity, a worldwide community of tremendously diverse people who yet have a sense of oneness in their spiritual outlook and ideals. They know, too, that they are part of an immense group that has been committed to trying to live lives of love, in imitation of Jesus Christ, for two thousand years.

The pope's role is something like that of the spiritual leader or symbol of humankind's highest strivings for unity, peace, and love. Though some disagree with him on matters outside of basic dogmas, they (and others) still take seriously the moral issues he raises. This is a visible sign for Catholics of their commitment to try to bring about a better world, now and forever. Mikhail Gorbachev testified that Pope John Paul II was responsible, more than anyone, for the downfall of Communism in Europe.

The Church, however, is not a privileged, exclusive club for those who have a sure way to salvation, as opposed to those who have not. The attitude of a Catholic can never be one of smugness or pride. It is only through God's goodness that one possesses what one does. If one knows more of the truth, one also has a greater responsibility for living up to it. Often those who are not Catholics put us to shame by their holiness and love.

While in the Catholic view there is available in Catholicism all that God has revealed to humankind, the fullness of his grace and truth, yet the expression of this truth may not be the best, and the communication of grace might be hindered by human weakness. For various reasons Catholics might not use, or might be unable to use, what is available. The Church known by an individual Catholic might be much more human than divine. Then, too, a Catholic might deliberately turn away from the Church's truth and grace. Others who are not Catholic might use better the truth and grace they have and thus be closer in faith and love to God and their fellow human beings.

God is present through all of creation and uses many ways to communicate his truth and grace. He works especially through those who are baptized—"Where two or three are gathered in my name, there am I in the midst of them" (Matthew 18, 20). All, however, can have access to his truth and grace. To be saved we must be united with Christ, but most people do not realize their union with him. Some other leaders, prophets, "gurus," have clearly been God's instruments to bring truth and grace to humankind. Christ is humankind's unique, divine savior and teacher, but others, too, show forth aspects of God.

The Church tries to discern God's truth, his revelation, in other religions and belief systems. Some years ago Pope John Paul II hosted a gathering at Assisi of representatives of the world's major religions, who came together to pray and share their hopes for peace and human unity. In this home of St. Francis, who has been called the most like Christ of anyone who ever lived, the pope symbolized the Church at its best.

The Church's purpose in the world is to bear witness in a special way to God's love among people. By its beliefs it wants to tell people that God has come among us and saved us, that he loves us infinitely and wants us to love one another. It is the way of salvation not for all of humankind but for those chosen to work more closely in a visible, communal way for the salvation of all—the minority whose purpose is to serve the majority by trying in their way to show God's love in the world. Its members are to proclaim—however inadequately—that the world has been saved and is filled with God's love.

The Church, therefore, is a sign set among the world's people to give them hope, to assure them that God and his love are ever with us, so that all in the world will continue to strive together to grow in love and not resort to unloving ways. The Church is there to tell us that none of our efforts—even the slightest—are ever in vain but are helping to bring about an eternal, perfect universe.

CATHOLIC CHRISTIAN EDUCATION—
SHARING THE GOOD NEWS AND A WAY OF LIFE

Catholics have maintained their own educational system because they wish to share the good news of their faith and pass on as well as possible a Christian way of life. Parochial schools try to communicate a Christian way of living as a day-by-day part of the students' lives. Parochial schools came into being, for the most part, to preserve and develop the religion of a largely immigrant people in an often anti-Catholic atmosphere and to help these people better integrate themselves into the American way of life. Over the years they have done a truly remarkable job.

In the past few decades they have been swamped by children—often as many non-Catholic as Catholic, and especially those of racial minorities—whose parents want them to receive an education based on firm values, caring discipline, and the motivation of each child as God's unique creation.

Today, ironically, when many others besides Catholics are using and appreciating Catholic schools, rising operating costs, coupled with parents de facto paying twice for their children's education, are forcing many to close.

Most Catholic education takes place in programs like the Confraternity of Christian Doctrine, where children come for a few hours a week to be educated by religious-education professionals, priests, religious, and laypeople—aided by numerous volunteer laymen and laywomen. The CCD educates at least two-thirds of the elementary school children whose parents want them to have some systematic training in the Catholic faith and in moral values; there is an even greater proportion of high school students enrolled in this. Considering that the CCD receives, on average, approximately one-fourth to one-fifth of a typical parish's financial outlay for education, this program has over the years done an amazing and outstanding job of religious educating.

Today, parents are more involved than ever in their children's education process under this program—in fact, in most cases active parent participation is a "must." But many parents feel ill-equipped in religious education matters or uneasy about taking part in what they have traditionally felt is the work of professional religious educators—though Vatican Council II, and countless documents since, stress again and again that parents are the primary educators of their children.

Many Catholics today have been finding that programs in adult/parent—and clergy—education are their greatest need. The American Catholic Church's National Catechetical Directory of 1977, the product of eight years' work and tens of thousands of contributions, says this strongly. Most parishes have a large number of laypeople who are better educated than ever before—except that they are woefully equipped in the matter of religious education. While many have taken courses in their parish, been in discussion groups, and so on, many more have only a bare knowledge of a few Catholic fundamentals and little appreciation for today's new, rich insights into theology, Scripture, and practical Christian living.

WHETHER OR NOT TO JOIN THE CHURCH

If one comes to know and believe in the Catholic Church, one should become a Catholic. If one comes to believe that this is the Church founded by Jesus Christ with his complete truth for salvation, and refuses to join it, he or she would be refusing to follow what conscience says is true. Christ said of such a person: "The one who does not believe will be condemned" (Mark 16, 17).

But if one has doubts about the truth of one or more of the Church's basic dogmas, or if one is satisfied with one's present belief, one should not become a Catholic. Some are able to accept the Church's teachings, and others of equally good faith are not. The ability to believe, as we have said, comes ultimately from God. All one can and must do is try to live up to one's conscience.

Our belief must always be a free response to God, with our conscience our supreme guide. If we try to inform ourselves about what

God wants, and sincerely try to live up to our conscience, we can rest content. In finding God's will for us, we must "enjoy immunity from external coercion, as well as psychological freedom" (*Declaration on Religious Freedom,* no. 2).

> All [people] have the duty, and therefore the right, to seek the truth in religious matters, in order that [they] may with prudence form for [themselves] right and true judgments of conscience. . . . However . . . the inquiry is to be free. . . . In all [their] activities [people] are bound to follow [their] consciences faithfully. . . . [They] are not to be forced to act in a manner contrary to [their] consciences. Nor, on the other hand, are [they] to be restrained from acting in accordance with [their] consciences, especially in religious matters (*Declaration on Religious Freedom,* no. 3).

One should never become a Catholic solely to have the same religion in a marriage or to please someone else. One may have come to investigate the Church because he or she intended marrying a Catholic, and then sees that sharing the same faith will be a great thing for the marriage and for the children—but now, to become a Catholic, one must believe on one's own. One must now feel that there is something more in Catholicism than what one already believes, something that one wants and feels should be a part of one's life. One may know that the help of a Catholic spouse will be needed to live one's new belief, but one can sincerely say that one is not becoming a Catholic only for the other, but rather on one's own.

> *If one is undecided, one should consider whether or not one has true doubts about the Church's basic teachings or dogmas.* If one doubts the truth of the divinity of Christ, his role as our savior, or that he somehow is with us in the eucharist, for example, one should not become a Catholic. But if one has problems with the "how" of his being both divine and human, or of his presence in the wafer of the eucharist, or how three Persons are one God, these should not be obstacles to joining the Church.
>
> Recall that some teachings—what we have called dogmas—are more basic, more important, than others. The truths about God as the Trinity and about Christ—including that he is somehow present in the Church and the sacraments—are much more important than, for example, papal infallibility or the Church's Marian doctrines. One becoming a Catholic might be sure about the former, but not so about the latter.

Also, one obviously does not have to accept, or practice, every Catholic belief with equal attention or enthusiasm. One might, for example, be unable to commit oneself with any enthusiasm to the teachings on Mary and the saints as our intercessors, realizing that these will probably never be very meaningful in one's life. Or something might be intellectually or emotionally repugnant, such as some Catholic devotions or some hierarchical/clerical attitudes toward, for example, women's equality in the Church.

There may be family opposition to one's becoming a Catholic: **Read Luke 12, 51-53, and Matthew 23, 34.** This can be particularly difficult. Usually later, when the family sees the convert is happy in his or her new faith, opposition is replaced by acceptance. Then, too, one should realize that after twenty or thirty years in another religious background, or with no religious background, it is only natural that one should take time to adjust to Catholicism. There may be little or no emotional enthusiasm about this step.

If one wonders whether there are doubts sufficient to keep one from becoming Catholic, one might consider whether or not one *wants* to live the life of a good Catholic. Despite the fact that some of the teachings may not yet be fully accepted intellectually, or one is simply not sure, is there the interior desire to live a Catholic Christian life? One might also ask oneself: Do I feel at home, comfortable here in this Catholic community? Do I best experience God here? Do I feel that Catholicism is helping me do God's will? Do I think that I am a better person because of my Catholic experience? Obviously, too, one who is thinking about this should consult a priest or other churchperson. One should never feel pressured to act; no priest ever would press anyone, and family and friends usually will—or should—have a like respect.

Finally, the way to the Catholic Church for any individual is a two-way street. One usually brings to it as much as one receives. The Church needs and profits by the things the convert has acquired from his or her own religious insights and moral strivings. The convert must try to be aware of what he or she can contribute, and patiently but perseveringly try to use one's special gifts within the Church. Many of the Church's best people have been those who found their way to it as adults.

CHRIST'S CHURCH IS HUMAN

The human beings Christ uses in his Church remain truly human, weak, and subject to sin. This is why he guides his Church through infallibility, to make sure it will never teach error because of human weakness. There have been bad popes, bishops, priests, and people throughout the Church's history. Christ warned us that this would happen. He compared the kingdom to a net containing good and bad fishes, a flock from which some sheep stray, a field containing both good and bad growths: **Read Matthew 13, 24-30.**

Of Christ's chosen apostles, Peter denied him, Judas betrayed him, and all but one deserted him in his most crucial hour. If these who were close to him could act so scandalously, we should expect scandals among their successors centuries later—"It must be that scandals come, but woe to the one through whom scandal does come!" (Matthew 18, 7). It is significant that the gospels tie in a personal reprimand of Peter with each conferral of power on him; this clearly shows the distinction between the man, who would be weak and sinful, and the office that would be divinely protected. Unworthy people are then to be expected in Christ's Church in all ages; logically, they should not cause us to have doubts about the truth of the Church, any more than one would have doubts about mathematics because some professors are poor teachers.

Many of the institutional elements of the Church particularly scandalize people and must be unrelentingly reformed. Some wonder why the Church cannot have the gospel simplicity of Christ's band of followers—but any human organization grows in complexity as it grows in size and its original ideals tend to be compromised. There are many things in the Church that cause some of the best people, both within and without, to draw back from it, while many within it work dedicatedly to improve them:

> *There is overcentralization and a tendency to stifle theological discussion.* Vatican Council II spurred a movement of decentralization, simplification, coresponsibility, and open sharing. But the attitude of many in authority today is one of "frozenness" toward almost any development of teachings and a suspicion of theologians and pastoral churchpeople who try to read the "signs of the times" and adapt to them—the very thing that the Council so strongly urged. In this process of retrenchment and recentralization, loyalty can become prized over competency and uniformity over an open discussion of issues, whether concerning marital morality or the role of women in the Church.

Rome's strength through the centuries has been its stability, its ability to preserve the good and treasured things of our Christian tradition. A desire for uniformity and control, then, is understandable in our time of ongoing change when almost everything seems up for questioning. But most theologians and churchpeople seeking to meet the very diverse pastoral needs of people today find that trying to achieve unity by requiring uniformity is much more harmful than it is helpful—and attempts to impose uniformity from above are bound to be ultimately counterproductive.

There is a lack of sufficient communication between people in various local churches, between local church authorities and people, and between various national churches and the central authorities of the Church. Sometimes people in a particular nation, culture, or group of nations can find that a universal, noninfallible ideal or norm, especially regarding morality, conflicts with their grasp of the total gospel preached by the Church and with their own consciences. Here continual communication, listening to one another, sincere attempts at discussion, and prayerful reflection are called for. Those in authority must be sensitive to the pastoral situation and theological reflection of those in particular cultures and nations—or their own credibility suffers in the long run. Unfortunately, those most zealous to communicate with the Church's central authority are often not representative of the Church in a particular culture or nation—sometimes called "Catholic fundamentalists," these people can exert influence far beyond their numbers.

People of various cultures must try to understand the fundamental intent of a universal teaching, that the Church is truly varied in its makeup, and that what is a problem for them might be quite the opposite elsewhere. The mature Christian knows that unity in a universal Church will not mean uniformity, but it should mean understanding and mutually open, sensitive love. The Church has a long memory, and its mature members know that patient love always wins out.

The Church, then, is in need of continual reformation and renewal. "While Christ, holy, innocent and undefiled, knew nothing of sin ... the Church, embracing sinners in her bosom, at the same time holy and always in need of being purified, follows the endless way of penance and renewal. Christ summons the Church to continual reformation as she goes her pilgrim way ... " (*Constitution on the Church,* no. 8; *Decree on*

Ecumenism, no. 6). God afflicts the Church so that it will never forget it is a pilgrim here below; he hammers and chisels at it so that it will remain a useful tool.

As a member of the Church, one is a part of its structure, with its strengths and its weaknesses, its certitude and formalism, its love and legalism. Many have suffered much in remaining loyal to the Church. Many of the theologians who wrote much of the Vatican Council II documents had previously had their work restricted or condemned. The great Teilhard de Chardin also suffered much from the same narrowness and short-sightedness, yet he wrote:

> Blessed are they who suffer at not seeing the Church so fair as they would wish, and are only the more submissive and prayerful for it. It is a profound grief, but of high spiritual value. It can never be repeated too often: the Catholic is the man who is sure of the existence of Jesus-Christ-God, for a number of reasons and in spite of many stumbling-blocks. Why is it that so many minds see nothing but the stumbling-blocks and wait until they are removed before they look at the reasons? (Teilhard de Chardin, *Making of a Mind,* p. 59).
>
> Franz Jagerstatter was an Austrian peasant who was beheaded in 1943 because he refused to serve in Hitler's army. A loyal Catholic to the end, he went against the advice of his compromising bishop, priest-friends, and family, and died like St. Thomas More. *In Solitary Witness* is the title of the inspiring book about his life and martyr's death. Like Joan of Arc was, he now has been proposed for canonization by some of the very churchmen who acquiesced in his death. Countless others have helped fulfill the Church's mission of redemption while yet suffering deeply from her inadequacies.

Our current age particularly is a time of crisis and change in which the Church is becoming less an institution and more a community— less a structure and more a place where truly human persons encounter Christ and one another—less a judge of the world and more a servant of the world. The work of renewal begun by Pope John XXIII and Vatican Council II is continuing, and this means critical reexamination, development, creativity—and also confusion, reaction, uncertainty.

Today, since Vatican Council II, the Church has come into difficult times, in the opinion of many. The hopeful, halcyon days that followed

Vatican II are over, and the Church in many places is divided and confused. Conservative Catholics are unhappy with many of the changes that have taken place; it has been very difficult for many to see cherished practices discarded and old certitudes universally questioned. Progressives, on the other hand, feel that the brakes have been put on the reforms begun by the Council, by some in leadership positions who are threatened, overly conservative, and sometimes insensitive.

Most Catholics clearly do not take the Church as seriously as they once did, especially regarding marriage and sexual morality and regarding social morality issues of justice and peace. Church attendance has fallen off only slightly, but many are "turned off" by inadequate sermons, the ongoing exclusion of women, and by what for some is the inadequacy of institutional religion to fulfill their spiritual aspirations.

Many of the Church's current difficulties are due to the era of rapid change in every field, and the consequent confusion and conflict through which we are now living. It was inevitable that the Church should suffer from the same stresses as the other institutions of our society. The Church particularly, as the great stabilizing influence of Western civilization for almost two thousand years, could not be expected to cope to everyone's satisfaction with the change that is all about us. It was inevitable that many people in the Church would be hurt and alienated.

But there are many hopeful signs as well: In many, many places the reforms of Vatican II have been slowly and quietly going forward; aging obstructionists are gradually disappearing from the scene, and in many parish councils, for example, conservatives and progressives are learning to dialogue and to work together. Many people have learned a new tolerance, an appreciation of other world religions, and can accept the fact that there are many theologies within the Church and that one can submit to the Church's guidance without giving up the inviolability of one's conscience. There is an increased moral awareness and sensitivity today, particularly in social matters. In many places, new, imaginative liturgical forms have emerged and often stir young and old alike.

The "people of God" are increasingly realizing that the Spirit is stirring among them, and that they need not wait for official leadership to act. Change usually begins from below and then is gradually accepted above. A new and deep interest in spirituality and prayer is manifesting itself.

New theological insights and practical social programs, sometimes upsetting at first, have been bit by bit revealing a profound and hopeful vision of God, humans, and a new world undreamed of before. Today the Church can no longer be triumphalistic and detached—it must be humble, poorer, simpler, more involved, and more honest—more like the way Jesus Christ himself envisioned it.

Many older Catholics remember the amazing event of Vatican Council II (1962-65), how it transformed what was then a complacent, often moribund Church. The bishops of the world gathered—together with scholars, leaders, and ordinary people of all the world's religions—to reform and renew the Church and "open it up" to the modern world. Otherwise bureaucratic and unimaginative prelates voted for progressive documents that they would previously have never dreamed of approving. For many who attended, the Spirit was almost palpably present—all the more so for those who thought the Church had stagnated or, worse, that it was meant to be otherworldly and largely detached from the daily concerns of people in the late twentieth century.

These older Catholics, and many younger ones as well, know that the Church can transform itself again. They know the Church's history is one of constant renewal and new life. They take confidence in the events of Vatican II and know that such a renewal and positive movement forward can happen again—probably, as with most things the Spirit accomplishes, when we least expect it.

Today, particularly, it seems to take maturity to be an active member of the Church. It is no longer as simple and unchallenging as it once was. All of us are challenged to examine our faith and find God for ourselves within the Church, instead of having him spoon-fed to us. The most authentic religious act of some will be to reject the caricatured God who never challenges, the comfortable, narrow God that was once given them.

In all this we recognize that the structures of the institutional Church, however inadequate and in need of continual reform, are necessary. Those who know the Church realize that Christ's message would have been lost to history had the institution not been there—however it obscures his message at times. They know that the institution is basically meant to be a ministry to serve the Christian people and all humankind, that it can never do this adequately, and that even when it fails

Christ goes on accomplishing his work in people. He brings success out of our human failures. This should not surprise us, for it is ultimately Christ who is working among us.

The Church reproduces the weakness and humiliation of Christ. Christ was sinless but accounted a sinner and traitor to his people. The Church is made up of sinners who are trying to bring Christ to all people. The Church must reproduce in itself the whole mystery of Christ, especially that of his cross—and no cross is greater for those who love Christ than the weaknesses of his Church. "Christ lives on in the Church, but he lives as crucified. . . . The imperfections of the Church are the cross of Christ" (Guardini).

Changes in the Church call for openness, patience, and charity among all. They also call for a deep faith—and psychological maturity. Some tend to resist almost any change, others want everything changed almost at once. Any significant change can be painful and confusing, but to refuse to undergo this pain is to remain underdeveloped, immature. The willingness to live with ambiguity and uncertainty is a sign of maturity, just as the inability to live with these indicates immaturity.

Vatican Council II recognized that Church members would disagree in carrying out its teachings—but, it said, "they should always try to enlighten one another through honest discussion, preserving mutual charity and caring above all for the common good" (*The Church in the Modern World,* no. 43).

RECONCILING THE DIVIDED CHURCH AND A DIVIDED WORLD

Through the centuries the unity of Christ's Church has been broken by individuals and groups. These splits within the Church have usually been caused, on the one hand, by the short-sightedness and sinfulness of the Church's members, particularly those in authority, and on the other by the understandable but divisive impatience of those who wanted to reform the Church.

Among those who split from the Church, a heresy is a denial of an infallible teaching of the Church, while a schism is a denial of the Church's authority. Both have existed from the beginning in the Church. John wrote the fourth gospel with those in mind who were even then denying the true nature of Christ. St. Paul was constantly harassed by those he calls "deceitful workers, disguising themselves as apostles of Christ" (2 Corinthians 11, 13). 1 John 2, 19, and 2 Peter 2 also refer to those who broke away from the teaching of the apostles. In the early centuries and into the Middle Ages there were many heresies, great and small; most of them have long since passed into history, and a few continue today in a weak form.

The Eastern Orthodox Churches came about when certain ancient Christian Churches, mostly of the Middle East, finally separated themselves in the eleventh century from the authority of the pope. The background of this split (touched on briefly in chapter 10) shows that the causes were more cultural and political than religious.

As the Christian Church developed, the four great patriarchates, particularly Rome and Constantinople, became the leading churches and centers of unity. In the East, the local churches gradually found a common unity—geographical, political, social, and cultural—under the same emperor, who came to consider himself the ultimate representative of Christ on earth. In the West, however, the unity of the Church was to be independent of all secular power, including that of the emperor. We have seen that while the Eastern Churches had little recourse to Rome during the first four centuries, their recognition of Rome's teaching as the criterion of orthodoxy became more frequent from the fifth century on; they were thus originally united with the Roman Church.

However, with the rising political power of Constantinople, an inevitable rivalry developed between it and Rome. The pope assumed a central role in uniting the Western world that was becoming more and more opposed to the Byzantine Empire. The Eastern emperors tried to browbeat the popes and sometimes imprisoned them, and the popes in turn showed a disdain for the legitimate leadership among the Eastern Churches of the patriarch of Constantinople. Then a ninth-century pope, who was particularly insensitive to the Eastern tradition of autonomy among the patriarchates, tried to impose upon them a strongly centralized papal authority. They reacted and eventually, in 1054, split with Rome.

A few times during the succeeding centuries these Churches were again united with Rome, but positions against one another gradually hardened: the Latins would not recognize the legitimate basis of the powers of the Eastern bishops and saw the uniformity of Western Catholics as the only ideal (positions reversed by Vatican Council II, incidentally). On the other hand, the Orthodox came to look on every development of dogma in the Western Church as a betrayal of apostolic tradition, and the Churches often became isolated nationalistic enclaves.

The causes of this schism were as much political and cultural as doctrinal—the Greek worldview versus the Roman, the isolation caused by Islam, and so on—furthered by a good deal of pride and lack of understanding on both sides. Today an ecumenical "thaw" has been taking place between the Churches, including regular theological discussions with the hopeful ultimate goal of unity. Conferences of the Orthodox Churches have also attempted to achieve more unity for this dialogue. Recent popes have encouraged and deepened the discussions. As Pope Paul VI did before him, Pope John Paul II went to Istanbul shortly after his installation and met with the new patriarch, and during recent years much progress has been made in talks regarding unity.

The Orthodox Churches have the same doctrines, basic moral code, Mass, sacraments, devotion to Mary and the saints, and so on as the Roman Catholic Church. They are the same as the Eastern Rites of the Roman Catholic Church in almost every respect, except that they do not recognize the authority and infallibility of the pope—thus they are considered in schism. They have suffered heroically for their Christianity, especially from the Turks and, from World War II until recently, from Communist domination; today those in Russia and other Eastern European countries have a new era of freedom. They also have been attaining a closer working unity among themselves.

The Eastern Rites of the Catholic Church are the groups among the Eastern Churches that are united with Rome. A "rite" is not just a particular way of worship but a whole unique, yet Catholic tradition, including schools of theology, devotions, spirituality, church discipline, art, architecture, music, and so on—in others words, a particular Catholic culture. We of the West must remember that the Christian Church was born in the East and that its life during the early centuries was centered in the East. From there originally came its basic theology, monasticism, and liturgy, and its greatest Fathers and Doctors.

The liturgies of the Eastern Christian Church—those united with Rome and those that are not—have many local differences, but this is what largely preserved their cultures and national unity during centuries of oppression. While the West developed an "incarnational" spirit, involved in present problems of Christian life on earth, Eastern Christianity expressed itself in a more mystical, "other-worldly" point of view; the institutional and juridical aspects of the Church were relegated to the emperor. The great autonomy of the Eastern Churches and their attitude of detachment from institutional concerns have obviously had both good and bad effects, as history shows. The same, of course, can be said of the West's more pragmatic approach.

Most people notice the obvious differences of the Eastern Churches from the West in discipline and ceremonies. They baptize by immersion, confirm infants at the time of their baptism, have a more elaborate Mass ritual, make greater use of sacred images (icons), and so on—and their priests, unless they are monks, can marry. Eastern liturgies have a great sense of sacredness and mystery, and they emphasize our openness in worship to God's majestic action, rather than our own action; they are less simple and orderly than those of the West, but may be participated in more fully and continually by the whole congregation. Increasingly, their liturgies are gradually undergoing a needed simplification.

The Protestant Reformation was the split in the Western Church in the sixteenth century. It is seen today that its effects were both bad and good. It was inevitable, we realize today, so many and so deep were its causes.

By the sixteenth century there had been for some time widespread evils in the Church. There was corruption and scandal in the lives of many churchmen. The prestige of the popes was seriously impaired by scandals and political maneuverings; during the great schism, two and even three men claimed to be pope. In many places, there was a superstitious overemphasis on externals and neglect of an inner religious spirit. At this time also the spirit of nationalism was growing and with it a spirit of political rebellion against any authority higher than a local one. A pagan spirit left from the Renaissance and a breakdown of the Church's scholastic scholarship contributed to the immorality and confusion.

However, the evils with the Church, bad as they were, should not be exaggerated. The basic doctrines of the Church were still there, though some churchmen were greatly distorting some of them. There were many holy men and women all over the Catholic world who had been working and praying for reform. Much of what happened was due to the fact that this period was a transitional one in history, much like our own, but the Church's leaders then were too blind, too ensconced in their positions, to see this and change their ways.

Martin Luther, a Catholic priest, joined others in protesting against some of the more flagrant abuses. He did not at first intend to break with the Catholic Church. His early teaching is a return to genuinely Catholic beliefs that were being largely overlooked. But, caught up in this changing period of history, faced with the intransigence and duplicity of the papal court, and encouraged by some of the German princes for their own purposes, he came to hold strong views of his own. Today we recognize that he had genuine and much-needed insights into the nature of Christianity and that his views were not as un-Catholic as was once thought.

But anathemas and counter-anathemas were hurled by both sides, and the split became an irreparable fact. Martin Luther was the first of the reformers. After Luther, others broke away—John Calvin in Switzerland, Henry VIII in England, John Knox in Scotland. Generally, as in Scandinavia, most people did not realize what was happening, but simply followed their rulers, whether Catholic or Protestant.

The result of the Reformation was that Christ's Church was split, dividing millions of Christians in the West, as the Eastern schism had done earlier. Within a short time numerous rival Christian groups sprang up. There was much religious anarchy, as even Luther deplored in his day. It led to much of the confusion we find in Christianity today with rival Christian Churches disputing among themselves. Then a significant start toward unity was made early in the twentieth century, leading to the formation of the World Council of Churches. Most of the "mainline" Protestant Churches and Orthodox Churches joined this group, which aimed at doctrinal dialogue and at joint social action. Intercommunion or "open communion" gradually became the practice among most Protestant Churches. Finally, today, four hundred years later, the movement for unity has been truly progressing since Vatican

Council II, with the entrance of the Roman Catholic Church into the dialogue and into cooperative efforts on every level.

The splitting of the Church at the Reformation was the fault of both "sides." If the reformers were sometimes extreme, Catholic leaders on the other hand had blinded themselves to how bad things were. As Cardinal Pole, the pope's representative at the reform Council of Trent, admitted:

> Before the tribunal of God's mercy we, the shepherds, should make ourselves responsible for all the evils now burdening the flock of Christ. The sins of all we should take upon ourselves, not in generosity but in justice; because the truth is that of these evils we are in great part the cause, and therefore we should implore the divine mercy through Jesus Christ (Henry S. John, *Essays on Christian Unity,* p. 20).

The Reformation spurred the Catholic Church to reform itself. History has shown that it was de facto necessary so that certain theological insights and other aspects of the Church might emerge and that abuses be shunted aside. While we feel that some teachings of Christianity have been neglected by our separated brethren, other aspects of Christ's teaching have been well developed and many new insights gained among them. They have "many elements of sanctification and truth" (*Constitution on the Church,* no. 8). We can learn much from each other, as we seek together to know Christ's will more fully and follow it (*Decree on Ecumenism,* no. 3).

We cannot see clearly why God has permitted divisions among Christians. But one thing seems obvious: They were brought about originally by the evil lives of Christians. When God's people of the Old Testament were unfaithful to him, Israel was split. So, too, among us. Hopefully, the confusion and pain of division will make us realize that unity must be earned by the good lives of us all.

Today we see that we deeply need one another. To Catholics, other Christians are our brothers and sisters; they come from the same family. There was a tragic family quarrel, and we split up. Today we see once again that our family, the Christian religion, is not what it should be because of our separateness. While, therefore, avoiding a "false irenicism" that pretends there are no real differences between us, we are trying to explain our teachings to one another, discuss our differences, and work to understand and share one another's insights. We should cooperate whenever we can, trying never to do separately what we can do together. Even though our communion is imperfect we are united in the most important things.

Vatican Council II stresses particularly our cooperation in social action:

> Cooperation among Christians vividly expresses the relationship which in fact already unites them, and sets in clearer relief the features of Christ the Servant. Such cooperation . . . should be developed more and more, particularly . . . where a social and technical evolution is taking place. It should contribute to a just evaluation of the dignity of the human person, to peace, the application of the gospel principles to social life, and the advancement of the arts and sciences in a truly Christian spirit. It should also be intensified in the use of every possible means to relieve the afflictions of our times, such as famine and natural disasters, illiteracy and poverty, lack of housing and the unequal distribution of wealth . . . (*Decree on Ecumenism,* no. 12).

Today the great movement for Christian unity, called ecumenism or the ecumenical movement, is well under way among almost all Christian Churches. The "siege mentality" that had developed during the centuries after the Reformation has finally been almost wholly dissipated, and a new appreciation of Christian Churches for one another has come about. Christian unity grew more in the four years of Vatican Council II than in the previous four hundred. Since the Council, despite occasional setbacks, it has been moving steadily forward.

We must continue to pray for unity, particularly with our fellow Christians. There is simply no substitute for praying together to make us realize the unity we have and to spur us to work for further unity. Recent popes have led the way in this on numerous occasions.

We should continually ask for a humble, open appreciation and love of our fellow Christians. "We should pray to the Holy Spirit for the grace to be genuinely self-denying, humble, and gentle in the service of others, and to have an attitude of brotherly generosity toward them . . . " (*Decree on Ecumenism,* no. 8).

Prayer and a gradual, interior change of heart are causing concerned Christians to be genuinely pained at our division, which "openly contradicts the will of Christ, scandalizes the world, and damages . . . the preaching of the gospel to every creature" (*Decree on Ecumenism,* no. 1). In many places, unfortunately, people have come to accept the presence of different Christian religions as they accept competing grocery chains or gas stations. Often it is only when one becomes personally involved, as for example when facing a possible interfaith marriage, that one realizes the true pain of division. Division hurts us all. It makes the faith and Christian life of all of us that much poorer, that much less truly catholic.

Next to the Orthodox Churches, the Anglican Church (the Episcopal Church in the United States) is the closest to Roman Catholicism in belief, sacraments, and church structure. Called a "Catholic" communion, it is considered to be, like the Orthodox, in schism.

The majority of Roman Catholic theologians who have examined the matter consider Anglican orders valid—and hence their sacraments—and the joint Roman Catholic-Anglican International Commission has asked for a reexamination of the Vatican's 1896 declaration of invalidity. A current problem regarding unity is the ordination of women to the priesthood and episcopacy by some of these churches (but, as we saw in chapter 22, this need not be the roadblock it has been considered).

Also drawing significantly closer are Catholicism and the "mainline" Protestant churches that hold to the Nicene Creed and have bishops and sacraments (baptism and the eucharist)—most notably the Lutherans, Presbyterians, and Methodists. Many Catholic theologians today consider these churches apostolic, not because their ministerial empowerment is traced back through a succession of laying on of bishops' hands going back to the early Church, but insofar as they maintain fidelity to the gospel and the teaching of the apostles.

Quietly progressing today are the "official" dialogues, periodic meetings among the scholars and theologians of the major Christian faiths. Amazing strides in understanding and agreement have been made, and some of these have been published as Documents on Anglican-Roman Catholic Relations, Lutheran-Roman Catholic Relations, Presbyterian Reformed-Roman Catholic Relations, and others.

Students for the priesthood and for the ministry of various denominations often study together in theological "unions" or "consortiums." Here all can take advantage of the scholarship and insights of professors of other faiths, of different theologies, and so on, thus broadening them all, and producing practical results of cooperation in ministries to the poor, to students, to business people, for peace and justice, and so on.

In a number of places, "sister parishes" have been coming together, sharing in their common Christian ministerial concerns for social justice and for spreading the gospel message—in a word, working together to more effectively bring Christian love to their particular neighborhood. Their common Christian concerns draw them to pray together periodically, anticipating the day when they can share together in the one eucharistic Body of Christ.

Honest dialogue with one another can be difficult and also rewarding. Gradually we learn what is meant by one another's theological terminology. Different, seemingly contradictory theological formulations can mask actual agreement, or at least views that are "complementary rather than conflicting"—this because of our "different methods and approaches in understanding and confessing divine things . . . " (cf. *Decree on Ecumenism, no. 17*). Pope John XXIII said, and Vatican Council II repeated, "The substance of the old doctrine of the deposit of faith is one thing, the formulation of its presentation another."

We do not want to do away with the spiritual insights and accomplishments of various Christian traditions in our search for unity. Different traditions have different things to offer to our common Christianity, and these should not be surrendered in our attempts at dialogue. Rather we should try to understand and appreciate one another's insights and spiritual principles, even when they seem to clash with our own—as just said, they are often complementary rather than conflicting. But when they do conflict, we should keep discussing, trying to understand, and praying, while being willing to live with unresolved paradoxes in these matters as in the rest of life.

We should remember especially that the Church's dogmas, while infallible and therefore irrevocable, can never express everything about their subjects, nor even begin to exhaust the fullness of truth that is in the mystery of Christianity. No formulation can ever adequately express the reality that we come to know in Christ. There is a wide and ever-open field for discussion, explanation, and development in clarifying even infallible definitions. We should also keep in mind that there is a "hierarchy of truths" in Catholic doctrine, that beliefs vary in their relationship to the foundation of the Christian faith, and therefore in their importance in the lives of Catholics. Also one must distinguish between the substance of a teaching and its formulation.

Pope John Paul II, in a significant 1995 encyclical, *That They May Be One,* invited other Christian churches, especially the Orthodox, to reflect on the office of the papacy, realizing that it can be an obstacle to unity as well as a center of unity.

Appreciation, cooperation, and love must also be shown to those of non-Christian religions, and of no formal religion, who so often have good will and seek to carry out their humanitarian ideals. Sometimes non-Christians and secular humanists shame us by the goodness and dedication of their lives; as St. Augustine said, "There are many outside who seem to be inside, and many inside who seem to be outside." There are aspects of truth and love that we can learn from one another; the Church has set up at Rome a Pontifical Council for Non-Christians to promote this dialogue and also one to dialogue with nonbelievers.

Vatican Council II exhorted us:

Prudently and lovingly, through dialogue and collaboration with the followers of other religions and in witness of Christian faith and life [we should] acknowledge, preserve and promote the spiritual and moral goods found among these [people], as well as the values in their society and culture (*Declaration on Non-Christian Religions,* no. 2).

While rejecting atheism, root and branch, the Church sincerely professes that all [people], believers and unbelievers alike, ought to work for the rightful betterment of this world in which all alike live; such an ideal cannot be realized, however, apart from sincere and prudent dialogue. . . . Respect and love ought to be extended also to those who think or act differently than we do in social, political, and even religious matters . . . to understand their ways of thinking through courtesy and love . . . (*The Church in the Modern World,* nos. 21 and 28).

We must remember that the Church is a mystery—it is continually developing, unfolding, growing in its understanding of itself. It is not just a static institution. It is a love relationship with Christ, the Trinity, and one another—and like any love relationship it is continually growing, sometimes painfully, revealing new depths and richness. This relationship, however, is unique because it is the mystery of Christ, God communicating himself to humans—and this has no bounds whatever.

This is why there will always be changes in the Church, new insights from various sources into its basic truths, and new ways of expressing our beliefs, that is, new ways of bringing God to women and men. The content, the "core" truths, of our faith remain the same, but what we understand of these grows and deepens. We can better understand and profit today from what was given us two thousand years ago if we are imaginatively open and can see how some truths can sometimes be better expressed in terms more understandable, more "living" for us today. If we are open, we let the Spirit expand our consciousness and give us new understanding, new insights, and renewed commitment to love, particularly when we gather to hear God's Word and share the eucharist.

Increasingly, the Church today is diverse and multicultural and no longer predominantly Western, European, or white in its liturgies, its pastoral practices, and even in its understanding of morality. Non-Christian nations were once looked on as "heathens" or "infidels" who were destined to be condemned forever unless they accepted Christianity in its European form. The Church was inculturated in Europe, built into Europe's social and political institutions, and while it brought much good when it spread to other lands, it was often narrowly self-focused and accompanied by those who sought only conquest and could be unbelievably greedy and cruel.

Today all this has changed, and the bulk of the Church's membership has been shifting to cultures other than European, white, or even Western. The Church is more and more inculturated in many places worldwide, using some of the local customs and traditions and vice versa, and it must be so "if the Gospel is to take flesh [and endure] in each people's culture" (*Catechism*, 854). It is still hard to figure out what is essential to the Catholic Christian faith and what is simply part of a European inculturation pattern.

Growth comes not only from the insights of other Christians but also from other world religions and from nonbelievers. The Church must look at these in the light of Christ's revelation, but it also must be truly and constantly open to the Spirit who breathes where she will and can use anyone as her prophet. The Spirit in this way also brings to light hitherto latent or unnoticed aspects of God's self-revelation in Jesus Christ.

Today Christians are coming to appreciate the religions of the East—Hinduism, Buddhism, Taoism—just as many Easterners are coming to appreciate more fully the teachings of Christ and the "active charity" of Western Christianity. We are learning much from the authentic religious teachers of the East—methods of meditation, self-discipline, detachment or "letting go" of material concerns, a "quieting" of one's inner self, a oneness with nature, an appreciation of intuitive or nonrational ways of arriving at truth, and so on. Often, through contact with Eastern religions, Christians come to appreciate more fully the deeply spiritual nature of their own tradition—just as Gandhi, for instance, was helped in formulating his history-changing way of nonviolent resistance by studying the teachings of Christ.

There have been problems for Christians in these Eastern traditions: pantheism, polytheism, reincarnation, a tendency toward fatalism or to denigrate the material world and the eternal uniqueness of each individual person. But as the dialogue between East and West continues, more similarities—complementarities rather than contraries—are continually coming to light.

Especially among contemplatives, those dedicated to a life of prayer, there is the realization that the different traditions may be saying much the same thing but using different words or cultural concepts. Recently, for instance, a Catholic monk-theologian, Joseph Wong, has shown that a similarity to the Christian Trinity, as well as other gospel teachings, can be found in the source of Taoist teachings, the *Tao-Te-Ching.*

Also making progress is the dialogue with Islam, the world's third great monotheistic religion (along with Judaism and Christianity), which also looks to the Bible as the basis of many of the teachings contained in its sacred book, the Koran. Islam strongly emphasizes the transcendence of God, his total "otherness" and utter holiness. It also stresses God's compassion; however, in the Christian view, because Islam does not believe that God has come among us as a human, in Jesus Christ, it could profit from the Christian revelation of God as closely caring and understanding, as One who has become one of us. Pope John Paul II has appealed that the request of Vatican Council II for dialogue and better understanding be accelerated on all levels, and that we put behind us the enmities of the past and work toward a future world of love and peace under our common Father.

In all this we should imitate Christ, who showed concretely how to treat those of other beliefs. He always recognized their dignity and treated them with respect. Though he was Jewish, he acceded to the faith of a Syro-Phoenician woman and worked a miracle for her (Mark 7, 25–30); he marveled at the faith of a Roman centurion and also worked a miracle for him (Matthew 8, 8–18). He welcomed Greeks and used the "heretical" Good Samaritan as his great example of love of neighbor. It does seem, then, that he would want all religions to be at peace with one another, instead of being exclusivistic and intolerant as has happened all too often throughout history.

THE CHURCH'S MISSION OF LOVING SERVICE IN TODAY'S WORLD

The Church rejoices in the world's accomplishments, not only in its own modest successes. Every achievement toward making this a better world helps carry out the plan of God, and the Church encourages its members to be a part of this.

> Christians, on pilgrimage toward the heavenly city, should seek and think of the things which are above. But this duty in no way decreases, rather it increases, the importance of their obligation to work with all [humankind] in the building of a more human world. Indeed the mystery of the Christian faith furnishes them with an excellent stimulant and aid to fulfill this duty more courageously and especially to uncover the full meaning of this activity. . . . When [humans] develop the earth by the work of [their] hands or with the aid of technology . . . [they] carry out the design of God manifested at the beginning of time, that [they] should subdue the earth, perfect creation and develop [themselves]. At the same time [they] obey the commandment of Christ that [they] place [themselves] at the service of [their] brethren (*The Church in the Modern World,* no. 57).

When we work we are carrying out God's plan, as surely as when we pray. There should be no dichotomy, though there will always be a "tension," between one's spiritual life and one's human accomplishments. Usually an integration is difficult to achieve, but as long as we try, whatever we do is used by God to fulfill his plan for the world's salvation. Vatican Council II said:

> Whoever labors . . . even though . . . unaware of the fact, is nevertheless being led by the hand of God . . . and can be a partner in the work of bringing divine creation to perfection. . . . Through labor . . . many are associated with the redemptive work of Jesus Christ, who conferred an eminent dignity on labor when at Nazareth he worked with his own hands (*The Church in the Modern World*, nos. 36 and 67).

The Church wants to work with all people to make our world a better place, to end war, poverty, and discrimination, to carefully develop and preserve the resources of the earth and give all people a share in them (cf. *The Church in the Modern World*, no. 55).

DAILY LIVING: THE COMPASSIONATE CHURCH

The Church's mission, and that of every Christian, must first of all be to the poor, underprivileged, and oppressed. We must desire for all what we desire for ourselves: civil rights, health, adequate education, development, civilization, and culture. Over half the world is deprived of some major need. Yet our American contribution to the economies of backward and starving nations is less than what we spend annually on cigarettes and chewing gum.

In our own country forty million people are poor or deprived, and twelve thousand of the world's people die each day from some form of starvation. In India, six million babies die each year because of malnutrition, and a third of the children in Africa will not live into adolescence. Several million families in Latin America must survive on the equivalent of a dollar a week. As we consider these facts we should also consider Christ's clear words about how we will be judged at the end: **Reread Matthew 25, 34–40.**

Vatican Council II spoke plainly of the scandal of so-called Christians who are unconcerned with the poor and deprived of the world: "Some nations with a majority of citizens who are counted as Christians have an abundance of this world's goods, while others are deprived of the necessities of life and are tormented with hunger, disease, and every kind of misery. This situation must not be allowed to continue, to the scandal of humanity. For the spirit of poverty and of charity is the glory and authentication of the Church of Christ" (*The Church in Modern World,* no. 88).

The Council reiterated that the Church must above all imitate the poor and persecuted Christ in carrying out its mission:

"Just as Christ carried out the work of redemption in poverty and oppression, so the Church is called to follow the same route. . . . Christ Jesus though he was by nature God . . . emptied himself, taking the nature of a slave, and 'being rich became poor' for our sakes. Thus the Church, although it needs human resources to carry out its mission, is not set up to seek earthly glory but to proclaim, and this by its own example, humility and self-sacrifice.

"Christ was sent by the Father 'to bring good news to the poor, to heal the contrite of heart' and 'to seek and to save what was lost. . . . ' Similarly, the Church encompasses with love all those who are poor and who suffer in the image of its poor and suffering founder. It does all it can to relieve their need and in them it strives to serve Christ" (*Constitution on the Church,* no. 8).

Put quite simply, the Church is on the side of the poor, the oppressed, and the neglected. Like Christ himself it prefers or opts for the poor. Those who are poor, underprivileged, the "marginalized," and wayward are the truly special members of the Church. They are "united with the suffering Christ in a special way for the salvation of the world" (*Constitution on the Church,* no. 41). They are the Church's real power—not its great universities or soaring cathedrals or well-scrubbed suburban multitudes.

Pope John XXIII once scandalized his entourage by insisting on visiting the worst prisoners in one of Rome's prisons, among them several murderers. After listening to the pope's brief talk, one of them said, "These words of hope that you have just given us—do they also apply to me, such a great sinner?" Pope John's only answer was to open his arms and clasp him to his heart.

Pope John Paul II went to an Italian prison to visit the man who attempted to assassinate him, forgiving him and also taking steps to provide for the care of his family.

SOME SUGGESTIONS FOR . . .

DISCUSSION

What advice would you give to someone becoming a convert to Catholicism?

If you are becoming a convert, can you perceive why God has chosen and called you to do this? What difficulties, as well as joys, might you expect as you continue your journey in the years ahead?

If you are returning to the Church after possibly many years away, what lessons have there been for you in your journey of alienation and return?

Throughout the Church's history many of its members whom it condemned and even persecuted have later been exonerated, even canonized as saints. What does this tell you about the Church's human aspect? About its divine side?

What, for you, most shows the Church's divine aspect? What most shows it humanness?

Regarding world poverty and disarmament, how would you, personally, apply Gandhi's words: "Your contribution is insignificant, but it is infinitely important that you make it"?

How do you think Christians might best contribute to making the world a better place for all today?

FURTHER READING

- *Catholicism Today: Survey of Catholic Belief and Practice,* Kohmescher (Paulist Press, 1980)—This is a good overview of the important aspects of Catholicism, with some helpful charts and graphs.
- • *Understanding Catholicism,* Hellwig (Paulist Press, 1981)—This book is particularly good for the more rationally, philosophically inclined.
- *Believing in Jesus,* Foley (St. Anthony Messenger Press, rev. ed., 1985)—Subtitled, "A Popular Overview of the Catholic Faith," this is a fine, relatively brief book for the average person who doesn't want to go too deeply.
- *Why Be Catholic?* O'Malley (Crossroad, 1993)—A wonderfully frank, no-holds-barred discussion of Catholicism through the centuries,

this book, for mature minds only, is enjoyable as well as enlightening reading.

- *Fundamentalism: A Catholic Perspective,* O'Meara (Paulist Press, 1990)—This small but superb book looks at the psychological as well as theological bases for ultraconservative attitudes, both without and especially within the Catholic Church.
- *Tensions in the Church: Facing the Challenges, Seizing the Opportunities,* Bacik (Sheed & Ward, 1993)—A priest-theologian and popular writer discusses in a positive way the four areas of tension regarding the Church that he has experienced in his university parish.
- *The Multicultural Church: A New Landscape in U.S. Theologies,* ed. Cenkner (Paulist Press, 1995)—A group of theologians, academic and pastoral, discuss how to live in today's sometimes confusingly multicultural Church, one in which our very diversity can give growth and enrichment to all.
- *Christian Foundations: An Introduction to Faith in Our Time,* Fischer and Hart, (Paulist Press, revised 1995)—A well-reviewed overview that tries to reduce the major issues of Christian life to their essential elements and to relate the core Christian message to the conditions of the modern world.
- *A Concise History of the Catholic Church,* Bokenkotter (Doubleday, 1990)—A very good survey of Catholic history that covers the essentials and distinguishes them from the nonessentials.
- *The Catholic Thing,* Haughton (Templegate, 1980)—A discerning writer pulls together the many things, including a good deal of history, that make up "the Catholic enterprise" for her.
- *The Catholic Experience,* Cunningham (Crossroad, 1985)—An excellent, balanced, and inspiring book that gives the many aspects of what for the author is Catholicism today.
- *Ecumenism: Striving for Unity amid Diversity,* Lowery (Twenty-Third Publications, 1986)—An excellent introduction to ecumenism for the person who is not a professional in this field.
- *Turning: Reflections on the Experience of Conversion,* Griffin (Doubleday, 1982)—A fine book in which a professional woman tells of her conversion, what led to it, and how it has affected her.
- • *Essential Catholicism,* Bokenkotter (Doubleday Image Books, 1986)—A "packed" book that gives a clear, concise, yet complete

look at the main matters of belief and morality in Catholicism, their history, and the diversity of theological thought within the Church.

•• *Catholicism,* McBrien (HarperSanFrancisco, 1994)—A thorough revision of the classic, 1,200-plus-page presentation of Catholic Christianity by one of the country's leading progressive theologians. Clearly written, with charts, diagrams, and updated references, this is a "must" for anyone seeking to understand Catholicism in any depth today.

•• *The HarperCollins Encyclopedia of Catholicism,* ed. McBrien (HarperSanFrancisco, 1995)—Edited by the same author, this is a monumental, comprehensive, one-volume guide to all aspects of current Catholicism. It has 4,200-plus entries by 280 leading experts from across the theological spectrum and is both mightily informative and wonderfully balanced.

•• *World Scripture: An Introduction to Comparative Religion,* Kramer (Paulist Press, 1986)—An excellent, very popular introduction to the world's great religions as seen through their sacred writings.

 • *The Cosmic Revelation,* Griffiths (Templegate, 1983)—A Catholic monk who spent twenty years in his own Indian "ashram" shows how the Hindu way to God relates to Christianity.

•• *The World's Religions,* Smith (HarperSanFrancisco, 1995)—This is a completely revised and updated version (with inclusive language and new material on the primal religions) of the author's classic *The Religions of Man.* It is also available as *The Illustrated World's Religions.*

•• *The History of God,* Armstrong (Ballantine Books, 1993)—A former nun and wide-ranging scholar discusses the three great monotheistic religions, Judaism, Christianity, and Islam. Clearly and interestingly written, and with some spiritual depth, this synthesis has been a bestseller since its publication.

•• *Jesus Christ at the Encounter of World Religion,* Dupuis (Orbis, 1991)—After many years in India, a Catholic theologian, in this highly praised book, examines how Jesus Christ is present in the world today, particularly in other religious traditions.

•• *Chinese Religion,* Ching (Orbis, 1993)—A small but highly recommended volume on the religious traditions of China—Taoism, Buddhism, and Confucianism.

PERSONAL REFLECTION

As a Christian and a human being, I must ask myself honestly: Do I desire for all people what I have and enjoy? Am I doing something, however small, to help end worldwide poverty and enlarge the "peace dividend"?

I might renew my resolution to help some individual poor person or family, someone retarded, forgotten, discriminated against, or underprivileged. I might join a group combating poverty or discrimination or working for peace—or I might regularly send help to some charity or peace project.

25

Living Daily the Christian Life

What should motivate a Christian to be "different" in her or his daily life? Should one do things out of fear, because one feels forced to? Conversely, when should one concretize the obligations that flow from love? What are some practical guidelines by which one can live daily a Christian life?

HOW DO WE KNOW HOW TO LIVE?

The way a Christian lives begins with a loving call from God. He invites us to share in a special way in his plan. We are free to respond or not. He reminds us, as he did the Israelites at Sinai, what he has done for us—and then he gives us commandments by which we can give him our response of love.

If we choose to accept God's loving invitation, we respond in and through Christ. The Christian life is an imitation of Christ, but it is more. It is being transformed into Christ, sharing his life, being here and now his hands and feet and eyes and ears. He lives in us and uses us to do now among people the things he did two thousand years ago. "It is no longer I who live, but Christ who lives in me" (Galatians 2, 20).

Each Christian, then, is Christ among us. Each is a new, special manifestation of Christ that will never exist again. Each of us in his or her own way must expect to undergo a "passover," a death and resurrection. We must struggle and suffer and die in order to be raised up to eternal happiness. It is not easy to live a life with Christ and in Christ. But once one tastes this life, nothing else can satisfy.

Christ guides us in living his life through his Spirit, who is within us. It is the Spirit who conforms us to Christ, who shows us what to do and who inspires and strengthens us to do it. The Holy Spirit, we recall, is the Person who is love—and in guiding us to live the Christian life the Spirit is simply showing us how to love—or, rather, how to let ourselves be loved by God, and then love in return.

The Spirit has been sent by Christ to form us into a community, his Church, to show us how to love and be loved. The Church is Christ among us as he works through his Spirit to unite and guide us so that we can witness his love among men and women. The Church is Christ among us doing the things he began to do two thousand years ago. The Church's role in the world is not to build itself as an institution of salvation, nor to enforce a series of moral laws, but always and only to help God's revelation of love reach people. Significantly, though the Church could do so, it has never solemnly defined as infallible a matter of morality.

The Church has laws, norms, and guides by which we live. (It should be evident by now that they are not nearly as numerous or as restrictive as might have been thought.) The purpose of the Church's laws is simply to show us how to let ourselves be loved by God and how to love him in return, particularly through our neighbor. All the Church's rules, and its every exercise of authority, are meant only to help us open ourselves freely and maturely to God's love.

> Those in love want to know, often in detail, what will please their beloved. They want to be told how to avoid upsetting their love relationship and how to grow in love day by day. They fear, with the wholesome fear of a lover, to hurt the one they love. And because they are mature, they know that if they hurt their beloved, if they upset their love relationship, they will only bring unhappiness upon themselves. Their lovingness itself will punish them for what they have done, and they cannot be happy until they have righted the wrong they have done to their beloved.

Christians know, too, that because they are human, they will sometimes be blinded—by emotion, greed, pride—or sometimes they will simply be bored with the whole process. People then may not want to show their love at all—they are faithful only from a sheer sense of duty—but they realize that faithfulness now is the real test of their love. To comply, to give up one's own way, to show one's love where it is hard, even very painful to do so, is the test of true love. So it is with our mature obedience to Christ in his Church. We know our weakness—that we will at times obey only reluctantly—but this can sometimes be the truest test of our love of God.

Of course, there is the ever-present temptation to legalism: to equate keeping the letter of the law with pleasing God. A servile fear or a comfortable, rationalized rule-keeping can take over our moral life. This is precisely what Christ came to dispel. He said, "Beware of the leaven of the Pharisees and Sadducees" (Matthew 16, 6); these had stressed the exact keeping of many observances to the detriment of the heart and spirit of the law, which is love. Some Christians, unfortunately, cannot yet realize that "perfect love casts out fear" (1 John 4, 18).

As we progress in the Christian life there is less and less need to consult the "rules." We gradually develop a Christian moral sense, come to "think with the Church." We take seriously the guidance of the Church in the formation of our conscience, but we do not expect of the Church answers that solve our moral dilemmas for us (although consultation with a spiritual guide is sometimes only wise and can keep us from self-deception). We try to grasp the Church's basic principles of morality, and with the guidance of the Spirit—received especially through time taken in receptive prayer—we apply them to our daily life.

> One realizes that many, perhaps most, moral situations are not clearly good or evil, that sometimes all one can do is choose what seems to be the lesser of two evils. But this is Christian maturity. As children must be given continual, explicit instructions when they are young, but have less and less need of guidance as they mature, so with maturing Christians in their moral development.

Here, then, in this chapter, are proposed not detailed rules of Christian morality but some general principles for daily living, suggestions for following the Spirit's guidance in our everyday life. But first we will see Christ's own program for living as one of his followers, the beatitudes.

THE BEATITUDES

Jesus' beatitudes tell us how to live to attain true happiness and the kingdom he came to bring us. Read Matthew 5, 3-12. They are called beatitudes because the one living according to them is "blessed" (which in older biblical translations means happy). They are "at the heart of Jesus' preaching" (*Catechism*, 1716). They give us his own principles for living a Christian life: like a plan or blueprint, they tell us what our attitudes and behavior should be as we go through our daily life.

The beatitudes tell us, briefly, that true happiness is not found in riches and material possessions, or in avoiding all pain and discomfort, or in attaining fame and power—especially at the expense of others. They tell us to hunger and thirst for "righteousness" or justice toward all, and to be peacemakers in our world. They ask us to be merciful and forgiving, and say that our hearts should be "pure" or single-minded in seeking God. Finally, they tell us to expect to be misunderstood, reviled, and even persecuted when we try to follow Christ and live like this.

The beatitudes confront us with tough moral choices. Reread Matthew 5, 3-12. They challenge us to live lives based on gospel values rather than on those of our materialistic society. They tell us wealth and power are, ultimately, not important—that, in effect, we can't take it with us—but that being an understanding and forgiving person is important. They say we should be concerned about justice, the poor and deprived, and concerned that peace reign in our world—all of which are surely not priorities in our present-day acquisitive, confrontative culture. Realistically, they conclude that we can expect to be put down, ignored, scorned, and perhaps even persecuted and killed if we try to live according to these values.

In the spirit of the beatitudes—of Christ's teaching—we will now try to apply the Church's moral teachings to four main areas of life: our home life, our work or school life, our social life, and our religious life.

OUR HOME LIFE

At home upon arising, Christians thank God for another day in which to live and to love, and ask his help, especially for some particular thing that they will have special need of that day. Realistically, some Christians, like a good proportion of humankind, will hardly feel alive, much less prayerful, when they arise; some would better delay their attempt at prayer until they are on the way to work, or later, as opportunities arise.

Our meals have always been associated in human custom with an awareness that it is ultimately God who gives us "our daily bread." Hence we begin them with some sort of brief prayer. All in the family might take their turns asking a blessing, or each can express his or her particular thanks. Our best prayers are usually those we compose ourselves.

Parents remember that they are God-models to their children, and while they realize their own weaknesses, they try to remember that God gives them special strength and insights. They *show* their love and affection toward their children, and they give example for their children's later life by expressing their love of one another—yet realizing that occasional inevitable conflicts also show their children that people can deeply love one another and yet be angry and at odds.

Parents remember that they are "by word and example . . . the first preachers of the faith to their children" (*Declaration on Christian Education,* no. 3).They try to make God real to their children, helping them express simple prayers, and praying with them (for example, at bedtime). To the extent they can, they regularly read with their children the Bible and stories that give examples of Christian living and attitudes the children can understand and relate to. Many good Bibles and imaginative, spiritually based books are available today for children. See "Further Reading" at the end of this chapter.

They try to give their children the vital sense of trust and security that can come only from showing mutual love, respect, and kindness. To the extent that they can, they love "unconditionally," that is, regardless of whether or not the children live up to their expectations. They try to give their children the "why" of anything they ask them to do, as far as this is possible. They know where their children are, and as best they can they try to make their home a center for the growing children's social life, a welcome place for them and their friends to come. They can and should talk things over with their children, such as the limited family budget, and let the children have a sense of shared responsibility for the family's decisions. They try to do things together with their children, as a family, and try to be imaginatively sensitive to their children's own growing preferences and skills. They help them make gradually more mature decisions on their own, letting them make choices as much as possible, but letting them know they are responsible and accountable for their choices.

Parents also are alert to helping their children prepare for the time when they will leave home and for their own marriage and/or job careers. They correct their children's faults unhesitantly, but also praise them for their accomplishments, however small. They use firm but loving discipline, and "hang tough," especially during their children's teens, against sometimes overwhelming peer pressure and other, perhaps inept, overly permissive parents. They do not yield to the temptation to give in and let their teenagers run their own lives. They use persistent love and continually try to consult, encourage, and share enthusiasms and interests with their emerging adults. They try to realize that adolescence today can extend into the midtwenties and beyond. They try to handle "boomerang children" who leave and return home, perhaps over and over, with understanding and yet firmness.

Mature Christian parents remember that they are the primary and principal educators of their children. Theirs is the primary duty of teaching their children, choosing schools and programs that will promote the child's spiritual and moral growth as well as their intellectual development. They take time to work with their child's teacher and demand accountability where education is inept or inefficient. The Catholic school, CCD, and other catechetical programs are only meant to help parents do *their* job more effectively. There is no duty of *both* parents more serious than this.

The Christian family will look beyond their immediate circle and try to be aware of the needs of others: the needs of their neighborhood, particularly people with few friends, children whose parents neglect them, the poor and underprivileged of their area—and of the world. Wise parents try to direct their children beyond the selfish and suffocating spiritual mediocrity that is often a danger (especially with materially well-off parents), and they give their children a broad, truly Christian worldview.

OUR WORK OR SCHOOL LIFE

Christians go to their job or profession with the knowledge that their work is helping to carry out God's plan for the universe. No act, however boring or seemingly fruitless, is ever wasted. They try to do their best because they realize that by their work they are spreading love and helping to bring the world to perfection.

Christians look for opportunities to help others in their office, factory, or classroom. They expect friction and conflicts and try to see the beam in their own eye before they point out the speck in their neighbor's. They try to be genuinely interested in even one other person who needs help in some way.

Christians give a full day's work for a full day's pay and try to take a constructive interest in their job. If they are employers, they provide safe and decent working conditions, give a living wage, avoid subtle perpetuations of sexual, racial, or age discrimination, and share profits and policy-making with employees to the extent that they can.

Christians in their business dealings practice honesty and justice. They realize that some things are fundamentally wrong: cheating, false advertising, dishonest business agreements, or taking profits from corporate investments in places and countries that violate human rights in the name of productivity. Selfish and greedy lobbying for one's particular interest to the detriment of the common good, avoiding one's justly owed taxes or debts, and bribery and "kickbacks" are plainly dishonest, avaricious, and un-Christian. Christians realize that if they have been dishonest, they owe restitution; if this cannot be made to those from whom it was stolen, it can be given to charity.

Christians give regularly—to the poor, disabled, aged, and underprivileged—of their money and whatever is possible of their time (and something, however small, always *is* possible, if we are honest with ourselves). They realize that they can quickly become caught up in the accumulation of material things that are not really necessary—while more than half the world is underfed, without decent clothing or housing, and with little or no education. Christians desire for all people the good things they themselves enjoy. They may come to realize that if they never refuse an appeal for help, they will themselves never be in want of anything essential.

Christians who are students are grateful for the opportunities they have for an education. They try to develop their God-given talents. If they do not succeed in one field, they imaginatively try another; they realize that they have something vital to contribute, in God's plan, to the world's development. They are honest and avoid cheating or taking advantage of those who are helping them attain an education. They steadily and coura-geously seek truth, realizing that this may sometimes cause them prob-lems of faith or problems with those interested only in learning for the material success and/or status it may bring.

OUR SOCIAL LIFE

Here again the Christian's basic attitude is one of universal love: "As you did it to one of the least of these my brethren you did it to me" (Matthew 25, 40). They try to reach out as Christ would to all people. They choose their friends and acquaintances not only from among those who are pleasant and personable but also from among those who are lonely, defensive, embittered.

Christians try to contribute to their country, their state, and their city by being good neighbors, joining some civic group, and voting for good candidates; perhaps they may feel qualified to run for office them-selves. They realize that patriotism is a virtue, and they support their country when it needs them. If they feel that they must witness by being conscientious objectors, they know that they must "agree to serve the human community in some other way" (*The Church in the Modern World,* no. 79).

Christians try to work for world peace—built on justice—realizing that this is an ongoing need of our time. They realize that they are Chris-tian citizens of the world, and they try to learn about and help those of other countries, particularly the needy, less-developed nations.

Christians appreciate their leisure time, but also realize that there are many things they can do to help others in their spare moments: visiting the sick, particularly those old, neglected, or mentally ill; giving time to a social or civic group working to help the homeless and others obtain adequate housing and jobs for those relatively unskilled. They are alert to speak out against immoral policies of government and demand ac-countability of elected officials. Better yet, they are alert to lawmakers' and other officials' achievements for the common good so that they can com-pliment and encourage them, even if only by dropping them a postcard.

Christians respect the person and dignity of their neighbor and their neighbor's right to his or her good reputation. Our neighbor, of course, is everyone. Neighbors avoid injuring another in any way, except in truly necessary self-defense; they keep to themselves information that, however true, would harm another's reputation. Christians realize that hatred, carrying a grudge, or injuring another's good name is usually seriously wrong. They recognize their neighbor's right to the truth, and particularly avoid lying that would do serious harm. They know, too, that they have an obligation in conscience to drive safely.

Christians remember their dignity and avoid injuring themselves and giving scandal by drunkenness, taking drugs, or smoking that harms their health. They realize that the disease of alcoholism, particularly, can get a hold on one without one's realizing it, and they are humble and realistic enough to recognize its warning signs.

Christians respect their own dignity and that of the one they profess to love by controlling their sexual desires, having and enjoying sex only within the marriage commitment. They recognize that they live in a sexually overstimulated society, and realistically take safeguards to avoid what they know are occasions of sin, temptations to use another or let oneself be used. If they fail, no matter how often, they return to seek forgiveness, and start over again, realizing that they are thereby building a disciplined and faithful love.

Christians realize that one's attitude toward those who are "different" because of race, nationality, sex, or old age is usually the real test of the genuineness of their Christianity. They recognize that an attitude of discrimination, segregation, or intrinsic superiority is seriously wrong; they try to do whatever they can to help bring about understanding and acceptance of all. Christians do not patronize a place, or live in housing, that excludes those of another race or ethnic background. They do what they can to obtain fair housing, education, and job opportunities for all. They try not to let apathy, fear, or disillusionment take over.

Christians recognize that prejudices are deep within us all and that overcoming these requires much perseverance and often great sacrifice. They may regard themselves as victims of "reverse discrimination," in, for example, an affirmative action program—but they are willing to endure some of this for the sake of a minority's long-denied right to justice and equality. They try to look on all men and women as individuals, to get to know them and appreciate them as human beings with strengths and weaknesses like themselves.

Christians expect that they will be mocked and sometimes harassed for living up to their beliefs. They remember Christ's words, "Behold, I send you as sheep in the midst of wolves. . . . If the world hates you, know that it has hated me before it hated you . . . " (Matthew 10, 16; John 15, 18).

OUR RELIGIOUS LIFE

Christians truly believe they can find God daily in their neighbors and that in their efforts to make this world even a bit better, they are working hand in hand with God. But they know, too, that they must pause periodically, try to be aware of God's presence, and recollect and remotivate themselves. They know that this is particularly necessary in our modern, materialistic, secularistic world, where things of the spirit are so easily forgotten.

Christians also pause to pray whenever they can, though it may be only once or twice during the day. They pray with confidence, no matter how sinful they have been, for they know that their poor prayer is joined with that of Christ and that it is the Spirit who is praying within them. Some sort of spiritual reading, particularly brief passages from the Bible, can be the "food" that makes meaningful these brief prayer-pauses. Some Christians find that prayerfully meditating on the Bible can open a new world for them. Some occasionally drop into a church, others meditate regularly and/or go out amid nature—to take time for silence and solitude.

Christians try to develop a sense of reverence, of worship, both personally and with others and do what they can to materially support their parish. They try to appreciate the sacred in others, in nature, as well as in places associated with their religion. They try to be active members of their parish, contributing their talents as well as financial support (Catholics contribute significantly less financially than other religious groups). They are realistically aware of today's prevalent temptations: passivity, not wanting to get involved, and/or selfishness in not wanting to give of one's time and money (unless someone one loves, or oneself, is personally affected).

Christians who are truly serious about growing in God's love know that they must set aside a time to spiritually "take inventory," if possible for a few days or more, at least once during the year. They might make a weekend retreat or take part in a cursillo or parish renewal mission or at least a day of recollection.

Christians also realize that they must join together with others in order to grow spiritually themselves and help others grow. They know that family prayer and religious discussions are only a start. They can usually find a group that they can join, whether an organized parish group or an informal one, to learn more about their faith, to contribute their own insights, or to do some ministering work. Some are not "joiners" by nature, but they can take advantage of special lectures, classes, and retreats.

Christians remember that a self-centered Christian is no Christian at all. They try to respond to opportunities to tactfully share their religious and moral convictions, especially with those who seem to need something in which to believe. But Christians also know that loving concern, a sensitivity to helping those in need of personal or material support, is the best way to bring Christ to others.

Christians know they need periodically to be reconciled, to seek God's and their neighbors' forgiveness, especially by the sacrament of reconciliation. They know life is a process of continual conversion, of making new starts—and they are not discouraged by it.

The weekly eucharistic family meal of their parish, the Mass, is the big spiritual event of the Christians' week. They know that if they deliberately neglect it, they must ask themselves how seriously they love Christ, or whether they appreciate what the Mass is. Christians should look forward to Mass and prepare a bit by reading that Sunday's Scriptures at home beforehand. They try to get at least one practical point out of the sermon, and above all take part in the communion meal as the great source of strength and ability to love during the coming week.

Christians realize their weakness and take advantage of the Church's reminders to do penance. They try to make Lent, for example, a time when they can do some positive good, particularly by way of self-discipline; they abstain from meat willingly and fast if they can, but they try particularly to make up for their sins by acts of kindness, patience, and interest in others.

Christians know that sometimes doubts will come, or the spiritual ennui in which they no longer seem to get anything out of their religion. They try to remember that God never forces himself upon us, but rather solicits our love in often hidden ways. They know that God's ways are not our ways.

Finally, Christians know that they must suffer and die with Christ in order to rise with him. They expect pain, frustration, and hardships during the day. But Christians try to offer them up with Christ's sufferings, realizing that this may ultimately be their greatest contribution to spreading love in the world.

SOME SUGGESTIONS FOR . . .

DISCUSSION

What do you think should most motivate a Christian's daily life? Your life?

Can you understand why one needs some "rules" to concretely and honestly live out one's commitment of love?

Which of the beatitudes is the most challenging for you? For our society today?

How do you think, concretely, the Church might help you in your personal life . . . spousal and family relationships . . . job or profession?

What do you consider your greatest need(s) in trying to live Christ's life in today's world?

FURTHER READING

- *Principles for a Catholic Morality,* O'Connell (Harper & Row, 1990)—This revised edition is a good summary of Catholic moral teaching in a popular style for students, clergy, and laypeople.
- • *Reason Informed by Faith: Foundations of Catholic Morality,* Gula (Paulist Press, 1989)—Perhaps the best contemporary book on fundamental morality, this covers sin, conscience, criteria for moral judgments, norms and decision-making, and discernment.
- • *What Are They Saying About Scripture and Ethics?* Spohn (Paulist Press, 1995)—In this revised, expanded edition of a popular book, a leading Catholic moral theologian discusses the renewed use of Scripture among Christian theologians, and then treats new questions regarding spirituality, feminist and Latin American liberation theologies, and character ethics.

- *Ethics in Pastoral Ministry,* Gula (Paulist Press, 1996)—In a conversational style, this highly regarded theologian offers help in dealing with some moral demands that arise from being pastoral as well as professional in one's ministry.
- *Where Do You Stand?* Higgins (Paulist Press, 1995)—Subtitled "Eight moral issues confronting today's Christians," this insightful book looks at the particulars behind eight of today's crucial moral issues, so that one might discerningly take a personal stand on them.
- The Harper/Hazelden Meditation Series (HarperSanFrancisco)—Several excellent little books provide practical spiritual support and guidance for modern problems such as loneliness, addiction, intimacy, relating to others, and more.

PERSONAL REFLECTION

If I believe in Christ, I am tremendously privileged. I can consciously live with him and in him each day, doing the things he did two thousand years ago. The Spirit within me will help my poor weakness and gradually form me into another Christ.

I might pick one or two areas in which I am particularly unlike Christ and ask the Spirit's daily help with these.

26

Fulfillment Forever

Why do we say that death is the climax of a Christian life? What will happen to us after death? What is the meaning of purgatory? What do we mean by saying that Christians expect a new heaven and a new earth? What, ultimately, is the difference in being a Christian?

OUR MEETING WITH CHRIST AT DEATH

Death is the climactic experience of our life. It is more than just a moment of time; it is an experience. We awaken to full consciousness and full freedom and encounter God himself. All our life has been lived for just this. But death usually has a fearfulness attached to it because of our sinfulness—men and women, even those otherwise strong, tend to shrink from it.

Christ by his death has changed the nature of our death. The Christian knows this: death is now our most meaningful act, the one to which we look forward as the climax and summation of our life. Someone has said, "The moment we are born we begin to die." None of us can avoid death, but committed Christians look ahead to it and live their life in the realization of its coming.

From here on we will be discussing eschatology, or the "last things," and how we will relate to these final, culminating events. Christ is called the "escaton" who, we will see, brings them about.

It is Christ whom we encounter after death face-to-face, in the clearest, most intimate way possible. Though the biblical imagery about this is apocalyptic, as we will see, Christian tradition from the beginning speaks of encountering Christ. He whom we have been reaching for in our prayers, whom we have dimly encountered in the sacraments, is now before us in the overwhelming fullness of his light and love and power.

Yet we also encounter ourselves, with total clarity and honesty—and we thus judge ourselves. In later tradition this came to be called the "particular (or individual) judgment." People sometimes tell how their life flashed before them as they faced death—perhaps this is a glimpse of our situation after death. We fully realize, now, whether our life's fundamental option or commitment has been toward God and others or toward ourselves.

We should often think of this moment. We know how we long to see someone whom we love and from whom we have been separated for some time—and on the other hand, how ashamed we are at meeting someone whom we have deeply offended. In these first moments of eternity, we shall be face-to-face with Christ whose love has always been with us, and for whom we should have been reaching all our life.

In this our last moment there is no in-between. The time of probation is over; there are no more chances. We are either saved or lost. This is the ultimate and only important distinction between people—either they have God's grace-presence with them or they do not—either they have chosen him and others or they have chosen only themselves.

Regarding reincarnation, Christianity has always rejected the notion of reincarnation, that one would be reborn, perhaps many times, until one has worked out one's "karma" from previous existences, or even endlessly. But some theologians today see the possibility of some sort of "reliving" for the relatively few individuals who never were able to make a fully human, free choice in this life, so that they might do so.

To prepare a person for death, the Church gives some or all of these sacraments, traditionally called the "last rites":

The sacrament of penance or reconciliation (conditional absolution or reconciliation if the person is unconscious).

The anointing of the sick.

Holy Communion, here called "Holy Viaticum"—the Church's sacrament for the dying. This is followed by a special blessing for the dying.

United in love with the dying one, during these rites those who are present should join in the prayers to the extent they can.

A priest should be called as soon as it becomes apparent that an illness is serious. We mentioned before the mistaken charity of not calling the priest for fear of frightening the patient. The sooner in a serious illness one receives the anointing of the sick, the better may be his or her chance of recovery, or at least the better the sick person can prepare for this final, all-important meeting with Christ at death.

If someone dies suddenly or is fatally injured, the priest should be called—even though it appears death has already taken place.

A word should be said about suicide: Most suicides were once denied a "Christian burial" because it was felt they were wrongfully taking on themselves God's ultimate right over life and death. Today the Church recognizes that those who commit suicide are usually not in full control of their reason and/or their will—and in cases of doubt pastoral compassion for the person should prevail.

The Christian's attitude toward death should be one of confidence and expectation. We know that God wants everyone to be saved, that he has surrounded us through life with the constant help of his love. We know Christ will be with us especially at death. No matter what sins we have committed, if we are sorry he forgives them all.

Because we look forward to an unending life of love and happiness, it usually makes little sense to use extraordinary or "heroic" means to prolong life, for example, that of a comatose loved one who is surviving only by continued use of a life-support system. Note, however, that this is not to be confused with wrongful "mercy killing." Some respected theologians would allow and even recommend cessation of feeding of those in a persistent vegetative state. In the often painful decisions about prolonging life, the previous wishes of our loved one, family consultation, sensitive counseling, and quiet prayer can all help.

PURGATORY: THE IDEA OF ACCOUNTABILITY

We have seen that we are responsible and accountable for our sins and have a need within ourselves to make up for them. If we do not do this

in our present life, we will have to do so after death. This has traditionally been called "purgatory," an attempt to express our need of eventual "purification"—the growth in needed love we must undergo before attaining union with God, who is Limitless Love, forever in heaven. This is essentially a way of saying we are responsible beings, ultimately accountable for our free actions and choices.

Purgatory is perhaps best described as the painful state or experience of encountering God after death, when we see him as he really is "face to face" (1 Corinthians 13, 12), and, by contrast, ourselves as we really are, as sinful humans. An encounter with the living God always is painfully, totally upsetting. God's manifestations of himself in Scripture show this:

> Moses veiled his face when he beheld the burning bush, for he was afraid to look on God (Exodus 3, 6). Elijah performed the same symbolic gesture of veiling his face on Mount Sinai (1 Kings 19, 13). In the vision in which God called Isaiah, even the seraphim veil their faces and the prophet exclaims with the terror of any creature menaced by the divine: "Woe is me! For I am lost . . . for my eyes have seen the King, the Lord of Hosts" (Isaiah 6, 5). Daniel saw God in a vision of fire and the proximity of God caused him to enter something like a mystical agony (Daniel 7, 9–10; 8, 17–18, 27). Ezekiel fell down before God, stricken with a strange paralysis and with dumbness (Ezekiel 3, 23–26). At Christ's transfiguration the disciples fell on their faces and were filled with awe (Matthew 17, 1–6).

We have seen that we will meet Christ after death, and in and through him, God himself. Without any more rationalizations or equivocation, we now face the One who has loved us totally, unconditionally. We now clearly realize how often we have hurt him and our fellow humans, and yet did nothing about it.

In this experience of purgation we make up for our sins by growing in love. Christ has made up for our sins and now accepts us totally, but we yet have the need of doing something about them ourselves, as when we hurt anyone we love. We experience this painful purgation because we have not loved enough. This is only reasonable. Most people realize they have not made up for all their sins, that they still are clinging to some faults, and they therefore could not expect to be perfectly happy immediately after death with the perfect, totally accepting Love we call God. On the other hand, they know that they are not evil enough to be damned. It is only logical, then, to believe in this experience, this situation or state of purgation.

Many theologians today do not accept the traditional notion of purgatory as a postdeath state, but see it rather as something undergone in this life—perhaps by unequivocal, painful times of facing and making up for our sins. Perhaps this takes place in the experience of dying. In any event, the concept of purgation after death is not in the New Testament, but the notion of accountability after death is an ancient one.

Parts of the Christian Church almost from the beginning believed in a state of purgation after death where the dead could not help themselves but could be helped by the prayers of those on earth. God's people of the Old Testament had only a vague notion of this, but a widespread Jewish tradition of the century before Christ held that it was a "holy and wholesome thought to pray for the dead that they may be loosed from their sins" (2 Maccabees 12, 46).

The concept of purgatory as a place of purification by "fire," before entering heaven, has been prevalent only since the thirteenth century. Archeology, however, shows that the earliest Christians prayed for their dead, who were sometimes said to be in a "place of tears" or a "place of darkness." The ancient liturgies of both East and West contain prayers for the dead, as in our Mass today. Many early Christian writers mention prayers for the dead.

Whatever the "when" and "how" of this purgatory state, those passing through it know that they are saved, are overwhelmed by God's love, and have a joy far more intense than anything on earth. The imagery of a place and of fire attempts to describe the paradox of purgatory—a state of joy and yet of suffering. The metaphors could still be apt, in that we all, at some time/place or other, submit ourselves to the penetrating, purifying power of God's love. We realize clearly our immature self-love, our attachment to sinful habits, and we "grow up" in love and break away from these. Our real self then emerges, totally absorbed in God, totally in love.

All our wayward habits and affections must be directed toward this one, true Love. One person may be clinging to material possessions, another to an overweening pride, and another has never disciplined his or her sex power.

All these must be purified, "burnt up" in an all-absorbing divine love. God wants nothing to interfere with his filling us with limitless love.

Thus there is pain in this purgatory-state. Any deep personality change is painful—and this is our final change for eternity. Growing in love can be particularly painful, especially when we contrast our imperfections with our beloved. A man with a destructive habit, for example, might meet a wonderful woman; he realizes he must conquer this habit if there is to be any permanent love between them—if he loves enough, he will strive painfully until he has the habit under control. In this purgation we come to love perfectly the perfect Lover.

Those in this state, therefore, want to be with God and yet do not want to be with him the way they are. We see clearly God's limitless goodness and our own faults by contrast. We want to be purified, and yet we burn with desire to be with God. The pain, however and wherever undergone, may be simply that we cannot be united with him quickly enough.

Those in this state can be helped by praying for them, offering Mass for them, offering our loving actions, sufferings, and so on. The power of love for one another with the Mystical Body knows no limits in this life, and it goes on after death as well. We can help others, even as we will be helped.

We should remember that we need not go through this purgatory state, if there is such after death, if we have loved sufficiently in this life. Some people by their great suffering seem to be going through their purgatory at present.

IN THE LITURGY

The Church treats the dead body with reverence, a sign of our belief that we will rise to eternal life. The body is brought to the church where a Mass of Christian Burial is offered; afterward, it is incensed, blessed with holy water, and brought to the cemetery, where after some final prayers it is buried, often in blessed ground.

The Church's liturgy for the dead emphasizes our confident hope of resurrection and eternal life. The prayers and songs speak of the fulfillment of life and eternal joy. A candle burns by the dead Christian's body, a sign of his or her eternal life with Christ, "the Light of the World" who came to lead us through the shadows and blackness of death to the indescribably dazzling eternal Light, God himself. White vestments are used, also a sign of resurrection and unending life.

The rite of funerals helps people take leave of a dead relative or friend and celebrates that person's entry into eternal life. Ordinarily, there are three "stations" or steps involved: the wake service preceding the funeral, then the Mass of Christian Burial described above, and the service at the cemetery.

At the weekly parish eucharist the priest or lector leads the parish family during the Prayer of the Faithful in praying for those who are deceased. In the Mass liturgy, during some of the eucharistic prayers there is a commemoration of our dead: the priest may pause as we pray for our dead.

Cremation is now allowed—and normally a Mass or service for our dead one is also held—because it is no longer seen as a denial of life after death. The gift of one's organs after death is not only allowed but recommended (*Catechism*, 2301).

During the month of November we particularly pray for the "holy souls" in purgatory. November 2 is the Feast of All Souls, "All Souls' Day," on which many Catholics take part in Mass for their dead.

People sometimes have Masses celebrated for deceased relatives and friends: they may give an offering, not to pay for the Mass, but to help the works of the Church.

AT THE END

When we speak of the end of the world we mean its completion, its consummation and transformation, not its destruction. Then the limitations of time and space, of disharmony and waste, will be over. A new order of things will begin.

We do not know when the end of the world is coming, and we know little about how it will take place. Christ says, "of that day or that hour no one knows . . . only the Father" (Mark 13, 32). The knowledge of this was not part of Christ's earthly mission, and we need not waste time uselessly speculating about it. There is too much to do with the wonderful, challenging world we have here and now.

There will be for all of us a resurrection, that is, we will be alive as full human beings and not just as spirits. The Apostles' Creed prays for the resurrection of the body, but the whole person is what is meant. In some sense, our world will be there, too, only it will be transformed (see the next section).

Christ will appear in judgment with all humankind before him: Read John 5, 25-30. This is imagery from Jewish apocalyptic literature, in which God strikingly vindicates his people and punishes their, and his, enemies. Christ is described as speaking in this way, familiar to his listeners, when he predicted the "last days" and the coming of the Messianic Age (cf. Mark 13, 3ff.; Matthew 24, 3ff.; Luke 21, 7ff.; also Revelation 20, 11-13).

> *Many today do not expect Christ's second coming (the parousia) to be an apocalyptic-type event in the future, but consider that it has already begun, that Christ's presence is gradually being realized in human history.* The end of the world, rather than being passively awaited, is actively being brought about by the love and labor of people. Christ who is among us will be revealed at the end, at the culmination of this unfolding, for all to see in power and glory.

> *Vatican Council II said this about Christ's presence among us now:* "Christ is now at work in the hearts of people through the energy of his Spirit, arousing not only a desire for the age to come, but by that very fact animating, purifying, and strengthening those noble longings by which the human family makes its life more human, and strives to render the whole earth submissive to his goal" (*The Church in the Modern World,* no. 38).

When Christ comes to us in judgment the whole of human history will be revealed. Then we will understand the "why" of everything, that all has worked out for God's glory and our happiness—even the crimes, wars, and countless cruelties throughout history. At present we are like someone with a few pieces of a jigsaw puzzle. Then we shall see the whole puzzle of history put together—and our faith tells us that it will be a picture of immense beauty and love.

Our existence immediately after death could already be something like that of the resurrected person. We will then be beyond time as we know it now. So we should not think of ourselves as separated spirits, having to "wait" until events on this earth have been completed before we begin our full human existence in eternity. There are many unanswered questions, of course, about this new existence; however, "a biology of our future life is impossible; at the most only a very restrained anthropology can be outlined" (Schoonenberg, *God's World in the Making*, p. 199).

THE NEW UNIVERSE TOWARD WHICH WE WORK

After the end there will be a new universe—a new heaven and a new earth. "But according to his promise we wait for a new heaven and a new earth in which righteousness dwells" (2 Peter 13). Since the material world has suffered from the disorder that has come from humankind's sin, it is only fitting that it should share in our final glory. The universe is now "in labor" toward this better state (cf. Romans 8, 20–22).

The new universe will be beautiful and perfect beyond imagining. We do not know the exact nature of this perfect universe, but we do know that nature will be in harmony with itself and with humankind; there will be no more devastating storms, tornadoes, earthquakes, and so on, and the immense power we have begun to discover in the subatomic world and throughout the universe will then be put to full use. There will be a vast cosmic renewal or glorification, and God will be revealed in all things, present among us in undreamed of ways.

It is up to us now to bring about this new universe. We said before that God has placed in our hands an unfinished universe, has entrusted to us the privilege of perfecting his work. Every step we take toward peacefully sharing nature's resources, toward preserving and not abusing nature continues creation and carries out God's plan of love. We are cocreators with God—and the more conscious we are of this the more we can contribute. Whenever we expend pain and love for others—working above all for justice and peace—we help to bring about the perfection of all things.

Christians and all who realize this have an especially great responsibility and privilege toward helping perfect the universe. We can never be satisfied with things as they are in their present state. We must be driven on to advance truth, peace, and love—for every "development" of the universe that does not help to spread love serves to strengthen tyranny and holds back the perfection of all things.

By their labor they are unfolding the Creator's work . . . and are contributing by their personal industry to the realization in history of the divine plan. . . . Therefore, the expectation of a new earth must not weaken but rather stimulate our concern for cultivating this one. For here grows the body of a new human family, a body which even now is able to give some kind of foreshadowing of the new age. . . . (*The Church in the Modern World*, nos. 34 and 39).

The writings of the scientist-mystic Teilhard de Chardin convey the insight adopted by Vatican Council II, that to do the work of the world is to contribute to the fulfillment and completion of Christ's redemption of the universe. The world of matter with which people work is "the divine milieu, charged with creative power . . . the ocean stirred by the Spirit . . . the clay molded and infused with life by the incarnate Word." As we work and love to perfect the world, we are helping to bring about the clear and full revelation of Christ as the center of all things. Then "the presence of Christ, which has been silently accruing in things, will suddenly be revealed—like a flash of light from pole to pole. Breaking through all the barriers which have seemingly kept it confined, it will invade the face of the earth . . . [and] the attraction exerted by [Christ] will lay hold of all the whirling elements in the universe so as to reunite them or subject them to his body. . . . Such will be the consummation of the divine milieu" (*The Divine Milieu*, pp. 7, 133–34).

Last but not least, Christians must be leaders in resolving the growing ecological crises of our time, brought on by humankind's abuse of our planet and its natural resources. Pope John Paul II has said that our earth is suffering, that the destruction of our environment is a serious moral issue for us all, and that every human being has a right to a safe environment. Peace in our world and the world we will hand on to our children, and our children's children, depends on our solidarity with nature's ecosystem, of which we are a part (World Day of Peace Message, Jan. 1, 1990).

The *Catechism* also reminds us that our dominion over the earth's resources cannot be separated from our moral obligations, "including those toward generations to come" (2456).

HEAVEN, OUR DESTINY

Heaven is perfect union with God and one another forever. It is not a place, not "here" or "there," but a state in which, while yet retaining our individuality, we will be caught up into the infinite God. While we can deduce next to nothing about the next life from Scripture, as today's scholars point out—it was not part of Christ's mission on earth to describe eternity, but rather to announce the good news of God's kingdom—yet the implications of Christ's teachings, the constant tradition of the Church, and the insights of the saints and mystics can tell us much.

> *We will love and be loved with an unimaginable, ever-increasing love.* We will be fully possessed, continually overwhelmed by God's beauty and goodness, and yet we will go on thirsting for more—even as we are filled to perfect contentment we yet seek and find still more and more.
>
> God will be able to totally give *himself* to us. No longer shall we have to intuit or reason to him from his works, speculate about him, or catch fleeting, unsatisfying "glimpses." We shall see him as he is, his very self, "face to face" (1 Corinthians 13, 12). Each of us will know God and be loved by him in the most intimate way possible, in a way no one or nothing in creation is or ever will be.

This will be incredible, unimaginable happiness. One cannot now begin to describe it. St. Paul who was caught up into its "outer fringes" was helpless to describe it; he could only quote Isaiah, who had also glimpsed it: "What no eye has seen, nor ear heard, nor the human heart conceived, [that is] what God has prepared for those who love him . . . " (1 Corinthians 2, 9).

In this heaven-state there will be no sorrow, no pain, no hardship, no struggle or temptation of any kind. We will understand everything we have ever wanted to—the secrets of the universe, the mysteries of our faith. We will have everything we want. And we will be secure in this eternal happiness, knowing that there is no possibility of ever losing it.

> He will dwell with them, and they shall be his people, and God himself will be with them; he will wipe away every tear from their eyes, and death shall be no more, neither shall there be mourning nor crying nor pain any more, for the former things have passed away (Revelation 21, 3–4).

An insight coming to the fore today is that none of us will fully arrive until we all arrive. In some mysterious way, we are all bound together, dependent on one another, so that in helping another we are ultimately helping ourselves. This comes from many sources, some of which are the biblical, Teilhardian, process, feminist, and liberation theology views of life, and the concept of Vatican Council II that we are one people journeying together toward our destiny because we are all the one interdependent Body of Christ. Strikingly, modern physical sciences and much of psychology, sociology, responsible politics, and even economics see humankind as increasingly interdependent on our "spaceship earth."

The liturgy calls heaven "eternal rest" to try to communicate to us its perfect peace, contentment, and security in knowing it will never be lost. For many people today, this security and peace has great meaning because they have spent most of their lives coping with the almost frantic, often meaningless work and contrived "relaxations" of our modern life. It will be comforting just to know there are no more "obligations," no more threats of loss of job, of savings, and especially no more wrenching loss of loved ones—not to mention the inbuilt anxiety that most people today are not fully conscious of but is still a part of the ground of their anxieties: the threat of nuclear destruction and terrorism.

Yet, paradoxically, this heaven-state is really living at last: a continual growth in knowledge and love, an endless expanding of our whole being, while in uttermost peace and contentment. Those who have had a brief glimpse of this state, the great mystics (including St. Paul), universally tell us in their different ways when they come out of their experiencing that our present life is, by comparison, like a dream, a "shadow life," a tiny foothold on what life really is. Thus they are unwilling to try to describe even their brief glimpses. As St. Paul says in the passage above, we have no concepts to even begin to conceive it. Or as the Zen masters are fond of repeating regarding their tiny glimpses of Nirvana: "One who says does not know, and one who knows does not say."

The Bible represents eternal life by images of activity and celebration, of feasts, joyous worship, and rewards for our service of God. We are to be the servants who because we have been faithful in little things during this life will enjoy not only the Lord's joy but all his goods (Luke 19, 17 and 19). Activity that is pained by anxiety and struggle will cease, and joyous celebration will go on forever. One modern author says, "If this sounds to us monotonous (perhaps), it is because we need to rid ourselves of a neurotic over-esteem for productive work, and of a not yet integrated and personalized use of our free time" (Schoonenberg, *God's World in the Making*, p. 8).

We will be ceaselessly growing in love and happiness, unendingly fulfilling our every power in the most intense activity imaginable. Even now we know how our consciousness can be expanded. Then we will have our full personality, alive to the depths of our being, fully ourselves, and have perfect love and friendship with others. We will be beyond time and space, able to transcend the whole universe in an instant, be wherever we want, and do whatever we want. We will be glorified like the resurrected Christ who is "the first-fruits of those who have fallen asleep" (1 Corinthians 15, 20).

In our heavenly state we will also know all those we have known and loved in this world, the saints and all the great people of history—in fact we will be strangers to no one, and we will delight in one another's perfections and in our mutual love. There will be no distracted turning away from God to others, or vice versa—the problem that so often disturbs us now—but rather we will then clearly see God in them, acting through them, giving himself and revealing himself through them. Everything will then be sacred, for God will be "all in all."

There will be degrees of love and happiness in heaven: the more we have loved in this life, the more of God's grace-presence we have with us now, the greater will be our love and happiness forever. The great sixteenth-century mystic, Teresa of Avila, said that she would remain on earth till the end of the world, suffering terribly, if she would love God just a bit more in heaven.

Christ's teaching assures us that heaven goes on forever (cf. Matthew 25, 46; 1 Corinthians 15, 52). This, of course, we cannot imagine. But we can try to appreciate its astounding privilege: in return for a lifetime of faithfulness on earth, God might have given us a thousand years of happiness in heaven, and this would be a wonderful reward; or he might have given us ten thousand, a million, or a billion years of happiness. But he does infinitely more, so great is his love: he gives us eternity, forever and ever and ever, with himself.

The only thing that can keep us from heaven is deliberately turning away from God. If we fully reject God by choosing a condition of mortal sin and die hardened in our sin, we have cut ourselves off from him, from love, from happiness, and have isolated ourselves forever in hell. However remote this possibility, it should make us better appreciate how much we need God's love, should make us work now with all our heart and strength to love him and our fellow human beings.

Above all, we should think often of being with God and Christ and one another in heaven, and have a great longing for this. The early Christians lived in constant expectation of Christ's reappearance, and they were spurred to astounding deeds of love and sacrifice. This present life is but a brief bridge between nothingness and eternity; when the crossing becomes too difficult, we should think of our real destiny on the other side. We should not hesitate to cry out with St. Paul, "Here indeed we groan and long to put on our heavenly dwelling" (2 Corinthians 5, 2). Or with John as he finished the last book of Scripture, "Amen—Come, Lord Jesus!"

DAILY LIVING:
THE DIFFERENCE IN BEING A CHRISTIAN

A special view of human history is what makes Christians different. They believe that it has an author and a plot and an end that gives it all meaning. They believe that all things will one day be perfected in Christ. Christians work and love with confidence that nothing ultimately is wasted, that they are carrying out God's plan, that the world can and will be perfected. They can fail, hurt their fellow humans, neglect to alleviate some of the pain they might, but they know that limitless fulfillment is on its way. They are convinced of what Christ said: "Anyone who hears my word and believes him who sent me, *has* eternal life [and] has passed from death to life" (John 5, 24).

Christians know that their lives are often no better than those of the unbeliever (and sometimes are worse), that they are weak, sinners, often confused, even capable of monstrous misdeeds. They know that only some Christians grasp and live their life with Christ at all fully, that the very name "Christian" is sometimes appropriated by those whose lives are narrow and un-Christian. But they believe that somehow God uses their poor efforts, takes them, and transfigures them into love that is changing the world. They believe that "he who has begun his work in you will complete it" (Philippians 1, 6). This is because they know that God has come among us in Jesus Christ, that they themselves are now joined to Christ, and that this gives even their poorest efforts a new power whose effect they will realize only in eternity.

By their lives Christians try to radiate Christ's love to the world. They try to show, especially in the union with their fellow Christians that is the Church, the love that animates them all. They know that they need the Church—its Word and its sacraments, particularly the eucharist—as their daily strength. They try not to expect visible results from their acts of love, and they realize that they must often live in a "dark night" where faith seems to be dead and God appears to have vanished.

They know that they must suffer and die with Christ in order to rise with him—that they also have to undergo suffering to open themselves fully to the love God has in store for them. They know that love must be more than a humanitarian service to one's fellows, that it must also express itself in humbly asking God's help, crying out in worship, in pure, human weakness, asking to know, to be able to do God's will—and not merely their own.

Committed Christians occasionally catch a glimpse of God, even in this age when God is often considered to have disappeared. They look at their fellow human beings and sometimes, perhaps only for an instant, see in them something divine. They look at nature, and on occasion it may cry out to them that there is a Creator. They occasionally have an insight, realize in retrospect how providence has watched over them, catch a bit of meaning behind it all—and perhaps they once may have personally experienced the great, shattering peace and joy that could only be God.

They hold the conviction, sometimes only mutely and obscurely, but with deep faith, "that neither death, nor life, nor angels, nor principalities, nor things present, nor things to come, nor powers, nor height nor depth, nor anything else in all creation, will be able to separate us from the love of God in Christ Jesus our Lord" (Romans 8, 38–39).

SOME SUGGESTIONS FOR . . .

DISCUSSION

Why should the Christian, however much he or she may naturally fear it, and however full life may be here and now, nevertheless have an attitude of expectation toward death?

Does purgatory—accountability—make sense to you? What in your life needs to be gotten rid of before meeting with the limitlessly loving God?

Do you feel you have any inkling, however small, of what heaven might be like?

What would you say is distinctive about being a Christian today?

What, for you, best sums up the way a Christian should live—however often he or she might fail at it?

FURTHER READING

- *Euthanasia: Moral and Pastoral Perspectives,* Gula (Paulist Press, 1994)—In this relatively small book the popular teacher and ethical consultant takes a clear look at what is involved in physician-assisted suicide and euthanasia, and offers a vision of humility, courage, and hope within a caring Christian community.
- *Critical Care Ethics: Treatment Decisions in American Hospitals,* Kelly (Sheed & Ward, 1991)—Another highly regarded ethicist discusses the consensus he and others see regarding foregoing medical treatment in some circumstances. He also treats pain, pain management, ethics committees, and problems of resource allocation.
- *Aging: The Fulfillment of Life,* Nouwen and Gaffney (Doubleday, 1976)—This is a fine book about making one's later years a hope-filled climax of one's life journey toward God.
- *What Are They Saying About Death and Christian Hope?* Hellwig (Paulist Press, 1978)—Brief and clearly written, this book by one of today's best theologians updates us on death and what will and what may follow.
- *Let Someone Hold You: The Journey of a Hospice Priest,* Morrissey (Crossroad, 1995)—A personal, very moving, very helpful account by someone long involved in this work.
- *Final Gifts: Understanding the Special Awareness, Needs, and Communications of the Dying,* Callahan and Kelley (Bantam Books, 1993)—In this moving and compassionate book two hospice nurses share the ways the dying communicate—including with those who have gone before them—and give some practical tips on how to best be with them.

- *How to Survive the Loss of a Love,* Colgrove, Bloomfield, and McWilliams (Prelude Press, 1991)—A simple, very popular little book that many survivors have found quietly, profoundly helpful.
- *The Birth of Purgatory,* LeGoff (University of Chicago Press, 1985)—An interesting and informative account of the development of the concept of purgatory, by an outstanding French medieval historian.
- • *Eternal Life?* Küng (Doubleday, 1984)—Subtitled "Life After Death as a Medical, Philosophical and Theological Problem," this frank, incisive book shows that one's opting to believe in unending life with God makes sense—that it is based on a "reasonable trust." This book can reinforce one's actively living a life of ever-deepening faith, and ever-increasing hope—or confident expectation—of eternal life.
- *The Coming of the Cosmic Christ,* Fox (Harper & Row, 1988)—A sweeping synthesis of the reemergence of wisdom, the feminine, creativity, mysticism, and Mother Earth; if occasionally enthusiastic, this is nonetheless deeply insightful and immensely hopeful.

FURTHER VIEWING/LISTENING

Dying to Live: Spiritual Care for the Dying and Their Families, Linn and Carr (Paulist Press)—These eight half-hour programs on two two-hour videotapes take one through the Carr's experience of facing death and seek to lead one to surrendering, bit by bit, everything to Jesus.

A FINAL REFLECTION

The story of Christ among us is now concluded. If you have been using this book regularly, during the past weeks or months you have been drawing closer to God, to Christ. In the gospels those who drew close to Christ were always changed—deeply changed.

Peter was an ordinary, simple fisherman—and he became the first leader of God's Church on earth. Mary Magdalene was a prostitute known far and wide—and she became a great saint. Judas was an ordinary businessman, and he became the prototype of all traitors.

If you have been following this story faithfully, you, too, are changed. You have had an open mind and heart and have been willing to risk this encounter with God. Whether you now classify yourself as a believer, an unbeliever, or one wavering between, you can be sure that you have been profoundly changed for the better—and the world has also, because of you.

May you be blessed for your generous effort!

Appendix

Using *Christ Among Us*
with the Rite of Christian Initiation
of Adults (RCIA)

Christ Among Us has been used with the RCIA in many places, and many suggestions have been made for its further implementation as a resource. Here are some possibilities:

The questions at the beginning and especially the "Discussion" questions at the end of each chapter are meant to help stimulate discussion—and to "tease out" further questions from catechumens.

During the Inquiry phase or Pre-Catechumenate, some use the chapters up to and including chapter 8, so that the inquirers might enter into the story of Christ at the beginning of their journey. Others use the chapters up to and including chapter 13. Sections of chapters that might be emphasized are:

To help introduce prayer, the Mass, and the liturgy: In chapter 1, "Daily Living: Prayer—Our Contact with God." In chapter 2, "Daily Living: Worshiping Our Creator."

The section of chapter 14 titled "Step by Step Through the Mass" and the part of chapter 15 on the liturgical year might be helpful at this point. The "In the Liturgy" sections of each chapter might also be emphasized. And since prayer is so basic to conversion, the section of chapter 16 entitled "Christian Prayer" might also be of help.

To help introduce the Bible (*note* that this book is structured to be used with a Bible): Chapter 2, "The Source of Our Story." All of chapter 11, especially the section entitled "An Outline of the Bible."

To help introduce the use of ritual, symbols, and the sacraments: chapter 12, "The Great Signs in Which We Meet God."

To help introduce the RCIA process: the section of chapter 13 on the RCIA gives the inquirer/catechumen a glimpse of what lies ahead. Sponsors and/or godparents might note what pertains to them.

To help those undecided about continuing: either here or before Election, the section entitled "Conversion" and the questions in the RCIA outline of chapter 13 might be helpful, as well as the chapter 24 section, "Whether or Not to Join the Church."

During the Catechumenate proper, some go through all the chapters to the end of the book. Some use all the chapters through chapter 24, and then use chapters 25 and 26 in the Mystagogia. Others save chapter 21 on marriage and chapter 22, "The Family that Is the Church," until the Mystagogia. One might also note again the suggestions given for the Inquiry phase.

For catechumens contemplating marriage and/or those who are divorced and remarried (or considering remarriage), the appropriate sections of chapter 21 should be helpful.

For some, the section in chapter 22, "The Emerging Role of Women in the Church," might be helpful and perhaps necessary—as well as these sections in chapter 7: "Our Father," "The Holy Spirit," and "Daily Living." The "Daily Living" section of chapter 10, "Our Attitude Toward Authority," might also be helpful and perhaps necessary, especially regarding dissent to noninfallible teachings.

The *Apostles' Creed* is given at the end of chapter 10. The *Nicene Creed* is in the "In the Liturgy" section of chapter 13, summarizing the faith into which the catechumens are being baptized and/or received.

As one moves through the catechumenate, chapters 16 and 17 can aid in making one's inward commitment and in trying to live it out daily in today's world. Some sections may be helpful to sponsors as well as to those catechumens who were formerly living a Christian life and now are seeking adult faith—the section "Renewing Our Baptismal Conversion" of chapter 13, and chapter 16 on the various aspects of faith, doubt, and returning—and for some, the section on hope.

The problem of undeserved suffering in one's life is treated, obviously inadequately, in the "Daily Living" section of chapter 8—but prayerful reflection on this might open some just a bit more to the God who came in Jesus Christ to show us he is always with us in our suffering.

For those trying to decide about Election, the section of chapter 24 titled "Whether or Not to Join the Church" (as well as those sections on the divine and human Church) can be of help—as well as the questions proposed in chapter 13 for those trying to discern regarding Election.

For some, the last section of the last chapter, "The Difference in Being a Christian," might help make a difference.

During the period of Election, special attention might be paid to chapter 16, and to going back over previous chapters—especially the sections on "Daily Living" and the "Personal Reflections." Chapter 8 should be reflected on as one prepares for the end of Lent and the Easter sacraments. Chapter 18 and 19 might be gone over again by one concerned with reconciliation. Chapter 25 tries to highlight some aspects of practical living as a Catholic Christian.

During the Mystagogia period, some go over again certain chapters that have been saved for this time. Chapter 22 can be particularly helpful to neophytes, as well as chapters 14 and 15 on the eucharist—and they might reflect more deeply on chapter 16 and on chapter 17, how they might make a contribution by their new Catholic Christian presence. Chapter 25 can be used as a way of reflecting on different aspects of living their Catholic Christian life.

Index